PEARSON   ALWAYS LEARNING

Intellectual Origins of the Contemporary West
Volume 1

Third Custom Edition Queen's University

Prepared by the Staff
Department of History
Queen's University
Kingston, Ontario

Pearson Learning Solutions, 501 Boylston Street, Suite 900, Boston, MA 02116
A Pearson Education Company
www.pearsoned.com

14 18

000200010271682405

BK/KD

ISBN 10: 1-256-82172-1
ISBN 13: 978-1-256-82172-4

COPYRIGHT ACKNOWLEDGMENTS

Christianson, reprinted from *Isis* 70 (1979), Copyright Clearance Center, Inc.

Introduction to "Galileo Galilei," reprinted from *Introduction to Contemporary Civilization in the West*, Third Edition (1960), Columbia University Press.

Translations of "The Assayer" and "Dialogue Concerning the Two Great World-Systems," by Galileo Galilei, reprinted from *Introduction to Contemporary Civilization in the West* (1960), Columbia University Press.

Introduction to "Isaac Newton," reprinted from *Introduction to Contemporary Civilization in the West*, Third Edition (1960), Columbia University Press.

TABLE OF CONTENTS

Early Hebrew and Greek Thought

All of Western thought begins with myth: not in the common modern sense of "falsehood," but in the sense of stories that contain deeper levels of significance. All the familiar branches of thought—philosophy, theology, natural science, law, social and political theory—began as interwoven strands of narrative. This course will explore their emergence from myth and their gradual differentiation from one another in the context of Western history.

The two myths at the foundations of Western civilization are Hebrew and Greek. They began in isolation from each other, and first collided when Alexander the Great united the Greek and Middle Eastern worlds in the fourth century B.C. The process of confrontation continued, sometimes respectfully, often in hostility, in the period of Roman domination that followed. One of the products of this contact was Christianity, which transformed and transmitted Classical culture through the thousand years that followed the end of the Roman Empire in the West in 476 A.D.

The central Hebrew myth is found in the readings from Genesis.[1] The world is created by a good God: it is broken and changed by humanity's wrong choices. This story, often referred to as the Fall, is at the core of Judaism and Christianity. Even outside religious thought, it retains a great deal of intellectual weight: we will meet it, in various forms, in thinkers as different as Marx, Freud and Camus.

The Hebrew concept of history develops this theme. Israel is chosen by God as his own people, and an agreement, or covenant, exists between the two.[2] Somehow Israel breaks this agreement, and God punishes them by disaster, whether failure of the harvest or national exile in Egypt or Babylon. Israel repents, and God restores the relationship and the nation's prosperity.

During the decades that followed Israel's mass deportation to Babylon (beginning in 587 B.C.), certain latent ideas began to emerge with more prominence in Hebrew thought. Israel's history had been cyclical: now, in the work of prophets like Isaiah, it seemed as though that history might have a linear direction, anticipating the coming of a redemptive hero (the Messiah) and climaxing in the reversal of the Fall. As this idea developed, it brought with it a sense that Israel was not only God's own people, but in some sense held this privileged position in trust for the rest of humanity.

If Hebrew thought claims its origins in direct divine revelation, Greek myth comes from more diffuse and varied sources. We can find the beginnings of Greek thinking in the works of the early poets who probably wrote during the 8th century B.C., notably those attributed to Homer and Hesiod. Hesiod systematized the Greek myths in his *Theogony*[3] and also composed the *Works and Days*,[4] a book which, although essentially about rural matters, echoes the social tensions of his own time. The stories attributed to Homer in the epic poems *The Iliad* and *The Odyssey* deal, however, with events in the Late Bronze Age, some 500 years earlier (13th century B.C.). The society described

---

[1] Selection from Genesis, Revised Standard Version

[2] Selection from Exodus, Revised Standard Version

[3] The *Theogony* is traditionally attributed to Hesiod, but, in its present form, represents various different recensions. The selection below is from Norman O. Brown, trans., Hesiod, *Theogony*, (Indianapolis: Bobbs-Merrill Co., 1953), pp. 56–59,66–67. The footnotes are omitted.

[4] Selection below from Mark P.O. Morford and Robert J. Lenardon, *Classical Mythology*, 2nd ed., (New York and London: Longman, 1977), pp. 41–43,47–48.

there is that of the old Indo-European warrior culture, found at various times in different forms from prehistoric India to medieval Iceland. The world is possibly created, and certainly controlled, by the Gods, with Zeus the Thunderer at their head. The gods have no clear connection with moral concerns, though they expect humanity to behave in accordance with their will. The ideal man—and he is a man—is the hero: a skilled warrior who lives by a code that values his own honour above all. The hero is distinguished not only by martial prowess, but by nobility of birth. At the top of the social scale is the king. Men and gods alike are ultimately subject to the impersonal forces of Fate.

Unlike Israel, the Greek world, by the time these early Greek poets were writing, was not a single political entity, but a set of independent states. Like the Hebrews, the Greeks distinguished themselves from all the peoples around them, but only on the basis of common language and customs. Local loyalties, like the family and the city, were more important than loyalty to a "Greece" that was only a notional unity.

Both Greeks and Hebrews continued to develop the ideas inherent in their fundamental stories. For the Hebrews, nature was Creation: it was ultimately ordered by God to his own ends, and thus not a subject of much independent investigation. Hebrew thought was most concerned with ethical problems, centring on the relationship between God and humanity, and the way people should behave toward each other. This sort of speculation characterizes the Wisdom books of the Hebrew scriptures (like Job, Proverbs and Sirach).

For the Greeks, nature was not so much part of the ethical sphere. It thus lent itself to the kind of reflection that marked the work of the first known Greek philosophers in the period of the 6th and 5th centuries B.C. These thinkers, such as Xenophanes, Thales, Heraclitus, and Melissus (from whose writings extracts are reproduced below),[5] together with some equally or even more notable contemporaries,[6] are known as the pre-Socratics, not because they form a definite school of philosophy, but simply because most of them lived before Socrates. In their efforts to understand the patterns underlying the appearances of nature, they used categories of thought taken from myth to organize their data into the beginnings of systematic, logical thought. Things as we see them are in constant change and motion, yet there is some kind of stability to them, as well. To change, they applied terms like "becoming," and to stability, terms like "being," and they tried to work out the relationship between the two poles. Was one real and the other only apparent? Or was there a form of balance between them? Similarly, the sensible universe was made up of many things, yet it could also be perceived as one thing, at least in thought. Which was real, the One or the Many?

Early Greek social and ethical thought down to the 5th century was conditioned by the tension between the values of a warrior culture and those necessary for life in a world where trading and farming were as important as war. A variety of political systems also developed in the Greek city-states, ranging from monarchy through oligarchy to democracy, but, whatever the type of political organisation, an ethic oriented around individual honour often proved divisive. In states that adopted a form of democratic constitution, like Athens which became the first democracy in 508 B.C., laws were supposed to be framed to benefit the city as a whole. But how were law-makers to balance the good of the state with the good of individuals when these appeared to conflict? Because so many legal issues were

---

[5] Selections below from Philip Wheelwright, ed. and trans., *The Presocratics*, (New York: The Odyssey Press, 1966), pp. 32–33, 44–47, 49, 70–72, 82–83, 85–87, 113–116.

[6] Such as Anaximander, Anaximenes, Parmenides, Zeno, Empedocles, Anaxagoras, Leucippus, Democritus, Pythagoras, Protagoras, Gorgias and Hippocrates.

decided by the votes of the majority in the law courts, the first systematic political thinkers were those who worked out strategies for convincing jurors, and trained others to do the same. But was a convincing argument the same as a moral one?

Thinkers like Schiller and Nietzsche have looked back on early Greek thought as the "morning of the world," and we could do the same with that of Israel. We begin with stories that encompass the whole of intellectual activity. The stories raise questions, which the first philosophers attempt to answer: at first almost at random, and later more systematically. In the process, new disciplines emerge and separate from one another. As we gain in knowledge of particular things, we lose something of our knowledge of the whole once contained in the narrative. For the rest of this course, we will be watching this process, and the attempts to recover the whole again from the mass of seemingly fragmented details.

From *Genesis*

1–3

In the beginning God created the heavens and the earth. The earth was without form and void, and darkness was upon the face of the deep; and the Spirit of God was moving over the face of the waters.

And God said, "Let there be light;" and there was light. And God saw that the light was good; and God separated the light from the darkness. God called the light Day, and the darkness he called Night. And there was evening and there was morning, one day.

And God said, "Let there be a firmament in the midst of the waters, and let it separate the waters from waters." And God made the firmament and separated the waters which were under the firmament from the waters which were above the firmament. And it was so. And God called the firmament Heaven. And there was evening and there was morning, a second day.

And God said, "Let the waters under the heavens be gathered together into one place, and let the dry land appear." And it was so. God called the dry land Earth, and the waters that were gathered together he called Seas. And God saw that it was good. And God said, "Let the earth put forth vegetation, plants yielding seed, and fruit trees bearing fruit in which is their seed, each according to its kind, upon the earth." And it was so. The earth brought forth vegetation, plants yielding seed according to their own kinds, and trees bearing fruit in which is their seed, each according to its kind. And God saw that it was good. And there was evening and there was morning, a third day.

And God said, "Let there be lights in the firmament of the heavens to separate the day from the night; and let them be for signs and for seasons and for days and years, and let them be lights in the firmament of the heavens to give light upon the earth." And it was so. And God made the two great lights, the greater light to rule the day, and the lesser light to rule the night; he made the stars also. And God set them in the firmament of the heavens to give light upon the earth, to rule over the day and over the night, and to separate the light from the darkness. And God saw that it was good. And there was evening and there was morning, a fourth day.

And God said, "Let the waters bring forth swarms of living creatures, and let birds fly above the earth across the firmament of the heavens." So God created the great sea monsters and every living creature that moves, with which the waters swarm, according to their kinds, and every winged bird according to its kind. And God saw that it was good. And God blessed them, saying, "Be fruitful and multiply and fill the waters in the seas, and let birds multiply on the earth." And there was evening and there was morning, a fifth day.

And God said, "Let the earth bring forth living creatures according to their kinds: cattle and creeping things and beasts of the earth according to their kinds." And it was so. And God made the beasts of the earth according to their kinds and the cattle according to their kinds, and everything that creeps upon the ground according to its kind. And God saw that it was good.

Then God said, "Let us make man in our image, after our likeness; and let them have dominion over the fish of the sea, and over the birds of the air, and over the cattle, and over all the earth, and over every creeping thing that creeps upon the earth." So God created man in his own image, in the image of God he created him; male and female he created them. And God blessed them, and God said to them, "Be fruitful and multiply, and fill the earth and subdue it; and have dominion over the fish of the sea and over the birds of the air and over every living thing that moves upon the earth." And God said, "Behold, I have given you every plant yielding seed which is upon the face of all the earth, and every tree with seed in its fruit; you shall have them for food. And to every beast of the earth, and to every bird of the air, and to everything that creeps on the earth, everything that has the breath of life, I have given every green plant for food." And it was so. And God saw everything that he had made, and behold, it was very good. And there was evening and there was morning, a sixth day.

Thus the heavens and the earth were finished, and all the host of them. And on the seventh day God finished his work which he had done and he rested on the seventh day from all his work which he had done. So God blessed the seventh day and hallowed it, because on it God rested from all his work which he had done in creation.

These are the generations of the heavens and the earth when they were created.

In the day that the LORD God made the earth and the heavens, when no plant of the field was yet in the earth and no herb of the field had yet sprung up—for the LORD God had not caused it to rain upon the earth, and there was no man to till the ground; but a mist went up from the earth and watered the whole face of the ground—then the LORD God formed man of dust from the ground, and breathed into his nostrils the breath of life; and man became a living being. And the Lord God planted a garden in Eden, in the east; and there he put the man whom he had formed. And out of the ground the LORD God made to grow every tree that is pleasant to the sight and good for food, the tree of life also in the midst of the garden, and the tree of the knowledge of good and evil.

A river flowed out of Eden to water the garden, and there it divided and became four rivers. The name of the first is Pishon; it is the one which flows around the whole land of Havilah, where there is gold; and the gold of that land is good; bdellium and onyx stone are there. The name of the second river is Gihon; it is the one which flows around the whole land of Cush. And the name of the third river is Tigris, which flows east of Assyria. And the fourth river is the Euphrates.

The LORD God took the man and put him in the garden of Eden to till it and keep it. And the LORD God commanded the man, saying, "You may freely eat of every tree of the garden; but of the tree of the knowledge of good and evil you shall not eat, for in the day that you eat of it you shall die."

Then the LORD God said, "It is not good that the man should be alone; I will make him a helper fit for him." So out of the ground the Lord God formed every beast of the field and every bird of the air, and brought them to the man to see what he would call them; and whatever the man called every living creature, that was its name. The man gave names to all cattle, and to the birds of the air, and to every beast of the field; but for the man there was not found a helper fit for him. So the Lord God caused a deep sleep to fall upon the man, and while he slept took one of his ribs and closed up its place with flesh; and the rib which the LORD God had taken from the man he made into a woman and brought her to the man.

Then the man said, "This at last is bone of my bones and flesh of my flesh; she shall be called Woman, because she was taken out of Man."

Therefore a man leaves his father and his mother and cleaves to his wife, and they become one flesh. And the man and his wife were both naked, and were not ashamed.

Now the serpent was more subtle than any other wild creature that the LORD God had made. He said to the woman, "Did God say, 'You shall not eat of any tree of the garden'?" And the woman said to the serpent, "We may eat of the fruit of the trees of the garden; but God said, 'You shall not eat of the fruit of the tree which is in the midst of the garden, neither shall you touch it, lest you die.' "But the serpent said to the woman, "You will not die. For God knows that when you eat of it your eyes will be opened, and you will be like God, knowing good and evil." So when the woman saw that the tree was good for food, and that it was a delight to the eyes, and that the tree was to be desired to make one wise, she took of its fruit and ate; and she also gave some to her husband, and he ate. Then the eyes of both were opened, and they knew that they were naked; and they sewed fig leaves together and made themselves aprons.

And they heard the sound of the LORD God walking in the garden in the cool of the day, and the man and his wife hid themselves from the presence of the LORD among the trees of the garden. But the LORD God called to the man, and said to him, "Where are you?" And he said "I heard the sound of thee in the garden, and I was afraid, because I was naked; and I hid myself." He said, "Who told you that you were naked? Have you eaten of the tree of which I commanded you not to eat?" The man said, "The woman whom thou gavest to be with me, she gave me fruit of the tree, and I ate." Then the LORD God said to the woman, "What is this that you have done?" The woman said, "The serpent beguiled me, and I ate." The LORD God said to the serpent,

> "Because you have done this,
> cursed are you above all cattle,
> and above all wild animals;
> upon your belly you shall go,
> and dust you shall eat
> all the days of your life.
> I will put enmity between you and the woman,
> and between your seed and her seed;
> he shall bruise your head,
> and you shall bruise his heel."
> To the woman he said,
> "I will greatly multiply your pain in childbearing;
> in pain you shall bring forth children,
> yet your desire shall be for your husband,
> and he shall rule over you."
> And to Adam he said,
> "Because you have listened to the voice of your wife,
> and have eaten of the tree
> of which I commanded you,'
> 'You shall not eat of it,'
> cursed is the ground because of you
> in toil you shall eat of it all the days of your life,

thorns and thistles it shall bring forth to you,
and you shall eat the plants of the field.
In the sweat of your face
you shall eat bread
till you return to the ground,
for out of it you were taken;
you are dust,
and to dust you shall return"

The man called his wife's name Eve, because she was the mother of all living. And the LORD God made for Adam and for his wife garments of skins, and clothed them.

Then the LORD God said, "Behold, the man has become like one of us, knowing good and evil; and now, lest he put forth his hand and take also of the tree of life, and eat, and live for ever'— therefore the LORD God sent him forth from the garden of Eden, to till the ground from which he was taken. He drove out the man; and at the east of the garden of Eden he placed the cherubim, and a flaming sword which turned every way, to guard the way to the tree of life.

11:1–9

Now the whole earth had one language and few words. And as men migrated from the east, they found a plain in the land of Shinar and settled there. And they said to one another, "Come, let us make bricks, and burn them thoroughly." And they had brick for stone, and bitumen for mortar. Then they said, "Come, let us build ourselves a city, and a tower with its top in the heavens, and let us make a name for ourselves, lest we be scattered abroad upon the face of the whole earth." And the LORD came down to see the city and the tower, which the sons of men had built. And the LORD said, "Behold, they are one people, and they have all one language; and this is only the beginning of what they will do; and nothing that they propose to do will now be impossible for them. Come, let us go down, and there confuse their language, that they may not understand one another's speech." So the LORD scattered them abroad from there over the face of all the earth, and they left off building the city. Therefore its name was called Babel, because there the LORD confused the language of all the earth; and from there the LORD scattered them abroad over the face of all the earth.

From *Exodus*

19:1–20:20

On the third new moon after the people of Israel had gone forth out of the land of Egypt, on that day they came into the wilderness of Sinai. And when they set out from Reph'idim and came into the wilderness of Sinai, they encamped in the wilderness; and there Israel encamped before the mountain. And Moses went up to God, and the LORD called to him out of the mountain, saying; "Thus you shall say to the house of Jacob, and tell the people of Israel: You have seen what I did to the Egyptians, and how, I bore you on eagles' wings and brought you to myself. Now therefore, if you will obey my voice and keep my covenant, you shall be my own possession among all peoples; for all the earth is mine, and you shall be to me a kingdom of priests and a holy nation. These, are the words which you shall speak to the children of Israel."

So Moses came and called the elders of the people, and set before them all these words which the LORD had commanded him. And all the people answered, together and said, "All that the LORD has spoken we will do;" And Moses reported the words of the people to the LORD. And the LORD said to Moses, "Lo, I am coming to you in a thick cloud, that the people may hear when I speak with you, and may also believe you for ever."

Then Moses told the words of the people to the LORD. And the LORD said to Moses, "Go to the people and consecrate them today and tomorrow, and let them wash their garments, and be ready by the third day; for on the third day the LORD will come down upon Mount Sinai in the sight of all the people. And you shall set bounds for the people round about, saying, 'Take heed that you do not go up into the mountain or touch the border of it; who ever touches the mountain shall be put to death; no hand shall touch him, but he shall be stoned or shot; whether beast or man, he shall not live.' When the trumpet sounds a long blast, they shall come up to the mountain." So Moses went down from the mountain to the people, and consecrated the people; and they washed their garments. And he said to the people, "Be ready by the third day; do not go near a woman."

On the morning of the third day there were thunders and lightnings, and a thick cloud upon the mountain, and a very loud trumpet blast, so that all the people who were in the camp trembled. Then Moses brought the people out of the camp to meet God; and they took their stand at the foot of the mountain. And Mount Sinai was wrapped in smoke, because the LORD descended upon it in fire; and smoke of it went up like the smoke of a kiln, and the whole mountain quaked greatly. And as the sound of the trumpet grew louder and louder, Moses spoke, and God answered him in thunder. And the LORD came down upon Mount Sinai, to the top of the mountain; and the LORD called Moses to the top of the mountain, and Moses went up. And the LORD said to Moses, "Go down and warn the people, lest they break through to the LORD to gaze and many of them perish. And also let the priests who come near to the LORD consecrate themselves, lest the LORD break out upon them." And Moses said to the LORD, "The people cannot come up to Mount Sinai; for thou thyself didst charge us, saying, 'Set bounds about the mountain, and consecrate it." And the LORD said to him, "Go down, and come up bringing Aaron with you; but do not let the priests and the people break through to come up to the LORD, lest he break out against them." So Moses went down to the people and told them.

And God spoke all these words, saying, "I am the LORD your God, who brought you out of the land of Egypt, out of the house of bondage.

"You shall have no other gods before me.

"You shall not make for yourself a graven image, or any likeness of anything that is in heaven above, or that is in the earth beneath, or that is in the water under the earth; you shall not bow down to them or serve them; for I the LORD your God am a jealous God, visiting the iniquity of the fathers upon the children to the third and fourth generation of those who hate me, but showing steadfast love to thousands of those who love me and keep my commandments.

"You shall not take the name of the LORD you God in vain; for the LORD will not hold him guilt-less who takes his name in vain.

"Remember the sabbath day, to keep it holy. Six days you shall labour, and do all your work; but the seventh day is a sabbath to the LORD your God; in it you shall not do any work; you, or your son, or your daughter, your manservant, or your maidservant, or your cattle, or the sojourner who is within your gates; for in six days the LORD made heaven and earth, the sea, and all that is in them, and rested the seventh day; therefore the LORD blessed the sabbath day and hallowed it.

"Honour your father and your mother, that your days may be long in the land which the Lord your God gives you.

"You shall not kill.

"You shall not commit adultery.

"You shall not steal.

"You shall not bear false witness against your neighbour.

"You shall not covet your neighbour's house; you shall not covet your neighbour's wife, or his manservant, or his maidservant, or his ox, or his ass, or anything that is your neighbour's."

Now when all the people perceived the thunderings and the lightnings and the sound of the trumpet and the mountain smoking, the people were afraid and trembled; and they stood afar off, and said to Moses, "You speak to us, and we will hear; but let not God speak to us, lest we die." And Moses said to the people, "Do not fear; for God has come to prove you, and that the fear of him may be before your eyes, that you may not sin."

From *Hesiod, Theogony*

II, 116–153

First of all, the Void came into being, next broad-bosomed Earth, the solid and eternal home of all, and Eros [Desire], the most beautiful of the immortal gods, who in every man and every god softens the sinews and overpowers the prudent purpose of the mind. Out of Void came Darkness and black Night, and out of Night came Light and Day, her Children conceived after union in love with Darkness. Earth first produced starry Sky, equal in size with herself, to cover her on all sides. Next she produced the tall mountains, the pleasant haunts of the gods, and also gave birth to the barren waters, sea with its raging surges—all this without the passion of love. Thereafter she lay with Sky and gave birth to Ocean with its deep current, Coeus and Crius and Hyperion and Iapetus; Thea and Rhea and Themis [Law] and Mnemosyne [Memory]; also golden-crowned Phoebe and lovely Tethys. After these came cunning Cronus, the youngest and boldest of her children; and he grew to hate the father who had begotten him.

Earth also gave Birth to the violent Cyclopes—Thunderer, Lightner, and bold Flash—who made and gave to Zeus the thunder and the lightning-bolt. They were like the gods in all respects except that a single eye stood in the middle of their foreheads, and their strength and power and skill were in their hands.

There were also born to Earth and Sky three more children, big, strong, and horrible, Cottus and Briareus and Gyes. This unruly brood had a hundred monstrous hands sprouting from their shoulders, and fifty heads on top of their shoulders growing from their sturdy bodies. They had monstrous strength to match their huge size.

III, 154–210

Of all the children born of Earth and Sky these were the boldest, and their father hated them from the beginning. As each of them was about to be born, Sky would not let them reach the light of day; instead he hid them all away in the bowels of Mother Earth. Sky took pleasure in doing this evil thing. In spite of her enormous size, Earth felt the strain within her and groaned. Finally she thought of an evil and cunning stratagem. She instantly produced a new metal, gray steel, and made a huge sickle. Then she laid the matter before her children; the anguish in her heart made her speak boldly: "My children, you have a savage father; if you will listen to me, we may be able to take vengeance for his evil outrage: he was the one who started using violence."

This was what she said; but all the children were gripped by fear, and not one of them spoke a word. Then great Cronus, the cunning trickster, took courage and answered his good mother with these words: "Mother, I am willing to undertake and carry through your plan. I have no respect for our infamous father, since he was the one who started using violence."

This was what he said, and enormous Earth was very pleased. She hid him in ambush and put in his hands the sickle with jagged teeth, and instructed him fully in her plot. Huge Sky came drawing night behind him and desiring to make love; he lay on top of Earth stretched all over her. Then from his ambush his son reached out with his left hand and with his right took the huge sickle with its long jagged teeth, and quickly sheared the organs from his own father and threw them away, backward over his shoulder. But that was not the end of them. The drops of blood that spurted from them were all taken in by Mother Earth, and in the course of the revolving years she gave birth to the powerful Erinyes [Spirits of Vengeance] and the huge Giants with shining armor and long spears. As for the organs themselves, for a long time they drifted round the sea just as they were when Cronus cut them off with the steel edge and threw them from the land into the waves of the ocean; then white foam issued from the divine flesh, and in the foam a girl began to grow. First she came near to holy Cythera, then reached Cyprus, the land surrounded by sea. There she stepped out, a goddess, tender and beautiful, and round her slender feet the green grass shot up. She is called Aphrodite by gods and men, because she grew in the *froth*, and also Cytherea, because she came near to Cythera, and the Cyprian, because she was born in watery Cyprus. Eros [Desire] and beautiful Passion were her attendants both at her birth and at her first going to join the family of the gods. The rights and privileges assigned to her from the beginning and recognized by men and gods are these: to preside over the whispers and smiles and tricks which girls employ, and the sweet delight and tenderness of love.

Great Father Sky called his children the Titans, because of his feud with them: he said that they blindly had *tightened* the noose and had done a savage thing for which they would have to pay in time to come.

IV, 211–336

Night gave birth to hateful Destruction and the black Specter and Death; she also bore Sleep and the race of Dreams—all these the dark goddess Night bore without sleeping with any male. Next she gave birth to Blame and painful Grief, and also the Fates and the pitiless Specters of Vengeance: it is these goddesses who keep account of the transgressions of men and of gods, and they never let their terrible anger end till they have brought punishment down on the head of the transgressor. Deadly Night also bore Retribution to plague men, then Deceit and Love and accursed Old Age and stubborn Strife.

Hateful Strife gave birth to painful Distress and Distraction and Famine and tearful Sorrow; also Wars and Battles and Murders and Slaughters; also Feuds and Lying Words and Angry Words; also Lawlessness and Madness—two sisters that go together—and the Oath, which, sworn with willful falsehood, brings utter destruction on men. . . .

VIII, 453–506

Rhea submitted to the embraces of Cronus and bore him children with a glorious destiny: Hestia, Demeter, and Hera, who walks on golden sandals; Hades, the powerful god whose home is underground and whose heart is pitiless; Poseidon, the god whose great blows make the earth quake; and Zeus the lord of wisdom, the father of gods and men, whose thunder makes the broad earth tremble. As each of these children came out of their mother's holy womb onto her knees, great Cronus swallowed them. His purpose was to prevent the kingship of the gods from passing to another one of the august descendants of Sky; he had been told by Earth and starry Sky that he was destined to be overcome by his own son. For that reason he kept a sleepless watch and waited for his own children to be born and then swallowed them. Rhea had no rest from grief so, when she was about to give birth to Zeus, the father of gods and men, she begged her own dear parents, Earth and starry Sky, to help her contrive a plan whereby she might bear, her child without Cronus' knowing it, and make amends to the vengeful spirits of her father Sky. Earth and Sky listened to their daughter and granted her request; they told her, what was destined to happen to King Cronus and to his bold son. When she was about to give birth to great Zeus, her youngest child, they sent her to the rich Cretan town of Lyctus. Huge Mother Earth undertook to nurse and raise the infant in the broad land of Crete. Dark night was rushing on as Earth arrived there carrying him, and Lyctus was the first place where she stopped. She took him and hid him in an inaccessible cave, deep in the bowels of holy earth, in the dense woods of Mount Aegeum. Then she wrapped a huge stone in baby blankets and handed it to the royal son of Sky, who then was king of the gods. He took the stone and swallowed it into his belly—the fool! He did not know that a stone had replaced his son, who survived, unconquered and untroubled, and who was going to overcome him by force and drive him from his office and reign over the gods in his place.

The young prince grew quickly in strength and stature. After years had passed Cronus the great trickster fell victim to the cunning suggestions of Mother Earth and threw up his own children again. The first thing he vomited was the stone, the last thing he had swallowed; Zeus set it up on the highways of the earth in holy Pytho under the slopes of Parnassus, to be a sign and a wonder to mankind thereafter.

Zeus also set free his father's brothers from the cruel chains in which their father Sky had in foolish frenzy bound them. They gratefully remembered his kindness and gave him the thunder and the lightning-bolt and flash, which huge Earth had kept hidden till then. In these weapons Zeus trusts; they make him master over gods and men.

From *Hesiod, Works and Days*

106–201

If you like, I shall offer a fine and skillful summary of another tale and you ponder it in your heart: how gods and mortal men came into being from the same origin. At the very first the immortals who have their homes on Olympus made a golden race of mortal men. They existed at the time when Cronus was king in heaven, and they lived as gods with carefree hearts completely without toil or trouble. Terrible old age did not come upon them at all, but always with vigor in their hands and their feet they took joy in their banquets removed from all evils. They died as though overcome by sleep. And all good things were theirs; the fertile land of its own accord bore fruit ungrudgingly in abundance. They in harmony and in peace managed their affairs with many good things, rich in flocks and beloved of the blessed gods.

But then the earth covered over this race. Yet they inhabit the earth and are called holy spirits, who are good and ward off evils, as the protectors of mortal men, and are providers of wealth, since they keep watch over judgments and cruel deeds, wandering over the whole earth wrapped in air. For they have these royal prerogatives. Then those who have their home on Olympus next made a second race of silver, far worse than the one of gold and unlike it both physically and mentally. A child was brought up by the side of his dear mother for a hundred years, playing in his house as a mere baby. But when they grew up and reached the measure of their prime they lived for only a short time and in distress because of their senselessness. For they could not restrain their wanton arrogance against one another and they did not wish to worship the blessed immortals or sacrifice at their holy altars, as is customary and right for men. Then in his anger Zeus the son of Cronus hid them away because they did not give the blessed gods who inhabit Olympus their due. Then the earth covered over this race, too, And they dwell under the earth and are called blessed by mortals, and although second, nevertheless honor attends them also.

Father Zeus made another race of mortal men, the third, of bronze and not at all like the one of silver; terrible and mighty because of their spears of ash, they pursued the painful and violent deeds of Ares. They did not eat bread at all but were terrifying and had dauntless hearts of adamant. Great was their might, and unconquerable hands grew upon their strong limbs out of their shoulders. Of bronze were their arms, of bronze were their homes, and they worked with bronze implements. Black iron there was not. When they had been destroyed by their own hands, they went down into the dark house of chill Hades without leaving a name. Black death seized them, although they were terrifying, and they left the bright light of the sun.

But when the earth covered over this race, too, again Zeus the son of Cronus made still another, the fourth on the nourishing earth, valiant in war and more just, a godlike race of heroic men, who are called demigods, and who preceded our own race on the vast earth. Some evil war and dread battle destroyed under seven-gated Thebes in the land of Cadmus as they battled for the flocks of Oedipus; the end of death closed about others after they had been led in ships over the great depths of the sea to Troy for the sake of Helen of the beautiful hair. Some father Zeus, the son of Cronus, sent to dwell at the ends of the earth where he has them live their lives; these happy heroes inhabit the Islands of the Blessed with carefree hearts by the deep swirling stream of Ocean. For them the fruitful earth bears honey-sweet fruit that ripens three times a year. Far from the immortals Cronus rules as king over them; for the father of gods and men released him from his bonds. Honor and glory attend these last in equal measure.

Far-seeing Zeus again made still another race of men who live on the nourishing earth. Oh, would that I were not a part of the fifth generation of men, but either had died before or had been born later. Now indeed the race is of iron. For they never cease from toil and woe by day, nor from being destroyed in the night. The gods will give them difficult troubles, but good will be mingled with their evils. Zeus will destroy this race of mortal men, too, whenever it comes to pass that they are born with gray hair on their temples. And a father will not be in harmony with his children nor his children with him, nor guest with host, nor friend with friend, and a brother will not be loved as formerly. As they grow old quickly they will dishonor their parents, and they will find fault, blaming them with harsh words and not knowing respect for the gods, since their right is might. They will not sustain their aged parents in repayment for their upbringing. One will destroy the city of another. No esteem will exist for the one who is true to an oath or just or good; rather men will praise the arrogance and evil of the wicked. Justice will be might and shame will not exist. The evil man will harm the better man, speaking against him unjustly and he will swear an oath besides. Envy, shrill and ugly and with evil delight, will attend all men in their woe. Then Aidos and Nemesis both will forsake mankind and go, their beautiful forms shrouded in white, from the wide earth to Olympus among the company of the gods. For mortal men sorry griefs will be left and there will be no defense against evil.

47–105

Zeus angered in his heart hid the means of human livelihood because wily Prometheus deceived him. And so he devised for men sorrowful troubles. He hid fire. Then the good son of Iapetus, Prometheus, stole it for men from wise Zeus in a hollow reed, without Zeus who delights in thunder seeing it. But then Zeus the cloud-gatherer was roused to anger and spoke to him: "Son of Iapetus, who know how to scheme better than all others, you are pleased that you stole fire and outwitted me—a great misery for you and men who are about to be. As recompense for the fire I shall give them an evil in which all may take delight in their hearts as they embrace it."

11

Thus he spoke and the father of gods and men burst out laughing. He ordered renowned Hephaestos as quickly as possible to mix earth with water and to implant in it a human voice and strength and to fashion the beautiful and desirable form of a maiden, with a face like that of an immortal goddess. But he ordered Athena to teach her the skills of weaving at the artful loom, and golden Aphrodite to shed grace about her head and painful longing and sorrows that permeate the body. And he commanded the guide Hermes, slayer of Argus, to put in her the mind of a bitch and the character of a thief.

Thus he spoke and they obeyed their lord Zeus, son of Cronus. At once the famous lame god molded out of earth the likeness of a modest maiden according to the will of Zeus. Bright-eyed Athena clothed and arrayed her, and the Graces and mistress Persuasion adorned her with golden necklaces. The beautiful-haired Seasons crowned her with spring flowers, and Pallas Athena fitted out her body with every adornment. Then the guide and slayer of Argus contrived in her breast lies and wheedling words and a thievish nature, as loud-thundering Zeus directed. And the herald of the gods put in her a voice, and named this woman Pandora, because all who have their homes on Olympus gave her a gift, a bane to men who work for their bread.

But when the Father had completed this sheer impossible trick he sent the swift messenger of the gods, the renowned slayer of Argus, to bring it as a gift for Epimetheus [brother of Prometheus]. And Epimetheus did not think about how Prometheus had told him never to accept a gift from Olympian Zeus but to send it back in case that in some way it turned out to be evil for mortals. But he received the gift and when indeed he had the evil he realized.

Previously the races of men used to live completely free from evils and hard work and painful diseases, which hand over men to the Fates. For morals soon grow old amidst evil. But the woman removed the great cover of the jar with her hands and scattered the evils within and for men devised sorrowful troubles. And Hope alone remained within there in the unbreakable home under the edge of the jar and did not fly out of doors. For the lid of the jar stopped her, before she could, through the will of the cloud-gatherer Zeus who bears the aegis. But the other thousands of sorrows wander among men, for the earth and the sea are full of evils. Of their own accord diseases roam among men some by day, others by night bringing evils to mortals in silence, since Zeus in his wisdom took away their voice. Thus it is not at all possible to escape the will of Zeus.

The *Theogony* Also Tells the Same Story, but Concludes (IX, 589–602) as Follows:

This was the origin of the damnable race of women—a plague which men must live with. They have no place where the curse of poverty is; they belong with luxury. Just as bees in their hollow hives support mischievous drones—the bees work busily all day till sunset making the white wax, while the drones sit at home in the shade of the hive and harvest into their bellies the fruits of another's labor—so Zeus the thunder-god made women mischievous in their ways and a curse for men: he dispensed a curse to go with a blessing.

Xenophanes (fl. 540–500 B.C.)

Fragments

God is one, supreme among gods and men, not at all like mortals in body or mind. (23)
It is the whole [of God] that sees, the whole that thinks, the whole that hears. (24)
Without effort he sets everything in motion by the thoughts of his mind. (25)
He always abides in the selfsame place, not moving at all; it is not appropriate to his nature to be in different places at different times. (26)

But mortals suppose that the gods have been born, that they have voices and bodies and wear clothing like men. (14)

If oxen or lions had hands which enabled them to draw and paint pictures as men do, they would portray their gods as having bodies like their own: horses would portray them as horses, and oxen as oxen. (15)

Aethiopians have gods with snub noses and black hair, Thracians have gods with gray eyes and red hair. (16)

Homer and Hesiod attributed to the gods all sorts of actions which when done by men are disreputable and deserving of blame—such lawless deeds as theft, adultery, and mutual deception. (11)

Quite evidently the gods have not revealed everything to mortals at the outset; for mortals are obliged, in the slow course of time, to discover what is best. (18)

No man has existed, nor will exist, who has plain knowledge about the gods and the questions I discuss. For even if someone happened by chance to say what is true, he still would not know that he did so. Yet everybody thinks he knows. (34)

Thales (ca. 636–ca. 546 B.C.)

Thales' Ideas as Described by Aristotle

When people had been mocking [Thales] for his poverty, insinuating that his philosophy was of no practical use to him, he drew upon his knowledge of the heavenly bodies to predict a large olive crop, and collecting some money while it was still winter he bought up all the olive presses in Miletus and Chius, securing them by partial payments very cheaply because of the absence of competing bids. When the proper time arrived there was a sudden demand for olive presses, which he then rented out on his own terms, making large profits for himself. (*Politics* 1259a 9)

As against those who say that the earth extends downward without limit there are those who say that the earth rests upon water. This is the oldest theory that has been preserved, and it is accredited to Thales of Miletus. The earth stays in place, he explained, because it floats like wood or some such substance of a nature to let it float upon water but not upon air. As if the same problem didn't logically arise for the water supporting the earth as for the earth itself! (*De Caelo* 294a 28)

Most of those who first engaged in philosophy supposed that the only principles of things were to be found as material elements. That of which all things consist, that from which they first arise and into which they finally vanish away, that of which the "basic being" (*ousia*) persists although the perceptible characteristics are changed,—this, they say, is the prime element and first-principle of things. There in they hold that nothing either comes-to-be or is destroyed, since this kind of "basic nature" (*physis*) always persists.

As to the nature of what is fundamental, however, and even as to whether it is one or many, there was much disagreement. Thales, the founder of this type of philosophy, declared the first-principle to be water, and for that reason he also held that the earth rests upon water. Probably the idea was suggested to him by the fact that the nutriment of everything contains moisture, and that heat itself is generated out of moisture and is kept alive by it. For of course it is assumed that whatever something is generated out of must be its first-principle. He drew his notion also from the fact that the seeds of everything have a moist nature; and of course the first-principle of moist things is water.

There are some who think that men of olden times—those who, long before the present era, first began to speculate about the gods—held similar views about basic nature. For they represented

Oceanus and Tethys as the parents of creation, and the gods as swearing their oaths by the River Styx, which is to say by water, the oldest and most honorable thing by which man swears. At any rate, while it is perhaps uncertain whether or not the view in question is really so ancient and venerable) it is generally accepted that Thales explained the primary cause in this way. (*Metaphysics* 983b 7)

From the stories that are told of him it would seem that Thales conceived of soul as somehow a motive power since he said that the magnetic stone has soul in it because it sets a piece of iron in motion. (*De Anima* 40Sa 19)

Some say that soul is diffused throughout the universe; and perhaps that is what Thales meant in saying that all things are full of gods. (*ibid.* 411a 7)

Thales' ideas as described by later Greek sources:

Thales was the first to go into Egypt and bring back scientific knowledge into Greece. He discovered a number of propositions himself, and he explained to his successors the underlying principles of many others. In some cases he employed deduction from universals, in others his approach was empirical.

Eudemus in his, treatise on geometry attributed to Thales this theorem [that triangles which are equal with respect to one side and its two adjacent angles are equal in all respects]; arguing that Thales must have employed the theorem in computing, as he is said to have done, the distance of ships at sea. (Proclus, *On Euclid*)

Thales is generally regarded as the first who taught the Greeks the investigation of nature. Although he had many predecessors, as Theophrastus has remarked, he surpassed them all to such a degree that they are forgotten. He is said by some to have left no writings except his so-called nautical star-guide. (Simplicius, *Commentaria*)

Heraclitus (ca. 540–ca. 475 B.C.)

Fragments on the Idea of Universal Flux

Everything flows and nothing abides; everything gives way and nothing stays fixed. (—)
You cannot step twice into the same river, for other waters and yet others go ever flowing on. (91, 12)
Cool things become warm, the warm grows cool; the moist dries, the parched becomes moist. (126)
It is in changing that things find repose. (84a)
Time is a child moving counters in a game; the royal power is a child's. (52)
War is both father and king of all; some he has shown forth as gods and others as men, some he has made slaves and others free. (53)
It should be understood that war is the common condition, that strife is justice, and that all things come to pass through the compulsion of strife. (80)
Homer was wrong in saying, "Would that strife might perish from amongst gods and men." For if that were to occur, then all things would cease to exist. (—)

Fragments on Processes of Nature

There is exchange of all things for fire and of fire for all things, as there is of wares for gold and of gold for wares. (90)

This universe, which is the same for all, has not been made by any god or man, but it always has been, is, and will be—an ever-living fire, kindling itself by regular measures and going out by regular measures. (30)

[The, phases of fire are] craving and satiety. (65)

It throws apart and then brings together again; it advances and retires. (91)

The transformations of fire: first, sea; and of sea, half becomes earth and half the lightning-flash. (31)

When earth has melted into sea, the resultant amount is the same as there had been before sea became hardened into earth. (31, ctd.)

Fire lives in the death of earth, air in the death of fire, water in the death of air, and earth in the death of water. (76)

The thunderbolt pilots all things. (64)

The sun is new each day. (6)

The sun is the breadth of a man's foot. (3)

If there were no sun, the other stars would not suffice to prevent its being night. (99)

The boundary line of evening and morning is the Bear; and opposite the Bear is the boundary of bright Zeus. (120)

The fairest universe is but a heap of rubbish piled up at random. (124)

Every beast is driven to pasture by a blow. (11)

Heraclitus' Ideas as Described by Later Greek Sources

Heraclitus' main tenets are these. Fire is the basic element. All things are interchangeable with fire, and they come-to-be by rarefaction and condensation, but how this occurs he has not clearly explained. All things come-to-be by conflict between opposites, and the universe in its entirety flows like a river. The All is limited, constituting a single world, which is alternately born from fire and dissolved into fire, and the succession of this endless cycle of alternating periods is fixed by Destiny. That phase of the cycle which involves a coming-to-be of things is called war and strife, while that which involves destruction by fire is called concord and peace. He refers to change as the road up-down, by which the cosmos comes-to-be.

Fire by compression becomes moist, by further compression it turns into water, and then the water as it stiffens is transformed into stone. This process he calls the downward road. Then the reverse process takes place, starting with earth, which, changes into water, and so on through the other phases [of the continuous process of liquefying, evaporating, and finally bursting into flame]. This process is the upward road.

Most of the phenomena [along the upward way] he explains by reference to exhalations from the sea. But there are exhalations from the earth also; those from the sea are bright and pure, while those from the earth are dark. Fire is nourished and increased by the bright exhalations, moisture by the dark ones.

Although he does not explain clearly the nature of the surrounding medium, he does say that it contains bowls with their hollow side turned toward us, and that bright exhalations collect in these concavities, where they are vaporized into flame. The resultant phenomena are the stars. The sun's flame is the brightest and hottest of these; the other stars are farther away from the earth, which is why we receive less light and heat from them. The moon is nearer to the earth, but it has to travel in a region that is impure. The sun, on the other hand, moves in a region that is transparent and unmixed, which is why it gives us more heat and light. Eclipses of the sun and moon occur when the bowls are turned upwards. The monthly phases of the moon take place as its bowl is gradually overturned. Day and night, months, and seasons of the year are due to different exhalations. Bright exhalations, when they have been vaporized into flame in the hollow orb of the sun, produce day; when dark exhalations win mastery there is night. The former cause an increase of warmth and summer; the latter, an increase of moisture and winter. His explanations of other natural phenomena are along much the same lines. (Diogenes Laertius, IX. 8–11)

In distinguishing the two instruments by which men seek to obtain a knowledge of truth—namely, sense and reason—Heraclitus holds that the findings of sense-experience are untrustworthy, and he sets up reason as the criterion. He expresses his criticisms of sense-experience in the statement [Fr. 13]; by which he means to say that to trust the non-rational appearances of sense is to be a barbarian soul. He declares that reason (logos) is the judge of truth—not just any kind of reason, but such as is sharable and divine. The meaning of this must be briefly explained.

One of his favorite tenets as a "philosopher of nature" (physikos) is that what encompasses us is rational and intelligent. . . . According to Heraclitus it is by inbreathing the divine Reason that we become intelligent. During sleep the pores of our senses are closed, so that the mind in us is shut off from what is akin to it in the surrounding world, and its connection with other things is then preserved only at the vegetative level through the pores of the skin. Being thus cut off it loses its formative power of memory. But when we wake up again it peers out through the pores of the senses, which serve as little windows, and by thus entering into relation with what surrounds us it regains its power of reason. Just as coals when brought close to the fire undergo a change which renders them incandescent, while if moved away they become extinguished; so likewise that portion of the surrounding milieu which is making a sojourn in the body, in losing contact with its source, therein loses its rational character by the separation, inasmuch as its only communion with the outer universe now takes place through the body's very numerous pores.

Heraclitus asserts, then, that the sharable and divine Reason (logos), by participating in which we become rational, is the criterion of truth. Hence that which appears to all men as a shared experience is trustworthy, inasmuch as it is perceived by the sharable and divine Reason; but what, affects only, a single individual is, on the contrary, untrustworthy. . . . This is nothing else but an explanation of how things are ordered in the All. Therefore, in so far as we share in the memory of it we say what is true, but when we utter our own private thoughts we speak false.

In this passage and in these words, then, he most explicitly declares that the sharable Reason is the criterion: i.e., that appearances are trustworthy when they are shared in common and are judged by the sharable Reason, whereas appearances which are private to a single individual are false. (Sextus Empiricus, *Against the Logicians* I. 126–134)

Melissus (mid-5th century B.C.)

Fragments

Anything that ever was must always have been and will always be. For if it had come into being, then before its coming-to-be it must have been nothing. But if ever there was nothing it would have been impossible out of nothing for anything to arise. (1)

Well then, since what is real could not have come into being, it not only now is but always was and always will be; and since it has neither beginning nor end it is [temporally] unlimited.

If it had come-to-be, then indeed it would have both a beginning and an end—a beginning, because its coming-to-be must have occurred at one moment of time rather than another; an end, because what has come-to-be will eventually terminate. Such is not the case, however. It never began and it never will terminate, but always was and always will be, without beginning or end; for it is impossible for anything really to be unless with utter completeness. (2)

Not only must it always be [and hence be unlimited in time], it must likewise always be unlimited in magnitude. (3)

Nothing that has a beginning and end is either eternal or unlimited. (4)

If it were not one, it would be bounded by something else. (5)

If it is real it would have to be one; for if it were two, it would be bounded by something else. (6)

Accordingly it is eternal and unlimited and everywhere alike. As it cannot perish, so it cannot become larger, nor undergo change, nor suffer pain or grief. For if it suffered any such modifications it would no longer be One. If it were altered in any respect, then necessarily it would not always be like itself; which would mean that something which once was had passed away and that something which once was not had come-to-be. If in ten thousand years it were to change by even so much as a hair's breadth, it would all perish for all time.

Even any reordering of it is not possible; for the order which it once had cannot perish, nor can any new order come-to-be. Since there cannot be any increase, nor any perishing, nor any alteration, how could there be any reordering of What Is? If anything at all were to be altered it would involve alteration of the entire cosmos.

It does not suffer pain. For a thing in pain lacks full being, and does not have the same power as a healthy thing does of continuing to be. Moreover, if it were in pain it would not always be alike, for to feel pain involves the addition or removal of something, and that would destroy its homogeneity. What is healthy cannot feel pain, for pain is a destroyer of health, and hence a destroyer of being and a producer of not-being. This same reasoning applies not only to pain but to grief as well.

There cannot be any emptiness; for what is empty is nothing, and what is nothing cannot be. Accordingly What is does not move; there is nowhere to which it can go, because everything is full. If there were some emptiness a thing could move into it, but since the empty does not exist there is nowhere for a thing to go. This means that neither can the dense and the rare exist; for to be rare is to be less full than to be dense, and is therefore to be comparatively empty. The difference between what is full and what is not full is simply this. If a thing has room to receive anything else into itself, it is not full, but if it has no room to do so it is full. What Is must necessarily be full, since the empty does not exist; and since it is full everywhere it cannot move. (7)

If there existed a many, the many existing things would have to be of the same kind as the One is. For suppose there existed, just as we see and hear them, such things as earth and water, air and fire, iron and gold, living and dead, black and white, and all the other different whatnesses which we speak of as existing: then each one of these perceived phenomena would be as it first appeared to us, perpetually just as it was at the first moment, without any alteration whatever.

Now in our everyday life we assume that we see and hear and understand more or less rightly; nevertheless we believe that what is warm becomes cool and what is cool becomes warm, that soft things become hard and hard things become soft, that what is living dies and that each new living thing is born out of non-living materials—in short, that all things are changed, and that there can be a vast difference between what they formerly were and what they are now. We suppose that even something as hard as iron gets worn away a little when rubbed; and we suppose the same of gold, stone, and other things that we regard as relatively durable. We suppose, too, that earth and stone come-to-be out of water. In such ways we show our ignorance of things as they are.

Our beliefs are not even consistent with one another. Having accepted many things as eternal and as possessing forms and durabilities of their own, we still imagine that all things undergo alteration, and that they become different from what we see on any given occasion. It follows, then, that we did not see correctly after all, and that we get no true apprehension of the things we believe to be many. For if [the appearances] were real, they would not change, but each of them would have to [continue to] be exactly such as it first appeared. For nothing is stronger than what is real.

In short, if there were any change, then what was has passed away and what was-not has come-to-be. Consequently even if many things existed they would have to be of the same nature as the One. (8)

If anything is, it would have to be one. Thus if something really is, it cannot have body, for if it had body it would, consist of parts and hence would no longer be one. (9)

If Being were divided it would be in motion, and if it were in motion it would, not Be. (10)

Plato

Plato (427?–347? B.C.) was born in Athens, the son of noble parents. As the pupil and friend of Socrates (469–399 B.C.), Plato adopted his tutor's technique of conversational questioning (dialectic); indeed, it is largely through the writings of Plato that we have any records at all of Socrates, for he left no known manuscripts and perhaps expressed himself only in talk with his students. Socrates was condemned to death for alleged impiety. Probably this was one of several reasons that influenced Plato to avoid an active political career and instead to found, in 388 B.C., his Academy in Athens, where he taught mathematics and philosophy. His work there was interrupted by two abortive efforts late in life to achieve a practical realization of his political ideals in Syracuse, a Greek city-state on the island of Sicily.

Plato wrote nearly thirty works in forty years, using the dialectical method. Among his early works are the *Apology* and *Crito*, concerning Socrates, and *Ion*, an investigation of the source of poetic ability. As he began to develop his views more explicitly, Plato wrote *Phaedrus*, a treatise on rhetoric, which contains his principal notions on the contemplation of the ideal. There followed *Gorgias*, on absolute morality, and *Meno*, on the acquisition of knowledge. Other works continued to dramatize opposing arguments as in the early Socratic dialogues. *Symposium* is on the love of beauty; *Phaedo* on immortality; *The Republic* an attempt to reconcile moral theory and political practice in the concepts of the ideal of justice and the rule of philosopher-kings.

In his *Seventh Epistle* Plato says that his philosophy has never been put into words and never will be. It is, indeed, difficult to summarize Plato's philosophy, or even briefly to sketch the system of thought he created as a setting for the moral faith of his older friend Socrates. Plato's writings include some of the boldest speculation in the history of philosophy; and his theories of knowledge, of love, nature, and human destiny; his political, moral, and psychological constructions; and his doctrine of Forms—implying as it does a vision of the universe at once moral and mathematical, esthetic and rational—have stimulated, and often intoxicated, a hundred generations of thinkers. One such thinker, Alfred North Whitehead, has said, "The safest general characterization of the European philosophical tradition is that it consists of a series of footnotes to Plato."

The following selections are from *The Republic* (translated from the Greek by John Llewelyn Davies and David James Vaughan).

Book VI (Excerpt)

And you are aware, my friend, that the advocates of this latter opinion are unable to explain what they mean by insight, and are compelled at last to explain it as insight into that which is good.

Yes, they are in a ludicrous difficulty.

They certainly are: since they reproach us with ignorance of that which is good, and then speak to us the next moment as if we knew what it was. For they tell us that the chief good is insight into good, assuming that we understand their meaning, as soon as they have uttered the term "good."

It is perfectly true.

Again: are not those, whose definition identifies pleasure with good, just as much infected with error as the preceding? For they are forced to admit the existence of evil pleasures, are they not?

19

Certainly they are.

From which it follows, I should suppose, that they must admit the same thing to be both good and evil. Does it not?

Certainly it does.

Then is it not evident that this is a subject often and severely disputed?

Doubtless it is.

Once more: is it not evident, that though many persons would be ready to do and seem to do, or to possess and seem to possess, what seems just and beautiful, without really being so; yet, when you come to things good, no one is content to acquire what only seems such; on the contrary, everybody seeks the reality, and semblances are here, if nowhere else, treated with universal contempt?

Yes, that is quite evident.

This good, then, which every soul pursues, as the end of all its actions, divining its existence, but perplexed and unable to apprehend satisfactorily its nature, or to enjoy that steady confidence in relation to it, which it does enjoy in relation to other things, and therefore doomed to forfeit any advantage which it might have derived from those same things;—are we to maintain that, on a subject of such overwhelming importance, the blindness we have described is a desirable feature in the character of those best members of the state in whose hands everything is to be placed?

Most certainly not.

At any rate, if it be not known in what way just things and beautiful things come to be also good, I imagine that such things will not possess a very valuable guardian in the person of him who is ignorant on this point. And I surmise that none will know the just and the beautiful satisfactorily till he knows the good.

You are right in your surmises.

Then will not the arrangement of our constitution be perfect, provided it be overlooked by a guardian who is scientifically acquainted with these subjects?

Unquestionably it will. But pray, Socrates, do *you* assert the chief good to be science or pleasure or something different from either?

Ho, ho, my friend! I saw long ago that you would certainly not put up with the opinions of other people on these subjects.

Why, Socrates, it appears to me to be positively wrong in one who has devoted so much time to these questions, to be able to state the opinions of others, without being able to state his own.

Well, I said, do you think it right to speak with an air of information on subjects on which one is not well-informed?

Certainly not with an air of information; but I think it right to be willing to state one's opinion for what it is worth.

Well, but have you not noticed that opinions divorced from science are all ill-favoured? At the best they are blind. Or do you conceive that those who, unaided by the pure reason, entertain a correct opinion, are at all superior to blind men, who manage to keep the straight path?

Not at all superior, he replied.

Then is it your desire to contemplate objects that are ill-favoured, blind, and crooked, when it is in your power to learn from other people about bright and beautiful things?

I implore you, Socrates, cried Glaucon, not to hang back, as if you had come to the end. We shall be content even if you only discuss the subject of the chief good in the style in which you discussed justice, temperance, and the rest.

Yes, my friend, and I likewise should be thoroughly content. But I distrust my own powers, and I feel afraid that my awkward zeal will subject me to ridicule. No, my good sirs: let us put aside, for the present at any rate, all inquiry into the real nature of the chief good. For, methinks, it is beyond the measure of this our enterprize to find the way to what is, after all, only my present opinion on the subject. But I am willing to talk to you about that which appears to be an off-shoot of the chief good, and bears the strongest resemblance to it, provided it is also agreeable to you; but if it is not, I will let it alone.

Nay, tell us about it, he replied. You shall remain in our debt for an account of the parent.

I wish that *I* could pay, and you receive, the parent sum, instead of having to content ourselves with the interest springing from it. However, here I present you with the fruit and scion of the essential good. Only take care that I do not involuntarily impose upon you by handing in a forged account of this offspring.

We will take all the care we can; only proceed.

I will do so, as soon as we have come to a settlement together, and you have been reminded of certain statements made in a previous part of our conversation, and renewed before now again and again.

Pray what statements?

In the course of the discussion we have distinctly maintained the existence of a multiplicity of things that are beautiful, and good, and so on.

True, we have.

And also the existence of an essential beauty, and an essential good, and so on;—reducing all those things which before we regarded as manifold, to a single form and a single entity in each case, and addressing each as an independent being.

Just so.

And we assert that the former address themselves to the eye, and not to the pure reason; whereas the forms address themselves to the reason, and not to the eye.

Certainly.

Now with what part of ourselves do we see visible objects?

With the eyesight.

In the same way we hear sounds with the hearing, and perceive everything sensible with the other senses, do we not?

Certainly.

Then have you noticed with what transcendent costliness the architect of the senses has wrought out the faculty of seeing and being seen?

Not exactly, he replied.

Well then, look at it in this light. Is there any other kind of thing, which the ear and the voice require, to enable the one to hear, and the other to be heard, in the absence of which third thing the one will not hear, and the other will not be heard?

No, there is not.

And I believe that very few, if any, of the other senses require any such third thing. Can you mention one that does?

No, I cannot.

But do you not perceive that, in the case of vision and visible objects, there is a demand for something additional?

How so?

Why, granting that vision is seated in the eye, and that the owner of it is attempting to use it, and that colour is resident in the objects, still, unless there be present a third kind of thing, devoted to this especial purpose, you are aware that the eyesight will see nothing, and the colours will be invisible.

Pray what is the third thing to which you refer?

Of course I refer to what you call light.

You are right.

Hence it appears, that of all the pairs aforesaid, the sense of sight, and the faculty of being seen, are coupled by the noblest link, whose nature is anything but insignificant, unless light is an ignoble thing.

No, indeed; it is very far from being ignoble.

To whom, then, of the gods in heaven can you refer as the author and dispenser of this blessing? And whose light is it that enables our sight to see so excellently well, and makes visible objects appear?

There can be but one opinion on the subject, he replied: your question evidently alludes to the sun.

Then the relation subsisting between the eyesight and this deity is of the following nature, is it not?

Describe it.

Neither the sight itself, nor the eye, which is the seat of sight, can be identified with the sun.

Certainly not.

And yet, of all the organs of sensation, the eye, methinks, bears the closest resemblance to the sun.

Yes, quite so.

Further, is not the faculty which the eye possesses dispensed to it from the sun, and held by it as something adventitious?

Certainly it is.

Then is it not also true, that the sun, though not identical with sight, is nevertheless the cause of sight, and is moreover seen by its aid?

Yes, quite true.

Well then, I continued, believe that I meant the sun, when I spoke of the offspring of the chief good, begotten by it in a certain resemblance to itself,—that is to say, bearing the same relation in the visible world to sight and its objects, which the chief good bears in the intellectual world to pure reason and its objects.

How so? Be so good as to explain it to me more at length.

Are you aware, that whenever a person makes an end of looking at objects, upon which the light of day is shedding colour, and looks instead at objects coloured by the light of the moon and stars, his eyes grow dim and appear almost blind, as if they were not the sea of distinct vision?

I am fully aware of it.

But whenever the same person looks at objects on which the sun is shining, these very eyes, I believe, see clearly, and are evidently the seat of distinct vision?

Unquestionably it is so.

Just in the same way understand the condition of the soul to be as follows. Whenever it has fastened upon an object, over which truth and real existence are shining, it seizes that object by an act of reason, and knows it, and thus proves itself to be possessed of reason: but whenever it has fixed upon objects that are blent with darkness,—the world of birth and death,—then it rests in *opinion*, and its sight grows dim, as its opinions shift backwards and forwards, and it has the appearance of being destitute of reason.

True, it has.

Now, this power, which supplies the objects of real knowledge with the truth that is in them, and which renders to him who knows them the faculty of knowing them, you must consider to be the essential Form of Good, and you must regard it as the origin of science, and of truth, so far as the latter comes within the range of knowledge: and though knowledge and truth are both very beautiful things, you will be right in looking upon good as something distinct from them, and even more beautiful. And just as, in the analogous case, it is right to regard light and vision as resembling the sun, but wrong to identify them with the sun; so, in the case of science and truth, it is right to regard both of them as resembling good, but wrong to identify either of them with good; because, on the contrary, the quality of the good ought to have a still higher value set upon it.

That implies an inexpressible beauty, if it not only is the source of science and truth, but also surpasses them in beauty; for, I presume, you do not mean by it pleasure.

Hush! I exclaimed, not a word of that. But you had better examine the illustration further, as follows.
Shew me how.

I think you will admit that the sun ministers to visible objects, not only the faculty of being seen, but also their vitality, growth, and nutriment, though it is not itself equivalent to vitality.

Of course it is not.

Then admit that, in like manner, the objects of knowledge not only derive from the good the gift of being known, but are further endowed by it with a real and essential existence; though the good, far from being identical with real existence, actually transcends it in dignity and power.

Hereupon Glaucon exclaimed with a very amusing air, Good heavens! what a miraculous superiority!

Well, I said, you are the person to blame, because you compel me to state my opinions on the subject.

Nay, let me entreat you not to stop, till you have at all events gone over again your similitude of the sun, if you are leaving anything out.

Well, to say the truth, I am leaving out a great deal.

Then pray do not omit even a trifle.

I fancy I shall leave much unsaid; however, if I can help it under the circumstances, I will not intentionally make any omission.

Pray do not.

Now understand that, according to us, there are two powers reigning, one over an intellectual, and the other over a visible region and class of objects;—if I were to use the term "firmament"[1] you might think I was playing on the word. Well then, are you in possession of these as two kinds,—one visible, the other intellectual?

Yes, I am.

Suppose you take a line divided into two unequal parts,—one to represent the visible class of objects, the other the intellectual,—and divide each part again into two segments on the same scale. Then, if you make the lengths of the segments represent degrees of distinctness or indistinctness, one of the two segments of the part which stands for the visible world will represent all images:—meaning by images, first of all, shadows; and, in the next place, reflections in water, and in close-grained, smooth, bright substances, and everything of the kind, if you understand me.

---

[1] The play upon τὸ ὀρατὸυ, "the visible," and ὀύ ρανὸς, "heaven," cannot be represented in English. The meaning apparently is,—"I do not use the term ονρανὸς, lest you should suppose that I wish to connect it etymologically with ὀράω."

Yes, I do understand.

Let the other segment stand for the real objects corresponding to these images,—namely, the animals about us, and the whole world of nature and of art.

Very good.

Would you also consent to say that, with reference to this class, there is, in point of truth and untruthfulness, the same distinction between the copy and the original, that there is between what is matter of opinion and what is matter of knowledge?

Certainly I should.

Then let us proceed to consider how we must divide that part of the whole line which represents the intellectual world.

How must we do it?

Thus: one segment of it will represent what the soul is compelled to investigate by the aid of the segments of the other part, which it employs as images, starting from hypotheses, and travelling not to a first principle, but to a conclusion. The other segment will represent the objects of the soul, as it makes its way from an hypothesis to a first principle[2] which is not hypothetical, unaided by those images which the former division employs, and shaping its journey by the sole help of real essential forms.

I have not understood your description so well as I could wish.

Then we will try again. You will understand me more easily when I have made some previous observations. I think you know that the students of subjects like geometry and calculation, assume by way of materials, in each investigation, all odd and even numbers, figures, three kinds of angles, and other similar data. These things they are supposed to know, and having adopted them as hypotheses, they decline to give any account of them, either to themselves or to others, on the assumption that they are self-evident; and, making these their starting point, they proceed to travel through the remainder of the subject, and arrive at last, with perfect unanimity, at that which they have proposed as the object of investigation.

I am perfectly aware of the fact, he replied.

Then you also know that they summon to their aid visible forms, and discourse about them, though their thoughts are busy not with these forms, but with their originals, and though they discourse not with a view to the particular square and diameter which they draw, but with a view to the absolute square and the absolute diameter, and so on. For while they employ by way of images those figures and diagrams aforesaid, which again have their shadows and images in water, they are really endeavouring to behold those abstractions which a person can only see with the eye of thought.

True.

This, then, was the class of things which I called intellectual; but I said that the soul is constrained to employ hypotheses while engaged in the investigation of them,—not travelling to a first principle, (because it is unable to step out of, and mount above, its hypotheses,) but using, as images, just the copies that are presented by things below,—which copies, as compared with the originals, are vulgarly esteemed distinct and valued accordingly.

I understand you to be speaking of the subject-matter of the various branches of geometry and the kindred arts.

[2] Omitting τὸ before ἐπαρχηύ.

Again, by the second segment of the intellectual world understand me to mean all that the mere reasoning process apprehends by the force of dialectic, when it avails itself of hypotheses not as first principles, but as genuine hypotheses, that is to say, as stepping-stones and impulses, whereby it may force its way up to something that is not hypothetical, and arrive at the first principle of every thing, and seize it in its grasp; which done, it turns round, and takes hold of that which takes hold of this first principle, till at last it comes down to a conclusion, calling in the aid of no sensible object whatever, but simply employing abstract, self-subsisting forms, and terminating in the same.

I do not understand you so well as I could wish, for I believe you to be describing an arduous task; but at any rate I understand that you wish to declare distinctly, that the field of real existence and pure intellect, as contemplated by the science of dialectic, is more certain than the field investigated by what are called the arts, in which hypotheses constitute first principles, which the students are compelled, it is true, to contemplate with the mind and not with the senses; but, at the same time, as they do not come back, in the course of inquiry, to a first principle, but push on from hypothetical premises, you think that they do not exercise pure reason on the questions that engage them, although taken in connexion with a first principle these questions come within the domain of the pure reason. And I believe you apply the term understanding, not pure reason, to the mental habit of such people as geometricians,—regarding understanding as something intermediate between opinion and pure reason.

You have taken in my meaning most satisfactorily; and I beg you will accept these four mental states, as corresponding to the four segments,—namely pure reason corresponding to the highest, understanding to the second, belief to the third, and conjecture to the last; and pray arrange them in gradation, and believe them to partake of distinctness in a degree corresponding to the truth of their respective objects.

I understand you, said he. I quite agree with you, and will arrange them as you desire.

Book VII

Now then, I proceeded to say, go on to compare our natural condition, so far as education and ignorance are concerned, to a state of things like the following. Imagine a number of men living in an underground cavernous chamber, with an entrance open to the light, extending along the entire length of the cavern, in which they have been confined, from their childhood, with their legs and necks so shackled, that they are obliged to sit still and look straight forwards, because their chains render it impossible for them to turn their heads round: and imagine a bright fire burning some way off, above and behind them, and an elevated roadway passing between the fire and the prisoners, with a low wall built along it, like the screens which conjurors put up in front of their audience, and above which they exhibit their wonders.

I have it, he replied.

Also figure to yourself a number of persons walking behind this wall, and carrying with them statues of men, and images of other animals, wrought in wood and stone and all kinds of materials, together with various other articles, which overtop the wall; and, as you might expect, let some of the passers-by be talking, and others silent.

You are describing a strange scene, and strange prisoners.

They resemble us, I replied. For let me ask you, in the first place, whether persons so confined could have seen anything of themselves or of each other, beyond the shadows thrown by the fire upon the part of the cavern facing them?

Certainly not, if you suppose them to have been compelled all their lifetime to keep their heads unmoved.

And is not their knowledge of the things carried past them equally limited?

Unquestionably it is.

And if they were able to converse with one another, do you not think that they would be in the habit of giving names to the objects which they saw before them?

Doubtless they would.

Again: if their prison-house returned an echo from the part facing them, whenever one of the passers-by opened his lips, to what, let me ask you, could they refer the voice, if not to the shadow which was passing?

Unquestionably they would refer it to that.

Then surely such persons would hold the shadows of those manufactured articles to be the only realities.

Without a doubt they would.

Now consider what would happen if the course of nature brought them a release from their fetters, and a remedy for their foolishness, in the following manner. Let us suppose that one of them has been released, and compelled suddenly to stand up, and turn his neck round and walk with open eyes towards the light; and let us suppose that he goes through all these actions with pain, and that the dazzling splendour renders him incapable of discerning those objects of which he used formerly to see the shadows. What answer should you expect him to make, if some one were to tell him that in those days he was watching foolish phantoms, but that now he is somewhat nearer to reality, and is turned towards things more real, and sees more correctly; above all, if he were to point out to him the several objects that are passing by, and question him, and compel him to answer what they are? Should you not expect him to be puzzled, and to regard his old visions as truer than the objects now forced upon his notice?

Yes, much truer.

And if he were further compelled to gaze at the light itself, would not his eyes, think you, be distressed, and would he not shrink and turn away to the things which he could see distinctly, and consider them to be really clearer than the things pointed out to him?

Just so.

And if some one were to drag him violently up the rough and steep ascent from the cavern, and refuse to let him go till he had drawn him out into the light of the sun, would he not, think you, be vexed and indignant at such treatment, and on reaching the light, would he not find his eyes so dazzled by the glare as to be incapable of making out so much as one of the objects that are now called true?

Yes, he would find it so at first.

Hence, I suppose, habit will be necessary to enable him to perceive objects in that upper world. At first he will be most successful in distinguishing shadows; then he will discern the reflections of men and other things in water, and afterwards the realities; and after this he will raise his eyes to encounter the light of the moon and stars, finding it less difficult to study the heavenly bodies and the heaven itself by night, than the sun and the sun's light by day.

Doubtless.

Last of all, I imagine, he will be able to observe and contemplate the nature of the sun, not as it *appears* in water or on alien ground, but as it *is* in itself in its own territory.

Of course.

His next step will be to draw the conclusion, that the sun is the author of the seasons and the years, and the guardian of all things in the visible world, and in a manner the cause of all those things which he and his companions used to see.

Obviously, this will be his next step.

What then? When he recalls to mind his first habitation, and the wisdom of the place, and his old fellow-prisoners, do you not think he will congratulate himself on the change, and pity them?

Assuredly he will.

And if it was their practice in those days to receive honour and commendations one from another, and to give prizes to him who had the keenest eye for a passing object, and who remembered best all that used to precede and follow and accompany it, and from these data divined most ably what was going to come next, do you fancy that he will covet these prizes, and envy those who receive honour and exercise authority among them? Do you not rather imagine that he will feel what Homer describes, and wish extremely

> To drudge on the lands of a master,
> Under a portionless wight,

and be ready to go through anything, rather than entertain those opinions, and live in that fashion?

For my own part, he replied, I am quite of that opinion. I believe he would consent to go through anything rather than live in that way.

And now consider what would happen if such a man were to descend again and seat himself on his old seat? Coming so suddenly out of the sun, would he not find his eyes blinded with the gloom of the place?

Certainly, he would.

And if he were forced to deliver his opinion again, touching the shadows aforesaid, and to enter the lists against those who had always been prisoners, while his sight continued dim, and his eyes unsteady,—and if this process of initiation lasted a considerable time,—would he not be made a laughingstock, and would it not be said of him, that he had gone up only to come back again with his eyesight destroyed, and that it was not worth while even to attempt the ascent? And if any one endeavoured to set them free and carry them to the light, would they not go so far as to put him to death, if they could only manage to get him into their power?

Yes, that they would.

Now this imaginary case, my dear Glaucon, you must apply in all its parts to our former statements, by comparing the region which the eye reveals, to the prison-house, and the light of the fire therein to the power of the sun: and if, by the upward ascent and the contemplation of the upper world, you understand the mounting of the soul into the intellectual region, you will hit the tendency of my own surmises, since you desire to be told what they are; though, indeed, God only knows whether they are correct. But, be that as it may, the view which I take of the subject is to the following effect. In the world of knowledge the essential Form of Good is the limit of our inquiries, and can barely be perceived; but, when perceived, we cannot help concluding that it is in every case the source of all that is bright and beautiful,—in the visible world giving birth to light and its master, and in the intellectual world dispensing, immediately and with full authority, truth and reason;—and that whosoever would act wisely, either in private or in public, must set this Form of Good before his eyes.

To the best of my power, said he, I quite agree with you.

That being the case, I continued, pray agree with me on another point, and do not be surprised, that those who have climbed so high are unwilling to take a part in the affairs of men, because their souls are ever loath to desert that upper region. For how could it be otherwise, if the preceding simile is indeed a correct representation of their case?

True, it could scarcely be otherwise.

Well: do you think it a marvellous thing, that a person, who has just quitted the contemplation of divine objects for the study of human infirmities, should betray awkwardness, and appear very ridiculous, when with his sight still dazed, and before he has become sufficiently habituated to the darkness that reigns around, he finds himself compelled to contend in courts of law, or elsewhere, about the shadows of justice, or images which throw the shadows, and to enter the lists in questions involving the arbitrary suppositions entertained by those who have never yet had a glimpse of the essential features of justice?

No, it is anything but marvellous.

Right: for a sensible man will recollect that the eyes may be confused in two distinct ways and from two distinct causes,—that is to say, by sudden transitions either from light to darkness, or from darkness to light. And, believing the same idea to be applicable to the soul, whenever such a person sees a case in which the mind is perplexed and unable to distinguish objects, he will not laugh irrationally, but he will examine whether it has just quitted a brighter life, and has been blinded by the novelty of darkness, or whether it has come from the depths of ignorance into a more brilliant life, and has been dazzled by the unusual splendour; and not till then will he congratulate the one upon its life and condition, and compassionate the other; and if he chooses to laugh at it, such laughter will be less ridiculous than that which is raised at the expense of the soul that has descended from the light of a higher region.

You speak with great judgment.

Hence, if this be true, we cannot avoid adopting the belief, that the real nature of education is at variance with the account given of it by certain of its professors, who pretend, I believe, to infuse into the mind a knowledge of which it was destitute, just as sight might be instilled into blinded eyes.

True; such are their pretensions.

Whereas, our present argument shews us that there is a faculty residing in the soul of each person, and an instrument enabling each of us to learn; and that, just as we might suppose it to be impossible to turn the eye round from darkness to light without turning the whole body, so must this faculty, or this instrument, be wheeled round, in company with the entire soul, from the perishing world, until it be enabled to endure the contemplation of the real world and the brightest part thereof, which, according to us, is the Form of Good. Am I not right?

You are.

Hence, I continued, this very process of revolution must give rise to an art, teaching in what way the change will most easily and most effectually be brought about. Its object will not be to generate in the person the power of seeing. On the contrary, it assumes that he possesses it, though he is turned in a wrong direction, and does not look towards the right quarter; and its aim is to remedy this defect.

So it would appear.

Hence, while, on the one hand, the other so-called virtues of the soul seem to resemble those of the body, inasmuch as they really do not pre-exist in the soul, but are formed in it in the course of time by habit and exercise; the virtue of wisdom, on the other hand, does most certainly appertain, as it would appear, to a more divine substance, which never loses its energy, but by change of position becomes useful and serviceable, or else remains useless and injurious. For you must, ere this, have noticed how keen-sighted are the puny souls of those who have the reputation of being clever but vicious, and how sharply they see through the things to which they are directed, thus proving that their powers of vision are by no means feeble, though they have been compelled to become the servants of wickedness, so that the more sharply they see, the more numerous are the evils which they work.

Yes, indeed it is the case.

But, I proceeded, if from earliest childhood these characters had been shorn and stripped of those leaden, earthborn weights, which grow and cling to the pleasures of eating and gluttonous enjoyments of a similar nature, and keep the eye of the soul turned upon the things below;—if, I repeat, they had been released from these snares, and turned round to look at objects that are true, then these very same souls of these very same men would have had as keen an eye for such pursuits as they actually have for those in which they are now engaged.

Yes, probably it would be so.

Once more: is it not also probable, or rather is it not a necessary corollary to our previous remarks, that neither those who are uneducated and ignorant of truth, nor those who are suffered to linger over their education all their life, can ever be competent overseers of a state,—the former because they have no single mark in life, which they are to constitute the end and aim of all their conduct both in private and in public; the latter, because they will not act without compulsion, fancying that, while yet alive, they have been translated to the islands of the blest.

That is true.

It is, therefore, our task, I continued, to constrain the noblest characters in our colony to arrive at that science which we formerly pronounced the highest, and to set eyes upon the good, and to mount that ascent we spoke of; and, when they have mounted and looked long enough, we must take care to refuse them that liberty which is at present permitted them.

Pray what is that?

The liberty of staying where they are, and refusing to descend again to those prisoners, or partake of their toils and honours, be they mean or be they exalted.

Then are we to do them a wrong, and make them live a life that is worse than the one within their reach?

You have again forgotten, my friend, that law does not ask itself how some one class in a state is to live extraordinarily well. On the contrary, it tries to bring about this result in the entire state; for which purpose it links the citizens together by persuasion and by constraint, makes them share with one another the benefit which each individual can contribute to the common weal, and does actually create men of this exalted character in the state, not with the intention of letting them go each on his own way, but with the intention of turning them to account in its plans for the consolidation of the state.

True, he replied; I had forgotten.

Therefore reflect, Glaucon, that far from wronging the future philosophers of our state, we shall only be treating them with strict justice, if we put them under the additional obligation of watching over their fellow-citizens, and taking care of them. We shall say; It is with good reason that your compeers elsewhere refuse to share in the labours of their respective states. For they take root in a city spontaneously, in defiance of the prevailing constitution; and it is but fair that a self-sown plant, which is indebted to no one for support, should have no inclination to pay to anybody wages for attendance. But in your case, it is we that have begotten you for the state as well as for yourselves, to be like leaders and kings of a hive,—better and more perfectly trained than the rest, and more capable of playing a part in both modes of life. You must therefore descend by turns, and associate with the rest of the community, and you must habituate yourselves to the contemplation of these obscure objects. For, when habituated, you will see a thousand times better than the residents, and you will recognize what each image is, and what is its original, because you have seen the realities of which beautiful and just and good things are copies. And in this way you and we shall find that the life of the state is a substances, and not a phantom like the life of our present states, which are mostly composed of men who fight among themselves for shadows, and are at feud for the administration of affairs, which they regard as a great boon. Whereas I conceive the truth stands thus: That city in which the destined rulers are least eager to rule, will inevitably be governed in the best and least factious manner, and a contrary result will ensue if the rulers are of a contrary disposition.

Plato on Contemporary Society

A good way to approach the *Republic* itself is to consider the actual types of Greek constitution of which Plato took account when he wrote it. These he deals with in Book VIII (Part IX in this edition), where he lists them as Timarchy, Oligarchy, Democracy, and Tyranny. The type of society which Plato calls timarchy is one which has no real parallel in modern experience, because it is, as he explicitly tells us, a sketch of the essential features of Spartan society. But for Plato Sparta was very important indeed, and some of the features of his own ideal society are borrowed from it. The Spartans were, briefly, a military aristocracy living among a subject population, the 'helots'. These helots were peasant serfs, cultivating the land for their Spartan masters; they could be called on to serve as light-armed troops in war, and might occasionally win their freedom, but in general they had neither rights nor privileges. Each year the magistrates declared war on them, so that to kill a Helot was an act of war and not of murder; and the Spartan secret police watched constantly for disaffection and killed mercilessly when they found it.

It was largely because they were a minority living thus in a subject population, which they always feared would revolt and which on several occasions did, that the Spartans followed their peculiar way of life. They were a military caste, in which the individual was rigidly subordinated to the community. Each citizen was a soldier, and education, marriage, and the details of daily life were all strictly regulated with a view to the maintenance of perfect military efficiency. 'When a child was born it was submitted to the inspection of the heads of the tribe, and if they judged it to be unhealthy or weak, it was exposed to die on the slopes of Mount Taygetos. At the age of seven years, the boy was consigned to the care of a state-officer, and the course of his education was entirely determined by the purpose of inuring him to bear hardships, training him to endure an exacting discipline, and instilling into his heart a sentiment of devotion to the State. The boys, up to the age of twenty, were marshalled in a huge school formed in the model of an army.' Here they were under the instruction of young men aged twenty to thirty, who were not yet of age to be admitted to full citizenship. At twenty they entered on military service and were permitted to marry; but they must still live in barracks, and could only pay fugitive and stolen visits to their wives. At thirty they became full citizens, but though they might live at home, they must still dine together in common messes, to which each made a fixed contribution from the 'lot' which each Spartan owned, which he might not alienate, and which was cultivated for him by his helot serfs. 'Spartan discipline extended itself to women too . . .

The girls, in common with the boys, went through a gymnastic training; and it was not considered immodest for them to practise their exercises almost nude. They enjoyed a freedom which was in marked contrast with the seclusion of women in other Greek states. They had a high repute for chastity; but if the government directed them to breed children for the State, they had no scruples in obeying the command, though it should involve a violation of the sanctity of the marriage-tie.'

No Spartan was allowed to possess wealth in the form of gold or silver, and they continued to use a clumsy iron coinage. Private luxury was forbidden, and Spartan simplicity was proverbial. The individual was entirely lost in the State; he had no life, no problems of his own. He lived in a camp, under military discipline, ready at any moment to fight for his country. It was not surprising that the Spartans were the most efficient soldiers in Greece, though they were not an aggressive people, but notoriously difficult to provoke to war.

These are the features of the Spartan system most relevant to a reader of the *Republic*. Its constitutional arrangements—a unique combination of hereditary kingship, popular election and magistrates, and council of elders—are comparatively unimportant, save perhaps in the respect paid to age and experience; membership of the Council was restricted to those over sixty, and in the *Republic* the status of full Guardianship cannot be reached till fifty. The Spartan system had many admirers in Greece; it had a completeness and aesthetic simplicity which appealed to the Greek mind, and made many Greeks admire it, though few would have wished to live under it. But if they admired they also criticized, and the criticisms Plato makes of timarchy are typical. He criticizes its exploitation of the lowest class as a wrong relation between ruler and ruled, liable to lead to serious disunity. He criticizes its intellectual limitations; Spartans thought little, and were proverbially slow-witted. They were also, in spite of their system, notoriously avaricious; and so timarchy is criticized for the institution of private property, forbidden in the ideal state, and the consequent growth of private greed. The Spartan and the timarchic society, in short, have the merits of discipline, respect for law, and courage, but are stupid, greedy, and brutal to their less privileged classes. Plato may to some extent have shared the admiration often felt by other Greeks for Sparta; but he was well aware of Spartan limitations.

The Spartan system was without parallel, except in Crete. But the other three types of social system which Plato mentions were common; indeed, one may generalize and say that in the fifth and fourth centuries BC the Greek cities were either democracies or oligarchies, interspersed here and there with tyrannies. During the Peloponnesian War the oligarchies had, on the whole, sided with Sparta, the democracies with Athens. And party differences, always acute in Greece, had been exacerbated by the suspicion that the other party was in league with the enemy. The suspicion was often justified, for both democrat and oligarch habitually put party first; and Plato's references to a party getting help against its opponents from outside (cf. 556e) and his deep horror of faction and disunity are a reflection of the bitterness of party strife, of which Thucydides has left the classic description. 'Both sides claimed to have the good of the community at heart, while both in fact aimed at political control, and in their struggle for ascendancy indulged in the worst excesses.'

To Plato an oligarchy was a society in which power and prestige went with wealth; and since the wealthy are normally few, where power goes with wealth political control is in the hands of a minority.

The days of hereditary aristocracy were long over, and though there were of course old families in most states (like Plato's own at Athens), birth had had to come to terms with wealth and, by itself, was, at the most, of limited political influence. So though Plato's characterization of oligarchy may be an over-simplification, it is not an unfair generalization to say that oligarchy in his day meant control by a wealthy minority. It was the controlling influence given to wealth that Plato particularly disliked. He had the deepest distrust of what would today be called the profit-motive and of the political influence of private wealth; and he thought that in an oligarchy (an 'acquisitive society') you were bound to get increasing exploitation of poor by rich, and an increasing degree of social maladjustment and disunity in consequence. He draws a picture of growing oppression met by growing bitterness and ending in revolution.

In his account of democracy Plato is drawing on his own experiences at Athens. And it is important to remember what a democracy in fifth- and fourth-century Greece was like. The Greeks lived in city-states, small communities consisting of a 'city' nucleus, with an area of agricultural land attached, from which the urban population drew all or most of its food-supply. The populations varied in size, but were all small by the standards of a modern city. The population of Athens when Plato was born was perhaps 200–300,000, including men, women, and slaves; and Athens was by Greek standards large. In a democracy the vote was confined to the adult male citizen population. At Athens slaves may have numbered some 60–80,000, and there were perhaps 35–40,000 'metics', that is, residents who because they had been born elsewhere did not qualify for citizenship. The total voting population was about 35–45,000. But within this body of voting citizens popular control was complete; for the Greeks never invented representative government, and the sovereign body at Athens was the Assembly, a mass meeting of all adult male citizens. Of course not all citizens bothered to attend regularly, and some whose homes were outside Athens itself found it difficult to do so. But in theory all could attend, and both in theory and in practice the Assembly was the sovereign body by which all political decisions must be taken. It was not practicable for it to meet too often (in theory it met ten times a year; in practice a good deal more often, though probably never more than once a week); and to carry on the business of state between meetings, to deal with much routine and financial business, and above all to draft business for meetings of the Assembly there was a Council of Five Hundred. This further sub-divided itself into Committees of fifty, each of which was responsible for carrying on public business during one-tenth of the year. But important as the Council's functions were, its powers were in practice limited by the rule that it should be chosen by lot from the citizen body, that membership was limited to one year, and that no citizen might hold membership more than twice. The Council thus never became a continuing body with a policy of its own: the Assembly remained supreme. Finally, the law-courts also were in popular control. Nearly all cases were tried before panels of jurors drawn by a system of mixed lot and election from the citizen body; and before these panels the magistrates could be tried for any irregularities committed during their year of office.

Such a complete system of popular control has never been known before or since. And it is important to remember that this, and not any form of modern representative government, is the background to Plato's comments on democracy. Its workings in fifth-century Athens and the criticisms then made of it have already been mentioned. It involved, said Thucydides, 'committing the conduct of state affairs to the whims of the multitude', and it has been described by a modern writer as government by perpetual plebiscite. But wide as the differences of background are, it would be quite wrong to dismiss Plato's criticisms of democracy as having no relevance today. If we are tempted to do so, we may perhaps remind ourselves that this is the first generation since his when a political leader can address and be seen by the whole electorate. What the ultimate effects of television will be we cannot yet say. But they have certainly brought political leaders far closer to the ordinary citizen, and opened up opportunities of a direct approach to the whole electorate that did not exist before in modern society.

What then are Plato's criticisms in the *Republic*? If we look first at the similes of the ship's captain (488*a*–*e*) and the large and powerful animal (493*b*–*e*), they seem to be twofold. First, that the people are bad judges in many political matters. The common man has no experience or expert knowledge of such things as foreign policy or economics, and to expect any very sensible judgment from him on such matters is to expect the impossible. He will judge on impulse, sentiment or prejudice, and though his heart may be sound (and Plato would have doubted whether even this was always true) his head will be muddled. This drawback might perhaps be overcome by good leadership. But here we come to the second criticism, that democracy encourages bad leadership. The people's judgement of their leaders is not always good, and they can't be trusted to make the best choice. But quite apart from that, the popular leader, dependent as he is for his position (and perhaps his income) on popular favour, will constantly be tempted to retain that favour by the easiest possible means. He will play on the likes and dislikes, the weaknesses and foibles of the public, will never tell them an unpleasant truth or advocate a policy that might make them uncomfortable. Like the modern advertiser and salesman, he is dependent on his public, and his position depends on selling them comfort and not telling them the truth. Sophist, salesman, and popular politician are on a par, and the people care little who their leaders are provided they 'profess themselves the people's friends' (558*c*). Popular leaders are as devoid of true knowledge as are the people they lead.

But that is not the whole story. The salient characteristic of democracy, we learn in Book VIII, is liberty—'every individual is free to do as he likes' (557*b*). This gives democratic society a diversity and variety that are very attractive, but its effect is extremely disintegrating. There is a growing dislike of any authority, political or moral; fathers pander to their sons, teachers to their pupils, 'and the minds of the citizens become so sensitive that the least vestige of restraint is resented as intolerable' (563*d*). Where there is so little social cohesion dissension inevitably grows. Politically, it takes the form of a struggle between rich and poor which finally degenerates into class-war. The poor have no use for the rich except to squeeze taxes out of them; the rich retaliate, and 'the freedom which the democrat claims will be a freedom of the *two nations,* the rich and the poor, to fight it out between themselves who shall have the larger slice of the cake.' Morally, it leads to greater and greater permissiveness; and Plato's description of a permissive society in Book VIII (562*b* ff.) has a particularly sharp-edged vividness.

There remains tyranny. Plato describes it as arising out of the chaos and dissension into which democracy degenerates; and though he would probably not have wished to maintain that this was an invariable rule, yet some tyrants, ancient and modern, have certainly started as popular leaders, and extreme social disunity may by reaction produce an extreme authoritarianism. Of Plato's treatment of tyranny three things may be said. (1) For him tyranny is essentially a personal rule. The tyrant needs followers, of course, and at a fairly early stage in his career he secures a 'personal body-guard', a private army bound to him by ties of common interest and guilt. But the basis of his power is a personal one; he is the Leader, and his rule is essentially the exercise of his own personal preferences, the arbitrary rule of an individual. (2) Tyranny has a peculiar self-destructiveness. The tyrant can brook no rival, which means that prominent personalities among his followers must be eliminated; anyone who can or will stand up to him will be swept away. And he needs constant wars, external crises, to distract attention from his internal misrule; which is another source of strain. (3) The tyrant is essentially what we should call a criminal type: the beginning of Book IX (571a) is an analysis of the similarity of the tyrant and the criminal, who are said to combine the characteristics of drunkard, sex-maniac, and madman. The tyrant, with his 'master passion', is barely sane, and his life is one of criminal indulgence. Fielding had the same thought in *Jonathan Wild*.

There is little need to comment on this analysis. The dominance of a dictator's personality, his private army, the purges among his followers are familiar. We might comment that his private life need not always be as wildly dissolute as Plato suggests; he is more formidable, though not necessarily less criminal or violent if it is not. But we still associate autocracy with repression and violence.

The purpose of this section has been to show, by reviewing Plato's analysis of contemporary forms of society, what he thought the major social evils of his time were; for it was to combat those evils that his own proposals were put forward. We may summarize as follows. In timarchy (Sparta) Plato saw two major evils. The evil of a split community in which one section exploits and holds down the remainder by force; and the evil of lack of intelligence—the Spartan might have many good qualities but he simply had not the intellectual capacity to know what he was doing; indeed he mistrusted the intellect and everything to do with it. In oligarchy the cardinal fault is desire for wealth (a fault which was already apparent in timarchy). Wealth as a social motive is to be mistrusted, and a ruling class which is devoted to its wealth, and which owes its position and power to wealth, will substitute exploitation for government. In democracy there is a radical lack of cohesion, because there is no proper respect for authority, moral or political. Democratic government is weak government, which plays on the weaknesses of the common man instead of giving him the leadership he needs; and it is liable to degenerate into a bitter class-struggle between haves and have-nots. Finally, in tyranny we see the danger that the violent and criminal instincts, normally kept under control, will get out of hand. The criminal is present in all societies (certainly in oligarchy and democracy); but in tyranny he has come into his own, and society is run by its criminal elements with the arch-criminal in charge. We may briefly sum up by saying that disunity, incompetence and violence, which he had seen at Athens and at Syracuse, were the main dangers against which Plato thought society must be protected.

Society and Politics

What Plato has to say on these topics can conveniently be considered under three headings: the Class System, Property and the Family, and the Philosopher Ruler.

The Class System

Plato arrives at this from the principle that in any society men will group themselves according to their occupations. In the economic sphere you will get producers, merchants, traders and so on. The economic structure of the society of which he was thinking, and in which he lived, is elementary; and he is thinking of occupations and not income-groups. But the principle is clear enough. He goes on to apply it in the sphere of war and government. The armies of Greece in the fifth century were citizen-armies; but the fourth century saw the rise of the professional soldier, and that may, in part, have suggested to Plato that his Guardians, who first appear as a military group, should be specialists in war. But it soon appears that they are to perform the functions not only of soldiering but also of government, and they are sub-divided into Rulers proper and Auxiliaries, who correspond, roughly, to Government and Army—Executive—Police (opening note to Part IV, section I), as opposed to the rest of the population, who make up the third class. Plato's three classes in fact are not so much three as two, one of which is further sub-divided.

Many object at once to this division of society into three distinct classes, with a definite order of subordination between them. The words 'hierarchic society' or 'caste system' are used to describe it disapprovingly. Plato might reply that the quarrel is to some extent about words. Any society, he might say, is bound to show economic groupings; few societies can do without their professional army; and in all societies someone has to give orders and someone obey, which means that in practice there will be a minority of people issuing orders or seeing they are obeyed (the government) and a majority obeying them (the rest). What people differ about is whether and to what extent these primary groupings should be complicated by further class-divisions based on birth or wealth, and how the governmental minority should in fact be chosen. To Plato's views on these last two topics, which are what the objectors really dislike, we shall return. Meanwhile it is important to see just what his three classes and their mutual relations are.

About his third class he does not tell us a great deal. They are not in any sense a proletariat or working class. They comprise all those engaged in economic activities—farmers, manufacturers, traders, rich or poor (for they are allowed to own property). Their function is to provide for the material and economic needs of the community. Their virtue is obedience, and it is pretty clear that they will be under strict control. The Guardians will see that there is no excessive wealth and poverty among them (422a), and will presumably direct and control all their activities. For they are the body of the governed whom the governing minority administers.

The governing minority, the Guardians, discharge between them, primarily, the functions of government and army. But that is, as already indicated, too narrowly imprecise a description. The function of the Rulers is to govern, that is to say, to take all those decisions of policy which it is the business of government to take. The Auxiliaries' function is 'to assist the Rulers in the execution of their decisions', or 'to enforce the decisions of the Rulers' (414b). We must think of them as combining the functions of civil service, military and police; as being, that is, charged with the execution and implementation (if necessary by force) of government decisions. And if we think of a society in which there is a government by full-time, trained experts, who are precluded by law from any other function, and who have a body of trained civil servants, together with the necessary police and military forces to assist them, we get some idea in modern terms of this part of Plato's proposals.

The two top classes are, as we have seen, really sub-divisions of a single class. They share the same way of life, and are put through the same elaborate system of training and promotion outlined in Part VII. There are a large number of promotion bars to be passed, quite enough to grade the Auxiliaries for their various functions, while leaving a small homogeneous Ruler class to emerge at the top; but all have started with equal opportunities. The third class have no say in matters of government; but Plato constantly emphasizes that the Rulers have their interests at heart (the difference between timarchy and the ideal is that in timarchy oppression has replaced benevolent government) and the Rulers govern with the willing consent of the governed (431e). This relationship is set out in the Foundation Myth (415a–c).

Two further criticisms may be considered here. First, Aristotle's criticism that we are not in fact told nearly enough about the third class. And although Plato is deliberate in his avoidance of detail, it is difficult not to agree that the criticism is just. There are too many essential questions left unanswered. The second criticism is that Plato's Guardians are a 'hereditary caste'. The critic, of course, assumes that this, if true, is itself a condemnation. But his interpretation is wrong. Plato emphatically asserts (415c) that promotion from the third class is not only possible but an important feature of his scheme, just as demotion from the two upper classes is also; and in Book VIII we are told that it is failure in this matter that leads to the change to timarchy. It is, of course, extremely hard to see how the scheme is to work, as Aristotle again remarks. Cornford suggests that all classes must share a common education up to the age of eighteen, in order that the Rulers can promote and demote; certainly the choice would have to be made by then, and this would be one way of making it, and would be in tune with Plato's views on the importance of education. But there is nothing in the text to suggest it, and we cannot speak with certainty. There is, however, no reason to doubt that Plato means what he says about promotion and demotion (see note on promotion, demotion and infanticide in Part VI, section 2). The real point is that what he wants is an aristocracy of talent. He thinks, as we shall see, that he can get this largely by breeding, as one breeds race-horses; but the breeding process is not infallible, and so there must be provision for both promotion and demotion, there must be both snakes and ladders, even though we don't know exactly what the rules are to be. Belief in an aristocracy of talent may be wicked; but it is not the same as belief in a hereditary caste.

The Philosopher Ruler

The Philosopher Ruler is the central theme of the *Republic*; it is the aim of its whole educational curriculum to produce him, and much that has already been said has dealt with him directly or by implication. At the end of the long course of training there is left a small class (how large we are not told) of those who have survived all tests and mastered the whole curriculum; they are the Philosopher Rulers. They represent the highest talent, are given the highest training and are put at the disposal of the state. They do not serve the state because they want to, they are philosophers who have seen the supreme vision and would prefer to spend their time in philosophy. But they have a duty to their fellow-men, and that they discharge by doing the work of government for which their training has fitted them; they are a dedicated minority ruling in the interests of all.

There is a perennial attraction in this conception of the highest talent put at the disposal of the community, of the ruler whose heart is in heaven dedicating himself to the service of society. We should respect Plato's vision, but not forget its dangers. We may ask first, on the plane of a humdrum realism, whether the long course of abstract studies which Plato proposes is really the best training for dealing with men and affairs; and whether the method of selection he proposes, based largely on proficiency in abstract subjects—examinations in mathematics, science and philosophy up to the age of thirty-five—is a sensible one. Is not this one of the fallacies to which educators are prone—the belief that people who do well in their courses will do well at everything, and that the longer they spend on them the better they will do? Is not a wider curriculum and a lot more practical experience more likely to produce a better ruler?

More important is the objection that government by a self-perpetuating minority of experts is in any case undesirable, and in particular 'undemocratic'. We have seen that recruits for the course which begins at the age of twenty are drawn from all the classes, though the vast majority of them come from the top two, because they are bred for the job. They are chosen by the Rulers on their merits: there is no question of democratic election, because, as we have seen, Plato thought that as bad a way of choosing rulers as choosing them by their wealth. And before we dismiss Plato's scheme out of hand, we should remember the methods we use today for picking people for administrative and managerial training, the tests of character and ability applied by the Civil Service Commissioners, for example, and reflect that those are the modern parallels to what he proposes. He is concerned to pick people for their competence for the job, and not for characteristics, such as wealth or persuasiveness, that have no necessary connection with that competence. Indeed he might well, at this point, put some questions to us. He would remind us that society today is infinitely more complicated than it was in his day. He would ask us how we think this increasingly complicated structure is to be administered if not by men and women who have the character and competence needed. He could then point out that the amount of ability available in any community is limited, and perhaps quote modern statistics in support of this. And if men are not equal in talent and abilities, surely no society can afford to work on the assumption that they are, least of all modern society. Must we not do our best to ensure that the available talent is most profitably employed, that differences of talent are recognized and the highest talent put to the best use? 'Which brings you back,' he might conclude, 'to the philosopher ruler.' For, as we have seen, what Plato wanted was an aristocracy of talent, and we must see the principles behind his detail. And if we want a modern brief description of his kind of society, 'Managerial Meritocracy' is perhaps the nearest we can get; it emphasizes the need for qualifications and competence in government, though it leaves out many of the other elements in the Platonic solution.

More fatal is the objection that the conception of a philosopher ruler encourages us to look for a degree of knowledge and integrity which are in fact not to be found. The knowledge of all human beings is limited, and for any group of them to think that they have the key to all human problems is presumptuous and absurd. But that is what the philosopher ruler is supposed to have; and certain types of doctrinaire are liable to a similar illusion. Yet to put the government of human affairs into the hands of any class of supposed experts is to ask from them more than they can possibly give. And quite apart from limitations of knowledge, there is the moral problem. Power is a corrupting influence, a corruption which few can resist; and on the whole political leaders are not men of more than average moral integrity—we are perhaps lucky if they are as good as that. It is better to act on that assumption, and to limit power lest it should be abused, than to look for the perfect ruler who needs no such limitation. The argument against Plato's system, in fact, is not that it trusts the common man too little but that it trusts his rulers too much.

Book IV: Part V
Justice in State and Individual

I. Justice in the State

The State which we have founded must possess the four 'cardinal virtues' of wisdom, courage, discipline, and justice. (Plato does not call them 'virtues', and the translation therefore uses the more neutral term 'qualities'.) It will have wisdom because of the knowledge possessed by the Rulers, courage because of the courage of the Auxiliaries, and self-discipline because of the harmony between all three Classes and their common agreement 'about who ought to rule'. Finally, justice is the principle which has in fact been followed throughout, the principle of one man one job, of 'minding one's own business', in the sense of doing the job for which one is naturally fitted and not interfering with other people.

[427]*d*   'Well, we seem to have got your city founded for you, Adeimantus,' I said. 'Now you must look at it and get your brother and Polemarchus and the rest of them to see if they can help you throw enough light on it for us to see where justice and injustice are to be found, how they differ from each other, and which of them anyone who is to be happy needs, irrespective of whether gods or men think he has it or not.'

  'Nonsense, Socrates,' said Glaucon. 'You promised to deal with the problem yourself, because
e you said it would be wicked for you not to give justice all the support of which you were capable.'

  'That's true,' I said; 'I remember. I must do as I said, but you must all help.'

  'Yes, we will,' he said.

  'I think we shall probably find what we want as follows. If we have founded it properly, our state is presumably perfect.'

  'It must be.'

  'Then it will obviously have the qualities of wisdom, courage, self-discipline, and justice.'

  'Obviously.'

  'Then if we can identify some of these qualities in it, the ones that are left will be the ones we are still looking for.'

428 *a*   'Yes.'

  'So suppose us to be looking first for one of any four things. If we find it, well and good. But if we find the other three before it, by so doing we have in effect identified the object of our search, which must obviously be the one left over.'

  'That's true.'

  'Should we not therefore follow this method in the present case, where again there are four things at issue?'

  'Obviously.'

b   'The first of the four that I can see clearly is wisdom, and there is one odd feature about it.'

'What?' he asked.

'The state we have described seems to me to be genuinely wise. For its judgement is good, isn't it?'

'Yes.'

'And the quality of good judgement is clearly a form of knowledge, as it is because of knowledge and not because of ignorance that we judge well.'

'Clearly.'

'But there are many different kinds of knowledge in our city.'

'Of course there are.'

'And do we say it has wisdom and judgement because of the knowledge of its carpenters?'

'Certainly not—that merely makes it good at carpentry.'   c

'So it's not called wise because of its knowledge of woodwork and the excellence of its designs?'

'No.'

'The same is presumably true of bronze and other materials.'

'The same is true,' he said.

'And I expect you would agree that knowledge of farming merely makes it good at agriculture.'

'Yes.'

'Well then,' I said, 'is there any form of knowledge to be found among any of the citizens in the state we've just founded which is exercised not on behalf of any particular interest but on behalf of the city as a whole, in such a way as to benefit the state both in its internal and external relations?'   d

'There is.'

'What is it, and where shall we find it?' I asked.

'It is the Guardians' knowledge,' he answered, 'and is to be found with those we called Guardians in the full sense.'

'And how do you describe the state because of it?'

'I say it has good judgement and wisdom.'

'And do you think that there will be more metal-workers in our state or Guardians in this sense?'   e

'Many more metal-workers,' he said.

'Won't the Guardians, in fact, be far fewer in number than any other group with special knowledge and name?'

'Yes.'

'So the state founded on natural principles is wise as a whole in virtue of the knowledge inherent in its smallest constituent part or class, which exercises authority over the rest. And it appears further that the naturally smallest class is the one which is endowed with that form of knowledge   429 a
which alone of all others deserves the title of wisdom.'

'That is all perfectly true,' he agreed.

'Well, then, we have somehow or other managed to find this one of our four qualities and its place in our society.'

'And as far as I'm concerned I'm quite satisfied with our findings,' he said.

'And it's not very difficult,' I went on, 'to see courage and the place of courage, which makes us call our state brave.'

'Tell me how.'

b   We shall say it's brave or cowardly with sole reference to the part which defends it and campaigns for it.'

'That is all that we need refer to.'

'Because I don't think that members of other classes have the power, by being cowardly or brave, to make the state one or the other.'

'No, they haven't.'

'Our city is therefore brave too in virtue of a part of itself. That part retains in all circumstances

c the power to judge, on the basis laid down by our lawgiver in its education, what and what sort of things are to be feared. For that, I take it, is what you mean by courage.'

'I didn't quite understand what you said,' he answered; 'say it again.'

'I say,' I replied, 'that courage is a sort of safe-keeping.'

'What sort?'

'The sort that will *safely keep* the opinion inculcated by the established education about what

d things and what kind of things are to be feared. And by retaining it in *all circumstances* I meant retaining it safely, without losing it in pleasure or pain, desire or fear. If you like, I'll give you an analogy.'

'Yes, do.'

'Well, take dyeing,' I said. 'You know that, when they want to dye wool purple, they are very particular about the natural colour of the material, which must be white; they then subject it to an elaborate process in order to prepare it to take the dye before they actually dip it. And the colour of anything

e dyed by this process remains fast, and the dye won't come out if you wash the material, whether you use soap or not; but if they start with wool of any other colour or don't give it this treatment— well, you know what happens to it.'

'Yes—the colour washes out and it looks silly,' he said.

'Assume, then,' I said, 'that this was the sort of result we were doing our best to achieve in choos-

430 *a* ing our soldier-class, and in educating them physically and mentally. Our whole object was to steep them in the spirit of our laws like a dye, so that nature and nurture might combine to fix in them indelibly their convictions about what is dangerous, and about all other topics, and prevent them being washed out by those most powerful detergents, pleasure, so much more effective than soap and

b soda, and pain and fear and desire, the most effective of all. This kind of ability to retain safely in all circumstances a judgement about what is to be feared, which is correct and in accord with law, is what I propose to call courage, unless you have any alternative to suggest.'

'No,' he replied, 'I haven't. For I imagine that you would not regard mere uninstructed judgement, such as an animal or slave might have on these matters, as being in accordance with law, even if right, and that you would use some other name for it.'

c 'You are quite right,' I said.

'Then I accept your description of courage.'

'Accept it as a description of the ordinary citizen's courage, and you won't be far wrong,' I replied; 'we will go into it more fully later, if you like. For the moment it's justice not courage we are looking for, and for this purpose I think the description's adequate.'

'That is fair enough.'

d 'Well, we are left with two qualities to look for in our state,' I said, 'self-discipline and the real object of our whole inquiry, justice.'

'Yes, we are.'

'I wonder if we could find justice without having to bother further about self-discipline.'

'Personally,' he said, 'I don't know, and I shouldn't want to find it, if it meant we were to give up looking for self-discipline. What I should like you to do is to look for self-discipline first.'

'And it would be wrong to refuse you,' I said.   *e*

'Then carry on,' he said.

'I will,' I replied, 'At first sight, self-discipline looks more like some sort of harmony or concord than the other virtues did.'

'In what way?'

'Self-discipline,' I said, 'is surely a kind of order, a control of certain desires and appetites. So people use "being master of oneself" (whatever that means) and similar phrases as indications of it. Isn't that so?'

'Certainly.'

'But "master of oneself" is an absurd phrase. For if you're master *of* yourself you're presumably also subject *to* yourself, and so *both* master *and* subject. For there is only one person in question   431 *a* throughout.'

'Undoubtedly.'

'What the expression is intended to mean, I think, is that there is a better and a worse element in the personality of each individual, and that when the naturally better element controls the worse then the man is said to be "master of himself", as a term of praise. But when (as a result of bad upbring-   *b* ing or bad company) the smaller forces of one's better element are overpowered by the numerical superiority of one's worse, then one is adversely criticized and said not to be master of oneself and to be in a state of indiscipline.'

'Which is quite reasonable.'

'Then look at our newly founded state,' I said, 'and you will find the first of these descriptions applies to it. For you will admit that it is right to call it master of itself, if we speak of self-discipline and self-mastery where the better part rules the worse.'

'Yes, I see; that's quite true.'

'And, what is more, the greatest number and variety of desires and pleasures and pains is gener-   *c* ally to be found in children and women and slaves, and in the less respectable majority of so-called free men.'

'Certainly.'

'While the simple and moderate desires, guided by reason and right judgement and reflection, are to be found in a minority who have the best natural gifts and best education.'

'True.'

'This feature too you can see in our state, where the desires of the less respectable majority are   *d* controlled by the desires and the wisdom of the superior minority.'

'Yes, I can see that.'

'And so if any city is to be said to be master of its pleasures and desires, and of itself, ours must be.'

'That is certainly true.'

'Then on all these counts we can surely say it is self-disciplined.'

'We can indeed,' he said.

e 'And of our state, if of any, it will be true that government and subjects will agree about who ought to rule. Or don't you think so?'

'I'm quite sure of it,' he said.

'In these circumstances, of which class do you think discipline is characteristic, rulers or subjects?'

'Of both, I suppose,' he replied.

'So you can see how right we were to guess just now that self-discipline was like a kind of concord.'

'Why?'

432 a 'Because, unlike courage and wisdom, which made our state brave and wise by being present in a particular part of it, self-discipline stretches across the whole scale. It produces a harmony between its strongest and weakest and middle elements, whether you measure by the standard of intelligence, or of strength, or of numbers or money or the like. And so we are quite justified in regarding self-discipline as this unanimity in which there is a natural concordance between higher and lower about which of them is to rule in state and individual.'

'I entirely agree.'

b 'Good,' said I; 'it looks as if we had spotted three of the qualities we are looking for in our state. What about the fourth of them, to which it will owe another form of excellence? It must obviously be justice.'

'Obviously.'

'Then we must stand like hunters round a covert and make sure that justice does not escape us

c and disappear from view. It must be somewhere about. Try and see if you can catch sight of it before I can, and tell me where it is.'

'I wish I could,' he said. 'All you can reasonably expect of me is to follow your lead and see things when you point them out.'

'Then follow me and hope for the best.'

'I will,' he said; 'lead on.'

'It looks to me,' I said, 'as if we were in a pretty impassable and obscure spot; it's certainly dark and difficult to find a way through. But we must push on all the same.'

d 'Yes, we must,' he agreed.

I cast about a bit and then cried, 'Tally ho, Glaucon! I think we are on the track, and our quarry won't altogether escape us.'

'That's good news.'

'We really are being a bit slow.'

'In what way?'

'Our quarry is lurking right under our feet all the time, and we haven't seen it but have been

e making perfect fools of ourselves. We are like people searching for something they have in their hands all the time; we're looking away into the distance instead of at the thing we want, which is probably why we haven't found it.'

'How do you mean?'

'I mean that it seems to me that we have failed to understand that we have in a sort of way been talking about it all through our discussion.'

'You are a long time leading up to what you've got to say; I'm getting impatient.'

'Well then, listen, and see if you think I'm talking sense. I believe justice is the requirement we   433 *a*
laid down at the beginning as of universal application when we founded our state, or else some particular form of it. We laid down, if you remember, and have often repeated, that in our state one
man was to do one job, the job he was naturally most suited for.'

'Yes, we did.'

'And further, we have often heard it said and often said ourselves that justice consists in minding   *b*
your own business and not interfering with other people.'

'Yes.'

'So perhaps justice is, in a certain sense, just this minding one's own business. Do you know my
grounds for so thinking?'

'No; what are they?'

'Because I think that the quality left over, now that we have discussed discipline, courage and
wisdom, must be what makes it possible for them to come into being in our state and preserves
them by its continued presence when they have done so. And we agreed that it would be justice   *c*
that was left over if we found the other three.'

'It must be.'

'Now, if we were asked to judge which of these qualities by its presence contributed most to the
goodness of our state, we should find it a difficult decision to make. Is it the agreement between rulers
and subjects? Is it the retention by our soldiers of a law-abiding judgement about what is and is not
to be feared? Is it the wisdom and watchfulness of our Guardians? Or is the greatest contribution to
its excellence made by the quality which makes each individual—child or woman, slave, free man   *d*
or artisan, ruler or subject—get on with his own job and not interfere with other people?'

'A difficult decision, I agree.'

'At any rate, wisdom, discipline, courage, and the ability to mind one's own business are all rivals
in this respect. And we can regard justice as making a contribution to the excellence of our city that   *e*
rivals that of the rest.'

'Yes, certainly.'

'Look at it again this way. I assume that you will make it the duty of our rulers to administer
justice?'

'Of course.'

'And won't they try to follow the principle that men should not take other people's belongings or
be deprived of their own?'

'Yes, they're bound to.'

'Their reason presumably being that it is *just*.'

'Yes.'

'So we reach again by another route the conclusion that justice is keeping what is properly one's   434 *a*
own and doing one's own job.'

'That is true.'

'There's another point on which I should like your agreement. Suppose a builder and a shoemaker tried to exchange jobs, or to take on the tools and the prestige of each other's trade, or suppose

alternatively the same man tried to do both jobs, would this and other exchanges of the kind do great harm to the state?'

'Not much.'

b   'But if someone who belongs by nature to the class of artisans and businessmen is puffed up by wealth or popular support or physical strength or any similar quality, and tries to enter our military class; or if one of our military Auxiliaries tries to get into the class of administering Guardians for which he is unfit, and they exchange tools and prestige; or if a single individual tries to do all these jobs at the same time—well, I think you'll agree that this sort of mutual interchange and interference spells destruction to our state.'

'Certainly.'

c   'Interference by the three classes with each other's jobs, and interchange of jobs between them, therefore, does the greatest harm to our state, and we are entirely justified in calling it the worst of evils.'

'Absolutely justified.'

'But will you not agree that the worst of evils for one's own community is injustice?'

'Of course.'

'So that is what injustice is. And conversely, when each of our three classes (businessmen, Auxiliaries, and Guardians) does its own job and minds its own business, that, by contrast, is justice and makes our state just.'

d   'I entirely agree with what you say,' he said.

'Don't let's be too emphatic about it yet,' I replied. 'If we find that the same pattern applies to the individual and is agreed to yield justice in him, we can finally accept it—there will be nothing to prevent us; if not, we shall have to think again. For the moment let us finish our investigation.'

2. The Elements in Mental Conflict

Plato starts by reasserting the parallel between state (society) and individual; 'since the qualities of a community are those of the component individuals, we may expect to find three corresponding elements in the individual soul. All three will be present in every soul; but the structure of society is based on the fact that they are developed to different degrees in different types of character.' After a warning that in what follows we must not expect too much philosophic precision, Plato proceeds to examine the conflict of motives in the individual, and concludes that we cannot, without contradiction, assume the existence of less than three types of motive or impulse in the mind. First there is reason, the faculty that calculates and decides: second there is desire or appetite, in the sense of bare physical and instinctive craving. There is also a third type of motive, covering such characteristics as pugnacity, enterprise, ambition, indignation, which are often found in conflict with unthinking impulse.

This is often referred to as Plato's doctrine of 'the three parts of the soul'. Two main questions arise in understanding it: (1) To what extent and in what sense does Plato think of separate 'parts' of the soul or mind? In the present passage the words he uses most commonly (eidos, genos) mean 'kinds', 'types', 'forms', though he does on occasion use the Greek word for part (meros); the words ('element', 'constituent') used in the translation are intended to be indeterminate.

Elsewhere Plato sometimes speaks as if the soul or mind had three distinct parts, as in the Phaedrus *and* Timaeus, *sometimes as if there were a single stream of mental energy manifesting itself in different activities, as in the* Symposium. *We perhaps do well, first, to remember that he has warned us that he is not speaking with scientific precision, but rather on the level of ordinary conversation; and, second, to bear in mind that he is concerned with morals and not with psychology, with a general classification of the main motives or impulses to action, rather than a scientific analysis of the mind. He is, in fact, probably always conscious that in speaking of 'parts' ('elements' or what not) of the soul he is using a metaphor. (2) What exactly are the three 'elements' that Plato describes? There is little difficulty with two of them. By 'appetite' Plato means the purely instinctive desires in their simplest form; it is easy enough, on a common-sense level, to recognize them. 'Reason' includes not only the ability to understand and to think before we act, the faculty of calculation and foresight, but also the ability to make up one's mind, the faculty of decision. The third element at first appears more miscellaneous, including, as we have seen, such qualities as indignation, courage, determination, spirit, and so on. Two illustrations may help us to understand it. First the distinction, still commonly made, between 'heart' and 'head'. When we make that distinction we do not include under 'heart' the mere animal instincts; we perhaps include more of the 'feelings' than Plato, but our meaning is not far from his second 'part of the soul'. (In the* Timaeus *reason is located in the head, 'spirit' in the breast, i.e. heart, and appetite in the belly.) Second, when Butler analysed the motives of moral action he found them threefold. Conscience, a rational faculty capable of judgement and having authority; particular passions, like hunger and thirst; and 'self-love', or, as we might call it today, the 'self-regarding instinct', or perhaps the instinct of self-preservation and self-assertion. Each of these two analyses recognizes a rational, controlling, authoritative part of the mind; each recognizes animal instinct; but each also recognizes a third element, one which is not easy to define, but which is perhaps most comprehensively described as self-regard, and which ranges from self-assertion, through self-respect, to our relations with others (Butler coupled 'self-love' and 'benevolence') and our concern for our reputation and good name.*

Plato uses two words, thumos *and* thumoeides, *for this element in the mind. Neither is easy to translate. I have used 'anger', 'indignation', 'spirit' as seemed to suit the context best.*

'We thought it would be easier to see justice in the individual if we looked for it first in some larger field which also contained it. We thought this larger field was the state, and so we set about founding an ideal state, being sure we should find justice in it because it was good. Let us therefore transfer our findings to the individual, and if they fit him, well and good; on the other hand, if we find justice in the individual is something different, we will return to the state and test our new definition. So by the friction of comparison we may strike a spark which will illuminate justice for us, and once we see it clearly we can fix it firmly in our own minds.' *e*

'That is the right method; let us follow it,' he said. *435 a*

'Then when we apply the same term to two things, one large and the other small, will they not be similar in respect of that to which the common term is applied?'

'Yes.'

'So there will be no difference between a just man and a just city, so far as the element of justice goes.' *b*

'None.'

'But we agreed that a state was just when its three natural constituents were each doing their job, and that it was self-disciplined and brave and wise in virtue of certain other states and dispositions of those constituents.'

'That is so,' he said.

c 'Well, then, my dear Glaucon,' I continued, 'we shall expect to find that the individual has the same three elements in his personality and to be justified in using the same language of him because he is affected by the same conditions.'

'That must follow.'

'Another nice little inquiry we've tumbled into!' I exclaimed. 'Has the personality these three constituents or not?'

'I shouldn't call it a little inquiry,' he said; 'but it's probably true enough, Socrates, that, as the saying goes, anything that's worth while is difficult.'

d 'So it seems. And I must tell you that in my opinion we shall never find an exact answer by the method of argument we are using in our present discussion—to get one we should have to go much further afield but we can probably find one that will be satisfactory by the standards we have so far used in our inquiry.'

'That's good enough,' he replied; 'at any rate, it would suit me for the present.'

'And it will be quite enough for me.'

'Then press on with the investigation.'

e 'Well, we are bound to admit that the elements and traits that belong to a state must also exist in the individuals that compose it. There is nowhere else for them to come from. It would be absurd to suppose that the vigour and energy for which northern people like the Thracians and Scythians have
436 a a reputation aren't due to their individual citizens; and similarly with intelligence, which can be said to be the main attribute of our own part of the world, or with the commercial instinct which one connects particularly with the Phoenicians and Egyptians.'

'That's perfectly true.'

'Here, then, we have a fact which is not particularly difficult to recognize.'

'Not at all difficult.'

'What is difficult is to see whether we perform all these functions with the same part of us, or
b each with a different part. Do we learn with one part of us, feel angry with another, and desire the pleasures of eating and sex and the like with another? Or do we employ our mind as a whole when our energies are employed in any of these ways? These are questions it's difficult to answer satisfactorily.'

'I agree,' he said.

Aristotle

(384–322 B.C.)

Whitehead regarded the whole European philosophical tradition as a series of footnotes to Plato, but Aristotle has been almost equally influential. Aristotle was Plato's pupil at the Academy for some years (366–347), but eventually, after a period as tutor to Philip of Macedon's son, Alexander, he returned to Athens and founded his own school, the Lyceum. In many ways Plato and Aristotle held similar philosophical views: neither was a sceptic, i.e. for both of them a real knowledge of a real universe was possible; for both the universe was ordered and had a design; for both the human soul was different from and more excellent than any other living being; both were very interested in the social and political life of their times. However, in other ways they were radically different, notably in their views on what reality is (metaphysics) and on how we acquire true knowledge (epistemology). The difference might be expressed in the following way.

Plato had inherited a problem. Parmenides had seen that what can be said to exist must have some stable and recognisable identity, which he took to imply that to *be* is to be *unchanging*. Heraclitus, on the other hand, had seen that the world we live in and experience is in a constant state of flux. The conclusion appears to be that we cannot know reality and that the world of the senses is unreal. Plato tried to solve this problem by making the changing, perceptible world a sort of imperfect reflection of an unchanging, intelligible world (the world of Forms or Ideas); true knowledge is of the world of Forms—of Man, for example, rather than of the individual man; but since the individual man fleetingly reflects the Form of Man, we do thus gain, not knowledge, but opinion, about the individual.

For Aristotle this view was mistaken. It placed the substantial reality of natural things outside the things themselves; it turned universal or common forms into super-individuals; and it made natural science impossible, for science deals with change, and there is, on Plato's theory, no knowledge of the changing. In fact, it made the world of change inexplicable.

In the first of the following passages, from the *Metaphysics*,[1] Aristotle shows that the knowledge of the form which each individual thing embodies arises in the mind not from our turning our attention away from the perceptible individual thing, but from reflection upon a class of similar individuals that we have experienced through the senses. In the second passage, from the *Categories*,[2] we find Aristotle insisting that the true reality (substance) is the individual; only in a secondary sense can the species *man* be regarded as a reality.

These contrasting metaphysical and epistemological doctrines will reappear later in the course, in the writings of thinkers influenced by classical philosophy, e.g. Augustine (Platonic), Aquinas (Aristotelean).

---

[1] Selection reprinted from J.A. Smith and W.D. Ross, eds., *The Works of Aristotle Translated into English,* Vol VIII, *Metaphysics.* (Oxford: The Clarendon Press, 1908), Book I (A) 980a 1.2l-981b 1.13.

[2] Selections reprinted from W.D. Ross, ed., E. M. Edgehill, trans., *The Works of Aristotle Translated into English,* Vol I, *Categories,* (Oxford: The Clarendon Press, 1928) 4: lb 1.25–2a 1.4; 5: 2a, 11.11–18, 2a, 1.33–2b 1.5, 3b 11.10–19, 4a 11.10–21.

Aristotle also wrote a number of works on natural science, for example biology, psychology and astronomy. The English title of the book from which the third selection is taken, *Physics*,[3] comes from the Greek word *physis* which means 'nature' (derived from *phyo*, meaning 'to grow'). In this selection Aristotle is discussing his doctrine of causation. He finds four types of cause: material, formal, efficient and final. In the fourth selection, taken from his work *On the Generation of Animals (de generatione animalium)*,[4] Aristotle's ideas about biological differences between male and female in the context of reproduction are set out.

Note: The word 'art' in the passage from the Metaphysics is a translation of the Greek *technē*, and it does not mean fine or literary art. Rather, it signifies the expertise, based on experience, which is involved in any *doing* (as in the practice of medicine, flute playing or government) or *making* (as in house building or painting a picture), when the practitioner possesses an insight into the general principle of what he is doing.

From *Metaphysics*

All men by nature desire to know. An indication of this is the delight we take in our senses; for even apart from their usefulness they are loved for themselves; and above all others the sense of sight. For not only with a view to action, but even when we are not going to do anything, we prefer sight to almost everything else. The reason is that this, most of all the senses, makes us know and brings to light many differences between things.

By nature animals are born with the faculty of sensation, and from sensation memory is produced in some of them, though not in others. And therefore the former are more intelligent and apt at learning than those which cannot remember; those which are incapable of hearing sounds are intelligent though they cannot be taught, e.g. the bee, and any other race of animals that may be like it; and those which besides memory have this sense of hearing, can be taught.

The animals other than man live by appearances and memories, and have but little of connected experience; but the human race lives also by art and reasonings. And from memory experience is produced in men; for many memories of the same thing produce finally the capacity for a single experience. Experience is almost identified with science and art, but really science and art come to men through experience; for 'experience made art', as Polus says, and rightly, 'but inexperience luck'. And art arises, when from many notions gained by experience one universal judgement about a class of objects is produced. For to have a judgement that when Callias was ill of this disease this did him good, and similarly in the case of Socrates and in many individual cases, is a matter of experience; but to judge that it has done good to all persons of a certain constitution, marked off in one class, when they were ill of this disease, e.g. to phlegmatic or bilious people when burning with fever,—this is a matter of art.

With a view to action experience seems in no respect inferior to art, and we even see men of experience succeeding more than those who have theory without experience. The reason is that experience is knowledge of individuals, art of universals, and actions and productions are all concerned with the individual; for the physician does not cure man, except in an incidental way, but Callias or Socrates or some other called by some such individual name, who happens to be a man. If, then, a man has the theory without the experience, and knows the universal but does not know the individual included in this, he will often fail to cure; for it is the individual that is to be cured. But yet we

[3] Selection from Aristotle's Physics, Book II, 3: 194b–165a: 7: 198a–198b, translated for this collection.

[4] Selection from A.L. Peck, trans., *Aristotle: Generation of Animals*, (London: Heinemann; and Cambridge, Mass.,: Harvard UP, 1963), pp. 91–93, 97, 101–103, 109, 173–175, 185, 459–461.

think that knowledge and understanding belong to art rather than to experience, and we suppose artists to be wiser than men of experience (which implies that Wisdom depends in all cases rather on knowledge); and this because the former know the cause, but the latter do not. For men of experience know that the thing is so, but do not know why, while the others know the 'why' and the cause. Hence we think that the master-workers in each craft are more honourable and know in a truer sense and are wiser than the manual workers, because they know the causes of the things that are done [we think the manual workers are like certain lifeless things which act indeed, but act without knowing what they do, as fire burns,—but while the lifeless things perform each of their functions by a natural tendency, the labourers perform them through habit]; thus we view them as being wiser not in virtue of being able to act, but of having the theory for themselves and knowing the causes. And in general it is a sign of the man who knows, that he can teach, and therefore we think art more truly knowledge than experience is; for artists can teach, and men of mere experience cannot.

Again, we do not regard any of the senses as Wisdom; yet surely these give the most authoritative knowledge of perticulars. But they do not tell us the 'why' of anything—e.g. why fire is hot; they only say that it is hot.

From *Categories*

Expressions which are in no way composite signify substance, quantity, quality, relation, place, time, position, state, action, or affection. To sketch my meaning roughly, examples of substance are 'man' or 'the horse'; of quantity, such terms as 'two cubits long;' of quality, such attributes as 'white,' 'grammatical'. 'Double,' 'half,' 'greater,' fall under the category of relation; 'in the market place,' 'in the Lyceum,' under that of place; 'yesterday,' 'last year,' under that of time. 'Lying,' 'sitting,' are terms indicating position; 'shod,' 'armed,' state; 'to lance,' 'to cauterize,' action; 'to be lanced,' 'to be cauterized,' affection. . . .

Substance, in the truest and primary and most definite sense of the word, is that which is neither predicable of a subject nor present in a subject; for instance, the individual man or horse. But in a secondary sense those things are called substances within which, as species, the primary substances are included; also those which, as genera, include the species. For instance, the individual man is included in the species 'man', and the genus to which the species belongs is 'animal'; these, therefore—that is to say, the species 'man' and the genus 'animal'—are termed secondary substances. . . .

Everything except primary substances is either predicable of a primary substance or present in a primary substance. This becomes evident by reference to particular instances which occur. 'Animal' is predicated of the species 'man,' therefore of the individual man, for if there were no individual man of whom it could be predicated, it could not be predicated of the species 'man' at all. Again, colour is present in body, therefore in individual bodies, for if there were no individual body in which it was present, it could not be present in body at all. Thus everything except primary substances is either predicated of primary substances, or is present in them, and if these last did not exist, it would be impossible for anything else to exist. . . .

All substance appears to signify that which is individual. In the case of primary substance this is indisputably true, for the thing is a unit. In the case of secondary substances, when we speak, for instance, of 'man' or 'animal', our form of speech gives the impression that we are here also indicating that which is individual, but the impression is not strictly true; for a secondary substance is not an individual, but a class with a certain qualification; for it is not one and single as a primary substance is; the words 'man', 'animal', are predicable of more than one subject. . . .

The most distinctive mark of substance appears to be that, while remaining numerically one and the same, it is capable of admitting contrary qualities. From among things other than substance, we should find ourselves unable to bring forward any which possessed this mark. Thus, one and the same colour cannot be white and black. Nor can the same one action be good and bad: this law holds good with everything that is not substance. But one and the self same substance, while retaining its identity, is yet capable of admitting contrary qualities. The same individual person is at one time white, at another black, at one time warm, at another cold, at one time good, at another bad.

From *Physics*

Book II

3. Now that we have established these distinctions, we must proceed to consider causes, and see what the various kinds of cause are and how many they are. Since knowledge is the object of our inquiry and since we do not think we know a thing until we can say why it is as it is—which in fact means grasping its (primary or proximate) cause—plainly we must try to achieve this with regard to coming-to-be and perishing and every kind of physical or natural change, in order that we may know what their principles are and may refer to these principles everything into which we inquire.

In one sense, what is described as a cause is that out of which a thing comes into being and that which remains present in it. Such, for instance, is bronze in the case of a statue, or silver in the case of a bowl, as well as the genera of which these materials, bronze and silver, are species.

In another sense, the form or the pattern, that is the statement of the essence, and its genera, are called causes; such, for example, in the case of the octave, are the ratio of two to one and, in general, number. The parts of the statement are a cause in this sense, too.

Thirdly, there is the proximate source of the change or the coming to rest: the adviser, for example, is a cause; the father is the cause of his child; and, in general, what produces is the cause of what is produced, and what does the changing is the cause of what is changed.

Fourthly, something is a cause insofar as it is an end, or the purpose for the sake of which a thing is done. In this sense, health, for example, is the cause of a man's going for a walk. "Why," someone asks, "is he going for a walk?" "For the good of his health," we reply, and, having said that, we think we have given the cause of his doing so. All the intermediate things, too, that are brought about through the agency of something else as means towards this same end have this as their cause: slimming, purging, drugs, and surgical instruments—all have the same purpose, health, as their cause, although they differ from one another in that some of them are activities, others instruments.

These are pretty well all the senses in which we use the term 'cause'. As the word has several senses it follows that there are many causes of the same thing, without any of them being accidental causes. Both the art of the sculptor and the bronze, for example, are causes of the statue. These are cause of the statue *qua* statue, not in virtue of anything else it may be [e.g. a gift]. They are, however, causes in different ways, the one being its matter or material cause, the other the source of the movement that produced it. Some things cause each other reciprocally; for example, hard work is a cause of fitness, and fitness is a cause of hard work; but again, they are not causes in the same way; the latter is an end, the former is a source of movement or change. Further, the same thing will be the cause of two contrary results. For that which by its presence brings about one result is sometimes blamed for bringing about the contrary by its absence. For instance, we describe the absence of the pilot as the cause of the ship's being wrecked, whereas his presence would have been the cause of its preservation.

But all the causes that we have just mentioned fall into the four most obvious groups. The letters of a syllable, the raw material of an article, fire and such things in bodies, the parts of a whole, and the premises of a syllogism—all these are causes in the sense of being what a thing comes from; but whereas the first of each pair is a cause in the sense of being a substratum (the parts of a whole, for example), the second of each pair is a cause by virtue of being a thing's essence: the whole, the combination, and the form. But the seed, the doctor, the adviser, and the producer, in general, are all sources of change or rest. Other things are causes by virtue of being the end and the good of everything else. For being the purpose, or 'that for the sake of which' means being the best of things and the end or goal of the things that lead up to it—and let us take it that it makes no difference whether we speak of the real or the apparent good.

7. It is clear, then, that there are causes, and that the number of them is what we have stated; for they correspond to the different ways in which we can answer the question "why?" The ultimate answer to that question can be reduced to saying what the thing is (as, for example, in mathematics, where any question ultimately leads to the definition of the straight or the commensurate or something else); or to saying what initiated a motion (if, for example, one is asked why certain people went to war, one replies, "Because they were raided") or to naming the purpose ('so that they could rule," for example); or, in the case of things that come into being, to naming the matter.

Clearly, then, these are the causes, and this is the number of them. Since there are four causes, it is the business of the natural scientist to know about them all, and he will give his answer to the question "why?" in the manner proper to his science if he refers what is being asked about to them all—to the matter, the form, the mover, and the purpose. The last three of these often coincide; for the essence and the purpose are one; and the proximate source of movement is of the same kind—for man generates man, and this is so in general with things that cause movement or change in other things by being moved themselves. Things that are not moved themselves are not the concern of natural science: for such things, without having any movement or any sources of movement in themselves, cause movement although remaining unmoved themselves. Hence there are three branches of study: one is concerned with things which are incapable of movement, the second with things that are in movement but are imperishable, and the third with perishable things.

Thus, the answer to the question "why?" is to be given by referring to the matter, the essence (or form), and to the proximate mover. In cases of coming-to-be it is mostly in this last way that people examine the causes; they ask what comes to be after what, what was the immediate thing that acted or was acted upon, and so on in order. The causes that move things in a physical or natural way are twofold; but of these, one is not a physical cause, since it has no principle of motion in itself (i.e., it has no capacity of being itself moved). A thing is in this position if it moves something else without being moved itself. This is the case with what is completely immovable and unchangeable and the first of all things. It is also the case with the essence or shape of that which is coming-to-be, since this is at the same time the end and purpose, or 'that for the sake of which'. Thus, since nature has a purpose, we must know this cause also. So, we must give our answer to the question "why?" in all these ways, namely (1) that from this, that must result (which will be either universally or usually true); (2) that if this is going to be so, there must also be that (just as there must be premises for a conclusion to come from); (3) that this is the thing's essence; and (4) that it is so because it is better so—not in any absolute sense, but with reference to the substance of whatever is in question.

From *On the Generation of Animals*
(De Generatione Animalium)

1. (726ᵇ) Semen is pretty certainly a residue from that nourishment which is in the form of blood and which, as being the final form of nourishment, is distributed to the various parts of the body. This, of course, is the reason why semen has great potency - the loss of it from the system is just as exhausting as the loss of pure healthy blood. . . .

2. Now (i) the weaker creature too must of necessity produce a residue, greater in amount and less thoroughly concocted; and (ii) this, if such is its character, must of necessity be a volume of bloodlike fluid. (iii) That which by nature has a smaller share of heat is weaker; and (iv) the female answers to this description. . . .

3. (727ᵃ) Now it is impossible that any creature should produce two seminal secretions at once, and as the secretion in females which answers to semen in males is the menstrual fluid, it obviously follows that the female does not contribute any semen to generation; for if there were semen, there would be no menstrual fluid; but as menstrual fluid is in fact formed, therefore there is no semen. . . .

4. (727ᵇ) By now it is plain that the contribution which the female makes to generation is the *matter* used therein, that this is to be found in the substance constituting the menstrual fluid, and finally that the menstrual fluid is a residue. (728a) . . . A woman is as it were an infertile male; the female, in fact, is female on account of inability of a sort, viz., it lacks the power to concoct semen out of the final state of nourishment . . . because of the coldness of its nature. . . .

5. (729ᵃ) The male provides the 'form' and the 'principle of the movement', the female provides the body, in other words, the material. Compare the coagulation of milk. Here, the milk is the body, and the fig-juice or the rennet contains the principle which causes it to set. . . .

6. 737ᵃ) When the semen has entered the uterus it 'sets' the residue produced by the female and imparts to it the same movement with which it is itself endowed. The female's contribution, of course, is a residue too,. . . and contains all the parts of the body *potentially*, though none in *actuality;* and 'all' includes those parts which distinguish the two sexes. Just as it sometimes happens that deformed offspring are produced by deformed parents, and sometimes not, so the off-spring produced by a female are sometimes female, sometimes not, but male. The reason is that the female is as it were a deformed male; and the menstrual discharge is semen, though in an impure condition; i.e. it lacks one constituent, and one only, the principle of Soul.

7. (738ᵇ) An animal is a living body, a body with Soul in it. The female always provides the material, the male provides that which fashions the material into shape; this, in our view, is the specific characteristic of each of the sexes: that is what it means to be male or female. Hence, necessity requires that the female should provide the physical part, i.e. a quantity of material, but not that the male should do so, since necessity does not require that the tools should reside in the product that is being made, not that the agent which uses them should do so. Thus the physical part, the body, comes from the female, and the Soul from the male, since the Soul is the essence of a particular body.

8. (775ᵃ) Once birth has taken place everything reaches its perfection sooner in females than in males—e.g. puberty, maturity, old age—because females are weaker and colder in their nature; and we should look upon the female state as being as it were a deformity, though one which occurs in the ordinary course of nature. While it is within the mother, then, it develops slowly on account of its coldness, since development is a sort of concoction, concoction is effected by heat, and if a thing is hotter its concoction is easy; when, however, it is free from the mother, on account of its weakness it quickly approaches its maturity and old age, since inferior things all reach their end more quickly.

From *Nicomachean Ethics*

I, 1. Every art or applied science and every systematic investigation, and similarly every action and choice, seem to aim at some good; the good, therefore, has been well defined as that at which all things aim. . . .

Since there are many activities, arts, and sciences, the number of ends is correspondingly large: of medicine the end is health, of shipbuilding a vessel, of strategy, victory, and of household management, wealth. In many instances several such pursuits are grouped together under a single capacity: the art of bridle-making, for example, and everything else pertaining to the equipment of a horse are grouped together under horsemanship; horsemanship in turn, along with every other military action, is grouped together under strategy; and other pursuits are grouped together under other capacities. In all these cases the ends of the master sciences are preferable to the ends of the subordinate sciences, since the latter are pursued for the sake of the former. This is true whether the ends of the actions lie in the activities themselves or, as is the case in the disciplines just mentioned, in something beyond the activities.

2. Now, if there exists an end in the realm of action which we desire for its own sake, an end which determines all our other desires . . . then obviously this end will be the good, that is, the highest good. Will not the knowledge of this good, consequently, be very important to our lives? Would it not better equip us, like archers who have a target to aim at, to hit the proper mark? If so, we must try to comprehend in outline at least what this good is and to which branch of knowledge or to which capacity it belongs.

This good, one should think, belongs to the most sovereign and most comprehensive master science, and politics clearly fits this description. For it determines which sciences ought to exist in states, what kind of sciences each group of citizens must learn, and what degree of proficiency each must attain. We observe further that the most honored capacities, such as strategy, household management, and oratory, are contained in politics. Since this science uses the rest of the science, and since, moreover, it legislates what people are to do and what they are not to do, its end seems to embrace the ends of the other sciences. Thus it follows that the end of politics is the good for man. For even if the good is the same for the individual and the state, the good of the state clearly is the greater and more perfect thing to attain and to safeguard. The attainment of the good for one man alone is, to be sure, a source of satisfaction; yet to secure it for a nation and for states is nobler and more divine.

In short, these are the aims of our investigation, which is in a sense an investigation of social and political matters. . . .

4. To resume the discussion: since all knowledge and every choice is directed toward some good, let us discuss what is in our view the aim of politics, i.e., the highest good attainable by action. As far as its name is concerned, most people would probably agree: for both the common run of people and cultivated men call it happiness, and understand by "being happy" the same as "living well" and "doing well." But when it comes to defining what happiness is, they disagree, and the account given by the common run differs from that of the philosophers. The former say it is some clear and obvious good, such as pleasure, wealth, or honor; some say it is one thing and others another, and often the very same person identifies it with different things at different times: when he is sick he thinks it is health, and when he is poor he says it is wealth; and when people are conscious of their own ignorance, they admire those who talk above their heads in accents of greatness. Some thinkers used to believe that there exists over and above these many goods another good, good in itself and by itself, which also is the cause of good in all these things. An examination of all the different opinions would perhaps be a little pointless. . . .

7. Let us return again to our investigation into the nature of the good which we are seeking. It is evidently something difficult in different actions and in each art: it is one thing in medicine, another in strategy, and another again in each of the other arts. What, then, is the good of each? Is it not that for the sake of which everything else is done? That means it is health in the case of medicine, victory in the case of strategy, a house in the case of building, a different thing in the case of different arts, and in all actions and choices it is the end. For it is for the sake of the end that all else is done. Thus, if there is some one end for all that we do, this would be the good attainable by action; if there are several ends, they will be the goods attainable by action.

Our argument has gradually progressed to the same point at which we were before, and we must try to clarify it still further. Since there are evidently several ends, and since we choose some of these—e.g., wealth, flutes, and instruments generally—as a means to something else, it is obvious that not all ends are final. The highest good, on the other hand, must be something final. Thus, if there is only one final end, this will be the good we are seeking; if there are several, it will be the most final and perfect of them. We call that which is pursued as an end in itself more final than an end which is pursued for the sake of something else; and what is never chosen as a means to something else we call more final than that which is chosen both as an end in itself and as a means to something else. What is always chosen as an end in itself and never as a means to something else is called final in an unqualified sense. This description seems to apply to happiness above all else: for we always choose happiness as an end in itself and never for the sake of something else. Honor, pleasure, intelligence, and all virtue we choose partly for themselves—for we would choose each of them even if no further advantage would accrue from them—but we also choose them partly for the sake of happiness, because we assume that it is through them that we will be happy. On the other hand, no one chooses happiness for the sake of honor, pleasure, and the like, nor as a means to anything at all.

I, 7. To call happiness the highest good is perhaps a little trite, and a clearer account of what it is, is still required. Perhaps this is best done by first ascertaining the proper function of man. For just as the goodness and performance of a flute player, a sculptor, or any kind of expert, and generally of anyone who fulfills some function or performs some action, are thought to reside in his proper function, so the goodness and performance of man would seem to reside in whatever is his proper function. Is it then possible that while a carpenter and a shoemaker have their own proper functions and spheres of action, man as man has none, but was left by nature a good-for-nothing without a function? Should we not assume that just as the eye, the hand, the foot, and in general each part of the body clearly has its own proper function, so man too has some function over and above the function of his parts? What can this function possibly be? Simply living? He shares that even with plants, but we are now looking for something peculiar to man. Accordingly, the life of nutrition and growth must be excluded. Next in line there is a life of sense perception. But this, too, man has in common with the horse, the ox, and every animal. There remains then an active life of the rational element. The rational element has two parts: one is rational in that it obeys the rule of reason, the other in that it possesses and conceives rational rules. . . .

The proper function of man, then, consists in an activity of the soul in conformity with a rational principle or, at least, not without it. In speaking of the proper function of a given individual we mean that it is the same in kind as the function of an individual who sets high standards for himself: the proper function of a harpist, for example, is the same as the function of a harpist who has set high standards for himself. The same applies to any and every group of individuals: the full attainment of excellence must be added to the mere function. In other words, the function of the harpist is to play the harp; the function of the harpist who has high standards is to play it well. On these assumptions, if we take the proper function of man to be a certain kind of life, and if this kind of life is an activity of the soul and consists in actions performed in conjunction with the rational element, and if a man of high standards is he who performs these actions well and properly, and if a function is well performed when it is performed in accordance with the excellence appropriate to it; we reach the conclusion that the good of man is an activity of the soul in conformity with excellence or virtue, and if there are several virtues, in conformity with the best and most complete.

But we must add "in a complete life." For one swallow does not make a spring, nor does one sunny day; similarly, one day or a short time does not make a man blessed and happy.

I, 13. Since happiness is a certain activity of the soul in conformity with perfect virtue, we must now examine what virtue or excellence is. For such an inquiry will perhaps better enable us to discover the nature of happiness. Moreover, the man who is truly concerned about politics seems to devote special attention to excellence, since it is his aim to make the citizens good and law-abiding. We have an example of this in the lawgivers of Crete and Sparta and in other great legislators. If an examination of virtue is part of politics, this question clearly fits into the pattern of our original plan.

There can be no doubt that the virtue which we have to study is human virtue. For the good which we have been seeking is a human good and the happiness a human happiness. By human virtue we do not mean the excellence of the body, but that of the soul, and we define happiness as an activity of the soul. . . .

Some things that are said about the soul in our less technical discussions are adequate enough to be used here; for instance, that the soul consists of two elements, one irrational and one rational. . . .

Of the irrational element, again, one part seems to be common to all living things and vegetative in nature: I mean that part which is responsible for nurture and growth. We must assume that some such capacity of the soul exists in everything that takes nourishment, in the embryonic stage as well as when the organism is fully developed; for this makes more sense than to assume the existence of some different capacity at the latter stage. The excellence of this part of the soul is, therefore, shown to be common to all living things and is not exclusively human. . . . But enough of this subject: we may pass by the nutritive part, since it has no natural share in human excellence or virtue.

In addition to this, there seems to be another integral element of the soul which, though irrational, still does partake of reason in some way . . . at any rate, in a mortally strong man it accepts the leadership of reason, and is perhaps more obedient still in a self-controlled and courageous man, since in him everything is in harmony with the voice of reason.

Thus we see that the irrational element of the soul has two parts: the one is vegetative and has no share in reason at all, the other is the seat of the appetites and of desire in general and partakes of reason insofar as it complies with reason and accepts its leadership; it possesses reason in the sense that we say it is "reasonable" to accept the advice of a father and of friends, not in the sense that we have a "rational" understanding of mathematical propositions. That the irrational element can be persuaded by the rational is shown by the fact that admonition and all manner of rebuke and exhortation are possible. If it is correct to say that the appetitive part, too, has reason, it follows that the rational element of the soul has two subdivisions: the one possesses reason in the strict sense, contained within itself, and the other possesses reason in the sense that it listens to reason as one would listen to a father.

Virtue, too, is differentiated in line with this division of the soul. We call some virtues "intellectual" and others "moral": theoretical wisdom, understanding, and practical wisdom are intellectual virtues, generosity and self-control moral virtues. In speaking of a man's character, we do not describe him as wise or understanding, but as gentle or self-controlled; but we praise the wise man, too, for his characteristics, and praiseworthy characteristics are what we call virtues.

II, 1. Virtue, as we have seen, consists of two kinds, intellectual virtue and moral virtue. Intellectual virtue or excellence owes its origin and development chiefly to teaching, and for that reason requires experience and time. Moral virtue, on the other hand, is formed by habit, *ethos*, and its name, *ēthikē*, is therefore derived, by a slight variation, from *ethos*. This shows, too, that none of the moral virtues is implanted in us by nature, for nothing which exists by nature can be changed by habit. For example, it is impossible for a stone, which has a natural downward movement, to become habituated to moving upward, even if one should try ten thousand times to inculcate the habit by throwing it in the air; nor can fire be made to move downward, nor can the direction of any nature-given tendency be changed by habituation. Thus, the virtues are implanted in us neither by nature nor contrary to nature: we are by nature equipped with the ability to receive them, and habit brings this ability to completion and fulfillment. . . .

Moreover, the same causes and the same means that produce any excellence or virtue can also destroy it, and this is also true of every art. It is by playing the harp that men become both good and bad harpists, and correspondingly with builders and all the other craftsmen: a man who builds well will be a good builder, one who builds badly a bad one. For if this were not so, there would be no need for an instructor, but everybody would be born as a good or a bad craftsman. The same holds true of the virtues: in our transactions with other men it is by action that some become just and others unjust, and it is by acting in the face of danger and by developing the habit of feeling fear or confidence that some become brave men and others cowards. The same applies to the appetites and feelings of anger: by reacting in one way or in another to given circumstances some people become self-controlled and gentle, and others self-indulgent and short-tempered. In a word, characteristics develop from corresponding activities. For that reason, we must see to it that our activities are of a certain kind, since any variations in them will be reflected in our characteristics. Hence it is no small matter whether one habit or another is inculcated in us from early childhood; on the contrary, it makes a considerable difference, or, rather, all the difference.

II, 6. It is not sufficient, however, merely to define virtue in general terms as a characteristic: we must also specify what kind of characteristic it is. It must, then, be remarked that every virtue or excellence (1) renders good the thing itself of which it is the excellence, and (2) causes it to perform its function well. For example, the excellence of the eye makes both the eye and its function good, for good sight is due to the excellence of the eye. Likewise, the excellence of a horse makes it both good as a horse and good at running, at carrying its rider, and at facing the enemy. Now, if this is true of all things, the virtue or excellence of man, too, will be a characteristic which makes him a good man, and which causes him to perform his own function well. . . .

Of every continuous entity that is divisible into parts it is possible to take the larger, the smaller, or an equal part, and these parts may be larger, smaller, or equal either in relation to the entity itself, or in relation to us. The "equal" part is something median between excess and deficiency. By the median of an entity I understand a point equidistant from both extremes, and this point is one and the same for everybody. By the median relative to us I understand an amount neither too large nor too small, and this is neither one nor the same for everybody. To take an example: . . . if ten pounds of food is much for a man to eat and two pounds too little, it does not follow that the trainer will prescribe six pounds, for this may in turn be much or little for him to eat; it may be little for Milo [the wrestler] and much for someone who has just begun to take up athletics. The same applies to running and wrestling. Thus we see that an expert in any field avoids excess and deficiency, but seeks the median and chooses it—not the median of the object but the median relative to us.

If this, then, is the way in which every science perfects its work, by looking to the median and by bringing its work up to that point—and this is the reason why it is usually said of a successful piece of work that it is impossible to detract from it or to add to it, the implication being that excess and deficiency destroy success while the mean safeguards it (good craftsmen, we say, look toward this standard in the performance of their work)—and if virtue, like nature, is more precise and better than any art, we must conclude that virtue aims at the median. I am referring to moral virtue: for it is moral virtue that is concerned with emotions and actions, and it is in emotions and actions that excess, deficiency, and the median are found. Thus we can experience fear, confidence, desire, anger, pity, and generally any kind of pleasure and pain either too much or too little, and in either case not properly. But to experience all this at the right time, toward the right objects, toward the right people, for the right reason, and in the right manner—that is the median and the best course, the course that is a mark of virtue.

Similarly, excess, deficiency, and the median can also be found in actions. Now virtue is concerned with emotions and actions; and in emotions and actions excess and deficiency miss the mark, whereas the median is praised and constitutes success. . . .

We may thus conclude that virtue or excellence is a characteristic involving choice, and that it consists in observing the mean relative to us, a mean which is defined by a rational principle, such as a man of practical wisdom would use to determine it. It is the mean by reference to two vices: the one of excess and the other of deficiency. It is, moreover, a mean because some vices exceed and others fall short of what is required in emotion and in action, whereas virtue finds and chooses the median.

X, 7. Now, if happiness is activity in conformity with virtue, it is to be expected that it should conform with the highest virtue, and that is the virtue of the best part of us. . . . That it is an activity concerned with theoretical knowledge or contemplation has already been stated.

This would seem to be consistent with our earlier statements as well as the truth. For this activity is not only the highest—for intelligence is the highest possession we have in us, and the objects which are the concern of intelligence are the highest objects of knowledge—but also the most continuous: we are able to study continuously more easily than to perform any kind of action. Furthermore, we think of pleasure as a necessary ingredient in happiness. Now everyone agrees that of all the activities that conform with virtue activity in conformity with theoretical wisdom is the most pleasant. At any rate, it seems that (the pursuit of wisdom or) philosophy holds pleasures marvelous in purity and certainty, and it is not surprising that time spent in knowledge is more pleasant than time spent in research. Moreover, what is usually called "self-sufficiency" will be found in the highest degree in the activity which is concerned with theoretical knowledge. Like a just man and any other virtuous man, a wise man requires the necessities of life; once these have been adequately provided, a just man still needs people toward whom and in company with whom to act justly, and the same is true of a self-controlled man, a courageous man, and all the rest. But a wise man is able to study even by himself, and the wiser he is the more is he able to do it. Perhaps he could do it better if he had colleagues to work with him, but he still is the most self-sufficient of all. Again, study seems to be the only activity which is loved for its own sake . . . it follows that the activity of our intelligence constitutes the complete happiness of man, provided that it encompasses a complete span of life; for nothing connected with happiness must be incomplete.

However, such a life would be more than human. A man who would live it would do so not insofar as he is human, but because there is a divine element within him. This divine element is as far above our composite nature as its activity is above the active exercise of the other (i.e., practical) kind of virtue. So if it is true that intelligence is divine in comparison with man, then a life guided by intelligence is divine in comparison with human life. We must not follow those who advise us to have human thoughts, since we are (only) men, and have mortal thoughts, as mortals should; on the contrary, we should try to become immortal as far as that is possible and do our utmost to live in accordance with what is highest in us. For though this is a small portion (of our nature), it far surpasses everything else in power and value. One might even regard it as each man's true self, since it is the controlling and better part. It would, therefore, be strange if a man chose not to live his own life but someone else's.

Moreover, what we stated before will apply here, too: what is by nature proper to each thing will be at once the best and the most pleasant for it. In other words, a life guided by intelligence is the best and most pleasant for man, inasmuch as intelligence, above all else, is man. Consequently, this kind of life is the happiest.

8. . . . A further indication that complete happiness consists in some kind of contemplative activity is this. We assume that the gods are in the highest degree blessed and happy. But what kind of actions are we to attribute to them? Acts of justice? Will they not look ridiculous making contracts with one another, returning deposits, and so forth? Perhaps acts of courage—withstanding terror and taking risks, because it is noble to do so? Or generous actions? . . . If we went through the whole list we would see that a concern with actions is petty and unworthy of the gods. Nevertheless, we all assume that the gods exist and, consequently, that they are active; for surely we do not assume them to be always asleep like Endymion. Now, if we take away action from a living being, to say nothing of production, what is left except contemplation? Therefore, the activity of the divinity which surpasses all others in bliss must be a contemplative activity, and the human activity which is most closely akin to it is, therefore, most conducive to happiness.

This is further shown by the fact that no other living being has a share in happiness, since they all are completely denied this kind of activity. The gods enjoy a life blessed in its entirety; men enjoy it to the extent that they attain something resembling the divine activity; but none of the other living beings can be happy, because they have no share at all in contemplation or study. So happiness is coextensive with study, and the greater the opportunity for studying, the greater the happiness, not as an incidental effect but as inherent in study; for study is in itself worthy of honor. Consequently, happiness is some kind of study or contemplation.

But we shall also need external well-being, since we are only human. Our nature is not self-sufficient for engaging in study: our body must be healthy and we must have food and generally be cared for. Nevertheless, if it is not possible for a man to be supremely happy without external goods, we must not think that his needs will be great and many in order to be happy. . . .

X, 9. . . . Surely, knowing about excellence or virtue is not enough: we must try to possess it and use it, or find some other way in which we may become good.

Now, if words alone would suffice to make us good, they would rightly "harvest many rewards and great," as Theognis says, and we would have to provide them. But as it is, while words evidently do have the power to encourage and stimulate young men of generous mind, and while they can cause a character well-born and truly enamored of what is noble to be possessed by virtue, they do not have the capacity to turn the common run of people to goodness and nobility. For the natural tendency of most people is to be swayed not by a sense of shame but by fear, and to refrain from acting basely not because it is disgraceful, but because of the punishment it brings. Living under the sway of emotion, they pursue their own proper pleasures and the means by which they can obtain them, and they avoid the pains that are opposed to them. But they do not even have a notion of what is noble and truly pleasant, since they have never tasted it. What argument indeed can transform people like that? To change by argument what has long been ingrained in a character is impossible or, at least, not easy. . . .

. . . For a man whose life is guided by emotion will not listen to an argument that dissuades him, nor will he understand it. How can we possibly persuade a man like that to change his ways? And in general it seems that emotion does not yield to argument but only to force. Therefore, there must first be a character that somehow has an affinity for excellence or virtue, a character that loves what is noble and feels disgust at what is base.

To obtain the right training for virtue from youth up is difficult, unless one has been brought up under the right laws. To live a life of self-control and tenacity is not pleasant for most people, especially for the young. Therefore, their upbringing and pursuits must be regulated by laws; for once they have become familiar, they will no longer be painful. But it is perhaps not enough that they receive the right upbringing and attention only in their youth. Since they must carry on these pursuits and cultivate them by habit when they have grown up, we probably need laws for this, too, and for the whole of life in general. For most people are swayed rather by compulsion than argument, and by punishments rather than by (a sense of) what is noble. . . .

Is it not, then, our next task to examine from whom and how we can learn to become legislators? . . .

Accordingly, since previous writers have left the subject of legislation unexamined, it is perhaps best if we ourselves investigate it and the general problem of the constitution of a state, in order to complete as best we can our philosophy of human affairs.

From *Politics*

Book I

Chapter I

Seeing that Every State is a sort of association and every association is formed for the attainment of some Good—for some presumed Good is the end of all action—it is evident that, as some Good is the object of all associations, so in the highest degree is the supreme Good the object of that association which is supreme and embraces all the rest, in other words, of the State or political association.

Now it is wrong to confound, as some do, the functions of the constitutional statesman, king, householder and slavemaster. They hold that the difference between them is not one of kind, but depends simply upon the number of persons ruled, i.e. that a man is a slavemaster, if he has but few subjects; if he has more, a householder; if still more, a constitutional statesman or king, there being no distinction between a large household and a small State; also that a man is either a king or a constitutional statesman according as he governs absolutely or in conformity to the laws of political science, being alternately ruler and subject. Such an opinion is erroneous. Our meaning will be clear, however, if we follow our usual method of investigation. For as in other cases we have to analyse a compound whole into the uncompounded elements which are its least parts, so in examining the constituents of a State we shall incidentally best ascertain the points of difference between the above-mentioned forms of government and the possibility of arriving at a scientific conclusion in regard to each of them.

Chapter II

Here, as elsewhere, the best system of examination will be to begin at the beginning and observe things in their growth.

There are certain primary essential combinations of those who cannot exist independently one of another. Thus male and female must combine in order to procreate children, nor is there anything deliberate or arbitrary in their so doing; on the contrary, the desire of leaving an offspring like oneself is natural to man as to the whole animal and vegetable world. Again, natural rulers and subjects combine for safety—*and when I say "natural,"* I mean that there are some persons qualified intellectually to form projects, and these are natural rulers or natural masters; while there are others qualified physically to carry them out, and these are subjects or natural slaves, so that the interest of master and slave are coincident.

Now Nature has differentiated females from slaves. None of Nature's products wears a poverty-stricken look like the Delphian knife[5] as it is called that cutlers make; each has a single definite object on the principle that any instrument admits of the highest finish, only if it subserves a single purpose rather than several. Among non-Greek peoples on the other hand females and slaves stand on one and the same footing. The reason is that natural rulers do not exist among them, and the association they form consists of none but slaves male and female; hence the poets say

'Tis meet Greeks rule barbarians,[6]

implying the natural identity of barbarians or non-Greeks and slaves.

But to resume: the associations of male and female, master and slave constitute the primary form of household, and Hesiod was right when he wrote

Get thee
First house and wife and ox to plough withal,

for an ox is to the poor what a servant is to the rich.

---

[5] The Delphian knife was a knife intended to serve more purposes than one, and therefore not especially suited to any.

[6] Euripides, *Iphigenia in Aulis*, 1400.

Thus the association naturally formed for the supply of everyday wants is a household; its members, according to Charondas, are "those who eat of the same store," or, according to the Cretan Epimenides "those who sit around the same hearth."

Again, the simplest association of several households for something more than ephemeral purposes is a village. It seems that the village in its most natural form is derived from the household, including all the children of certain parents and the children's children, or, as the phrase sometimes is, "all who are suckled upon the same milk."

This is the reason why States were originally governed by kings as is still the case with uncivilized peoples; they were composed of units accustomed to this form of government. For as each household is under the kingly government of its eldest member, so were also the offshoot-households as comprising none but blood-relations. It is this condition of things that Homer means when he describes *the Cyclopes* as

> law-givers each
> Of his own wives and children,

in allusion to their want of corporate life. This patriarchal government was universal in primitive times; in fact the reason why all nations represent the polity of the Gods as monarchical is that such originally was, if it is not still, their own polity, and men assimilate the lives no less than the bodily forms of the Gods to their own.

Lastly, the association composed of several villages in its complete form is the State, in which the goal of full independence may be said to be first attained. For as the State was formed to make life possible, so it exists to make life good. Consequently if it be allowed that the simple associations, *i.e. the household and the village*, have a natural existence, so has the State in all cases; for in the State they attain complete development, and Nature implies complete development, as the nature of anything, e.g. of a man, a house or a horse, may be defined to be its condition when the process of production is complete. Or *the naturalness of the State may be proved in another way*: the object proposed or the complete development of a thing is its highest Good; but independence *which is first attained in the State* is a complete development or the highest Good *and is therefore natural.*

Thus we see that the State is a natural institution, that Man is naturally a political animal and that one who is not a citizen of any State, if the cause of his isolation be natural and not accidental, is either a superhuman being or low *in the scale of civilization*, as he stands alone like a "blot" on the backgammon board. The "clanless, lawless, heartless" man so bitterly described by Homer[7] is a case in point; for he is naturally a citizen of no state and a lover of war. Also that Man is a political animal in a higher sense than a bee or any other gregarious creature is evident from the fact that Nature, as we are fond of asserting, creates nothing without a purpose and Man is the only animal endowed with speech. Now mere sounds serve to indicate sensations of pain and pleasure and are therefore assigned to other animals as well as to Man; for their nature does not advance beyond the point of perceiving pain and pleasure and signifying these perceptions to one another. The object of speech on the other hand is to indicate advantage and disadvantage and therefore also justice and injustice. For it is a special characteristic which distinguishes Man from all other animals that he alone

---

[7] *Iliad*, ix, 63, 64.

enjoys perception of good and evil, justice and injustice and the like. But these are the principles of that association which constitutes a household or a State.

Again, in the order of Nature the State is prior to the household or the individual. For the whole must needs be prior to its part. For instance, if you take away *the body which is* the whole, there will not remain any such thing as a foot or a hand, unless we use the same word in a different sense as when we speak of a stone hand as a hand. For a hand separated from the body will be a disabled hand; whereas it is the function or faculty of a thing which makes it what it is, and therefore when things lose their function or faculty it is not correct to call them the same things but rather homonymous, *i.e. different things having the same name.*

We see then that the State is a natural institution, and also that it is prior to the individual. For if the individual as a separate unit is not independent, he must be a part and must bear the same relation to the State as other parts to their wholes; and one who is incapable of association with others or is independent and has no need of such association is no member of a State, in other words he is either a brute or a God. Now the impulse to political association is innate in all men. Nevertheless the author of the first combination whoever he was was a great benefactor of human kind. For man, as in his condition of complete development, *i.e. in the State*, he is the noblest of all animals, so apart from law and justice he is the vilest of all. For injustice is always most formidable when it is armed; and Nature has endowed Man with arms which are intended to subserve the purposes of prudence and virtue but are capable of being wholly turned to contrary ends. Hence if Man be devoid of virtue, no animal is so unscrupulous or savage, none so sensual, none so gluttonous. Just action on the other hand is bound up with the existence of a State; for the administration of justice is an ordinance of the political association and the administration of justice is nothing else than the decision of what is just.

Chapter III

Having now ascertained the constituent elements of the State, as every State is composed of households we must begin with a discussion of Domestic Economy.

There are various parts of Domestic Economy corresponding to the constituent parts of a household, which in its complete form comprises slaves and free persons. But as the right method of investigating anything is to reduce it to its elements and the primary or elementary parts of a household are master and slave, husband and wife, parent and children, we have to examine the true nature and character of these three relations, i.e. the relations of a slavemaster to his slaves, of a husband to his wife and a of a parent to his children. These three we may lay down as certain. But there is another part which is sometimes regarded as equivalent to the whole of Domestic Economy and sometimes as its principal part, and the truth is well worthy of investigation. I mean the so-called Art of Finance.

We will first consider the relations of master and slave in order to arrive at a practical conclusion and also, if possible, to frame some theory of the subject better than those now in vogue. There are some thinkers, as I said at the beginning of this treatise, who hold that the ownership of slaves is a science and identify the functions of the householder, the slavemaster, the constitutional statesman and the king. Others again regard slaveowning as doing violence to Nature on the ground that the distinction of slave and free man is wholly conventional and has no place in Nature, and is therefore void of justice, as resting on mere force.

Chapter IV

Property then is a part of the household and the Art of acquiring property a part of Domestic Economy, inasmuch as without certain necessaries it is impossible to live happily or indeed to live at all. Nor can the art of the householder any more than any definite art dispense with its proper instruments, if its work is to be adequately performed. Instruments however may be animate or inanimate. In the case e.g. of a pilot, the tiller is an inanimate instrument, the "lookout" an animate one; in fact in every art an assistant is virtually an instrument. Thus we conclude that any given property is an instrument conducing to life, property as a whole is a mass of instruments, a slave is an animate property, and every assistant may be described as a single instrument doing the work of several. For suppose that every instrument could obey a person's orders or anticipate his wishes and so fulfil its proper function like the legendary figures of Daedalus or the tripods of Hephaestus which, if we may believe the poet,

Entered self-moved the conclave of the Gods,

suppose, I say, that in like manner combs were in the habit of combing and quills of playing the cithern of themselves, mastercraftsmen would have no need of assistants nor masters of slaves. While then instruments in the common use of the term are instruments of production, a property is an instrument of action; that is to say, while a comb is not only used but produces something else, a coat or a bed can only be used. And as there is this difference of kind between production and action and instruments are necessary to both, it follows that there must be a corresponding difference in the instruments. Now life consists not in production but in action; and as *every property is an instrument conducing to existence, and a slave is an animate property*, it follows that a slave is an assistant in the sphere of action.

The term "property" may be compared to the term "member," in that a member is not only a member of something else but belongs wholly to that something, and the same is true of a property. Thus while a master is master of his slave but in no sense belongs to him, a slave is not only the slave of a certain master but belongs wholly to his master.

These facts clearly prove the nature and faculty of the slave. A natural slave is one who, although a human being, is naturally not his own master but belongs to someone else. Now this is the case with a human being when he is nothing more than a property, and a property means any instrument of action which has a separate existence, *i.e. is not a mere part of the person who uses it.*

Chapter VI[8]

This being determined, we have next to consider whether it is right to assume a single polity or several, and, if several, what is the nature of each, and how many there are, and what are the points of distinction between them. A polity may be defined as an order of the State in respect of its offices generally and especially of the supreme office. For the governing class is everywhere supreme in the State, and the nature of the polity is determined by the governing class. I mean e.g. that it is the commons who are supreme in a Democracy and the Few on the other hand in an Oligarchy, and *accordingly* we call their polities distinct. The same remark may be extended to all the rest; *if the governing class is different, so is the polity.*

---

[8] In the preceding chapter Aristotle determines that eligibility to the honors of the state and to public office are the most exact marks of citizenship.

We must begin by laying down (1) the object for which a State is framed and (2) the various kinds of rule which may be exercised over man in his social existence.

It has been stated at the very outset of our treatise in the discussion of Domestic Economy and the government of slaves that Man is naturally a political animal, and consequently, even where there is no need of mutual service, men are none the less anxious to live together. Still it cannot be denied that the common advantage of all is also a motive of union, *more or less operative* according to the degree in which each individual is capable of the higher life. Although to the citizens, both collectively and individually, this higher life is emphatically the end proposed, yet life itself is also an object for which they unite and maintain the corporate political association; for it is probable that some degree of the higher life is necessarily implied in merely living, unless there is a great preponderance of hardship in the life. Certain it is that the majority of men endure much suffering without ceasing to cling to life—a proof that a certain happiness or natural sweetness resides in it.

But *to proceed to the second point*: it is not difficult to distinguish the forms of rule which are generally recognized; for even in our unscientific discourses we often discuss and determine their character. In the government of slaves, although the interests of natural salve and natural master are really identical, yet the object of the rule is nevertheless the interest of the master and is that of the slave only incidentally, because, if the slave is destroyed, it is impossible that the master's government should be maintained. On the other hand, in the rule of children or a wife or a whole household, which in our terminology is economic rule, the end is either the good of the subjects or some common good of rulers and subjects alike, i.e. it is essentially the good of the subjects, as we see in the other arts such as Medicine and Gymnastic, although it may perhaps incidentally be also the good of the rulers themselves. For there is no reason why the gymnastic trainer should not himself be occasionally one of the gymnasts, as the pilot is invariably one of the crew. And thus while the trainer or pilot has in view *not his own interest but* the interest of those who are under him, yet in any case where he himself shares their position he enjoys incidentally the same benefit as they do; for the one becomes a sailor and the other one of the gymnasts, although he is a trainer. *It is because the object of political rule is the benefit of the subjects* that in any State framed on the principle of equality and similarity among the citizens a claim is put forward for an alteration of rule. It was originally claimed, as is natural enough, that all should serve the State in turn, and that, as each citizen during his period of rule of office had already paid regard to the interest of another, so that other should in turn pay regard to his. But nowadays the profits derivable from the public service and an official status create a desire for perpetuity of office; it is as though the officers of State, being invalids, were to enjoy good health *during all their term of power*, in which case it is probable that they would be equally eager for office.

It is evident then that all such polities as regard the good of the community are really normal according to the principle of abstract justice, while such as regard the private good of the rulers are all corruptions of perversions of the normal polities; for the relations of rulers to the subjects in them are like the relations of a master to his slaves, whereas the State is *properly* a society of free persons.

Chapter VII

Having now settled these points, we have next to consider the number of different polities and their nature. We will begin with the normal polities; for when they are determined the perverted forms will be evident at once.

As in any State the polity and the governing class are virtually the same, *i.e. the polity is determined by the governing class*, as the governing class is the supreme authority in a State, and as supreme power must be vested either in an individual or in a Few or in the Many, it follows that, when the rule of the individual or the Few or the Many is exercised for the benefit of the community at large, the polities are normal, whereas the polities which subserve the private interest either of the individual or the Few or the masses are perversions; for either the members of the State do not deserve the name of citizens, or they ought to have a share in its advantages. The form of Monarchy in which regard is paid to the interest of the community is commonly known as Kingship, and the government of the Few, although of a number exceeding one, for the good of all, as Aristocracy, whether because the rule is in the hands of the best citizens (οἵ ἄριστοι) or because they exercise it for the best interests (τὸ ἄριστον) of the State and all its members; while when it is the masses who direct public affairs for the interest of the community, the government is called by the name which is common to all the polities, viz. a Polity. The result in this case is such as might have been expected. For although it is possible to find an individual or a few persons of eminent virtue, it can hardly be the case that a large number are perfectly accomplished in every form of virtue; at the best they will be accomplished only in military virtue, as it is the only one of which the masses are capable. The consequence is that in this polity, *viz. the Polity proper*, the military class is supreme, and all who bear arms enjoy full political privileges.

As perverted forms of the polities just mentioned we have Tyranny by the side of Kingship, Oligarchy of Aristocracy and Democracy of Polity. For Tyranny is monarchical rule for the good of the monarch, Oligarchy *the rule of a Few* for the good of the wealthy, and Democracy *the rule of the Many* for the good of the poor; none of them subserves the interest of the community at large.

Chapter VIII

But we ought to describe at rather greater length the nature of the several polities, as the matter is one which presents certain difficulties, and it is proper that a philosophical inquirer in any subject, who looks at something more than the merely practical side, should not ignore or omit any point but should bring to light the actual truth in all.

Tyranny is, as has been said, a form of Monarchy corresponding in the political association to the rule of a master over his slaves; Oligarchy a government where the supreme power in the polity is vested in the propertied classes; Democracy, on the contrary, a government where it is vested in those who possess no considerable property, i.e. the poor. But there is an initial difficulty in this definition. Democracy being defined as a polity in which the masses are supreme, suppose the supreme authority in the State were to reside in the majority who are rich; or similarly, to take the converse case, the polity being called an Oligarchy where a small number of persons are supreme, suppose it happens somewhere or other that the supreme power is in the hands of the poor who are stronger although less numerous than the rich; it would seem that our definition of the polities is unsatisfactory in these cases. On the other hand, if we combine numerical minority with wealth and numerical majority with poverty, and designate the polities accordingly as an Oligarchy where the offices of State are in the hands of the rich being a minority, and a Democracy where they are in the hands of the poor being a majority, there is here another difficulty. How are we to describe the polities we mentioned just now, viz. where the rich being a majority or the poor being a minority are respectively supreme in the State? For there is no other polity besides those we have named. It seems then to be proved by our argument that the small or large number of the class which is supreme in the State is only an accident of Oligarchies on the one hand and Democracies on the other, owing to the fact that the rich are few and the poor numerous all the world over. Accordingly the polities above mentioned, *viz. where the rich are a majority or the poor a minority*, do not in fact constitute exceptions. The really distinctive characteristics of Democracy and Oligarchy are poverty and wealth; and it is a necessary law that wherever wealth constitutes the title to rule, whether the rulers are a minority or a majority, the polity is an Oligarchy, whereas, if the poor are rulers, it is a Democracy. But as a matter of fact it happens, as we said, that in the case rulers are few and in the other many; for there are only few people who are wealthy, whereas liberty is enjoyed by all alike, and wealth and liberty are the grounds upon which the two parties respectively base their claim to be masters of the polity.

Book IV

Chapter II

As at the beginning of our treatise we divided polities into the normal polities, which are three in number, viz. Kingship, Aristocracy and Polity, and the perversions of these which are also three, viz. Tyranny the perversion of Kingship, Oligarchy of Aristocracy and Democracy of Polity; as Aristocracy and Kingship have been already discussed—for the consideration of the best polity is nothing else than a discussion of the polities which bear these names, as in theory each of them is constituted on the basis of virtue furnished with external means—and as further the points of difference between Aristocracy and Kingship and the occasions when a polity is to be regarded as regal have been determined, it remains to describe the form which is called by the general name of all polities, *viz. the Polity*, and the remaining forms, Oligarchy, Democracy and Tyranny.

It is evident, if we consider these perversions, which is the worst and which is the next worst. For the perversion of the primary or most divine form must be the worst; and as Kingship must either be a mere name and not a reality or must have its justification in the vast superiority of the reigning king, it follows that Tyranny is the form which is worst and farthest removed from a constitutional government, Oligarchy the next worst—for Aristocracy, *it must be remembered*, is widely different from Oligarchy—and Democracy the least bad. An earlier writer[9] has already expressed himself in this sense, although not from the same point of view as ours. For *he recognized a good and a bad form of each of these polities and* held that of all the polities when they are good, i.e. of good Oligarchy and the like, Democracy is the worst, but that when they are bad it is the best. We maintain on the contrary that these polities are wholly vitiated, and it is not right to speak of one Oligarchy as being better than another but only as being less bad. . . .

Chapter XI

But what is the best polity and the best life for the great majority of States and persons, as tested by the standard not of a virtue which is beyond the attainment of ordinary human beings, nor of such an education as requires natural advantages and the external resources which Fortune alone can give, nor again of the ideally constructed polity, but of such a life as the majority of people are capable of realizing in a political association and such a polity as the majority of States are capable of enjoying? For as the so-called Aristocracies of which we recently spoke lie in some respects beyond the reach of ordinary States and in others approximate to the Polity in the limited sense of the term, we may speak of the two forms, *viz. Aristocracy and Polity*, as one and the same.

In the determination of all these questions we may start from the same principles. If it has been correctly stated in the *Ethics* that the happy is a life which is unimpeded in the exercise of virtue, and

---

[9] Plato, *The Statesman.*

that virtue is a mean between two extremes, it follows that the mean life, viz. the attainment of the mean condition possible to the citizens of any State, is the best. And further the same canons of virtue and vice necessarily hold good for a State and for its polity, as the polity is, so to say, the life of a State.

In every State without exception there are three parts, viz. the very rich, the very poor and thirdly the intermediate class. As it is admitted then that the moderate or intermediate condition is best, it is evident that the possession of Fortune's gifts in an intermediate degree is the best thing possible. For this is the condition in which obedience to reason is easiest; whereas one who is excessively beautiful, strong, noble or wealthy, or on the contrary excessively poor or weak or deeply degraded cannot easily live a life conformable to reason. Such persons are apt in the first case to be guilty of insolence and criminality on a large scale, and in the second to become rogues and petty criminals. But all crimes are the results either of insolence or of roguery, both which are conditions prejudicial to the interests of States. And further persons, who are in the enjoyment of an extraordinary amount of Fortune's gifts, strength, wealth, friends and so on, have neither the disposition nor the knowledge necessary for submission to authority—a fault which they derive from their home-training in early years, as they are educated amidst such indulgence that they do not get the habit of submitting even to their masters— while persons who suffer from too great deficiency of these blessings are reduced to a state of mental degradation. Thus while the latter do not understand how to rule, but only how to be ruled like slaves, the former do not understand how to submit to any rule, but only to exercise the rule of slave-masters. The result is a State composed exclusively of slaves and slave-masters instead of free men, with sentiments of envy on the one side and of contempt on the other. But such sentiments are the very negation of friendship and political association; for all association implies friendship, as is proved by the fact that people do not choose even to walk on the same road with their enemies. But in theory at least the State is composed as far as possible of persons who are equal and similar, and this is especially the condition of the middle class. And from this it follows that, if we take the parts of which the State in our conception is composed, it is a State of this kind, *viz. composed largely of the middle class*, which enjoys the best political constitution. Further it is this middle class of citizens which runs the least risk of destruction in a State. For as they do not like paupers lust after the goods of others, nor do others lust after theirs, as paupers after the property of the rich, they pass an existence void of peril, being neither the objects nor the authors of conspiracies. Hence it was a wise prayer of Phocylides

> The middle class within the State
> Fares best, I ween;
> May I be neither low nor great
> But e'en between.

It is clear then that the best political association is the one which is controlled by the middle class, and that the only States capable of a good administration are those in which the middle class is numerically large and stronger, if not than both the other classes, yet at least than either of them, as in that case the addition of its weight turns the scale and prevents the predominance of one extreme or the other. Accordingly it is an immense blessing to a State that the active citizens should possess an intermediate and sufficient amount of property; for where there is a class of extremely wealthy people on the one hand and a class of absolute paupers on the other, the result is either an extreme Democracy or an untempered Oligarchy, or, as the outcome of the predominance of either extreme, a Tyranny. For Tyranny results from the most violent form of Democracy or from Oligarchy, but is far less likely to result from a polity in which the middle class is strong and the citizens all stand much on the same level. The reason of this we will state hereafter when we treat of the revolutions of polities. It is evident however that the intermediate form of polity is best, as it is the only one which is free from political disturbances. For it is where the middle class is large that there is the least danger of disturbances and dissensions among the citizens. And this too, viz. the largeness of the middle class, is the reason why great States are comparatively little liable to political disturbances; whereas in small States it is easy to divide the whole population into two camps, leaving no intermediate class, and all the citizens in them are practically either poor or rich. It is the middle class too which imparts to Democracies a more secure and permanent character than to Oligarchies, as the middle class are more numerous and enjoy a larger share of the honours of State in Democracies than in Oligarchies; for if there is no middle class, and the poor in virtue of their numbers are preponderant, the consequence is failure and speedy destruction of the State.

We may fairly regard it as an indication *of the same fact, viz. of the superiority of the middle class*, that the best legislators belong to the middle class of citizens, e.g. Solon, as is evident from his poems, Lycurgus—for he was not king—Charondas and most others.

We see too from these facts why it is that the great majority of polities are either democratical or oligarchical. The reason is that, as the middle class is generally small in them, whichever of the two other classes enjoys the superiority in any case, whether it be the propertied class or the commons, it is a party which transgresses the rule of the mean that imparts its own bias to the polity, and thereby produces either Democracy or Oligarchy. And there is the further fact that in consequence of the political disturbances and contentions between the commons on the one hand and the rich on the other whichever party happens to get the better of its opponents, instead of establishing a polity of a broad and equal kind, assumes political supremacy as a prize of the victory and sets up either a Democracy or an Oligarchy. We may add that the two States, which have attained an imperial position in Greece, having regard solely to their own respective polities always established either Democracies or Oligarchies in the different States, not out of any consideration for the interests of the States in question, but simply for their own interest. And the result of all these circumstances is that the intermediate polity is either never realized at all or only seldom and in a few States; for among all who have hitherto attained a commanding position there has been only a single individual who was prevailed upon to restore this political system, *viz. a Polity*. And indeed it has become a settled habit among the citizens of Greek States not even to desire the principle of equality but to seek a position either of rule or of patient submission to a dominant power.

The nature of the best polity and the reason why it is the best are now clear. But taking the general list of polities and remembering that according to our former statement there are several varieties of Democracy and Oligarchy, we shall not after our determination of the best polity find a difficulty in discerning what kind of polity is to be placed first, second and so on in due order according to their comparative excellence and inferiority. For the nearer a polity is to the best polity, the better of course it will be, and the further it is removed from the mean, the worse it will be, unless indeed it is tried with reference to an arbitrary standard. And when I speak of an arbitrary standard, I mean that there are many cases in which one of two polities is preferable *in itself*, but the other may well be more advantageous to a certain State.

Chapter XII

The nature and character of the polities suited to particular natures and characters is the next question which we have to consider.

It is necessary to begin by assuming a principle of general application, viz. that the part of the State which desires the continuance of the polity ought to be stronger than that which does not. But in every State there is a qualitative and a quantitative element. By the former I mean freedom, wealth, culture and nobility; by the latter mere numerical superiority. But it is possible that of the parts of which the State is composed the quality may belong to one and the quantity to another, e.g. that the ignoble classes may be numerically larger than the noble or the poor than the rich, but that their superiority in quantity may not be commensurate with their inferiority in quality. It is necessary therefore to institute a comparison between the two elements.

Where the numerical superiority of the poor bears the proportion we have indicated *to the qualitative superiority of the rich, i.e. is vastly superior to it,* it is natural that the polity established should be a Democracy, and that the species of Democracy should be determined by the character of the commons to whom the superiority belongs, i.e. that, if it is the agricultural population which is predominant, it should be the primary form of Democracy, if the mechanical and wage-earning population, the latest development of Democracy, and so for all the intermediate forms. Where on the other hand the superiority of the rich or upper classes in quality is greater than its inferiority in quantity, it is natural that the polity should be an Oligarchy, and as in the last case that the species of Oligarchy should be determined by the character of the oligarchical population in whom the superiority resides.

But the legislator in his political system ought always to secure the support of the middle class. For if the laws which he enacts are oligarchical, he should aim at *the satisfaction of* the middle class; if democratical, he should engage their support in behalf of the laws. But it is only where the numbers of the middle class preponderate either over both the extremes or over only one of them that there is a possibility of a permanent polity. For there is no danger of a conspiracy among the rich and the poor against the middle class, as neither rich nor poor will consent to a condition of slavery, and if they try to find a polity which is more in the nature of a compromise, they will not discover any other than this, *viz. the polity which rests upon the middle class.* For the mutual distrustfulness *of the Oligarchs and Democrats* will prevent them from consenting to an alternation of rule. All the world over on the other hand there is nobody so thoroughly trusted as an arbitrator, and the middle class occupies a position of arbitration *between the rich and the poor.*

But the permanence of the polity will depend upon the excellence of the fusion. It is a common and serious mistake made even by those who desire to set up aristocratical polities not only to give an undue share of power to the rich but to endeavour to deceive the commons. For the spurious advantages are sure in time to produce a real evil, as the usurpations of the rich are more fatal to the polity than those of the commons.

Stoic Thought

Stoic thought first developed in the early 3rd century B.C. with Zeno of Citium (335–263 B.C.), deriving its name from the Stoa Poikile (or Painted Stoa) in Athens where he used to lecture. Along with Zeno, Early Stoicism owed its formulation and development in the 3rd century to his successors Cleanthes of Assos (c. 301–232 B.C.) (best remembered for his *Hymn to Zeus*)[1] and Chrysippus of Soli (280–207 B.C.). Thereafter, in the 2nd and 1st centuries B.C. Stoic thought passed into the Roman world where it flourished, particularly as a result of the teaching of Panaetius (d.109 B.C.) and Poseidonius of Rhodes (135–47 B.C.). Stoic philosophy of this period is known as that of the Middle Stoa. Both Panaetius and Poseidonius were influential on Cicero (106–43 B.C.), who studied under the latter on Rhodes and at Rome. Cicero, who is perhaps better known for his role in the politics of the Late Roman Republic and for the exemplary Latin style of his speeches, probably followed the ideas of his teacher quite closely in his philosophical works such as the *De Republica (On the Republic)* (54–52 B.C.), the *De Legibus (On the Laws)* (52–46 B.C.), the *De Finibus Bonorum et Malorum (On the Chief End of Man)* (45 B.C.), the *De Natura Deorum (On the Nature of the Gods)* (45 B.C.) and the *Tusculan Disputations* (44 B.C.).[2] In the first two centuries A.D. Stoic philosophy (the Late Stoa) continued to be of great importance at Rome. The thought and writings of men such as Lucius Seneca (4 B.C.–A.D. 65), Epictetus (c.A.D. 55–c.135) (whose *Encheiridion or Manual* was probably compiled by his pupil and friend Arrian),[3] and the emperor Marcus Aurelius (A.D. 121–180), demonstrate the lasting appeal of this school of philosophy.

Indeed, Stoic ideas persisted in their popularity in Late Antiquity and exercised a considerable influence in the development of some areas of Christian thought, particularly morality; clear traces may be found in some passages in the New Testament, as well as in the writings of many early Church fathers (e.g. Ambrose of Milan in the 4th century A.D.). Some elements drawn from Stoic philosophy continued to find their way into medieval writings but it was not until the late 16th and early 17th centuries that Stoic ideas again came to be well known and developed in the Western tradition. The Enlightenment, with its stress on the importance and power of reason, borrowed heavily from the Stoic tradition in all manner of ways, while traces of its influence continue to be discernible in some branches of modern philosophy.

Stoicism began as an attempt to come to terms with the significant changes and disruptions which marked the passing of the relative stability and the widely shared values of classical Greek society and culture in the Hellenistic era following the death of Alexander (323 B.C.). Seen by its proponents as a 'striving after wisdom', it did so by presenting a coherent explanation of the nature of the material world and human existence which depends on the concept of an all pervading Reason. For the Stoics, right reason, which was conceived of as divine fire, governs all things; it

---

[1] Cleanthes *Hymn to Zeus*, trans., J. Adams, in W. J. Oates, ed., *The Stoic and Epicurean Philosophers*, (New York: 1940).

[2] Extracts from Cicero, trans., Paul MacKendrick, in P. MacKendrick and Herbert M. Howe, eds., *Classics in Translation*, II, (Madison, Wisconsin: 1952), pp. 150–151, 165–170, 173–175, 181–185.

[3] Extracts from Epictetus, trans., P.E. Matheson in J. L. Saunders, ed., *Greek and Roman Philosophy after Aristotle* (New York: 1966), pp. 133–137, 140–141, 145–146, 149–150.

is responsible for (and evidenced in) the orderly pattern visible throughout the universe, despite the constantly changing from of all material things. The goal of human beings, who are distinguished from all other form of life by their possession of rationality, is thus to live in accordance with the natural, rational order which unites the cosmos. Stoic political and moral thought stems from this one basic principle. The individual who follows the precepts of reason will necessarily be virtuous, will act rightly, and so will be truly happy; a strong sense of duty and of natural justice thus mark Stoic morality. At the same time, human affairs are seen as being those of one great city inhabited by the universal brotherhood of mankind; the individual, as a world citizen endowed with reason, has both a right and a duty to participate actively in its functioning. In its more complex presentations, Stoic philosophy divides into three distinguishable but necessarily interlinked fields: those of logic, physics, and ethics. In one common metaphor these are depicted as the garden wall, the fruitful soil of the garden, and the crop the garden produces.

Over the centuries of its existence, and as it was presented by individual thinkers in widely differing circumstances, many features of Stoic philosophy underwent development and significant shifts in emphasis; in its Roman phases, for instance, there was a particular stress on moral and practical aspects, and on the application of its teaching to the individual. The fundamental features of Stoic thought remained recognisable, however, and came to form a crucial part of the general stock of ideas which later Western thought inherited from Antiquity.

Cicero

From *On the Nature of the Gods*

Stoic Theology: The Hierarchy of Nature

II. 33. BALBUS. And even if we want to proceed from primitive and incomplete natures to the ultimate and perfect ones, we arrive of necessity at the nature of the gods. For we notice, first, that nature supports the fruits of the earth, to which she grants simply protection while they take root and grow. **34** Next, she has given animals sense-perception and motion, and appetite, which attracts them to healthful food and repels them from what is poisonous. She has given more than this to man, for she has added reason, whereby the soul's appetites are regulated, being sometimes allowed to run free, and sometimes reined in. The fourth and highest level includes those who are born naturally good and wise, in whom there is innate from the beginning a self-consistent right reason, which must be considered higher than man, attributable to God, and therefore to the universe, in which that perfect and absolute reason must inhere. **35** For it cannot be said that in any ordered arrangement something in the nature of an end and finishing touch does not exist. For just as in the vine or in cattle, unless some force interferes, we see nature take its own course to an end; just as a picture or an artifact or any other product of human skill has an effect as of a finished piece of work, so also in nature as a whole, and to a much greater degree, some end is necessarily accomplished and brought to perfection. This is all the more certain because, while many external forces can prevent particular natural objects from reaching perfection, nothing can stand in the way of universal Nature, because it contains and controls all natural objects. Therefore that fourth and highest level must exist, since no force can attack it. This is the level at which we suppose the Nature of all things to exist; since it naturally excels all things, and since nothing can stand in its way, it follows necessarily that a universe endowed with mind and with practical wisdom exists.

Balbus passes to the divine nature. God is not made in man's image; He is spherical, and revolves. Nature operates creatively, artistically, and providentially because God is in it. The gods the people worship are personified abstractions, or heroes, or natural forces. Pure religion and undefiled is this: to worship one divine being in holiness and purity, and without superstition. He then proceeds to his third point, the divine governance of the universe, of which the chief proof is the famous "argument from Design," which deduces the existence of the watchmaker from the existence of the watch. The world's order is too marvellous to be the result of a fortuitous concourse of atoms. Only familiarity, as Aristotle tells us, blinds us to the divine marvels of the universe.

The Stoic Argument from Design

95. Suppose that beings existed who lived underground in fine, well-lighted houses, adorned with statues and pictures, and equipped with every convenience which ostensibly happy people enjoy in abundance. Suppose further that they had never gone above ground, but had it on hearsay that a divine force existed. Then suppose that one day the jaws of the earth yawned open and they were able to make their way out from their hidden dwellings to the regions which we inhabit. Suppose there suddenly burst upon them the sight of the earth, the sea, and the sky, that they saw for the first time mighty clouds and blustering winds, and the size, the beauty, and the efficiency of the sun, making daylight with its rays spread all over heaven. Imagine next that night cast its shadows over the earth, and they saw the whole of heaven studded and adorned with stars, and the varied light of the waxing and the waning moon, the risings and the settings of the heavenly bodies and their orbits, fixed and unchangeable through all eternity. At the sight of these, surely their first thought would be that the gods exist and that all these wonderful works are the works of God. . . .

98. Let us look first at the whole earth, set in the midpoint of the universe, solid, spherical, and made into a ball by the gravitation of all its parts, clothed in a garment of flowers and plants and trees and fruits, in number beyond belief, in diversity that cannot cloy. Think too of springs flowing cool in all seasons, of rivers with their pellucid waters, of river banks clothed in grass-green, of high vaulted caves, rough rocks, tall mountains looming up, fields stretching away to the horizon; and think of the hidden veins of silver and gold, and the limitless supply of marble.

99. How many different kinds of animals there are, both tame and wild! Think of the birds, flying and singing, the flocks feeding, and the life of the beasts of the forest! And what shall I say of the race of men, who, appointed as it were as custodians of the earth, suffer it not to breed too many wild beasts nor to turn into an uncultivated wilderness of weeds; men, by whose labors the countryside, the islands, and the seashore gleam with the bright pattern of houses and cities? If we could see all this with our souls as we see it with our eyes, no one could look at the whole earth and still be of two minds about divine reason.

[Balbus describes the sea and the sky in the same ecstatic vein, quoting at length from Cicero's translation of the astronomical poet Aratus. The whole of these wonders is held together, he says, by a sort of cosmic sympathy.]

From On the Republic

In a dream, Scipio's father Paulus gives him an overview of the universe, illustrating the small part humans occupy . . .

"'But, like your grandfather here, like me who begot you, Scipio, practise justice and loyalty, virtues which, important as they are in the case of parents and kinsfolk, are most important of all as they affect the fatherland. Such a life is the road to heaven and to this assemblage of those who have finished with mortal life, and, released from the body, dwell in the place which you see.'

16. "Pointing to a ring of light blazing with uncommon splendor among the other flames he continued, 'And this, as the Greeks have taught you, you call the Galaxy or Milky Way.' As I looked at it, it seemed to make the rest of the heavens wondrous bright. Moreover there were stars there such as we never see from the earth, and all of a size beyond our wildest conjecture: the smallest of these was the moon, farthest from the sphere of heaven, closest to the earth, shining with a borrowed light Furthermore, the stellar spheres were far larger than the earth. The result was that the earth itself seemed to me so small that I was vexed at the small size of our empire, which gives us access to the merest pinpoint, as it were, of earth.

17. "As I kept looking down, my grandfather said, "How long, pray, will you mind remain earthbound? Do you not see that you have come into the temple of the sky? The universe, you must know, is built of nine circles or rather hollow spheres, one within the other, of which one is the sphere of heaven, the outermost, embracing all the rest, identical with God himself, the all-highest, limiting and containing the others; studded in this heavenly sphere are the eternal rolling orbits of the fixed stars; and beneath it are the seven spheres which revolve the opposite way from the heavenly sphere; one of these spheres is occupied by that planet which on earth men call Saturn. Next comes the glow of that good-omened and health-bringing planet called Jupiter; next below is Mars, red and hateful to the earth; next, about half-way between heaven and earth, comes the sun, the leader, chief, and regulator of all other sources of light, the mind and guiding principle of the universe, so large that it surveys and fills all things with its light. One of the two orbits that follows close upon the sun is Venus, the other Mercury, and in the inmost sphere the moon turns, lit by the sun's rays. Beneath the sphere of the moon there is nothing that is not mortal and frail, except the souls granted as a gift of the gods to the race of men, but above the moon all things ae eternal. For the core of all the hollow spheres, the ninth, the earth, does not move, but is the lowest, so that all heavy objects gravitate toward it of their own weight.'

18. "After I had collected myself following the amazement with which I viewed the spheres, I asked, 'What is this music, so mighty and so sweet, that fills my ears?' "It is the driving motion of the spheres themselves that produces it, he replied; 'though the intervals that separate them are unequal, yet the spheres are arranged in an exact proportion; the harmony of bass and treble makes a series of matched chords. For so mighty a motion cannot proceed in silence, and naturally at one extreme of the universe the sound is high, at the other low. That is, that outermost orbit, the heavenly one that carries the stars, because it moves the fastest, moves with a high-pitched, lively sound, while this lowest, or lunar, sphere moves with a deep bass note. I leave the ninth, the earth, out of account, for it remains forever fixed, and motionless in one place, occupying the midpoint of the universe. But the other eight orbits, two of which (Mercury and Venus) move at the same speed, strike seven notes with fixed intervals. This number is the key of almost everything; imitating this music with stringed instrument and the voice, expert musicians have opened for themselves a pathway back to heaven, just as others have whose massive intellects have followed divine pursuits in the midst of this human life.

19. "'When the ears of mere mortals are filled with this music, they grow deaf; indeed, hearing is the dullest of your senses. Just as the people who dwell in the high mountains at the cataracts of the Nile have lost their sense of hearing entirely, because the roar is so deafening, even so this music, resulting from the turning of the whole universe at high velocity, is so great a thing that men's ears cannot hear it, just as you cannot look straight at the sun without its rays blinding your eyes.'

"Marvel as I did at this, I could not keep my eyes from perpetually looking at the earth.

20. "Just then my grandfather said, 'I perceive that you still cannot take your mind off the habitat and abode of men; but if it seems to you to be as small as it really is, keep this heavenly sphere ever in view, and despise that mortal one. For what reputation can you gain from the converse of mere men, or what glory that is worth the striving? You see from here that the earth is inhabited only here and there in confined spaces, and that desert wastes lie between these inhabited blots or patches. You see too that dwellers on earth are not only so cut off from one another that there can be no intercommunication; but that some live in the same longitude as you but in the opposite latitude, others in the same latitude but in the opposite longitude, while still others live at the antipodes. Surely you cannot expect your reputation to spread among any of these.

21. "From here also you can see that this same earth is girdled round, as it were, by several zones, two of which, as far apart as possible, and supported by the opposite poles of the heavens, you see to be frozen solid, while the middle and widest zone is parched by the heat of the sun. Only the remaining two are habitable. The south Temperate Zone, where, from your point of view, men walk upside down, has nothing to do with Romans; this other, buffeted by the north wind, where you live—see how small a part of it belongs to you. For the whole territory you inhabit, narrowly limited from north to south, wider from east to west, is nothing but a sort of tiny island, surrounded by that sea which though on earth you call it the Atlantic, the Great Sea, the Ocean, or some grandiose name, is really, as you see, quite infinitesimal.

22. "'Out of the area of this known and inhabited world, small as it is, how likely is it that your name, or that of any one of us, can climb the Caucasus which you see here, or swim the Ganges there? Who at the other ends of the earth, east or west, north or south, will hear your name? When you have lopped off these areas, surely you see what narrow limits your fame would have to spread itself in. As for those who actually do talk about us, how long will they do so?

23. "'And this is not all. Even if *our* posterity should want to hand on to theirs the eulogy of any one of us which they received as a heritage from their fathers, the floods and conflagrations which must occur at fixed intervals would make it impossible for us to achieve a temporal, much less an eternal glory. In any case what does it matter that posterity will talk about you, when you consider that your ancestors never did? And yet those same ancestors are at least as numerous as posterity, and they were certainly better men.

Epictetus

From *The Manual (Encheiridion)*

1. Of all existing things some are in our power, and others are not in our power. In our power are thought, impulse, will to get and will to avoid, and, in a word, everything which is our own doing. Things not in our power include the body, property, reputation, office, and in a word, everything which is not our own doing. Things in our power are by nature free, unhindered, untrammelled; things not in our power are weak, servile, subject to hindrance, dependent on others. Remember then that if you imagine that what is naturally slavish is free, and what is naturally another's is your own, you will be hampered, you will mourn, you will be put to confusion, you will blame gods and men; but if you think that only your own belongs to you, and that what is another's is indeed another's no one will ever put compulsion or hindrance on you, you will blame none, you will accuse none, you will do nothing against your will, no one will harm you, you will have no enemy, for no harm can touch you.

Aiming then at these high matters, you must remember that to attain them requires more than ordinary effort; you will have to give up some things entirely, and put off others for the moment. And if you would have these also—office and wealth—it may be that you will fail to get them, just because your desire is set on the former, and you will certainly fail to attain those things which alone bring freedom and happiness.

Make it your study then to confront every harsh impression with the words, 'You are but an impression, and not at all what you seem to be'. Then test it by those rules that you possess; and first by this—the chief test of all—'Is it concerned with what is in our power or with what is not in our power?' And if it is concerned with what is not in our power, be ready with the answer that it is nothing to you.

2. Remember that the will to get promises attainment of what you will and will to avoid promises escape from what you avoid; and he who fails to get what he wills is unfortunate, and he who does not escape what he wills to avoid is miserable. If then you try to avoid only what is unnatural in the region within your control, you will escape from all that you avoid; but if you try to avoid disease or death or poverty you will be miserable.

Therefore let your will to avoid have no concern with what is not in man's power; direct it only to things in man's power that are contrary to nature. But for the moment you must utterly remove the will to get; for if you will to get something not in man's power you are bound to be unfortunate; while none of the things in man's power that you could honourably will to get is yet within your reach. Impulse to act and not to act, these are your concern; yet exercise them gently and without strain, and provisionally.

3. When anything, from the meanest thing upwards, is attractive or serviceable or an object of affection, remember always to say to yourself, 'What is its nature?' If you are fond of a jug, say you are fond of a jug; then you will not be disturbed if it be broken. If you kiss your child or your wife, say to yourself that you are kissing a human being, for then if death strikes it you will not be disturbed.

4. When you are about to take something in hand, remind yourself what manner of thing it is. If you are going to bathe put before your mind what happens in the bath—water pouring over some, others being jostled, some reviling, others stealing; and you will set to work more securely if you say to yourself at once: 'I want to bathe, and I want to keep my will in harmony with nature,' and so in each thing you do; for in this way, if anything turns up to hinder you in your bathing, you will be ready to say, 'I did not want only to bathe, but to keep my will in harmony with nature, and I shall not so keep it, if I lose my temper at what happens'.

5. What disturbs men's minds is not events but their judgements on events. For instance, death is nothing dreadful, or else Socrates would have thought it so. No, the only dreadful thing about it is men's judgement that it is dreadful. And so when we are hindered, or disturbed, or distressed, let us never lay the blame on others, but on ourselves, that is, on our own judgements. To accuse others for one's own misfortunes is a sign of want of education; to

75

accuse oneself shows that one's education has begun; to accuse neither oneself nor others shows that one's education is complete.

6. Be not elated at an excellence which is not your own. If the horse in his pride were to say, 'I am handsome', we could bear with it. But when you say with pride, 'I have a handsome horse', know that the good horse is the ground of your pride. You ask then what you can call your own. The answer is—the way you deal with your impressions. Therefore when you deal with your impressions in accord with nature, then you may be proud indeed, for your pride will be in a good which is your own.

7. When you are on a voyage, and your ship is at anchorage, and you disembark to get fresh water, you may pick up a small shellfish or a truffle by the way, but you must keep your attention fixed on the ship, and keep looking towards it constantly, to see if the Helmsman calls you; and if he does, you have to leave everything, or be bundled on board with your legs tied like a sheep. So it is in life. If you have a dear wife or child given you, they are like the shellfish or the truffle, they are very well in their way. Only, if the Helmsman call, run back to your ship, leave all else, and do not look behind you. And if you are old, never go far from the ship, so that when you are called you may not fail to appear.

8. Ask not that events should happen as you will, but let your will be that events should happen as they do, and you shall have peace.

9. Sickness is a hindrance to the body, but not to the will, unless the will consent. Lameness is a hindrance to the leg, but not to the will. Say this to yourself at each event that happens, for you shall find that though it hinders something else it will not hinder you.

10. When anything happens to you, always remember to turn to yourself and ask what faculty you have to deal with it. If you see a beautiful boy or a beautiful woman, you will find continence the faculty to exercise there; if trouble is laid on you, you will find endurance; if ribaldry, you will find patience. And if you train yourself in this habit your impressions will not carry you away.

11. Never say of anything, 'I lost it,' but say, 'I gave it back.' Has your child died? It was given back. Has your wife died? She was given back. Has your estate been taken from you? Was not this also given back? But you say, 'He who took it from me is wicked.' What does it matter to through whom the Giver asked it back? As long as He gives it you, take care of it, but not as your own; treat it as passers-by treat an inn.

12. If you wish to make progress, abandon reasonings of this sort: 'If I neglect my affairs I shall have nothing to live on'; 'If I do not punish my son, he will be wicked.' For it is better to die of hunger, so that you be free from pain and free from fear, than to live in plenty and be troubled in mind. It is better for your son to be wicked than for you to be miserable. Wherefore begin with little things. Is your drop of oil spilt? Is your sup of wine stolen? Say to yourself, 'This is the price paid for freedom from passion, this is the price of a quiet mind." Nothing can be had without a price. When you call your slave-boy, reflect that he may not be able to hear you, and if he hears you, he may not be able to do anything you want. But he is not so well off that it rests with him to give you peace of mind.

13. If you wish to make progress, you must be content in external matters to seem a fool and a simpleton; do not wish men to think you know anything, and if any should think you to be somebody, distrust yourself. For know that it is not easy to keep your will in accord with nature and at the same time keep outward things.

14. It is silly to want your children and your wife and your friends to live for ever, for that means that you want what is not in your control to be in your control, and what is not your own to be yours. In the same way if you want your servant to make no mistakes, you are a fool, for you want vice not to be vice but something different. But if you want not to be disappointed in your will to get, you can attain to that.

Exercise yourself then in what lies in your power. Each man's master is the man who has authority over what he wishes or does not wish, to secure the one or to take away the other. Let him then who wishes to be free not wish for anything or avoid anything that depends on others; or else he is bound to be a slave.

15. Remember that you must behave in life as you would at a banquet. A dish is handed round and comes to you; put out your hand and take it politely. It passes you; do not stop it. It has not reached you; do not be impatient to get it, but wait till your turn comes. Bear yourself thus towards children, wife, office, wealth, and one day you will be worthy to banquet with the gods. But if when they are set before you, you do not take them but despise them, then you shall not only share the gods' banquet, but shall share their rule. For by so doing Diogenes and Heraclitus and men like them were called divine and deserved the name.

16. When you see a man shedding tears in sorrow for a child abroad or dead, or for loss of property, beware that you are not carried away by the impression that it is outward ills that make him miserable. Keep this thought by you: 'What distresses him is not the event, for that does not distress another, but his judgement on the event' Therefore do not hesitate to sympathize with him so far as words go, and if it so chance, even to groan with him; but take heed that you do not also groan in your inner being.

17. Remember that you are an actor in a play, and the Playwright chooses the manner of it: if he wants it short, it is short; if long, it is long. If he wants you to act a poor man you must act the part with all your powers; and so if your part be a cripple or a magistrate or a plain man. For your business is to act the character that is given you and act it well; and choice of the cast is Another's.

29. In everything you do consider what comes first and what follows, and so approach it. Otherwise you will come to it with a good heart at first because you have not reflected on any of the consequences, and afterwards, when difficulties have appeared, you will desist to your shame. Do you wish to win at Olympia? So do I, by the gods, for it is a fine thing. But consider the first steps to it, and the consequences, and so lay your hand to the work. You must submit to discipline, eat to order, touch no sweets, train under compulsion, at a fixed hour, in heat and cold, drink no cold water, nor wine, except by order; you must hand yourself over completely to your trainer as you would to a physician, and then when the contest comes you must risk getting hacked, and sometimes dislocate your hand, twist your ankle, swallow plenty of sand, sometimes get a flogging, and with all this suffer defeat. When you have considered all this well, then enter on the athlete's course, if you still wish it. If you act with out thought you will be behaving like children, who one day play at wrestlers, another day at gladiators, now sound the trumpet, and next strut the stage. Like them you will be now an athlete, now a gladiator, then orator, then philosopher, but nothing with all your soul. Like an ape, you imitate every sight you see, and one thing after another takes your fancy. When you undertake a thing you do it casually and half-heartedly, instead of considering it and looking at it all round. In the same way some people, when they see a philosopher and hear a man speaking like Euphrates (and indeed who can speak as he can?), wish to be philosophers themselves.

Man, consider first what it is you are undertaking, then look at your own powers and see if you can bear it. Do you want to compete in the pentathlon or in wrestling: Look to your arms, your thighs, see what your loins are like. For different men are born for different tasks. Do you suppose that if you do this you can live as you do now—eat and drink as you do now, indulge desire and discontent just as before? Nay, you must sit up late, work hard, abandon your own people, be looked down on by a mere slave, be ridiculed by those who meet you, get the worst of it in everything—in honour, in office, in justice, in every possible thing. This is what you have to consider: whether you are willing to pay this price for peace of mind, freedom, tranquillity. If not, do not come near; do not be, like the children, first a philosopher, then a tax-collector, then an orator, then one of Caesar's procurators. These callings do not agree. You must be one man, good or bad; you must develop either your Governing Principle, or your outward endowments; you must study either your inner man, or outward things—in a work, you must choose between the position of a philosopher and that of a mere outsider.

44. It is illogical to reason thus, 'I am richer than you, therefore I am superior to you,' 'I am more eloquent than you, therefore I am superior to you.' It is more logical to reason, 'I am richer than you, therefore my property is superior to yours,' 'I am more eloquent than you, therefore my speech is superior to yours.' You are something more than property or speech.

45. If a man washes quickly, do not say that he washes badly, but that he washes quickly. If a man drinks much wine, do not say that he drinks badly, but that he drinks much. For till you have decided what judgement prompts him, how do you know that he acts badly? If you do as I say, you will assent to your apprehensive impressions and to none other.

46. On no occasion call yourself a philosopher, nor talk at large of your principles among the multitude, but act on your principles. For instance, at a banquet do not say how one ought to eat, but eat as you ought. Remember that Socrates had so completely got rid of the thought of display that when men came and wanted an introduction to philosophers he took them to be introduced; so patient of neglect was he. And if a discussion arise among the multitude on some principle, keep silent for the most part; for you are in great danger of blurting out some undigested thought. And when someone says to you, 'You know nothing,' and you do not let is provoke you, then know that you are really on the right road. For sheep do not bring grass to their shepherds and show them how much they have eaten, but they digest their fodder and then produce it in the form of wool and milk. Do the same yourself; instead of displaying your principles to the multitude, show them the results of the principles you have digested.

47. When you have adopted the simple life, do not pride yourself upon it, and if you are a water-drinker do not say on every occasion, 'I am a water-drinker.' And if you ever want to train laboriously, keep it to yourself and do not make a show of it. Do not embrace statues. If you are very thirsty take a good draught of cold water, and rinse your mouth and tell no one.

48. The ignorant man's position and character is this: he never looks to himself for benefit or harm, but to the world outside him. The philosopher's position and character is that he always look to himself for benefit and harm.

The signs of one who is making progress are: he blames none, praises none, complains of none, accuses none, never speaks of himself as if he were somebody, or as if he knew anything. And if any-one compliments him he laughs in himself at his compliment; and if one blames him, he makes no defence. He goes about like a convalescent, careful not to disturb his constitution on its road to recovery, until it has got firm hold. He has got rid of the will to get, and his will to avoid is directed no longer to what is beyond our power but only to what is in our power and contrary to nature. In all things he exercises his will without strain. If men regard him as foolish or ignorant he pays no heed. In one word, he keeps watch and guard on himself as his own enemy, lying in wait for him.

Cicero

The Laws

With respect to the true principle of justice, many learned men have maintained that it springs from Law. I hardly know if their opinion be not correct, at least, according to their own definition; for "Law (say they) is the highest reason, implanted in nature, which prescribes those things which ought to be done, and forbids the contrary." This, they think, is apparent from the converse of the proposition; because this same reason, when it is confirmed and established in men's minds, is the law of all their actions.

They therefore conceive that the voice of conscience is a law, that moral prudence is a law, whose operation is to urge us to good actions, and restrain us from evil ones. They think, too, that the Greek name for law ($\nu o \mu o \varsigma$), which is derived from $\nu \acute{\epsilon} \mu \omega$, to distribute, implies the very nature of the thing, that is, to give every man his due. For my part, I imagine that the moral essence of law is better expressed by its Latin name, (*lex*), which conveys the idea of selection or discrimination. According to the Greeks, therefore, the name of law implies an equitable distribution of goods: according to the Romans, an equitable discrimination between good and evil.

The true definition of law should, however, include both these characteristics. And this being granted as an almost self-evident proposition, the origin of justice is to be sought in the divine law of eternal and immutable morality. This indeed is the true energy of nature, the very soul and essence of wisdom, the test of virtue and vice. But since every discussion must relate to some subject, whose terms are of frequent occurrence in the popular language of the citizens, we shall be sometimes obliged to use the same terms as the vulgar, and to conform to that common idiom which signifies by the word law, all the arbitrary regulations which are found in our statute books, either commanding or forbidding certain actions.

We should seek for justice in its native source, which being discovered, we shall afterwards be able to speak with more authority and precision respecting our civil laws, that come home to the affairs of our citizens.

I shall endeavour to describe a system of Laws adapted to the Commonwealth, which Scipio declares to be most desirable in those Six Books which I have written under that title. All our laws, therefore, are to be accommodated to that mixed kind of political government there recommended. We shall also treat of the general principles of morals and manners, which appear most appropriate to such a constitution of society, but without descending to particular details.

Grant me that the entire universe is overruled by the power of God, that by his nature, reason, energy, mind, divinity, or some other word of clearer signification, all things are governed and directed. . . . Since you grant me the existence of God, and the superintendence of Providence, I maintain that he has been especially beneficent to man. This human animal—prescient, sagacious, complex, acute, full of memory, reason and counsel, which we call man,—is generated by the supreme God in a more transcendent condition than most of his fellow-creatures. For he is the only creature among the earthly races of animated beings endued with superior reason and thought, in which the rest are deficient. And what is there, I do not say in man alone, but in all heaven and earth, more divine than reason, which, when it becomes ripe and perfect, is justly termed wisdom?

There exists, therefore, since nothing is better than reason, and since this is the common property of God and man, a certain aboriginal rational intercourse between divine and human natures. This reason, which is common to both, therefore, can be none other than right reason; and since this *right reason* is what we call *Law*, God and men are said by Law to be consociated. Between whom, since there is a communion of law, there must be also a communication of Justice.

Law and Justice being thus the common rule of immortals and mortals, it follows that they are both the fellow-citizens of one city and commonwealth. And if they are obedient to the same rule, the same authority and denomination, they may with still closer propriety be termed fellow-citizens, since one celestial regency, one divine mind, one omnipotent Deity then regulates all their thoughts and actions.

This universe, therefore, forms one immeasurable Commonwealth and city, common alike to gods and mortals. And as in earthly states, certain particular laws, which we shall hereafter describe, govern the particular relationships of kindred tribes; so in the nature of things doth an universal law, far more magnificent and resplendent, regulate the affairs of that universal city where gods and men compose one vast association.

When we thus reason on universal nature, we are accustomed to reason after this method. We believe that in the long course of ages and the uninterrupted succession of celestial revolutions, the seed of the human race was sown on our planet, and being scattered over the earth, was animated by the divine gift of souls. Thus men retained from their terrestrial origin, their perishable and mortal bodies, while their immortal spirits were ingenerated by Deity. From which consideration we are bold to say that we possess a certain consanguinity and kindred fellowship with the celestials. And so far as we know, among all the varieties of animals, man alone retains the idea of the Divinity. And among men there is no nation so savage and ferocious as to deny the necessity of worshipping God, however ignorant it may be respecting the nature of his attributes. From whence we conclude that every man must recognize a Deity, who considers the origin of his nature and the progress of his life.

Now the law of virtue is the same in God and man, and cannot possibly be diverse. This virtue is nothing else than a nature perfect in itself, and developed in all its excellence. There exists therefore a similitude between God and man; nor can any knowledge be more appropriate and sterling than what relates to this divine similitude.

Nature, attentive to our wants, offers us her treasures with the most graceful profusion. And it is easy to perceive that the benefits which flow from her are true and veritable gifts, which Providence has provided on purpose for human enjoyment, and not the fortuitous productions of her exuberant fecundity. Her liberality appears, not only in the fruits and vegetables which gush from the bosom of the earth, but likewise in cattle and the beasts of the field. It is clear that some of these are intended for the advantage of mankind, a part for propagation, and a part for food. Innumerable arts have likewise been discovered by the teaching of nature; for her doth reason imitate, and skilfully discover all things necessary to the happiness of life.

With respect to man this same bountiful nature hath not merely allotted him a subtle and active spirit, but moreover favoured him with physical senses, like so many guardians and messengers. Thus has she improved our understanding in relation to many obscure principles, and laid the foundation of practical knowledge; and in all respects moulded our corporeal faculties to the service of our intellectual genius. For while she has debased the forms of other animals, who live to eat rather than eat to live, she has bestowed on man an erect stature, and an open countenance, and thus prompted him to the contemplation of heaven, the ancient home of his kindred immortals. So exquisitely, too, hath she fashioned the features of the human race, as to make them symbolic of the most recondite thoughts and sentiments. As for our too eloquent eyes (*oculi nimis arguti*), do they not speak forth every impulse and passion of our souls? And that which we call *expression*, in which we infinitely excel all the inferior animals, how marvellously it delineates all our speculations and feelings! Of this the Greeks well knew the meaning, though they had no word for it.

I will not enlarge on the wonderful faculties and qualities of the rest of the body, the modulation of the voice, and the power of oratory, which is perhaps the greatest instrument of our influence over human society. These matters do not belong to the occasion of our present discourse, and I think that Scipio has already sufficiently explained them in those books of mine which you have read.

As the Deity, therefore, was pleased to create man as the chief and president of all terrestrial creatures, so it is evident, without further argument, that human nature has made the greatest advances by its intrinsic energy; that nature, which without any other instruction than her own, has developed the first rude principles of the understanding, and strengthened and perfected reason to all the appliances of science and art.

You may well describe these topics as grand, which we are now briefly discussing. For of all the questions on which our philosophers argue, there is none which it is more important thoroughly to understand than this, *that man is born for justice, and that law and equity are not a mere establishment of opinion, but an institution of nature*. This truth will become still more apparent if we investigate the nature of human association and society.

There is no one thing more like to another, more homogeneous and analogous, than man is to man. And if the corruption of customs, and the variation of opinions, had not induced an imbecility of minds, and turned them aside from the course of nature, no one would more nearly resemble himself than all men would resemble all men. Therefore whatever definition we give of man, it must include the whole human race. And this is a good argument, that no portion of mankind can be heterogeneous or dissimilar from the rest; because, if this were the case, one definition could not include all men.

In fact, reason, which alone gives us so many advantages over beasts, by means of which we conjecture, argue, refute, discourse, and accomplish and conclude our designs, is assuredly common to all men; for the faculty of acquiring knowledge is similar in all human minds, though the knowledge itself may be endlessly diversified. By the same senses we all perceive the same objects, and that which strikes the sensibilities of the few, cannot be indifferent to those of the many. Those first rude elements of intelligence which, as I before observed, are the earliest developments of thought, are similarly exhibited by all men; and that faculty of speech which is the soul's interpreter, agrees in the ideas it conveys, though it may differ in the syllables that express them. And therefore there exists not a man in any nation, who, adopting his true nature for his true guide, may not improve in virtue.

Nor is this resemblance which all men bear to each other remarkable in those things only which accord to right reason. For it is scarcely less conspicuous in those corrupt practices by which right reason is most cruelly violated. For all men alike are captivated by voluptuousness, which is in reality no better than disgraceful vice, though it may seem to bear some natural relations to goodness; for by its delicious delicacy and luxury it insinuates error into the mind, and leads us to cultivate it as something salutary, forgetful of its poisonous qualities.

An error, scarcely less universal, induces us to shun death, as if it were annihilation; and to cling to life, because it keeps us in our present stage of existence, which is perhaps rather a misfortune than a desideratum. Thus, likewise, we erroneously consider pain as one of the greatest evils, not only on account of its present asperity, but also because it seems the precursor of mortality. Another common delusion obtains, which induces all mankind to associate renown with honesty, as if we are necessarily happy when we are renowned, and miserable when we happen to be inglorious.

In short, our minds are all similarly susceptible of inquietudes, joys, desires and fears; and if opinions are not the same in all men, it does not follow, for example, that the people of Egypt who deify dogs and cats, do not labour under superstition in the same way as other nations, though they may differ from them in the forms of its manifestation.

But in nothing is the uniformity of human nature more conspicuous than in its respect for virtue. What nation is there, in which kindness, benignity, gratitude, and mindfulness of benefits are not recommended? What nation in which arrogance, malice, cruelty, and unthankfulness, are not reprobated and detested! This uniformity of opinions, invincibly demonstrates that mankind was intended to compose one fraternal association. And to affect this, the faculty of reason must be improved till it instructs us in all the arts of well-living. . . .

It follows, then, in the line of our argument, *that nature made us just that we might participate our goods with each other, and supply each other's wants.* You observe in this discussion whenever I speak of nature, I mean *nature in its genuine purity*, and not in the corrupt state which is displayed by the depravity of evil custom, which is so great, that the natural and innate flame of virtue is often almost extinguished and stifled by the antagonist vices, which are accumulated around it.

But if our true nature would assert her rights, and teach men the noble lesson of the poet, who says, "I am a man therefore no human interest can be indifferent to me,"—then would justice be administered equally by all and to all. For nature hath not merely given us reason, but right reason, and consequently that law, which is nothing else than right reason enjoining what is good, and forbidding what is evil.

Now if nature hath given us law, she hath also given us justice,—for as she has bestowed reason on all, she has equally bestowed the sense of justice on all. And therefore did Socrates deservedly execrate the man who first drew a distinction between the law of nature and the law of morals, for he justly conceived that this error is the source of most human vices.

It is to this essential union between the naturally honourable, and the politically expedient, that this sentence of Pythagoras refers:—"Love is universal: let its benefits be universal likewise." From whence it appears that when a wise man is attached to good man by that friendship whose rights are so extensive, that phenomenon takes place which is altogether incredible to worldlings, and yet it is a necessary consequence, that he loves himself not more dearly than he loves his friend. For how can a difference of interests arise where all interests are similar? If there could be such a difference of interests, however minute, it would be no longer a true friendship, which vanishes immediately when, for the sake of our own benefit, we would sacrifice that of our friend. . . .

[I will add a few considerations] in conformity with the method of the philosophers. I do not mean the older sages of philosophy, but those modern philosophers who keep a magazine of arguments in reserve, on every imaginable topic, and who, instead of discussing questions freely and unconstrainedly, will permit us to speak only in accordance with their logical arrangements and dialectical distinctions. These gentlemen will never allow that we have done justice to our subject, unless we demonstrate that nature is just, and justice is natural, in a distinct and scientific disputation. . . .

Was it the fear of punishment, and not the nature of the thing itself that ought to restrain mankind from wickedness, what, I would ask, could give villains the least uneasiness, abstracting from all fears of this kind? And yet none of them was ever so audaciously impudent, but he endeavoured to justify what he had done by some law of nature, denied the fact, or else pretended a just sorrow for it. Now if the wicked have the confidence to appeal to these laws, with what profound respect ought good men to treat them?

There is the greater need, therefore, of insisting on the natural and unavoidable penalties of conscience. For if either direct punishment, or the fear of it, was what deterred from a vicious course of life, and not the turpitude of the thing itself, then none could be guilty of injustice, in a moral sense, and the greatest offenders ought rather to be called imprudent than wicked.

On the other hand, if we are determined to the practice of goodness, not by its own intrinsic excellence, but for the sake of some private advantage, we are cunning, rather than good men. What will not that man do in the dark who fears nothing but a witness and a judge? Should be meet a solitary individual in a desert place, with a large sum of money about him, and altogether unable to defend himself from being robbed, how would he behave? In such a case the man whom we have represented to be honest from principle, and the nature of the thing itself, would converse with the stranger, assist him, and show him the way. But as to the man who does nothing for the sake of another, and measures everything by the advantage it brings to himself, it is obvious, I suppose, how such a one would act; and should he deny that he would kill the man or rob him of his treasure, his reason for this cannot be that he apprehends there is any moral turpitude in such actions, but only because he is afraid of a discovery, and the bad consequences that would thence ensue. A sentiment this, at which not only learned men, but even clowns must blush.

It is therefore an absurd extravagance in some philosophers to assert that all things are necessarily just, which are established by the civil laws and the institutions of the people. Are then the laws of tyrants just, simply because they are laws? If the thirty tyrants of Athens imposed certains laws on the Athenians, and if these Athenians were delighted with these tyrannical laws, are we therefore bound to consider these laws as just? For my own part, I do not think such laws deserve any greater estimation than that passed during our own interregnum, which ordained, that the dictator should be empowered to put to death with impunity, whatever citizens he pleased, without hearing them in their own defence.

There can be but one essential justice, which cements society, and one law which establishes this justice. This law is right reason, which is the true rule of all commandments and prohibitions. Whoever neglects this law, whether written or unwritten, is necessarily unjust and wicked.

But if justice consists in submissions to written laws and national customs, and if, as the Epicureans persist in affirming, everything must be measured by utility alone, he who wishes to find an occasion of breaking such laws and customs, will be sure to discover it. So that real justice remains powerless if not supported by nature, and this pretended justice is overturned by that very utility which they call its foundation.

But this is not all. If nature does not ratify law, all the virtues lose their sway. What becomes of generosity, patriotism, or friendship? Where should we find the desire of benefitting our neighbours, or the gratitude that acknowledges kindness? For all these virtues proceed from our natural inclination to love and cherish our associates. This is the true basis of justice, and without this, not only the mutual charities of men, but the religious service of the gods, would become obsolete; for these are preserved, as I imagine, rather by the natural sympathy which subsists between divine and human beings, than by mere fear and timidity.

If the will of the people, the decrees of the senate, the adjudications of magistrates, were sufficient to establish justice, the only question would be how to gain suffrages, and to win over the votes of the majority, in order that corruption and spoliation, and the falsification of wills, should become lawful. But if the opinions and suffrages of foolish men had sufficient weight to outbalance the nature of things, might they not determine among them, that what is essentially bad and pernicious should henceforth pass for good and beneficial? Or why should not a law able to enforce injustice, take the place of equity? Would not this same law be able to change evil into good, and good into evil?

As far as we are concerned, we have no other rule capable of distinguishing between a good or a bad law, than our natural conscience and reason. These, however, enable us to separate justice from injustice, and to discriminate between the honest and the scandalous. For common sense has impressed in our minds the first principles of things, and has given us a general acquaintance with them, by which we connect with Virtue every honourable and excellent quality, and with Vice all that is abominable and disgraceful.

Now we must entirely take leave of our senses, ere we can suppose that law and justice have no foundation in nature, and rely merely on the transient opinions of men. We should not venture to praise the virtue of a tree or a horse, in which expression there is an abuse of terms, were we not convinced that this virtue was in their nature, rather than in our opinion. For a stronger reason, it is mainly with respect to the moral nature of things, that we ought to speak of honour and shame among men.

If opinion could determine respecting the character of universal virtue, it might also decide respecting particular or partial virtues. But who will dare to determine that a man is prudent and cautious in his moral disposition, from any external appearances? For virtue evidently lies in perfect rationality, and this resides in the inmost depths of our nature. The same remark applies to all honour and honesty, for we judge of true and false, creditable and discreditable, rather by their essential qualities, than their external relations. Thus we judge according to their intrinsic nature, that rationality of life, which is virtue, must be ever constant and perpetual, and that inconstancy must necessarily be vicious.

We form an estimate of the opinions of youths, but not by their opinions. Those virtues and vices which reside in their moral natures, must not be measured by opinions. And so of all moral qualities, we must discriminate between honourable and dishonourable by reference to the essential nature of the things themselves.

The good we commend, must needs contain in itself something commendable. For as I before stated, goodness is not a mode of opinion: it is what it is, by the force of its very essence. If it were otherwise, opinion alone might constitute virtue and happiness, which is the most absurd of suppositions. And since we judge of good and evil by their nature, and since good and evil are the true constituents of honour and shame, we should judge in the same manner all honourable and all shameful qualities, testing them by the law of nature, without prejudice or passion. But our steady attention to this moral law of nature is often too much disturbed by the dissension of men and the variation of opinions. We might perhaps obey this law of nature more exactly, if we attended more accurately to the evidence of our senses, which being absolutely natural, are less likely to be deceived by artificial objects. Those objects, indeed, which sometimes present to us one appearance, sometimes another, we term fictions of the senses; but it is far otherwise. For neither parent, nor nurse, nor master, nor poet, nor drama, deceive our senses; nor do popular prejudices seduce them. But our delusions are connected with corruption of our mental opinions. And this corruption is either superinduced by those causes of error I have enumerated, which, taking possession of the young and uneducated, betray them into a thousand perversities, or by that voluptuousness which is the mimic of goodness, implicated and interfused through all our senses—the prolific mother of all human disasters. For she so corrupts us by her bewitching blandishments that we no longer perceive that things may be essentially excellent, though they have none of this deliciousness and pruriency.

From what I have said on this subject, it may then easily be concluded, that Justice and Equity are desirable for their own sake. For all virtuous men love Justice and Equity, for what they are in themselves; and we cannot believe that such virtuous men should delude themselves by loving something which does not deserve their affection. Justice and Right are therefore desirable and amiable in themselves; and if this is true of Right, it must be true of all the moral virtues with which it is connected. What then shall we say of liberality? Is it to be exercised gratuitously, or does it covet some reward and recompense? If a man does good without expecting any recompense for his kindness, then it is gratuitous: if he does expect compensation, it is a mere matter of traffic. Doubtless, he who truly deserves the reputation of a generous and good-natured man, performs his philanthropical duties without consulting his secular interests. In the same way the virtue of justice demands neither emolument nor salary, and therefore we desire it for its own sake, because it is its own reward. And for this reason we should entertain the same estimate of all moral virtues.

Besides this, if we weigh virtue by the mere utility and profit that attend it, and not by its own merit, the virtue which results will be in fact a species of vice (*malitia rectissime decitur*). For the more a man's views are self-interested, the further he recedes from probity. It therefore necessarily happens, that those who measure virtue by profit, acknowledge no other virtue than this usurious vice. For who could be called benevolent, if none endeavoured to do good for the love of others? Where could we find the grateful person, if those who are disposed to gratitude could meet no benefactor disinterested enough to deserve it? What would become of sacred friendship, if we were not to love our friends for their own sake with all our heart and soul? In pursuance of this pseudo-benevolence, we must desert our friend, as soon as we can derive no further assistance from him. What can be more inhuman! But if friendship ought rather to be cultivated on its own account, for the same reason are society, equality, and justice, desirable for themselves. If this were not so, there could be no justice at all, since nothing is more opposite to the very essence of virtue than selfish interest.

What then shall we say of temperance, sobriety, continence, modesty, bashfulness, and chastity? Is it the fear of laws, or the dread of judgments and penalties, which restrain intemperance and dissoluteness? Do we then live in innocence and moderation, only to acquire a certain secular reputation? And when we blush at licentious discourse, is it only through a squeamish prudery, lest our reputation should be stained? How I am ashamed at those philosophers, who assert that there are no vices to be avoided but those which the laws have branded with infamy. Can it be said that those are truly chaste, who abstain from adultery, merely for the fear of public exposure, and that disgrace which is only one of its many evil consequences? Indeed, what can you praise or blame with reason, if you depart from that great law and rule of nature, which makes the difference between right and wrong? Shall corporal defects, if they are remarkable, shock our sensibilities, and shall those of the soul make no impression on us?—Of the soul, I say, whose turpitude is so evidently proved by its vices. For what is there more hideous than avarice, more ferocious than lust, more contemptible than cowardice, more base than stupidity and folly? Well, therefore, may we style unhappy, those persons in whom any one of these vices is conspicuous, not on account of the disgraces or losses to which they are exposed, but on account of the moral baseness of their sins.

We may apply the same ethical test to those who are distinguished for their virtue. For if virtue be not the highest excellence to which we aspire, it necessarily follows that there is something better than virtue. Is it money, fame, beauty, health? All these appear of little value to us when we possess them, especially when we consider that the duration of their enjoyment is altogether uncertain. Is it that basest of all things, voluptuousness? Certainly not; for nothing gives so much dignity to virtue, as its capacity of overruling and despising all the gratifications of secular and sensual life. . . .

I should say, that Cato, and municipal citizens like him, have two countries, one, that of their birth, and the other, that of their choice. Cato being born at Tusculum, was elected a citizen of Rome, so that a Tusculan by extraction, and a Roman by election, he had, besides his native country, a rightful one. So among your Athenians, before Theseus urged them to quit their rural territories, and assembled them at Athens, those that were natives of Sunium, were reckoned as Sunians and Athenians at the same time. In the same way, we may justly entitle as our country, both the place from where we originated, and that to which we have been associated. It is necessary, however, that we should attach ourselves by a preference of affection to the latter, which, under the name of the Commonwealth, is the common country of us all. For this country it is, that we ought to sacrifice our lives; it is to her that we ought to devote ourselves without reserve; and it is for her that we ought to risk and hazard all our riches and our hopes. Yet this universal patriotism does not prohibit us from preserving a very tender affection for the native soil that was the cradle of our infancy and our youth.

Therefore I will never disown Arpinum as my country, at the same time acknowledging that Rome will always secure my preference, and that Arpinum can only deserve the second place in my heart. . . .

Let us once more examine, before we descend to particulars, what is the essence and moral obligation of law; lest, when we come to apply it to its subordinate relations, we should not exactly understand each other for want of explanation; and lest we should be ignorant of the force of those terms which are usually employed in jurisprudence.

This . . . hath been the decision of the wisest philosophers; that law was neither excogitated by the genius of men, nor is it anything discovered in the progress of society; but a certain eternal principle, which governs the entire universe; wisely commanding what is right, and prohibiting what is wrong. Therefore, that aboriginal and supreme law is the Spirit of God himself; enjoining virtue, and restraining vice. For this reason it is, that this law, which the gods have bestowed on the human race, is so justly applauded. For it is the reason and mind of Wisdom, urging us to good, and deterring us from evil.

From little children have we learned such phrases as this, "that a man appeals to justice, and goes to law;" and a great many municipal laws have we heard mentioned; but we should not understand that such commandments and prohibitions have sufficient moral power to make us practise virtue and avoid vice.

The moral power of law, is not only far more ancient than these legal institutions of states and peoples, but it is coeval with God himself, who beholds and governs both heaven and earth. For it is impossible that the divine mind should exist without reason; and divine reason must necessarily be possessed of a power to determine what is virtuous and what is vicious. Nor, because it was nowhere written, that one man should maintain the pass of a bridge against the enemy's whole army, and that he should order the bridge behind him to be cut down, are we therefore to imagine that the valiant Cocles did not perform this great exploit, agreeably to the laws of nature and the dictates of true bravery. Again, though in the reign of Tarquin there was no written law concerning adultery, it does not therefore follow that Sextus Tarquinius did not offend against the eternal law when he committed a rape on Lucretia, daughter of Tucipitinus. For, even then he had the light of reason deduced from the nature of things, that incites to good actions and dissuades from evil ones. And this has the force of a law, not from the time it was written, but from the first moment it began to exist. Now, this existence of moral obligation is coeternal with that of the divine mind. Therefore the true and supreme law, whose commands and prohibitions are equally infallible, is the right reason of the Sovereign Deity.

Therefore, as the Divine Mind, or reason, is the supreme law, so it exists in the mind of the sage, so far as it can be perfected in man. With respect to civil laws, which differ in all ages and nations, the name of law belongs to them not so much by right as by the favour of the people. For every law which deserves the name of a law ought to be morally good and laudable, as we might demonstrate by the following arguments. It is clear, that laws were originally made for the security of the people, for the preservation of cities, for the peace and benefit of society. Doubtless, the first legislators persuaded the people that they would write and publish such laws only as should conduce to the general morality and happiness, if they would receive and obey them. Such were the regulations, which being settled and sanctioned, they justly entitled *Laws*. From which we may reasonably conclude, that those who made unjustifiable and pernicious enactments for the people, counteracted their own promises and professions; and established anything rather than *laws*, properly so called, since it is evident that the very signification of the word *law*, comprehends the essence and energy of justice and equity.

I would therefore interrogate you on this point like our inquisitive philosophers. If a state wants something, wanting which it is reckoned no state, must not that something be something good? [And furthermore, if] a state has no law, is it not for that reason to be reckoned no state? We must therefore reckon law among the very best things.

If then in the majority of nations, many pernicious and mischievous enactments are made, as far removed from the law of justice we have defined as the mutual engagements of robbers, are we bound to call them laws? For as we cannot call the recipes of ignorant empirics, who give poisons instead of medicines, the prescriptions of a physician, we cannot call that the true law of the people, whatever be its name, if it enjoins what is injurious, let the people receive it as they will. For law is the just distinction between right and wrong, conformable to nature, the original and principal regulator of all things, by which the laws of men should be measured, whether they punish the guilty or protect the innocent. [Consequently] no law but that of justice should either be proclaimed as a law or enforced as a law. [Therefore] regard as nullable and voidable the laws of Titius and Apuleius, because they are unjust. You may say the same of the laws of Livius, so much the more, since a single vote of the senate would be sufficient to abrogate them in an instant. But that law of justice, which I have explained, can never be rendered obsolete or inefficacious.

[Therefore, we require the] laws of justice the more ardently, because they would be durable and permanent, and would not require those perpetual alterations which all injudicious enactments demand. . . .

Let this, therefore, be a fundamental principle in all societies, that the gods are the supreme lords and governors of all things,—that all events are directed by their influence and wisdom, and that they are loving and benevolent to mankind. They likewise know what every person really is; they observe his actions, whether good or bad; they discern whether our religious professions are sincere and heartfelt, and are sure to make a difference between good men and the wicked.

When once our minds are confirmed in these views, it will not be difficult to inspire them with true and useful sentiments,—such as this, that no man should be so madly presumptuous as to believe that he has either reason or intelligence, if he does not believe that the heaven and the world possess them likewise, or in other words, that there is no Supreme Mind which keeps the universe in motion. The presumption is the more excessive in man, who with his best philosophy, can hardly understand what the universe means.

In truth, we can scarcely reckon him a man, whom neither the regular courses of the stars, nor the alternations of day and night, nor the temperature of the seasons, nor the productions that nature displays for his use, do not urge to gratitude towards heaven.

As the beings furnished with reason are incomparably superior to those who want it, and we cannot say, without impiety, that anything transcends the universal Nature, we must therefore confess that divine reason is contained within her. Who will dispute the utility of these sentiments, when he shall reflect how many cases of the greatest importance are decided by oaths; how much the sacred rites performed in making treaties tend to assure peace and tranquility; also, what numbers the fear of divine punishment has reclaimed from a vicious course of life; and how sacred the social rights must be in a society where a firm persuasion obtains of the immediate intervention of the immortal gods, both as witnesses and judges of our actions? Such is the "preamble of the law," to use the expression of Plato.

Lucretius

Epicurean Philosophy at Rome

The Nature of Happiness

What joy it is, when out at sea the stormwinds are lashing the waters, to gaze from the shore at the heavy stress some other man is enduring! Not that anyone's afflictions are in themselves a source of delight; but to realize from what troubles you yourself are free is joy indeed. What joy, again, to watch opposing hosts marshalled on the field of battle when you have yourself no part in their peril! But this is the greatest joy of all: to stand aloof in a quiet citadel, stoutly fortified by the teaching of the wise, and to gaze down from that elevation on others wandering aimlessly in a vain search for the way of life, pitting their wits one against another, disputing for precedence, struggling night and day with unstinted effort to scale the pinnacles of wealth and power. O joyless hearts of men! O minds without vision! How dark and dangerous the life in which this tiny span is lived away! Do you not see that nature is clamoring for two things only, a body free from pain, and a mind released from worry and fear for the enjoyment of pleasurable sensations?

So we find that the requirements of our bodily nature are few indeed, no more than is necessary to banish pain. To heap pleasure upon pleasure may heighten man's enjoyment at times. But what matter if there are no golden images of youths about the house, holding flaming torches in their right hands to illumine banquets prolonged into the night? What matter if the hall does not sparkle with silver and gleam with gold, and no carved and gilded rafters ring to the music of the lute? Nature does not miss these luxuries when men recline in company on the soft grass by a running stream under the branches of a tall tree and refresh their bodies pleasurably at small expense. Better still if the weather smiles upon them and the season of the year stipples the green herbage with flowers. Burning fevers flee no swifter from your body if you toss under figured counterpanes and coverlets of crimson than if you must lie in rude homespun.

If our bodies are not profited by treasures or titles or the majesty of the kingship, we must go on to admit that neither are our minds. Or tell me, Memmius, when you see your legions thronging the Campus Martius in the ardor of mimic warfare, supported by ample auxiliaries, magnificently armed and fired by a common purpose, does that sight scare the terrors of superstition from your mind? Does the fear of death retire from your breast and leave it carefree at the moment when you sight your warships ranging far and wide? Or do we not find such resources absurdly ineffective? The fears and anxieties that dog the human breast do not shrink from the clash of arms or the fierce rain of missiles. They stalk unabashed among princes and potentates. They are not awe-struck by the gleam of gold or the bright sheen of purple robes.

Can you doubt then that this power rests with reason alone? ...

Reprinted with permission of the publisher from Ronald Latham's translation of *Lucretius: On the Nature of the Universe*, I, 62–126, 136–158, 215–224, 265–297; II, 1–52, 80–128, 216–293; III, 417–458, 799–805, 830–869, 912–930, 964–977; IV, 1058–1070, 1089–1192. (Penguin Books Ltd.: 1951).

Praise of Epicurus

When human life lay grovelling in all men's sight, crushed to the earth under the dead weight of superstition whose grim features lowered menacingly upon mortals from the four quarters of the sky, a man of Greece was first to raise mortal eyes in defiance, first to stand erect and brave the challenge. Fables of the gods did not crush him, nor the lightning flash and the growling menace of the sky. Rather, they quickened his manhood, so that he, first of all men, longed to smash the constraining locks of nature's doors. The vital vigor of his mind prevailed. He ventured far out beyond the flaming ramparts of the world and voyaged in mind throughout infinity. Returning victorious, he proclaimed to us what can be and what cannot: how a limit is fixed to the power of everything and an immovable frontier post. Therefore superstition in its turn lies crushed beneath his feet, and we by his triumph are lifted level with the skies.

Superstition Is the Mother of Sinful Deeds

One thing that worries me is the fear that you may fancy yourself embarking on an impious course, setting your feet on the path of sin. Far from it. More often it is this very superstition that is the mother of sinful and impious deeds. Remember how at Aulis the altar of the Virgin Goddess was foully stained with the blood of Iphigeneia by the leaders of the Greeks, the patterns of chivalry. The headband was bound about her virgin tresses and hung down evenly over both her cheeks. Suddenly she caught sight of her father standing sadly in front of the altar, the attendants beside him hiding the knife and her people bursting into tears when they saw her. Struck dumb with terror, she sank on her knees to the ground. Poor girl, at such a moment it did not help her that she had been first to give the name of father to a king. Raised by the hands of men, she was led trembling to the altar. Not for her the sacrament of marriage and the loud chant of Hymen. It was her fate in the very hour of marriage to fall a sinless victim to a sinful rite, slaughtered to her greater grief by a father's hand, so that a fleet might sail under happy auspices. Such are the heights of wickedness to which men are driven by superstition.

You yourself, if you surrender your judgment at any time to the bloodcurdling declamations of the prophets, will want to desert our ranks. Only think what phantoms they can conjure up to overturn the tenor of your life and wreck your happiness with fear. And not without cause. For, if men saw that a term was set to their troubles, they would find strength in some way to withstand the hocus-pocus and intimidations of the prophets. As it is, they have no power of resistance, because they are haunted by the fear of eternal punishment after death. They know nothing of the nature of the spirit. Is it born, or is it implanted in us at birth? Does it perish with us, dissolved by death, or does it visit the murky depths and dreary sloughs of Hades? Or is it transplanted by divine power into other creatures, as described in the poems of our own Ennius, who first gathered on the delectable slopes of Helicon an ever-green garland destined to win renown among the nations of Italy? Ennius indeed in his immortal verses proclaims that there is also a Hell, which is peopled not by our actual spirits or bodies but only by shadowy images, ghastly pale. It is from this realm that he pictures the ghost of Homer, of unfading memory, as appearing to him, shedding salt tears and revealing the nature of the universe. . . .

First Principles

I am well aware that it is not easy to elucidate in Latin verse the obscure discoveries of the Greeks. The poverty of our language and the novelty of the theme compel me often to coin new words for the purpose. But your merit and the joy I hope to derive from our delightful friendship encourage me to face any task however hard. This it is that leads me to stay awake through the quiet of the night, studying how by choice of words and the poet's art I can display before your mind a clear light by which you can gaze into the heart of hidden things.

This dread and darkness of the mind cannot be dispelled by the sunbeams the shining shafts of day, but only by an understanding of the outward form and inner workings of nature. In tackling this theme, our starting-point will be this principle: *Nothing can ever be created by divine power out of nothing.* The reason why all mortals are so gripped by fear is that they see all sorts of things happening on the earth and in the sky with no discernible cause, and these they attribute to the will of God. Accordingly, when we have seen that nothing can be created out of nothing, we shall then have a clearer picture of the path ahead, the problem of how things are created and occasioned without the aid of the gods. . . .

The second great principle is this: *nature resolves everything into its component atoms and never reduces anything to nothing.* If anything were perishable in all its parts, anything might perish all of a sudden and vanish from sight. There would be no need of any force to separate its parts and loosen their links. In actual fact, since everything is composed of indestructible seeds, nature obviously does not allow anything to perish till it has encountered a force that shatters it with a blow or creeps into chinks and unknits it. . . .

Well, Memmius, I have taught you that things cannot be created out of nothing nor, once born, be summoned back to nothing. Perhaps, however, you are becoming mistrustful of my words, because these atoms of mine are not visible to the eye. Consider, therefore, this further evidence of *bodies whose existence you must acknowledge though they cannot be seen.* First, wind, when its force is roused, whips up waves, founders tall ships and scatters cloud-rack. Sometimes scouring plains with hurricane force it strews them with huge trees and batters mountain peaks with blasts that hew down forests. Such is wind in its fury, when it whoops aloud with a mad menace in its shouting. Without question, therefore, there must be invisible particles of wind which sweep sea and land and the clouds in the sky, swooping upon them and whirling them along in a headlong hurricane. In the way they flow and the havoc they spread they are no different from a torrential flood of water when it rushes down in a sudden spate from the mountain heights, swollen by heavy rains, and heaps together wreckage from the forest and entire trees. Soft though it is by nature, the sudden shock of oncoming water is more than even stout bridges can withstand, so furious is the force with which the turbid, storm-flushed torrent surges against their piers. With a mighty roar it lays them low, rolling huge rocks under its waves and brushing aside every obstacle from its course. Such, therefore, must be the movement of blasts of wind also. When they have come surging along some course like a rushing river, they push obstacles before them and buffet them with repeated blows; and sometimes, eddying round and round, they snatch them up and carry them along in a swiftly circling vortex. Here then is proof upon proof that winds have invisible bodies, since in their actions and behavior they are found to rival great rivers, whose bodies are plain to see. . . .

. . . It follows that nature works through the agency of invisible bodies. . . .

All Particles of Matter Are on the Move

If you think that the atoms can stop and by their stopping generate new motions in things, you are wandering far from the path of truth. Since the atoms are moving freely through the void, they must all be kept in motion either by their own weight or on occasion by the impact of another atom. For it must often happen that two of them in their course knock together and immediately bounce apart in opposite directions, a natural consequence of their hardness and solidity and the absence of anything behind to stop them.

As a further indication that all particles of matter are on the move, remember that the universe is bottomless: there is no place where the atoms could come to rest. As I have already shown by various arguments and proved conclusively, space is without end or limit and spreads out immeasurably in all directions alike.

It clearly follows that no rest is given to the atoms in their course through the depths of space. Driven along in an incessant but variable movement, some of them bounce far apart after a collision while others recoil only a short distance from the impact. From those that do not recoil far, being driven into a closer union and held there by the entanglement of their own interlocking shapes, are composed firmly rooted rock, the stubborn strength of steel and the like. Those others that move freely through larger tracts of space, springing far apart and carried far by the rebound—these provide for us thin air and blazing sunlight. Besides these, there are many other atoms at large in empty space which have been thrown out of compound bodies and have nowhere even been granted admittance so as to bring their motions into harmony.

This process, as I might point out, is illustrated by an image of it that is continually taking place before our very eyes. Observe what happens when sunbeams are admitted to a building and shed light on its shadowy places. You will see a multitude of tiny particles mingling in a multitude of ways in the empty space within the light of the beam, as though contending in everlasting conflict, rushing into battle rank upon rank with never a moment's pause in a rapid sequence of unions and disunions. From this you may picture what it is for the atoms to be perpetually tossed about in the illimitable void. To some extent a small thing may afford an illustration and an imperfect image of great things. Besides, there is a further reason why you should give your mind to these particles that are seen dancing in a sunbeam: their dancing is an actual indication of underlying movements of matter that are hidden from our sight. . . .

The Atoms Swerve

In this connection there is another fact that I want you to grasp. *When the atoms are traveling straight down through empty space by their own weight, at quite indeterminate times and places they swerve ever so little from their course*, just so much that you can call it a change of direction. If it were not for this swerve everything would fall downwards like raindrops through the abyss of space. No collision would take place and no impact of atom on atom would be created. Thus nature would never have created anything.

If anyone supposes that heavier atoms on a straight course through empty space could outstrip lighter ones and fall on them from above, thus causing impacts that might give rise to generative motions, he is going far astray from the path of truth. The reason why objects falling through water or thin air vary in speed according to their weight is simply that the matter composing water or air cannot obstruct all objects equally, but is forced to give way more speedily to heavier ones. But empty space can offer no resistance to any object in any quarter at any time, so as not to yield free passage as its own nature demands. Therefore through undisturbed vacuum all bodies must travel at equal speed though impelled by unequal weights. The heavier will never be able to fall on the lighter from above or generate of themselves impacts leading to that variety of motions out of which nature can produce things. We are thus forced back to the conclusion that the atoms swerve a little—but only a very little, or we shall be caught imagining slantwise movements, and the facts will prove us wrong. For we see plainly and palpably that weights, when they come tumbling down, have no power of their own to move aslant, so far as meets the eye. But who can possibly perceive that they do not diverge in the very least from a vertical course?

Again, . . . what is the source of the free will possessed by living things throughout the earth? What, I repeat, is the source of that willpower snatched from the fates, whereby we follow the path along which we are severally led by pleasure, swerving from our course at no set time or place but at the bidding of our hearts? There is no doubt that on these occasions the will of the individual originates the movements that trickle through his limbs. Observe, when the starting barriers are flung back, how the racehorses in the eagerness of their strength cannot break away as suddenly as their hearts desire. For the whole supply of matter must first be mobilized throughout every member of the body: only then, when it is mustered in a continuous array, can it respond to the prompting of the heart. So you may see that the beginning of movement is generated by the heart; starting from the voluntary action of the mind, it is then transmitted throughout the body and the limbs. Quite different is our experience when we are shoved along by a blow inflicted with compulsive force by someone else. In that case it is obvious that all the matter of our body is set going and pushed along involuntarily, till a check is imposed through the limbs by the will. Do you see the difference? Although many men are driven by an external force and often constrained involuntarily to advance or to rush headlong, yet there is within the human breast something that can fight against this force and resist it. At its command the supply of matter is forced to take a new course through our limbs and joints or is checked in its course and brought once more to a halt. So also in the atoms you must recognize the same possibility: besides weight and impact there must be a third cause of movement, the source of this inborn power of ours, since we see that nothing can come out of nothing. For the weight of an atom prevents its movements from being completely determined by the impact of other atoms. But the fact that the mind itself has no internal necessity to determine its every act and compel it to suffer in helpless passivity—this is due to the slight swerve of the atoms at no determinate time or place. ...

Spirit Is Mortal

My next point is this: you must understand that the *minds of living things and the light fabric of their spirits are neither birthless nor deathless.* To this end I have long been mustering and inventing verses with a labor that is also a joy. Now I will try to set them out in a style worthy of your career.

Please note that both objects are to be embraced under one name. When, for instance, I proceed to demonstrate that "spirit" is mortal, you must understand that this applies equally to "mind" since the two are so conjoined as to constitute a single substance.

First of all, then, I have shown that spirit is flimsy stuff composed of tiny particles. Its atoms are obviously far smaller than those of swift-flowing water or mist or smoke, since it far outstrips them in mobility and is moved by a far slighter impetus. Indeed, it is actually moved by images of smoke and mist. So, for instance, when we are sunk in sleep, we may see altars sending up clouds of steam and giving off smoke; and we cannot doubt that we are here dealing with images.

Now, we see that water flows out in all directions from a broken vessel and the moisture is dissipated, and mist and smoke vanish into thin air. Be assured, therefore, that spirit is similarly dispelled and vanishes far more speedily and is sooner dissolved into its component atoms once it has been let loose from the human frame. When the body, which served as a vessel for it, is by some means broken and attenuated by loss of blood from the veins, so as to be no longer able to contain it, how can you suppose that it can be contained by any kind of air, which must be far more tenuous than our bodily frame?

Again, we are conscious that mind and body are born together, grow up together and together decay. With the weak and delicate frame of wavering childhood goes a like infirmity of judgment. The robust vigor of ripening years is accompanied by a steadier resolve and a maturer strength of mind. Later, when the body is palsied by the potent forces of age and the limbs begin to droop with blunted vigor, the understanding limps, the tongue falters and the mind totters: everything weakens and gives way at the same time. It is thus natural that the vital spirit should all evaporate like smoke, soaring into the gusty air, since we have seen that it shares the body's birth and growth and wearies with the weariness of age. . . .

. . . You must admit, therefore, that when the body has perished there is an end also of the spirit diffused through it. It is surely crazy to couple a mortal object with an eternal and suppose that they can work in harmony and mutually interact. What can be imagined more incongruous, what more repugnant and discordant, than that a mortal object and one that is immortal and everlasting should unite to form a compound and jointly weather the storms that rage about them? . . .

Nothing to Fear in Death

From all this it follows that *death is nothing to us* and no concern of ours, since our tenure of the mind is mortal. In days of old, we felt no disquiet when the hosts of Carthage poured in to battle on every side—when the whole earth, dizzied by the convulsive shock of war, reeled sickeningly under the high ethereal vault, and between realm and realm the empire of mankind by land and sea trembled in the balance. So, when we shall be no more—when the union of body and spirit that engenders us has been disrupted—to us, who shall then be nothing, nothing by any hazard will happen any more at all. Nothing will have power to stir our senses, not though earth be fused with sea and sea with sky.

If any feeling remains in mind or spirit after it has been torn from our body, that is nothing to us, who are brought into being by the wedlock of body and spirit, conjoined and coalesced. Or even if the matter that composes us should be reassembled by time after our death and brought back into its present state—if the light of life were given to us anew—even that contingency would still be no concern of ours once the chain of our identity had been snapped. We who are now are not concerned with ourselves in any previous existence: the sufferings of those selves do not touch us. When you look at the immeasurable extent of time gone by and the multiform movements of matter, you will readily credit that these same atoms that compose us now must many a time before have entered into the self-same combinations as now. But our mind cannot recall this to remembrance. For between then and now is interposed a breach in life, and all the atomic motions have been wandering far astray from sentience.

If the future holds travail and anguish in store, the self must be in existence, when that time comes, in order to experience it. But from this fate we are redeemed by death, which denies existence to the self that might have suffered these tribulations. Rest assured, therefore, that we have nothing to fear in death. One who no longer is cannot suffer, or differ in any way from one who has never been born, when once this mortal life has been usurped by death the immortal. . . .

Here, again, is the way men often talk from the bottom of their hearts when they recline at a banquet, goblet in hand and brows decked with garlands: "How all too short are these good times that come to us poor creatures! Soon they will be past and gone, and there will be no recalling them." You would think the crowning calamity in store for them after death was to be parched and shrivelled by a tormenting thirst or oppressed by some other vain desire. But even in sleep, when mind and body alike are at rest, no one misses himself or sighs for life. If such sleep were prolonged to eternity, no longing for ourselves would trouble us. And yet the vital atoms in our limbs cannot be far removed from their sensory motions at a time when a mere jolt out of sleep enables a man to pull himself together. Death, therefore, must be regarded, so far as we are concerned, as having much less existence than sleep, if anything can have less existence than what we perceive to be nothing. For death is followed by a far greater dispersal of the seething mass of matter: once that icy breach in life has intervened, there is no more waking.

... The old is always thrust aside to make way for the new, and one thing must be built out of the wreck of another. There is no murky pit of Hell awaiting anyone. There is need of matter, so that later generations may arise; when they have lived out their span, they will all follow you. Bygone generations have taken your road, and those to come will take it no less. So one thing will never cease to spring from another. To none is life given in freehold; to all on lease. Look back at the eternity that passed before we were born, and mark how utterly it counts to us as nothing. This is a mirror that Nature holds up to us, in which we may see the time that shall be after we are dead. Is there anything terrifying in the sight—anything depressing—anything that is not more restful than the soundest sleep? ...

The Thing Called Love—Be on Your Guard

This, then, is what we term Venus. This is the origin of the thing called love—that drop of Venus' honey that first drips into our heart, to be followed by numbing heartache. Though the object of your love may be absent, images of it still haunt you and the beloved name chimes sweetly in your ears. If you find yourself thus passionately enamoured of an individual, you should keep well away from such images. Thrust from you anything that might feed your passion, and turn your mind elsewhere. Vent the seed of love upon other objects. By clinging to it you assure yourself the certainty of heartsickness and pain. ...

This is the one thing of which the more we have, the more our breast burns with the evil lust of having. Food and fluid are taken into our body: since they can fill their allotted places, the desire for meat and drink is thus easily appeased. But a pretty face or a pleasing complexion gives the body nothing to enjoy but insubstantial images, which all too often fond hope scatters to the winds.

When a thirsty man tries to drink in his dreams but is given no drop to quench the fire in his limbs, he clutches at images of water with fruitless effort and while he laps up a rushing stream he remains thirsty in the midst. Just so in the midst of love Venus teases lovers with images. They cannot glut their eyes by gazing on the beloved form, however closely. Their hands glean nothing from those dainty limbs in their aimless roving over all the body. Then comes the moment when with limbs entwined they pluck the flower of youth. Their bodies thrill with the presentiment of joy, and it is seed-time in the fields of Venus. Body clings greedily to body; moist lips are pressed on lips, and deep breaths are drawn through clenched teeth. But all to no purpose. One can glean nothing from the other, nor enter in and be wholly absorbed, body in body; for sometimes it seems that that is what they are craving and striving to do, so hungrily do they cling together in Venus' fetters, while their limbs are unnerved and liquefied by the intensity of rapture. At length, when the spate of lust is spent, there comes a slight intermission in the raging fever. But not for long. Soon the same frenzy returns. The fit is upon them once more. They ask themselves what it is they are craving for, but find no device that will master their malady. In aimless bewilderment they waste away, stricken by an unseen wound.

Add to this that they spend their strength and fail under the strain. Their days are passed at the mercy of another's whim. Their wealth slips from them, transmuted to Babylonian brocades. Their duties are neglected. Their reputation totters and goes into a decline. It is all very well for dainty feet to sparkle with gay slippers of Sicyon; for settings of gold to enclasp huge emeralds aglow with green fire, and sea-tinted garments to suffer the constant wear and stain of Venus. A hard-won patrimony is metamorphosed into bonnets and tiaras or, it may be, into Grecian robes, masterpieces from the looms of Elis or of Ceos. No matter how lavish the décor and the cuisine—drinking parties (with no lack of drinks), entertainments, perfumes, garlands, festoons and all—they are still to no purpose.

From the very heart of the fountain of delight there rises a jet of bitterness that poisons the fragrance of the flowers. Perhaps the unforgetting mind frets itself remorsefully with the thought of life's best years squandered in sloth and debauchery. Perhaps the beloved has let fly some two-edged word, which lodges in the impassioned heart and glows there like a living flame. Perhaps he thinks she is rolling her eyes too freely and turning them upon another, or he catches in her face a hint of mockery.

And these are the evils inherent in love that prospers and fulfills its hopes. In starved and thwarted love the evils you can see plainly without even opening your eyes are past all counting. How much better to be on your guard beforehand, as I have advised, and take care that you are not enmeshed!

To avoid enticement into the snares of love is not so difficult as, once entrapped, to escape out of the toils and snap the tenacious knots of Venus. And yet, be you never so tightly entangled and embrangled, you can still free yourself from the curse unless you stand in the way of your own freedom. First, you should concentrate on all the faults of mind or body of her whom you covet and sigh for. For men often behave as though blinded by love and credit the beloved with charms to which she has no valid title. How often do we see blemished and unsightly women basking in a lover's adoration! One man scoffs at another and urges him to propitiate Venus because he is the victim of such a degrading passion; yet as like as not the poor devil is in the same unhappy plight himself, all unaware. A sallow wench is acclaimed as a nut-brown maid. A sluttish slattern is admired for her "sweet disorder." Her eyes are never green, but grey as Athene's. If she is stringy and woody, she is lithe as a gazelle. A stunted runt is a sprite, a sheer delight from top to toe. A clumsy giantess is "a daughter of the gods divinely tall." She has an impediment in her speech—a charming lisp, of course. She's as mute as a stockfish— what modesty! A waspish, fiery-tempered scold—she "burns with a gem-like flame." She becomes "svelte" and "willowy" when she is almost too skinny to live; "delicate" when she is half-dead with coughing. Her breasts are swollen and protuberant: she is "Ceres suckling Bacchus." Her nose is snub— "a Faun," then, or "a child of the Satyrs." Her lips bulge: she is "all kiss." It would be a wearisome task to run through the whole catalogue. But suppose her face in fact is all that could be desired and the charm of Venus radiates from her whole body. Even so, there are still others. Even so, we lived without her before. Even so, in her physical nature she is no different, as we well know, from the plainest of her sex. She is driven to use foul-smelling fumigants. Her maids keep well away from her and snigger behind her back. The tearful lover, shut out from the presence, heaps the threshold with flowers and garlands, anoints the disdainful door-posts with perfume, and plants rueful kisses on the door. Often enough, were he admitted, one whiff would promptly make him cast around for some decent pretext to take his leave. His fond complaint, long-pondered and far-fetched, would fall dismally flat. He would curse himself for a fool to have endowed her with qualities above mortal imperfection.

To the daughters of Venus themselves all this is no secret. Hence they are at pains to hide all the back-stage activities of life from those whom they wish to keep fast bound in the bonds of love. But their pains are wasted, since your mind has power to drag all these mysteries into the daylight and get at the truth behind the sniggers.

The New Testament

While Roman and Jewish sources refer to Jesus of Nazareth, the only detailed account we have of his life and teaching between 4 B.C. and A.D. 30 comes from his followers, who compiled the Gospels with the intention that the reader "believing might have eternal life" (John 20:31, also Luke 1:1–4). Though Luke employs critical methods reminiscent of Thucydides, the Gospels portray Jesus as his followers saw him. Matthew, perhaps with an eye to Jewish readers, stressed the coming of the long awaited "Kingdom of God", and how Jesus fulfilled Old Testament Messianic prophecy. John focused on the mystery of Jesus as the one sent by God the Father to be Saviour of the World, emphasizing Jesus' claim that he was God become man. Luke apparently directed his account to non-Jewish inquirers, portraying the universal kindness of Jesus to the poor, sick and needy.

For over a century religious and non-religious scholars have disagreed concerning the dates when the texts were composed, the method of compilation, and whether or not authentic authorship can be proven. Most agree that the present received manuscripts were copied between A.D. 200 and 330, but fragments of the Gospels and Acts dating from 130 also have been found. Few would dispute that earlier versions and oral accounts existed in the first Christian communities. During the nineteenth century influential German scholars argued that no Gospel could have been written before A.D. 130. In the light of recent research, however, current scholars suggest that the Gospel of Matthew probably was written in Antioch between A.D. 70 and 85, Luke either in Caesarea or western Greece between 60 and 80, and John in Antioch or Ephesus between 90 and 96. Whatever the academic controversy, these selections contain the classic doctrinal sources of Christian ethics, the Incarnation, the Passion-Crucifixion and the Resurrection.

In 1774 the German scholar J.J. Griesbach classified Mathew, Mark and Luke as "Synoptic Gospels" ("with the same eye"), since the narratives frequently echo one another. John records many different incidents and discusses the implications of some of Jesus' teachings at greater length. Though the diction of each Gospel reflects the Aramaic spoken in Palestine during the first century, the surviving manuscripts are written in the vernacular Greek (*koine*) used throughout the eastern Roman Empire.

In addition to the Gospel stories, the New Testament provides an account of what happened within the Christian community in the first years after Jesus' departure and tells of how Christian beliefs began to be spread outside Judaism and across the Roman world in the late First Century (so the Acts of the Apostles). Other material, primarily in the form of letters to developing Churches in such places as Rome, Corinth, and Thessalonica, represents the initial stage in the gradual elaboration of Early Christian theology. Many of these letters (or Epistles) are attributed to Paul of Tarsus (on whom see further, *CC*, I, p. 77), others to other leading figures in the Primitive Church. As Christianity sought to distinguish itself from the contemporary beliefs and practices not only of Judaism, but also of other Near Eastern and Greco-Roman sects and religions, it became increasingly important for it to define what exactly it believed. At the same time it sought to express its ideas in language which was accessible and acceptable not only to ordinary men and women but also to members of the Greco-Roman intellectual elite, something which meant a growing interaction with the principal pagan philosophies (such as Platonism and Stoicism). The last book of the New

Testament, the Revelation of John, takes the form of an apocalypse. In this highly allegorical work an attempt is made both to come to terms with the hostility and persecution the Early Church encountered from the political organisation of the Roman world and to present an account of the anticipated end of the world and the final judgement. The New Testament Canon was formed in the period from the second to the fourth century A.D.

The selections which follow are taken from the 1946 Revised Standard Version (in turn based on the 1611 Authorized King James Version) of the Bible.

Matthew 1:18–24

Now the birth of Jesus Christ took place in this way. When his mother Mary had been betrothed to Joseph, before they came together she was found to be with child of the Holy Spirit; and her husband Joseph, being a just man and unwilling to put her to shame, resolved to divorce her quietly. But as he considered this, behold, an angel of the Lord appeared to him in a dream, saying, "Joseph, son of David, do not fear to take Mary your wife, for that which is conceived in her is of the Holy Spirit; she will bear a son, and you shall call his name Jesus, for he will save his people from their sins." All this took place to fulfil what the Lord had spoken by the prophet:

"Behold, a virgin shall conceive and bear a son,
and his name shall be called Emmanu-el"

(which means, God with us). When Joseph woke from sleep, he did as the angel of the Lord commanded him; he took his wife, but knew her not until she had borne a son; and he called his name Jesus.

John 1:1–34

In the beginning was the Word, and the Word was with God, and the Word was God. He was in the beginning with God; all things were made through him, and without him was not anything made that was made. In him was life, and the life was the light of men. The light shines in the darkness, and the darkness has not overcome it.

There was a man sent from God, whose name was John. He came for testimony, to bear witness to the light, that all might believe through him. He was not the light, but came to bear witness to the light.

The true light that enlightens every man was coming into the world. He was in the world, and the world was made through him, yet the world knew him not. He came to his own home, and his own people received him not. But to all who received him, who believed in his name, he gave power to become children of God; who were born, not of blood nor of the will of the flesh nor of the will of man, but of God.

And the Word became flesh and dwelt among us, full of grace and truth; we have beheld his glory, glory as of the only Son from the Father. (John bore witness to him, and cried, "This was he of whom I said, 'He who comes after me ranks before me, for he was before me.'") And from his fullness have we all received, grace upon grace. For the law was given through Moses; grace and truth came through Jesus Christ. No one has ever seen God; the only Son, who is in the bosom of the Father, he has made him known.

And this is the testimony of John, when the Jews sent priests and Levites from Jerusalem to ask him, "Who are you?" He confessed, he did not deny, but confessed, "I am not the Christ." And they asked him, "What then? Are you Elijah?" He said, "I am not." "Are you the prophet?" And he answered,

"No." They said to him then, "Who are you? Let us have an answer for those who sent us. What do you say about yourself?" He said, "I am the voice of one crying in the wilderness, 'Make straight the way of the Lord,' as the prophet Isaiah said."

Now they had been sent from the Pharisees. They asked him, "Then why are you baptizing, if you are neither the Christ, nor Elijah, nor the prophet?" John answered them, "I baptize with water; but among you stands one whom you do not know, even he who comes after me, the thong of whose sandal I am not worthy to untie." This took place in Bethany beyond the Jordan, where John was baptizing.

The next day he saw Jesus coming toward him, and said, "Behold, the Lamb of God, who takes away the sin of the world! This is he of whom I said, 'After me comes a man who ranks before me, for he was before me.' I myself did not know him; but for this I came baptizing with water, that he might be revealed to Israel." And John bore witness, "I saw the Spirit descend as a dove from heaven, and it remained on him. I myself did not know him; but he who sent me to baptize with water said to me, 'He on whom you see the Spirit descend and remain, this is he who baptizes with the Holy Spirit.' And I have seen and have borne witness that this is the Son of God."

Matthew 4:23–25; 5–7

And he went about all Galilee, teaching in their synagogues and preaching the gospel of the kingdom and healing every disease and every infirmity among the people. So his fame spread throughout all Syria, and they brought him all the sick, those afflicted with various diseases and pains, demoniacs, epileptics, and paralytics, and he healed them. And great crowds followed him from Galilee and the Decapolis and Jerusalem and Judea and from beyond the Jordan.

Seeing the crowds, he went up on the mountain, and when he sat down his disciples came to him. And he opened his mouth and taught them, saying:
"Blessed are the poor in spirit, for theirs is the kingdom of heaven.
"Blessed are those who mourn, for they shall be comforted.
"Blessed are the meek, for they shall inherit the earth.
"Blessed are those who hunger and thirst for righteousness, for they shall be satisfied.
"Blessed are the merciful, for they shall obtain mercy.
"Blessed are the pure in heart, for they shall see God.
"Blessed are the peacemakers, for they shall be called sons of God.
"Blessed are those who are persecuted for righteousness' sake, for theirs is the kingdom of heaven.
"Blessed are you when men revile you and persecute you and utter all kinds of evil against you falsely on my account. Rejoice and be glad, for your reward is great in heaven, for so men persecuted the prophets who were before you.
"You are the salt of the earth; but if salt has lost its taste, how shall its saltness be restored? It is no longer good for anything except to be thrown out and trodden under foot by men.
"You are the light of the world. A city set on a hill cannot be hid. Nor do men light a lamp and put it under a bushel, but on a stand, and it gives light to all in the house. Let your light so shine before men, that they may see your good works and give glory to your Father who is in heaven.
"Think not that I have come to abolish the law and the prophets; I have come not to abolish them but to fulfil them. For truly, I say to you, till heaven and earth pass away, not an iota, not a dot, will pass from the law until all is accomplished. Whoever then relaxes one of the least of these

commandments and teaches men so, shall be called least in the kingdom of heaven; but he who does them and teaches them shall be called great in the kingdom of heaven. For I tell you, unless your righteousness exceeds that of the scribes and Pharisees, you will never enter the kingdom of heaven.

"You have heard that it was said to the men of old. 'You shall not kill; and whoever kills shall be liable to judgment.' But I say to you that every one who is angry with his brother shall be liable to judgment; whoever insults his brother shall be liable to the council, and whoever says, 'You fool!' shall be liable to the hell of fire. So if you are offering your gift at the altar, and there remember that your brother has something against you, leave your gift there before the altar and go; first be reconciled to your brother, and then come and offer your gift. Make friends quickly with your accuser, while you are going with him to court, lest your accuser hand you over to the judge, and the judge to the guard, and you be put in prison; truly, I say to you, you will never get out till you have paid the last penny.

"You have heard that it was said, 'You shall not commit adultery.' But I say to you that every one who looks at a woman lustfully has already committed adultery with her in his heart. If your right eye causes you to sin, pluck it out and throw it away; it is better that you lose one of your members than that your whole body be thrown into hell. And if your right hand causes you to sin, cut it off and throw it away; it is better that you lose one of your members than that your whole body go into hell.

"It was also said, 'Whoever divorces his wife, let him give her a certificate of divorce.' But I say to you that every one who divorces his wife, except on the ground of unchastity, makes her an adulteress; and whoever marries a divorced woman commits adultery.

"Again you have heard that it was said to the men of old, 'You shall not swear falsely, but shall perform to the Lord what you have sworn.' But I say to you, Do not swear at all, either by heaven, for it is the throne of God, or by the earth, for it is his footstool, or by Jerusalem, for it is the city of the great King. And do not swear by your head, for you cannot make one hair white or black. Let what you say be simply 'Yes' or 'No'; anything more than this comes from evil.

"You have heard that it was said, 'An eye for an eye and a tooth for a tooth. But I say to you, Do not resist one who is evil. But if any one strikes you on the right cheek, turn to him the other also; and if any one would sue you and take your coat, let him have your cloak as well; and if any one forces you to go one mile, go with him two miles. Give to him who begs from you, and do not refuse him who would borrow from you.

"You have heard that it was said, 'You shall love your neighbor and hate your enemy.' But I say to you, Love your enemies and pray for those who persecute you, so that you may be sons of your Father who is in heaven; for he makes his sun rise on the evil and on the good, and sends rain on the just and on the unjust. For if you love those who love you, what reward have you? Do not even the tax collectors do the same? And if you salute only your brethren, what more are you doing than others? Do not even the Gentiles do the same? You, therefore, must be perfect, as your heavenly Father is perfect.

"Beware of practicing your piety before men in order to be seen by them; for then you will have no reward from your Father who is in heaven.

"Thus, when you give alms, sound no trumpet before you, as the hypocrites do in the synagogues and in the streets, that they may be praised by men. Truly, I say to you, they have their reward. But when you give alms, do not let your left hand know what your right hand is doing, so that your alms may be in secret; and your Father who sees in secret will reward you.

"And when you pray, you must not be like the hypocrites; for they love to stand and pray in the synagogues and at the street corners, that they may be seen by men. Truly, I say to you, they have their reward. But when you pray, go into your room and shut the door and pray to your Father who is in secret; and your Father who sees in secret will reward you.

"And in praying do not heap up empty phrases as the Gentiles do; for they think that they will be heard for their many words. Do not be like them, for your Father knows what you need before you ask him. Pray then like this:

Our Father who art in heaven,
Hallowed be thy name.
Thy kingdom come,
Thy will be done,
On earth as it is in heaven.
Give us this day our daily bread;
And forgive us our debts,
As we also have forgiven our debtors;
And lead us not into temptation,
But deliver us from evil.

For if you forgive men their trespasses, your heavenly Father also will forgive you; but if you do not forgive men their trespasses, neither will your Father forgive your trespasses.

"And when you fast, do not look dismal, like the hypocrites, for they disfigure their faces that their fasting may be seen by men. Truly, I say to you, they have their reward. But when you fast, anoint your head and wash your face, that your fasting may not be seen by men but by your Father who is in secret; and your Father who sees in secret will reward you.

"Do not lay up for yourselves treasures on earth, where moth and rust consume and where thieves break in and steal, but lay up for yourselves treasures in heaven, where neither moth nor rust consumes and where thieves do not break in and steal. For where your treasure is, there will your heart be also.

"The eye is the lamp of the body. So, if your eye is sound, your whole body will be full of light; but if your eye is not sound, your whole body will be full of darkness. If then the light in you is darkness, how great is the darkness!

"No one can serve two masters; for either he will hate the one and love the other, or he will be devoted to the one and despise the other. You cannot serve God and mammon.

"Therefore I tell you, do not be anxious about your life, what you shall eat or what you shall drink, nor about your body, what you shall put on. Is not life more than food, and the body more than clothing? Look at the birds of the air: they neither sow nor reap nor gather into barns, and yet your heavenly Father feeds them. Are you not of more value than they? And which of you by being anxious can add one cubit to his span of life? And why are you anxious about clothing? Consider the lilies of the field, how they grow; they neither toil nor spin; yet I tell you, even Solomon in all his glory was not arrayed like one of these. But if God so clothes the grass of the field, which today is alive and tomorrow is thrown into the oven, will he not much more clothe you, O men of little faith? Therefore do not be anxious, saying, 'What shall we eat?' or 'What shall we drink?' or 'What shall we wear?' For the Gentiles seek all these things; and your heavenly Father knows that you need them all. But seek first his kingdom and his righteousness, and all these things shall be yours as well.

"Therefore do not be anxious about tomorrow, for tomorrow will be anxious for itself. Let the day's own trouble be sufficient for the day.

"Judge not, that you be not judged. For with the judgment you pronounce you will be judged, and the measure you give will be the measure you get. Why do you see the speck that is in your brother's eye, but do not notice the log that is in your own eye? Or how can you say to your brother, 'Let me take the speck out of your eye,' when there is the log in your own eye? You hypocrite, first take the log out of your own eye, and then you will see clearly to take the speck out of your brother's eye.

"Do not give dogs what is holy; and do not throw your pearls before swine, lest they trample them underfoot and turn to attack you.

"Ask, and it will be given you; seek, and you will find; knock, and it will be opened to you. For every one who asks receives, and he who seeks finds, and to him who knocks it will be opened. Or what man of you, if his son asks him for a loaf, will give him a stone? Or if he asks for a fish, will give him a serpent? If you then, who are evil, know how to give good gifts to your children, how much more will your Father who is in heaven give good things to those who ask him! So whatever you wish that men would do to you, do so to them; for this is the law and the prophets.

"Enter by the narrow gate; for the gate is wide and the way is easy, that leads to destruction, and those who enter by it are many. For the gate is narrow and the way is hard, that leads to life, and those who find it are few.

"Beware of false prophets, who come to you in sheep's clothing but inwardly are ravenous wolves. You will know them by their fruits. Are grapes gathered from thorns, or figs from thistles? So, every sound tree bears good fruit, but the bad tree bears evil fruit. A sound tree cannot bear evil fruit, nor can a bad tree bear good fruit. Every tree that does not bear good fruit is cut down and thrown into the fire. Thus you will know them by their fruits.

"Not every one who says to me, 'Lord, Lord,' shall enter the kingdom of heaven, but he who does the will of my Father who is in heaven. On that day many will say to me, 'Lord, Lord, did we not prophesy in your name, and cast out demons in your name, and do many mighty works in your name?' And then will I declare to them, 'I never knew you; depart from me, you evildoers.'

"Every one then who hears these words of mine and does them will be like a wise man who built his house upon the rock; and the rain fell, and the floods came, and the winds blew and beat upon that house, but it did not fall, because it had been founded on the rock. And every one who hears these words of mine and does not do them will be like a foolish man who built his house upon the sand; and the rain fell, and the floods came, and the winds blew and beat against that house, and it fell; and great was the fall of it.

And when Jesus finished these sayings, the crowds were astonished at his teaching, for he taught them as one who had authority, and not as their scribes.

Luke 23:1–5, 13–25, 32–34, 44–49

Then the whole company of them arose, and brought him before Pilate. And they began to accuse him, saying, "We found this man perverting our nation, and forbidding us to give tribute to Caesar, and saying that he himself is Christ a king." And Pilate asked him, "Are you the King of the Jews?" And he answered him, "You have said so." And Pilate said to the chief priests and the multitudes, "I find no crime in this man." But they were urgent, saying, "He stirs up the people, teaching throughout all Judea, from Galilee even to this place." . . .

Pilate then called together the chief priests and the rulers and the people, and said to them, "You brought me this man as one who was perverting the people; and after examining him before you, behold, I did not find this man guilty of any of your charges against him; neither did Herod, for he sent him back to us. Behold, nothing deserving death has been done by him; I will therefore chastise him and release him."

But they all cried out together, "Away with this man, and release to us Barabbas"—a man who had been thrown into prison for an insurrection started in the city, and for murder. Pilate addressed them once more, desiring to release Jesus; but they shouted out, "Crucify, crucify him!" A third time he said to them, "Why, what evil has he done? I have found in him no crime deserving death; I will therefore chastise him and release him." But they were urgent, demanding with loud cries that he should be crucified. And their voices prevailed. So Pilate gave sentence that their demand should be granted. He released the man who had been thrown into prison for insurrection and murder, whom they asked for; but Jesus he delivered up to their will. . . .

Two others also, who were criminals, were led away to be put to death with him. And when they came to the place which is called The Skull, there they crucified him, and the criminals, one on the right and one on the left. And Jesus said, "Father, forgive them; for they know not what they do." And they cast lots to divide his garments. . . .

It was now about the sixth hour, and there was darkness over the whole land until the ninth hour, while the sun's light failed; and the curtain of the temple was torn in two. Then Jesus, crying with a loud voice, said, "Father, into thy hands I commit my spirit!" And having said this he breathed his last. Now when the centurion saw what had taken place, he praised God, and said, "Certainly this man was innocent!" And all the multitudes who assembled to see the sight, when they saw what had taken place, returned home beating their breasts. And all his acquaintances and the women who had followed him from Galilee stood at a distance and saw these things.

Matthew 28:1–10, 16–20

Now after the sabbath, toward the dawn of the first day of the week, Mary Magdalene and the other Mary went to see the sepulchre. And behold, there was a great earthquake; for an angel of the Lord descended from heaven and came and rolled back the stone, and sat upon it. His appearance was like lightning, and his raiment white as snow. And for fear of him the guards trembled and became like dead men. But the angel said to the women, "Do not be afraid; for I know that you seek Jesus who was crucified. He is not here; for he has risen, as he said. Come, see the place where he lay. Then go quickly and tell his disciples that he has risen from the dead, and behold, he is going before you to Galilee; there you will see him. Lo, I have told you." So they departed quickly from the tomb with fear and great joy, and ran to tell his disciples. And behold, Jesus met them and said, "Hail!" And they came up and took hold of his feet and worshiped him. Then Jesus said to them, "Do not be afraid; go and tell my brethren to go to Galilee, and there they will see me." . . .

Now the eleven disciples went to Galilee, to the mountain to which Jesus had directed them. And when they saw him they worshiped him; but some doubted. And Jesus came and said to them, "All authority in heaven and on earth has been given to me. Go therefore and make disciples of all nations, baptizing them in the name of the Father and of the Son and of the Holy Spirit, teaching them to observe all that I have commanded you; and lo, I am with you always, to the close of the age."

Acts of the Apostles 2; 6:8–15; 7:54–8:3; 9:1–29; 17:16–34

When the day of Pentecost had come, they were all together in one place. And suddenly a sound came from heaven like the rush of a mighty wind, and it filled all the house where they were sitting. And there appeared to them tongues as of fire, distributed and resting on each one of them. And they were all filled with the Holy Spirit and began to speak in other tongues, as the Spirit gave them utterance.

Now there were dwelling in Jerusalem Jews, devout men from every nation under heaven. And at this sound the multitude came together, and they were bewildered, because each one heard them speaking in his own language. And they were amazed and wondered, saying, "Are not all these who are speaking Galileans? And how is it that we hear, each of us in his own native language? Parthians and Medes and Elamites and residents of Mesopotamia, Judea and Cappadocia, Pontus and Asia, Phrygia and Pamphylia, Egypt and the parts of Libya belonging to Cyrene, and visitors from Rome, both Jews and proselytes, Cretans and Arabians, we hear them telling in our own tongues the mighty works of God."

And all were amazed and perplexed, saying to one another, "What does this mean?" But others mocking said, "They are filled with new wine."

But Peter, standing with the eleven, lifted up his voice and addressed them, "Men of Judea and all who dwell in Jerusalem, let this be known to you, and give ear to my words. For these men are not drunk, as you suppose, since it is only the third hour of the day; but this is what was spoken by the prophet Joel:

'And in the last days it shall be, God declares,
that I will pour out my Spirit upon all flesh,
and your sons and your daughters shall prophesy,
and your young men shall see visions,
and your old men shall dream dreams;
yea, and on my menservants and my maidservants in those days
I will pour out my Spirit; and they shall prophesy.
And I will show wonders in the heaven above
and signs on the earth beneath,
blood, and fire, and vapour of smoke;
the sun shall be turned into darkness
and the moon into blood,
before the day of the Lord comes,
the great and manifest day.
And it shall be that whoever calls on the name of the Lord shall be saved.'

"Men of Israel, hear these words: Jesus of Nazareth, a man attested to you by God with mighty works and wonders and signs which God did through him in your midst, as you yourselves know— this Jesus, delivered up according to the definite plan and foreknowledge of God, you crucified and killed by the hands of lawless men. But God raised him up, having loosed the pangs of death, because it was not possible for him to be held by it. For David says concerning him,

'I saw the Lord always before me,
for he is at my right hand that I may not be shaken;
therefore my heart was glad, and my tongue rejoiced;

105

moreover my flesh will dwell in hope.
For thou wilt not abandon my soul to Hades,
Nor let thy Holy One see corruption.
Thou hast made known to me the ways of life;
thou wilt make me full of gladness with thy presence.'

"Brethren, I may say to you confidently of the patriarch David that he both died and was buried, and his tomb is with us to this day. Being therefore a prophet, and knowing that God had sworn with an oath to him that he would set one of his descendants upon his throne, he foresaw and spoke of the resurrection of the Christ, that he was not abandoned to Hades, nor did his flesh see corruption. This Jesus God raised up, and of that we all are witnesses. Being therefore exalted at the right hand of God, and having received from the Father the promise of the Holy Spirit, he has poured out this which you see and hear. For David did not ascend into the heavens; but he himself says,

'The Lord said to my Lord, Sit at my right hand,
till I make thy enemies a stool for thy feet.'

Let all the house of Israel therefore know assuredly that God has made him both Lord and Christ, this Jesus whom you crucified."

Now when they heard this they were cut to the heart, and said to Peter and the rest of the apostles, "Brethren, what shall we do?" And Peter said to them, "Repent, and be baptized every one of you in the name of Jesus Christ for the forgiveness of your sins; and you shall receive the gift of the Holy Spirit. For the promise is to you and to your children and to all that are far off, every one whom the Lord our God calls to him." And he testified with many other words and exhorted them, saying, "Save yourselves from this crooked generation." So those who received his word were baptized, and there were added that day about three thousand souls. And they devoted themselves to the apostles' teaching and fellowship, to the breaking of bread and the prayers.

And fear came upon every soul; and many wonders and signs were done through the apostles. And all who believed were together and had all things in common; and they sold their possessions and goods and distributed them to all, as any had need. And day by day, attending the temple together and breaking bread in their homes, they partook of food with glad and generous hearts, praising God and having favour with all the people. And the Lord added to their number day by day those who were being saved.

And Stephen, full of grace and power, did great wonders and signs among the people. Then some of those who belonged to the synagogue of the Freedmen (as it was called), and of the Cyrenians, and of the Alexandrians, and of those from Cilicia and Asia, arose and disputed with Stephen. But they could not withstand the wisdom and the Spirit with which he spoke. Then they secretly instigated men, who said, "We have heard him speak blasphemous words against Moses and God." And they stirred up the people and the elders and the scribes, and they came upon him and seized him and brought him before the council, and set up false witnesses who said, "This man never ceases to speak words against this holy place, and the law; for we have heard him say that this Jesus of Nazareth will destroy this place and will change the customs which Moses delivered to us." And gazing at him, all who sat in the council saw that his face was like the face of an angel. . . .

Now when they heard these things they were enraged, and they ground their teeth against him [Stephen]. But he, full of the Holy Spirit, gazed into heaven and saw the glory of God, and Jesus standing at the right hand of God; and he said, "Behold, I see the heavens opened, and the Son of man standing at the right hand of God." But they cried out with a loud voice and stopped their ears and rushed together upon him. Then they cast him out of the city and stoned him; and the witnesses laid down their garments at the feet of a young man named Saul. And as they were stoning Stephen, he prayed, "Lord Jesus, receive my spirit." And he knelt down and cried with a loud voice, "Lord, do not hold this sin against them." And when he had said this, he fell asleep. And Saul was consenting to his death.

And on that day a great persecution arose against the church in Jerusalem; and they were all scattered throughout the region of Judea and Samaria, except the apostles. Devout men buried Stephen, and made great lamentation over him. But Saul laid waste the church, and entering house after house, he dragged off men and women and committed them to prison. . . .

But Saul, still breathing threats and murder against the disciples of the Lord, went to the high priest and asked him for letters to the synagogues at Damascus, so that if he found any belonging to the Way, men or women, he might bring them bound to Jerusalem. Now as he journeyed he approached Damascus, and suddenly a light from heaven flashed about him. And he fell to the ground and heard a voice saying to him, "Saul, Saul, why do you persecute me?" And he said, "Who are you, Lord?" And he said, "I am Jesus whom you are persecuting; but rise and enter the city, and you will be told what you are to do." The men who were travelling with him stood speechless, hearing the voice but seeing no one. Saul arose from the ground; and when his eyes were opened, he could see nothing; so they led him by the hand and brought him into Damascus. And for three days he was without sight, and neither ate nor drank.

Now there was a disciple at Damascus named Ananias. The Lord said to him in a vision, "Ananias." And he said, "Here I am, Lord." And the Lord said to him, "Rise and go to the street called Straight, and inquire in the house of Judas for a man of Tarsus named Saul; for behold, he is praying, and he has seen a man named Ananias come in and lay his hands on him so that he might regain his sight." But Ananias answered, "Lord, I have heard from many about this man, how much evil he has done to thy saints at Jerusalem; and here he has authority from the chief priests to bind all who call upon thy name." But the Lord said to him, "Go, for he is a chosen instrument of mine to carry my name before the Gentiles and kings and the sons of Israel; for I will show him how much he must suffer for the sake of my name." So Ananias departed and entered the house. And laying his hands on him he said, "Brother Saul, the Lord Jesus who appeared to you on the road by which you came, has sent me that you may regain your sight and be filled with the Holy Spirit." And immediately something like scales fell from his eyes and he regained his sight. Then he rose and was baptized, and took food and was strengthened.

For several days he was with the disciples at Damascus. And in the synagogues immediately he proclaimed Jesus, saying, "He is the Son of God." And all who heard him were amazed, and said, "Is not this the man who made havoc in Jerusalem of those who called on this name? And he has come here for this purpose, to bring them bound before the chief priests." But Saul increased all the more in strength, and confounded the Jews who lived in Damascus by proving that Jesus was the Christ.

When many days had passed, the Jews plotted to kill him, but their plot became known to Saul. They were watching the gates day and night, to kill him; but his disciples took him by night and let him down over the wall, lowering him in a basket.

And when he had come to Jerusalem he attempted to join the disciples; and they were all afraid of him, for they did not believe that he was a disciple. But Barnabas took him, and brought him to the apostles, and declared to them how on the road he had seen the Lord, who spoke to him, and how at Damascus he had preached boldly in the name of Jesus. So he went in and out among them at Jerusalem, preaching boldly in the name of the Lord. And he spoke and disputed against the Hellenists; but they were seeking to kill him.

Now while Paul was waiting for them [Silas and Timothy] at Athens, his spirit was provoked within him as he saw that the city was full of idols. So he argued in the synagogue with the Jews and the devout persons, and in the market place every day with those who chanced to be there. Some also of the Epicurean and Stoic philosophers met him. And some said, "What would this babbler say?" Others said, "He seems to be a preacher of foreign divinities'—because he preached Jesus and the resurrection. And they took hold of him and brought him to the Areopagus, saying, "May we know what this new teaching is which you present? For you bring some strange things to our ears; we wish to know therefore what these things mean." Now all the Athenians and the foreigners who lived there spent their time in nothing except telling or hearing something new.

So Paul, standing in the middle of the Areopagus, said: "Men of Athens, I perceive that in every way you are very religious. For as I passed along, and observed the objects of your worship, I found also an altar with this inscription, 'To an unknown god.' What therefore you worship as unknown, this I proclaim to you. The God who made the world and everything in it, being Lord of heaven and earth, does not live in shrines made by man, nor is he served by human hands, as though he needed anything, since he himself gives to all men life and breath and everything. And he made from one every nation of men to live on all the face of the earth, having determined allotted periods and the boundaries of their habitation, that they should seek God, in the hope that they might feel after him and find him. Yet he is not far from each one of us, for

'In him we live and move and have our being';
as even some of your poets have said,
'For we are indeed his offspring.'

Being then God's offspring, we ought not to think that the Deity is like gold, or silver, or stone, a representation by the art and imagination of man. The times of ignorance God overlooked, but now he commands all men everywhere to repent, because he has fixed a day on which he will judge the world in righteousness by a man whom he has appointed, and of this he has given assurance to all men by raising him from the dead."

Now when they heard of the resurrection of the dead, some mocked; but others said, "We will hear you again about this." So Paul went out from among them. But some men joined him and believed, among them Dionysius the Areopagite and a woman named Damaris and others with them.

First Letter of Paul to the Corinthians 12–13; 15:1–28

Now concerning spiritual gifts, brethren, I do not want you to be uninformed. You know that when you were heathen, you were led astray to dumb idols, however you may have been moved. Therefore I want you to understand that no one speaking by the Spirit of God ever says "Jesus be cursed!" and no one can say "Jesus is Lord" except by the Holy Spirit.

Now there are varieties of gifts, but the same Spirit; and there are varieties of service, but the same Lord; and there are varieties of working, but it is the same God who inspires them all in every one. To each is given the manifestation of the Spirit for the common good. To one is given through the Spirit the utterance of wisdom, and to another the utterance of knowledge according to the same Spirit, to another faith by the same Spirit, to another gifts of healing by the one Spirit, to another the working of miracles, to another prophecy, to another the ability to distinguish between spirits, to another various kinds of tongues, to another the interpretation of tongues. All these are inspired by one and the same Spirit, who apportions to each one individually as he wills.

For just as the body is one and has many members, and all the members of the body, though many, are one body, so it is with Christ. For by one Spirit we were all baptized into one body—Jews or Greeks, slaves or free—and all were made to drink of one Spirit.

For the body does not consist of one member but of many. If the foot should say, "Because I am not a hand, I do not belong to the body," that would not make it any less a part of the body. And if the ear should say, "Because I am not an eye, I do not belong to the body," that would not make it any less a part of the body. If the whole body were an eye, where would be the hearing? If the whole body were an ear, where would be the sense of smell? But as it is, God arranged the organs in the body, each one of them, as he chose. If all were a single organ, where would the body be? As it is, there are many parts, yet one body. The eye cannot say to the hand, "I have no need of you," nor again the head to the feet, "I have no need of you." On the contrary, the parts of the body which seem to be weaker are indispensable, and those parts of the body which we think less honourable we invest with the greater honour, and our unpresentable parts are treated with greater modesty, which our more presentable parts do not require. But God has so adjusted the body, giving the greater honour to the inferior part, that there may be no discord in the body, but that the members may have the same care for one another. If one member suffers, all suffer together; if one member is honoured, all rejoice together.

Now you are the body of Christ and individually members of it. And God has appointed in the church first apostles, second prophets, third teachers, then workers of miracles, then healers, helpers, administrators, speakers in various kinds of tongues. Are all apostles? Are all prophets? Are all teachers? Do all work miracles? Do all possess gifts of healing? Do all speak with tongues? Do all interpret? But earnestly desire the higher gifts.

And I will show you a still more excellent way.

If I speak in the tongues of men and of angels, but have not love, I am a noisy gong or a clanging cymbal. And if I have prophetic powers, and understand all mysteries and all knowledge, and if I have all faith, so as to remove mountains, but have not love, I am nothing. If I give away all I have, and if I deliver my body to be burned, but have not love, I gain nothing.

Love is patient and kind; love is not jealous or boastful; it is not arrogant or rude. Love does not insist on its own way; it is not irritable or resentful; it does not rejoice at wrong, but rejoices in the right. Love bears all things, believes all things, hopes all things, endures all things.

Love never ends, as for prophecies, they will pass away; as for tongues, they will cease; as for knowledge, it will pass away. For our knowledge is imperfect and our prophecy is imperfect; but when the perfect comes, the imperfect will pass away. When I was a child, I spoke like a child, I thought like a child, I reasoned like a child; when I became a man, I gave up childish ways. For now we see in a mirror dimly, but then face to face. Now I know in part; then I shall understand fully, even as I have been fully understood. So faith, hope, love abide, these three; but the greatest of these is love.

Now I would remind you, brethren, in what terms I preached to you the gospel, which you received, in which you stand, by which you are saved, if you hold it fast—unless you believed in vain.

For I delivered to you as of first importance what I also received, that Christ died for our sins in accordance with the scriptures, that he was buried, that he was raised on the third day in accordance with the scriptures, and that he appeared to Cephas, then to the twelve. Then he appeared to more than five hundred brethren at one time, most of whom are still alive, though some have fallen asleep. Then he appeared to James, then to all the apostles. Last of all, as to one untimely born, he appeared also to me [Paul]. For I am the least of the apostles, unfit to be called an apostle, because I persecuted the church of God. But by the grace of God I am what I am, and his grace toward me was not in vain. On the contrary, I worked harder than any of them, though it was not I, but the grace of God which is with me. Whether then it was I or they, so we preach and so you believed.

Now if Christ is preached as raised from the dead, how can some of you say that there is no resurrection of the dead? But if there is no resurrection of the dead, then Christ has not been raised; if Christ has not been raised, then our preaching is in vain and your faith is in vain. We are even found to be misrepresenting God, because we testified of God that he raised Christ, whom he did not raise if it is true that the dead are not raised. For if the dead are not raised, then Christ has not been raised. If Christ has not been raised, your faith is futile and you are still in your sins. Then those also who have fallen asleep in Christ have perished. If for this life only we have hoped in Christ, we are of all men most to be pitied.

But in fact Christ has been raised from the dead, the first fruits of those who have fallen asleep. For as by a man came death, by a man has come also the resurrection of the dead. For as in Adam all die, so also in Christ shall all be made alive. But each in his own order: Christ the first fruits, then at his coming those who belong to Christ. Then comes the end, when he delivers the kingdom to God the Father after destroying every rule and every authority and power. For he must reign until he has put all his enemies under his feet. The last enemy to be destroyed is death. "For God has put all things in subjection under his feet." But when it says, "All things are put in subjection under him," it is plain that he is excepted who put all things under him. When all things are subjected to him, then the Son himself will also be subjected to him who put all things under him, that God may be everything to every one.

The First Letter of John 2.1–25

My little children, I am writing this to you so that you may not sin; but if any one does sin, we have an advocate with the Father, Jesus Christ the righteous; and he is the expiation for our sins, and not for ours only but also for the sins of the whole world. And by this we may be sure that we know him, if we keep his commandments. He who says "I know him" but disobeys his commandments is a liar, and the truth is not in him; but whoever keeps his word, in him truly love for God is perfected. By this we may be sure that we are in him: he who says he abides in him ought to walk in the same way in which he walked.

Beloved, I am writing you no new commandment, but an old commandment which you had from the beginning; the old commandment is the word which you have heard. Yet I am writing you a new commandment, which is true in him and in you, because the darkness is passing away and the true light is already shining. He who says he is in the light and hates his brother is in the darkness still. He who loves his brother abides in the light, and in it there is no cause for stumbling. But he who hates his brother is in the darkness and walks in the darkness, and does not know where he is going, because the darkness has blinded his eyes.

I am writing to you, little children, because your sins are forgiven for his sake. I am writing to you, fathers, because you know him who is from the beginning. I am writing to you, young men, because you have overcome the evil one. I write to you, children, because you know the Father. I write to you, fathers, because you know him who is from the beginning. I write to you, young men, because you are strong, and the word of God abides in you, and you have overcome the evil one.

Do not love the world or the things in the world. If any one loves the world, love for the Father is not in him. For all that is in the world, the lust of the flesh and the lust of the eyes and the pride of life, is not of the Father but is of the world. And the world passes away, and the lust of it; but he who does the will of God abides for ever.

Children, it is the last hour; and as you have heard that antichrist is coming, so now many antichrists have come; therefore we know that it is the last hour. They went out from us, but they were not of us; for if they had been of us, they would have continued with us; but they went out, that it might be plain that they all are not of us. But you have been anointed by the Holy One, and you all know. I write to you, not because you do not know the truth, but because you know it, and know that no lie is of the truth. Who is the liar but he who denies that Jesus is the Christ? This is the antichrist, he who denies the Father and the Son. No one who denies the Son has the Father. He who confesses the Son has the Father also. Let what you heard from the beginning abide in you. If what you heard from the beginning abides in you, then you will abide in the Son and in the Father. And this is what he has promised us, eternal life.

The Revelation to John 1:1–20; 4–6; 21:1–14

The revelation of Jesus Christ, which God gave him to show to his servants what must soon take place; and he made it known by sending his angel to his servant John, who bore witness to the word of God and to the testimony of Jesus Christ, even to all that he saw. Blessed is he who reads aloud the words of the prophecy, and blessed are those who hear, and who keep what is written therein; for the time is near.

John to the seven churches that are in Asia:

Grace to you and peace from him who is and who was and who is to come, and from the seven spirits who are before his throne, and from Jesus Christ the faithful witness, the firstborn of the dead, and the ruler of kings on earth.

To him who loves us and has freed us from our sins by his blood and made us a kingdom, priests to his God and Father, to him be glory and dominion for ever and ever. Amen. Behold, he is coming with the clouds, and every eye will see him, every one who pierced him; and all tribes of the earth will wail on account of him. Even so. Amen.

"I am the Alpha and the Omega," says the Lord God, who is and who was and who is to come, the Almighty.

I John, your brother, who share with you in Jesus the tribulation and the kingdom and the patient endurance, was on the island called Patmos on account of the word of God and the testimony of Jesus. I was in the Spirit on the Lord's day, and I heard behind me a loud voice like a trumpet saying, "Write what you see in a book and send it to the seven churches, to Ephesus and to Smyrna and to Pergamum and to Thyatira and to Sardis and to Philadelphia and to Laodicea."

Then I turned to see the voice that was speaking to me, and on turning I saw seven golden lampstands, and in the midst of the lampstands one like a son of man, clothed with a long robe and with a golden girdle round his breast; his head and his hair were white as white wool, white as snow; his eyes were like a flame of fire, his feet were like burnished bronze, refined as in a furnace, and his voice was like the sound of many waters; in his right hand he held seven stars, from his mouth issued a sharp two-edged sword, and his face was like the sun shining in full strength.

When I saw him, I fell at his feet as though dead. But he laid his right hand upon me, saying, "Fear not, I am the first and the last, and the living one; I died, and behold I am alive for evermore, and I have the keys of Death and Hades. Now write what you see, what is and what is to take place

111

hereafter. As for the mystery of the seven stars which you saw in my right hand, and the seven golden lampstands, the seven stars are the angels of the seven churches and the seven lampstands are the seven churches. . . .

After this I looked, and lo, in heaven an open door! And the first voice, which I had heard speaking to me like a trumpet, said, "Come up hither, and I will show you what must take place after this." At once I was in the Spirit, and lo, a throne stood in heaven, with one seated on the throne! And he who sat there appeared like jasper and carnelian, and round the throne was a rainbow that looked like an emerald. Round the throne were twenty-four thrones, and seated on the thrones were twenty-four elders, clad in white garments, with golden crowns upon their heads. From the throne issue flashes of lightning, and voices and peals of thunder, and before the throne burn seven torches of fire, which are the seven spirits of God; and before the throne there is as it were a sea of glass, like crystal.

And round the throne, on each side of the throne, are four living creatures, full of eyes in front and behind: the first living creature like a lion, the second living creature like an ox, the third living creature with the face of a man, and the fourth living creature like a flying eagle. And the four living creatures, each of them with six wings, are full of eyes all round and within, and day and night they never cease to sing.

"Holy, holy, holy, is the Lord God Almighty,
who was and is and is to come!"

And whenever the living creatures give glory and honour and thanks to him who is seated on the throne, who lives for ever and ever, the twenty-four elders fall down before him who is seated on the throne and worship him who lives for ever and ever; they cast their crowns before the throne, singing,

"Worthy art thou, our Lord and God,
to receive glory and honour and power,
for thou didst create all things,
and by thy will they existed and were created."

And I saw in the right hand of him who was seated on the throne a scroll written within and on the back, sealed with seven seals; and I saw a strong angel proclaiming with a loud voice, "Who is worthy to open the scroll and break its seals?" And no one in heaven or on earth or under the earth was able to open the scroll or to look into it, and I wept much that no one was found worthy to open the scroll or to look into it. Then one of the elders said to me, "Weep not; lo, the Lion of the tribe of Judah, the Root of David, has conquered, so that he can open the scroll and its seven seals."

And between the throne and the four living creatures and among the elders, I saw a Lamb standing, as though it had been slain, with seven horns and with seven eyes, which are the seven spirits of God sent out into all the earth; and he went and took the scroll from the right hand of him who was seated on the throne. And when he had taken the scroll, the four living creatures and the twenty-four elders fell down before the Lamb, each holding a harp, and with golden bowls full of incense, which are the prayers of the saints; and they sang a new song, saying,

"Worthy art thou to take the scroll and to open its seals,
for thou wast slain and by thy blood didst ransom men for God
from every tribe and tongue and people and nation,

and hast made them a kingdom and priests to our God,
and they shall reign on earth."

Then I looked, and I heard around the throne and the living creatures and the elders the voice of many angels, numbering myriads of myriads and thousands of thousands, saying with a loud voice, "Worthy is the Lamb who was slain, to receive power and wealth and wisdom and might and honour and glory and blessing!" And I heard every creature in heaven and on earth and under the earth and in the sea, and all therein, saying, "To him who sits upon the throne and to the Lamb be blessing and honour and glory and might for ever and ever!" And the four living creatures said, "Amen!" and the elders fell down and worshipped.

Now I saw when the Lamb opened one of the seven seals, and I heard one of the four living creatures say, as with a voice of thunder, "Come!" And I saw, and behold, a white horse, and its rider had a bow; and a crown was given to him, and he went out conquering and to conquer.

When he opened the second seal, I heard the second living creature say, "Come!" And out came another horse, bright red; its rider was permitted to take peace from the earth, so that men should slay one another; and he was given a great sword.

When he opened the third seal, I heard the third living creature say, "Come!" And I saw, and behold, a black horse, and its rider had a balance in his hand; and I heard what seemed to be a voice in the midst of the four living creatures saying, "A quart of wheat for a denarius, and three quarts of barley for a denarius; but do not harm oil and wine!"

When he opened the fourth seal, I heard the voice of the fourth living creature say, "Come!" And I saw, and behold, a pale horse, and its rider's name was Death, and Hades followed him; and they were given power over a fourth of the earth, to kill with sword and with famine and with pestilence and by wild beasts of the earth.

When he opened the fifth seal, I saw under the altar the souls of those who had been slain for the word of God and for the witness they had borne; they cried out with a loud voice, "O Sovereign Lord, holy and true, how long before thou wilt judge and avenge our blood on those who dwell upon the earth?" Then they were each given a white robe and told to rest a little longer, until the number of their fellow servants and their brethren should be complete, who were to be killed as they themselves had been.

When he opened the sixth seal, I looked, and behold, there was a great earthquake; and the sun became black as sackcloth, the full moon became like blood, and the stars of the sky fell to the earth as the fig tree sheds its winter fruit when shaken by a gale; the sky vanished like a scroll that is rolled up, and every mountain and island was removed from its place. Then the kings of the earth and the great men and the generals and the rich and the strong, and every one, slave and free, hid in the caves and among the rocks of the mountains, calling to the mountains and rocks, "Fall on us and hide us from the face of him who is seated on the throne, and from the wrath of the Lamb; for the great day of their wrath has come, and who can stand before it?"

Then I saw a new heaven and a new earth; for the first heaven and the first earth had passed away, and the sea was no more. And I saw the holy city, new Jerusalem, coming down out of heaven from God, prepared as a bride adorned for her husband; and I heard a great voice from the throne saying, "Behold, the dwelling of God is with men. He will dwell with them, and they shall be his people, and God himself will be with them; he will wipe away every tear from their eyes, and death shall be no more, neither shall there be mourning nor crying nor pain any more, for the former things have passed away."

And he who sat upon the throne said, "Behold, I make all things new." Also he said, "Write this, for these words are trustworthy and true." And he said to me, "It is done! I am the Alpha and the Omega, the beginning and the end. To the thirsty I will give water without price from the fountain of the water of life. He who conquers shall have this heritage, and I will be his God and he shall be my son. But as for the cowardly, the faithless, the polluted, as for murders, fornicators, sorcerers, idolaters, and all liars, their lot shall be in the lake that burns with fire and brimstone, which is the second death."

Then came one of the seven angels who had the seven bowls full of the seven last plagues, and spoke to me, saying, "Come, I will show you the Bride, the wife of the Lamb." And in the Spirit he carried me away to a great, high mountain, and showed me the holy city Jerusalem coming down out of heaven from God, having the glory of God, its radiance like a most rare jewel, like a jasper, clear as crystal. It had a great, high wall, with twelve gates, and at the gates twelve angels, and on the gates the names of the twelve tribes of the sons of Israel were inscribed; on the east three gates, on the north three gates, on the south three gates, and on the west three gates. And the wall of the city had twelve foundations, and on them the twelve names of the twelve apostles of the Lamb. . . .

Some Additional Passages from the New Testament on Women, Marriage, and Slavery

Mark 10:2–12

And Pharisees came up and in order to test him asked, "Is it lawful for a man to divorce his wife?" He answered them, "What did Moses command you?" They said, "Moses allowed a man to write a certificate of divorce, and to put her away." But Jesus said to them, "For your hardness of heart he wrote you this commandment. But from the beginning of creation, 'God made them male and female.' 'For this reason a man shall leave his father and mother and be joined to his wife, and the two shall become one.' So they are no longer two but one. What therefore God has joined together, let not man put asunder."

Luke 10:38–42

Now as they went on their way, he entered a village; and a woman named Martha received him into her house. And she had a sister called Mary, who sat at the Lord's feet and listened to his teaching. But Martha was distracted with much serving; and she went to him and said, "Lord, do you not care that my sister has left me to serve alone? Tell her then to help me." But the Lord answered her, "Martha, Martha, you are anxious and troubled about many things; one thing is needful. Mary has chosen the good portion, which shall not be taken away from her."

John 8:2–11

Early in the morning he came again to the temple; all the people came to him, and he sat down and taught them. The scribes and the Pharisees brought a woman who had been caught in adultery, and placing her in the midst they said to him, "Teacher, this woman has been caught in the act of adultery. Now in the law Moses commanded us to stone such. What do you say about her?" This they said to test him, that they might have some charge to bring against him. Jesus bent down and wrote with his finger on the ground. And as they continued to ask him, he stood up and said to them, "Let him who is without sin among you be the first to throw a stone at her." And once more he bent down and wrote with his finger on the ground. But when they heard it, they went away, one by one, beginning with the eldest, and Jesus was left alone with the woman standing before him. Jesus looked up and said to her, "Woman, where are they? Has no one condemned you?" She said, "No one, Lord." And Jesus said, "Neither do I condemn you; go, and do not sin again."

I Corinthians 7

Now concerning the matters about which you wrote. It is well for a man not to touch a woman. But because of the temptation to immorality, each man should have his own wife and each woman her own husband. The husband should give to his wife her conjugal rights, and likewise the wife to her husband. For the wife does not rule over her own body, but the husband does; likewise the husband does not rule over his own body, but the wife does. Do not refuse one another except perhaps by agreement for a season, that you may devote yourselves to prayer; but then come together again, lest Satan tempt you through lack of self-control. I say this by way of concession, not of command. I wish that all were as I myself am. But each has his own special gift from God, one of one kind and one of another.

To the unmarried and the widows I say that it is well for them to remain single as I do. But if they cannot exercise self-control, they should marry. For it is better to marry than to be aflame with passion.

To the married I give charge, not I but the Lord, that the wife should not separate from her husband (but if she does, let her remain single or else be reconciled to her husband) and that the husband should not divorce his wife.

To the rest I say, not the Lord, that if any brother has a wife who is an unbeliever, and she consents to live with him, he should not divorce her. If any woman has a husband who is an unbeliever, and he consents to live with her, she should not divorce him. For the unbelieving husband is consecrated through his wife, and the unbelieving wife is consecrated through her husband. Otherwise, your children would be unclean, but as it is they are holy. But if the unbelieving partner desires to separate, let it be so; in such a case the brother or sister is not bound. For God has called us to peace. Wife, how do you know whether you will save your husband? Husband, how do you know whether you will save your wife?

Only, let every one lead the life which the Lord has assigned to him, and in which God has called him. This is my rule in all the churches. Was any one at the time of his call already circumcised? Let him not seek to remove the marks of circumcision. Was any one at the time of his call uncircumcised? Let him not seek circumcision. For neither circumcision counts for anything nor uncircumcision, but keeping the commandments of God. Every one should remain in the state in which he was called. Were you a slave when called? Never mind. But if you can gain your freedom, avail yourself of the opportunity. For he who was called in the Lord as a slave is a freedman of the Lord. Likewise he who was free when called is a slave of Christ. You were bought with a price; do not become slaves of men. So, brethren, in whatever state each was called, there let him remain with God.

Now concerning the unmarried, I have no command of the Lord, but I give my opinion as one who by the Lord's mercy is trustworthy. I think that in view of the impending distress it is well for a person to remain as he is. Are you bound to a wife? Do not seek to be free. Are you free from a wife? Do not seek marriage. But if you marry, you do not sin, and if a girl marries she does not sin. Yet those who marry will have worldly troubles, and I would spare you that. I mean, brethren, the appointed time has grown very short; from now on, let those who have wives live as though they had none, and those who mourn as though they were not mourning, and those who rejoice as though they were not rejoicing, and those who buy as though they had no goods, and those who deal with the world as though they had no dealings with it. For the form of this world is passing away.

I want you to be free from anxieties. The unmarried man is anxious about the affairs of the Lord, how to please the Lord; but the married man is anxious about worldly affairs, how to please his wife, and his interests are divided. And the unmarried woman or girl is anxious about the affairs of the Lord, how to be holy in body and spirit; but the married woman is anxious about worldly affairs, how to please her husband. I say this for your own benefit, not to lay any restraint upon you, but to promote good order and to secure your undivided devotion to the Lord.

If any one thinks that he is not behaving properly toward his betrothed, if his passions are strong, and it has to be, let him do as he wishes: let them marry—it is no sin. But whoever is firmly established in his heart, being under no necessity but having his desire under control, and has determined this in his heart, to keep her as his betrothed, he will do well. So that he who marries his betrothed does well; and he who refrains from marriage will do better.

A wife is bound to her husband as long as he lives. If the husband dies, she is free to be married to whom she wishes, only in the Lord. But in my judgment she is happier if she remains as she is. And I think that I have the Spirit of God.

Galatians 3:19–29

Why then the law? It was added because of transgressions, till the offspring should come to whom the promise had been made; and it was ordained by angels through an intermediary. Now an intermediary implies more than one; but God is one.

Is the law then against the promises of God? Certainly not; for if a law had been given which could make alive, then righteousness would indeed be by the law. But the scripture consigned all things to sin, that what was promised to faith in Jesus Christ might be given to those who believe.

Now before faith came, we were confined under the law, kept under restraint until faith should be revealed. So that the law was our custodian until Christ came, that we might be justified by faith. But now that faith has come, we are no longer under a custodian; for in Christ Jesus you are all sons of God, through faith. For as many of you as were baptized into Christ have put on Christ. There is neither Jew nor Greek, there is neither slave nor free, there is neither male nor female; for you are all one in Christ Jesus. And if you are Christ's, then you are Abraham's offspring, heirs according to promise.

I Timothy 2:8–15

I desire then that in every place the men should pray, lifting holy hands without anger or quarrelling; also that women should adorn themselves modestly and sensibly in seemly apparel, not with braided hair or gold or pearls or costly attire but by good deeds, as befits women who profess religion. Let a woman learn in silence with all submissiveness. I permit no woman to teach or to have authority over men; she is to keep silent. For Adam was formed first, then Eve; and Adam was not deceived, but the woman was deceived and became a transgressor. Yet woman will be saved through bearing children, if she continues in faith and love and holiness, with modesty.

Titus 2:1–10

But as for you, teach what befits sound doctrine. Bid the older men be temperate, serious, sensible, sound in faith, in love, and in steadfastness. Bid the older women likewise to be reverent in behaviour, not to be slanderers or slaves to drink; they are to teach what is good, and so train the young women to love their husbands and children, to be sensible, chaste, domestic, kind, and submissive to their husbands, that the word of God may not be discredited. Likewise urge the younger men to control themselves. Show yourself in all respects a model of good deeds, and in your teaching show integrity, gravity, and sound speech that cannot be censured, so that an opponent may be put to shame, having nothing evil to say of us. Bid slaves to be submissive to their masters and to give satisfaction in every respect; they are nor to be refractory, not to pilfer, but to show entire and true fidelity, so that in everything they may adorn the doctrine of God our Saviour.

Paul of Tarsus

Born in Tarsus, Cilicia (present-day Turkey), of an orthodox Jewish family who were also Roman citizens, Saul or Paul (in the latinized version of his name) was as a youth trained as a tentmaker and sent to Jerusalem to study rabbinic law under the sage Gamaliel. Initially a zealous, nationalistic Jew, Paul assisted and applauded at a riot against the young Christian community of Jerusalem after the first post-crucifixion Pentecost. The Jewish High Priest thereupon commissioned him in the year 35 to suppress incipient Christianity in Damascus. As he approached that Syrian city Paul experienced a vision of Jesus and was converted to Christianity, subsequently becoming it energetic missionary throughout the Mediterranean world and the leading formulator of its theology. Vigorously attacking those apostles who wished to retain the Judaic character of the young Christian community, Paul successfully insisted that it not commit itself to Jewish law and ritual. His victory in this controversy enabled the Christian church, spearheaded by his proselytizing activities, to convert to its doctrine vast numbers of gentiles. His doctrine stated that Jesus was and is God's son, whose crucifixion made possible forgiveness of sin and salvation to all true believers. Paul was executed during the persecutions of Nero, *c.*6$_7$.

These letters of Paul come from the Revised Standard Version of the Bible. (New York, Thomas Nelson & Sons, 1952).

The Letter of Paul to the Romans

Chapter I

1. Paul, a servant of Jesus Christ, called to be an apostle, set apart for the gospel of God which he promised beforehand through his prophets in the holy scriptures, the gospel concerning his Son, who was descended from David according to the flesh and designated Son of God in power according to the Spirit of holiness by his resurrection from the dead, Jesus Christ our Lord, through whom we have received grace and apostleship to bring about obedience to the faith for the sake of his name among all the nations, including yourselves who are called to belong to Jesus Christ;

7. To all God's beloved in Rome, who are called to be saints:

Grace to you and peace from God our Father and the Lord Jesus Christ.

8. First, I thank my God through Jesus Christ for all of you, because your faith is proclaimed in all the world. For God is my witness, whom I serve with my spirit in the gospel of his Son, that without ceasing I mention you always in my prayers, asking that somehow by God's will I may now at last succeed in coming to you. For I long to see you, that I may impart to you some spiritual gift to strengthen you, that is, that we may be mutually encouraged by each other's faith, both yours and mine. I want you to know, brethren, that I have often intended to come to you (but thus far have been prevented), in order that I may reap some harvest among you as well as among the rest of the Gentiles. I am under obligation both to Greeks and to barbarians, both to wise and to the foolish: so I am eager to preach the gospel to you also who are in Rome.

16. For I am not ashamed of the gospel: it is the power of God for salvation to every one who has faith, to the Jew first and also to the Greek. For in it the righteousness of God is revealed through faith for faith; as it is written, "He who through faith is righteous shall live."

18. For the wrath of God is revealed from heaven against all ungodliness and wickedness of men who by their wickedness suppress the truth. For what can be known about God is plain to them, because God has shown it to them. Ever since the creation of the world his invisible nature, namely, his eternal power and deity, has been clearly perceived in the things that have been made. So they are without excuse; for although they knew God they did not honor him as God or give thanks to him, but they became futile in their thinking and their senseless minds were darkened. Claiming to be wise, they became fools, and exchanged the glory of the immortal God for images resembling mortal man or birds or animals or reptiles.

24. Therefore God gave them up in the lust of their hearts to impurity to the dishonoring of their bodies among themselves, because they exchanged the truth about God for a lie and worshiped and served the creature rather than the Creator, who is blessed forever! Amen.

26. For this reason God gave them up to dishonorable passions. Their women exchanged natural relations for unnatural, and the men likewise gave up natural relations with women and were consumed with passion for one another, men committing shameless acts with men and receiving in their own persons the due penalty for their error.

28. And since they did not see fit to acknowledge God, God gave them up to a base mind and to improper conduct. They were filled with all manner of wickedness, evil, covetousness, malice. Full of envy, murder, strife, deceit, malignity, they are gossips, slanderers, haters of God, insolent, haughty, boastful, inventors of evil, disobedient to parents, foolish, faithless, heartless, ruthless. Though they know God's decree that those who do such things deserve to die, they not only do them but approve those who practice them.

Chapter II

Therefore you have no excuse, O man, whoever you are, when you judge another; for in passing judgment upon him you condemn yourself, because you, the judge, are doing the very same things. We know that the judgment of God rightly falls upon those who do such things. Do you suppose, O man, that when you judge those who do such things and yet do them yourself, you will escape the judgment of God? Or do you presume upon the riches of his kindness and forbearance and patience? Do you not know that God's kindness is meant to lead you to repentance? But by your hard and impenitent hear you are storing up wrath for yourself on the day of wrath when God's righteous judgment will be revealed. For he will render to every man according to his works: to those who by patience in well-doing seek for glory and honor and immortality, he will give eternal life; but for those who are factious and do not obey the truth, but obey wickedness, there will be wrath and fury. There will be tribulation and distress for every human being who does evil, the Jew first and also the Greek, but glory and honor and peace for every one who does good, the Jew first and also the Greek. For God shows no partiality.

12. All who have sinned without the law will also perish without the law, and all who have sinned under the law will be judged by the law. For it is not the hearers of the law who are righteous before God, but the doers of the law who will be justified. When Gentiles who have not the law do by nature what the law requires, they are a law of themselves, even though they do not have the law. They show that what the law requires is written on their hearts, while their conscience also bears witness and their conflicting thought accuse or perhaps excuse them on that day when, according to my gospel, God judges the secrets of men by Christ Jesus.

17. But if you call yourself a Jew and rely upon the Law and boast of your relation of God and know his will and approve what is excellent, because you are instructed in the law, and if you are sure that you are a guide to the blind, a light to those who are in darkness, a corrector of the foolish, a teacher of children, having in the law the embodiment of knowledge and truth—you then who teach others, will you not teach yourself? While you preach against stealing, do you steal? You who say that one must not commit adultery, do you commit adultery? You who abhor idols, do you rob temples? You who boast in the law, do you dishonor god by breaking the law? For, as it is written,

"The name of God is blasphemed among the Gentiles because of you."

25. Circumcision indeed is of value if you obey the law; but if you break the law, your circumcision becomes uncircumcision. So, if a man who is uncircumcised keeps the precepts of the law, will not his uncircumcision be regarded as circumcision? Then those who are physically uncircumcised but keep the law will condemn you who have the written code and circumcision but break the law. For he is not a real Jew who is one outwardly, nor is true circumcision something external and physical. He is a Jew who is one inwardly, and real circumcision is a matter of the heart, spiritual and not literal. His praise is not from men but from God.

Chapter III

Then what advantage has the Jew? Or what is the value of circumcision? Much in every way. To begin with, the Jews are entrusted with the oracles of God. What if some were unfaithful? Does their faithlessness nullify the faithfulness of God? By no means! Let God be true though every man be false, as it is written,

"That thou mayest be justified in thy words, and prevail when thou art judged."

5. But if our wickedness serves to show the justice of God, what shall we say? That God is unjust to inflict wrath on us? (I speak in a human way.) By no means! For then how could God judge the world? But if through my falsehood God's truthfulness abounds to his glory, why am I still being condemned as a sinner? And why not do evil that good may come?—as some people slanderously charge us with saying. Their condemnation is just.

9. What then? Are we Jews any better off? No, not at all; for I have already charged that all men, both Jews and Greeks, are under the power of sin, as it is written:

"None is righteous, no, not one; no one understands, no one seeks for God.

12. All have turned aside, together they have gone wrong; no one does good, not even one."

13. "Their throat is an open grave, they use their tongues to deceive." "The venom of asps is under their lips."

14. "Their mouth is full of curses and bitterness."

15. "Their feet are swift to shed blood,

16. in their paths are ruin and misery,

17. and the way of peace they do not know."

18. "There is no fear of God before their eyes."

19. Now we know that whatever the law says it speaks to those who are under the law, so that every mouth may be stopped, and the whole world may be held accountable to God. For no human being will be justified in his sight by works of the law since through the law comes knowledge of sin.

21. But now the righteousness of God has been manifested apart from law, although the law and the prophets bear witness to it, the righteousness of God through faith in Jesus Christ for all who believe. For there is no distinction; since all have sinned and fall short of the glory of God, they are justified by his grace as a gift, through the redemption which is in Christ Jesus, whom God put forward as an expiation by his blood, to be received by faith. This was to show God's righteousness, because in his divine forbearance he had passed over former sins; it was to prove at the present time that he himself is righteous and that he justifies him who has faith in Jesus.

27. Then what becomes of our boasting? It is excluded. On what principle? On the principle of works? No, but on the principle of faith. For we hold that a man is justified by faith apart from works of law. Or is God the God of Jews only? Is he not the God of Gentiles also? Yes, of Gentiles also, since God is one; and he will justify the circumcised on the ground of their faith and the uncircumcised because of their faith. Do we then overthrow the law by this faith? By no means! On the contrary, we uphold the law.

Chapter IV

What then shall we say about Abraham, our forefather according to the flesh? For if Abraham was justified by works, he has something to boast about, but not before God. For what does the scripture say? "Abraham believed God, and it was reckoned to him as righteousness." Now to one who works, his wages are not reckoned as a gift but as his due. And to one who does not work but trusts him who justifies the ungodly, his faith is reckoned as righteousness. So also David pronounces a blessing upon the man to whom God reckons righteousness apart from works:

7. "Blessed are those whose iniquities are forgiven, and whose sins are covered; blessed is the man against whom the Lord will not reckon his sin."

9. Is this blessing pronounced only upon the circumcised, or also upon the uncircumcised? We say that faith was reckoned to Abraham as righteousness. How then was it reckoned to him? Was it before or after he had been circumcised? It was not after, but before he was circumcised. He received circumcision as a sign or seal of the righteousness which he had by faith while he was still uncircumcised. The purpose was to make him the father of all who believe without being circumcised and who thus have righteousness reckoned to them, and likewise the father of the circumcised who are not merely, circumcised but also follow the example of the faith which our father Abraham had before he was circumcised.

13. The promise to Abraham and his descendants, that they should inherit the world, did not come through the law but through the righteousness of faith. If it is the adherents of the law who are to be the heirs, faith is null and the promise is void. For the law brings wrath, but where there is no law there is no transgression.

16. That is why it depends on faith, in order that the promise may rest on grace and be guaranteed to all his descendants—not only to the adherents of the law but also to those who share the faith of Abraham, for he is the father of us all, as it is written, "I have made you the father of many nations"—in the presence of the God in whom he believed, who gives life to the dead and calls into existence the things that do not exist. In hope he believed against hope, that he should become the father of many nations; as he had been told, "So shall your descendants be." He did not weaken in faith when he considered his own body, which was as good as dead because he was about a hundred years old, or when he considered the barrenness of Sarah's womb. No distrust made him waver concerning the promise of God, but he grew strong in his faith as he gave glory to God, fully convinced that God was able to do what he had promised. That is why his faith was "reckoned to him as righteousness." But the words, "it was reckoned to him," were written not for his sake alone, but for ours also. It will be reckoned to us who believe in him that raised from the dead Jesus our Lord, who was put to death for our trespasses and raised for our justification.

Chapter V

Therefore, since we are justified by faith, we have peace with God through our Lord Jesus Christ. Through him we have obtained access to this grace in which we stand, and we rejoice in our hope of sharing the glory of God. More than that, we rejoice in our sufferings, knowing that suffering produces endurance, and endurance produces character, and character produces hope, and hope does not disappoint us, because God's love has been poured into our hearts through the Holy Spirit which has been given to us.

6. While we were yet helpless, at the right time Christ died for the ungodly. Why, one will hardly die for a righteous man—though perhaps for a good man one will dare even to die. But God shows his love for us in that while we were yet sinners Christ died for us. Since, therefore, we are now justified by his blood, much more shall we be saved by him from the wrath of God. For if while we were enemies we were reconciled to God by the death of his Son, much more, now that we are reconciled, shall we be saved by his life. Not only so, but we also rejoice in God through our Lord Jesus Christ, through whom we have now received our reconciliation.

12. Therefore as sin came into the world through one man and death through sin, and so death spread to all men because all men sinned—sin indeed was in the world before the law was given, but sin is not counted where there is no law. Yet death reigned from Adam to Moses, even over those whose sins were not like the transgression of Adam, who was a type of the one who was to come.

15. But the free gift is not like the trespass. For if many died through one man's trespass, much more have the grace of God and the free gift in the grace of that one man Jesus Christ abounded for many. And the free gift is not like the effect of that one man's sin. For the judgment following one trespass brought condemnation, but the free gift following many trespasses brings justification. If, because of one man's trespass, death reigned through that one man, much more will those who receive the abundance of grace and the free gift of righteousness reign in life through the one man Jesus Christ.

18. Then as one man's trespass led to condemnation for all men, so one man's act of righteousness leads to acquittal and life for all men. For as by one man's disobedience many were made sinners, so by one man's obedience many will be made righteous. Law came in, to increase the trespass; but where sin increased, grace abounded all the more, so that, as sin reigned in death, grace also might reign through righteousness to eternal life through Jesus Christ our Lord.

Chapter VI

What shall we say then? Are we to continue in sin that grace may abound? By no means! How can we who died to sin still live in it? Do you not know that all of us who have been baptized into Christ Jesus were baptized into his death? We were buried therefore with him by baptism into death, so that as Christ was raised from the dead by the glory of the Father, we too might walk in newness of life.

5. For if we have been united with him in a death like his, we shall certainly be united with him in a resurrection like his. We know that our old self was crucified with him so that the sinful body might be destroyed, and we might no longer be enslaved to sin. But if we have died with Christ, we believe that we shall also live with him. For we know that Christ being raised from the dead will never die again; death no longer has dominion over him. The death he died he died to sin, once for all, but the life he lives he lives to God. So you also must consider yourselves dead to sin and alive to God in Christ Jesus.

12. Let not sin therefore reign in your mortal bodies, to make you obey their passions. Do not yield your members to sin as instruments of wickedness, but yield yourselves to God as men who have been brought from death to life, and your members to God as instruments of righteousness. For sin will have no dominion over you, since you are not under law but under grace.

15. What then? Are we to sin because we are not under law but under grace? By no means! Do you not know that if you yield yourselves to any one as obedient slaves, you are slaves of the one whom you obey, either of sin, which leads to death, or of obedience, which leads to righteousness? But thanks be to God, that you who were once slaves of sin have become obedient from the heart to the standard of teaching to which you were committed, and, having been set free from sin, have becomes slaves of righteousness. I am speaking in human terms, because of your natural limitations. For just as you once yielded your members to impurity and to greater and greater iniquity, so now yield your members to righteousness for sanctification.

20. When you were slaves of sin, you were free in regard to righteousness. But then what return did you get from the things of which you are now ashamed? The end of those things is death. But now that you have been set free from sin and have become slaves of God, the return you get is sanctification and its end, eternal life. For the wages of sin is death, but the free gift of God is eternal life in Christ Jesus our Lord.

Chapter VII

Do you not know, brethren—for I am speaking to those who know the law—that the law is binding on a person only during his life? Thus a married woman is bound by law to her husband as long as he lives; but if her husband dies she is discharged from the law concerning the husband. Accordingly, she will be called an adulteress if she lives with another man while her husband is alive. But if her husband dies she is free from that law, and if she marries another man she is not an adulteress.

4. Likewise, my brethren, you have died to the law through the body of Christ, so that you may belong to another, to him who has been raised from the dead in order that we may bear fruit for God. While we were living in the flesh, our sinful passions, aroused by the law, were at work in our members to bear fruit for death. But now we are discharged from the law, dead to that which held us captive, so that we serve not under the old written code but in the new life of the Spirit.

7. What then shall we say? That the law is sin? By no means! Yet, if it had not been for the law, I should not have known sin. I should not have known what it is to covet if the law had not said, "You shall not covet." But sin, finding opportunity in the commandment, wrought in me all kinds of covetousness. Apart from the law sin lies dead. I was once alive apart from the law, but when the commandment came, sin revived and I died; the very commandment which promised life proved to be death for me. For sin, finding opportunity in the commandment, deceived me and by it killed me. So the law is holy and the commandment is holy and just and good.

13. Did that which is good, then, bring death to me? By no means! It was sin, working death in me through what is good, in order that sin might be shown to be sin, and through the commandment might become sinful beyond measure. We know that the law is spiritual; but I am carnal, sold under sin. I do not understand my own actions. For I do not do what I want, but I do the very thing I hate. Now if I do what I do not want, I agree that the law is good. So then it is no longer I that do it, but sin which dwells within me. For I know that nothing good dwells within me, that is, in my flesh. I can will what is right, but I cannot do it. For I do not do the good I want, but the evil I do not want is what I do. Now if I do what I do not want, it is no longer I that do it, but sin which dwells within me.

21. So I find it to be a law that when I want to do right, evil lies close at hand. For I delight in the law of God, in my inmost self, but I see in my members another law at war with the law of my mind and making me captive to the law of sin which dwells in my members. Wretched man that I am! Who will deliver me from this body of death? Thanks be to God through Jesus Christ our Lord! So then, I of myself serve the law of God with my mind, but with my flesh I serve the law of sin.

Chapter VIII

There is therefore now no condemnation for those who are in Christ Jesus. For the law of the Spirit of life in Christ Jesus has set me free from the law of sin and death. For God has done what the law, weakened by the flesh, could not do: sending his own Son in the likeness of sinful flesh and for sin, he condemned sin in the flesh and for sin, in order that the just requirement of the law might be fulfilled in us, who walk not according to the flesh but according to the Spirit. For those who live according to the flesh set their minds on the things of the flesh, but those who live according to the Spirit set their minds on the things of the Spirit. To set the mind on the flesh is death, but to set the mind on the Spirit is life and peace. For the mind that is set on the flesh is hostile to God; it does not submit to God's law, indeed it cannot; and those who are in the flesh cannot please God.

9. But you are not in the flesh, you are in the Spirit, if the Spirit of God really dwells in you. Any one who does not have the Spirit of Christ does not belong to him. But if Christ is in you, although your bodies are dead because of sin, your spirits are alive because of righteousness. If the Spirit of him who raised Jesus from the dead dwells in you, he who raised Christ Jesus from the dead will give life to your mortal bodies also through his Spirit which dwells in you.

12. So then, brethren, we are debtors, not to the flesh, to live according to the flesh—for if you live according to the flesh you will die, but if by the Spirit you put to death the deeds of the body you will live. For all who are led by the Spirit of God are sons of God. For you did not receive the spirit of slavery to fall back into fear, but you have received the spirit of sonship. When we cry, "Abba! Father!" it is the Spirit himself bearing witness with our spirit that we are children of God, and if children, then heirs, heirs of God and fellow heirs with Christ, provided we suffer with him in order that we may also be glorified with him.

18. I consider that the sufferings of this present time are not worth comparing with the glory that is to be revealed to us. For the creation awaits with eager longing for the revealing of the sons of God; for the creation was subjected to futility, not of its own will but by the will of him who subjected it in hope; because the creation itself will be set free from its bondage to decay and obtain the glorious liberty of the children of God. We know that the whole creation has been groaning in travail together until now; and not only the creation, but we ourselves, who have the first fruits of the Spirit, groan inwardly as we wait for adoption as sons, the redemption of our bodies. For in this hope we were saved. Now hope that is seen is not hope. For who hopes for what he sees? But if we hope for what we do not see, we wait for it with patience.

26. Likewise the Spirit helps us in our weakness; for we do not know how to pray as we ought, but the Spirit himself intercedes for us with sighs too deep for words. And he who searches the hearts of men knows what is the mind of the Spirit, because the Spirit intercedes for the saints according to the will of God.

28. We know that in everything God works for good with those who love him, who are called according to his purpose. For those whom he foreknew he also predestined to be conformed to the image of his Son, in order that he might be the first-born among many brethren. And those whom he predestined he also called; and those whom he called he also justified; and those whom he justified he also glorified.

31. What then shall we say to this? If God is for us, who is against us? He who did not spare his own Son but gave him up for us all, will he not also give us all things with him? Who shall bring any charge against God's elect? It is God who justifies; who is to condemn? Is it Christ Jesus, who died, yes, who was raised from the dead, who is at the right hand of God, who indeed intercedes for us? Who shall separate us from the love of Christ? Shall tribulation, or distress, or persecution, or famine, or nakedness, or peril, or sword? As it is written,

"For thy sake we are being killed all the day long; we are regarded as sheep to be slaughtered."

No, in all these things we are more than conquerors through him who loved us. For I am sure that neither death, nor life, nor angels, nor principalities, nor things present, nor things to come, nor powers, nor height, nor depth, nor anything else in all creation, will be able to separate us from the love of God in Christ Jesus our Lord.

Chapter IX

I am speaking the truth in Christ, I am not lying; my conscience bears me witness in the Holy Spirit, that I have great sorrow and unceasing anguish in my heart. For I could wish that I myself were accursed and cut off from Christ for the sake of my brethren, my kinsmen by race. They are Israelites, and to them belong the sonship, the glory, the covenants, the giving of the law, the worship, and the promises; to them belong the patriarchs, and of their race, according to the flesh, is the Christ. God who is over all be blessed for ever. Amen.

6. But it is not as though the word of God had failed. For not all who are descended from Israel belong to Israel, and not all are children of Abraham because they are his descendants; but "Through Isaac shall your descendants be named." This means that it is not the children of the flesh who are the children of God, but the children of the promise are reckoned as descendants. For this is what the promise said, "About this time I will return and Sarah shall have a son." And not only so, but also when Rebecca had conceived children by one man, our forefather Isaac, though they were not yet born and had done nothing either good or bad, in order that God's purpose of election might continue, not because of works but because of his call, she was told, "The elder will serve the younger." As it is written, "Jacob I loved, but Esau I hated."

14. What shall we say then? Is there injustice on God's part? By no means! For he says to Moses, "I will have mercy on whom I have mercy, and I will have compassion on whom I have compassion." So it depends not upon man's will or exertion, but upon. God's mercy. For the scripture says to Pharaoh, "I have raised you up for the very purpose of showing my power in you, so that my name may be proclaimed in all the earth." So then he has mercy upon whomever he wills, and he hardens the heart of whomever he wills.

19. You will say to me then, "Why does he still find fault? For who can resist his will?" But, who are you, a man, to answer back to God? Will what is molded say to its molder, "Why have you made me thus?" Has the potter no right over the clay, to make out of the same lump one vessel for beauty and another for menial use? What if God, desiring to show his wrath and to make known his power, has endured with much patience the vessels of wrath made for destruction, in order to make known the riches of his glory for the vessels of mercy, which he has prepared beforehand for glory, even us whom he has called, not from the Jews only but also from the Gentiles? As indeed he says in Hosea, "Those who were not my people I will call 'my people,' and her who was not beloved I will call 'my beloved.'" "And in the very place where it was said to them, 'You are not my people,' they will be called 'sons of the living God.'"

27. And Isaiah cries out concerning Israel: "Though the number of the sons of Israel be as the sand of the sea, only a remnant of them will be saved; for the Lord will execute his sentence upon the earth with rigor and dispatch." And as Isaiah predicted, "If the Lord of hosts had not left us children, we would have fared like Sodom and have been made like Gomorrah."

30. What shall we say, then? That Gentiles who did not pursue righteousness have attained it, that is, righteousness through faith; but that Israel who pursued the righteousness which is based on law did not succeed in fulfilling that law. Why? Because they did not pursue it through faith, but as if it were based on works. They have stumbled over the stumbling-stone, as it is written, "Behold I am laying in Zion a stone that will make men stumble, a rock that will make them fall; and he who believes in him will not be put to shame."

Chapter X

Brethren, my heart's desire and prayer to God for them is that they may be saved. I bear them witness that they have a zeal for God, but it is not enlightened. For, being ignorant of the righteousness that comes from God, and seeking to establish their own, they did not submit to God's righteousness. For Christ is the end of the law, that every one who has faith may be justified.

5. Moses writes that the man who practices the righteousness which is based on the law shall live by it. But the righteousness based on faith says, Do not say in your heart, "Who will ascend into heaven?" (that is, to bring Christ down) or "Who will descend into the abyss?" (that is, to bring Christ up from the dead). But what does it say? The word is near you, on your lips and in your heart (that is, the word of faith which we preach); because, if you confess with your lips that Jesus is Lord and believe in your heart that God raised him from the dead, you will be saved. For man believes with his heart and so is justified, and he confesses with his lips and so is saved. The scripture says, "No one who believes in him will be put to shame." For there is no distinction between Jew and Greek; the same Lord is Lord of all and bestows his riches upon all who call upon him. For, "every one who calls upon the name of the Lord will be saved."

14. But how are men to call upon him in whom they have not believed? And how are they to believe in him of whom they have never heard? And how are they to hear without a preacher? And how can men preach unless they are sent? As it is written, "How beautiful are the feet of those who preach good news!" But they have not all heeded the gospel; for Isaiah says, "Lord, who has believed what he has heard from us?" So faith comes from what is heard, and what is heard comes by the preaching of Christ.

18. But I ask, have they not heard? Indeed they have; for

"Their voice has gone out to all the earth, and their words to the ends of the world."

Again I ask, did Israel not understand? First Moses says,

"I will make you jealous of those who are not a nation; with a foolish nation I will make you angry."

Then Isaiah is so bold as to say,

"I have been found by those who did not seek me; I have shown myself to those who did not ask for me."

21. But of Israel he says, "All day long I have held out my hands to a disobedient and contrary people."

Chapter XI

I ask, then, has God rejected his people? By no means! I myself am an Israelite, a descendant of Abraham, a member of the tribe of Benjamin. God has not rejected his people whom he foreknew. Do you not know what the scripture says of Elijah, how he pleads with God against Israel? "Lord, they have killed thy prophets, they have demolished thy alters, and I alone am left, and they seek my life." But what is God's reply to him? "I have kept for myself seven thousand men who have not bowed the knee to Baal." So too at the present time there is a remnant, chosen by grace. But if it is by grace, it is no longer on the basis of works; otherwise grace would no longer be grace.

7. What then? Israel failed to obtain what it sought. The elect obtained it, but the rest were hardened, as it is written.

"God gave them a spirit of stupor, eyes that should not see, and ears that should not hear, down to this very day."

And David says, "Let their feast become a snare and a trap, a pitfall and a retribution for them; let their eyes be darkened so that they cannot see, and bend their backs for ever."

11. So I ask, have they stumbled so as to fall? By no means! But through their trespass salvation has come to the Gentiles, so as to make Israel jealous. Now if their trespass means riches for the world, and if their failure means riches for the Gentiles, how much more will their full inclusion mean!

13. Now I am speaking to you Gentiles. Inasmuch then as I am an apostle to the Gentiles, I magnify my ministry in order to make my fellow Jews jealous, and thus save some of them. For if their rejection means the reconciliation of the world, what will their acceptance mean but life from the dead? If the dough offered as first fruits is holy, so is the whole lump; and if the root is holy, so are the branches.

17. But if some of the branches were broken off, and you, a wild olive shoot, were grafted in their place to share the richness of the olive tree, do not boast over the branches. If you do boast, remember it is not you that support the root, but the root that supports you. You will say, "Branches were broken off so that I might be grafted in." That is true. They were broken off because of their unbelief, but you stand fast only through faith. So do not become proud, but stand in awe. For if God did not spare the natural branches, neither will he spare you. Note then the kindness of and the severity of God: severity toward those who have fallen, but God's kindness to you, provided you continue in his kindness; otherwise you too will be cut off. And even the others, if they do not persist in their unbelief, will be grafted in, for God has the power to graft them in again. For if you have been cut from what is by nature a wild olive tree, and grafted, contrary to nature, into a cultivated olive tree, how much more will these natural branches be grafted back into their own olive tree.

25. Lest you be wise in your own conceits, I want you to understand this mystery, brethren: a hardening has come upon part of Israel, until the full number of the Gentiles come in, and so all Israel will be saved: as it is written,

"The Deliverer will come from Zion, he will banish ungodliness from Jacob"; "and this will be my covenant with them when I take away their sins."

As regards the gospel they are enemies of God, for your sake; but as regards election they are beloved for the sake of their forefathers. For the gifts and the call of God are irrevocable. Just as you were once disobedient to God but now have received mercy because of their disobedience, so they have now been disobedient in order that by the mercy shown to you they also may receive mercy. For God has consigned all men to disobedience, that he may have mercy upon all.

33. O the depth of the riches and wisdom and knowledge of God! How unsearchable are his judgments and how inscrutable his ways!

"For who has known the mind of the Lord, or who has been his counselor?"

"Or who has given a gift to him that he might be repaid?"

For from him and through him and to him are all things. To him be glory forever. Amen.

Augustine

(354–430)

Augustine began his treatise *On Free Choice of the Will (De libero arbitrio voluntatis)* in 387, two years after his conversion to Christianity, and completed it in 395. In this work Augustine is attempting to reach a solution to the problem of evil: If God is omnipotent and all-loving, how can there be evil in the world? The Manichaean answer was that evil comes from the existence in the universe of a second power, the principle of darkness. Thus, for the Manichee, God, though He is benevolent, is not omnipotent. For about a decade, while he was a member of the Manichaean sect, Augustine accepted this doctrine. But gradually Manichaean dualism became unsatisfactory to him and eventually, with the help of Neoplatonism, he reached a solution to the problem of evil that was compatible with his Christianity. He argued that evil was not a positive reality at all but rather a lack of goodness. All things that existed were created by God and as such were good. But some things failed to reach the perfection of their kind. In man, moral evil arose when the will, instead of fulfilling its potential, turned away from higher things to lower, from the eternal to the temporal, from the spiritual to the material. Thus evil was not created by some rival power to God, nor was God Himself anything but benevolent. Rather, evil was the result of man's abuse of his free will. Whether this argument is consistent with Augustine's later, fully-developed doctrine of grace is open to question.

The passages selected here illustrate very well the influence of Platonism on the thought of Augustine.[1] In them he is presenting his argument for the existence of God, an argument that rests on the evidence of reason alone, without any appeal to revelation. He presents it in the form of a dialogue between himself (Augustine) and a young man (Evodius).

From On Free Choice of the Will

II. 6 Reason is the highest and most excellent faculty of man. God and that which is more excellent than reason.

Augustine: Since the nature which merely exists and does not live or understand (for example, the inanimate body) is inferior to the nature that not only exists, but also lives, though it does not understand (for example, the soul of beasts); and since this in turn is inferior to that which at once exists, lives, and understands (for example, the rational mind in man)—you do not think then, do you, that anything can be found in us more excellent (that is, among those things by which our nature is perfected so that we are men) than this which we put in the third place? Clearly we have a body,

---

[1] Selections from A. S. Benjamin and L. H. Hackstaff, trans., *On Free Choice of the Will,* (Indianapolis: The Bobbs Merrill Co., 1964), pp. 48–49, 53–67, 71–77.

From St. Augustine, *Confessions,* I, 9, 13, 14; II, 1, 3, 4, 6, 9; III, 1–7; IV, 3; V, 10, 13, 14; VII, 9, 20; VIII, 3, 4, 6, 8, 11, 12; based on the translation by E. B. Pusey.

Source: City of God, translated by Marcus Dods (Edinburgh: T. & T. Clark, 1872), 2, pp. 1–2, 6–8, 9–12, 15–29.

and a kind of life that makes the body live and grow. We recognize these two conditions in beasts as well. We have also a third thing: a head or eye of our soul, as it were, or whatever term can be more aptly applied to our reason and understanding. This is what the nature of a beast does not have. Please see whether you can find anything in man's nature which is more noble than reason.

Evodius: I see absolutely nothing more noble.

A: What if we should be able to find something which you would not doubt not only exists, but even is more excellent than our reason? Will you hesitate to say that, whatever it is, this is our God?

E: If I could find something better than what is best in my nature, I would not immediately say that this is God. I am not inclined to call God that to which my reason is inferior, but rather that to whom no one is superior.

A: Clearly. And God Himself has given your reason the power to think so devoutly and truly about Him. But, I ask you, if you find that there is nothing superior to our reason except what is eternal and immutable, will you hesitate to say that this is God? You know that bodies are mutable and that life itself, which animates the body in its varying conditions, is plainly subject to change. Reason itself is clearly proven to be mutable, now struggling to arrive at truth, now ceasing to struggle, sometimes reaching it and sometimes not. If, without the aid of any organ of the body or of any sense inferior to it, either touch, taste, smell, hearing, or sight, reason discerns that it is inferior and through its own power discerns something eternal and immutable, reason should at the same time admit that it is inferior and that this is its God.

E: I shall admit that this is God to which nothing is granted to be superior.

A: Good! It will be sufficient, then, for me to prove that there is something of this nature which you will admit to be God; or, if there is anything superior, you will grant that this superior being is God. Therefore, whether there is something superior or not, it will be proven that God exists when, as I promised, I show with God's aid that there is something superior to reason.

E: Prove then what you promise.

II. 8 The order of numbers, known as one and unchangeable, is not known by the bodily senses.

A: Come! Listen and tell me whether we may find anything that all reasoning men see with their reason and mind in common with all others, while what is seen is present in all and, unlike food or—drink, is not transformed into some use by those to whom it is present, instead remaining uncorrupted and complete whether or not men discern it. Perhaps you think that nothing like this exists?

E: On the contrary, I see that many such things exist, one of which is quite enough to mention: the order and the truth of number [*ratio et veritas numeri*] are present to all who think. Everyone who calculates tries to understand the truth of number with his own reason and understanding. Some can do this rather easily; others have more difficulty. Yet the truth of number offers itself to all alike who are able to grasp it. When a man understands it, it is not changed into a kind of nourishment for him; when he fails to grasp it, the truth of number does not disappear; rather, it remains true and permanent, while man's failure to grasp it is commensurate with the extent of his error.

A: Correct! I see that you are not inexperienced in this, and have quickly found your answer. If someone were to say to you that numbers were impressed upon our spirit not as a result of their own nature, but as a result of those objects which we experience with the bodily senses, what answer would you make? Or do you agree with this?

E: No, I do not. Even if I did perceive numbers with the bodily sense, I would not be able to perceive with the bodily senses the meaning of division and addition. It is with the light of the mind that I would prove wrong the man who makes an error in addition or subtraction. Whatever I may experience with my bodily senses, such as this air and earth and whatever corporeal matter they contain, I cannot know how long it will endure. But seven and three are ten, not only now, but forever. There has never been a time when seven and three were not ten, nor will there ever be a time when they are not ten. Therefore, I have said that the truth of number is incorruptible and common to all who think.

A: I do not disagree with your answer, for you spoke truly and clearly. But you will easily see that numbers themselves are not drawn from the bodily senses, if you realize how any number you please multiplied by one is that number. For example, two times one is two; three times one is three; ten times one is ten; any number times one is that number. Anyone who really thinks about the number one realizes that he cannot perceive it through the bodily senses, for whatever we experience through a sense is proven to be many, not one. This follows because it is a body and is therefore infinitely divisible. But I need not concentrate upon each small and indistinct part; however small such a bodily part may be, it has a right, left, upper, and lower side, or a farther and nearer side, or ends and a middle. These, we admit, must be in a body, however small it is; thus, we concede that no body is truly and purely one. Yet all these parts could not be counted, if they had not been distinguished by the concept of one. When, therefore, I look for one in a body, I do not doubt that I will not find it. I know what I am seeking there and what I shall not find there. I know that I cannot find one, or rather that it does not exist in a body at all. How do I know that a body is not one? If I did not know what one is, I could not count the many parts of the body. Moreover, however I may know one, I do not know it through the bodily senses, because through the bodily senses I know nothing except a body which, we have proven, is not really and simply one. Furthermore, if we have not perceived one through a sense of the body, we have not perceived by a sense any number of those numbers which we discern only through the understanding. There exists no number which does not get its name from the number of times it contains one. The perception of one does not occur through any bodily sense. The half of any body whatsoever, although the whole body consists of two halves, also has its own half; therefore, there are two parts of a body which are not simply two. Moreover, the number which is called two because it is twice what is irreducibly one, cannot be two parts of one, in other words, that which is simply one cannot again have a half or a third or whatever part you please, since it is simply and truly one. In observing the order of numbers, we see after one the number two, which is twice one. Twice two does not follow next in order; rather, three comes next, and then four, which is twice two. This order [ratio] continues throughout all the rest of the numbers by a fixed and unchangeable law. Thus after one, the first of all numbers, when one itself is excepted, the first number is the double of one, for two comes next. After this second number, that is, after two, when two is excepted, the second number is the double of two; for after two the first number is three, and the second number is four, the double of two. After the third, that is, after the number three, when it is itself excepted, the third number is the double of three; for after the third number, that is, after three, the first number is four, the second five, and the third six, which is the double of three. So after the fourth number, when it is itself excepted, the fourth number is the double of four; for after the fourth number, after four, the first number is five, the second is six, the third is seven, and the fourth number is eight, which is the double of four. Through all of the rest of the numbers you will find the same thing that is found in the first pair of number, one and two, namely, the double of any number is as many times after this number as such a number is from the beginning.

How do we discern that this fact which holds for the whole number series is unchangeable, fixed, and incorruptible? No one perceives all the numbers by any bodily sense, for they are innumerable. How do we know that this is true for all numbers? Through what fantasy or vision do we discern so confidently the firm truth of number throughout the innumerable series, unless by some inner light unknown to bodily sense?

Men to whom God has given ability in argument, and whom stubbornness does not lead into confusion, are forced to admit that the order and truth of numbers have nothing to do with the bodily senses, but are unchangeable and true and common to all rational beings. Therefore, although many other things could occur to us that are common and, as it were, public for rational beings, things that are seen by each individual with his mind and reason and still remain inviolate and unchanged, nevertheless, I am not unwilling to accept the fact that the order and truth of number are the best possible examples that you could have given when you wished to answer my question. Not without reason was number joined to wisdom in the Holy Scriptures where it is said, "I and my heart have gone round to know and to consider and to search out wisdom and number."[2]

II. 9 Is wisdom, which is necessary for human happiness, one and the same in all men who are wise?

A: Nevertheless, I beg you, what opinion should we have in the case of wisdom itself? Do you think that each man has his own individual wisdom? Or is there one wisdom that exists alike for all men, such that the more a man partakes of this wisdom, the wiser he is?

E: I do not know what wisdom you mean. I see that men have various opinions as to what is said or done wisely. Men who serve as soldiers think that they are acting wisely, while men who despise military service, devoting their energy and effort to agriculture, praise agriculture and claim that this is wisdom. Men who are shrewd in devising ways of acquiring wealth think that they are wise. Men who disregard all this or put aside temporal things of this sort, devoting their whole effort to the search for truth so that they may know themselves and God—these men judge that this is the great gift of wisdom. Those who are not willing to devote themselves to the leisure of seeking and contemplating truth, but prefer toilsome business and official duties so that they may advise men and engage in the just government and management of human affairs—these men think that they are wise. Men who do both of these things and live some of the time in the contemplation of truth, and some of the time amid toilsome official duties which they think they owe to human society, think that they hold the prize of wisdom. I pass over innumerable sects, all of which rank their own followers over others and claim that they alone are wise. Therefore, since we are discussing the problem between us in such a way that we must assert, not our beliefs, but only what we clearly understand, I cannot answer your question unless I know by reflection and reasoning what wisdom itself is.

A: You don't think, do you, that wisdom is anything other than the truth in which the highest good is discerned and held? All the different sects that you mentioned seek good and avoid evil. Their doctrines vary because different things appear to them to be good. Whoever, then, seeks what he should not seek, errs, even though he would not seek it if he did not think it good, The man who seeks nothing cannot err, nor can the man who seeks what he ought to seek. Insofar as all men seek the happy life, they do not err. Insofar as each man fails to follow the road of life that leads to happiness, although he may confess and profess that he is unwilling to arrive anywhere except at happiness, he is in error. His error is that he follows something that does not lead where he wishes to arrive. The greater his error on the road of life, the less his wisdom, and the farther he is from the truth in which the highest good is discerned and grasped. Moreover, when the highest good has been pursued and obtained, each man becomes happy—which beyond a doubt is what we all wish. Just as it is

---

[2] Eccles. 7:26 (Eccles. 7:25).

agreed that we all wish to be happy, so it is agreed that we all wish to be wise, since no one without wisdom is happy. No man is happy except through the highest good, which is to be found and included in that truth which we call wisdom. Just as the idea of happiness is impressed upon our minds before we are happy—through this idea we know confidently and say without hesitation that we wish to be happy—so, before we are wise, we have an idea of wisdom in our minds. Through this idea each one of us, if asked whether or not he wants to be wise, answers without any confusion or doubt that he does so wish.

If it is, therefore, agreed between us what wisdom is, although perhaps you could not explain wisdom in words—for if you did not discern wisdom at all with your spirit, you would not know either that you wish to be wise or that you ought to wish to be wise, which I do not think you will deny—I want you to tell me whether you think that wisdom offers itself alike to all who think, just as the order and truth of number do. Or since there are as many minds as there are men, so that I discern nothing in your mind and you discern nothing in mine, do you think that there can be as many wisdoms as there are wise men?

E: If the highest good is one for all men, the truth in which it is discerned and grasped—that is, wisdom—must be one and common to all men.

A: Do you doubt that the highest good, whatever it is, is one for all men?

E: Yes, I do, because I see different men rejoicing in different things as their highest goods.

A: Indeed, I wish that no one had any doubt about the highest good, just as no one has any doubt that a man cannot be happy without obtaining the highest good. Since the question is important, and may demand a long explanation, let us imagine that the highest goods are as many as the different things which are sought by various men as the highest good. It does not follow, does it, that wisdom itself is not common alike to all men, just because the goods which men discern in it and choose are many and varied? If you think this, you may also doubt that the light of the sun is one, because we see many different things in it. From these many things, each man chooses according to his will what he may enjoy through his sight. One man willingly looks at the height of a mountain and rejoices to see it; another at the level fields; another at the hollow of valleys; another at the greenness of the woods; another at the flickering surface of the sea; another compares all or some of these things at the same time, for the delight of seeing them. Just as the objects which men see in the sunlight and choose to enjoy are many and varied, yet the light in which the sight of each man watching sees and holds what he enjoys is one; so even if the goods are many and varied from which each man may choose what he wishes, determining to discern, grasp, and enjoy the highest good rightly and truly, nevertheless it is possible that the very light of wisdom, in which these goods can be discerned and grasped, is one wisdom common to all wise men.

E: I grant that this can be so and that nothing is opposed to the existence of one wisdom common to all, even if there are many different highest goods. But I would like to know whether or not this is so; for when we grant that this may possibly be so, we do not necessarily grant that it *is* so.

A: Meanwhile, we maintain that wisdom exists. But whether it is one and common to all men, or whether each individual has his own wisdom as he has his own soul or mind, we do not yet know.

E: Yes.

II. 10 The rules of wisdom are the same for all wise men.

A: How, then, do we see the truth of what we are maintaining: that wisdom and wise men exist, and that all men wish to be happy? I do not doubt that you see this and see that it is true. Do you see that this is true in the same way that you see your own thoughts, of which I am completely ignorant, unless you disclose them to me? Or do you see it in the same way that you understand, that is, in such a way that I too can see the truth, even though you do not disclose it to me?

E: I do not doubt that you can see the truth also, even though I might not want you to.

A: Is not the one truth which we both see in our individual minds common to both of us?

E: Clearly.

A: Likewise, I believe, you do not deny the truth that we should seek after wisdom.

E: I do not doubt it.

A: Can we deny that this fact is true and one, yet common for all who know it? Each man sees it with his own mind, not with mine, yours, or anyone else's; yet what is seen, is present for all to see in common. We cannot deny this, can we?

E: Of course not.

A: Won't you also admit the following to be absolutely true: that we should live justly; that the worse should be subordinate to the better; that equals should be compared with equals and to each should be given his own; and that each of these truths is present for you, me and all to see in common?

E: Yes.

A: Will you deny that the incorrupt is better than the corrupt, the *eternal* better than the temporal, the inviolable better than the violable?

E: Who can deny this?

A: Can anyone call truth his own, when it is present unchangingly, for all to meditate upon who have the power to meditate?

E: No one can truly call truth his own. Truth is one and common to all, just as much as it is true.

A: Likewise, who can deny that the spirit should be turned away from corruption and toward incorruption, and that incorruption, not corruption, should be loved? When a man grants something to be true, does he not also understand that it is changeless, and does he not see that it is present in common for all minds that have the power to behold it?

E: True.

A: Will anyone doubt that the life which cannot be moved by any opposition from a sure and honest judgement is better than the one which is easily broken and overcome by the troubles of this life?

E: Who would doubt it?

A: I shall not ask any more questions of this kind. It is sufficient that you see and grant, as I do, that it is certain that these judgements are rules and, as it were, lights of virtue; and that true and unchangeable things, whether individually or all together, are present in common for all men to meditate upon who have the power to perceive with mind and reason. I do ask this however: Do you think that these things are a part of wisdom? I believe that you think that the man who has gained wisdom is wise.

E: Yes.

A: Could a man who lives justly live this way if he did not see which are the inferior things that he subordinates to superior ones, or the equals that he joins to equals, or the particular things that he assigns to their own particular places?

E: He could not.

A: You won't deny, will you, that the man who sees these things sees wisely?

E: No.

A: Likewise, doesn't the man who lives prudently choose incorruption and judge that incorruption is to be preferred to corruption?

E: Most clearly.

A: Therefore, when he chooses to turn his spirit to that which no one doubts should be chosen, it cannot be denied, can it, that he chooses wisely?

E: Of course not.

A: When, therefore, he turns his mind to a wise choice, he does so wisely.

E: Certainly.

A: And he acts wisely who is not turned by fear or punishment from what he chooses or turns to wisely.

E: Without a doubt.

A: It is very clear, then, that all that we have called the rules and lights to virtue are a part of wisdom, inasmuch as the more a man uses them in leading his life, the more wisely he acts and lives. Moreover, whatever is done wisely cannot rightly be said to be separate from wisdom.

E: Yes.

A: The true and immutable rules of wisdom are as true and immutable as the rules of number, whose order and truth, you have said, are unchangeably present and common to all who see them. When asked about a few of these rules of wisdom individually, you replied that they were evidently true, and you admitted that they are present and common for all to see who have the power to see them.

II. 11 How are the rules of number and wisdom related?

E: I cannot doubt this. But I would very much like to know whether these two things, wisdom and number, are members of any single class. You recall that they have been placed together in the Holy Scriptures. Does one depend on the other, or is the one included in the other? Does number, for example, depend upon wisdom, or is it included in wisdom? I do not dare to say that wisdom depends upon number, or is included in number; this could hardly be the case, since I have known many accountants and men skilled in numbers (whatever name is applied to men who use numbers well and accurately), yet I have known few wise men—perhaps none. Wisdom seems by far more worthy than number.

A: You have mentioned something at which I too often wonder. When I think about the unchanging truth of numbers, and when I consider the province of numbers—their room or sanctuary, as it were, or whatever suitable name can be found by which we may designate the home or seat of numbers—I am far removed from my body. I may, perhaps, find something about which I can think, but it is nothing that I can express in words; as though exhausted, I return to familiar things, so as to be able to speak, and I speak of objects before my eyes, objects that it is usual to speak of. The same thing happens to me when I think as carefully and intently as I can about wisdom. Besides, I am very much amazed because these two things lie in the most secret and yet most certain truth—even by the testimony of the Scriptures, where number and wisdom are placed together. I wonder greatly, as I said before, why number is generally regarded as of little value while wisdom is thought precious. Yet number and wisdom are somehow one and the same thing, since the Divine Writings say of wisdom that it "reaches from end to end powerfully and disposes all things sweetly."[3] The power that "reaches from end to end powerfully" is perhaps called "number"; while the power which "disposes all things sweetly" is now thought of as wisdom proper, though both of these belong to the same wisdom. Because wisdom gave numbers to all objects, even the lowliest objects that have been placed at the very end; because all objects, even the least ones, have their own numbers; because, moreover, wisdom did not grant, either to corporeal objects or to all spirits, the power to know, but granted it only to rational beings, as if it made in them a home for itself, from which it could arrange everything, including even the least object to which it has assigned number; because we easily make judgments about corporeal objects as things which have been placed in a lower order than ours and which we see are beneath us, even though numbers have been stamped upon them—for these reasons, we consider these numbers to be inferior to ourselves and therefore regard them as baser.

But when we begin, as it were, to ascend along the path, we discover that numbers transcend our minds and remain unchangeable in their own truth. Because few men can know, but even stupid men can count, men admire wisdom and despise numbers. Yet the further removed learned students are from the filth of the earth, the more clearly do they apprehend both numbers and wisdom in truth itself, and they hold both of them to be precious. For them, not only do silver, gold, and the other things for which we strive bear no comparison with this truth, but even they themselves appear worthless when compared to it. Therefore, do not marvel that, while wisdom has appeared precious to men, number has seemed base: it has seemed so because men can count more easily than they can know. You see that men consider gold more precious than the golden light of a lamp, in comparison with which gold is to be scorned. Yet the lesser object receives more honor because even a beggar may light a lamp for himself, while few men have gold. The comparison suggests that wisdom, since it is rare, is inferior to number—which is impossible, since they are identical; but it requires an eye capable of discerning it. Brightness and heat are perceived consubstantially, so to speak, in the one fire; they cannot be separated. Yet the heat is communicated to objects which are placed near to the fire, while brightness is diffused far and wide. In the same way, the power of intelligence, which lies in wisdom, warms things (such as rational souls) that lie near it. But the power of intelligence does not affect things that are farther away, (for instance, corporeal objects) with the heat of knowing; it floods them, rather, with the light of numbers. This comparison may be somewhat obscure to you, for no analogy from visible things can be made applicable in every respect to that which is invisible.

Yet attend to the following point which is sufficient for our question as is clear enough, even to humble minds like ours. Although it is not clear to us whether number is a part of or separate from wisdom, or whether wisdom is a part of or separate from number, or whether they are the same, it is clear that both are true, and immutably true.

II. 12 One immutable truth, common to all who know, exists, and is more excellent than the minds that know it

A: You will not deny, therefore, that immutable truth, comprising everything that is immutably true, exists; and you cannot say that immutable truth is yours, or mine, or anyone else's. It is present and shows itself as a kind of miraculously secret, yet public, light for all who see what is immutably

---

[3] Wisd. Of Sol. 8:1.

true. Who would say, then, that anything which is present for all who think and know belongs exclusively to the nature of anyone of these?

You remember, I imagine, that we have already given some discussion to the senses of the body. The objects which we perceive in common by means of the sense of the eyes or ears—colours and sounds, for example, which you and I can see and hear at the same time—these objects do not belong to the nature of our eyes or ears, but are common for both of us to perceive. You will not, therefore, say that the objects which you and I perceive together, each with our own mind, belong to the natures of either of us. We cannot say that the object seen by the eyes of two people belongs to either of the two. It is, instead, some third object, upon which the sight of each of the two is directed.

E: This is evidently the case.

A: Do you think that the truth of which we have been talking for so long, and in which, though it is one, we see so many things—do you think that this truth is more excellent than our minds, or equally so, or less? If it were less excellent, we would make judgments *about* it, not *according to* it. In the same way, we make judgments about corporeal objects because they are below us, and we say not only that they are or are not this way, but also that they ought to be this way, or ought not to be. It is likewise concerning our spirits: we know not only that the spirit *is*, but often also that it *ought to be*, such and such. When we speak about corporeal objects, we make the following judgments: this is less bright than it should be; or, it is not so square; and so forth. We speak, however, the following way, according to the nature of our character [*morum ratio*], about spirits: this is less apt than it ought to be: or, less gentle; or, less forceful. We make these judgments according to the inner rules of truth which we perceive in common. But no one makes judgment about the rules themselves. When a man says that the eternal is more powerful that the temporal, and that seven plus three are ten, he does not say that it ought to be so; he knows it is this way, and does not correct it as an examiner would, but he rejoices as if he has made a discovery.

If truth were equal to our minds, it would be subject to change. Our minds sometimes see more and sometimes less, and because of this we acknowledge that they are mutable. Truth, remaining in itself, does not gain anything when we see it, or lose anything when we do not see it. It is whole and uncorrupted. With its light, truth gives joy to the men who turn to it, and punishes with blindness those who turn away from it.

What of the fact that in accordance with truth we make judgments about our minds, yet we cannot make judgements about the truth? We say that a mind knows less than it ought to, or as much as it should. Moreover, the nearer the mind can get to immutable truth and the more closely it can cling to the truth, the more the mind ought to know. Therefore, if truth is neither inferior nor equal to our minds, it follows that it is superior to them, and more excellent.

II. 15 God, that which is more excellent than reason, demonstrably exists.

A: You granted, moreover, that if I showed you something higher than our minds, you would admit, assuming that nothing existed which was still higher, that God exists. I accepted your conditions and said that it was enough to show this. For if there is something more excellent than truth, this is God. If there is not, then truth itself is God. Whether or not truth is God, you cannot deny that God exists, and this was the question with which we agreed to deal. If it disturbs you that we accept on faith that God is the "Father of Wisdom" in the Sacred Teaching of Christ, remember that we also accept on faith that wisdom born of the eternal is equal to the Father. This is not the question at hand, but it is to be maintained with unshakable faith. For God exists, truly and in the highest degree. This indubitable fact we maintain, I think, not only by faith, but also by a sure though somewhat tenuous form of reasoning, which is sufficient for the immediate question. Thus we can explain the other points pertinent to our discussion, unless you have some objection to raise about the preceding parts.

E: I can scarcely find words for the unbelievable joy that fills me. I accept these arguments, crying out that they are most certain. And my inner voice shouts, for truth itself to hear, that I cling to this: not only does good exist, but indeed the highest good—and this is the source of happiness.

A: Fine. I too am happy. But, I ask you, we are not now wise and happy, are we? Rather, do we not strive toward attaining this goal?

E: I think that we are striving toward the goal.

A: How do you understand that these are certain truths, so that you cry out that you are happy? You admit that this joy comes from wisdom. Can a foolish man know wisdom?

E: Not so long as he is foolish.

A: Then you are wise, or else you do not yet know wisdom.

E: I am not yet wise, but I would not say that I am foolish insofar as I know wisdom, for I cannot deny that the things I know are certain, and that they belong to wisdom.

A: Please tell me, don't you admit that the man who is not just is unjust? And he who is not prudent is imprudent? He who is not temperate is intemperate? Or do you have any doubts about this?

E: I admit that, when a man is not just, he is unjust. I would also give the same answer in regard to the prudent or the temperate man.

A: Why, then, is a man not foolish when he is not wise?

E: I admit this too. When someone is not wise, he is foolish.

A: Now which of these are you?

E: Whichever you want to call me. I do not dare say that I am wise; and from what I have just admitted I must indubitably conclude that I am foolish.

A: Therefore, the foolish man knows wisdom. As we have already said, he would not be sure that he wanted to be wise and that he ought to be wise, unless the idea of wisdom [*notio sapientiae*] was inherent in his mind. So it is with those individual things that belong to wisdom itself, about which I have just questioned you, and in the knowledge of which you rejoice.

E: It is as you say.

II. 16 Wisdom shows itself to the seeker in the guise of numbers embodied in all things of this world

A: When we are eager to be wise, we simply, and as quickly as we can, find some means of concentrating our whole soul on the object; when it is attained by the mind, we fix it there firmly, not so that the soul may rejoice in its own private pleasure—which involves only fleeting pleasures—but so that the soul, free of all inclination toward the things of time and space, may grasp that which is one, the same and eternal. As the soul is the whole life of the body, so God is the happy life of the soul. This is the undertaking in which we are engaged, and toward which we will strive until we have completed it. It has been granted to us to enjoy these true and certain goods which gleam before us, however obscured they may have been until this stage of our journey. Is this not what was written of wisdom's treatment of its lovers, when they approach and seek it? It is said, "In the ways it will show itself to them joyfully and in all providence it will meet them."[4] Wherever you turn, wisdom speaks to you through the imprint it has stamped upon

---

[4] Wisd. Of Sol. 6:17.

its works. When you begin to slip toward outward things, wisdom calls you back, by means of their very forms, so that when something delights you in body and entices you through the bodily senses, you may see that it has number and may ask whence it comes. Thus you return to yourself: you know that you cannot approve or disapprove of what you touch with the bodily senses, unless you have within you certain laws of beauty to which you refer the beautiful objects that you perceive outside of you.

Look at the sky, the earth, and the sea, and at whatever in them shines from above or crawls, flies, or swims below. These have form because they have number. Take away these forms and there will be nothing. Whence are these except from number? Indeed, they exist only insofar as they have number.

In art, the makers of all bodily forms have numbers by which they organize their works. They move their hands and instruments in producing their works until what has been formed externally achieves completion by corresponding as closely as possible to the inward light; and when it has been communicated by the intermediaries of the senses, it delights the inner judge who gazes upward upon numbers. Ask next what moves the limbs of the artist himself, and it will be number, for his limbs also are moved according to number. If you take the work from his hands and take the purpose of creating the work from his spirit, and if you say that pleasure causes the motion of the limbs, it will be called "dancing." If you ask what is pleasant in dancing, number will answer you, "Behold, it is I." Look closely at the beauty of the graceful body and you will see that numbers are held in space. Then look closely at the beauty of motion in a body and you will see that numbers are involved in time. Enter into the art from which the numbers come, and ask there for time and space. Neither will exist; yet number lives there. Number has no location in space [*regio spatiorum*], no duration of time. Nevertheless, when the men who wish to become artists adapt themselves to the art to be learned, they move their bodies through time and space. They move their spirits through time; indeed, their skill increases with the passage of time.

Go beyond even the spirit of an artist, that you may see eternal number. Then wisdom will shine upon you from its inner abode and from the shrine of truth. If your sight is still too weak and is repelled from this vision, turn the eye of your mind to the road where wisdom used to reveal itself for your delight. Then remember that you have postponed a vision which you may seek again when you are stronger and sounder.

Woe to men who forsake you as their leader, O Wisdom, and wander from your footsteps! Woe to those who love not you, but the signs you show, and who forget your meaning! o sweetest light of the purified mind! Wisdom! You do not cease to suggest to us what you are. Your beckoning is all the beauty of creation.

By the very beauty of his work the artist somehow beckons the spectator, instead of fixing his eyes wholly on the beauty of the work he has made, to pass over this beauty and to look in fondness at him who made it. In the same way, the men who love not you, but what you make, are like those who hear an eloquent wise man and, while they listen avidly to the sweetness of his voice and the formation of his well-placed syllables, lose what is most important—the meaning of the ideas, of which the words were merely signs.

Woe to the men who turn from your light and cling complacently to their own darkness! When they turn their back to you, they are fixed in the work of flesh, as in their own shadows; yet even there, they receive what delights them from the encompassing brightness of your light. But love of the shadow causes the soul's eye to become too lazy and weak to endure the splendor of the sight of you. Besides, the more willingly and more indulgently a man follows and accepts something very weak, the more he becomes covered with darkness, and gradually he becomes unable to see what is supreme. He begins to think that some evil is deceiving him in his blindness, or attracts him in his poverty, or has captured and is torturing him. Yet he is really suffering deservedly because he has turned from the light of wisdom; what is just cannot be evil.

Therefore, Evodius, if you look at something mutable, you cannot grasp it either with the bodily senses or the consideration of the mind, unless it possesses some numerical form. If this form is removed, the mutable dissolves into nothing; do not, then, doubt that there is some eternal and immutable Form which prevents mutable objects from being destroyed and allows them to complete their temporal course, as it were, by measured movements and in a distinct variety of forms. This eternal Form is neither contained by nor, as it were, spread out in space, neither prolonged nor changed by time. Through eternal Form every temporal thing can receive its form and, in accordance with its kind, can manifest and embody number in space and time.

II. 17 All good things come from God.

A: Just as we say that something which can be changed is "changeable," so I call that which can receive form "formable," and say that everything that is changeable must also be formable. Nothing can give itself form, since nothing can give to itself what it does not have. And surely a thing receives form so that it may have form.

Therefore, if anything whatever has a form, it does not need form. But, if something does not have form, it cannot receive from itself what it does not have. Nothing, therefore, as we said, can give itself form.

What more should we say concerning the mutability of body and spirit? Enough has been said above. We have established that body and spirit are given form by an immutable and eternal Form. To this Form it has been said, "Thou shalt change them and they will be changed; but thou art the same, and thy years fail not."[5] The speech of the prophet has used "years without fail" to mean "eternity". Concerning this Form, it has been said also that it is "permanent in itself, it renews all things"[6]

We understood from this that everything is governed by providence. If all existing things cease to exist when form is completely taken away, immutable Form itself—through which all mutable things subsist, so that they manifest and embody number appropriate to their forms—this immutable Form is their providence, for if it did not exist, they would not exist either.

As he gazes attentively at the whole of creation, he who travels the road to wisdom perceives how delightfully wisdom reveals itself to him on the way, and meets him in all providence. The more beautiful is the road to the wisdom toward which he hastens, the more ardently he burns to complete the journey,

If you can find any other kind of creature except (1) that which exists and does not live, or (2) that which lives and does not understand, or (3) that which exists, lives, and understands—only then can you tell me that there exists some good which does not come from God. These three kinds of things can be expressed as well by the two terms, "body" and "life," for what only lives, but does not understand—for example, a beast—and what understands—for example, man—are both properly spoken of as "life." These two, therefore, body and life, which are considered creatures (for one even speaks of the life of the Creator, and this is the highest life)—these two creatures, body and

---

[5] Ps. 101:27–28 (Ps. 102:26–27).
[6] Wisd. Of Sol. 7:27.

life, since, as we have shown above, they are both formable, and since they dissolve into nothing if form is completely lost, prove that they exist as a result of that Form which is always of the same nature. Therefore, all good things, whether great or small, can come only from God.

What is greater in creatures than life that has understanding? What can be less than body? No matter how much creatures may lack, and however much they tend toward nonexistence by virtue of their deficiency, nevertheless some form remains in them, so that they somehow exist. Moreover, whatever form remains in a deficient object comes from that Form which knows no lack and which does not allow the motions of things, whether they be growing or decaying, to exceed the laws of their own numbers.

Therefore, whatever we find to be praiseworthy in nature, whether we judge that its value be great or small, must be referred to the most excellent and ineffable praise of the Creator. Do you have any objections to raise on these points?

From *Confessions*

"Our heart is restless until it rests in You."

Schooldays

O God, my God, what miseries and mockeries did I now experience, when obedience to my teachers was proposed to me as proper in a boy in order that in this world I might prosper and excel in rhetorical learning, which would obtain for me the praise of men and deceitful riches. Then I was put to school to get learning, in which I (poor child) knew not what use there was; and yet, if idle in learning, I was beaten. For this was considered right by our forefathers; and many, passing the same way before us, had built for us a weary path along which we were compelled to go, multiplying toil and grief upon the sons of Adam.

Yet we noticed, Lord, that men prayed to You, and we learned from them to think of You (according to our capacities) as some great One, who, though hidden from our senses, could hear and help us. So as a boy I began to call upon You, my Aid and Refuge; though small, yet with no small earnestness, I broke the fetters of my tongue to call on You, praying to You that I might not be beaten at school. And when You did not hear me (not thereby encouraging my folly), my elders, yes, even my parents, who yet wished me no harm, laughed at my stripes, which were a great and grievous ill to me. . . .

It was not that we lacked, O Lord, memory or capacity; You gave us enough of these for our age. But our sole delight was play, and for this we were punished by those who were themselves doing the same thing. But older folks' idleness is called "business"; the idling of boys, though really the same, is punished by these older folks; and no one is sorry for either boys or men. For will anyone of sound discretion approve of my being beaten as a boy because, by playing ball, I made less progress in studies which, by learning, I might as a man play some more unbecoming game? . . .

Why I so much hated Greek, which I had to study as a boy, I do not fully understand. For I loved Latin; not the elementary grammar, but the literature. As for the rudiments—reading, writing, and arithmetic—I found them as hard and hateful as Greek. . . .

Why then did I hate Greek literature? . . . The difficulty of learning a foreign language sprinkled bitterness over all the sweetness of the Greek stories. For not one word of it did I understand, and to make me understand I was urged vehemently with cruel threats and punishments. There was a time also (as an infant) when I knew no Latin; but I learned it without fear or suffering, by mere observation, amid the caresses of my nurses and the jests of friends, whose smiles and laughter encouraged me. I learned it without any pressure or punishment to urge me on, for my heart urged me to give birth to thoughts which I could only do by learning words not from instructors but from those who talked with me and for whom I was able to express what I was feeling. There is no doubt, then, that free curiosity has more value in learning languages than harsh enforcement. . . .

To Whom Am I Telling This? and to What Purpose?

I will now call to mind my past foulness and the carnal corruptions of my soul, not because I love them but that I may love You, O my God. For love of Your love I do it, reviewing my most wicked ways in the very bitterness of my remembrance, that You may grow sweet to me (O sweetness never failing, blissful and assured sweetness). And I gather myself together out of that dissipated state, in which I was torn to pieces while turned from You, the One Good, while losing myself among a multiplicity of things.

Having arrived at adolescence, I was on fire to take my fill of hell. I became like an animal, pursuing various and shady lusts: *my beauty consumed away* and I stank in Your sight; pleasing myself and desirous to please in the sight of men. . . .

To whom am I telling this? Not to You, my God, but in Your presence to my own kind, to that small portion of mankind as may come upon these writings of mine. And to what purpose? Simply that I and whoever reads this may think *out of what depths we are to cry unto Thee.* For what is nearer to Your ears than a confessing heart and a life of faith? . . .

An Act of Vandalism: Seeking Only to Be Wicked

Theft is punished by Your law, O Lord, and the law written in the hearts of men. . . . Yet I wanted to steal, and did steal, compelled not by hunger or poverty but because I lacked a sense of justice and was filled with iniquity. For I stole that of which I had plenty, and of much better quality. Nor cared I to enjoy what I stole; I enjoyed the theft itself, and the sin.

There was a pear tree near our vineyard, laden with fruit but tempting neither in color or taste. To shake it and rob it, I and some lewd young fellows went late one night (having according to our depraved custom prolonged our sports in the street till then) and took huge loads, not for eating— we barely tasted them—but to fling to the hogs. Our real pleasure in doing this was that it was forbidden. Such was my heart, O God, such was my heart which You had pity on when it was at the bottom of the bottomless abyss. Now let my heart tell You what it sought there, when I was evil for no purpose, having no reason for wrongdoing except wrongdoing itself. It was foul, and I loved it; I loved destroying myself; I loved my sin, not the thing for which I had sinned but the sin itself. Foul soul, falling from Your firmament to utter destruction; not seeking profit from wickedness, but seeking only to be wicked! . . .

Did I find pleasure in appearing to break Your law, doing so by stealth since I had no real power to do so? Was I, like a prisoner, making a small show of liberty by doing unpunished what I was not allowed to do and so getting a false sense of omnipotence? Behold Your servant, fleeing from his Lord and pursuing a shadow! What rottenness! What monstrosity of life and abyss of death! Could I enjoy what was forbidden only because it was forbidden? . . .

See, my God, this vivid memory of my soul. Yet I could not have committed that theft alone. . . . When someone cries "Come on, let's do it," we are ashamed to be ashamed. . . .

Loving a Vagrant Liberty

I came to Carthage, where there sang all around me in my ears a cauldron of unholy loves. I was not yet in love, yet I loved the idea of love, and out of a deep-seated want I hated myself for not wanting more. I sought for something to love, being in love with loving, and I hated security and a life without snares. For within me was a famine of that spiritual food, Yourself, my God. . . . To love then, and to be loved, was sweet to me; but more so when I obtained the enjoyment of the body of the person I loved. Thus I defiled the spring of friendship with the filth of physical desire and beclouded its brightness with the hell of lust. . . .

Stage plays also carried me away, full of images of my miseries and of fuel for my fire. Why is it that man desires to be made sad, beholding miserable and tragic things which he himself would by no means wish to suffer? Yet he desires as a spectator to feel sorrow, and this sorrow is his pleasure. . . .

O my God, my exceeding great mercy, my refuge from those terrible destroyers, among whom I wandered in my arrogance, withdrawing further from You, loving my own ways and not Yours, loving a vagrant liberty.

Aroused to Seek Wisdom Whatever It Might Be

These studies of mine also, which were considered commendable, were designed to fit me to excel in the law courts—the more craftier I was, the more famous I should become. Such is men's blindness, that blindness itself should become a source of pride! And by now I was a leader in the school of rhetoric, which I proudly enjoyed, swelling with arrogance, though (Lord, You know) I was far quieter and entirely removed from the subvertings of those "Subverters" (for this cruel and devilish name was their badge of sophistication) among whom I lived, with a shameless shame that I was not like them. With them I went about and sometimes I enjoyed their friendship, although I always hated their actions—that is, their "subvertings," when they wantonly persecuted the modesty of freshmen whom they disturbed by mocking and jeering for no reason whatever, feeding thereby their own malicious mirth. Nothing can be more like the behavior of devils than this. They were rightly called "subverters," being themselves subverted and perverted by the same deceiving spirits which secretly derided and seduced them when they amused themselves by jeering and deceiving others.

Among such companions, in that unsettled age of mine, I studied books of eloquence, wherein I desired to be eminent for a damnable and vainglorious end—joy in human vanity. In the normal course of study I fell upon a certain book by Cicero, whose style almost all admire, though not his heart. This book of his contains an exhortation to philosophy, and is called *Hortensius*. But this book altered my mind; it turned my prayers to You, O Lord, and gave me other purposes and desires. Every vain hope suddenly became worthless to me; I longed with an incredibly burning desire for an immortality of wisdom, and I began now to rise, so that I might return to You. For not to sharpen my tongue (which was the goal of the education I was purchasing with my mother's allowances, in my nineteenth year, my father having died two years before), not to sharpen my tongue did I use that book; what moved me was not its style, but its content.

How did I burn then, my God, how did I burn to fly from earthly things to You. But I did not know what You would do with me; for with You is wisdom. But the love of wisdom is in Greek called "philosophy," and it was with wisdom that that book inflamed me. . . . And since at that time

(You, O light of my heart, know this) Apostolic Scripture was not known to me, the one thing that delighted me in Cicero's exhortation was that I was greatly aroused, kindled, and inflamed to love, seek, obtain, hold, and embrace not this sect but wisdom itself, whatever it might be. And this alone checked my ardent desire, that the name of Christ was not there. For this name, O Lord, this name of my Savior, Your Son, had my tender heart, even with my mother's milk, devoutly drunk in and deeply treasured; and whatsoever was without that name, however learned, polished, or true, could not hold me entirely.

The Holy Scriptures Seemed to Me Unworthy

I resolved then to direct my attention to the Holy Scriptures, that I might see what they were like. And what I saw was something not understood by the proud nor laid open to children; and I was not one who could enter into it, or stoop my neck to follow its path. For not as I now write did I feel when I first turned to those Scriptures; they seemed to me unworthy to be compared to the stateliness of Cicero. My swelling pride shunned their style, nor could my sharp wit pierce their depths. Yet they were such as would grow up with a little child; but I disdained to be a little child, and, swollen with pride, took myself to be grown-up.

The Manichaeans: Foolish Deceivers

Therefore I fell among men who were proudly raving, exceedingly carnal and wordy, in whose mouths were the snares of the Devil, smeared with a mixture of the syllables of Your name and of our Lord Jesus Christ and of the Holy Ghost, the Paraclete, our Comforter. These names were always in their mouths, but only as sounds and the noise of the tongue, for their hearts were void of truth. Yet they cried out "Truth, Truth" and spoke much thereof to me, yet the truth was not in them. . . . Yet because I thought them to be You, I fed upon them; not eagerly, for You did not in them taste to me as You are; for You are not these empty falsehoods, nor was I nourished by them, but exhausted rather. . . .

For that which really is, I knew not; and I was through my sharpness of wit persuaded to assent to foolish deceivers when they asked me, "What is the origin of evil?" "Is God bounded by a bodily shape and has he hair and nails?" "Are those [patriarchs of the Old Testament] to be esteemed righteous who had many wives at the same time and killed men and sacrificed living creatures?" At which I, in my ignorance, was much troubled and, while departing from the truth, seemed to myself to be drawing towards it. This was because as yet I did not know that evil is nothing but an absence of good. . . . I did not even know that God is a spirit, having no parts extended in length and breadth. . . .

Those Imposters Called Astrologers

Thus I did not hesitate to consult those imposters called astrologers, because they offered no sacrifices and prayed to no spirit to assist their divinations. Yet true Christian piety necessarily rejects and condemns their art. For *it is a good thing to confess unto Thee*, and to say, *Have mercy upon me, heal my soul, for I have sinned against Thee*, and not to misuse Your mercy as a license, but to remember the Lord's words, *Behold, thou art made whole, sin no more, lest a worse thing happen to thee*. All this wholesome truth the astrologers strive to destroy, saying: "The cause of your sin is inevitably determined in the heavens" and "This did Venus do, or Saturn or Mars." As though man, who is flesh and blood and proud corruption, should be blameless, while the Creator and Ruler of heaven and the stars is to bear the blame. And who is He but our God? . . .

The governor of the province in those days was a wise man, skillful and renowned in medicine. . . . When I told him that I was much given to reading the books of the horoscope-casters, he kindly and in a fatherly way advised me to throw them away and not to waste on such nonsense care and attention that could be put to better use. . . . When I asked him why it was that many things were foretold by astrology, he reasoned that it was due to the force of chance, which is diffused throughout the whole order of things. Thus while haphazardly paging through a book of poetry, one often comes upon a line which is wondrously appropriate to some matter on one's mind, though the poet was singing and thinking of something quite different. So, he said, it is not to be wondered at if a man's mind should unconsciously by some instinct, and by chance rather than by art, produce an answer that would seem to correspond with the affairs and actions of the inquirer. . . .

Skepticism: Men Ought to Doubt Everything

At Rome I again associated with those false and deceiving "holy ones" [Manichaeans], not only with the "hearers" (one of whom was the man in whose house I had fallen sick and recovered), but also with those whom they call "the elect." For I still held the belief that it is not we who sin but some other nature sinning in us; it gratified my pride to think myself free of blame when I had done anything evil. . . . However, I now despaired of finding any profit in that false doctrine, and I began to hold laxly and carelessly even those ideas with which I had decided to rest content if I could find nothing better.

The thought occurred to me that those philosophers whom they call Academics were wiser than the rest because they held that men ought to doubt everything and had concluded that no truth can be comprehended by man [see p. 334]. For so I was clearly convinced that they thought (as is commonly believed), though I did not yet understand their real meaning. And I did openly discourage my host from that overconfidence which I perceived him to have in those fables of which the books of Manes are full. Yet I lived on more friendly terms with them than with others who were not of this heresy. I no longer defended it with my former eagerness; still my friendship with that sect (Rome secretly harboring many of them) made me slower to seek any other belief, especially since I despaired of finding the truth in Your Church, O Lord of heaven and earth, Creator of all things visible and invisible. For they had turned me against it, and it seemed to me degrading to believe that You had the shape of human flesh and were bounded by the bodily outlines of our limbs. . . .

Ambrose

To Milan I came, to Ambrose the bishop, known to the whole world as among the best of men, Your devout servant whose eloquence did then plentifully dispense to *Thy people the fatness of Thy wheat, the gladness of Thy oil and the sober intoxication of Thy wine.* To him was I unknowingly led by You, that I might knowingly be led to You by him. That man of God received me as a father, and as bishop welcomed my coming. I began to love him, at first indeed not as a teacher of the truth (which I utterly despaired of finding in Your Church), but as a person who was kind to me. I listened diligently to him preaching to the people, not with the right intent but, as it were, judging his eloquence, whether it was equal to his fame or flowed higher or lower than was reported. So I hung intently on his words, but of what he said I was a careless and scornful onlooker. I was delighted with the charm of his discourse; it was more learned, yet less winning and harmonious than that of Faustus. Of the actual matter, however, there was no comparison; Faustus was merely wandering amid Manichaean delusions, while Ambrose was soundly teaching salvation.

But salvation is far from sinners such as I then was. Yet I was drawing nearer little by little, though unconsciously.

For though I took no pains to learn what he said but only to hear how he said it, . . . yet together with the words which I liked came also into my mind the subject matter to which I was indifferent, for I could not separate them. And while I opened my heart to admit how eloquently he spoke, it also occurred to me gradually how truly he spoke. The things he said now began to appear to me capable of being defended. The Catholic faith, for which I had thought nothing could be said against the Manichaean objections, I now thought might be maintained on sound grounds—especially after I had heard one or two passages of the Old Testament explained figuratively, which, when I had taken them literally, I was slain spiritually. Many passages then of those books having been explained in a spiritual sense, I now blamed my conceit for having believed that no answer could be given to those who hated and scoffed at the Law and the Prophets. Yet I did not then feel that the Catholic way was to be followed merely because it also could find learned maintainers who could at length and with some show of reason answer objections, nor that the faith which I held was to be condemned because both faiths could be defended. Thus the Catholic cause seemed to me not vanquished, nor not as yet victorious.

Then I earnestly bent my mind to see if in any way I could by any certain proof convict the Manichaeans of falsehood. Could I only have been able to conceive of a spiritual substance, all their strongholds would have collapsed and been cast out of my mind. But I could not. However, concerning the body of this world and the whole of nature which our senses can reach to, as I more and more considered and compared things, I judged the views of most of the philosophers to be much more probable. So then after the supposed manner of the Academics, doubting everything and wavering between all, I decided that I must leave the Manichaeans. I judged that, while in a state of doubt, I could not continue in that sect to which I now preferred some of the philosophers. These philosophers, however, because they were without the saving name of Christ, I utterly refused to commit the cure of my sick soul. I determined therefore to be a catechumen in the Catholic Church, which my parents had encouraged me to join, until something certain should dawn upon me by which I might steer my course. . . .

Some Books of the Platonists

By means of a man puffed up with the most exaggerated pride, You brought to my attention some books of the Platonists translated from Greek into Latin. And therein I read, not of course in the same words but to the very same effect and supported by many sorts of reasons, that *In the beginning was the Word, and the Word was with God, and the Word was God: the same was in the beginning with God. All things were made by Him, and without Him was nothing made: that which was made by Him is life, and the life was the light of men, and the light shineth in the darkness, and the darkness comprehended it not.* And that the soul of man, though it *bears witness to the light,* yet itself *is not that light;* but the Word of God, being God, *is that true light that lighteth every man that cometh into the world.* Also that *He was in the world, and the world was made by Him, and the world knew Him not.* But I did not read there that *He came unto His own, and His own received Him not; but as many as received Him, to them gave He power to become the sons of God, as many as believed in His name.*

I also read there that *God the Word was born not of flesh, nor of blood, nor of the will of man, nor of the will of the flesh, but of God.* But I did not find there that *the Word was made flesh, and dwelt among us.* . . .

And You have called the Gentiles into Your inheritance. I myself had come to You from the Gentiles, and I set my mind upon the gold which You willed Your people to take from Egypt, since it was Yours, wherever it was. And to the Athenians You said by Your Apostle, that in You we live, move, and have our being, as one of their own poets had said. And certainly these books came from Athens. . . .

Having then read those books of the Platonists, which taught me to search for incorporeal truth, I came to see Your *invisible things, understood by those things which are made.* And though I fell back from this point, I still perceived what that was which, through the darkness of my mind, I was unable to contemplate; I was certain that You are and that You are infinite, yet not being diffused in space whether finite or infinite: that You truly are and are ever the same, in no part or motion varying; and that all other things are from You, as is proved by the sure fact that they exist. . . . I believe it was Your will that I should come upon these books before I studied Your Scriptures, that it might be imprinted on my memory how I was affected by them; and that afterwards when my spirits were tamed through Your books, and my wounds dressed by Your healing fingers, I might be able to distinguish between presumption and confession, between those who see the goal but not the way—the way that leads us not only to see but to dwell in the country of blessedness. . . .

Christians Are Made, Not Born

Good God! what takes place in man that he should more rejoice at the salvation of a soul despaired of or freed from a great peril, than if there had always been hope or the peril had been less? . . .

What is it in the soul, then, which makes it more delighted at finding or recovering the things it loves than if it had always had them? Indeed, other creatures bear the same witness; everywhere all things cry out, "So it is." The conquering general has his triumph; yet he would not have conquered if he had not fought; and the more peril there was in the battle, the more joy there is in the triumph. The storm tosses the sailors and threatens shipwreck; all are pale at the approach of death; then the sky and sea are calmed, and they are as exceedingly joyful as they had been fearful. A friend is sick and his pulse threatens danger; all who long for his recovery are sick in mind with him. He recovers, though as yet he walks not with his former strength; yet there is more joy than there was before when he walked sound and strong. Even the ordinary pleasures of human life men acquire through pain, not only those pains which fall upon us unlooked for and against our will, but also self-chosen and pleasure-seeking pain. Eating and drinking give no pleasure unless they are preceded by the pains of hunger and thirst. Drunkards eat certain salty things to procure an uncomfortable dryness which drink alleviates, thus causing pleasure. It is also customary that the engaged girl should not at once give herself, lest the husband later should hold her cheap whom, as betrothed, he no longer sighed after. . . .

Do not many, out of a deeper hell of blindness. . . , come back to You and are enlightened by that light which *they who receive, receive power from Thee to become Thy sons?*" . . .

Antony the Egyptian Monk

One day there came to see Alypius and me a certain Ponticianus, our countryman, an African holding high office in the emperor's court. What he wanted of us I did not know, but we sat down to converse. It chanced that he noticed a book on a gaming table beside us. He took it, opened it, and contrary to his expectation—he thought it would be one of those books which I was wearying myself in teaching—found that it was the Apostle Paul. Smiling and looking at me, he expressed his joy and wonder that he had come suddenly upon this book, and only this book, beside me. For he was a Christian, and baptized. He often bowed himself before You, our God, in Church, in long and frequent prayers. When I then told him that I gave great attention to these works of Scripture, a conversation began, suggested by him, about Antony the Egyptian monk, whose name was very well known among Your servants, though up to that hour unknown to Alypius and me. When he discovered this he talked all the more about him, informing us and wondering at our ignorance of one so eminent. And we were amazed to hear of Your wonderful works so fully attested in times so recent—almost in our own time—and done in the true Faith and Catholic Church. All three of us were filled with wonder; we because the deeds were so great, and he because they had not reached us.

He spoke next of the flocks of men in the monasteries, of their holy ways full of the sweet fragrance of You, and of the fruitful deserts in the wilderness, about which we knew nothing. There was actually a monastery at Milan outside the walls, full of good brothers under the care of Ambrose, and we knew nothing of it. He went on speaking, and we listened in intense silence.

Ponticianus' Story: The Burden of the World

He told us how one afternoon at Triers, when the emperor was at the chariot races in the Circus, he and three companions went for a walk in the gardens near the city walls. They happened to walk in pairs, one of the three going with him and the other two wandering off by themselves. As the latter two strolled along, they came upon a cottage inhabited by some of Your servants, *poor in spirit, of whom is the kingdom of heaven,* and there they found a little book containing the life of Antony. This one of them began to read. He became full of wonder and excitement, and as he read on he began to think of taking up such a life, giving up his secular service to serve You. For these two men were state officials called "agents for public affairs." Then, suddenly filled with a holy love and a sober shame, in anger with himself he turned to his friend and said: "Tell me now, what do we expect to attain by all these labors of ours? What do we aim at? Why do we serve the state? Can our hopes at court rise higher than to be the emperor's favorites? And is that not a difficult position to hold, and full of dangers? And how many dangers must we survive before we reach a position that is even more dangerous? And how long before we arrive there? But a friend of God, if I wish it, I can become now at once." So he spoke. And in pain with the birth of a new life, he turned his eyes again upon the book. He read on and was changed inwardly, where You alone could see; and his mind, it soon appeared, threw off the burden of the world. For as he read and the waves of his heart rolled up and down, he stormed at himself awhile, then saw the better course and chose it for his own. Being now Yours, he said to his friend, "Now I have broken loose from those hopes we had and have decided to serve God; and I begin this service at this moment, in this place. If you do not wish to imitate me, at least do not oppose me." The other answered that he would stay with him and be his comrade in so glorious a service and for so glorious a reward. . . . This was the story Ponticianus told us. . . .

Sick at Heart and Tormented

Then in this great tumult of my inner dwelling, which I had stirred up against my soul in the chamber of my heart, troubled in mind and countenance, I turned toward Alypius. "What ails us?" I exclaimed. "What is this that you have just heard? The unlearned rise up and take heaven by force, and we with all our learning wallow in flesh and blood! Are we ashamed to follow because others have gone before us? And do we feel no shame at not following?" Some such words I uttered, and then my feverish mind tore me away from him while he stared silently at me in astonishment. For it was not my usual voice; my forehead, cheeks, eyes, color, and tone of voice spoke my mind more than the words I uttered.

There was a garden next to our lodging, and we used it as well as the whole house; for the owner of the house, our landlord, did not live there. The tumult in my breast drove me into this garden, for there no one could intervene in this ardent suit I had brought against myself until it should end as You knew, but I did not. But there I was, going mad in order to become sane, dying in order to have life, knowing how evil I was, not knowing how good I was soon to become. I retired then into the garden, Alypius following my steps. . . .

Thus was I sick at heart and tormented, accusing myself much more bitterly than ever, rolling and turning in my chain till I could break free. I was held only slightly, but I was still held. . . . I kept saying within myself, "Let it be done now, let it be done now!" and as I spoke the words I began to do it. I almost made it, but not quite. . . .

Those toys and trifles and vanities of vanities, my old mistresses, held me back. They pulled at my garment of flesh and whispered softly: "Are you casting us off?" and "From this moment shall we be no more with you forever?" and "From this moment shall you not be allowed to do this or that forever?" . . . What defilements did they suggest! What shame! And now I only half heard them; they no longer openly showed themselves to contradict me, but they were muttering behind my back and stealthily pulling on me, as I departed, to make me look back at them. Yet they did retard me, so that I hesitated to tear myself free from them and leap in the direction I was called; and the strong force of habit kept saying to me, "Do you think you can live without them?" . . .

All the Darkness of Doubt Vanished Away

But when my searching thought had from the secret depths of my soul drawn up all my misery and heaped it in the sight of my heart, a mighty storm rose up within me, bringing a mighty shower of tears. I stood up and left Alypius so that I might weep and cry to my heart's content, solitude seeming more suited for the business of weeping. I moved away far enough so that his presence would not embarrass me. . . . Somehow I flung myself down under a fig tree and gave way to my tears. . . . And in my misery I kept crying, "How long shall I go on saying 'tomorrow, tomorrow'? Why not now? Why not make an end of my ugly sins at this moment?"

Such things I said, weeping all the while with the most bitter sorrow in my heart. Suddenly I heard the sing-song voice of a child in a nearby house. Whether it was the voice of a boy or a girl I cannot say, but again and again it repeated the refrain, "Take it and read, take it and read." Instantly I looked up, thinking hard whether there was any kind of game in which children chanted such words, but I could not remember ever hearing anything like it before. I checked my tears and stood up, telling myself that this could only be a command from God to open my book of Scripture and read the first passage I should find. For I had heard the story of Antony, and I remembered how he had entered a church during the reading of the Gospel and had taken it as an admonition addressed to him when he heard the words: *Go, sell all that thou hast, and give to the poor, and thou shalt have treasure in heaven, and come and follow me.* And by such an oracle he had been immediately converted to You. Eagerly then I returned to the place where Alypius was sitting, for there I had put down the volume of the Apostle Paul when I arose. I snatched it up, opened it, and in silence read the first passage on which my eyes fell: *Not in rioting and drunkenness, not in chambering and wantonness, not in strife and envying, but put ye on the Lord Jesus Christ, and make not provision for the flesh, to fulfill the lusts thereof.* I had no wish to read more and no need to do so. For instantly, as I came to the end of that sentence, it was as though the light of confidence streamed into my heart, and all the darkness of doubt vanished away.

· · · · · · · · · · · ·

12. My answer to those who ask 'What was God doing before he made heaven and earth?' is not 'He was preparing Hell for people who pry into mysteries'. This frivolous retort has been made before now, so we are told, in order to evade the point of the question. But it is one thing to make fun of the questioner and another to find the answer. So I shall refrain from giving this reply. For in matters of which I am ignorant I would rather admit the fact than gain credit by giving the wrong answer and making a laughing-stock of a man who asks a serious question.

Instead of this I will say that you, my God, are the Creator of all creation, and if we mean the whole of creation when we speak of heaven and earth, I unreservedly say that before he made heaven and earth, God made nothing. For if he did make anything, could it have been anything but a creature of his own creation? I only wish I knew everything that I could profit by knowing with as much certainty as I know that no creature was made before any creation took place.

13. A fickle-minded man, whose thoughts were all astray because of his conception of time past, might wonder why you, who are God almighty, Creator of all, Sustainer of all, and Maker of heaven and earth, should have been idle and allowed countless ages to elapse before you finally undertook the vast work of creation. My advice to such people is to shake off their dreams and think carefully, because their wonder is based on a misconception.

How could those countless ages have elapsed when you, the Creator, in whom all ages have their origin, had not yet created them? What time could there have been that was not created by you? How could time elapse if it never was?

You are the Maker of all time. If, then, there was any time before you made heaven and earth, how can anyone say that you were idle? You must have made that time, for time could not elapse before you made it.

But if there was no time before heaven and earth were created, how can anyone ask what you were doing 'then'? If there was no time, there was no 'then'.

From *Enchiridion*

Chapter IX: What We Are to Believe. In Regard to Nature It Is Not Necessary for the Christian to Know More than That the Goodness of the Creator Is the Cause of All Things

When . . . the question is asked what we are to believe in regard to religion, it is not necessary to probe into the nature of things, as was done by those whom the Greeks call *physici*; nor need we be in alarm lest the Christian should be ignorant of the force and number of the elements,—the motion, and order, and eclipses of the heavenly bodies; the form of the heavens; the species and the natures of animals, plants, stones, fountains, rivers, mountains; about chronology and distances; the signs of coming storms; and a thousand other things which those philosophers either have found out, or think they have found out. For even these men themselves, endowed though they are with so much genius, burning with zeal, abounding in leisure, tracking some things by the aid of human conjecture, searching into others with the aids of history and experience, have not found out all things; and even their boasted discoveries are oftener mere guesses than certain knowledge. It is enough for the Christian to believe that the only cause of all created things, whether heavenly or earthly, whether visible or invisible, is the goodness of the Creator, the one true God; and that nothing exists but Himself that does not derive its existence from Him; and that He is the Trinity—to wit, the Father, and the Son begotten of the Father, and the Holy Spirit proceeding from the same Father, but one and the same Spirit of Father and Son.

Chapter XXV: God's Judgments Upon Fallen Men and Angels. The Death of the Body Is Man's Peculiar Punishment

. . . There is one form of punishment peculiar to man—the death of the body. God had threatened him with this punishment of death if he should sin, leaving him indeed to the freedom of his own will, but yet commanding his obedience under pain of death; and He placed him amid the happiness of Eden, as it were in a protected nook of life, with the intention that, if he preserved his righteousness, he should thence ascend to a better place.

Chapter XXVI: Through Adam's Sin His Whole Posterity Were Corrupted, and Were Born Under the Penalty of Death, Which He Had Incurred

Thence, after his sin, he was driven into exile, and by his sin the whole race of which he was the root was corrupted in him, and thereby subjected to the penalty of death. And so it happens that all descended from him, and from the woman who had led him into sin, and was condemned at the same time with him,—being the offspring of carnal lust on which the same punishment of disobedience was visited,—were tainted with the original sin, and were by it drawn through divers errors and sufferings into that last and endless punishment which they suffer in common with the fallen angels, their corrupters and masters, and the partakers of their doom. And thus "by one man sin entered into the world, and death by sin; and so death passed upon all men, for that all have sinned." By "the world" the apostle, of course, means in this place the whole human race.

Chapter XXVII: The State of Misery to Which Adam's Sin Reduced Mankind, and the Restoration Effected through the Mercy of God

Thus, then, matters stood. The whole mass of the human race was under condemnation, was lying steeped and wallowing in misery, and was being tossed from one form of evil to another, and, having joined the faction of the fallen angels, was paying the well-merited penalty of that impious rebellion. For whatever the wicked freely do through blind and unbridled lust, and whatever they suffer against their will in the way of open punishment, this all evidently pertains to the just wrath of God. But the goodness of the Creator never fails either to supply life and vital power to the wicked angels (without which their existence would soon come to an end); or, in the case of mankind, who spring from a condemned and corrupt stock, to impart form and life to their seed, to fashion their members, and through the various seasons of their life, and in the different parts of the earth, to quicken their senses, and bestow upon them the nourishment they need. For He judged it better to bring good out of evil, than not to permit any evil to exist. And if He had determined that in the case of men, as in the case of the fallen angels, there should be no restoration to happiness, would it not have been quite just, that the being who ~~~elled against God, who in the abuse of his freedom spurned and transgressed the com~~~ ~~~eator when he could so easily have kept it, who defaced in himself the ima~~~ ~~~bbornly turning away from His light, who by an evil use of his free-wil~~~ ~~~some bondage to the Creator's laws,—would it not have been just that~~~ ~~~n wholly and to all eternity deserted by God, and left to suffer the eve~~~ ~~~so richly earned? Certainly so God would have done, had He been on~~~ ~~~and had He not designed that His unmerited mercy should shine forth t~~~ ~~~ast with the unworthiness of its objects.

[handwritten note:] Every single person in my class is morally depraved and I, personally, cannot deal. God off :(

Chapter XXX: Men Are Not Saved by Good Works, nor by the Free Determination of Their Own Will, but by the Grace of God through Faith

But this part of the human race to which God has promised pardon and a share in His eternal kingdom, can they be restored through the merit of their own works? God forbid. For what good work can a lost man perform, except so far as he has been delivered from perdition? Can they do anything by the free determination of their own will? Again I say, God forbid. For it was by the evil use of his free-will that man destroyed both it and himself. For, as a man who kills himself must, of course, be alive when he kills himself, but after he has killed himself ceases to live, and cannot restore himself to life; so, when man by his own free-will sinned, then sin being victorious over him, the freedom of his will was lost. "For of whom a man is overcome, of the same is he brought in bondage." This is the judgment of the Apostle Peter. And as it is certainly true, what kind of liberty, I ask, can the bondslave possess, except when it pleases him to sin? For he is freely in bondage who does with pleasure the will of his master. Accordingly, he who is the servant of sin is free to sin. And hence he will not be free to do right, until, being freed from sin, he shall begin to be the servant of righteousness. And this is true liberty, for he has pleasure in the righteous deed; and it is at the same time a holy bondage, for he is obedient to the will of God. But whence comes this liberty to do right to the man who is in bondage and sold under sin, except he be redeemed by Him who has said, "If the Son shall make you free, ye shall be free indeed?" And before this redemption is wrought in a man, when he is not yet free to do what is right, how can he talk of the freedom of his will and his good works, except he be inflated by that foolish pride of boasting which the apostle restrains when he says, "By grace are ye saved, through faith."

Chapter XXXI: Faith Itself Is the Gift of God; and Good Works Will Not Be Wanting in Those Who Believe

And lest men should arrogate to themselves the merit of their own faith at least, not understanding that this too is the gift of God, this same apostle, who says in another place that he had "obtained mercy of the Lord to be faithful," here also adds: "and that not of yourselves; it is the gift of God: not of works, lest any man should boast." And lest it should be thought that good works will be wanting in those who believe, he adds further: "For we are His workmanship, created in Christ Jesus unto good works, which God hath before ordained that we should walk in them." We shall be made truly free, then, when God fashions us, that is, forms and creates us anew, not as men—for He has done that already—but as good men, which His grace is now doing, that we may be a new creation in Christ Jesus, according as it is said: "Create in me a clean heart, O God." For God had already created his heart, so far as the physical structure of the human heart is concerned; but the psalmist prays for the renewal of the life which was still lingering in his heart.

Chapter XXXII: The Freedom of the Will Is Also the Gift of God, for God Worketh in Us Both to Will and to Do

And further, should any one be inclined to boast, not indeed of his works, but of the freedom of his will, as if the first merit belonged to him, this very liberty of good action being given to him as a reward he had earned, let him listen to this same preacher of grace, when he says: "For it is God which worketh in you, both to will and to do of His own good pleasure"; and in another place: "So, then, it is not of him that willeth, nor of him that runneth, but of God that showeth mercy." Now as, undoubtedly, if a man is of the age to use his reason, he cannot believe, hope, love, unless he will to do so, nor obtain the prize of the high calling of God unless he voluntarily run for it; and what sense is it "not of him that willeth, nor of him that runneth, but of God that showeth mercy," except that, as it is written, "the preparation of the heart is from the Lord?". . . The true interpretation of the saying, "It is not of him that willeth, nor of him that runneth, but of God that showeth mercy," is that the whole work belongs to God, who both makes the will of man righteous, and thus prepares it for assistance, and assists it when it is prepared. For the man's righteousness of will precedes many of God's gifts, but not all; and it must itself be included among those which it does not precede. We read in Holy Scripture, both that God's mercy "shall meet me," and that His mercy "shall follow me." It goes before the un-willing to make him willing; it follows the willing to make his will effectual. Why are we taught to pray for our enemies, who are plainly unwilling to lead a holy life, unless that God may work willingness in them? And why are we ourselves taught to ask that we may receive, unless that He who has created in us the wish, may Himself satisfy the wish? We pray, then, for our enemies, that the mercy of God may prevent them, as it has prevented us: we pray for ourselves that His mercy may follow us.

Chapter XLV: In Adam's First Sin, Many Kinds of Sin Were Involved

However, even in that one sin, which "by one man entered into the world, and so passed upon all men," and on account of which infants are baptized, a number of distinct sins may be observed, if it be analyzed as it were into its separate elements. For there is in it pride, because man chose to be under his own dominion, rather than under the dominion of God; and blasphemy, because he did not believe God; and murder, for he brought death upon himself; and spiritual fornication, for the purity of the human soul was corrupted by the seducing blandishments of the serpent; and theft, for man turned to his own use the food he had been forbidden to touch; and avarice, for he had a craving for more than should have been sufficient for him; and whatever other sin can be discovered on careful reflection to be involved in this one admitted sin.

Chapter L: Christ Took Away Not Only the One Original Sin, but All the Other Sins That Have Been Added to It

... The first man brought one sin into the world, but this man took away not only that one sin, but all that He found added to it. Hence the apostle says: "And not as it was by one that sinned, so is the gift: for the judgment was by one to condemnation, but the free gift is of many offenses unto justification." For it is evident that the one sin which we bring with us by nature would, even if it stood alone, bring us under condemnation; but the free gift justifies man from many offenses: for each man, in addition to the one sin which, in common with all his kind, he brings with him by nature, has committed many sins that are strictly his own. ...

Chapter LVI: The Holy Spirit and the Church. The Church Is the Temple of God

And now, having spoken of Jesus Christ, the only Son of God, our Lord, with the brevity suitable to a confession of our faith, we go on to say that we believe also in the Holy Ghost,—thus completing the Trinity which constitutes the Godhead. Then we mention the Holy Church. And thus we are made to understand that the intelligent creation, which constitutes the free Jerusalem, ought to be subordinate in the order of speech to the Creator, the Supreme Trinity: for all that is said of the man Christ Jesus has reference, of course, to the unity of the person of the Onlybegotten. Therefore the true order of the Creed demanded that the Church should be made subordinate to the Trinity, as the house to Him who dwells in it, the temple to God who occupies it, and the city to its builder. And we are here to understand the whole Church, not that part of it only which wanders as a stranger on the earth, praising the name of God from the rising of the sun to the going down of the same, and singing a new song of deliverance from its old captivity; but that part also which has always from its creation remained steadfast to God in heaven, and has never experienced the misery consequent upon a fall. This part is made up of the holy angels, who enjoy uninterrupted happiness; and (as it is bound to do) it renders assistance to the part which is still wandering among strangers: for these two parts shall be one in the fellowship of eternity, and now they are one in the bonds of love, the whole having been ordained for the worship of the one God. Wherefore, neither the whole Church, nor any part of it, has any desire to be worshipped instead of God, nor to be God to any one who belongs to the temple of God—that temple which is built up of the saints who were created by the uncreated God. ... The temple of God, then, that is, of the Supreme Trinity as a whole, is the Holy Church, embracing in its full extent both heaven and earth.

Chapter LXV: God Pardons Sins, but on Condition of Penitence, Certain Times for Which Have Been Fixed by the Law of the Church

... Crimes themselves, however great, may be remitted in the Holy Church; and the mercy of God is never to be despaired of by men who truly repent, each according to the measure of his sin. And in the act of repentance, where a crime has been committed of such a nature as to cut off the sinner from the body of Christ, we are not to take account so much of the measure of time as of the measure of sorrow; for a broken and a contrite heart God does not despise. But as the grief of one heart is frequently hid from another, and is not made known to others by words or other signs, when it is manifest to Him of whom it is said, "My groaning is not hid from Thee," those who govern the Church

153

have rightly appointed times of penitence, that the Church in which the sins are remitted may be satisfied; and outside the Church sins are not remitted. For the Church alone has received the pledge of the Holy Spirit, without which there is no remission of sins—such, at least, as brings the pardoned to eternal life.

Chapter LXI: The Pardon of Sin Has Reference Chiefly to the Future Judgment

Now the pardon of sin has reference chiefly to the future judgment. For, as far as this life is concerned, the saying of Scripture holds good: "A heavy yoke is upon the sons of Adam, from the day that they go out of their mother's womb, till the day that they return to the mother of all things." So that we see even infants, after baptism and regeneration, suffering from the infliction of divers evils: and thus we are given to understand, that all that is set forth in the sacraments of salvation refers rather to the hope of future good, than to the retaining or attaining of present blessings. For many sins seem in this world to be overlooked and visited with no punishment, whose punishment is reserved for the future (for it is not in vain that the day when Christ shall come as Judge of quick and dead is peculiarly named the day of judgment); just as, on the other hand, many sins are punished in this life, which nevertheless are pardoned, and shall bring down no punishment in the future life.

Chapter XCVIII: Predestination to Eternal Life Is Wholly of God's Free Grace

And, moreover, who will be so foolish and blasphemous as to say that God cannot change the evil wills of men, whichever, whenever, and wheresoever He chooses, and direct them to what is good? But when He does this, He does it of mercy; when He does it not, it is of justice that He does it not; for "He hath mercy on whom He will have mercy, and whom He will He hardeneth." And when the apostle said this, he was illustrating the grace of God, in connection with which he had just spoken of the twins in the womb of Rebecca, "who being not yet born, neither having done any good or evil, that the purpose of God according to election might stand, not of works, but of Him that calleth, it was said unto her, The elder shall serve the younger." And in reference to this matter he quotes another prophetic testimony: "Jacob have I loved, but Esau have I hated." But perceiving how what he had said might affect those who could not penetrate by their understanding the depth of this grace: "What shall we say then?" he says: "Is there unrighteousness with God? God forbid." For it seems unjust that, in the absence of any merit or demerit, from good or evil works, God should love the one and hate the other. Now, if the apostle had wished us to understand that there were future good works of the one, and evil works of the other, which of course God foreknew, he would never have said, "not of works," but, "of future works," and in that way would have solved the difficulty, or rather there would then have been no difficulty to solve. As it is, however, after answering, "God forbid"; that is, God forbid that there should be unrighteousness with God; he goes on to prove that there is no unrighteousness in God's doing this, and says: "For He saith to Moses, I will have mercy on whom I have mercy, and I will have compassion on whom I will have compassion." Now, who but a fool would think that God was unrighteous, either in inflicting penal justice on those who had earned it, or in extending mercy to the unworthy? Then he draws his conclusion: "So then it is not of him that willeth, nor of him that runneth, but of God that showeth mercy." Thus both the twins were born children of wrath, not on account of any works of their own, but because they were bound in the fetters of that original condemnation which came through Adam. But He who said,

"I will have mercy on whom I will have mercy," loved Jacob of His undeserved grace, and hated Esau of His deserved judgment. And as this judgment was due to both, the former learnt from the case of the latter that the fact of the same punishment not falling upon himself gave him no room to glory in any merit of his own, but only in the riches of the divine grace; because "it is not of him that willeth, nor of him that runneth, but of God that showeth mercy." And indeed the whole face, and, if I may use the expression, every lineament of the countenance of Scripture conveys by a very profound analogy this wholesome warning to every one who looks carefully into it, that he who glories should glory in the Lord.

Chapter XCIX: As God's Mercy Is Free, So His Judgments Are Just, and Cannot Be Gainsaid

Now after commending the mercy of God, saying, "So it is not of him that willeth, nor of him that runneth, but of God that showeth mercy," that he might commend His justice also (for the man who does not obtain mercy finds, not iniquity, but justice, there being no iniquity with God), he immediately adds: "For the scripture saith unto Pharaoh, Even for this same purpose have I raised thee up, that I might show my power in thee, and that my name might be declared throughout all the earth." And then he draws a conclusion that applies to both, that is, both to His mercy and His justice: "Therefore hath He mercy on whom He will have mercy, and whom He will He hardeneth." "He hath mercy" of His great goodness, "He hardeneth" without any injustice; so that neither can he that is pardoned glory in any merit of his own, nor he that is condemned complain of anything but his own demerit. For it is grace alone that separates the redeemed from the lost, all having been involved in one common perdition through their common origin. Now if any one, on hearing this, should say, "Why doth He yet find fault? for who hath resisted His will?" as if a man ought not to be blamed for being bad, because God hath mercy on whom He will have mercy, and whom He will He Hardeneth, God forbid that we should be ashamed to answer as we see the apostle answered: "Nay, but, O man, who art thou that repliest against God? Shall the thing formed say to Him that formed it, Why hast Thou made me thus? Hath not the potter power over the clay, of the same lump to make one vessel unto honor, and another unto dishonor?" Now some foolish people think that in this place the apostle had no answer to give; and for want of a reason to render, rebuked the presumption of his interrogator. But there is great weight in this saying: "Nay, but, O man, who art thou?" and in such a matter as this it suggests to a man in a single word the limits of his capacity, and at the same times does in reality convey an important reason. For if a man does not understand these matters, who is he that he should reply against God? And if he does understand them, he finds no further room for reply. For then he perceives that the whole human race was condemned in its rebellious head by a divine judgment so just, that if not a single member of the race had been reedeemed, no one could justly have questioned the justice of God; and that it was right that those who are redeemed should be redeemed in such a way as to show, by the greater number who are unredeemed and left in their just condemnation, what the whole race deserved, and whither the deserved judgment of God would lead even the redeemed, did not His undeserved mercy interpose, so that every mouth might be stopped of those who wish to glory in their own merits, and that he that glorieth might glory in the Lord."

Chapter CXVII: Love, Which Is Greater than Faith and Hope, Is Shed Abroad in Our Hearts by the Holy Ghost

And now as to *love,* which the apostle declares to be greater than the other two graces, that is, than faith and hope, the greater the measure in which it dwells in a man, the better is the man in whom it dwells. For when there is a question as to whether a man is good, one does not ask what he believes, or what he hopes, but what he loves. For the man who loves aright no doubt believes and hopes aright; whereas the man who has not love believes in vain, even though his beliefs are true; and hopes in vain, even though the objects of his hope are a real part of true happiness; unless, indeed, he believes and hopes for this, that he may obtain by prayer the blessing of love. For, although it is not possible to hope without love, it may yet happen that a man does not love that which is necessary to the attainment of his hope; as, for example, if he hopes for eternal life (and who is there that does not desire this?) and yet does not love righteousness, without which no one can attain to eternal life. Now this is the true faith of Christ which the apostle speaks of, "which worketh by love"; and if there is anything that it does not yet embrace in its love, asks that it may receive, seeks that it may find, and knocks that it may be opened unto it. For faith obtains through prayer that which the law commands. For without the gift of God, that is, without the Holy Spirit, through whom love is shed abroad in our hearts, the law can command, but it cannot assist; and, moreover, it makes a man a transgressor, for he can no longer excuse himself on the plea of ignorance. Now carnal lust reigns where there is not the love of God. . . .

Chapter CXXI: Love Is the End of All the Commandments, and God Himself Is Love

All the commandments of God, then, are embraced in love, of which the apostle says: "Now the end of the commandment is charity, out of a pure heart, and of a good conscience, and of faith unfeigned." Thus the end of every commandment is charity, that is, every commandment has love for its aim. But whatever is done either through fear of punishment or from some other carnal motive, and has not for its principle that love which the Spirit of God sheds abroad in the heart, is not done as it ought to be done, however it may appear to men. For this love embraces both the love of God and the love of our neighbor, and "on these two commandments hang all the law and the prophets." We may add the Gospel and the apostles. For it is from these that we hear this voice: The end of the commandment is charity, and God is love. Wherefore, all God's commandments, one of which is "Thou shalt not commit adultery," and all those precepts which are not commandments but special counsels, one of which is, "It is good for a man not to touch a woman," are rightly carried out only when the motive principle of action is the love of God, and the love of our neighbor in God. And this applies both to the present and the future life. We love God now by faith, then we shall love Him through sight. Now we love even our neighbor by faith; for we who are ourselves mortal know not the hearts of mortal men. But in the future life, the Lord "both will bring to light the hidden things of darkness, and will make manifest the counsels of the hearts, and then shall every man have praise of God"; for every man shall love and priase in his neighbor the virtue which, that it may not be hid, the Lord Himself shall bring to light. Moreover, lust diminishes as love grows, till the latter grows to such a height that it can grow no higher here. For "greater love hath no man than this, that a man lay down his life for his friends." Who then can tell how great love shall be in the future world, when there shall be no lust for it to restrain and conquer? For that will be the perfection of health when there shall be no struggle with death.

Averroës

(1126–1198)

Introduction

We maintain that the business of philosophy is nothing other than to look into creation and to ponder over it in order to be guided to the Creator—in other words, to look into the meaning of existence. For the knowledge of creation leads to the cognizance of the Creator, through the knowledge of the created. The more perfect becomes the knowledge of creation, the more perfect becomes the knowledge of the Creator. The Law encourages and exhorts us to observe creation. Thus, it is clear that this is to be taken either as a religious injunction or as something approved by the Law. But the Law urges us to observe creation by means of reason and demands the knowledge thereof through reason. This is evident from different verses of the Qur'an. For example, the Qur'an says: "Wherefore take example from them, you who have eyes" [Qur'an 49.2]. That is a clear indication of the necessity of using the reasoning faculty, or rather both reason and religion, in the interpretation of things. Again it says: "Or do they not contemplate the kingdom of heaven and earth and the things which God has created" [Qur'an 7.184]. This is in plain exhortation to encourage the use of observation of creation. And remember that one whom God especially distinguishes in this respect, Abraham, the prophet. For He says: "And this did we show unto Abraham: the kingdom of heaven and earth" [Qur'an 6.75]. Further, He says: "Do they not consider the camels, how they are created; and the heaven, how it is raised" [Qur'an 88.17]. Or, still again: "And (who) meditate on the creation of heaven and earth, saying, O Lord you have not created this in vain" [Qur'an 3.176]. There are many other verses on this subject: too numerous to be enumerated.

Now, it being established that the Law makes the observation and consideration of creation by reason obligatory—and consideration is nothing but to make explicit the implicit—this can only be done through reason. Thus we must look into creation with the reason. Moreover, it is obvious that the observation which the Law approves and encourages must be of the most perfect type, performed with the most perfect kind of reasoning. As the Law emphasizes the knowledge of God and His creation by inference, it is incumbent on any who wish to know God and His whole creation by inference, to learn the kinds of inference, their conditions and that which distinguishes philosophy from dialectic and exhortation from syllogism. This is impossible unless one possesses knowledge beforehand of the various kinds of reasoning and learns to distinguish between reasoning and what is not reasoning. This cannot be done except one knows its different parts, that is, the different kinds of premises.

Hence, for a believer in the Law and a follower of it, it is necessary to know these things before he begins to look into creation, for they are like instruments for observation. For, just as a student discovers by the study of the law, the necessity of knowledge of legal reasoning with all its kinds and distinc-

From *On the Harmony of Religions and Philosophy.*

157

tions, a student will find out by observing the creation the necessity of metaphysical reasoning. Indeed, he has a greater claim on it than the jurist. For if a jurist argues the necessity of legal reasoning from the saying of God: "Wherefore take example *from them* O you who have eyes" [Qur'an 59.2], a student of divinity has a better right to establish the same from it on behalf of metaphysical reasoning.

One cannot maintain that this kind of reasoning is an innovation in religion because it did not exist in the early days of Islam. For legal reasoning and its kinds are things which were invented also in later ages, and no one thinks they are innovations. Such should also be our attitude towards philosophical reasoning. There is another reason why it should be so, but this is not the proper place to mention it. A large number of the followers of this religion confirm philosophical reasoning, all except a small worthless minority, who argue from religious ordinances. Now, as it is established that the Law makes the consideration of philosophical reasoning and its kinds as necessary as legal reasoning, if none of our predecessors has made an effort to enquire into it, we should begin to do it, and so help them, until the knowledge is complete. For if it is difficult or rather impossible for one person to acquaint himself single-handed with all things which it is necessary to know in legal matters, it is still more difficult in the case of philosophical reasoning. And, if before us, somebody has enquired into it, we should derive help from what he has said. It is quite immaterial whether that man is our co-religionist or not; for the instrument by which purification is perfected is not made uncertain in its usefulness by its being in the hands of one of our own party, or of a foreigner, if it possesses the attributes of truth. By these latter we mean those Ancients who investigated these things before the advent of Islam.

Now, such is the case. All that is wanted in an enquiry into philosophical reasoning has already been perfectly examined by the Ancients. All that is required of us is that we should go back to their books and see what they have said in this connection. If all that they say be true, we should accept it and if there be something wrong, we should be warned by it. Thus, when we have finished this kind of research we shall have acquired instruments by which we can observe the universe, and consider its general character. For so long as one does not know its general character one cannot know the created, and so long as he does not know the created, he cannot know its nature.

All things have been made and created. This is quite clear in itself, in the case of animals and plants, as God has said "Verily the idols which you invoke, beside God, can never create a single fly, though they may all assemble for that purpose" [Qur'an 22.72]. We see an inorganic substance and then there is life in it. So we know for certain that there is an inventor and bestower of life, and He is God. Of the heavens we know by their movements, which never become slackened, that they work for our benefit by divine solicitude, and are subordinate to our welfare. Such an appointed and subordinate object is always created for some purpose. The second principle is that for every created thing there is a creator. So it is right to say from the two foregoing principles that for every existent thing there is an inventor. There are many arguments, according to the number of the created things, which can be advanced to prove this premise. Thus, it is necessary for one who wants to know God as He ought to be known to acquaint himself with the essence of things, so that he may get information about the creation of all things. For who cannot understand the real substance and purpose of a thing, cannot understand the minor meaning of its creation. It is to this that God refers in the following verse "Or do they not contemplate the heaven and the earth, and the things which God has created?" [Qur'an 7.184]. And so a man who would follow the purpose of philosophy in investigating the existence of things, that is, would try to know the cause which led to its creation, and the purpose of it would know the argument of kindness most perfectly. These two arguments are those adopted by Law.

The verses of the Qur'an leading to a knowledge of the existence of God are dependent only on the two foregoing arguments. It will be quite clear to anyone who will examine closely the verses, which occur in the Divine Book in this connection. These, when investigated, will be found to be of three kinds: either they are verses showing the "arguments of kindness," or those mentioning the "arguments of creation," or those which include both the kinds of arguments. The following verses may be taken as illustrating the argument of kindness. "Have we not made the earth for a bed, and the mountains for stakes to find the same? And have we not created you of two sexes; and appointed your sleep for rest; and made the night a garment to cover you; and destined the day to the gaining of your livelihood and built over you seven solid heavens; and placed therein a burning lamp? And do we not send down from the clouds pressing forth rain, water pouring down in abundance, that we may thereby produce corn, and herbs, and gardens planted thick with trees?" [Qur'an 77.6–16] and, "Blessed be He Who has placed the twelve signs in the heavens; has placed therein a lamp by day, and the moon which shines by night" [Qur'an 25.62] and again, "Let man consider his food" [Qur'an 80.24].

The following verses refer to the argument of invention, "Let man consider, therefore of what he is created. He is created of the seed poured forth, issuing from the loins, and the breast bones" [Qur'an 86.6]; and, "Do they not consider the camels, how they are created; the heaven, how it is raised; the mountains, how they are fixed; the earth how it is extended" [Qur'an 88.17]; and again "O man, a parable is propounded unto you; wherefore hearken unto it. Verily the idols which they invoke, besides God, can never create a single fly, though they may all assemble for the purpose" [Qur'an 22.72]. Then we may point to the story of Abraham, referred to in the following verse, "I direct my face unto Him Who has created heaven and earth; I am orthodox, and not of the idolaters" [Qur'an 6.79]. There may be quoted many verses referring to this argument. The verses comprising both the arguments are also many, for instance, "O men, of Mecca, serve your Lord, Who has created you, and those who have been before you: peradventure you will fear Him; Who has spread the earth as a bed for you, and the heaven as a covering, and has caused water to descend from heaven, and thereby produced fruits for your sustenance. Set not up, therefore, any equals unto God, against your own knowledge [Qur'an 2.19]. His words, "Who has created you, and those who have been before you," lead us to the argument of creation; while the words, "who has spread the earth" refer to the argument of divine solicitude for man. Of this kind also are the following verses of the Qur'an, "One sign of the resurrection unto them is the dead earth; We quicken the same by rain, and produce therefrom various sorts of grain, of which they eat" [Qur'an 36.32]; and, "Now in the creation of heaven and earth, and the vicissitudes of night and day are signs unto those who are endowed with understanding, who remember God standing, and sitting, and lying on their sides; and meditate on the creation of heaven and earth, saying O Lord, far be it from You, therefore deliver us from the torment of hellfire" [Qur'an 3.188]. Many verses of this kind comprise both the kinds of arguments.

This method is the right path by which God has invited men to a knowledge of His existence, and informed them of it through the intelligence which He has implanted in their nature. The followin verse refers to this fixed and innate nature of man, "And when the Lord drew forth their posterity from the loins of the sons of Adam, and took them witness against themselves, Am I not your Lord? They answered, Yes, we do bear witness" [Qur'an 7.171]. So it is incumbent for one who intends to obey God, and follow the injunction of His Prophet, that he should adopt this method, thus making himself one of those learned men who bear witness to the divinity of God, with His own witness, and that of His angels, as He says, "God has borne witness, that there is no God but He, and the angels, and those who are endowed with wisdom profess the same; who execute righteousness; there is no God but He; the Mighty, the Wise" [Qur'an 3.16]. Among the arguments for both of themselves is the praise which God refers to in the following verse, "Neither is there anything which does not celebrate his praise; but you understand not their celebration thereof" [Qur'an 17.46].

It is evident from the above arguments for the existence of God that they are dependent upon two categories of reasoning. It is also clear that both of these methods are meant for particular people; that is, the learned. Now as to the method for the masses. The difference between the two lies only in details. The masses cannot understand the two above-mentioned arguments but only what they can grasp by their senses; while the learned men can go further and learn by reasoning also, besides learning by sense. They have gone so far that a learned man has said, that the benefits the learned men derive from the knowledge of the members of human and animal body are a thousand and one. If this be so, then this is the method which is taught both by Law and by Nature. It is the method which was preached by the Prophet and the divine books. The learned men do not mention these two lines of reasoning to the masses, not because of their number, but because of a want of depth of learning on their part about the knowledge of a single thing only. The example of the common people, considering and pondering over the universe, is like a man who looks into a thing, the manufacture of which he does not know. For all that such a man can know about it is that it has been made, and that there must be a maker of it. But, on the other hand, the learned look into the universe, just as a man knowing the art would do; try to understand the real purpose of it. So it is quite clear that their knowledge about the Maker, as the maker of the universe, would be far better than that of the man who only knows it as made. The atheists, who deny the Creator altogether, are like men who can see and feel the created things, but would not acknowledge any Creator for them, but would attribute all to chance alone, and that they come into being by themselves.

Now, then, if this is the method adopted by the Law, it may be asked: What is the way of proving the unity of God by means of the Law; that is, the knowledge of the religious formula that "there is no god, but God." The negation contained in it is an addition to the affirmative, which the formula contains, while the affirmative has already been proved. What is the purpose of this negation? We would say that the method, adopted by the Law, of denying divinity to all but God is according to the ordinance of God in the Qur'an. . .

If you look a little intently it will become clear to you, that in spite of the fact that the Law has not given illustration of those things for the common people, beyond which their imagination cannot go, it has also informed the learned men of the underlying meanings of those illustrations. So it is necessary to bear in mind the limits which the Law has set about the instruction of every class of men, and not to mix them together. For in this manner the purpose of the Law is multiplied. Hence it is that the Prophet has said, "We, the prophets, have been commanded to adapt ourselves to the conditions of the people, and address them according to their intelligence." He who tries to instruct all the people in the matter of religion, in one and the same way, is like a man who wants to make them alike in actions too, which is quite against apparent laws and reason.

From the foregoing it must have become clear to you that the divine vision has an esoteric meaning in which there is no doubt, if we take the words of the Qur'an about God as they stand, that is, without proving or disproving the anthropomorphic attribute of God. Now since the first part of the Law has been made quite clear as to God's purity, and the quantity of the teaching fit for the common people; it is time to begin the discussion about the actions of God, after which our purpose in writing this treatise will be over.

In this section we will take up five questions around which all others in this connection revolve. In the first place a proof of the creation of the universe; secondly, the advent of the prophets; thirdly, predestination and fate; fourthly, Divine justice and injustice; and fifthly, the Day of Judgment.

Problem First: the Creation of the Universe

The Law teaches that the universe was invented and created by God, and that it did not come into being by chance or by itself. The method adopted by the Law for proving this is not the one upon which the Asharites have depended. For we have already shown that those methods are not specially certain for the learned, nor common enough to satisfy all the classes of men. The methods which are really serviceable are those which have a very few premises, and the results of which fall very near to the commonly known ideas. But in instructing the common people the Law does not favor statements composed of long and complete reasoning, based upon different problems. So everyone who, in teaching them, adopts a different course, and interprets the Law according to it, has lost sight of its purpose and gone astray from the true path. And so also, the Law in giving illustrations for its reasoning uses only those which are present before us.

Whatever has been thought necessary for the common people to know, has been explained to them by the nearest available examples, as in the case of the day of Judgment. But whatever was unnecessary for them to know, they have been told that it was beyond their knowledge, as the words of God about the Soul [Qur'an 22.85]. Now that we have established this, it is necessary that the method adopted by the Law for teaching the creation of the universe to the common people be such as would be acknowledged by all. It is also necessary that since there cannot be found anything present to illustrate the creation of the universe the Law must have used the examples of the creation of things in the visible world.

So the method adopted by Law is that the universe was made by God. If we look intently into the verse pertaining to this subject we shall see that the method adopted is that of divine solicitude, which we know to be one of those which prove the existence of God. When a man sees a thing made in a certain shape, proportion and fashion, for a particular advantage is derived from it, and purpose which is to be attained, so that it becomes clear to him, that had it not been found in that shape, and proportion, then that advantage would have been wanting in it, he comes to know for certain that there is a maker of that thing, and that he had made it in that shape and proportion, for a set purpose. For it is not possible that all those qualities serving that purpose be collected in that thing by chance alone. For instance, if a man sees a stone on the ground in a shape fit for sitting, and finds its proportions and fashion of the same kind, then he would come to know that it was made by a maker, and that he had made it and placed it there. But when he sees nothing in it which may have made it fit for sitting then he becomes certain that its existence in the place was by chance only, without its being fashioned by any maker.

Such is also the case with the whole of the universe. For when a man sees the sun, the moon, and all the stars, which are the cause of the four seasons; of days and nights, of rain, water and winds, of the inhabitation of the parts of the earth, of the existence of man, and of the being of all the animals and the plants and of the earth being fit for the habitation of a man, and other animals living in it; and the water fit for the animals living in it; and the air fit for birds, and if there be anything amiss in this creation and edifice, the whole world would come to confusion and disorder, then he would come to know with certainty that it is not possible that this harmony in it for the different members of the universe—man, animals, and plants—be found by chance only.

He will know that there is one who determined it, and so one who made it by intention, and that is God, exalted and magnified may He be. He would know with certainty that the universe is a created thing, for he would necessarily think that it is not possible that in it should be found all this harmony, if it be not made by someone, and had come into existence by chance alone. This kind of argument, is quite definite and at the same time clear, and some have mentioned it here. It is based upon two principles which are acknowledged by all. One of them being, that the universe, with all its component parts, is found fit for the existence of man and things; secondly, that which is found suitable in all its parts, for a single purpose, leading to a single goal, is necessarily a created thing. So those two principles lead us naturally to admit that the universe is a created thing, and that there is a maker of it. Hence "the argument of analogy" leads to two things at one and the same time, and that is why it is the best argument for proving the existence of God. This kind of reasoning is also found in the Qur'an in many verses in which the creation of the universe is mentioned.

For instance, "Have We not made the earth a bed, and the mountains for shelter to fix the same? And have We not created you of two sexes; and appointed your sleep for rest and made the night a garment to cover you, and destined the day to a gaining of a livelihood; and built over you seven heavens, and placed therein a burning lamp? And do We not send down from the clouds pressing forth rain, water pouring down in abundance, that We may hereby produce corn and herbs, and gardens planted thick with trees" [Qur'an 77.3ff]. If we ponder over this verse it would be found that our attention has been called to the suitability of the different parts of the universe for the existence of man. In the very beginning we are informed of a fact well-known to all—and that is that the earth has been created in a way which has made it suitable for our existence. Had it been unstable, or of any other shape, or in any other place, or not of the present proportion, it would not have been possible to be here, or at all created on it. All this is included in the words, "Have We not made the earth a bed for you"? for in a bed are collected together all the qualities of shape, tranquility, and peace, to which may be added those of smoothness and softness.

So how strange is this wonderful work and how excellent this blessedness, and how wonderful this collection of all the qualities! This is so because in the word *mihad* (bed) are brought together all those qualities, which are found in the earth, rendering it suitable for the existence of man. It is a thing which becomes clear to the learned after much learning and a long time, "But God will appropriate His mercy unto whom He pleases [Qur'an 2.99]. Then as to the divine words, "And the mountains for stakes,"—they tell us of the advantage to be found in the tranquility of the earth on account of the mountains. For had the earth been created smaller than it is now, that is, without mountains, it would have been quivered by the motion of other elements, the water and the air, and would have been shaken and thus displaced. This would naturally have been the cause of the destruction of the animal world. So when its tranquility is in harmony with those living on it, it did not come into being by chance alone, but was made by someone's intention, and determination. Certainly it was made by One who intended it, and determined it, for the sake of those living on it.

Then He calls our attention to the suitability of the existence of night and day for animals. He says "And made the night a garment to cover you; and destined the day to a gaining of your livelihood. " He means to say that He has made the night like a covering and clothing for all the things, from the heat of the sun. For had there been no setting of the sun at night, all the things, whose life has been made dependent upon the sun, would have perished—that is, the animals and the plants. As clothing protects the people from the heat of the sun, in addition to its being a covering, so God likened the night to it. This is one of the most beautiful of the metaphors. There is also another advantage in the night for the animals: their sleep in it is very deep, after the setting of the sun, which keeps faculties in motion, that is, wide awake. So God has said, "And appointed your sleep for rest," on account of the darkness of the night. Then He says, "And built over you seven heavens, and placed therein a burning lamp." Here by the word building He means their creation, and their harmony with the created things, and their arrangement and system. By strength He means that power of revolution and motion which is never slackened, and never overtaken by fatigue; and they never fall like other roofs and high edifices. To this refer the words of God, "And made the heaven a roof well-supported" [Qur'an 21.33]. By all this He shows their fitness in number, shape, fashion, and movement, for the existence of those who live on the earth round it. Were one of the heavenly bodies, not to speak of all, to stop for a moment all would be chaos on the face of the earth. Some people think the blast of the last trumpet, which will be the cause of the thunderbolt, will be nothing but a stop in the revolution of the heavenly bodies.

Then He tells us of the advantage of the sun for those living on the earth and says, "And placed therein a burning lamp. " He calls it a lamp because in reality it is all darkness, and light covers the darkness of the night, and if there be no lamp, man can get no advantage out of his sense of sight at nighttime; and in the same way if there were no sun the animals can have no benefit of their sense of seeing. He calls our attention to this advantage of the suns ignoring others because it is the noblest of all the advantages and the most-apparent of all. Then He tells us of His kindness in sending down rain, for the sake of the plants and the animals. The coming down of rain in an appointed proportion, and at an appointed season, for the cultivated fields cannot be by chance alone, but is the result of divine solicitude for us all. So He says, "And do We not send down from the clouds pressing forth rain, water pouring down in abundance that We may hereby produce corn and herbs, and gardens planted thick with trees."

There are many verses of the Qur'an on this subject. For instance, He says, "Do you not see how God has created the seven heavens, one above another, and has placed the moon therein for a light, and has appointed the sun for a taper? God has also provided and caused you to bring forth wheat from the earth" [Qur'an 71.14–16]. If we were to count all such verses and comment upon them showing the kindness of the Creator for the created, it would take too many volumes. We do not intend to do it in this book. If God should grant us life and leisure we shall write a book to show the kindness of God to which He has called our attention.

It should be known that this kind of argument is just contrary to that which the Asharites think leads to the knowledge of God. They think that the creation does not lead us to the knowledge of God through any of His goodness, but through possibility, that is, the possibility which is found in all things, which we can understand to be of his shape or of quite a contrary one. But if this possibility be found alike in both the cases, then there is no wisdom in the creation of the universe, and there is found no harmony between man and the parts of it. For, as they think, if it is possible for the things to have any other form than they have now, then there can exist no harmony between man and other existent things by the creation of which God has obliged man and commanded him to be thankful to Him. This opinion, by which the creation of man, as a part of the universe, is just as possible, for instance, as his creation in the void, is like the opinion of those who say that man exists but he could have been created in quite a different shape, and yet could perform actions like a man. According to them it is also possible that he may have formed the part of another universe quite different from the existing one. In that case the blessing of the universe can have no obligation for man, for they are not necessary for his purpose. Hence man is quite careless of them and they of him. So their existence is no blessing to him. This is all against the nature of man.

On the whole, a man who denies the existence of the effects arranged according to the causes in the question of arts, or whose wisdom cannot understand it, then he has no knowledge of the art of its Maker. So also a man who denies the existence of an order of effects in accordance with causes in this universe, denies the existence of the Creator altogether. Their saying that God is above these causes, and that they cannot have any bearing on the effects by His command, is very far from the true nature of philosophy, nay, it is a destroyer of it. For if it is possible to have the same effects with other than the prescribed causes just in the same degree as by them, then where is the greatness in producing the effects from the known Causes? It is so because the effects from the causes have one of the following three reasons. Either the existence of the causes will be in place of the effects by compulsion, as a man's taking his food; or their being more perfect, that is, the effect becoming better and more perfect through them, as a man's having two eyes, or they may have neither a better nor a more compulsive effect. In this case the existence of the effect and the cause would be by chance, without any intention at all; and, hence, there would be no greatness found in it.

For instance, if the shape of a human hand, the number of the fingers, and their length be neither necessary nor adding any perfection in its work in seizing things of different kind, then the actions of the hand from this shape, and number of parts, would be by chance alone. If it be so, then it makes no difference whether a man is given a hand or a hoof, or something else, like the different animals, for their particular actions. On the whole, if we ignore the causes and their effects, then there remains nothing to refute the arguments of those who believe in the creation of the universe by chance alone, that is, those who say that there is no Creator at all, and that which has come into being in this universe is the result of material causes. For taking one of the two alternatives it is not more possible that it may have happened by chance, than done by an independent Actor. So when the Asharites say that the existence of one or more possibilities shows that there is a particular Maker of these things, they can answer and say that the existence of things by one of these possibilities was by chance alone, for intention works as one of the causes, and that which happens without any means or cause is by chance. We see that many things come into being in this way. For example, the elements mix together by chance, and then by this unintentional mixing there is produced a new thing. They mix again, and this quite unintentionally produces quite a new thing. In this way every kind of creation may be said to have come into existence by chance.

We say that it is necessary that there be found order and arrangement, the more perfect and finished than what can be imagined. This mixing together of elements is limited and prearranged, and things produced by them are sure to happen, and no disorder has ever happened in them. But all this could not happen by chance alone, for that which happens in this way by chance is of the least value. It is to this that God refers, "It is the work of the Lord, who has rightly disposed all things" [Qur'an 27.90]. I would like to know what completeness can be found in things made by chance, for such things are by no means better than their opposites. To this God refers in the following words, "You cannot see in the Creation of the most Merciful any unfitness or disproportion. Lift your eyes again to heaven, and look whether you see any flaw" [Qur'an 67.3]. But what defect can be greater than that all the things can be found with any other quality than they really possess. For the non-existent quality may be better than the existing one. In this way, if one thinks that were the Eastern movement to become Western and vice-versa, there would be no difference in the universe then he has destroyed philosophy altogether. He is like a man who thinks that were the right side of the animals to become left, and vice-versa, there would be no difference at all, for one of the two alternatives is there. For as it is possible to say that it is made according to one alternative by an independent Maker, so it is possible to assert that it was all made by chance alone. For we see so many things coming into being by themselves.

It is quite clear to you that all the people see that lower kinds of creation could have been made in a different way from that in which they really are, and as they see this lower degree in many things they think that they must have been made by chance. But in the higher creation they know that it is impossible to have been made in a more perfect and excellent form than that given to it by the Creator. So this opinion, which is one of the opinions of the Mutakallimun is both against the Law and philosophy. What we say is that the opinion of possibility in creation is closer to a complete denial of God, than leading us nearer to Him. At the same time it falsifies philosophy. For if we do not understand that there is a mean between the beginnings and ends of the Creation, upon which is based the ends of things, then there can neither be any order nor any method in it. And if they be wanting then there can be no proof of the existence of an intelligent and knowing Maker; for taking them together with cause and effect we are led to the fact that they must have been created by wisdom and knowledge.

But, on the other hand, the existence of either of two possibilities shows that they may have been performed by a not-knowing Maker and by chance alone. Just as a stone falling on the earth may fall in any place, on any side, and in any form. It will show the want of the existence either of a creator at all or at least of a wise and knowing Creator. The thing which has compelled the Mutakallimun of the Asharites to adopt this opinion is a denial of the action of those natural forces which God has put in all things, as He has endowed them with life, power and so forth. They avoided the opinion that there was any other creator but God, and God forbid that there be any other, for he is the only creator of the causes and they are made effective by His command only. We will talk of this in detail when discoursing on Fate and Predestination. They were also afraid that by admitting the natural causes they might be accused of saying that the universe came into being by chance only. They would have known that a denial of it means a denial of a great part of the arguments, which can be advanced for a proof of the existence of God. One who denies any part of God's creation denies His work, which falls very near to a denial of a part of His attributes.

On the whole as their opinion is based upon hasty conclusions, which come to the mind of a man by superficial thought and as apparently it appears that the word "intention" can be applied to one who has power to do bad or otherwise, they saw that if they did not admit that all the creation is possible, they would not be able to say that it came into existence by the action of an intending creator. So they say that all the creation is possible so that they may prove that the creator is an intelligent one. They never thought of the order which is necessary in things made, and with that their coming from an intelligent creator. These people have also ignored the blame they will have to bear in thus denying wisdom to the creator; or maintaining that chance should be found governing creation. They know, as we have said, that it is necessary, on account of the order existent in nature, that it must have been brought into being by some knowing creator, otherwise the order found in it would be by chance. When they were compelled to deny the natural forces they had to deny with them a large number of those forces which God has made subservient to His command for the creation and preservation of things. For God has created some things from causes which He has produced from outside, these are the heavenly bodies; there are other things which He has made by causes placed in the things themselves, that is; the soul, and other natural forces, by which he preserves those things. So how wicked is the man who destroys philosophy, and "invented a lie about God" [Qur'an 3.88].

This is only a part of the change which has taken place in the Law, in this and other respects, which we have already mentioned, and will mention hereafter. From all this it must have become clear to you that the method which God had adopted for teaching His creatures that the universe is made and created by Him is the method of kindness and wisdom, towards all His creatures and especially towards man. It is a method which bears the same relation to our intellect, as the sun bears to our senses. The method which it has adopted towards the common people about this problem is that of illustration from things observed. But as there was nothing which could be given as an illustration, and as the common people cannot understand a thing, an illustration of which they cannot see, God tells us that the universe was created in a certain time out of a certain thing, which He made. He tells us his condition before the creation of the universe, "His throne was above the waters" [Qur'an 11.9]. He also says, "Verily your Lord is God who created the heavens and the earth in six days" [Qur'an 7.52], and "Then He set His mind to the creation of the heavens, and it was smoke" [Qur'an 12.10]. In addition to these there are other verses of the Book, pertaining to this subject. So it is incumbent that nothing out of them should be interpreted for the common people, and nothing should be presented to them in explaining it but this illustration. For one who changes it, makes the wisdom of the Law useless. If it be said that the Law teaches about the universe that it is created, and made out of nothing and in no time, then it is a thing which even the learned cannot understand, not to speak of the common people. So we should not deviate in this matter of the Law. . . .

Problem Second: The Advent of the Prophets

If we admit the existence of the prophetic mission, by putting the idea of possibility, which is in fact ignorance, in place of certainty, and make miracles a proof of the truth of man who claims to be a prophet it becomes necessary that they should not be used by a person, who says that they can be performed by others than prophets, as the Mutakallimun do. They think that the miracles can be performed by the magicians and saints. The condition which they attach with them is that miracles prove a man to be a prophet, when he at the same time claims to be so, for the true prophet can perform them as opposed to the false ones. This is an argument without any proof, for it can be understood either by hearing or reason That is, it is said that one whose claims to prophecy are wrong, cannot perform miracles, but as we have already said, when they cannot be performed by a liar, then they can only be done by the good people, whom God has meant for this purpose. These people, if they speak a lie, are not good, and hence cannot perform the miracles. But this does not satisfy the people who think miracles to be possible from the magicians, for they certainly are not good men. It is here that the weakness of the argument lies. Hence some people have thought that the best thing is to believe that they cannot be performed but by the prophets.

It is clear to you from the life of the prophet, peace be upon him, that he never invited any man or community to believe in his prophecy, and that which he has brought with him from God, by means of the performance of any miracles in support of his claim, such as changing one element into another. Whatever miracles did appear from him were only performed in the natural course of things, without on his part any intention of contention or competition. The following words of the Qur'an will make this clear "And they say: We will by no means believe in you, until you cause a spring of water to gush forth for us out of the earth, and you have a garden of palm-trees and vines, and you cause rivers to spring forth from the midst thereof in abundance; or you cause the heaven to fall down in pieces upon us, as you have given out, or you bring down God and the angels to vouch for you; or you have a house of gold, or you ascend by a ladder to heaven; neither will we believe your ascending there alone, until you cause a book to descend unto us, bearing witness of you which we may read. Answer: My Lord be praised, Am I other than a man sent as an apostle?" [Qur'an 17.92-95]. Then again, "Nothing hindered us from sending you with miracles, except that the former nations have charged them with imposture" [Qur'an 17.61].

The thing by which we invited the people to believe in him, and with which he vied with them is the Qur'an. For, says God, "Say, verily, if men and *jinn* were purposely assembled, that they might produce a book like this Qur'an, they could not produce one like unto it, although the one of them assigned the other" [Qur'an 17.90]. Then further, he says, "will they say, He hath forged the Qur'an? Answer, bring therefore ten chapters like unto it forged by yourself" [Qur'an 11.16]. This being the case the miracle of the Prophet with which he vied with the people and which he advanced as an argument for the truth of his claim to the prophetic mission, was the Qur'an. If it be said that this is quite clear, but how does it appear that the Qur'an is a mirage, and that it proves his prophecy, while just now we have proved the weakness of the proof of prophecy by means of miracles without any exceptions in the case of any prophet. Besides, the people have differed in taking the Qur'an to be a miracle at all. For in their opinion one of the conditions of a miracle is that it should be quite different from any act which may have become habitual. But the Qur'an is of this sort, because it is only words, though it excels all created words. So it becomes a miracle by its superiority only, that is, the impossibility for people bringing anything like it, on account of its being highly eloquent. This being the case, it differs from the habitual, not in *genus* but in details only, and that which differs in this way is of the same genus.

Some people say that it is a miracle by itself, and not by its superiority. They do not lay it down as a condition for miracles that they should be quite different from the habitual, but think that it should be such a habitual act, as men may fall short of accomplishing. We would reply that it is as the objectors say, but the thing about it is not as they have thought. That the Qur'an is an evidence of his prophecy, is based, we believe, upon two principles, which are found in the Book itself. The first being that the existence of the class of men called prophets and apostles is well-known. They are the men who lay down laws for the people by divine revelation, and not by human education. Their existence can be denied only by the people who deny repeated action, as the existence of all things which we have not seen—the lives of the famous thinkers and so forth. All the philosophers, and other men are agreed, except those who pay no regard to their words, (and they are the Materialists), that there are men to whom have been revealed many commandments for the people, to perform certain good actions, by which their beatitude may be perfected; and to make them give up certain wrong beliefs and vicious actions. This is the business of divine apostles.

The second principle is, that everyone who does this work, that is, lays down laws by revelation, is a prophet. This principle is also quite in accordance with human nature. For as it is known that the business of medicine is to cure a disease, and one who can cure is a physician, so it is also known that the business of the prophets is to give law to the people by divine revelation, and one who does so is a prophet. The Book mentions the first principle in the following: "Verily We have revealed Our will unto you, as We have revealed it unto Noah, and the prophets who succeeded him, and We have revealed it unto Abraham, and Ishmael, and Isaac and Jacob, and the tribes, and unto Jesus, and Job, and Jonas, and Aaron and Solomon; and we have given you the Qur'an as We gave the Psalms unto David; some apostles have We sent, whom We have mentioned unto you, and God spoke unto Moses discoursing with him" [Qur'an 4.161–162], and again: "Say, I am not alone among the apostles" [Qur'an 46.8].

The second principle is that Mohammed, peace be upon him, has done the work of a prophet, that is, has given Law to the people by divine revelation. This also can be known from the Qur'an, where God mentions it. He says, "O men, now is an evident proof come unto you from your Lord, and We have sent down unto you manifest light" [Qur'an 4.173]. By manifest light is meant the Qur'an. Again He says, "O men, now is the apostle come unto you from your Lord; believe, therefore, it will be better for you" [Qur'an 4.168], and again, "But those among them who are well-grounded in knowledge, and faithful, who believe in that which has been sent down unto you, and that which has been sent down unto the prophets before you" [Qur'an 4.160]; and again "God is the witness of the revelation which He has sent down unto you; He sent it down with his special knowledge; the angels are also witness thereof; but God is a sufficient witness" [Qur'an 4.164].

Problem Third: Of Fate And Predestination

This is one of the most intricate problems of religion. For if you look into the traditional arguments (*Hadith*) about this problem you will find them contradictory; such also being the case with arguments of reason. The contradiction in the arguments of the first kind is found in the Qur'an and the *Hadith*. There are many verses of the Qur'an, which by their universal nature teach that all the things are predestined and that man is compelled to do his acts; then there are verses which say that man is free in his acts and not compelled in performing them. The following verses tell us that all the things are by compulsion, and are predestined, "Everything have We created bound by a fixed degree" [Qur'an 56.49]; again, "With Him everything is regulated according to a determined measure" [Qur'an 13.9]. Further, He says, "No accident happened in the earth, nor in your persons, but the same was entered in the Book verily it is easy with God" [Qur'an 57.22]. There may be quoted many other verses on this subject.

Now, as to the verses which say that man can acquire deeds by free will, and that things are only possible and not necessary, the following may be quoted: "Or He destroys them (by ship-wreck), because of that which their crew have merited; though He pardons many things" [Qur'an 42.32]. And again, "Whatever misfortune befalls you is sent you by God, for that which your hands have deserved" [Qur'an 42.32]. Further, He says, "But they who commit evil, equal thereunto" [Qur'an 10.28]. Again, He says, "It shall have the good which it gains, and it shall have the evil which it gains" [Qur'an 2.278]. And, "And as to Thamud, We directed them, but they loved blindness better than the true directions" [Qur'an 41.16].

Sometimes contradiction appears even in a single verse of the Qur'an. For instance, He says, "After a misfortune has befallen you (you had already attained two equal advantages), do you say, whence comes this? Answer, This is from yourselves" [Qur'an 3.159]. In the next verse, He says, "And what happened unto you, on the day whereon the two armies met, was certainly by permission of the Lord" [Qur'an 3.160]. Of this kind also is the verse, "Whatever good befalls you, O man, it is from God; and whatever evil befalls you, it is from yourself" [Qur'an 4.81]; while the preceding verse says, "All is from God" [Qur'an 4.80].

Such is also the case with the *hadith*. The Prophet says, "Every child is born in the true religion; his parents afterwards turn him into a Jew or a Christian." On another occasion he said, "The following people have been created for hell, and do the deeds of those who are fit for it. These have been created for heaven, and do deeds fit for it." The first *hadith* says that the cause of disbelief is one's own environments; while faith and belief are natural to man. The other *hadith* says that wickedness and disbelief are created by God, and man is compelled to follow them.

This condition of things has led Muslims to be divided into two groups. The one believed that man's wickedness or virtue is his own acquirement, and that according to these he will be either punished or rewarded. These are the Mutazilites. The belief of the other party is quite opposed to this. They say that man is compelled to do his deeds. They are the Jabarites. The Asharites have tried to adopt a mean between these two extreme views. They say that man can do action, but the deeds done, and the power of doing it, are both created by God. But this is quite meaningless. For if the deed and the power of doing it be both created by God, then man is necessarily compelled to do the act. This is one of the reasons of the difference of opinion about this problem.

As we have said there is another cause of difference of opinion about this problem, than the traditional one. This consists of the contradictory arguments advanced. For if we say that man is the creator of his own deeds, it would be necessary to admit that there are things which are not done according to the will of God, or His authority. So there would be another creator besides God, while the Muslims are agreed that there is no creator but He. If, on the other hand, we were to suppose that man cannot act freely, we admit thus he is compelled to do certain acts, for there is no mean between compulsion and freedom. Again, if man is compelled to do certain deeds, then on him has been imposed a task which he cannot bear; and when he is made to bear a burden, there is no difference between his work and the work of inorganic matter. For inorganic matter has no power, neither has the man the power for that which he cannot bear. Hence all people have made capability one of the conditions for the imposition of a task, such as wisdom. We find Abul Maali, saying in his *Nizamiyyah*, that man is free in his own deeds and has the capability of doing them. He has established it upon the impossibility of imposing a task which one cannot bear, in order to avoid the principle formerly disproved by the Mutazilites, on account of its being unfit by reason. The succeeding Asharites have opposed them. Moreover, if man had no power in doing a deed, then it will be only by chance that he may escape from evil, and that is meaningless. Such also would be the case with acquiring goodness. In this way all those arts which lead to happiness, as agriculture, etc., would become useless. So also would become useless all those arts the purpose of which is protection from, and repulsion of danger, as the sciences of war, navigation, medicine, etc. Such a condition is quite contrary to all that is intelligible to man.

Now it may be asked that if the case is so, how is this contradiction which is to be found both in *hadith* and reason to be reconciled we would say, that apparently the purpose of religion in this problem is not to divide it into two separate beliefs, but to reconcile them by means of a middle course, which is the right method. It is evident that God has created in us power by which we can perform deeds which are contradictory in their nature. But as this cannot be complete except by the cause which God has furnished for us, from outside, and the removal of difficulties from them, the deeds done are only completed by the conjunction of both these things at the same time. This being so, the deeds attributed to use are done by our intention, and by the fitness of the causes which are called the *Predestination* of God, which He has furnished for us from outside. They neither complete the works which we intend nor hinder them, but certainly become the cause of our intending them— one of the two things. For intention is produced in us by our imagination, or for the verification of a thing, which in itself is not in our power, but comes into being by causes outside us. For instance, if we see a good thing, we like it, without intention, and move towards acquiring it. So also, if we happen to come to a thing which it is better to shun, we leave it without intention. Hence our intentions are bound and attached to causes lying outside ourselves.

To this the following words of God refer: "Each of them have angels, mutually succeeding each other, before him and behind him; they watch him by the command of God" [Qur'an 13.12]. As these outside causes take this course according to a well-defined order and arrangement, and never go astray from the path which their Creator has appointed for them, and our own intentions can neither be compelled, nor ever found, on the whole, but by *their* fitness, so it is necessary that actions too should also be within well-defined limits, that is, they be found in a given period of time and in a given quantity. This is necessary because our deeds are only the effects of causes, lying outside us; and all the effects which result from limited and prearranged causes are themselves limited, and are found in a given quantity only. This relation does not exist only between our actions and outside causes, but also between them and the causes which God has created in our body, and the well-defined order existing between the inner and outer causes. This is what is meant by Fate and predestination, which is found mentioned in the Qur'an and is incumbent upon man. This is also the "Preserved Tablet" [Qur'an 85.22]. God's knowledge of these causes, and that which pertains to them, is the cause of their existence. So no one can have a full knowledge of these things except God, and hence He is the only Knower of secrets, which is quite true; as God has said, "Say, None either in heaven or earth, know that which is hidden besides God" [Qur'an 27.67].

A knowledge of causes is a knowledge of secret things, because the secret is a knowledge of the existence of a thing, before it comes into being, and as the arrangement and order of causes bring a thing into existence or not at a certain time, there must be a knowledge of the existence or non-existence of a thing at a certain time. A knowledge of the causes as a whole is the knowledge of what things would be found or not found at a certain moment of time. Praised be He, Who has a complete knowledge of creation and all of its causes. This is what is meant by the "keys of the secret," in the following words of God, "with Him are the keys of secret things; none know them besides Himself" [Qur'an 6.59].

All that we have said being true, it must have become evident how we can acquire our deeds, and how far they are governed by predestination and fate. This very reconciliation is the real purpose of religion by those verses and *hadith* which are apparently contradictory. When their universal nature be limited in this manner, those contradictions should vanish by themselves, and all the doubts which were raised before, about the contradictory nature of reason, would disappear. The existent things from our volition are completed by two things, our intention and the other causes. But when the deeds are referred to only by one of these agencies, doubts would rise. It may be said is a good answer, and here reason is in perfect agreement with religion, but it is based upon the principles that these are agreed that there are creative causes bringing into existence other things; while the Muslims are agreed that there is no Creator but God. We would say that whatever they have agreed upon is quite right, but the objection can be answered in two ways. One of them is that this objection itself can be understood in two ways; one of them being that there is no Creator but God, and all those causes which He has created, cannot be called creators, except speaking figuratively.

Their existence also depends upon Him. He alone has made them to be causes, nay, He only preserves their existence as creative agents, and protects their effects after their actions. He, again, produces their essences at the moment when causes come together. He alone preserves them as a whole. Had there been no divine protection they could not have existed for the least moment of time. Abu Hamid (Al-Ghazzali) has said that a man who makes any of the causes to be co-existent with God is like a man who makes the pen share the work of a scribe in writing; that is, he says that the pen is a scribe and the man is a scribe too. He means that "writing" is a word which may be applied to both, but in reality they have no resemblance in anything but word, for otherwise there is no difference between them. Such is also the case with the word *Creator*, when applied to God and the Causes. We say that in this illustration there are doubts. It should have been clearly shown, whether the scribe was the Creator of the essence (*Jawhar*) of pen, a preserver of it, as long as it remains a pen, and again a preserver of the writing after it is written, a Creator of it after it has come in touch with the pen, as we have just explained that God is the Creator of the essences (*Jawahir*) of everything which comes into contact with its causes, which are so called only by the usage. This is the reason why there is no creator but God—a reason which agrees with our feelings, reason and religion. Our feelings and reason see that there are things which produce others.

The order found in the universe is of two kinds: that which God has put in the nature and disposition of things; and that which surround the universe from outside. This is quite clear in the movement of the heavenly bodies. For it is evident that the sun and the moon, the day and night, and all other stars are obedient to us; and it is on this arrangement and order which God has put in their movements that our existence and that of all other things depends. So even if we imagine the least possible confusion in them, with them in any other position, size and rapidity of movement which God has made for them, all the existent things upon the earth would be destroyed. This is so because of the nature in which God has made them and the nature of the things which are effected by them. This is very clear in the effects of the sun and the moon upon things of this world; such also being the case with the rains, winds, seas and other tangible things. But the greater effect is produced upon plants, and upon a greater number, or all, on the animals. Moreover, it is apparent that had there not been those faculties which God has put in our bodies, as regulating them that could not exist even for a single moment after birth. But, we say, had there not been the faculties found in all the bodies of the animals, and plants and those found in the world by the movement of the heavenly bodies, then they would not have existed at all, not even for a twinkling of the eye.

So praised be the "Sagacious, the Knowing" [Qur'an 67.14]. God has called our attention to this fact in His book, "And He has subjected the night and the day to your service; and the sun and the moon and the stars, which are compelled to serve by His Command" [Qur'an 77.14]; again, "Say, what think you, if God should cover you with perpetual night, until the day of Resurrection" [Qur'an 16.12]; and again, "Of His mercy, He has made you night and the day, that you may rest in the one, and may seek to obtain provision for yourselves of His abundance, by your industry; in the other" [Qur'an 28.71]; and, "And He obliges whatever is in heaven or on earth to serve you" [Qur'an 18.73]. Further He says, "He likewise compels the sun and the moon, which diligently perform their courses, to serve you; and have subjected the day and night to your service" [Qur'an 45.12]. There may be quoted many other verses on the subject. Had there been any wisdom in their existence by which God has favored us, and there would not have been those blessings for which we are to be grateful to Him.

The second answer to the objection is that we say that the things produced out of it are of two kinds: essences and substances; and movements, hardness, coldness and all other accidents. The essences and substances are not created by any but God. Their causes effect the accidents of those essences, and not the essences themselves. For instance, man and woman are only the agents, while God is the real creator of the child, and the life in it. Such is also the case with agriculture. The earth is prepared and made ready for it, and the seed scattered in it. But it is God who produces the ear of the grain. So there is no creator but God, while created things are but essences. To this refer the words of God. "O men, a parable is propounded unto you, therefore, hearken unto it. Verily the idols which you invoke, besides God, can never create a single fly, although they may all assemble for the purpose; and if the fly snatch anything from them they cannot turn the same from it. Weak is the petitioner and the petitioned" [Qur'an 22.72]. This is where the unbeliever wanted to mislead Abraham, when he said, "I give life and kill" [Qur'an 22.260]. When Abraham saw that he could understand it, he at once turned to the conclusive argument and said, "Verily, God brings the sun from the east; do you bring it from the west."

On the whole, if the matter about the creator and the doer be understood on this wise, there would be no contradiction, either in *Hadith* or in reason. So we say that the word "Creator" does not apply to the created things by any near or far-fetched metaphor, for the meaning of the creator is the inventor of the essences. So God has said, "God created you, and that which you know" [Qur'an 2.260]. It should be known that one who denies the effect of the causes on the results of them, also denies philosophy and all the sciences. For science is the knowledge of the things by their causes, and philosophy is the knowledge of hidden causes. To deny the causes altogether is a thing which is unintelligible to human reason. It is to deny the Creator, not seen by us. For the unseen in this matter must always be understood by a reference to the seen.

So those men can have no knowledge of God, when they admit that for every action there is an actor. It being so, the agreement of the Muslims on the fact that there is no Creator but God cannot be perfect, if we understand by it the denial of the existence of an agent in the visible world. For from the existence of the agent in it, we have brought an argument for the Creator in the invisible world. But when we have once admitted the existence of the Creator in the invisible world, it becomes clear that there is no Creative agent except one by His command and will. It is also evident that we can perform our own deeds, and that one who takes up only one side of the question is wrong, as is the case with the Mutazilites and the Jabarites. Those who adopt the middle course, like the Asharites, for discovering the truth cannot find it. For they make no difference for a man between the trembling and the movement of his hand by intention. There is no meaning in their admitting that both the movements are not by ourselves. Because if they are not by ourselves we have no power to check them, so we are compelled to do them. Hence there is no difference between trembling of hand and voluntary movement, which they could call acquired. So their is no difference between them, except in their names, which never effect the things themselves. This is all clear by itself.

Problem Fourth: Divine Justice and Injustice

The Asharites have expressed a very peculiar opinion, both with regard to reason and religion; about this problem they have explained it in a way in which religion has not, but have adopted quite an opposite method. They say that in this problem the case of the invisible world is quite opposed to the visible. They think that God is just or unjust within the limits of religious actions. So when a man's action is just with regard to religion, he also is just; and whatever religion calls it to be unjust, He is unjust. They say that whatever has not been imposed as a divinely ordained duty upon men, does not come within the four walls of religion. He is neither just or unjust, but all His actions about such things are just. They have laid down that there is nothing in itself which may be called just or unjust. But to say that there is nothing which may in itself be called good or bad is simply intolerable. Justice is known as good, and injustice as bad. So according to them, polytheism is in itself neither injustice nor evil, but with regard to religion, and had religion ordained it, it would have been just and true. Such also would have been the case with any kind of sin. But all this is quite contrary to our *hadith* and reason.

As to *hadith* God has described himself as just, and denied injustice to himself. He says "God has borne witness that there is no God but He; and the angels and those who are endowed with wisdom profess the same, who execute righteousness" [Qur'an 3.16]; and "Your God is not unjust towards His servants;" and again, "Verily, God will not deal unjustly with men in any respect; but men deal unjustly with their own souls" [Qur'an 41.46]. It may be asked, What is your opinion about misleading the people, whether it is just or unjust, for God has mentioned in many a verse of the Qur'an, "That He leads as well as misleads the people?" [Qur'an 10.45]. He says, "God causes to err whom He pleases, and directs whom He pleases" [Qur'an 14.4]; and, "If we had pleased, we had certainly given every soul its direction" [Qur'an 32.11]. We would say that these verses cannot be taken esoterically, for there are many verses which apparently contradict them—the verses in which God denies injustice to himself.

For instance, He says, "He likes not ingratitude (*Kufr*) in His servant" [Qur'an 39.9]. So it is clear that as He does not like ingratitude even from them, He certainly cannot cause them to err. As to the statement of the Asharites that God sometimes does things which He does not like, and orders others which He does not want, God forbid us from holding such a view about him, for it is pure infidelity. That God has not misled the people and has not caused them to err will be clear to you from the following verses: "Wherefore be you orthodox and set your face towards true religion, the institution of God, to which He has created man kindly disposed" [Qur'an 30.29]; and, "when your Lord drew forth their posterity from the lions of the sons of Adam" [Qur'an 7.171]. A *hadith* of the Prophet says "Every child is born according to the divine constitution."

These being contradictions in this problem we should try to reconcile them so that they may agree with reason. The verse, "Verily, God will cause to err whom He pleases, and will direct whom He pleases" [Qur'an 14.4] refers to the prearranged divine will, with which all things have been endowed. They have been created erring, that is, prepared to go astray by their very nature, and led to it by inner and outer causes. The meaning of the verse, "If We had pleased, We have given unto every soul its direction" [Qur'an 35.9], is that He thought of not creating people ready to err, by their nature, or by the outer causes, or by both, though He could have done so. But as the dispositions of men are different the words may mislead the one and direct the other. For these are the verses which speak of misleading the people. For instance, "He will thereby mislead many, and will direct many thereby: but He will not mislead any thereby except the transgressors" [Qur'an 2.24]; and, "We have appointed the vision which We showed you" [Qur'an 17.62], and also the tree cursed in the Qur'an, and the verses about the number of angels of hell. "Thus does God cause to err whom He pleases and He directs whom He pleases" [Qur'an 74.34]. It means that for evil natures, these verses are misleading, as for the sick bodies even good drugs are injurious. . . .

Problem Fifth: The Day of Judgment

Come the Day of Judgment, some believe that the body will be different from our present body. This is only transient, that will be eternal. For this also there are religious arguments. It seems that even Abdullah ben-Abbas held this view. For it is related of him that he said, "There is nought in this world of the hereafter, but names." It seems that this view is better suited to the learned men because its possibility is based upon principles, in which there is no disagreement according to all men: the one being that the soul is immortal, and the second is that the return of the souls into other bodies does not look so impossible as the return of the bodies themselves. It is so because the material of the bodies here is found following and passing from one body to another, *i.e.*, one and the same matter is found in many people and in many different times. The example of bodies cannot be found, for their matter is the same. For instance a man dies and his body becomes dissolved into earth. The earth ultimately becomes dissolved into vegetable, which is eaten by quite a different man from whom another man comes into being. If we suppose them to be different bodies, then our aforesaid view cannot be true.

The truth about this question is this question is that man should follow that which he himself has thought out but anyhow it should not be the view which may deny the fundamental principle altogether. For this would be denying its existence. Such a belief leads to infidelity, on account of a distinct knowledge of this condition being given to man, both by religion and by human reason, which is all based upon the eternal nature of the soul. If it be said whether there is any argument or information in the Law about this eternal nature of the soul, we would say that it is found in the Qur'an itself, where God says, "God takes unto himself the souls of men at the time of their death; and those which die not He also takes in their sleep" [Qur'an 39.43]. In this verse sleep and death have been placed upon the same level, on account of the change in its instrument, and in sleep on account of a change in itself. For had it not been so it would not have come to its former condition after awakening. By this means we know that this cession does not effect its essence, but was only attached to it on account of change in its instrument. So it does not follow that with a cessation of the work of the instrument, the soul also ceases to exist. Death is only a cessation of work, so it is clear that its condition should be like that of sleep. As someone has said that if an old man were to get the eyes of the young, he would begin to see like him.

This is all that we thought of in an exposition of the beliefs of our religion, Islam. What remains for us is to look into things of religion in which interpretation is allowed and not allowed. And if allowed, then who are the people to take advantage of it? With this thing we would finish our discourse.

The things found in the Law can be divided into five kinds. But in the first place there are only two kinds of things: indivisible and the divisible. The second one is divided into four kinds. The first kind which is mentioned in the Qur'an, is quite clear in its meanings. The second is that in which the thing mentioned is not the thing meant but is only an example of it. This is again divided into four kinds. First, the meanings which it mentions are only illustrations such that they can only be known by the far-fetched and compound analogies, which cannot be understood, but after a long time and much labor. None can accept them but perfect and excellent natures; and it cannot be known that the illustration given is not the real thing; except by this far-fetched way. The second is just the opposite of the former: they can be understood easily, and it can be known that the example is just what is meant here. Thirdly, it can be easily known that it is merely an illustration, but what it is the example of is difficult to comprehend. The fourth kind is quite opposite to the former. The thing of which it is an example, is easily understood; while it is difficult to know that it is an example at all.

The interpretation of the first kind is wrong without doubt. The kind in which both the things are far-fetched: its interpretation particularly lies with those who are well-grounded in knowledge; and an exposition of it is not fit for any but the learned. The interpretation of its opposite—that which can be understood on both the sides—is just what is wanted, and an exposition of it is necessary. The case of the third kind is like the case of the above. For in it illustration has not been mentioned because of the difficulty for the common people to understand it: it only incites the people to action. Such is the case with the *hadith* of the prophet, "The black stone is God's action on Earth," etc., etc. That which can be easily known that is an example, but difficult to know of which it is an example, should not be interpreted but for the sake of particular persons and learned men. Those who understand that it is only an illustration, but are not learned enough to know the thing which it illustrates, should be told either that it is allegorical and can be understood by the well-established learned men; or the illustration should be changed in a way which might be near to their understanding. This would be the best plan to dispel doubts from their minds.

The law about this should be that which has been laid down by Abu Hamid (Al Ghazzali) in his book, *Al Tafriga bainal Islam wal Zindiga*. It should be understood that one thing has five existences which he calls by the name of essential (*Zati*); sensual (*Hissi*); rational (*Agli*); imaginative (*Khayali*); and doubtful (*Shilbhi*). So at the time of doubt it should be considered which of these five kinds would better satisfy the man who has doubts. If it be that which he has called essential than an illustration would best satisfy their minds. In it is also included the following *hadith* of the Prophet, "Whatever the earlier prophets saw I have seen it from my place here, even heaven and hell;" "Between my cistern of water and the pulpit there is a garden of paradise;" and "The earth will eat up the whole of a man except the extremity of the tail." All these, it can easily be known are but illustrations, but what is the thing which they illustrate it is difficult to comprehend. So it is necessary in this case to give an instance to the people which they may easily understand. This kind of illustration, when used on such an occasion, is allowable; but when used irrelevantly it is wrong. Abu Hamid has not decided about the occasion when both the sides of the question—the illustration and the illustrated—be both far-fetched and difficult to understand. In this case there would apparently be a doubt, but a doubt without any foundation. What should be done is to prove that the doubt has no basis, but no interpretation should be made, as we have shown in many places in our present book against the Mutakallimun, Asharites and the Mutazilites.

The fourth kind of occasion is quite opposite to the former. In this it is very difficult to understand that it is an example, but when once understood, you can easily comprehend the thing illustrated. In the interpretation of this also, there is a consideration: about those people who know that if it is an example, it illustrates such and such a thing; but they doubt whether it is an illustration at all. If they are not learned people, the best thing to do with them is not to make any interpretation, but only to prove the fallacy of the views which they hold about its being an illustration at all. It is also possible that an interpretation may make them still distant from the truths on account of the nature of the illustration and the illustrated. For these two kinds of occasions, if an interpretation is given, they give rise to strange beliefs, far from the law which when disclosed are denied by the common people. Such has been the case with the Sufis, and those learned men who have followed them. When this work of interpretation was done by people who could not distinguish between these occasions, and made no distinction between the people for whom the interpretation is to be made, there arose differences of opinion, at last forming into sects, which ended in accusing one another with unbelief. All this is pure ignorance of the purpose of the Law.

From what we have already said the amount of mischief done by interpretation must have become clear to you. We always try to acquire our purpose by knowing what should be interpreted, and what not; and when interpreted, how it should be done; and whether all the difficult portions of the Law and *Hadith* are to be explained or not. These are all included in the four kinds which have already been enumerated.

The purpose of our writing this book is now completed. We took it up because we thought that it was the most important of all purposes—connected with God and the Law.

Thomas Aquinas

(1225–1274)

After 1278 the official scholar of the Dominican Order, canonized by Pope John XXII in 1323, Thomas Aquinas was certainly one of the greatest and one of the most influential intellects of the Middle Ages. As a young Dominican Friar he studied under Albertus Magnus at Paris and Rome. Thereafter most of his life was spent at Paris and in Italy pursuing scholarly activities. His greatest single contribution to medieval thought lay in his assimilation of Aristotelian ideas into the Christian context. This can be seen clearly in the following passage, taken from his *Summa Contra Gentiles* (written during the period 1259 and 1264).[1] Horrified by the excesses of the radical Aristotelians such as Siger of Brabant on the left, and dissatisfied with conservatives such as Bonaventure on the right, he attempts to find a solution to the reason-revelation controversy that will do justice to both human reason and divine revelation at the same time.

From *Summa Contra Gentiles*

Book I: Of God as He Is in Himself

Chapter I—The Function of the Wise Man

My mouth shall discuss truth, and my lips shall detest the ungodly. (proverbs 8. 7)

According to established popular usage, which the Philosopher considers should be our guide in the naming of things, they are called 'wise' who put things in their right order and control them well. Now, in all things that are to be controlled and put in order to an end, the measure of control and order must be taken from the end in view; and the proper end of everything is something good. Hence we see in the arts that art A governs and, as it were, lords it over art B, when the proper end of art B belongs to A. Thus the art of medicine lords it over the art of the apothecary, because health, the object of medicine, is the end of all drugs that the apothecary's art compounds. These arts that lord it over others are called 'master-building,' or 'masterful arts'; and the 'master-builders' who practise them arrogate to themselves the name of 'wise men.' But because these persons deal with the ends in view of certain particular things, without attaining to the general end of all things, they are called 'wise in this or that particular thing,' as it is said, *As a wise architect I have laid the foundation* (I Cor. 3: 10); while the name of 'wise' without qualification is reserved for him alone who deals with the last end of the universe, which is also the first beginning of the order of the universe. Hence, according to the Philosopher, it is proper to the wise man to consider the highest causes.

---

[1] Book I Chs. 1–8 and Book II Chs. 1 and 4 have been reproduced from Joseph Rickaby, S.J., trans., Saint Thomas Aquinas, *Summa Contra Gentiles*, (London: Burns and Oates Ltd., 1908), pp. 1–8, 79–80. Book II Chs. 2 and 3 have been reproduced from the English Dominican Fathers, trans., Saint Thomas Aquinas, *Summa Contra Gentiles*, (London: Burns and Oates Ltd., 1923). The biblical references in Book II Chs. 2 and 3 have been deleted.

Now the last end of everything is that which is intended by the prime author or mover thereof. The prime author and mover of the universe is intelligence, as will be shown later (B. II, Chaps. XXIII, XXIV). Therefore the last end of the universe must be the good of the intelligence, and that is truth. Truth then must be the final end of the whole universe; and about the consideration of that end wisdom must primarily be concerned. And therefore the Divine Wisdom, clothed in flesh, testifies that he came into the world for the manifestation of truth: *For this was I born, and unto this I came into the world, to give testimony to the truth* (John 28:37). The Philosopher also rules that the first philosophy is the science of truth, not of any and every truth, but of that truth which is the origin of all truth, and appertains to the first principle of the being of all things; hence its truth is the principle of all truth, for things are in truth as they are in being.

It is one and the same function to embrace either of two contraries and to repel the other. Hence, as it is the function of the wise man to discuss truth, particularly of the first beginning, so it is his also to impugn the contrary error. Suitably therefore is the double function of the wise man displayed in the words above quoted from the Sapiential Book, namely, to study, and upon study to speak out the truth of God, which of all other is most properly called truth, and this is referred to in the words, *My mouth shall discuss truth*, and to impugn error contrary to truth, as referred to in the words, *And my lips shall detest the ungodly.*

Chapter II—Of the Author's Purpose

Of all human pursuits, the pursuit of wisdom is the more perfect, the more sublime, the more useful, and the more agreeable. The more perfect, because in so far as a man gives himself up to the pursuit of wisdom, to that extent he enjoys already some portion of true happiness. *Blessed is the man that shall dwell in wisdom* (Eccles. 14:22). The more sublime, because thereby man comes closest to the likeness of God, *who hath made all things in wisdom* (Ps. 103:24). The more useful, because by this same wisdom we arrive at the realm of immortality. *The desire of wisdom shall lead to an everlasting kingdom* (Wisd. 6:21). The more agreeable, *because her conversation hath no bitterness, nor her company any weariness, but gladness and joy* (Wisd. 8:16).

But on two accounts it is difficult to proceed against each particular error: first, because the sacrilegious utterances of our various erring opponents are not so well known to us as to enable us to find reasons, drawn from their own words, for the confutation of their errors: for such was the method of the ancient doctors in confuting the errors of the Gentiles, whose tenets they were readily able to know, having either been Gentiles themselves, or at least having lived among Gentiles and been instructed in their doctrines. Secondly, because some of them, as Mohammedans and Pagans, do not agree with us in recognising the authority of any scripture, available for their conviction, as we can argue against the Jews from the Old Testament, and against heretics from the New. But these receive neither: hence it is necessary to have recourse to natural reason, which all are obliged to assent to. But in the things of God natural reason is often at a loss.

Chapter III—That the Truths Which We Confess Concerning God Fall under Two Modes or Categories

Because not every truth admits of the same mode of manifestation, and "a well-educated man will expect exactness in every class of subject, according as the nature of the thing admits," as is very well remarked by the Philosopher (*Eth. Nicom. I, 1094b*), we must first show what mode of proof is possible for the truth that we have now before us. The truths that we confess concerning God fall under two modes. Some things true of God are beyond all the competence of human reason, as that

God is Three and One. Other things there are to which even human reason can attain, as the existence and unity of God, which philosophers have proved by a demonstration under the guidance of the light of natural reason. That there are points of absolute intelligibility in God altogether beyond the compass of human reason, most manifestly appears. For since the leading principle of all knowledge of any given subject-matter is an understanding of the thing's innermost being, or substance—according to the doctrine of the Philosopher, that the essence is the principle of demonstration -it follows that the mode of our knowledge of the substance must be the mode of knowledge of whatever we know about the substance. Hence if the human understanding comprehends the substance of anything, as of a stone or triangle, none of the points of intelligibility about that thing will exceed the capacity of human reason. But this is not our case with regard to God. The human understanding cannot go so far of its natural power as to grasp. His substance, since under the conditions of the present life the knowledge of our understanding commences with sense; and therefore objects beyond sense cannot be grasped by human understanding except so far as knowledge is gathered of them through the senses. But things of sense cannot lead our understanding to read in them the essence of the Divine Substance, inasmuch as they are effects inadequate to the power that caused them. Nevertheless our understanding is thereby led to some knowledge of God, namely, of His existence and of other attributes that must necessarily be attributed to the First Cause. There are, therefore, some points of intelligibility in God, accessible to human reason, and other points that altogether transcend the power of human reason.

The same thing may be understood from consideration of degrees of intelligibility. Of two minds, one of which has a keener insight into truth than the other, the higher mind understands much that the other cannot grasp at all, as is clear in the 'plain man' (*in rustico*), who can in no way grasp the subtle theories of philosophy. Now the intellect of an angel excels that of a man more than the intellect of the ablest philosopher excels that of the plainest of plain men (*rudissimi idiotoe*). The angel has a higher standpoint in creation than man as a basis of his knowledge of God, inasmuch as the substance of the angel, whereby he is led to know God by a process of natural knowledge, is nobler and more excellent than the things of sense, and even than the soul itself, whereby the human mind rises to the knowledge of God. But the Divine Mind exceeds the angelic much more than the angelic the human. For the Divine Mind of its own comprehensiveness covers the whole extent of its substance, and therefore perfectly understands its own essence, and knows all that is knowable about itself; but an angel of his natural knowledge does not know the essence of God, because the angel's own substance, whereby it is led to a knowledge of God, is in effect inadequate to the power of the cause that created it. Hence not all things that God understands in Himself can be grasped by the natural knowledge of an angel; nor is human reason competent to take in all that an angel understands of his own natural ability. As therefore it would be the height of madness in a 'plain man' to declare a philosopher's propositions false, because he could not understand them, so and much more would a man show exceeding folly if he suspected of falsehood a divine revelation given by the ministry of angels, on the mare ground that it was beyond the investigation of reason.

The same thing manifestly appears from the incapacity which we daily experience in the observation of nature. We are ignorant of very many properties of the things of sense; and of the properties that our senses do apprehend, in most cases we cannot perfectly discover the reason. Much more is it beyond the competence of human reason to investigate all the points of intelligibility in that supreme excellent and transcendent substance of God. Consonant with this is the saying of the

Philosopher, that "as the eyes of bats are to the light of the sun, so is the intelligence of our soul to the thinks most manifest by nature" (Aristotle, *Metaphysics* I, min. 1).

To this truth Holy Scripture also bears testimony. For it is said: *Perchance thou wilt seize upon the traces of God, and fully discover the Almighty* (Job 11:7). And, *Lo, God is great, and surpassing our knowledge* (Job 36:26). And, *We know in part* (I Cor. 13:9). Not everything, therefore, that is said of God, even though it be beyond the power of reason to investigate, is at once to be rejected as false.

Chapter IV—*That It Is an Advantage for the Truths of God Known by Natural Reason to Be Proposed to Men to Be Believed on Faith*

If a truth of this nature were left to the sole enquiry of reason, three disadvantages would follow. One is that the knowledge of God would be confined to few. The discovery of truth is the fruit of studious enquiry. From this very many are hindered. Some are hindered by a constitutional unfitness, their natures being ill-disposed to the acquisition of knowledge. They could never arrive by study to the highest grade of human knowledge, which consists in the knowledge of God. Others are hindered by the needs of business and the ties of the management of property. There must be in human society some men devoted to temporal affairs. These could not possibly spend time enough in the learned lessons of speculative enquiry to arrive at the highest point of human enquiry, the knowledge of God. Some again are hindered by sloth. The knowledge of the truths that reason can investigate concerning God presupposes much previous knowledge. Indeed almost the entire study of philosophy is directed to the knowledge of God. Hence, of all parts of philosophy, that part stands over to be learnt last, which consists of metaphysics dealing with points of Divinity. Thus, only with great labour of study is it possible to arrive at the searching out of the aforesaid truth; and this labour few are willing to undergo for sheer love of knowledge.

Another disadvantage is that such as did arrive at the knowledge or discovery of the aforesaid truth would take a long time over it, on account of the profundity of such truth, and the many prerequisites to the study, and also because in youth and early manhood, the soul, tossed to and fro on the waves of passion, is not fit for the study of such high truth: only in settled age does the soul become prudent and scientific, as the Philosopher says. Thus, if the only way open to the knowledge of God were the way of reason, the human race would dwell long in thick darkness of ignorance: as the knowledge of God, the best instrument for making men perfect and good, would accrue only to a few, and to those few after a considerable lapse of time.

A third disadvantage is that, owing to the infirmity of our judgement and the perturbing force of imagination, there is some admixture of error in most of the investigations of human reason. This would be a reason to many for continuing to doubt even of the most accurate demonstrations, not perceiving the force of the demonstration, and seeing the divers judgements of divers persons who have the name of being wise men. Besides, in the midst of much demonstrated truth there is sometimes an element of error, not demonstrated but asserted on the strength of some plausible and sophistic reasoning that is taken for a demonstration. And therefore it was necessary for the real truth concerning divine things to be presented to men with fixed certainty by way of faith. Wholesome therefore is the arrangement of divine clemency, whereby things even that reason can investigate are commanded to be held on faith, so that all might easily be partakers of the knowledge of God, and that without doubt and error.

Hence it is said: Now ye walk not as the Gentiles walk in the vanity of their own notions, having the understanding darkened (Eph. 4:17,18); and, I will make all thy sons taught of the Lord (Isa. 54:15).

Chapter V—That It Is an Advantage for Things that Cannot Be Searched Out by Reason to Be Proposed as Tenets of Faith

Some may possibly think that points which reason is unable to investigate ought not to be proposed to man to believe, since Divine Wisdom provides for every being according to the measure of its nature; and therefore we must show the necessity of things even that transcend reason being proposed by God to man for his belief.

1. One proof is this. No one strives with any earnestness of desire after anything, unless it be known to him beforehand. Since, then, as will be traced out in the following pages (B. Ill, Chap. CXL VIII), Divine Providence directs men to a higher good than human frailty can experience in the present life, the mental faculties ought to be evoked and led onward to something higher than our reason can attain at present, learning thereby to desire something and earnestly to tend to something that transcends the entire state of the present life. And such is the special function of the Christian religion, which stands alone in its promise of spiritual and eternal goods, whereas the Old Law, carrying temporal promises, proposed few tenets that transcended the enquiry of human reason.

2. Also another advantage is thence derived, to wit, the repression of presumption, which is the mother of error. For there are some so presumptuous of their own genius as to think that they can measure with their understanding the whole nature of the Godhead, thinking all that to be true which seems true to them, and that to be false which does not seem true to them. In order then that the human mind might be delivered from this presumption, and attain to a modest style of enquiry after truth, it was necessary for certain things to be proposed to man from God that altogether exceeded his understanding.

3. There is also another evident advantage in this, that any knowledge, however imperfect, of the noblest objects confers a very high perfection on the soul. And therefore, though human reason cannot fully grasp truths above reason, nevertheless it is much perfected by holding such truths after some fashion at least by faith. And therefore it is said: *Many things beyond the understanding of man are shown to thee* (Eccles. 3:23). And, *The things that are of God, none knoweth but the Spirit of God: but to us God hath revealed them through his Spirit* (I Cor. 2:10–11).

Chapter VI—That There Is No Lightmindedness in Assenting to Truths of Faith, Although They Are above Reason

The Divine Wisdom, that knows all things most fully, has deigned to reveal these her secrets to men, and in proof of them has displayed works beyond the competence of all natural powers, in the wonderful cure of diseases, in the raising of the dead, and what is more wonderful still, in such inspiration of human minds as that simple and ignorant persons, filled with the gift of the Holy Ghost, have gained in an instant the height of wisdom and eloquence. By force of the aforesaid proof, without violence of arms, without promise of pleasures, and, most wonderful thing of all, in the midst of the violence of persecutors, a countless multitude, not only of the uneducated but of the wisest men, flocked to the Christian faith, wherein doctrines are preached that transcend all human understanding, pleasures of sense are restrained, and a contempt is taught of all worldly possessions. That mortal minds should assent to such teaching is the greatest of miracles, and a manifest work of divine inspiration leading men to despise the visible and desire only invisible goods. Nor did this happen suddenly nor by chance, but by a divine disposition, as is manifest from the fact that God foretold by many oracles of His prophets that He intended to do this. The books of those prophets are still venerated amongst us, as bearing testimony to our faith. This argument is touched upon in the text: *Which* [salvation] *having begun to be uttered by the Lord, was confirmed by them that heard him even unto us, God joining in the testimony by signs and portents and various distributions of the Holy Spirit* (Heb. 2:3, 4). This so wonderful conversion of the world to the Christian faith is so certain a sign of past miracles, that they need no further reiteration, since they appear evidently in their effects. It would be more wonderful than all other miracles, if without miraculous signs the world had been induced by simple and low-born men to believe truths so arduous, to do works so difficult, to hope for reward so high. And yet even in our times God ceases not through His saints to work miracles for the confirmation of the faith.

Chapter VII—That the Truth of Reason Is Not Contrary to the Truth of Christian Faith

The natural dictates of reason must certainly be quite true: it is impossible to think of their being otherwise. Nor again is it permissible to believe that the tenets of faith are false, being so evidently confirmed by God. Since therefore falsehood alone is contrary to truth, it is impossible for the truth of faith to be contrary to principles known by natural reason.

1. Whatever is put into the disciple's mind by the teacher is contained in the knowledge of the teacher, unless the teacher is teaching dishonestly, which would be a wicked thing to say of God. But the knowledge of principles naturally known is put into us by God, seeing that God Himself is the author of our nature. Therefore these principles also are contained in the Divine Wisdom. Whatever therefore is contrary to these principles is contrary to Divine Wisdom, and cannot be of God.

2. Contrary reasons fetter our intellect fast, so that it cannot proceed to the knowledge of the truth. If therefore contrary informations were sent us by God, our intellect would be thereby hindered from knowledge of the truth: but such hindrance cannot be of God.

3. What is natural cannot be changed while nature remains. But contrary opinions cannot be in the same mind at the same time: therefore no opinion or belief is sent to man from God contrary to natural knowledge.

And therefore the Apostle says: *The word is near in thy heart and in thy mouth, that is, the word of faith which we preach* (Rom. 10:8). But because it surpasses reason it is counted by some as contrary to reason, which cannot be. To the *same* effect is the authority of Augustine (*Gen. ad litt. ii, 18*): "What truth reveals can nowise be contrary to the holy books either of the Old or of the New Testament." Hence the conclusion is evident, that any arguments alleged against the teachings of faith do not proceed logically from first principles of nature, principles of themselves known. and so do not amount to a demonstration; but are either probable reasons or sophistical; hence room is left for refuting them.

Chapter VIII—Of the Relation of Human Reason to the First Truth of Faith

The things of sense, from whence human reason takes its beginning of knowledge, retain in themselves some trace of imitation of God, inasmuch as they *are*, and are *good*; yet so imperfect, is this trace that it proves wholly insufficient to declare the substance of God Himself. Since every agent acts to the producing of its own likeness, effects in their several ways bear some likeness to their causes: nevertheless the effect does not always attain to the perfect likeness of the agent that produces it. In regard then to knowledge of the truth of faith, which can only be thoroughly known to those who behold the substance of God, human reason stands so conditioned as to be able to argue some true likenesses to it: which likenesses however are not sufficient for any sort of demonstrative or intuitive comprehension of the aforesaid truth. Still it is useful for the human mind to exercise itself in such reasonings, however feeble, provided there be no presumptuous hope of perfect comprehension or demonstration.

With this view the authority of Hilary agrees, who says (*De Trinitate*, ii, 10), speaking of such truth: *In this belief start, run, persist; and though I know that you will not reach the goal, still I shall congratulate you as I see you making progress. But intrude not into that sanctuary, and plunge not into the mystery of infinite truth; entertain no presumptuous hope of comprehending the height of intelligence, but understand that it is incomprehensible.*

Book II: God the Origin of Creatures

Chapter I—Connexion of What Follows with What Has Gone Before

There can be no perfect knowledge of anything, unless its activity be known: for from the mode of activity proper to a thing, and the species to which it belongs, the measure and quality of its power is estimated; and the power shows the nature of the thing, for each thing is naturally active according to the nature with which it is actually endowed. But there is a twofold activity: one immanent in the agent, and a perfection of his, as feeling, understanding and willing; the other passing out to an exterior thing, and a perfection of the thing made and Constituted thereby, as warming, cutting and building. Both of these acts are proper to God: the first, inasmuch as He understands, wills, rejoices and loves; the second, inasmuch as He produces and brings things into being, conserves and governs them. Of the first act of God we have spoken in the previous book, treating of the divine knowledge and will. It remains now to treat of the second action, whereby things are produced and governed by God.

Chapter II—That the Consideration of Creatures Is Useful for Building Up Our Faith

This meditation on the divine works is indeed necessary in order to build up man's faith in God.

First, because through meditating on His works we are able somewhat to admire and consider the divine wisdom. For things made by art are indications of the art itself, since they are made in likeness to the art. Now God brought things into being by His wisdom: for which reason it is said in the Psalm: *Thou hast made all things in wisdom.* Hence we are able to gather the wisdom of God from the consideration of His works, since by a kind of communication of His likeness it is spread abroad in the things He has made. For it is said; *He poured her out,* namely wisdom, *upon all His works*: wherefore the psalmist after saying: *Thy knowledge is become wonderful to me: it is high, and I can not reach to it,* and after referring to the aid of the divine enlightening, when he says: *Night shall be my light,* etc., confesses himself to have been helped to know the divine wisdom by the consideration of the divine works, saying: *Wonderful are Thy works, and my soul knoweth right well.*

Secondly, this consideration leads us to admire the sublime power of God, and consequently begets in men's hearts a reverence for God. For we *must* needs conclude that the, power of the maker transcends the things made. Wherefore it is said: *If they*, the philosophers, to wit, *admired their power and their effects*, namely of the heavens, stars, and elements of the world, *let them understand . . . that He that made them is mightier than they*. Also it is written: *The invisible things of God . . . are clearly seen, being understood by the things that are made: His eternal power also and divinity*. And this admiration makes us fear and reverence God. Hence it is said: *Great is Thy name in might. Who shall not fear Thee, O King of nations?*

Thirdly, this consideration inflames the souls of men to the love of the divine goodness. For whatever goodness and perfection is generally apportioned among various creatures is all united together in Him universally, as in the source of all goodness, as we proved in the First Book. Wherefore if the goodness, beauty, and sweetness of creatures are so alluring to the minds of men, the fountainhead of the goodness of God Himself, in comparison with the rivulets of goodness which we find in creatures, will draw the entranced minds of men wholly to itself. Hence it is said in the psalm, *Thou has given me, O Lord, a delight in Thy doings; and in the works of Thy hands I shall rejoice*: and elsewhere it is said of the children of men: *They shall be inebriated with the plenty of Thy house*, that is of all creatures, *and Thou shalt make them drink of the torrent of Thy pleasure. For with Thee is the fountain of life*. Again it is said against certain men: *By these good things that are seen*, namely creatures that are good by participation, *they could not understand Him that is*, good to wit, nay more, that is goodness itself, as we have shown in the First Book.

Fourthly, this consideration bestows on man a certain likeness to the divine perfection. For it was shown in the First Book that God, by knowing Himself, beholds all other things in Himself. Since then the Christian faith teaches man chiefly about Cod, and makes him to know creatures by the light of divine revelation, there results in man a certain likeness to the divine wisdom. Hence it is said: *But we all beholding the glory of the Lord with open face, are transformed into the same image*.

Accordingly it is evident that the consideration of creatures helps to build up the Christian faith. Wherefore it is said: *I will . . . remember the works of the Lord, and I will declare the things I have seen: by the words of the Lord are His works*.

Chapter III—That the Knowledge of the Nature of Creatures Avails for Refuting Errors against God

The consideration of creatures is likewise necessary not only for the building up of faith, but also for the destruction of errors. For errors about creatures sometimes lead one astray from the truth of faith, in so far as they disagree with true knowledge of God. This happens in several ways.

First, because through ignorance of the nature of creatures men are sometimes so far misled as to deem that which can but derive its being from something else to be the first cause and God, for they think that nothing exists besides visible creatures. Such were those who thought that any kind of body was God: of whom it is said: *Who... have imagined either the fire, or the wind, or the swift air, or the circle of the stars, or the great water, or the sun and moon to be the gods*.

Secondly, because they ascribe to certain creatures that which belongs to God alone. This also results from error about creatures: for one does not ascribe to a thing that which is incompatible with its nature, unless one is ignorant of its nature: for instance if we were to ascribe three feet to a man. Now that which belongs to God alone is incompatible with the nature of a creature: even as that which belongs to man alone is incompatible with another thing's nature. Hence the forgoing error arises from ignorance of the creature's nature. Against this error it is said: *They gave the incommunicable name to stones and wood.* Into this error fell those who ascribe the creation of things, or the knowledge of the future, or the working of miracles to causes other than God.

Thirdly, because something is withdrawn from the divine power in its working on creatures, through ignorance of the creature's nature. This is evidenced in those who ascribe to things a twofold principle, and in those who aver that things proceed from God, not by the divine will, but by natural necessity, and in those who withdraw either all or some things from divine providence, or who deny that it can work outside the ordinary course of things. For all these are derogatory to the divine power. Against these it is said: *Who... looked upon the Almighty as if He could do nothing, and Thou showest Thy power, when men will not believe Thee to be absolute in power.*

Fourthly, Man, who is led by faith to God as his last end, through ignoring the natures of things, and consequently the order of his place in the universe, thinks himself to be beneath certain creatures above whom he is placed: as evidenced in those who subject man's will to the stars and against these it is said: *Be not afraid of the signs of heaven, which the heathens fear*; also in those who deem the angels to be the creators of souls, the human souls to be mortal; and in those who hold any like opinions derogatory to the dignity of man.

Accordingly it is clear that the opinion is false of those who asserted that it mattered not to the truth of faith what opinions one holds about creatures, so long as one has a right opinion about God, as Augustine relates in his book *De Origine Animae*: since error concerning creatures by subjecting the human mind to causes other than God amounts to a false opinion about God, and misleads the minds of men from God, to Whom faith strives to lead them.

Wherefore Scripture threatens punishment to those who err about creatures, as to unbelievers, in the words of the psalm: *Because they have not understood the works of the Lord and the operations of His hands, Thou shalt destroy them, and shalt not build them up; and: These things they thought and were deceived, and further on: They esteemed not the honour of holy souls.*

Chapter IV—That the Philosopher and the Theologian View Creatures from Different Standpoints

Human philosophy considers creatures as they are in themselves: hence we find different divisions of philosophy according to the different classes of things. But Christian faith considers them, not in themselves, but inasmuch as they represent the majesty of God, and in one way or another are directed to God, as it is said: *Of the glory of the Lord his work is full: hath not the Lord made his saints to tell of his wonders?* (Eccles. 42: 16, 17). Therefore the philosopher and the faithful Christian (*fidelis*) consider different points about creatures: the philosopher considers what attaches to them in their proper nature: the faithful Christian considers about creatures only what attaches to them in their relation to God, as that they are created by God, subject to God, and the like. Hence it is not to be put down as an imperfection in the doctrine of faith, if it passes unnoticed many properties of things, as the configuration of the heavens, or the laws of motion. And again such points as are considered by philosopher and faithful Christian alike, are treated on different principles: for the philosopher takes his stand on the proper and immediate causes of things; but the faithful Christian argues from the First Cause, showing that so the matter is divinely revealed, or that this makes for the glory of God, or that God's power is infinite. Hence this speculation of the faithful Christian ought to be called the highest wisdom, as always regarding the highest cause, according to the text: *This is your wisdom and understanding before the nations* (Deut. 4:6). And therefore human philosophy is subordinate to this higher wisdom; and in sign of this subordination divine wisdom sometimes draws conclusions from premises of human philosophy. Further, the two systems do not observe the same order of procedure. In the system of philosophy, which considers creatures in themselves and from them leads on to the knowledge of God, the first study is of creatures and the last of God; but in the system of faith, which studies creatures only in their relation to God, the study first of God and afterwards of creatures; and this is a more perfect view, and more like to the knowledge of God, who, knowing Himself, thence discerns other beings. Following this latter order, after what has been said in the first book about God in Himself, it remains for us to treat of the beings that come from God.

From *Summa Theologica*

First Article: Whether, Besides the Philosophical Sciences, Any Further Doctrine Is Required?

We Proceed Thus to the First Article

Objection 1. It seems that, besides the philosophical sciences, we have no need of any further knowledge. For man should not seek to know what is above reason: *Seek not the things that are too high for thee.* But whatever is not above reason is sufficiently considered in the philosophical sciences. Therefore any other knowledge besides the philosophical sciences is superfluous.

Obj. 2. Further, knowledge can be concerned only with being, for nothing can be known, save the true, which is convertible with being. But everything, that is, is considered in the philosophical sciences—even God Himself; so that there is a part of philosophy called theology, or the divine science, as is clear from Aristotle. Therefore, besides the philosophical sciences, there is no need of any further knowledge.

On the contrary, It is written: *All Scripture inspired of God is profitable to teach, to reprove, to correct, to instruct in justice.* Now Scripture, inspired of God, is not a part of the philosophical sciences discovered by human reason. Therefore it is useful that besides the philosophical sciences there should be another science—*i.e.*, inspired of God.

I answer that, It was necessary for man's salvation that there should be a knowledge revealed by God, besides the philosophical sciences investigated by human reason. First, because man is directed to God as to an end that surpassed the grasp of his reason: *The eye hath not seen, O God, besides Thee, what things Thou hast prepared for them, that wait for Thee.* But the end must first be known by men who are to direct their thoughts and actions to the end. Hence it was necessary for the salvation of man that certain truths which exceed human reason should be made known to him by divine revelation. Even as regards those truths about God which human reason can investigate, it was necessary that man be taught by a divine revelation. For the truth about God, such as reason can know it, would only be known by a few, and that after a long time, and with the admixture of many errors; whereas man's whole salvation, which is in God, depends upon the knowledge of this truth. Therefore, in order that the salvation of men might be brought about more fitly and more surely, it was necessary that they be taught divine truths by divine revelation. It was therefore necessary that, besides the philosophical sciences investigated by reason, there should be a sacred science by way of revelation.

Reply Obj. 1. Although those things which are beyond man's knowledge may not be sought for by man through his reason, nevertheless, what is revealed by God must be accepted through faith. Hence the sacred text continues, *For many things are shown to thee above the understanding of man.* And in such things sacred science consists.

Reply Obj. 2. Sciences are diversified according to the diverse nature of their knowable objects. For the astronomer and the physicist both prove the same conclusion—that the earth, for instance, is round; the astronomer by means of mathematics (*i.e.*, abstracting from matter), but the physicist by means of matter itself. Hence there is no reason why those things which are treated by the philosophical sciences, so far as they can be known by the light of natural reason, may not also be treated by another science so far as they are known by the light of the divine revelation. Hence the theology included in sacred doctrine differs in genus from that theology which is part of philosophy.

· · · · · · · · · · · ·

Question II: The Existence of God

Third Article: Whether God Exists?
We Proceed Thus to the Third Article

Objection 1. It seems that God does not exist; because if one of two contraries be infinite, the other would be altogether destroyed. But the Name *God* means that He is infinite goodness. If, therefore, God existed, there would be no evil discoverable; but there is evil in the world. Therefore God does not exist.

Obj. 2. Further, it is superfluous to suppose that what can be accounted for by a few principles has been produced by many. But it seems that everything we see in the world can be accounted for by other principles, supposing God did not exist. For all natural things can be reduced to one principle which is nature; and all voluntary things can be reduced to one principle, which is human reason, or will. Therefore there is no need to suppose God's existence.

On the contrary, It is said in the person of God: *I am Who am.*
I answer that, The existence of God can be proved in five ways.

The first and more manifest way is the argument from motion. It is certain, and evident to our senses, that in the world some things are in motion. Now whatever is moved is moved by another, for nothing can be moved except it is in potentiality to that towards which it is moved; whereas a thing moves inasmuch as it is an act. For motion is nothing else than the reduction of something from potentiality to actuality. But nothing can be reduced from potentiality to actuality, except by something in a state of actuality. Thus that which is actually hot, as fire, makes wood, which is potentially hot, to be actually hot, and thereby moves and changes it. Now it is not possible that the same thing should be at once in actuality and potentiality in the same respect, but only in different respects. For what is actually hot cannot simultaneously be potentially hot; but it is simultaneously potentially cold. It is therefore impossible that in the same respect and in the same way a thing should be both mover and moved, i.e., that it should move itself. Therefore, whatever is moved must be moved by another. If that by which it is moved be itself moved, then this also must needs be moved by another, and that by another again. But this cannot go on to infinity, because then there would be no first mover, and, consequently, no other mover, seeing that subsequent movers move only inasmuch as they are moved by the first mover; as the staff moves only because it is moved by the hand. Therefore it is necessary to arrive at a first mover moved by no other; and this everyone understands to be God.

The second way is from the nature of efficient cause. In the world of sensible things we find there is an order of efficient causes. There is no case known (neither is it, indeed, possible) in which a thing is found to be the efficient cause of itself; for so it would be prior to itself, which is impossible. Now in efficient causes it is not possible to go on to infinity, because in all efficient causes following in order, the first is the cause of the intermediate cause, and the intermediate is the cause of the ultimate cause, whether the intermediate cause be several, or one only. Now to take away the cause is to take away the effect. Therefore, if there be no first cause among efficient causes, there will be no ultimate, nor any intermediate, cause. But if in efficient causes it is possible to go on to infinity, there will be no first efficient cause, neither will there be an ultimate effect, nor any intermediate efficient causes; all of which is plainly false. Therefore it is necessary to admit a first efficient cause, to which everyone gives the name of God.

The third way is taken from possibility and necessity, and runs thus. We find in nature things that are possible to be and not to be, since they are found to be generated, and to be corrupted, and consequently, it is possible for them to be and not to be. But it is impossible for these always to exist, for that which can not-be at some time is not. Therefore, it everything can not-be, then at one time there was nothing in existence. Now if this were true, even now there would be nothing in existence, because that which does not exist begins to exist only through something already existing. Therefore, if at one time nothing was in existence, it would have been impossible for anything to have begun to exist; and thus even now nothing would be in existence—which is absurd. Therefore, not all beings are merely possible, but there must exist something the existence of which is necessary. But every necessary thing either has its necessity caused by another, or not. Now it is impossible to go on to infinity in necessary things which have their necessity caused by another, as has been already proved in regard to efficient causes. Therefore we cannot but admit the existence of some being having of itself its own necessity, and not receiving it from another, but rather causing in others their necessity. This all men speak of as God.

The fourth way is taken from the gradation to be found in things. Among beings there are some more and some less good, true, noble, and the like. But *more* and *less* are predicted of different things according as they resemble in their different ways something which is the maximum, as a thing is said to be hotter according as it more nearly resembles that which is hottest; so that there is something which is truest, something best, something noblest, and consequently, something which is most being, for those things that are greatest in truth are greatest in being, as it is written in *Metaph.* ii. Now the maximum in any genus is the cause of all in that genus, as fire, which is the maximum of heat, is the cause of all hot things, as is said in the same book. Therefore there must also be something which is to all beings the cause of their being, goodness, and every other perfection; and this we call God.

The fifth way is taken from the governance of the world. We see that things which lack knowledge, such as natural bodies, act for an end, and this is evident from their acting always, or nearly always, in the same way, so as to obtain the best result. Hence it is plain that they achieve their end, not fortuitously, but designedly. Now whatever lacks knowledge cannot move towards an end, unless it be directed by some being endowed with knowledge and intelligence; as the arrow is directed by the archer. Therefore some intelligent being exists by whom all natural things are directed to their end; and this being we call God.

Reply Obj. I. As Augustine says: *Since God is the highest good. He would not allow any evil to exist in His works, unless His omnipotence and goodness were such as to bring good even out of evil.* This is part of the infinite goodness of God, that He should allow evil to exist, and out of it produce good.

Reply Obj. 2. Since nature works for a determinate end under the direction of a higher agent, whatever is done by nature must be traced back to God as to its first cause. So likewise whatever is done voluntarily must be traced back to some higher cause other than human reason and will, since these can change and fail; for all things that are changeable and capable of defect must be traced back to an immovable and self-necessary first principle, as has been shown.

On the Governance of Rulers

Chapter II: It Is More Expedient that a Multitude of Men Living Together Be Ruled by One Man Rather than by Many

Having set forth . . . preliminary points we must now inquire what is better for a province or a city; whether to be ruled by one man or by many. Now this may be considered from the very purpose of government. For the aim of any ruler should be directed towards securing the welfare of whatever he undertakes to rule. The duty of the pilot, for instance, is to preserve his ship amidst the perils of the sea and to bring it unharmed to the port of safety. Now, the welfare and safety of a multitude formed into a society is the preservation of its unity, which is called peace, and which, if taken away, the benefit of social life is lost and moreover the multitude in its disagreement becomes a burden to itself. The chief concern of the ruler of a multitude, therefore, should be to procure the unity of peace: and it is not legitimate for him to deliberate whether he shall establish peace in the multitude subject to him, just as a physician does not deliberate whether he shall heal the sick man encharged to him. For no one should deliberate about an end which he is obliged to seek, but only about the means to attain that end. Wherefore, the Apostle, having commended the unity of the faithful people, says: "Be ye careful to keep the unity of the spirit in the bond of peace."[1] The more efficacious, therefore, a government is in keeping the unity of peace, the more useful it will be. For we call that more useful which leads the better to the end. Now it is manifest that what is itself one can more efficaciously bring about unity than several: just as the most efficacious cause of heat is that which is by its nature hot. Therefore the rule of one man is more useful than the rule of many.

Furthermore, it is evident that several persons could by no means keep a multitude from harm (*conservant*) if they totally disagreed. For a certain union is necessary among them if they are to rule at all: several men, for instance, could not pull a ship in one direction unless joined together in some fashion. Now several are said to be united according as they come closer to being one. So one man rules better than several who come near being one.

Again, whatever is in accord with nature is best: for in all things nature does what is best. Now, every natural governance is governance by one. In the multitude of bodily members there is one which moves them all, namely, the heart; and among the powers of the soul one power presides as chief,

---

[1] Eph. iv, 3.

namely, the reason. Even among bees there is one queen (*rex*) and in the whole universe there is One God, Maker and Ruler of all things. And this is reasonable. For every multitude is derived from unity. Wherefore, artificial things imitate natural things and since a work of art is better according as it attains a closer likeness to what is in nature, it necessarily follows that it is best, in the case of a human multitude, that it be ruled by one person.

This is also evident from experience; for provinces or cities which are not ruled by one person are torn with dissensions and are tossed about without peace so that the complaint seems to be fulfilled which the Lord uttered through the Prophet: "Many pastors have destroyed my vineyard."[2] But, on the contrary, provinces and cities which are ruled under one king enjoy peace, flourish in justice and delight in prosperity. Hence, the Lord by His prophets promises to His people as a great reward that He will give them one head and that one Prince will be in the midst of them.

Chapter V: That in a Government by Many, Tyrannical Government Occurs More Frequently than in a Government by One: Therefore the Rule of One Man is Better

When a choice is to be made between two things from both of which danger impends, that one must by all means be chosen from which the lesser evil follows. Now, lesser evil follows from a monarchy if it be changed into a tyranny, than from the government of several nobles, when it becomes corrupt. For the dissension which commonly follows upon the government of several, runs counter to the good of peace, which is the principal thing in a social group; which good, indeed, is not done away with by a tyranny, unless there be an excess of tyranny which rages against the whole community, but certain goods of particular men are hindered. The rule of one man is therefore to be preferred to the rule of many, although perils follow from both. Further, that from which great dangers may more often follow is, it would seem, the more to be avoided; but the greatest dangers to the multitude follow more frequently from the rule of many than from the rule of one. For, it commonly happens that one out of the many turns from the pursuit of the common good more than does one man ruling alone. Now when any one among several leaders turns aside from the pursuit of the common good, danger of internal dissension threatens the multitude of subjects, because when the chiefs quarrel, the consequence is that dissension in the multitude follows. If, however, one man is in command, he usually, indeed, looks to the common good; or if he turn his attention away from the common good, it does not immediately follow that he turns his attention to the oppression of his subjects, which is an excess of tyranny and holds the highest degree of wickedness in government, as has been shown above. The dangers which arise from the government of many are more to be avoided, therefore, than those which arise from the government of one. Moreover, it happens that the rule of many is changed into a tyranny not less, but perhaps more, frequently than the rule of one. For once dissension arises through the rule of several, it often happens that one triumphs over the others and usurps the government of the multitude for himself alone; and this indeed may be clearly seen from what has come about in such circumstances. For the rule of almost all groups of many has ended in tyranny, as is plainly seen in the Roman Republic. When it had been administered for a long time by several magistrates, dissensions and civil wars arose and it fell into the power of the most cruel tyrants. And, in general, if one carefully considers what has happened in the past and what is happening in the present, he will discover that more men practised tyranny in lands ruled by many than in those governed by one. If, therefore, kingly rule, which is the best government, seems chiefly to be avoided because of tyranny, and, on the other hand, tyranny is wont to occur not

---

[2] Jer. xii, 10.

less, but more, in the rule of many than in the rule of one, it follows that it is simply more expedient to live under one king than under the rule of several.

Chapter VI: Conclusion, that the Rule of One Man Is Simply the Best. It Shows How the Multitude Must be Disposed in Regard to Him, Because the Opportunity of Tyrannizing Must be Removed from Him, and that He Should be Tolerated even in His Tyranny on Account of the Greater Evil to be Avoided

Therefore, since the rule of one man, which is the best, is to be preferred, and since it may happen that it be changed into a tyranny, which is the worst, it is clear from what has been said that diligent zeal must be exercised in order that the interests of the multitude be so safeguarded with regard to their king that they may not fall under a tyrant. First it is necessary that the man who is raised up to be king by those to whom this office belongs, should be of such character that it is improbable he should fall into tyranny. Wherefore, Daniel, commending the Providence of God with respect to the establishment of the king says: "The Lord hath sought him a man according to his own heart."[3] Then, once the king is established, the government of the kingdom must be so arranged that opportunity to tyrannize be removed. At the same time his power should be so tempered that he cannot easily fall into tyranny. How these things may be done we must consider in what follows. Finally, provision must be made for facing the situation should the king turn aside into tyranny.

Indeed, if there be not an excess of tyranny it is more expedient to tolerate for a while the milder tyranny than, by acting against the tyrant, to be involved in many perils which are more grievous than the tyranny itself. For it may happen that those who act against the tyrant are unable to prevail and the tyrant, thus provoked, rages the more. Even if one should be able to prevail against the tyrant, from this fact itself very grave dissensions among the people frequently ensue: the multitude may be broken up by factions either during their revolt against the tyrant, or, concerning the organization of the government, after the tyrant has been overthrown. It also happens that sometimes, while the multitude is driving out the tyrant by the help of some man, he, having received the power, seizes the tyranny, and fearing to suffer from another what he did to his predecessor, oppresses his subjects with a more grievous slavery. For this is wont to happen in tyranny, namely, that the second becomes more grievous than the one preceding, inasmuch as, without abandoning the previous oppressions, he himself thinks up fresh ones from the malice of his heart: whence, in Syracuse, when there was a time that everybody desired the death of Dionysius, a certain old woman kept constantly praying that he might be unharmed and that he might survive her. When the tyrant learned this he asked why she did it. Then she said, "When I was a girl we had a harsh tyrant and I wished for his death; when he was killed, there succeeded him one who was somewhat harsher: I was very eager to see the end of his dominion also: then we began to have a third ruler still more harsh—that was you. So if you should be taken away a worse would succeed in your place."

Now some have been of opinion that if the excess of tyranny is unbearable, it would be an act of virtue for strong men to slay the tyrant and to expose themselves to dangers of death in order to set the multitude free. An example of this occurs even in the Old Testament. For a certain Aioth (*Aod*) slew Eglon, King of Moab, who was oppressing the people of God under harsh slavery, with the dagger fastened to his thigh; and he was made a judge of the people. But this opinion is not in accord with apostolic teaching. For Peter admonishes us to be reverently subject to our masters, not only to

---

[3] I Kings xiii, 14.

the good and gentle but also to the froward: "For if one who suffers unjustly bear his trouble for conscience sake, this is a grace."[4] Wherefore, when many Roman emperors tyrannically persecuted the faith of Christ, a great multitude both of the nobility and of the populace was converted to the faith and they were praised, not for resisting, but for patiently and courageously bearing death for Christ. This is plainly manifested in the case of the holy legion of Thebans. Aioth (*Aod*), then, must be considered rather as having slain a foe, than as having assassinated a ruler of the people, though a tyrannical one. Hence even in the Old Testament we read that they who killed Joas, the king of Juda, although he had fallen away from the worship of God, were slain and their children spared according to the precept of the law. It would, moreover, be dangerous both for the multitude and for their rulers if certain persons should attempt on their own private presumption, to kill their governors, even tyrants. For to dangers of this kind, usually the wicked expose themselves more than the good. For the rule of a king, no less than that of a tyrant, is burdensome to the wicked because, according to the words of Solomon,[5] "A wise king scattereth the wicked." Consequently, by presumption of this kind, danger to the people from the loss of their king would be more imminent than relief through the removal of the tyrant.

Furthermore it rather seems, that to proceed against the cruelty of tyrants is an action to be undertaken, not through the private presumption of a few, but by public authority. First of all, if to provide itself with a king belong to the right of any multitude, it is not unjust that the king set up by that multitude be destroyed or his power restricted, if he tyrannically abuse the royal power. It must not be thought that such a multitude is acting unfaithfully in deposing the tyrant, even though it had previously subjected itself to him in perpetuity; because he himself has deserved that the covenant with his subjects should not be kept, since, in ruling the multitude, he did not act faithfully as the office of a king demands. Thus did the Romans cast out from the kingship, Tarquin the Proud, whom they had accepted as their king, because of his tyranny and the tyranny of his sons; and they set up in their place a lesser power, namely; the consular power. So too Domitian, who had succeeded those most moderate Emperors, Vespasian, his father, and Titus, his brother, was slain by the Roman senate when he exercised tyranny, and all that he had wickedly done to the Romans, was justly and profitably, by a decree of the senate, declared null and void.

Thus it came about that Blessed John the Evangelist, the beloved disciple of God, who had been exiled to the island of Patmos by that very Domitian, was sent back to Ephesus by a decree of the senate.

If, however, it pertains to the right of some higher authority to provide a king for a certain multitude, a remedy against the wickedness of a tyrant is to be looked for from him. Thus when Archelaus, who had already begun to reign in Judaea in the place of Herod, his father, was imitating his father's wickedness, a complaint against him having been laid before Caesar Augustus by the Jews, his power was, first of all, diminished by depriving him of his title of king and by dividing one half of his kingdom between his two brothers; later, since he was not restrained from tyranny even by this means, Tiberius Caesar sent him into exile in Lyons, a city of Gaul.

Should no human aid whatsoever against a tyrant be forthcoming, recourse must be had to God, the King of all, who is a helper in due time in tribulation. "For, it lies within His power to turn the

---

[4] I Peter ii, 18, 19.

[5] Prov. xx, 26.

cruel heart of the tyrant to mildness."[6] In the words of Solomon:[7] "The heart of the king is in the hand of the Lord, whithersoever He will He shall turn it." He it was who turned into mildness the cruelty of King Assuerus, who was preparing death for the Jews. He it was who so transformed the cruel king Nabuchodonosor that he became a proclaimer of the divine power. "Therefore," he said, "I, Nabuchodonosor, do now praise and magnify and glorify the King of Heaven: because all his works are true and His ways judgments, and them that walk in pride He is able to abase."[8] Those tyrants, however, whom he deems unworthy of conversion he is able to put out of the way or reduce them to the lowest degree, according to the words of the Wise Man: "God hath overturned the thrones of proud princes: and hath set up the meek in their stead." He it was who, seeing the afflicting of his people in Egypt and hearing their cry, hurled the tyrant Pharaoh with his army into the sea. He it was who not only banished from his kingly throne the above mentioned Nabuchodonosor in his former pride, but also cast him from the fellowship of men and changed him into the likeness of a beast. For also His hand is not shortened that He cannot free His people from tyrants. For by Isaias He promises to give his people rest from their labour and trouble and harsh slavery in which they had formerly served; and by Ezechiel He says, "I will deliver my flock from their mouth,"[9] that is from the mouth of shepherds who feed themselves. But to deserve to secure this benefit from God, the people must desist from sin; because by divine permission wicked men receive power to rule as a punishment for sin, as the Lord says by the Prophet Osee:[10] "I will give thee a king in my wrath"; and it is said in Job that he "maketh a man that is a hypocrite to reign for the sins of the people."[11] Sin must therefore be done away with that the scourge of tyrants may cease.

Chapter VIII: Here the Doctor Declares of What Sort Is the True End of the King, the End Which Should Move Him to Rule Well

Therefore, since worldly honour and human glory are not a sufficient reward for royal cares it remains to enquire what sort of reward is sufficient. Now, it is proper that a king look to God for his reward, for a servant looks to his master for the reward of his service. Now, in governing his people a king is the minister of God, as the Apostle says: All power is from the Lord God and God's minister is "an avenger to execute wrath upon him that doth evil";[12] and in the Book of Wisdom, kings are described as being ministers of God. Consequently, kings ought to look to God for the reward of their ruling. Now, God sometimes rewards kings for their service by temporal goods. But such rewards are common to both the good and the wicked. Wherefore the Lord says: "Nabuchodonosor, king of Babylon, hath made his army to undergo hard service against Tyre . . . and there hath been no reward given him nor his army, for Tyre, for the service he rendered me against it,"[13] for that service, namely, by which power is the minister of God, according to the Apostle, and the avenger to execute wrath upon him that doth evil: and afterwards he adds, regarding the reward, "Therefore, thus saith the Lord God: 'I will set Nabuchodonosor the king of Babylon in the land of Egypt, and he shall rifle the spoils thereof . . . and it shall be wages for his army.'" Therefore, if God recompenses wicked kings who fight against the enemies of God, though not with the intention of serving God, but to execute their own

---

[6] Prov. ix, 10.
[7] Prov. xxi, 1.
[8] Dan. iv, 4.
[9] Ez. xxxiv, 10.
[10] Hos. xiii, 11.
[11] Job xxxiv, 30.
[12] Rom. xiii, 1, 4.
[13] Ez. xxix, 18.

hatred and cupidity, by giving them such great rewards as to yield them victory over their foes, to subject kingdoms to their sway and to grant them spoils to rifle, what will he do for good kings who rule the people of God and assail his enemies from a holy motive? He promises them not an earthly reward indeed but an everlasting one and in none other than in Himself, as Peter says, to the shepherds of the people, "Feed the flock of God that is among you and when the prince of pastors shall appear," that is the King of kings, Christ, "you shall receive a neverfading crown of glory,"[14] concerning which Isaias says, "The Lord shall be a crown of glory and a garland of joy to his people."[15]

This is also clearly shown by reason. For it is implanted in the minds of all who have the use of reason that the reward of virtue is happiness. The virtue (*virtus*) of anything whatsoever is explained to be that which makes its possessor good and renders his deed good. Moreover, everyone strives by working well to attain that which is most deeply implanted in desire: namely, to be happy. This, no one is able not to will. It is therefore, fitting to expect as a reward for virtue that which makes man happy. Now, if to work well is a virtuous deed and the king's work is to rule his people well, then that which makes him happy will be the king's reward. But what that is has now to be considered.

Happiness we say is the ultimate end of our desires. Now the movement of desire does not go on to infinity, else natural desire would be vain for infinity cannot be traversed. Since, then, the desire of an intellectual nature is for universal good, that good alone can make it truly happy, which, when attained, leaves no further good to be desired, Whence, happiness is called the perfect good inasmuch as it comprises in itself all things desirable. But no earthly good is such a good. For they who have riches desire to have more, and the like is clear for the rest: and if they do not seek more, they at least desire that those they have should abide or that others should follow in their stead, for nothing permanent is found in earthly things. Consequently there is nothing earthly which can calm desire. And so nothing earthly can make man happy, that it may be a fitting reward for a king.

Again, the last perfection and perfect good of anything you choose depends upon something higher, for even bodily things are made better by the addition of better things, but worse by being mixed with baser things. For if gold is mingled with silver, the silver is made better, while by an admixture of lead it is rendered impure. Now, it is manifest that all earthly things are beneath the human mind; but happiness is the last perfection and the perfect good of man, which all men desire to reach. Therefore, there is no earthly thing which could make man happy, nor is any earthly thing a sufficient reward for a king. For, as Augustine says,[16] we do not call Christian princes happy merely because they have reigned a long time, or because after a peaceful death they have left their sons to rule or because they subdued the enemies of the state, or because they were able to guard against or to suppress citizens who rose up against them; but we call them happy if they rule justly, if they prefer to rule their passions rather than any nations whatsoever, if they do all things not through the ardour of vain glory but for the love of eternal happiness. Such Christian rulers we say are happy, now in hope, afterwards in very fact when that which we await shall come to pass. But there is not any other created thing which would make a man happy and which could be set up as the reward for a king. For the desire of each thing tends toward its source, whence is the cause of its being. But the

---

[14] I Peter v, 2, 4.
[15] Isa. xiii, 5.
[16] *City of God*, V, 24.

cause of the human soul is none other than God who made it to His own image. Therefore, it is God alone Who can still the desires of man and make man happy and be the fitting reward for a king.

Furthermore, the human mind knows universal good through understanding and desires it through will: but universal good is not found except in God. Therefore there is nothing which could make man happy, fulfilling his every desire, but God, of whom it is said in the Psalm, "Who satisfieth thy desire with good things."[17] In this therefore, should the king place his reward. Accordingly King David, with this in mind, said, "What have I in heaven? And besides Thee what do I desire upon earth?"[18] and he afterwards adds in answer to this question, "It is good for me to adhere to my God and to put my hope in the Lord God." For it is He who gives salvation to kings, not merely temporal salvation by which He saves both men and beasts together, but also that salvation of which He says by the mouth of Isaias, "But my salvation shall be for ever," that salvation by which He saves men and makes them equal to the angels. Therefore, it can thus be verified that the reward of the king is honour and glory. But what worldly and frail honour can be likened to this honour that a man be made a citizen and a kinsman of God, numbered among the sons of God and obtain the inheritance of the heavenly kingdom with Christ? This is the honour of which King David in desire and wonder says, "Thy friends, O God, are made exceedingly honourable."[19] And further, what glory of human praise can be compared to this, not uttered by the false tongue of flatterers nor the fallacious opinion of men, but issuing from the witness of our inmost conscience and confirmed by the testimony of God, who promises to those who confess Him that he will confess them before the Angels of God in the glory of the Father? They who seek this glory will find it and they will win the glory of men which they do not seek; witness Solomon, who not only received from the Lord wisdom which he sought, but was made glorious above other kings.

Chapter XII: He Proceeds to Show the Office of a King, Wherein According to the Ways of Nature, He Points Out that the King Is in the Kingdom, as the Soul Is in the Body, in the Same Manner as God Is in the Universe

The next point to be considered is the nature of the kingly office and what sort of man a king must be. Now, because things which are in accordance with art imitate the things which are in accordance with nature (from which, in fact, we must receive in order that we may work according to reason), it appears that the best kingly administration will be one which is patterned after the regime of nature. In things of nature, however, there is found to be both a universal and a particular rulership; universal, by the fact that everything is embraced under the rulership of God, who governs all things by His providence. The particular rulership which is found in man is most like the Divine rulership. For this reason man is called a smaller world, since in him there is found the form of universal rulership. For, just as the universe of corporeal creatures and all spiritual powers come under the Divine government, in like manner are the members of the body and the other powers of the soul controlled by reason, and thus, in a certain proportionate manner, reason is to man what God is to the world. Since man is by nature a social animal living in a group, as we have pointed out above, a likeness of the divine rulership is found in him, not only in this, that a single man is ruled by reason, but also in that a multitude is governed through the reason of one man. This appertains above all to the office of a king, although among certain animals that live socially a likeness of this rulership is to

---

[17] Ps. cii, 5.
[18] Ps. lxxii, 25.
[19] Ps. xvii, 138.

be found. For example, we likewise say there are queens (*reges*) among bees, not that among them rulership is exercised through reason, but through natural instinct implanted in them by the Great Ruler, who is the author of nature. Therefore let the king recognize that such is the office which he undertakes, namely, that he is to be in the kingdom what the soul is in the body, and what God is in the world. If he reflect seriously upon this, from one motive, a zeal for justice will be enkindled in him, when he contemplates that he has been appointed to this position in place of God, to exercise judgment in his kingdom; from another, he acquires the gentleness of clemency and mildness, when he considers as his own members, those individuals who are subject to his rulership.

Chapter XIV: What Manner of Government Is Possible for a King, Seeing that It Imitates the Divine Providence; This Method of Government Had Its Origin in the Guidance of a Ship; and a Comparison Is Set Up Between Sacerdotal and Royal Dominion

Just as the founding of a city or a kingdom may suitably be learned from the way the world was created, so too the way to govern may be learned from the governing of the world. Before going into that, however, we should consider that to govern is to bring the thing governed in a suitable way to its proper end. Thus a ship is said to be governed, when, through the skill of the sailor, it is brought by a direct route and unharmed to harbour. Consequently, if anything is ordained to an end outside itself (as a ship to a harbour), it is the governor's duty, not only to preserve the thing unharmed, but further to bring it to its end. If on the contrary, there should be anything whose end is not outside itself, then the governor's endeavours would merely tend to preserve the thing itself undamaged in its proper perfection. Although nothing of this kind is found in the world, except God Himself, Who is the end of all, yet the care of that which is ordained to something outside itself, is hindered by many things and in different ways. For, perhaps, one person may have the duty of preserving a thing in existence, and another the duty of bringing it to a higher state of perfection. This is clearly the case in the example of the ship, from which the idea (*ratio*) of government is derived. For it is the carpenter's duty to repair anything that is broken in the ship, but the sailor bears the anxiety of bringing the ship to port. It is the same with man. The doctor sees to it that a man's life is preserved in health, the tradesman supplies the necessities of life, the teacher takes care that he learns the truth, and the tutor sees that he lives according to reason. If a man were not ordained to any other end outside himself, the above mentioned cares would be sufficient for him.

But as long as a man's moral life endures there is some good extraneous to him, namely, final beatitude which is looked for after death, in the enjoyment of God, for as the Apostle says:[20] "As long as we are in the body we are far from the Lord." Consequently the Christian man, for whom that beatitude has been purchased by the blood of Christ, and who in order to attain it, has received the earnest of the Holy Ghost, needs an additional spiritual care to direct him to the harbour of eternal salvation, and this care is provided for the faithful by the ministers of the Church of Christ.

We must form the same judgment about the end of society as a whole as we do concerning the end of one man. If, therefore, the end of man were some good that exists in himself, then the ultimate end of the multitude to be governed would likewise be for the multitude to acquire such good and persevere in its possession. If such an ultimate end either of an individual man or a multitude, were a corporeal one, namely, life and health of body, to govern would then be a physician's charge.

---

[20] II Cor. v, 6.

If that ultimate end were an abundance of wealth, then some financier would be king of the multitude. If the good of the knowledge of truth were of such a kind that the multitude might attain to it, the king would have the duty of teacher. But it is clear, that the end of any multitude gathered together, is to live virtuously. For, men form groups for the purpose of living well together, a thing which the individual man living alone could not attain. But a good life is a virtuous life. Therefore a virtuous life is the end for which men form groups.

The evidence for this lies in the fact that only those who render mutual assistance to one another in living well truly form part of an assembled multitude. For if men assembled merely to *live,* then animals and serfs would form a part of the civil body. And if men assembled only to acquire wealth, then all those who traded together, would belong to one city. Thus we see that only those are regarded as forming one society who are directed by the same laws and the same government, to live well. Therefore, since man, by living virtuously, is ordained to a higher end, which consists of the enjoyment of God, as we have said above, then human society must have the same end as the individual man. Therefore, it is not the ultimate end of an assembled multitude to live virtuously, but through virtuous living to attain to the possession of God. Furthermore if it could attain this end by the power of human nature, then the duty of a king would have to include the direction of men to this end. We are supposing that he is called "king" to whom the supreme power of governing in human affairs is entrusted. Now the higher the end to which a government is ordained, the loftier is that government; for we always find that the one to whom it pertains to achieve the final end, commands those who execute the things that are ordained to that end. For example, the captain, whose business it is to regulate navigation, tells the man who builds the ship what kind of a ship he must build in order that it be suitable to navigation; and the citizen who bears arms, tells the blacksmith what kind of arms to make. But, because a man does not attain his end which is the possession of God, by human power, but by Divine power, according to the words of the Apostle: "By the grace of God life everlasting,"[21] therefore the task of leading him to that end does not pertain to human government but to divine.

Consequently, government of this kind pertains to that king who is not only a man, but also God, namely to our Lord Jesus Christ, Who by making men sons of God, brought them to the glory of Heaven.

This then is the government which has been delivered to Him and which shall not be destroyed, on account of which He is called, in Holy Writ, not Priest only, but King, as Jeremias says: "The king shall reign and he shall be wise."[22] Hence a royal priesthood is derived from Him, and what is more, all those who believe in Christ, in so far as they are His members, are called kings and priests. Consequently, in order that spiritual things might be distinguished from earthly things, the ministry of this kingdom has been entrusted not to earthly kings, but to priests, and in the highest degree to the chief priest, the successor of St. Peter, the Vicar of Christ, the Roman Pontiff, to whom all the kings of Christian peoples are to be subject as to our Lord Jesus Christ Himself. For those to whom pertains the care of intermediate ends should be subject to him to whom pertains the care of the ultimate end, and be directed by his rule. Because the priesthood of the gentiles, and the whole worship of their Gods existed merely for the acquisition of temporal goods (which were all ordained to the common good of the multitude, whose care devolved upon a king), the priests of the gentiles

---

[21] Rom. vi, 23.
[22] Jer. xxiii, 5.

were very properly subject to the kings. Similarly, because in the old law earthly goods were promised to a religious people (not indeed by demons but by the true God), the priests of the old law, we read, were also subject to the kings. But in the new law there is a higher priesthood by which men are guided to heavenly goods. Consequently in the law of Christ, kings must be subject to priests.

Therefore, it was a marvelous effect of Divine Providence that in the city of Rome, which God had foreseen would be the principal seat of the Christian people, the custom was gradually established that the rulers of the city should be subject to the priests, for as Valerius Maximus relates: "Our City has always considered that everything should yield precedence to religion, even those things in which it aimed to display the splendor of supreme majesty. Wherefore our governments did not hesitate to minister to religion, considering that they would thus hold control of human affairs if they faithfully and constantly were submissive to divine authority." Because it was to come to pass that the religion of the Christian priesthood should especially thrive in France, God permitted that among the Gauls too, their tribal priests, called Druids, should lay down the law of all Gaul, as Julius Caesar relates in the book which he wrote about the Gallic war.[23]

Chapter XV: . . . Here We Note Those Things Which Dispose Towards a Proper Life, and Those Which Hinder, and Also the Remedy Which the King Must Apply Against These Hindrances

. . . For an individual man to lead a good life two things are required. The first and most important is to act in a virtuous manner (for virtue is that by which one lives well); the second, which is secondary, and, as it were, instrumental, is a sufficiency of those bodily goods whose use is necessary for an act of virtue. Yet the unity of man is brought about by nature, while the unity of a society, which we call peace, must be procured through the efforts of the ruler. Therefore, to establish virtuous living in a multitude three things are necessary. First of all, that the multitude be established in the unity of peace. Second, that the multitude thus united in the bond of peace, be guided to good deeds. For just as a man can do nothing well unless unity within his members be presupposed, so a multitude of men which lacks the unity of peace, is hindered from virtuous action, by the fact that it fights against its very existence as a group. In the third place, it is necessary that there be at hand a sufficient supply of the things required for proper living, procured by the ruler's efforts. Then, when virtuous living is set up in society by the efforts of the king, it remains for him to look to its conservation.

Now there are three things which prevent permanence in public virtue. One of these arises from nature. For the good of society should not be established for one time only; it should be in a sense perpetual. Men, on the other hand, cannot abide forever because they are mortal. Even while they are alive they do not always preserve the same vigor, for the life of man is subject to many changes. So a man is not equally suited to the performance of the same duties throughout the whole span of his life. A second impediment to the preservation of public good which comes from within, consists in the perversity of the wills of man, inasmuch as they are either too lazy to perform what the state demands, or, still further, they are harmful to the peace of society, because, by transgressing justice, they disturb the peace of their neighbors. The third hindrance to the preservation of the state comes from without, namely, when peace is destroyed through the attacks of enemies, or, as it sometimes happens, the kingdom or city is completely blotted out. In regard to these three dangers, a triple charge

---

[23] De Bello Gallico, VI, 13.

is laid upon the king. First of all, he must take care of the appointment of men to succeed or replace others in charge of the various offices, just as, by the providence of God, provision is made for the succession and replacement of corruptible things, which cannot last forever the same, by the generation of things to take their place. Thus just as the integrity of the universe is maintained so too, the good of the multitude subject to the king will be maintained by his care, provided he carefully attend to the appointment of new men to fill the place of those who drop out. In the second place, by his law and orders, punishments and rewards, he restrains the men subject to him from wickedness, and encourages them to works of virtue, following the example of God, Who gave His law to man and requites those who observe it with rewards, and those who transgress it with punishments. The king's third charge is to keep the multitude entrusted to him safe from the enemy. For it would be useless to prevent internal dangers if the multitude could not be defended against external dangers.

So, for the proper direction of the multitude, there remains the third duty of the kingly office, namely, that he be solicitous for its improvement. He performs this duty when, in each of the things we have mentioned, he corrects what is out of order, and supplies what is lacking, and, if any of them can be done better he tries to do it. This is why the Apostle[24] exhorts the faithful to be zealous for the better gifts. These then are the duties of the kingly office, each of which must now be treated in greater detail.

---

[24] I Cor. xii, 31.

Moses Maimonides

(1135–1204)

Moses Ben Maimon (1135–1204) was born in Cordova. He was instructed by his father in the Bible, the Talmud, and mathematics; Arab teachers gave him his education in Philosophy and the natural sciences, especially medicine.

About 1160 his family, with most of the rest of the Jewish community of Cordova, fled to Fez, in Morocco, to escape the pressure to convert to Islam. In Fez, too, the Jews were forced to attend the Mosques, and in 1165 the family emigrated to Palestine and then to Egypt.

Maimonides set up as a physician in Old Cairo and gave public lectures on philosophy. In 1171 Sultan Saladin made Egypt a refuge for persecuted Jews. Maimonides' fame grew, both as a physician and, on the strength of his commentary on the *Mishnah* (1168), as a rabbinical authority. In 1180 appeared the great religious code, the *Mishnah Torah*, which unified the Talmud and explained the Law from the standpoint of Aristotelianism; in 1990 he finished his masterpiece, the *Moreh Nebuchim,* a philosophical defense of Judaism.

During the remainder of his life Maimonides was personal physician to Alafdel, the eldest son of Saladin, and he did much medical work, including treatises used for many generations in European medical schools.

Maimonides' philosophical writings are among those works which attempted to reconcile traditional religious teachings with reason, that is, with Aristotle; and like Averroës and Thomas Aquinas, his counterparts in Islam and the Christian world, he was bitterly opposed by many of his own faith. Nevertheless, all subsequent attempts to fix the basic doctrines of Judaism have proceeded from his work.

Although Maimonides lived a thousand years later than Paul, his Letter to Yemen is one of the clearest statements of the central beliefs of Judaism as answers to the claims of Christianity. It draws the distinction between Jew and Christian much more sharply and more directly than most previous Jewish literature. It makes clear the Jewish conceptions of righteousness and of the moral law that Pauline Christianity at various times claimed to have canceled, subsumed into itself, or universalized into a call for faith in Christ as the Messiah and for love for all men as equals before God.

From *The Guide of the Perplexed*

Introduction

One of seven causes should account for the contradictory or contrary statements to be found in any book or compilation.

The first cause: The author has collected the remarks of various people with differing opinions, but has omitted citing his authorities and has not attributed each remark to the one who said it. Contradictory or contrary statements can be found in such compilations because one of

The following selection is taken from Salomon Pines, trans., Moses Maimonides, *The Guide of the Perplexed*, (Chicago: University of Chicago Press, 1963). pp. 244–45, 252–55, 270–74, 278–82.

the two propositions is the opinion of one individual while the other proposition is the opinion of another individual.

The second cause: The author of a particular book has adopted a certain opinion that he later rejects; both his original and later statements are retained in the book.

The third cause: Not all the statements in question are to be taken in their external sense; some are to be taken in their external sense, while some others are parables and hence have an inner content. Alternatively, two apparently contradictory propositions may both be parables and when taken in their external sense may contradict, or be contrary to, one another.

The fourth cause: There is a proviso that, because of a certain necessity, has not been explicitly stated in its proper place; or the two subjects may differ, but one of them has not been explained in its proper place, so that a contradiction appears to have been said, whereas there is no contradiction.

The fifth cause: Arises from the necessity of teaching and making someone understand. For there may be a certain obscure matter that is difficult to conceive. One has to mention it or to take it as a premise in explaining something that is easy to conceive and that by rights ought to be taught before the former, since one always begins with what is easier. The teacher, accordingly, will have to be lax and, using any means that occur to him or gross speculation, will try to make that first matter somehow understood. He will not undertake to state the matter as it truly is in exact terms, but rather will leave it so in accord with the listener's imagination that the latter will understand only what he now wants him to understand. Afterward, in the appropriate place, that obscure matter is stated in exact terms and explained as it truly is.

The sixth cause: The contradiction is concealed and becomes evident only after many premises. The greater the number of premises needed to make the contradiction evident, the more concealed it is. It thus may escape the author, who thinks there is no contradiction between his two original propositions. But if each proposition is considered separately, a true premise being joined to it and the necessary conclusion drawn—and this is done to every conclusion: a true premise being joined to it and the necessary conclusion drawn—after many syllogisms the outcome of the matter will be that the two final conclusions are contradictory or contrary to each other. That is the kind of thing that escapes the attention of scholars who write books. If, however, the two original propositions are evidently contradictory, but the author has simply forgotten the first when writing down the second in another part of his compilation, this is a very great weakness, and that man should not be reckoned among those whose speeches deserve consideration.

The seventh cause: In speaking about very obscure matters it is necessary to conceal some parts and to disclose others. Sometimes in the case of certain dicta this necessity requires that the discussion proceed on the basis of a certain premise, whereas in another place necessity requires that the discussion proceed on the basis of another premise contradicting the first one. In such cases the vulgar must in no way be aware of the contradiction; the author accordingly uses some device to conceal it by all means. . . .

. . . Divergences that are to found in this treatise are due to the fifth cause and the seventh. Know this, grasp its true meaning, and remember it very well so as not to become perplexed by some of its chapters.

Chapter 31

Know that the human intellect has objects of apprehension that it is within its power and according to its nature to apprehend. On the other hand, in that which exits there also are existents and matters that, according to its nature, it is not capable of apprehending in any way or through any cause; the gates of their apprehension are shut before it. There are also in that which exists things of which the intellect may apprehend one state while not being cognizant of other states. The fact that it apprehends does not entail the conclusion that it can apprehend all things—just as the senses have apprehensions but it is not within their power to apprehend at whatever distance the objects of apprehension may happen to be. Similarly with regard to all other bodily faculties, for the fact that a man is able to carry two hundred-weights does not mean that he is able to carry ten. The difference in capacity existing between the individuals of the species with regard to sensory apprehensions and all the other bodily faculties is manifest and clear to all men. However, it has a limit, inasmuch as these capacities cannot attain to every distance however far away nor to every degree however great it may happen to be. The identical rule obtains with regard to human intellectual apprehensions. There are great differences in capacity between the individuals of the species. This also is manifest and very clear to the men of knowledge. It many thus happen that whereas one individual discovers a certain notion by himself through his speculation, another individual is not able ever to understand that notion. Even if it were explained to him for a very long time by means of every sort of expression and parable, his mind would not penetrate to it in any way, but would turn back without understanding it. This difference in capacity is likewise not infinite, for man's intellect indubitably has a limit at which it stops. There are therefore things regarding which it has become clear to man that it is impossible to apprehend them. And he will not find that his soul longs for knowledge of them, inasmuch as he is aware of the impossibility of such knowledge and of there being no gate through which one might enter in order to attain it. Of this nature is our ignorance of the number of the stars of heaven and whether that number is even or odd, as well as our ignorance of the number of the species of living beings, minerals, plants, and other similar things.

On the other hand, there are things for the apprehension of which man will find that he has a great longing. The sway of the intellect endeavouring to seek for, and to investigate, their true reality exists at every time and in every group of men engaged in speculation. With regard to such things there is a multiplicity of opinions, disagreement arises between the men engaged in speculation, and doubts crop up; all this because the intellect is attached to an apprehension of these things, I mean to say because of its longing for them; and also because everyone thinks that he has found a way by means of which he will know the true reality of the matter. Now it is not within the power of the human intellect to give a demonstration of these matters. For in all things whose true reality is known through demonstration there is no tug of war and no refusal to accept a thing proven—unless indeed such refusal comes from an ignoramus who offers a resistance that is called resistance to demonstration. Thus you can find groups of people who dispute the doctrine that the earth is spherical and that the sphere has a circular motion and with regard to other matters of this kind. These folk do not enter into our purpose. The things about which there is this perplexity are very numerous in divine matters, few in matters pertaining to natural science, and nonexistent in matters pertaining to mathematics.

Alexander of Aphrodisias* says that there are three causes of disagreement about things. One of them is love of domination and love of strife, both of which turn man aside from the apprehension of truth as it is. The second cause is the subtlety and the obscurity of the object of apprehension in itself and the difficulty of apprehending it. And the third cause is the ignorance of him who apprehends and

---

*Greek commentator Aristotle.

his inability to grasp things that it is possible to apprehend. That is what Alexander mentioned. However, in our times there is a fourth cause that he did not mention because it did not exist among them. It is habit and upbringing. For man has in his nature a love of, and an inclination for, that to which he is habituated. Thus you can see that the people of the desert—notwithstanding the disorderliness of their life, the lack of pleasures, and the scarcity of food—dislike the towns, do not hanker after their pleasures, and prefer the bad circumstances to which they are accustomed to good ones to which they are not accustomed. Their souls accordingly would find no repose in living in palaces, in wearing silk clothes, and in the enjoyment of baths, ointments, and perfumes. In a similar way, man has love for, and the wish to defend, opinions to which he is habituated and in which he has been brought up and has a feeling of repulsion for opinions other than those. For this reason also man is blind to the apprehension of the true realities and inclines toward the things to which he is habituated. This happened to the multitude with regard to the belief in His corporeality and many other metaphysical subjects as we shall make clear. All this is due to people being habituated to, and brought up on, texts that it is an established usage to think highly of and to regard as true and whose external meaning is indicative of the corporeality of God and of other imaginings with no truth in them, for these have been set forth as parables and riddles. This is so for reasons that I shall mention further on.

Do not think that what we have said with regard to the insufficiency of the human intellect and its having a limit at which it stops is a statement made in order to conform to Law. For it is something that has already been said and truly grasped by the philosophers without their having concern for a particular doctrine or opinion. And it is a true thing that cannot be doubted except by an individual ignorant of what has already been demonstrated. We have put this chapter before others and with a view to its serving as an introduction to that which shall come after it.

Chapter 32

You who study my treatise know that something similar to what happens to sensory apprehensions happens likewise to intellectual apprehensions in so far as they are attached to matter. For when you see with your eye, you apprehend something that is within the power of your sight to apprehend. If, however, your eyes are forced to do something they are reluctant to do—if they are made to gaze fixedly and are set the task of looking over a great distance, too great for you to see, or if you contemplate very minute writing or a minute drawing that is not within your power to apprehend—and if you force your eye, in spite of its reluctance, to find out the true reality of the thing, your eye shall not only be too weak to apprehend that which you are unable to apprehend, but also too weak to apprehend that which is within your power to apprehend. Your eye shall grow tired, and you shall not be able to apprehend what you could apprehend before having gazed fixedly and before having been given this task. A similar discovery is made by everyone engaging in the speculative study of some science with respect to his state of reflection. For if he applies himself to reflection and sets himself a task demanding his entire attention, he becomes dull and does not then understand even that which is within his scope to understand. For the condition of all bodily faculties is, in this respect, one and the same. Something similar can happen to you with regard to intellectual apprehensions. For if you stay your progress because of a dubious point; if you do not deceive yourself into believing that there is a demonstration with regard to matters that have not been demonstrated; if you do not hasten to reject and categorically to pronounce false any assertions whose contradictories have not been demonstrated; if, finally, you do not aspire to apprehend that which you are unable to apprehend—you will have achieved human perfection and attained the rank of Rabbi Akiva, peace be on him, who "entered in peace and went out in peace" (Hagigah 14b) when engaged in the theoretical study of these metaphysical matters. If, on the other hand, you aspire to apprehend things that are beyond your apprehension; or if you hasten to pronounce false assertions, the contradictories of which have not been demonstrated or that are possible, though very remotely so—you will have joined Elisha Aher. That is, you will not only not be perfect, but will be the most deficient among the deficient; and it shall so fall out that you will be overcome by imaginings and by an inclination toward things defective, evil, and wicked—this resulting from the intellect's being preoccupied and its light's being extinguished. In a similar way, various species of delusive imaginings are produced in the sense of sight when the visual spirit is weakened, as in the case of sick people and of such as persist in looking at brilliant or minute objects.

Chapter 59

... As everyone is aware that it is not possible, except through negation, to achieve an apprehension of that which is in our power to apprehend and that, on the other hand, negation does not give knowledge in any respect of the true reality of the thing with regard to which the particular matter in question has been negated—all men, those of the past and those of the future, affirm clearly that God, may He be exalted, cannot be apprehended by the intellects, and that none but He Himself can apprehend what He is, and that apprehension of Him consists in the inability to attain the ultimate term in apprehending Him. Thus all the philosophers say: We are dazzled by His beauty, and He is hidden from us because of the intensity with which He becomes manifest, just as the sun is hidden to eyes that are too weak to apprehend it. This has been expatiated upon in words that it would serve no useful purpose to repeat here. The most apt phrase concerning this subject is the dictum occurring in the Psalms, "Silence is praise to You" (Ps. 65:2), which interpreted signifies: silence with regard to You is praise. This is a most perfectly put phrase regarding this matter. For of whatever we say intending to magnify and exalt, on the one hand we find that it can have some application to Him, may He be exalted, and on the other we perceive in it some deficiency. Accordingly, silence and limiting oneself to the apprehensions of the intellects are more appropriate—just as the perfect ones have enjoined when they said: "Commune with your own heart upon your bed, and be still" (Ps. 4:5).

You also know their famous dictum—would that all dicta were like it. I shall quote it to you textually, even though it is well remembered, so as to draw your attention to the various significations it expresses. They have said: "Someone who came into the presence of Rabbi Hanina said [in prayer]: God the Great, the Valiant, the Terrible, the Mighty, the Strong, the Tremendous, the Powerful. Thereupon [Rabbi Hanina] said to him: Have you finished all the praises of your Teacher? Even as regards the first three epithets [used by you] we could not have uttered them if Moses our Teacher had not pronounced them in the Law (Deut. 10: 17) and if the men of the Great Synagogue had not [subsequently] come and established [their use] in prayer. And you come and say all this. What does this resemble? It is as if a mortal king who had millions of gold pieces were praised for possessing silver. Would this not be an offense to him?" (Berakhot 33b). Here ends the dictum of this perfect one. Consider in the first place his reluctance and unwillingness to multiply the affirmative attributes. Consider also that he has stated clearly that if we were left only to our intellects we should never have mentioned these attributes or stated a thing appertaining to them. Yet the necessity to address men in such terms as would make them achieve some representation—in accordance with the dictum of the sages: "The Torah speaks in the language of the sons of man" (Yevamot 71a; Bava Metzia 31b)—obliged resort to predicting of God their own perfections when speaking to them. It must then be our purpose to draw a line at using these expressions and not to apply them to Him except only in reading the Torah. However, as the men of the Great Synagogue, who were prophets, appeared in their turn and inserted the mention of these attributes in the prayer, it is our purpose to pronounce only these attributes when saying our prayers. According to the spirit, this dictum makes it clear that, as it happened, two necessary obligations determined our naming these attributes in our prayers: one of them is that they occur in the Torah, and the other is that the prophets in question used them in the prayer they composed. Accordingly, we should not have mentioned these attributes at all but for the first necessary obligation; and but for the second necessity, we should not have taken them out of their context and should not have had recourse to them in our prayers. As you continue to consider the attributes, it will become clear to you from this statement that we are not permitted in our prayers to use and to cite all the attributes ascribed to God in the books of the prophets. For [Rabbi Hanina] not only says: "If Moses our Teacher had not pronounced them, we could not have uttered them," but poses a second condition: "And if the men of the Great Synagogue had not [subsequently] come and established [their use] in prayer" (Berakhot 33b)— whereupon we are permitted to use them in our prayers.

Thus what we do is not like what is done by the truly ignorant who spoke at great length and spent great efforts on prayers that they composed and on sermons that they compiled and through which they, in their opinion, came nearer to God. In these prayers and sermons they predicate of God qualificative attributions that, if predicated of a human individual, would designate a deficiency in him. For they do not understand those sublime notions that are too strange for the intellects of the vulgar and accordingly took God, may He be magnified and glorified, for an object of study for their tongues; they predicated attributes of Him and addressed Him in all the terms that they thought permitted and expatiated at such length in this way that in their thoughts they made Him move on account of an affection. They did this especially when they found the text of a prophet's speech regarding these terms. Thereupon they had full license to bring forward texts that ought to be interpreted in every respect, and to take them according to their external meaning, to derive from them inferences and secondary conclusions, and to found upon them various kinds of discourses. This kind of license is frequently taken by poets and preachers or such as think that what they speak is poetry, so that the utterances of some of them constitute an absolute denial of faith, while other utterances contain such rubbish and such perverse imaginings as to make men laugh when they hear them, on account of the nature of these utterances, and to make them weep when they consider that these utterances are applied to God, may he be magnified and glorified. If I were not unwilling to set out the deficiencies of those who make these utterances, I should have quoted to you something of the latter in order that you should give heed to the points in which they may be impugned. However, the deficiencies in these utterances are most manifest to him who understands. It also behooves you to consider and say that in view of the fact that speaking ill and defamation are acts of great disobedience, how much all the more so is the loosening of the tongue with regard to God, may He be exalted, and the predicating of His qualificative attributions above which He is exalted. But I shall not say that this is an act of disobedience, but rather that it constitutes unintended obloquy and vituperation on the part of the multitude who listen to these utterances and on the part of the ignoramus who pronounces them. As for him who apprehends the deficiency of those speeches and yet uses those speeches, he belongs in my opinion to the category of people of whom it is said, "And the children of Israel did impute things that were not right to the Lord their God" (II Kings 17:9), and is said elsewhere, "And to utter error against the Lord" (Is. 32:6). Accordingly if you are one "who has regard for the honour of his Creator," (Hagigah 11b) you ought not to listen in any way to these utterances, let alone give expression to them and still less make up others like them. For you know the extent of the sin of him who "makes vituperative utterances against what is above." (Sukkah 53a; Taanit 25a) You accordingly ought not to set forth in any respect the attributes of God in an affirmative way—with a view, as you think, to magnifying Him—and ought not to go beyond that which has been inserted in the prayers and benedictions by the men of the Great Synagogue. For this is sufficient from the point of view of necessity; in fact, as Rabbi Hanina said, it is amply sufficient. But regarding the other attributes that occur in the books of the prophets and are recited during the perusal of these books, it is believed, as we have made clear, that they are attributes of action or that they indicate the negation of their nonexistence in God. This notion concerning them also should not be divulged to the vulgar. For this kind of speculation is more suitable for the elite who consider that the magnification of God does not consist in their saying improper things but in their understanding properly.

Hereupon I shall return to completing the indications concerning the dictum of Rabbi Hanina and to giving it correct interpretation. He does not say, for example: "What does this resemble? It is as if a mortal king who had millions of gold pieces were praised for possessing one hundred pieces." For this example would have indicated that the perfections of Him, may He be exalted, while more perfect than the perfections that are ascribed to Him, still belong to the same species as the latter. As we have demonstrated, this is not so. But the wisdom manifest in this parable lies in his saying: "gold pieces and were praised for possessing silver." He says this in order to indicate that in God, may He be exalted, there is nothing belonging to the same species as the attributes that are regarded by us as perfections, but that all these attributes are deficiencies with regard to God, just as he made clear in this parable when he said: "Would this not be an offense to Him?" I have then already made it known to you that everything in these attributes that you regard as a perfection is a deficiency with regard to Him, may he be exalted, as it belongs to a species to which the things that are with us belong. Solomon, peace be on him, has rightly directed us with regard to this subject, in words that should be sufficient for us, when he said: "For God is in heaven and you upon the earth; therefore let your words be few" (Eccles. 5: 1).

Part Two

Chapter 13

There are three opinions of human beings, namely, of all those who believe that there is an existent Deity, with regard to the eternity of the world or its production in time.

The first opinion, which is the opinion of all who believe in the Law of Moses our Teacher, is that the world as a whole—I mean to say, every existent other than God, may He be exalted—was brought into existence by God after having been purely and absolutely nonexistent, and that God, may He be exalted, had existed alone, and nothing else—neither an angel nor a sphere nor what subsists within the sphere. Afterward, through His will and His volition, He brought into existence out of nothing all the beings as they are, time itself being one of the created things. For time is consequent upon motion, and motion is an accident in what is moved. Furthermore, what is moved—that is, that upon the motion of which time is consequent—is itself created in time and came to be after not having been. Accordingly, one's saying: God "was" before He created the world—where the word "was" is indicative of time—and similarly all the thoughts that are carried along in the mind regarding the infinite duration of His existence before the creation of the world, are all of them due to a supposition regarding time or to an imagining of time and not due to the true reality of time. For time is undubitably an accident. According to us it is one of the created accidents, as are blackness and whiteness. And though it does not belong to the species of quality, it is nevertheless, generally stated, an accident necessarily following upon motion, as is made clear to whoever has understood the discourse of Aristotle on the elucidation of time and on the true reality of its existence. . . .

This is one of the opinions. And it is the undoubtedly a basis of the law of Moses our Teacher. And it is second to the basis that is the belief in the unity [of God]. Nothing other than this should come to your mind. It was Abraham our Father who began to proclaim in public this opinion to which speculation had led him. For this reason he made his proclamation "in the name of the Lord, God of the world" (Gen. 21:33);** he had also explicitly stated this opinion in saying: "Maker of heaven and earth" (Gen. 14:22).

The second opinion is that of all the philosophers of whom we have heard reports and whose discourses we have seen. They say that it is absurd that God would bring a thing into existence out of nothing. Furthermore, according to them, it is likewise not possible that a thing should pass away into nothing; I mean to say that it is not possible that a certain being, endowed with matter and form, should be generated out of the absolute nonexistence of that matter, or that it should pass away into the absolute nonexistence of that matter. To predicate of God that He is able to do this is, according to them, like predicating of Him that He is able to bring together two contraries in one instant of time; or that He is able to create something that is like Himself, may He be exalted, or to make Himself corporeal, or to create a square whose diagonal is equal to its side, and similar impossibilities. What may be understood from their discourse is that they say that just as His not bringing impossible things into existence does not argue a lack of power on His part—since what is impossible has a firmly established nature that is not produced by an agent and that consequently cannot be changed—it likewise is not due to lack of power on His part that He is not able to bring into existence a thing out of nothing, for his belongs to the class of all the impossible things. Hence they believe that there exists a certain matter that is eternal as the Deity is eternal; and that He does not exist without it, nor does it exist without Him. They do not believe that it has the same rank in what exists as He, may He be exalted, but that He is the cause of its existence; and that it has the same relation toward Him as, for instance, clay has toward a potter or iron toward a smith; and that He creates in it whatever He wishes. Thus He sometimes forms out of it a heaven and an earth, and sometimes He forms out of it something else. The people holding this opinion believe that the heaven too is subject to generation and passing-away, but that it is not generated out of nothing and does not pass away into nothing. For it is generated and passes away just as the individuals that are animals are generated from existent matter and pass away into existent matter. The generation and passing-away of the heaven is thus similar to that of all the other existents that are below it.

The people belonging to this sect are in their turn divided into several sects. But it is useless to mention their various sects and opinions in this treatise. However, the universal principle held by this sect is identical with what I have told you. This is also the belief of Plato. For you will find that Aristotle in the *Akroasis* (*Physics*) relates of him that he, I mean Plato, believed that the heaven is subject to generation and passing-away. And you likewise will find his doctrine plainly set forth in his book to Timaeus. But he does not believe what we believe, as is thought by him who does not examine opinions and is not precise in speculation; he (the interpreter) imagines that our opinion and his (Plato's) opinion are identical. But this is not so. As for us, we believe that the heaven was

---

**This is the invocation with which Maimonides begins each of the three parts of the *Guide of the Perplexed*.

generated out of nothing after a state of absolute nonexistence, whereas he believes that it has come into existence and has been generated from some other thing. This then is the second opinion.

The third opinion is that of Aristotle, his followers, and the commentators of his books. He asserts what also is asserted by the people belonging to the sect that has just been mentioned, namely, that something endowed with matter can by no means be brought into existence out of that which has no matter. He goes beyond this by saying that the heaven is in no way subject to generation and passing-away. His opinion on this point may be summed up as follows. He thinks that this being as a whole, such as it is, has never ceased to be and will never do so; that the permanent thing not subject to generation and passing-away, namely, the heaven, likewise does not cease to be; that time and motion are perpetual and everlasting and not subject to generation and passing-away; and also that the thing subject to generation and passing-away, namely, that which is beneath the sphere of the moon, does not cease to be. I mean to say that its first matter is not subject in its essence to generation and passing-away, but that various forms succeed each other in it in such a way that it divests itself of one form and assumes another. He thinks, furthermore, that this whole higher and lower order cannot be corrupted and abolished, that no innovation can take place in it that is not according to its nature, and that no occurrence that deviates from what is analogous to it can happen in it in any way. He asserts—though he does not do so textually, but this is what his opinion comes to—that in his opinion it would be an impossibility that will should change in God or a new volition arise in Him; and that all that exists has been brought into existence, in the state in which it is at present, by God through His volition; but that it was not produced after having been in a state of nonexistence. He thinks that just as it is impossible that the Deity should become nonexistent or that His essence should undergo a change, it is impossible that a volition should undergo a change in Him or a new will arise in Him. Accordingly, it follows necessarily that this being as a whole has never ceased to be as it is at present and will be as it is in the future eternity.

This is a summary and the truth of these opinions. They are the opinions of those according to whom the existence of the Deity for this world has been demonstrated. Those who have no knowledge of the existence of the Deity, may He be held sublime and honored, but think that things are subject to generation and passing-away through conjunction and separation due to chance and that there is no one who governs and orders being, are Epicurus, his following, and those like him, as is related by Alexander. It is useless for us to mention these sects. For the existence of the Deity has already been demonstrated, and there can be no utility in our mentioning the opinions of groups of people who built their doctrine upon a foundation the reverse of which has been demonstrated as true. Similarly it is useless for us to wish to prove as true the assertion of the people holding the second opinion, I mean that according to which the heaven is subject to generation and passing-away. For they believe in eternity; and there is, in our opinion, no difference between those who believe that heaven must of necessity be generated from a thing and pass away into a thing or the belief of Aristotle who believed that it is not subject to generation and corruption. For the purpose of every follower of the Law of Moses and Abraham our Father or of those who go the way of these two is to believe that there is nothing eternal in any way at all existing simultaneously with God; to believe also that the bringing into existence of a being out of nonexistence is for the Deity not an impossibility, but rather an obligation, as is deemed likewise by some of the men of speculation.

After we have expounded those opinions, I shall begin to explain and summarize the proofs of Aristotle in favor of his opinion and the motive that incited him to adopt it.

Petrarch

(1304–1374)

Francesco Petrarca, or Petrarch (1304-74), is famous as a humanist poet and scholar, and to his own age he was no less renowned as a man of the world. An Italian by birth, Petrarch was educated in France and studied law in Italy. Although his interests centered around literature, he was the friend and political adviser of popes and princes and an educational reformer. Serving Cardinal Colonna, Petrarch became a canon and traveled throughout Europe. After a period of retirement writing at Vaucluse in southeastern France, he received the laurel crown at Rome in 1341 for his Italian poetry. Diplomatic services took him to Italy; he then spent time at Avignon. After the death of Cardinal Colonna, Petrarch served the Visconti family before his final retirement to Arquà, where he died.

A major figure in Italian literature and often called "the father of humanism," Petrarch shows the mutual attraction of ascetic and secular values so characteristic of modern man. His works in Latin, which he felt to be still the literary language *par excellence*, include: an epic, *Africa; Metrical Epistles; On Contempt for the Worldly Life; On Solitude*; and the *Letters*. His Italian works include the *Trionfi* (Triumphs) and the *Canzoniere* (Song Book). The latter is responsible for his fame as a love poet; inspired by a young girl, Laura, whom he first saw in 1327, Petrarch wrote the lyrics which, especially in the sonnet and ode forms, established a model for generations of European poets.

The following letter, originally in Latin (1336), is taken from Robinson and Rolfe, *Petrarch* (New York, G.P. Putnam's Sons, 1898; 2d ed., 1914).

The Letter to Posterity provides an autobiographical introduction to Petrarch's life and work. The two short examples of his poetry reveal Petrarch's feelings about love and his attitude toward the corruption evident in the church of his day.[1]

The Ascent of Mount Ventoux

(Letter to Dionisio da Borgo San Sepolcro)

TO-DAY I made the ascent of the highest mountain in this region, which is not improperly called Ventosum. My only motive was the wish to see what so great an elevation had to offer. I have had the expedition in mind for many years; for, as you know, I have lived in this region from infancy, having been cast here by that fate which determines the affairs of men. Consequently the mountain, which is visible from a great distance, was ever before my eyes, and I conceived the plan of some time doing what I have at last accomplished to-day. The idea took hold upon me with especial force when, in re-reading Livy's *History of Rome*, yesterday, I happened upon the place where Philip of Macedon, the same who waged war against the Romans, ascended Mount Haemus in Thessaly, from whose summit he was able, it is said, to see two seas, the Adriatic and the Euxine. Whether this be true or false I have not been able to determine, for the mountain is too far away, and writers disagree. Pomponius Mela, the cosmographer—not to mention others who have spoken of this

---

[1] Both selections are taken from Mark Musa, trans., *Petrarch*, World's Classics Series, (Oxford University Press, 1985), pp. 1–10, 50–51.

occurrence—admits its truth without hesitation; Titus Livius, on the other hand, considers it false. I, assuredly, should not have left the question long in doubt, had that mountain been as easy to explore as this one. Let us leave this matter one side, however, and return to my mountain here'—it seems to me that a young man in private life may well be excused for attempting what an aged king could undertake without arousing criticism.

When I came to look about for a companion I found, strangely enough, that hardly one among my friends seemed suitable, so rarely do we meet with just the right combination of personal tastes and characteristics, even among those who are dearest to us. This one was too apathetic, that one over-anxious; this one too slow, that one too hasty; one was too sad, another over-cheerful; one more simple, another more sagacious, than I desired. I feared this one's taciturnity and that one's loquacity. The heavy deliberation of some repelled me as much as the lean incapacity of others. I rejected those who were likely to irritate me by a cold want of interest, as well as those who might weary me by their excessive enthusiasm. Such defects, however grave, could be borne with at home, for charity suffereth all things, and friendship accepts any burden; but it is quite otherwise on a journey, where every weakness becomes much more serious. So, as I was bent upon pleasure and anxious that my enjoyment should be unalloyed, I looked about me with unusual care, balanced against one another the various characteristics of my friends, and without committing any breach of friendship I silently condemned every trait which might prove disagreeable on the way. And—would you believe it?—I finally turned homeward for aid, and proposed the ascent to my only brother, who is younger than I, and with whom you are well acquainted. He was delighted and gratified beyond measure by the thought of holding the place of a friend as well as of a brother.

At the time fixed we left the house, and by evening reached Malaucène, which lies at the foot of the mountain, to the north. Having rested there a day, we finally made the ascent this morning, with no companions except two servants; and a most difficult task it was. The mountain is a very steep and almost inaccessible mass of stony soil. But, as the poet has well said, "Remorseless toil conquers all." It was a long day, the air fine. We enjoyed the advantages of vigour of mind and strength and agility of body, and everything else essential to those engaged in such an undertaking, and so had no other difficulties to face than those of the region itself. We found an old shepherd in one of the mountain dales, who tried, at great length, to dissuade us from the ascent, saying that some fifty years before he had, in the same ardour of youth, reached the summit, but had gotten for his pains nothing except fatigue and regret, and clothes and body torn by the rocks and briars. No one, so far as he or his companions knew, had ever tried the ascent before or after him. But his counsels increased rather than diminished our desire to proceed, since youth is suspicious of warnings. So the old man, finding that his efforts were in vain, went a little way with us, and pointed out a rough path among the rocks, uttering many admonitions, which he continued to send after us even after we had left him behind. Surrendering to him all such garments or other possessions as might prove burdensome to us, we made ready for the ascent, and started off at a good pace. But as usually happens, fatigue quickly followed upon our excessive exertion, and we soon came to a halt at the top of a certain cliff. Upon starting on again we went more slowly, and I especially advanced along the rocky way with a more deliberate step. While my brother chose a direct path straight up the ridge, I weakly took an easier one which really descended. When I was called back, and the right road was shown me, I replied that I hoped to find a better way round on the other side, and that I did not mind going farther if the path were only less steep. This was just an excuse for my laziness; and when the others had already reached a considerable height I was still wandering in the valleys. I had failed to find an easier path, and had only increased the distance and difficulty of the ascent. At last I became disgusted with the intricate way I had chosen, and resolved to ascend without more ado. When I reached my brother, who while waiting for me, had had ample opportunity for rest, I was tired and irritated. We walked along together for a time, but hardly had we passed the first spur when I forgot about the circuitous route which I had just tried, and took a lower one again. Once more I followed an easy, roundabout path through winding valleys, only to find myself soon in my old difficulty. I was simply trying to avoid the exertion of the ascent; but no human ingenuity can alter the nature of things, or cause anything to reach a height by going down. Suffice it to say that, much to my vexation and my brother's amusement, I made this same mistake three times or more during a few hours.

After being frequently misled in this way, I finally sat down in a valley and transferred my winged thoughts from things corporeal to the immaterial, addressing myself as follows:—"What thou hast repeatedly experienced to-day in the ascent of this mountain, happens to thee, as to many, in the journey toward the blessed life. But this is not so readily perceived by men, since the motions of the body are obvious and external while those of the soul are invisible and hidden. Yes, the life which we call blessed is to be sought for on a high eminence, and strait is the way that leads to it. Many, also, are the hills that lie between; and we must ascend, by a glorious stairway, from strength to strength. At the top is at once the end of our struggles and the goal for which we are bound. All wish to reach this goal, but, as Ovid says, 'To wish is little; we must long with the utmost eagerness to gain our end.' Thou certainly dost ardently desire, as well as simply wish, unless thou deceivest thyself in this matter, as in so many others. What, then, doth hold thee back? Nothing, assuredly, except that thou wouldst take a path which seems, at first thought, more easy, leading through low and worldly pleasures. But nevertheless in the end, after long wanderings, thou must perforce either climb the steeper path, under the burden of tasks foolishly deferred, to its blessed culmination, or lie down in the valley of thy sins, and (I shudder to think of it!), if the shadow of death overtake thee, spend an eternal night amid constant torments." These thoughts stimulated both body and mind in a wonderful degree for facing the difficulties which yet remained. Oh, that I might traverse in spirit that other road for which I long day and night, even as to-day I overcome material obstacles by my bodily exertions! And I know not why it should not be far easier, since the swift immortal soul can reach its goal in the twinkling of an eye, without passing through space, while my progress to-day was necessarily slow, dependent as I was upon a failing body weighed down by heavy members.

One peak of the mountain, the highest of all, the country people call "Sonny," why, I do not know, unless by antiphrasis, as I have sometimes suspected in other instances; for the peak in question would seem to be the father of all the surroundings ones. On its top is a little level place, and here we could at last rest our tired bodies.

Now, my father, since you have followed the thoughts that spurred me on in my ascent, listen to the rest of the story, and devote one hour, I pray you, to reviewing the experiences of my entire day. At first, owing to the unaccustomed quality of the air and the effect of the great sweep of view spread out before me, I stood like one dazed. I beheld the clouds under our feet, and what I had read of Athos and Olympus seemed less incredible as I myself witnessed the same things from a mountain of less fame. I turned my eyes toward Italy, whither my heart most inclined. The Alps, rugged and snow-capped, seemed to rise close by, although they were really at a great distance; the very same Alps through which that fierce enemy of the Roman name once made his way, bursting the rocks, if we may believe the report, by the application of vinegar. I signed, I must confess, for the skies of Italy, which I beheld rather with my mind than with my eyes. An inexpressible longing came over me to see once more my friend and my country. At the same time I reproached myself for this double weakness, springing, as it did, from a soul not yet steeled to manly resistance. And yet there were excuses for both of these cravings, and a number of distinguished writers might be summoned to support me.

Then a new idea took possession of me, and I shifted my thoughts to a consideration of time rather than place. "To-day it is ten years since, having completed thy youthful studies, thou didst leave Bologna. Eternal God! In the name of immutable wisdom, think what alterations in thy character this intervening period has beheld! I pass over a thousand instances. I am not yet in a safe harbour where I can calmly recall past storms. The time may come when I can review in due order all the experiences of the past, saying with St. Augustine, 'I desire to recall my foul actions and the carnal corruption of my soul, not because I love them, but that I may the more love thee, O my God.' Much that is doubtful and evil still clings to me, but what I once loved, that I love no longer. And yet what am I saying? I still love it, but with shame, but with heaviness of heart. Now, at last, I have confessed the truth. So it is. I love, but love what I would not love, what I would that I might hate. Though loath to do so, though constrained, though sad and sorrowing, still I do love, and I feel in my miserable self the truth of the well known words, 'I will hate if I can; if not, I will love against my will.' Three years have not yet passed since that perverse and wicked passion which had a firm gasp upon me and held undisputed sway in my heart began to discover a rebellious opponent, who was unwilling longer to yield obedience. These two adversaries have joined in close combat for the supremacy, and for a long time now a harassing and doubtful war has been waged in the field of my thoughts."

Thus I turned over the last ten years in my mind, and then, fixing my anxious gaze on the future, I asked myself, "If, perchance, thou shouldst prolong this uncertain life of thine for yet two lustres, and shouldst make and advance toward virtue proportionate to the distance to which thou hast departed from thine original infatuation during the past two years, since the new longing first encountered the old, couldst thou, on reaching thy fortieth year, face death, if not with complete assurance, at least with hopefulness, calmly dismissing from thy thoughts the residuum of life as it faded into old age?"

These and similar reflections occurred to me, my father. I rejoiced in my progress, mourned my weakness, and commiserated the universal instability of human conduct. I had well-nigh forgotten where I was and our object in coming; but at last I dismissed my anxieties, which were better suited to other surroundings, and resolved to look about me and see what we had come to see. The sinking sun and the lengthening shadows of the mountain were already warning us that the time was near at hand when we must go. As if suddenly wakened from sleep, I turned about and gazed toward the west. I was unable to discern the summits of the Pyrenees, which form the barrier between France and Spain; not because of any intervening obstacle that I know of but owing simply to the insufficiency of our mortal vision. But I could see with the utmost clearness, off to the right, the mountains of the region about Lyons, and to the left the bay of Marseilles and the waters that lash the shores of Aigues Mortes, altho' all these places were so distant that it would require a journey of several days to reach them. Under our very eyes flowed the Rhone.

While I was thus dividing my thoughts, now turning my attention to some terrestrial object that lay before me, now raising my soul, as I had done my body, to higher planes, it occurred to me to look into my copy of St. Augustine's *Confessions*, a gift that I owe to your love, and that I always have about me, in memory of both the author and the giver. I opened the compact little volume, small indeed in size, but of infinite charm, with the intention of reading whatever came to hand, for I could happen upon nothing that would be otherwise than edifying and devout. Now it chanced that the tenth book presented itself. My brother, waiting to hear something of St. Augustine's from my lips, stood attentively by. I call him, and God too, to witness that where I first fixed my eyes it was written: "And men go about to wonder at the heights of the mountains, and the mighty waves of the sea, and the wide sweep of rivers, and the circuit of the ocean, and the revolution of the stars, but themselves they consider not." I was abashed, and, asking my brother (who was anxious to hear more), not to annoy me, I closed the book, angry with myself that I should still be admiring earthly things who might long ago have learned from even the pagan philosophers that nothing is wonderful but the soul, which, when great itself, finds nothing great outside itself. Then, in truth, I was satisfied that I had seen enough of the mountain; I turned my inward eye upon myself, and from that time not a syllable fell from my lips until we reached the bottom again. Those words had given me occupation enough, for I could not believe that it was by a mere accident that I happened upon them. What I had there read I believed to be addressed to me and to no other, remembering that St. Augustine had once suspected the same thing in his own case, when, on opening the book of the Apostle, as he himself tell us, the first words that he saw there were, "Not in rioting and drunkenness, not in chambering and wantonness, not in strife and envying. But put ye on the Lord Jesus Christ, and make not provision for the flesh, to fulfil the lusts thereof."

The same thing happened earlier to St. Anthony, when he was listening to the Gospel where it is written, "If thou wilt be perfect, go and sell that thou hast, and give to the poor, and thou shalt have treasure in heaven: and come and follow me." Believing this scripture to have been read for his especial benefit, as his biographer Athanasius says, he guided himself by its aid to the Kingdom of Heaven. And as Anthony on hearing these words waited for nothing more, and as Augustine upon reading the Apostle's admonition sought no farther, so I concluded my reading in the few words which I have given. I thought in silence of the lack of good counsel in us mortals, who neglect what is noblest in ourselves, scatter our energies in all directions, and waste ourselves in a vain show, because we look about us for what is to be found only within. I wondered at the natural nobility of our soul, save when it debases itself of its own free will, and deserts its original estate, turning what God has given it for its honour into dishonour. How many times, think you, did I turn back that day, to glance at the summit of the mountain, which seemed scarcely a cubit high compared with the range of human contemplation,—when it is not immersed in the foul mire of earth? With every downward step I asked myself this: If we are ready to endure so much sweat and labour in order that we bring our bodies a little nearer heaven, how can a soul struggling toward God, up the steeps of human pride and human destiny, fear any cross or prison or sting of fortune? How few, I thought, but are diverted from their path by the fear of difficulties or the love of ease! How happy the lot of those few, if any such there be! Is it of them, assuredly, that the poet was thinking, when he wrote:

Happy the man who is skilled to understand
Nature's hid causes; who beneath his feet
All terrors casts, and death's relentless doom,
And the loud orar of greedy Acheron.

How earnestly should we strive, not to stand on mountain-tops, but to trample beneath us those appetites which spring from earthly impulses.

With no consciousness of the difficulties of the way, amidst these preoccupation which I have so frankly revealed, we came, long after dark, but with the full moon lending us its friendly light, to the little inn which we had left that morning before dawn. The time during which the servants have been occupied in preparing our supper, I have spent in a secluded part of the house, hurriedly jotting down these experiences on the spur of the moment, lest, in case my task were postponed, my mood should change on leaving the place, and so my interest in writing flag.

You will see, my dearest father, that I wish nothing to be concealed from you, for I am careful to describe to you not only my life in general but even my individual reflections. And I beseech you, in turn, to pray that these vague and wandering thoughts of mine may some time become firmly fixed, and, after having been vainly tossed about from one interest to another, may direct themselves at last toward the single, true, certain, and everlasting good.

Letter to Posterity

You may, perhaps, have heard tell of me, though even this is doubtful, since a poor and insignificant name like mine will hardly have travelled far in space or time. If, however, you have heard of me, you may wish to know the kind of man I was or about the fruit of my labours, especially those you may have heard of or, at any rate, of those whose titles at least may have reached you.

To begin with myself, then, what men say about me will differ widely, since in passing judgement almost everyone is influenced not so much by truth as by whim; there is no measure for praise and blame. I was, in truth, one of your own, a poor mortal, neither of high origin, nor, on the other hand, of too humble birth, but belonging, as Augustus Caesar says of himself, to an old family. As for my disposition, I am not by nature evil or wanting in modesty except as contagious custom may have infected me. My youth was gone before I realized it; young manhood carried me away; but a maturer age brought me to my senses and taught me by experience the truth I had read in books long before: that youth and pleasure are vain—the lesson of that Author of all times and ages, Who permits wretched mortals, puffed with emptiness, to wander for a time until at last, becoming mindful of their sins, they learn to know themselves. In my youth I was blessed with an agile, active body, though not particularly strong, and while I cannot boast of being very handsome, I was good looking enough in my younger days. I had a clear complexion, between light and dark, lively eyes, and for many years sharp vision, which, however, unexpectedly deserted me when I passed my sixtieth birthday, and forced me, reluctantly, to resort to the use of glasses. Although I had always been perfectly healthy, old age assailed me with its usual array of discomforts.

My parents were good people, Florentine in origin, and not too well off; in fact, I may as well admit it, they were on the edge of poverty. Since they had been expelled from their native city, I was born to exile, at Arezzo, in the year 1304 of the age beginning with Christ's birth, July the twentieth, on a Monday, at dawn. I have always had great contempt for money; not that I wouldn't like to be rich, but because I hate the work and care which are invariably associated with wealth. I have never liked to give great feasts; on the contrary, I have led a happier life with a plain diet and ordinary foods than all the followers of Apricius, with their elaborate dinners. So-called banquets, those vulgar bouts, hostile to sobriety and good manners, I have always found to be repugnant. I have always thought it tiresome and useless to invite others to such affairs, and no less so to be invited to them myself by others. On the other hand, to dine with one's friends I find most pleasant, and nothing has ever given me more delight than the unannounced arrival of a friend— nor have I ever willingly sat down to table without a friend. And nothing annoys me more than display, not only because it is bad in itself, and opposed to humility, but because it is disturbing and distracting.

In my younger days I struggled constantly with an overwhelming but pure love-affair—my only one, and I would have struggled with it longer had not premature death, bitter but salutary for me, extinguished the cooling flames. I certainly wish I could say that I have always been entirely free from desires of the flesh, but I would be lying if I did. I can, however, surely say this: that, while I was being carried away by the ardour of my youth and by my temperament, I always detested such sins from the depth of my soul. When I was nearing the age of forty, and my vigour and passions were still strong, I renounced abruptly not only those bad habits, but even the very recollection of them—as if I had never looked at a woman. This I consider to be among my greatest blessings, and I thank God, who freed me while I was still sound and vigorous from that vile slavery which I always found hateful. But let us turn to other matters now.

I have taken pride in others but never in myself, and insignificant as I was, I have always considered myself to be even more so. As for anger, it very often did harm to me but never to others. I have always been most desirous of honourable friendships, and have cherished them faithfully. And I boast without fear, since I know I speak sincerely, that while I am prone to take offence, I am equally quick to forget offences and have a good memory for benefits received. I had the good fortune of associating with kings and princes, and having the friendship of nobles to the point of exciting envy. But it is the cruel fate of the elderly that sooner or later they must weep for friends who have passed away. Some of the greatest kings of this age have loved me and cultivated my friendship. They may know why; I certainly do not. I was on such terms with some of them that in a certain sense they seemed to be more my guests than I theirs; their eminence in no way made me uncomfortable; on the contrary, it brought with it many advantages. I kept aloof, however, from many of whom I was very fond; such was my innate spirit for freedom that I carefully avoided those whose high standing seemed to threaten the freedom I loved so much.

I had a well balanced mind rather than a keen one, one adapted to all kinds of good and wholesome study, but especially inclined to moral philosophy and poetry. In the course of time I neglected the latter and found pleasure in sacred literature, finding in it a hidden sweetness which I had previously taken lightly, and I came to regard the works of the poets as mere amenities. Though I was interested in many subjects, I devoted myself especially to the study of antiquity, for I always disliked our own age—so much so, that had it not been for the love of those dear to me, I would have preferred to have been born in any other time than our own. In order to forget my own times, I have always tried to place myself mentally in another age; thus I delighted in history—though I was troubled by the conflicting statements, but when in doubt I accepted what appeared to me most probable or else yielded to the authority of the writer.

Many people have said that my style is clear and compelling; but to them it seems weak and obscure. In fact, in ordinary conversation with friends, or acquaintances, I never worried about my language, and I have always marvelled at the fact that Augustus Caesar took such pains in this respect. When, however, the subject-matter or the circumstances or the listener seemed to demand otherwise, I have given some attention to style, with what success, however, I cannot say. Let those to whom I spoke be the judges. If only I have lived well, I care little how well I spoke. Mere elegance of language can result at best in an empty reputation.

My life up to now has, through circumstances or my own choice, been disposed as follows. Some of my first year was spent at Arezzo, where I first saw the light of day; the following six years were, since my mother had by this time been recalled from exile, spent at my father's estate at Ancisa, about fourteen miles above Florence. My eighth year was spent at Pisa, the ninth and later years in Transalpine Gaul, at Avignon, on the left bank of the Rhone, where the Roman Pontiff holds and has long held the Church of Christ in shameful exile—though a few years ago it seemed as if Urban V was on the point of restoring the church to its ancient seat. But clearly nothing is coming of this effort and, what is worst of all, the Pope, while he was still living, seemed to repent of his good deed. If he had lived a little longer, he certainly would have learned what I thought of his return. My pen was in my hand when suddenly he gave up both his exalted office and his life. Unhappy man! To think he could have died before St. Peter's altar and in his own home! Had his successors remained in their capital he would have been looked upon as the cause of this fortunate change or, had they left Rome, his virtue would have been all the more conspicuous as their fault, in contrast, would have been more evident But such lamentations here stray too far from my subject.

So then, on the windy banks of the river Rhone I spent my boyhood, under the care of my parents, and then, my entire youth under the direction of my own vanities. There were, however, long intervals spent elsewhere, for at that time I spent four full years in the little town of Carpentras, a little to the east of Avignon. In these two places I learned as much grammar, logic, and rhetoric as my age permitted, or rather, as much as is usually taught in school, and how little that is, dear reader, you well know. Then I went to Montpellier to study law, and spent four years there, and then to Bologna for three years where I attended lectures on civil law, and many thought I would have done very well had I continued my studies. But I gave up the subject altogether as soon as it was no longer necessary to follow the wishes of my parents. It was not because I disliked the power and authority of the law, which is undoubtedly very great, or because of the endless references it contains to Roman antiquity, which I admired so, but rather because I felt it was being continuously degraded by those who practice it. I hated the idea of learning an art which I would not practise dishonestly, and could hardly hope to practise otherwise. Had I made the latter attempt, my scrupulousness would undoubtedly have been ascribed to incompetence.

So at the age of twenty-two I returned home. Since habit has nearly the force of nature, I call home my Avignon exile for I had lived there since childhood. I was already beginning to become known there, and my friendship was sought out by prominent men. Why, I do not know. I must confess that this is a source of surprise to me now, although it seemed natural enough at an age when we are used to considering ourselves worthy of the highest respect. I was courted first and foremost by that eminent and noble Colonna family which at that period adorned the Roman Curia with their presence. While I might be now, at that time I was certainly unworthy of the esteem in which that family held me. I was especially welcomed and taken to Gascony by the incomparable Giacomo Colonna, then bishop of Lombez, the like of whom I doubt that I have ever seen or ever shall see. There in the shade of the Pyrenees I spent a heavenly summer in delightful conversation with my master and the members of our company, and never do I recall the experience without a sigh of regret.

Returning, I spent many years in the house of Giacomo's brother, Cardinal Giovanni Colonna, not as if I were a servant and he my lord but rather as if he were my father, or better, a most affectionate brother. It was as though I were in my very own home. About this time, youthful curiosity impelled me to visit France and Germany. And while I invented other reasons to gain the approval of my elders for the journey, the real reason was burning desire for new sights. First I visited Paris, as I was anxious to discover what was true and what fictitious in the accounts I had heard of that city. After my return from this journey I went to Rome, which I had ardently desired to visit since I was a child. There I soon came to be a great admirer of Stefano, the noble head of the Colonna family, who was an ancient hero, and I was in turn so welcomed by him in every respect that it was as though I were his son. The affection and good will which this excellent man showed me persisted until the end of his life, and it lives with me still, and never will it fade, not until I myself cease to be.

Having returned I experienced the innate repugnance I have always felt for city life, and especially for that disgusting city of Avignon which I truly abhorred. Seeking some means of escape, I fortunately discovered a delightful valley, narrow and secluded, called Vaucluse, about fifteen miles from Avignon, where the Sorgue, the prince of streams, has its source. Captured by the charms of the place, I transferred myself and my books there. If I were to tell you what I did there during those many years, it would prove to be a long story. Indeed, almost every bit of writing I did was either done or begun or at least conceived there, and my undertakings were so numerous that even to the present day they keep me busy and weary. My mind, like my body, is more agile than strong, so that while it was easy for me to conceive of many projects, I would drop them because they were too difficult to execute. The aspect of my surroundings suggested my undertaking the composition of a sylvan bucolic song, my *Bucolicum carmen*. I also composed a work in two books on *The Life of Solitude (De vita solitaria),* which I dedicated to Philip, now exalted to the Cardinal and Bishop of Sibina. He was always a great man, but at the time of which I speak, he was only the humble Bishop of Cavaillon. He is the only one of my old friends who is still left, and he has always loved and treated me not episcopally, as Ambrose did Augustine, but as a brother.

One Friday in Holy Week while I was wandering in those mountains, I had the strong urge to write an epic poem about Scipio Africanus the Great, whose name had been dear to me since childhood. While I began the project with great enthusiasm, I soon, owing to a variety of distractions, put it aside. The poem was called *Africa,* after its hero, and by some fate, whether the book's or my own, it did not fail to arouse the interest of many even before its publication.

While leading a leisurely existence there, on one and the same day, remarkable as it may seem, I received letters from both the Roman Senate and the Chancellor at the University of Paris, summoning me to appear in Rome and Paris, respectively to receive the poet's laurel crown. In my youthful elation I convinced myself that I was quite worthy of this honour and recognition which came from such eminent judges, and I measured my own merit by the judgement of others. But I hesitated for a time over which invitation I should accept, and sent a letter to the Cardinal Giovanni Colonna, of whom I have already spoken, asking his opinion. He was so nearby that, having written to him late in the day, I had his reply before nine the next morning. I followed his advice, and recognized the claims of Rome as superior to all others (I still have the two letters I wrote to him on that occasion showing that I took his advice). So I set off for Rome. And although, as is the way of youth, I was a most indulgent judge of my own work, I was still uneasy about accepting my own estimation of myself as well as the verdict even of such men as those who summoned me, despite the fact that they would certainly not have honoured me with such an offer, if they had not believed me worthy.

So I decided to visit Naples first, and there I went to see that celebrated king and philosopher, Robert, who was as illustrious a ruler as he was a man of letters. He was, in truth, the only monarch of our times who was both a friend of learning and of virtue, and I asked him to examine me in such things as he found to criticize in my work. The warmth of his reception and judgement remains to this day a source of astonishment to me, and also undoubtedly to the reader who happens to know something of the matter. When he learned the reason for my coming, the king seemed very pleased. He was gratified by my youthful faith in him, and felt, perhaps, that he shared in a way the glory of my coronation, since I had chosen him above all men as my qualified critic. After talking over a great many things, I showed him my *Africa,* which pleased him so much that he asked me as a great favour to dedicate it to him. This was a request I certainly could not refuse, nor, in fact, would I have wished to refuse, even had it been in my power. He then set a day during which he would consider the object of my visit. He kept me busy from noon until evening, and since the time proved too short, with one discussion leading to another, we spent the two following days in the same way. Thus, having tested my ignorance for three days, the king finally pronounced me worthy of the laurel. He wanted to bestow the honour on me at Naples, and urged me to agree to this, but my love for Rome was stronger than the insistence of even so great a monarch as Robert. At length, finding me inflexible in my purpose, he sent me on my way with royal escorts and letters to the Roman Senate in which he enthusiastically expressed his flattering opinion of me. This royal judgement was in accord with that of many others, and especially with my own, but today I cannot accept either of those verdicts. In his case there was more affection and encouragement of youth than devotion to truth.

So then, I went to Rome, and continuing in spite of my unworthiness to rely upon the judgement of so eminent a critic, I who had been merely a simple student, received the laurel crown to the great joy of the Romans who attended the ceremony. This occasion is described elsewhere in my letters, both in prose and verse. The laurel, however, in no way gave me more wisdom, though it did arouse some envy—but that is a tale too long to be told here.

Leaving Rome, I went to Parma, and spent some time with the members of the Correggio family who were very good men and most generous to me but much at odds with each other. They gave Parma such a good government as it had never before had within the memory of man, and such as it is not likely ever to enjoy again.

I was most conscious of the honour I had just received, and worried for fear that I might seem to be unworthy of the distinction; consequently, as I was walking one day in the mountains and happened to cross the river Enza in the region of Reggio Selvapiana, I was struck by the beauty of the spot and began to write again the *Africa,* which I had put aside. In my enthusiasm, which had appeared to be dead, I wrote some lines that very day, and some more each day that followed until I returned to Parma. Here I happened to find a quiet and secluded house (which I later bought, and which is still my own), and I continued my task with such ardour and completed the work in so short a time, that the fact I did so still amazes me to this day. I was already thirty-four years old when I returned to the fountain of the Sorgue, and to my transalpine solitude. I had stayed long both in Parma and Verona, and I am thankful to say that everywhere I went I was treated with much greater esteem than I merited.

Some time after this, my growing reputation attracted the kindness of Giacomo the Younger of Carrara, a very fine man whose equal, I doubt, cannot be found among the rulers of his time. For years, when I was beyond the Alps, or whenever I happened to be in Italy, he constantly sent messengers and letters, and with his petitions he urged me to accept his friendship. At last, though I expected little satisfaction from the venture, I made up my mind to go to him and see what this insistence on the part of so eminent a person, and one who was a stranger to me, was all about. Then, after some time I went to Padua, where I was received by that man of illustrious memory not as a mere mortal might be received, but as the blessed are received in heaven—with such joy and such unbelievable affection and respect that I cannot adequately describe it is words and must, therefore, be silent. Among other things, when he learned that I had been a cleric from boyhood, he had me made a canon of Padua in order to bind me closer to himself and to his city. In short, if his life had been longer, that would have put an end to all my wanderings. But alas! Nothing mortal is enduring, and there is nothing sweet which sooner or later does not become bitter. He had scarcely given two years to me, to his country, and to the world before God, Who had given him to us, took him away. And it is not my blind love for him that makes me feel that neither I, nor his country, nor the world was worthy of him. Although the son, who succeeded him, was a very sensible and distinguished man, who like his father was always very cordial and respectful to me, I could stay no longer after the death of this man to whom I was so closely linked (even by the similarity of our ages) and I returned to France, not so much from desire to see again what I had already seen a thousand times, as from hope of getting rid of my misfortunes (the way a sick man does) with a change of scene. . . .

From the *Canzoniere*

134

I FIND no peace, and I am not at war,
I fear and hope, and burn and I am ice;
I fly above the heavens, and lie on earth,
and I grasp nothing and embrace the world.

One keeps me jailed who neither locks nor opens,
nor keeps me for her own nor frees the noose;
love does not kill, nor does he loose my chains;
he wants me lifeless but won't loosen me.

I see with no eyes, shout without a tongue;
I yearn to perish, and I beg for help;
I hate myself and love somebody else.

I thrive on pain and laugh with all my tears;
I dislike death as much as I do life;
because of you, lady, I am this way.

136

MAY heaven's fire pour down on your tresses,
since doing evil gives you so much pleasure,
impious one, who after streams and acorns
got fat and rich by starving other people,

you nest of treachery in which is hatched
all evil that today spreads through the world,
you slave of wine, of bedrooms, and of food,
high testing-ground for every kind of lust!

In all your rooms young girls and older men
are romping round, the devil in the middle
with bellows and his fire and his mirrors.

You were not raised on cushions in cool shade
but naked to the wind, barefoot in thorns.
May God smell all the stink from how you live!

Christine de Pizan

(c. 1365–c. 1430)

CRISTINA DA PIZZANO or Christine de Pizan was born in Venice, the daughter of Tommaso di Benvenuto da Pizzano, a physician with a doctoral degree from the University of Bologna. When she was three years old, King Charles V of France invited de Pizan's father to assume the post of court physician and astrologer. Tommaso brought his family to France, and despite his wife's opposition taught his daughter Latin, philosophy, and the sciences. When de Pizan was fifteen she married Éstienne de Castel, a royal secretary ten years her senior. Her marriage was extremely happy, and she continued her studies with Éstienne's encouragement. Unfortunately, tragedy struck the family. Charles V died in 1380 and Tommaso lost favour at court, dying in about 1385; subsequently de Pizan's husband died in an epidemic in 1389, leaving her a widow in her mid-twenties with three small children, a mother, and two brothers to support.

De Pizan turned to writing to make a living, and dedicated her works to nobles or members of the royal family, who provided the author and her relatives with gifts and patronage. Often writing on commission, she employed scribes to copy and lavishly illuminate her works, which were sumptuously bound at the request of wealthy nobles. Inspired by the Italian humanist Dante Alighieri, who wrote in Italian rather than Latin, de Pizan wrote in a French vernacular modelled upon Latin prose. She made no attempt to hide her intelligence, boldly engaging in debates with male academics and vigorously attacking male myths about women. During her career she wrote an important defence of women and courtly love, an official biography of Charles V, a treatise on the Roman and modern art of war, a political manual for the dauphin, lamentations on the Hundred Years' War, and numerous poems. The selection that follows is drawn from *The Book of the City of Ladies* (1405), the work for which she is most well known in modern times.[1] In part a feminist recasting of Giovanni Boccaccio's book on famous and infamous women of Antiquity, its title was inspired by St. Augustine's *City of God.* A companion work, *The Book of Three Virtues* (1405), instructed women of all classes in virtuous behaviour.

Following the disastrous French defeat at Agincourt and the Burgundian massacres in Paris in 1418, de Pizan retired to a convent and ceased to write for eleven years. However, after Joan of Arc defeated the English at Orléans and Troyes in 1429, de Pizan broke her silence to compose a lengthy poem in honour of this heroic member of her sex. The popular author died several months later, when she was about sixty-five years old. Although copies of her manuscripts circulated for over a century in France and England, her writings eventually fell into obscurity. Scholars only rediscovered Christine de Pizan's works in the twentieth century, and are now coming to appreciate her remarkably innovative feminist perspective, her contribution in spreading Renaissance learning beyond the confines of Italy, and experiments in developing a literary French vernacular.

---

[1] Selection reprinted from Earl Jeffrey Richards, trans., *The Book of the City of Ladies,* (New York: Persea Books, 1982), pp. 3–8, 62–64, 117–120, 153–155, 160–162, 217–218, 254–257.

From *The Book of the City of Ladies*

I.1.1. Here begins the Book of the City of Ladies, whose first chapter tells why and for what purpose this book was written.

One day as I was sitting alone in my study surrounded by books on all kinds of subjects, devoting myself to literary studies, my usual habit, my mind dwelt at length on the weighty opinions of various authors whom I had studied for a long time. I looked up from my book, having decided to leave such subtle questions in peace and to relax by reading some light poetry. With this in mind, I searched for some small book. By chance a strange volume came into my hands, not one of my own, but one which had been given to me along with some others. When I held it open and saw from its title page that it was by Mathéolus, I smiled, for though I had never seen it before, I had often heard that like other books it discussed respect for women. I thought I would browse through it to amuse myself. I had not been reading for very long when my good mother called me to refresh myself with some supper, for it was evening. Intending to look at it the next day, I put it down. The next morning, again seated in my study as was my habit, I remembered wanting to examine this book by Mathéolus. I started to read it and went on for a little while. Because the subject seemed to me not very pleasant for people who do not enjoy lies, and of no use in developing virtue or manners, given its lack of integrity in diction and theme, and after browsing here and there and reading the end, I put it down in order to turn my attention to more elevated and useful study. But just the sight of this book, even though it was of no authority, made me wonder how it happened that so many different men—and learned men among them—have been and are so inclined to express both in speaking and in their treatises and writing so many wicked insults about women and their behavior. Not only one or two and not even just this Mathéolus (for this book had a bad name anyway and was intended as a satire) but, more generally, judging from the treatises of all philosophers and poets and from all the orators—it would take too long to mention their names—it seems that they all speak from one and the same mouth. They all concur in one conclusion: that the behavior of women is inclined to and full of every vice. Thinking deeply about these matters, I began to examine my character and conduct as a natural woman and, similarly, I considered other women whose company I frequently kept, princesses, great ladies, women of the middle and lower classes, who had graciously told me of their most private and intimate thoughts, hoping that I could judge impartially and in good conscience whether the testimony of so many notable men could be true. To the best of my knowledge, no matter how long I confronted or dissected the problem, I could not see or realize how their claims could be true when compared to the natural behavior and character of women. Yet I still argued vehemently against women, saying that it would be impossible that so many famous men—such solemn scholars, possessed of such deep and great understanding, so clear-sighted in all things, as it seemed—could have spoken falsely on so many occasions that I could hardly find a book on morals where, even before I had read it in its entirety, I did not find several chapters or certain sections attacking women, no matter who the author was. This reason alone, in short, made me conclude that, although my intellect did not perceive my own great faults and, likewise, those of other women because of its simpleness and ignorance, it was however truly fitting that such was the case. And so I relied more on the judgment of others than on what I myself felt and knew. I was so transfixed in this line of thinking for such a long time that it seemed as if I were in a stupor. Like a gushing fountain, a series of authorities, whom I recalled one after another, came to mind, along with their opinions on this topic. And I finally decided that God formed a vile creature when He made woman, and I wondered how such a worthy artisan could have deigned to make such an abominable work which, from what they say, is the vessel as well as the refuge and abode of every evil and vice. As I was thinking this, a great unhappiness and sadness welled up in my heart, for I detested myself and the entire feminine sex, as though we were monstrosities in nature. And in my lament I spoke these words: "Oh, God, how can this be? For unless I stray from my faith, I must never doubt that Your infinite wisdom and most perfect goodness ever created anything which was not good. Did You yourself not create woman in a very special way and since that time did You not give her all those inclinations which it pleased You for her to have? And how could it be that You could go wrong in anything? Yet look at all these accusations which have been judged, decided, and concluded against women. I do not know how to understand this repugnance. If it is so, fair Lord God, that in fact so many abominations abound in the female sex, for You Yourself say that the testimony of two or three witnesses lends credence, why shall I not doubt that this is true? Alas, God, why did You not let me be born in the world as a man, so that all my inclinations would be to serve You better, and so that I would not stray in anything and would be as perfect as a man is said to be? But since Your kindness has not been extended to me, then forgive my negligence in Your service, most fair Lord God, and may it not displease You, for the servant who receives fewer gifts from his lord is less obliged in his service." I spoke these words to God in my lament and a great deal more for a very long time in sad reflection, and in my folly I considered myself most unfortunate because God had made me inhabit a female body in this world.

I.2. Here Christine describes how three ladies appeared to her and how the one who was in front spoke first and comforted her in her pain.

I.2.1 So occupied with these painful thoughts, my head bowed in shame, my eyes filled with tears, leaning on the pommel of my chair's armrest, I suddenly saw a ray of light fall on my lap, as though it were the sun. I shuddered then, as if wakened from sleep, for I was sitting in a shadow where the sun could not have shone at that hour. And as I lifted my head to see where this light was coming from, I saw three crowned ladies standing before me, and the splendor of their bright faces shone on me and throughout the entire room. Now no one would ask whether I was surprised, for my doors were shut and they had still entered. Fearing that some phantom had come to tempt me and filled with great fright, I made the Sign of the Cross on my forehead.

I.2.2 Then she who was the first of the three smiled and began to speak, "Dear daughter, do not be afraid, for we have not come here to harm or trouble you but to console you, for we have taken pity on your distress, and we have come to bring you out of the ignorance which so blinds your own intellect that you shun what you know for a certainty and believe what you do not know or see or recognize except by virtue of many strange opinions. You resemble the fool in the prank who was dressed in women's clothes while he slept; because those who were making fun of him repeatedly told him he was a woman, he believed their false testimony more readily than the certainty of his own identity. Fair daughter, have you lost all sense? Have you forgotten that when fine gold is tested in the furnace, it does not change or vary in strength but becomes purer the more it is hammered and handled in different ways? Do you not know that the best things are the most debated and the most discussed? If you wish to consider the question of the highest form of reality, which consists in ideas or celestial substances, consider whether the greatest philosophers who have lived and whom you support against your own sex have ever resolved whether ideas are false and contrary to the truth. Notice how these same philosophers contradict and criticize one another, just as you have seen in the *Metaphysics* where Aristotle takes their opinions to task and speaks similarly of Plato and other philosophers. And note, moreover, how even Saint Augustine and the Doctors of the Church have criticized Aristotle in certain passages, although he is known as the prince of philosophers in whom both natural and moral philosophy attained their highest level. It also seems that you think that all the words of the philosophers are articles of faith, that they could never be wrong. As far as the poets of whom you speak are concerned, do you not know that they spoke on many subjects in a fictional way and that often they mean the contrary of what their words openly say? One can interpret them according to the grammatical figure of *antiphrasis,* which means, as you know, that if you call something bad, in fact, it is good, and also vice versa. Thus I advise you to profit from their works and to interpret them in the manner in which they are intended in those passages where they attack women. Perhaps this man, who called himself Mathéolus in his own book, intended it in such a way, for there are many things which, if taken literally, would be pure heresy. As for the attack against the estate of marriage—which is a holy estate, worthy and ordained by God—made not only by Mathéolus but also by others and even by the *Romance of the Rose* where greater credibility is averred because of the authority of its author, it is evident and proven by experience that the contrary of the evil which they posit and claim to be found in this estate through the obligation and fault of women is true. For where has the husband ever been found who would allow his wife to have authority to abuse and insult him as a matter of course, as these authorities maintain? I believe that, regardless of what you might have read, you will never see such a husband with your own eyes, so badly colored are these lies. Thus, in conclusion, I tell you, dear friend, that simplemindedness has prompted you to hold such an opinion. Come back to yourself, recover your senses, and do not trouble yourself anymore over such absurdities. For you know that any evil spoken of women so generally only hurts those who say it, not women themselves."

I.27. Christine asks reason whether God has ever wished to ennoble the mind of woman with the loftiness of the sciences; and reason's answer.

I.27.1 After hearing these things, I replied to the lady who spoke infallibly: "My lady, truly has God revealed great wonders in the strength of these women whom you describe. But please enlighten me again, whether it has ever pleased this God, who has bestowed so many favors on women, to honor the feminine sex with the privilege of the virtue of high understanding and great learning, and whether women ever have a clever enough mind for this. I wish very much to know this because men maintain that the mind of women can learn only a little"

She answered, "My daughter, since I told you before, you know quite well that the opposite of their opinion is true, and to show you this even more clearly, I will give you proof through examples. I tell you again—and don't doubt the contrary—if it were customary to send daughters to school like sons, and if they were then taught the natural sciences, they would learn as thoroughly and understand the subtleties of all the arts and sciences as well as sons. And by chance there happen to be such women, for, as I touched on before, just as women have more delicate bodies than men, weaker and less able to perform many tasks, so do they have minds that are freer and sharper whenever they apply themselves."

"My lady, what are you saying? With all due respect, could you dwell longer on this point, please. Certainly men would never admit this answer is true, unless it is explained more plainly, for they believe that one normally sees that men know more than women do."

She answered, "Do you know why women know less?"

"Not unless you tell me, my lady."

"Without the slightest doubt, it is because they are not involved in many different things, but stay at home, where it is enough for them to run the household, and there is nothing which so instructs a reasonable creature as the exercise and experience of many different things."

"My lady, since they have minds skilled in conceptualizing and learning, just like men, why don't women learn more?"

She replied, "Because, my daughter, the public does not require them to get involved in the affairs which men are commissioned to execute, just as I told you before. It is enough for women to perform the usual duties to which they are ordained. As for judging from experience, since one sees that women usually know less than men, that therefore their capacity for understanding is less, look at men who farm the flatlands or who live in the mountains. You will find that in many countries they seem completely savage because they are so simple-minded. All the same, there is no doubt that Nature provided them with the qualities of body and mind found in the wisest and most learned men. All of this stems from a failure to learn, though, just as I told you, among men and women, some possess better minds than others. Let me tell you about women who have possessed great learning and profound understanding and treat the question of the similarity of women's minds to men's."

II. 13. Christine asks Lady Rectitude whether what the books and men say is true, that married life is so hard to endure because of women and the wrong they cause. Rectitude answers and begins to speak of the great love shown by women for their husbands.

II. 13.1 Then, as we were searching for these women by order of Lady Rectitude, I spoke these words as we went along, "My lady, truly you and Reason have solved and settled all the problems and questions which I could not answer, and I consider myself very well informed about what I asked. I have learned a great deal from you: how all things which are feasible and knowable, whether in the area of physical strength or in the wisdom of the mind and every virtue, are possible and easy for women to accomplish. But could you now please confirm for me whether what men claim, and what so many authors testify, is true—a topic about which I am thinking very deeply—that life within the institution of marriage is filled and occupied with such great unhappiness for men because of women's faults and impetuosity, and because of their rancorous ill-humour, as is written in so many books? Many assert that these women care so little for their husbands and their company that nothing else annoys them as much? For this reason, in order to escape and avoid such inconveniences, many authorities have advised wise men not to marry, affirming that no women—or very few—are loyal to their mates. Valerius wrote to Rufus along similar lines, and Theophrastus remarked in his book that no wise man should take a wife, because there are too many worries with women, too little love, and too much gossip, and that, if a man marries in order to be better taken care of and nursed in sickness, a loyal servant could better and more loyally care for him and serve him and would not cost him nearly as much, and that if the wife becomes sick, the languishing husband does not dare budge from her side. But enough of such things, which would take too long to recite in full, therefore I say to you, dear lady, that if these remarks are true, so evil are these faults that all the other graces and virtues which women could possess are wiped out and canceled by them."

"Certainly, friend," she replied, "just as you yourself once said regarding this question, whoever goes to court without an opponent pleads very much at his ease. I assure you that women have never done what these books say. Indeed, I have not the slightest doubt that whoever cared to investigate the debate on marriage in order to write a new book in accordance with the truth would uncover other data. How many women are there actually, dear friend—and you yourself know—who because of their husbands' harshness spend their weary lives in the bond of marriage in greater suffering than if they were slaves among the Saracens? My God! How many harsh beatings—without cause and without reason—how many injuries, how many cruelties, insults, humiliations, and outrages have so many upright women suffered, none of whom cried out for help? And consider all the women who die of hunger and grief with a home full of children, while their husbands carouse dissolutely or go on binges in every tavern all over town, and still the poor women are beaten by their husbands when they return, and *that* is their supper! What do you say to that?

Am I lying? Have you never seen any of your women neighbors so decked out?"

And I said to her, "Certainly, my lady, I have seen many, and I feel very sorry for them."

"I believe you, and to say that these husbands are so unhappy with their wives' illnesses! Please, my friend, where are they? Without my having to say any more to you, you can easily see that such foolishness spoken and written against women was and is an arbitrary fabrication which flies in the fact of the truth. For men are masters over their wives, and not the wives mistresses over their husbands, who would never allow their wives to have such authority. But let me hasten to assure you that not all marriages are conducted with such spite, for there are those who live together in great peacefulness, love, and loyalty because the partners are virtuous, considerate, and reasonable. And although there are bad husbands, there are also very good ones, truly valiant and wise, and the women who meet them were born in a lucky hour, as far as the glory of the world is concerned, for what God has bestowed upon them. You know this perfectly well from your own experience, for you had such a good husband that, given a choice, you could not have asked for better, whom no other man in your judgment could surpass in kindness, peacefulness, loyalty, and true love, and for whose sake the remorse over Fate's having taken him from you will never leave your heart. In spite of what I have told you—and it is true that there are many women greatly mistreated by their husbands—realize, however, that there are very different kinds of women, and some unreasonable, for if I claimed that they were all good, I could easily be proven a liar, but that is the least part. I will not meddle with evil women, for such women are like creatures alienated from their own nature.

II. 13.2 "But to speak of good women, as for this Theophrastus, whom you have mentioned, and who says that a man can be cared for by his servant as loyally and as carefully as by his wife—ha! How many good women there are who are so conscientious in caring for their husbands, healthy or sick, with a loyal love as though their husbands were gods! I do not think that you will ever find such a servant. And since we have taken up this question, let me give you numerous examples of the great love and loyalty shown by women for their husbands. Now we have come back to our City, thank God, with all the noble company of fair and upright women whom we will lodge there. Here is the noble queen Hypsicratea, long ago the wife of the rich king Mithridates. We will lodge her first of all in the noble residence and palace which has been readied for her because she is from such an ancient time and of such worthiness."

II. 36. Against those men who claim it is not good for women to be educated.

Following these remarks, I, Christine, spoke, "My lady, I realize that women have accomplished many good things and that even if evil women have done evil, it seems to me, nevertheless, that the benefits accrued and still accruing because of good women—particularly the wise and literary ones and those educated in the natural sciences whom I mentioned above—outweigh the evil. Therefore, I am amazed by the opinions of some men who claim that they do not want their daughters, wives, or kinswomen to be educated because their mores would be ruined as a result."

She responded, "Here you can clearly see that not all opinions of men are based on reason and that these men are wrong. For it must not be presumed that mores necessarily grow worse from knowing the moral sciences, which teach the virtues, indeed, there is not the slightest doubt that moral education amends and ennobles them. How could anyone think or believe that whoever follows good teaching or doctrine is the worse for it? Such an opinion cannot be expressed or maintained. I do not mean that it would be good for a man or a woman to study the art of divination or those fields of learning which are forbidden—for the holy Church did not remove them from common use without good reason—but it should not be believed that women are the worse for knowing what is good.

"Quintus Hortensius, a great rhetorician and consummately skilled orator in Rome, did not share this opinion. He had a daughter, named Hortensia, whom he greatly loved for the subtlety of her wit. He had her learn letters and study the science of rhetoric, which she mastered so thoroughly that she resembled her father Hortensius not only in wit and lively memory but also in her excellent delivery and order of speech—in fact, he surpassed her in nothing. As for the subject discussed above, concerning the good which comes about through women, the benefits realized by this woman and her learning were, among others, exceptionally remarkable. That is, during the time when Rome was governed by three men, this Hortensia began to support the cause of women and to undertake what no man dared to undertake. There was a question whether certain taxes should be levied on women and on their jewelry during a needy period in Rome. This woman's eloquence was so compelling that she was listened to, no less readily than her father would have been, and she won her case.

II. 36.3 "Similarly, to speak of more recent times, without searching for examples in ancient history, Giovanni Andrea, a solemn law professor in Bologna not quite sixty years ago, was not of the opinion that it was bad for women to be educated. He had a fair and good daughter, named Novella, who was educated in the law to such an advanced degree that when he was occupied by some task and not at leisure to present his lectures to his students, he would send Novella, his daughter, in his place to lecture to the students from his chair. And to prevent her beauty from distracting the concentration of her audience, she had a little curtain drawn in front of her. In this manner, she could on occasion supplement and lighten her father's occupation. He loved her so much that, to commemorate her name, he wrote a book of remarkable lectures on the law which he entitled *Novella super Decretalium,* after his daughter's name.

II. 36.4 "Thus, not all men (and especially the wisest) share the opinion that it is bad for women to be educated. But it is very true that many foolish men have claimed this because it displeased them that women knew more than they did. Your father, who was a great scientist and philosopher, did not believe that women were worth less by knowing science; rather, as you know, he took great pleasure from seeing your inclination to learning. The feminine opinion of your mother, however, who wished to keep you busy with spinning and silly girlishness, following the common custom of women, was the major obstacle to your being more involved in the sciences. But just as the proverb already mentioned above says, "No one can take away what Nature has given, your mother could not hinder in you the feeling for the sciences which you, through natural inclination, had nevertheless gathered together in little droplets. I am sure that, on account of these things, you do not think you are worth less but rather that you consider it a great treasure for yourself; and you doubtless have reason to."

And I, Christine, replied to all of this, "Indeed, my lady, what you say is as true as the Lord's Prayer."

II.44. Refuting those men who claim women want to be raped, rectitude gives several examples, and first of all, Lucretia.

II. 44.1 Then I, Christine, spoke as follows, "My lady, I truly believe what you are saying, and I am certain that there are plenty of beautiful women who are virtuous and chaste and who know how to protect themselves well from the entrapments of deceitful men. I am therefore troubled and grieved when men argue that many women want to be raped and that it does not bother them at all to be raped by men even when they verbally protest. It would be hard to believe that such great villainy is actually pleasant for them."

She answered, "Rest assured, dear friend, chaste ladies who live honestly take absolutely no pleasure in being raped. Indeed, rape is the greatest possible sorrow for them. Many upright women have demonstrated that this is true with their own credible examples, just like Lucretia, the noblest Roman woman, supreme in chastity among Roman women, wife of a nobleman named Tarquin Collatinus. Now, when another man, Tarquin the Proud, son of King Tarquin, was greatly taken with love for this noble Lucretia, he did not dare to tell her because of the great chastity he saw in her, and, despairing of achieving his goal with presents or entreaties, he considered how he could have her through ruse. Claiming to be a close friend of her husband, he managed to gain entrance into her house whenever he wished, and once, knowing her husband was not at home, he went there and the noble lady received him with the honors due to someone whom she thought to be a close friend of her husband. However, Tarquin, who had something altogether different on his mind, succeeded in entering Lucretia's bedroom and frightened her terribly. Put briefly, after trying to coax her for a long time with promises, gifts, and favors, he saw that entreaties were getting him nowhere. He drew his sword and threatened to kill her if she made a sound and did not submit to his will. She answered that he should go ahead and kill her, for she would rather die than consent. Tarquin, realizing that nothing would help him, concocted a great malice, saying that he would publicly declare that he had found her with one of his sergeants. In brief, he so scared her with this threat (for she thought that people would believe him) that finally she suffered his rape. Lucretia, however, could not patiently endure this great pain, so that when daylight came she sent for her husband, her father, and her close relatives who were among the most powerful people in Rome, and, weeping and sobbing, confessed to them what had happened to her. Then, as her husband and relatives, who saw that she was overwhelmed with grief, were comforting her, she drew a knife from under her robe and said, "This is how I absolve myself of sin and show my innocence. Yet I cannot free myself from the torment nor extricate myself from the pain. From now on no woman will ever live shamed and disgraced by Lucretia's example." Having said this, she forcibly plunged the knife into her breast and collapsed dead before her husband and friends. They rushed like madmen to attack Tarquin. All Rome was moved to this cause, and they drove out the king and would have killed his son if they had found him. Never again was there a king in Rome. And because of this outrage perpetrated on Lucretia, so some claim, a law was enacted whereby a man would be executed for raping a woman, a law which is fitting, just, and holy."

Here begins the Third Part of the Book of the City of Ladies, which tells how the high roofs of the towers were completed and by whom and which noble ladies were chosen to reside in the great palaces and lofty mansions.

III. 1.1 The First Chapter tells how Justice led the Queen of Heaven to live in the City of Ladies.
Lady Justice then turned to me in her sublime manner and said, "Christine, to tell the truth, it seems to me that you have worked extraordinarily well on building the City of Ladies, according to your capacities and with the aid of my sisters which you have put to excellent use. Now it is time for me to undertake the rest, just as I promised you. That is, to bring and to lodge here the most excellent Queen,

blessed among women, with her noble company, so that she may rule and govern the City, inhabited by the multitude of noble ladies from her court and household, for I see the palaces and tall mansions ready and furnished, the streets paved to receive her most excellent and honorable company and assembly. Let princesses, ladies, and all women now come forward to receive her with the greatest honor and reverence, for she is not only their Queen but also has ministry and dominion over all created powers after the only Son whom she conceived of the Holy Spirit and carried and who is the Son of God the Father. And it is right that the assembly of all women beg this most lofty and excellent sovereign princess to reside here below in her humility with them in their City and congregation without disdain or spite because of their insignificance compared to her highness. Yet, there is no need to fear that her humility, which surpasses all others, and her more than angelic goodness will allow her to refuse to inhabit and reside in the City of Ladies, and above all, in the palace already prepared for her by my sister Rectitude, which is constructed solely of glory and praise. Let all women now accompany me, and let us say to her:

III. 1.2 "We greet you, Queen of Heaven, with the greeting which the Angel brought you, when he said, *Hail Mary,* which pleased you more than all other greetings. May all the devout sex of women humbly beseech you that it please you well to reside among them with grace and mercy, as their defender, protector, and guard against all assaults of enemies and of the world, that they may drink from the fountain of virtues which flows from you and be so satisfied that every sin and vice be abominable to them. Now come to us, Heavenly Queen, Temple of God, Cell and Cloister of the Holy Spirit, Vessel of the Trinity, Joy of the Angels, Star and Guide to those who have gone astray, Hope of the True Creation. My Lady, what man is so brazen to dare think or say that the feminine sex is vile in beholding your dignity? For if all other women were bad, the light of your goodness so surpasses and transcends them that any remaining evil would vanish. Since God chose His spouse from among women, most excellent Lady, because of your honor, not only should men refrain from reproaching women but should also hold them in great reverence."

III. 1.3 The Virgin replied as follows: "O Justice, greatly beloved by my Son, I will live and abide most happily among my sisters and friends, for Reason, Rectitude, and you, as well as Nature, urge me to do so. They serve, praise, and honor me unceasingly, for I am and will always be the head of the feminine sex. This arrangement was present in the mind of God the Father from the start, revealed and ordained previously in the council of the Trinity."

Here Justice answered, while all the women knelt with their heads bowed, "My Lady, may honor and praise be given to you forever. Save us, our Lady, and pray for us to your Son who refuses you nothing."

III. 19. The end of the book: Christine addresses the ladies.

III. 19.1 My most honored ladies, may God be praised, for now our City is entirely finished and completed, where all of you who love glory, virtue, and praise may be lodged in great honor, ladies from the past as well as from the present and future, for it has been built and established for every honorable lady. And my most dear ladies, it is natural for the human heart to rejoice when it finds itself victorious in any enterprise and its enemies confounded. Therefore you are right, my ladies, to rejoice greatly in God and in honest mores upon seeing this new City completed, which can be not only the refuge for you all, that is, for virtuous women, but also the defense and guard against your enemies and assailants, if you guard it well. For you can see that the substance with which it is made is entirely of virtue, so resplendent that you may see yourselves mirrored in it, especially in the roofs built in the last part as well as in the other parts which concern you. And my dear ladies, do not misuse this new inheritance like the arrogant who turn proud when their prosperity grows and their wealth multiplies, but rather follow the example of your Queen, the sovereign Virgin, who, after the extraordinary honor of being chosen Mother of the Son of God was announced to her, humbled herself all the more by calling herself the hand-maiden of God. Thus, my ladies, just as it is true that a creature's humility and kindness wax with the increase of its virtues, may this City be an occasion for you to conduct yourselves honestly and with integrity and to be all the more virtuous and humble.

And you ladies who are married, do not scorn being subject to your husbands, for sometimes it is not the best thing for a creature to be independent. This is attested by what the angel said to Ezra: Those, he said, who take advantage of their free will can fall into sin and despise our Lord and deceive the just, and for this they perish. Those women with peaceful, good, and discreet husbands who are devoted to them, praise God for this boon, which is not inconsiderable, for a greater boon in the world could not be given them. And may they be diligent in serving, loving, and cherishing their husbands in the loyalty of their heart, as they should, keeping their peace and praying to God to uphold and save them. And those women who have husbands neither completely good nor completely bad should still praise God for not having the worst and should strive to moderate their vices and pacify them, according to their conditions. And those women who have husbands who are cruel, mean, and savage should strive to endure them while trying to overcome their vices and lead them back, if they can, to a reasonable and seemly life. And if they are so obstinate that their wives are unable to do anything, at least they will acquire great merit for their souls through the virtue of patience. And everyone will bless them and support them.

So, my ladies, be humble and patient, and God's grace will grow in you, and praise will be given to you as well as the Kingdom of Heaven. For Saint Gregory has said that patience is the entrance to Paradise and the way of Jesus Christ. And may none of you be forced into holding frivolous opinions nor be hardened in them, lacking all basis in reason, nor be jealous or disturbed in mind, nor haughty in speech, nor outrageous in your acts, for these things disturb the mind and lead to madness. Such behavior is unbecoming and unfitting for women.

III. 19.4 And you, virgin maidens, be pure, simple, and serene, without vagueness, for the snares of evil men are set for you. Keep your eyes lowered, with few words in your mouths, and act respectfully. Be armed with the strength of virtue against the tricks of the deceptive and avoid their company.

III. 19.5 And widows, may there be integrity in your dress, conduct, and speech; piety in your deeds and way of life; prudence in you bearing; patience (so necessary!), strength, and resistance in tribulations and difficult affairs; humility in your heart, countenance, and speech; and charity in your works.

III. 19.6 In brief, all women—whether noble, bourgeois, or lower-class—be well-informed in all things and cautious in defending your honor and chastity against your enemies! My ladies, see how these men accuse you of so many vices in everything. Make liars of them all by showing forth your virtue, and prove their attacks false by acting well, so that you can say with the Psalmist, "the vices of the evil will fall on their heads." Repel the deceptive flatterers who, using different charms, seek with various tricks to steal that which you must consummately guard, that is, your honor and the beauty of your praise. Oh my ladies, flee, flee the foolish love they urge on you! Flee it, for God's sake, flee! For no good can come to you from it Rather, rest assured that however deceptive their lures, their end is always to your detriment. And do not believe the contrary, for it cannot be otherwise. Remember, dear ladies, how these men call you frail, unserious, and easily influenced but yet try hard, using all kinds of strange and deceptive tricks, to catch you, just as one lays traps for wild animals. Flee, flee, my ladies, and avoid their company—under these smiles are hidden deadly and painful poisons. And so may it please you, my most respected ladies, to cultivate virtue, to flee vice, to increase and multiply our City, and to rejoice and act well. And may I, your servant, commend myself to you, praying to God who by His grace has granted me to live in this world and to persevere in His holy service. May He in the end have mercy on my great sins and grant to me the joy which lasts forever, which I may, by His grace, afford to you. Amen.

Here ends the Third and Last Part of the Book of the City of Ladies.

Isotta Nogarola

Born in 1418 in Verona, Isotta Nogarola became perhaps the most learned woman of the fifteenth century in Italy. She studied Latin and Greek with a pupil of Guarino, and at the age of 18 she began her own humanist correspondence, writing to Guarino himself. However, the scorn shown her by many hostile men drove her to stop writing in 1438, just two years later.

Nogarola moved temporarily to Venice in that year but returned to Verona in 1441 and decided neither to marry nor to become a nun but to dedicate herself to sacred studies. This she did, and she managed to achieve some considerable distinction. In the early 1450s she became close to Venetian diplomat and humanist Lodovico Foscarini. The dialogue that follows represents a literary discussion between them on the relative sinfulness of Adam and Eve.

Isotta Nogarola died in 1466.

Of the Equal or Unequal Sin of Adam and Eve

An honorable disputation between the illustrious Lord Ludovico Foscarini, Venetian doctor of arts and both laws, and the noble and learned and divine lady Isotta Nogarola of Verona, regarding this judgment of Aurelius Augustine: They sinned unequally according to sex, but equally according to pride.

Ludovico begins : If it is in any way possible to measure the gravity of human sinfulness, then we should see Eve's sin as more to be condemned than Adam's [for three reasons]. [First], she was assigned by a just judge to a harsher punishment than was Adam. [Second], she believed that she was made more like God, and that is in the category of unforgiveable sins against the Holy Spirit. [Third], she suggested and was the cause of Adam's sin—not he of hers; and although it is a poor excuse to sin because of a friend, nevertheless none was more tolerable than the one by which Adam was enticed.

Isotta: But I see things—since you move me to reply—from quite another and contrary viewpoint. For where there is less intellect and less constancy, there there is less sin; and Eve [lacked sense and constancy] and therefore sinned less. Knowing [her weakness] that crafty serpent began by tempting the woman, thinking the man perhaps invulnerable because of his constancy. [For it says in] *Sentences* 2: Standing in the woman's presence, the ancient foe did not boldly persuade, but approached her with a question: "Why did God bid you not to eat of the tree of paradise?" She responded: "Lest perhaps we die." But seeing that she doubted the words of the Lord, the devil said: "You shall not die," but "you will be like God, knowing good and evil."

[Adam must also be judged more guilty than Eve, secondly] because of his greater contempt for the command. For in Genesis 2 it appears that the Lord commanded Adam, not Eve, where it says: "The Lord God took the man and placed him in the paradise of Eden to till it and to keep it," (and it does not say, "that they might care for and protect it") ". . . and the Lord God commanded the man" (and not "them"): "From every tree of the garden you may eat" (and not "you" [in the plural sense]),

Source: M. King and A. Rabil, eds. & trans., *Her Immaculate Hand: Selected, Works By and About The Women Humanists of 1400 Italy* [Binghamton, N.Y.: MARTS, 1983], pp. 59–69. Reprinted by permission of the publisher.

and, [referring to the forbidden tree], "for the day you eat of it, you must die," [again, using the singular form of "you"] [God directed his command to Adam alone] because he esteemed the man more highly than the woman.

Moreover, the woman did not [eat from the forbidden tree] because she believed that she was made more like God, but rather because she was weak and [inclined to indulge in] pleasure. Thus: "Now the woman saw that the tree was good for food, pleasing to the eyes, and desirable for the knowledge it would give. She took of its fruit and ate it, and also gave some to her husband and he ate," and it does not say [that she did so] in order to be like God. And if Adam had not eaten, her sin would have had no consequences. For it does not say: "If Eve had not sinned Christ would not have been made incarnate," but "If Adam had not sinned," Hence the woman, but only because she had been first deceived by the serpent's evil persuasion, did indulge in the delights of paradise; but she would have harmed only herself and in no way endangered human posterity if the consent of the first-born man had not been offered. Therefore Eve was no danger to posterity but [only] to herself; but the man Adam spread the infection of sin to himself and to all future generations. Thus Adam, being the author of all humans yet to be born, was also the first cause of their perdition. For this reason the healing of humankind was celebrated first in the man and then in the woman, just as [according to Jewish tradition], after an unclean spirit has been expelled from a man, as it springs forth from the synagogue, the woman is purged [as well].

Moreover, that Eve was condemned by a just judge to a harsher punishment is evidently false, for God said to the woman: "I will make great your distress in childbearing; in pain shall you bring forth children; for your husband shall be your longing, though he have dominion over you." But to Adam he said: "Because you have listened to your wife and have eaten of the tree of which I have commanded you not to eat" (notice that God appears to have admonished Adam alone [using the singular form of "you"] and not Eve) "Cursed be the ground because of you; in toil shall you eat of it all the days of your life; thorns and thistles shall it bring forth to you, and you shall eat the plants of the field. In the sweat of your brow you shall eat bread, till you return to the ground, since out of it you were taken; for dust you are and unto dust you shall return." Notice that Adam's punishment appears harsher than Eve's; for God said to Adam: "to dust you shall return," and not to Eve, and death is the most terrible punishment that could be assigned. Therefore it is established that Adam's punishment was greater than Eve's.

I have written this because you wished me to. Yet I have done so fearfully, since this is not a woman's task. But you are kind, and if you find any part of my writing clumsy you will correct it.

Ludovico: You defend the cause of Eve most subtly, and indeed defend it so [well] that, if I had not been born a man, you would have made me your champion. But sticking fast to the truth, which is attached by very strong roots, I have set out [here] to assault your fortress with your own weapons. I shall begin by attacking its foundations, which can be destroyed by the testimony of Sacred Scripture, so that there will be no lack of material for my refutation.

Eve sinned from ignorance and inconstancy, from which you conclude that she sinned less seriously. [But] ignorance—especially of those things which we are obligated to know—does not excuse us. For it is written: "If anyone ignores this, he shall be ignored." The eyes which guilt makes blind punishment opens. He who has been foolish in guilt will be wise in punishment, especially when the sinner's mistake occurs through negligence. For the woman's ignorance, born of arrogance, does not excuse her, in the same way that Aristotle and the [lawyers], who teach a true philosophy, find the drunk and ignorant deserving of a double punishment. Nor do I understand how in the world you, so many ages distant from Eve, fault her intellect, when her knowledge, divinely created by the highest craftsman of all things, daunted that clever serpent lurking in paradise. For, as you write, he was not bold enough to attempt to persuade her but approached her with a question.

But the acts due to inconstancy are even more blameworthy [than those due to ignorance]. For to the same degree that the acts issuing from a solid and constant mental attitude are more worthy and distinct from the preceding ones, so should those issuing from inconstancy be punished more severely, since inconstancy is an evil in itself and when paired with an evil sin makes the sin worse.

Nor is Adam's companion excused because Adam was appointed to protect her, [contrary to your contention that] thieves who have been trustingly employed by a householder are not punished with the most severe punishment like strangers or those in whom no confidence has been placed. Also, the woman's frailty was not the cause of sin, as you write, but her pride, since the demon promised her knowledge, which leads to arrogance and inflates [with pride], according to the apostle. For it says in Ecclesiasticus: "Pride was the beginning of every sin." And though the other women followed, yet she was the first since, when man existed in a state of innocence, the flesh was obedient to him and [did not struggle] against reason. The first impulse [of sin], therefore, was an inordinate appetite for seeking that which was not suited to its own nature, as Augustine wrote to Orosius: "Swollen by pride, man obeyed the serpent's persuasion and disdained God's commands." For the adversary said to Eve: "Your eyes will be opened and you will be like God, knowing good and evil." Nor would the woman have believed the demon's persuasive words, as Augustine says [in his commentary] on Genesis, unless a love of her own power had overcome her, which [love is] a stream sprung from the well of pride. [I shall continue to follow Augustine in his view that at the moment] when Eve desired to capture divinity, she lost happiness. And those words: "If Adam had not sinned, etc." confirm me in my view. For Eve sinned perhaps in such a way that, just as the demons did not merit redemption, neither perhaps did she. I speak only in jest, but Adam's sin was fortunate, since it warranted such a redeemer.

And lest I finally stray too far from what you have written, [I shall turn to your argument that Adam's punishment was more severe than Eve's and his sin, accordingly, greater. But] the woman suffers all the penalties [inflicted on] the man, and since her sorrows are greater than his, not only is she doomed to death, condemned to eat at the cost of sweat, denied by the cherubim and flaming swords entry to paradise, but in addition to all these things which are common [to both], she alone must give birth in pain and be subjected to her husband. [Her punishment is thus harsher than Adam's, as her sin is greater].

But because in such a matter it is not sufficient to have refuted your arguments without also putting forward my own, [I shall do so now]. Eve believed that she was made similar to God and, out of envy, desired that which wounds the Holy Spirit. Moreover, she must bear responsibility for every fault of Adam because, as Aristotle testifies, the cause of a cause is the cause of that which is caused. Indeed, every prior cause influences an outcome more than a secondary cause, and the principle of any genus, according to the same Aristotle, is seen as its greatest [component]. In fact, [it] is considered to be more than half the whole. And in the *Posterior Analytics* he writes: "That on account of which any thing exists is that thing and more greatly so." Now [since] Adam sinned on account of Eve, it follows that Eve sinned much more than Adam. Similarly, just as it is better to treat others well than to be well-treated, so it is worse to persuade another to evil than to be persuaded to evil. For he sins less who sins by another's example, inasmuch as what is done by example can be said to be done according to a kind of law, [and thus justly]. For this reason it is commonly said that "the sins that many commit are [without fault]." [Thus Eve, who persuaded her husband to commit an evil act, sinned more greatly than Adam, who merely consented to her example.] And if Adam and Eve both had thought that they were worthy of the same glory, Eve, who was inferior [by nature], more greatly departed from the mean, and consequently sinned more greatly. Moreover, as a beloved companion she could deceive her husband [vulnerable to her persuasion because of his love for her] more easily than the shameful serpent could deceive the woman. And she persevered longer [in sin] than Adam, because she began first, and offenses are that much more serious (according to Gregory's decree) in relation to the length of time they hold the unhappy soul in bondage. Finally, to bring my discourse to a close, Eve was the cause and the example of sin, and Gregory greatly increases the guilt in the case of the example. And Christ, who could not err, condemned more severely the pretext of the ignorant Jews, because it came first, than he did the sentence of the learned Pilate, when he said: "They who have betrayed me to you have greater sin, etc." All who wish to be called Christians have always agreed with this judgment, and you, above all most Christian, will approve and defend it. Farewell, and do not fear, but dare to do much, because you have excellently understood so much and write so learnedly.

Isotta: I had decided that I would not enter further into a contest with you because, as you say, you assault my fortress with my own weapons. [The propositions] you have presented me were so perfectly and diligently defended that it would be difficult not merely for me, but for the most learned men, to oppose them. But since I recognize that this context is useful for me, I have decided to obey your honest wish. Even though I know I struggle in vain, yet I will earn the highest praise if I am defeated by so mighty a man as you.

Eve sinned out of ignorance and inconstancy, and hence you contend that she sinned more gravely, because the ignorance of those things which we are obligated to know does not excuse us, since it is written: "He who does not know will not be known." I would concede your point if that ignorance were crude or affected. But Eve's ignorance was implanted by nature, of which nature God himself is the author and founder. In many people it is seen that he who knows less sins less, like a boy who sins less than an old man or a peasant less than a noble. Such a person does not need to know explicitly what is required for salvation, but implicitly, because [for him] faith alone suffices. The question of inconstancy proceeds similarly. For when it is said that the acts which proceed from inconstancy are more blameworthy, [that kind of] inconstancy is understood which is not innate but the product of character and sins.

The same is true of imperfection. For when gifts increase, greater responsibility is imposed. When God created man, from the beginning he created him perfect, and the powers of his soul perfect, and gave him a greater understanding and knowledge of truth as well as a greater depth of wisdom. Thus it was that the Lord led to Adam all the animals of the earth and the birds of heaven, so that Adam could call them by their names. For God said: "Let us make mankind in our image and likeness, and let them have dominion over the fish of the sea, and the birds of the air, the cattle, over all the wild animals and every creature that crawls on the earth," making clear his own perfection. But of the woman he said: "It is not good that the man is alone; I will make him a helper like himself." And since consolation and joy are required for happiness, and since no one can have solace and joy when alone, it appears that God created woman for man's consolation. For the good spreads itself, and the greater it is the more it shares itself. Therefore, it appears that Adam's sin was greater than Eve's. [As] Ambrose [says]: "In him to whom a more indulgent liberality has been shown is insolence more inexcusable."

"But Adam's companion," [you argue], "is not excused because Adam was appointed to protect her, because thieves who have been trustingly employed by a householder are not punished with the most severe punishment like strangers or those in whom the householder placed no confidence." This is true, however, in temporal law, but not in divine law, for divine justice proceeds differently from temporal justice in punishing [sin].

[You argue further that] "the fragility of the woman was not the cause of sin, but rather her inordinate appetite for seeking that which was not suited to her nature," which [appetite] is the product, as you write, of pride. Yet it is clearly less a sin to desire the knowledge of good and evil than to transgress against a divine commandment, since the desire for knowledge is a natural thing, and all men by nature desire to know. And even if the first impulse [of sin] were this inordinate appetite, which cannot be without sin, yet it is more tolerable than the sin of transgression, for the observance of the commandments is the road which leads to the country of salvation. [It is written]: "But if thou wilt enter into life, keep the commandments;" and likewise: "What shall I do to gain eternal life? Keep the commandments." And transgression is particularly born of pride, because pride is nothing other than rebellion against divine rule, exalting oneself above what is permitted according to divine rule, by disdaining the will of God and displacing it with one's own. Thus Augustine [writes] in *On Nature and Grace:* "Sin is the will to pursue or retain what justice forbids, that is, to deny what God wishes." Ambrose agrees with him in his *On Paradise:* "Sin is the transgression against divine law and disobedience to the heavenly commandments." Behold! See that the transgression against and disobedience to the heavenly commandments is the greatest sin, whereas you have thus defined sin: "Sin is the inordinate desire to know." Thus clearly the sin of transgression against a command is greater than [the sin of] desiring the knowledge of good and evil. So even if inordinate desire be a sin, as with Eve, yet she did not desire to be like God in power but only in the knowledge of good and evil, which by nature she was actually inclined to desire.

[Next, as to your statement] that those words, "if Adam had not sinned," confirm you in your view [of Eve's damnability], since Eve may have so sinned that, like the demons, she did not merit redemption, I reply that she also was redeemed with Adam, because [she was] "bone of my bone and flesh of my flesh." And if it seems that God did not redeem her, this was undoubtedly because God held her sin as negligible. For if man deserved redemption, the woman deserved it much more because of the slightness of the crime. For the angel cannot be excused by ignorance as can the woman. For the angel understands without investigation or discussion and has an intellect more in the likeness of God's—to which it seems Eve desired to be similar—than does man. Hence the angel is called intellectual and the man rational. Thus where the woman sinned from her desire for knowledge, the angel sinned from a desire for power. While knowledge of an appearance in some small way can be partaken of by the creature, in no way can it partake in the power of God and of the soul of Christ. Moreover, the woman in sinning thought she would receive mercy, believing certainly that she was committing a sin, but not one so great as to warrant God's inflicting such a sentence and punishment. But the angel did not think [of mercy]. Hence Gregory [says in the] fourth book of the *Moralia:* "The first parents were needed for this, that the sin which they committed by transgressing they might purge by confessing." But that persuasive serpent was never punished for his sin, for he was never to be recalled to grace. Thus, in sum, Eve clearly merited redemption more than the angels.

[As to your argument] that the woman also suffers all the penalties inflicted on the man, and beyond those which are common [to both] she alone gives birth in sorrow and has been subjected to man, this also reinforces my earlier point. As I said, the good spreads itself, and the greater it is the more it shares itself. So also evil, the greater it is the more it shares itself, and the more it shares itself the more harmful it is, and the more harmful it is the greater it is. Furthermore, the severity of the punishment is proportional to the gravity of the sin. Hence Christ chose to die on the cross, though this was the most shameful and horrible kind of death, and on the cross he endured in general every kind of suffering by type. Hence Isidore writes concerning the Trinity: "The only-born Son of God in executing the sacrament of his death, in himself bears witness that he consummated every kind of suffering when, with lowered head, he gave up his spirit." The reason was that the punishment had to correspond to the guilt. Adam took the fruit of the forbidden tree; Christ suffered on the tree and so made satisfaction [for Adam's sin]. [As] Augustine [writes]: "Adam disdained God's command" [and he does not say Eve] "accepting the fruit from the tree, but whatever Adam lost Christ restored." [For Christ paid the penalty for sin he had not committed, as it says in] Psalm 64: "For what I have not taken, then I atoned." Therefore, Adam's sin was the greatest [possible], because the punishment corresponding to his fault was the greatest [possible] and was general in all men. [As the] apostle [says]: "All sinned in Adam."

"Eve," [you say], "must bear responsibility for every fault of Adam because, as Aristotle shows, whatever is the cause of the cause is the cause of the thing caused." This is true in the case of things which are, as you know better [than I], in themselves the causes of other things, which is the case for the first cause, the first principle, and "that on account of which anything is what it is." But clearly this was not the case with Eve, because Adam either had free will or he did not. If he did not have it, he did not sin; if he had it, then Eve forced the sin [upon him], which is impossible. For as Bernard says: "Free will, because of its inborn nobility, is forced by no necessity," not even by God, because if that were the case it would be to concede that two contradictories are true at the same time. God cannot do, therefore, what would cause an act proceeding from free will and remaining free to be not free but coerced. [As] Augustine [writes in his commentary] on Genesis: "God cannot act against that nature which he created with a good will." God could himself, however, remove that condition of liberty from any person and bestow some other condition on him. In the same way fire cannot, while it remains fire, not burn, unless its nature is changed and suspended for a time by divine force. No other creature, such as a good angel or devil can do this, since they are less then God; much less a woman, since she is less perfect and weaker than they. Augustine clarifies this principle [of God's supremacy] saying: "Above our mind is nothing besides God, nor is there anything intermediary between God and our mind." Yet only something which is superior to something else can coerce it; but Eve was inferior to Adam, therefore she was not herself the cause of sin. [In] Ecclesiasticus 15 [it says]: "God from the beginning created man and placed him in the palm of his counsel and made clear his commandments and precepts. If you wish to preserve the commandments, they will preserve you and create in you pleasing faith." Thus Adam appeared to accuse God rather than excuse himself when he said: "The woman you placed at my side gave me fruit from the tree and I ate it."

[Next you argue] that the beloved companion could have more easily deceived the man than the shameful serpent the woman. To this I reply that Eve, weak and ignorant by nature, sinned much less by assenting to that astute serpent, who was called "wise," than Adam—created by God with perfect knowledge and understanding—in listening to the persuasive words and voice of the imperfect woman.

[Further, you say] that Eve persevered in her sin a longer time and therefore sinned more, because crimes are that much more serious according to the length of time they hold the unhappy soul in bondage. This is no doubt true, when two sins are equal, and in the same person or in two similar persons. But Adam and Eve were not equals, because Adam was a perfect animal and Eve imperfect and ignorant. [Therefore, their sins were not comparable, and Eve, who persevered longer in sin, was not on that account more guilty than Adam].

Finally, if I may quote you: "The woman was the example and the cause of sin, and Gregory emphatically extends the burden of guilt to [the person who provided] an example, and Christ condemned the cause of the ignorant Jews, because it was first, more than the learned Pilate's sentence when he said: 'Therefore he who betrayed me to you has greater sin.'" I reply that Christ did not condemn the cause of the ignorant Jews because it was first, but because it was vicious and devilish due to their native malice and obstinacy. For they did not sin from ignorance. The gentile Pilate was more ignorant about these things than the Jews, who had the law and the prophets and read them and daily saw signs concerning [Christ]. For John 15 says: "If I had not come and spoken to them, they would have no sin. But now they have no excuse for their sin." Thus they themselves said: "What are we doing? for this man is working signs." And: "Art thou the Christ, the Son of the Blessed One?" For the [Jewish] people was special to God, and Christ himself [said]: "I was not sent except to the lost sheep of the house of Israel. It is not fair to take the children's bread and cast it to the dogs." Therefore the Jews sinned more, because Jesus loved them more.

Let these words be enough from me, an unarmed and poor little woman.

Niccolò Machiavelli

NICCOLÒ MACHIAVELLI (1469–1527) was a Florentine who came from the class of impoverished gentry that was losing caste before the rapid rise of the bourgeoisie. He served Florence in various diplomatic posts for fourteen years, serving on missions requiring at once the utmost in finesse and in tough-mindedness. When in 1512 the pope was victorious over France and its Florentine ally and the antirepublican Medici were returned to power, Machiavelli was one of those forced into exile. It was during this period of exile that he wrote *The Prince* (1513), the *Discourses on Livy* (1517–19), and his other books. Machiavelli's energies found no adequate release merely in writing books, however, and like that other Florentine exile, Dante, he was ill at ease away from his native city. He made many attempts to get back into public life. The victorious revolution of the popular party in Florence in 1527 seemed to Machiavelli to be his opportunity. He returned to Florence, but the Florentine Council, some of whom had read *The Prince*, decided against trusting him as a public official. Machiavelli, however, died before he had heard of this decision.

Machiavelli's *The Prince*, written while he was in exile, describes the nature of the strong ruler and the methods best calculated to keep him in office. The *Discourses on Livy* reveal Machiavelli's republicanism, his belief that widespread public virtue is necessary to preserve the state. Machiavelli also wrote a *History of Florence, On the Art of War*, poetry, and some sardonic drama.

The Prince

Chapter I: The Various Kinds of Government and the Ways by Which They Are Established

ALL STATES AND DOMINIONS which hold or have held sway over mankind are either republics or monarchies. Monarchies are either hereditary in which the rulers have been for many years of the same family, or else they are of recent foundation. The newly founded ones are either entirely new, as was Milan to Francesco Sforza, or else they are, as it were, new members grafted on to the hereditary possessions of the prince that annexes them, as is the kingdom of Naples to the King of Spain. The dominions thus acquired have either been previously accustomed to the rule of another prince, or else have been free states, and they are annexed either by force of arms of the prince himself, or of others, or else fall to him by good fortune or special ability.

Chapter II: Of Hereditary Monarchies

I will not here speak of republics, having already treated of them fully in another place. I will deal only with monarchies, and will discuss how the various kinds described above can be governed and

The translation of sections of *The Prince* from the Italian is by Luigi Ricci (1903), revised by E. R. P. Vincent. The excerpt from *The Discourses on Livy* is from *The Portable Machiavelli*, edited and translated by Peter Bondella and Mark Musa (New York: Penguin Books, 1979), pp. 168–71, 175–81, 193–96, 200–213, 281–90. © 1979 by Viking Penguin, Inc. Some footnotes deleted. Reprinted by permission of Viking Penguin, Inc.

maintained. In the first place, the difficulty of maintaining hereditary states accustomed to a reigning family is far less than in new monarchies; for it is sufficient not to transgress ancestral usages, and to adapt one's self to unforeseen circumstances; in this way such a prince, if of ordinary assiduity, will always be able to maintain his position, unless some very exceptional and excessive force deprives him of it; and even if he be thus deprived, on the slightest mischance happening to the new occupier, he will be able to regain it.

We have in Italy the example of the Duke of Ferrara, who was able to withstand the assaults of the Venetians in 1484 and of Pope Julius in 1510, for no other reason than because of the antiquity of his family in that dominion. In as much as the legitimate prince has less cause and less necessity to give offence, it is only natural that he should be more loved; and, if no extraordinary vices make him hated, it is only reasonable for his subjects to be naturally attached to him, the memories and causes of innovations being forgotten in the long period over which his rule has extended; whereas one change always leaves the way prepared for the introduction of another.

Chapter III: Of Mixed Monarchies

But it is in the new monarchy that difficulties really exist. First, if it is not entirely new, but a member as it were of a mixed state, its disorders spring at first from a natural difficulty which exists in all new dominions, because men change masters willingly, hoping to better themselves; and this belief makes them take arms against their rulers, in which they are deceived, as experience later proves that they have gone from bad to worse. This is the result of another very natural cause, which is the inevitable harm inflicted on those over whom the prince obtains dominion, both by his soldiers and by an infinite number of other injuries caused by his occupation.

Thus you find enemies in all those whom you have injured by occupying that dominion, and you cannot maintain the friendship of those who have helped you to obtain this possession, as you will not be able to fulfil their expectations, nor can you use strong measures with them, being under an obligation to them; for which reason, however strong your armies may be, you will always need the favour of the inhabitants to take possession of a province. It was from these causes that Louis XII of France, though able to occupy Milan without trouble, immediately lost it, and the forces of Ludovico alone were sufficient to take it from him the first time, for the inhabitants who had willingly opened their gates to him, finding themselves deluded in the hopes they had cherished and not obtaining those benefits they had anticipated, could not bear the vexatious rule of their new prince.

It is indeed true that, after reconquering rebel territories they are not so easily lost again, for the ruler is now, by the fact of the rebellion, less averse to secure his position by punishing offenders, unmasking suspects, and strengthening himself in weak places. So that although the mere appearance of such a person as Duke Ludovico on the frontier was sufficient to cause France to lose Milan the first time, to make her lose her grip of it the second time was only possible when all the world was against her, and after her armies had been defeated and driven out of Italy; which was the result of the causes above mentioned. Nevertheless it was taken from her both the first and the second time. The general causes of the first loss have been already discussed; it remains now to be seen what were the causes of the second loss and by what means France could have avoided it, or what measures might have been taken by another ruler in that position which were not taken by the King of France. Be it observed, therefore, that those states which on annexation are united to a previously existing state may or may not be of the same nationality and language. If they are, it is very easy to hold them, especially if they are not accustomed to freedom; and to possess them securely it suffices that the family of the princes which formerly governed them be extinct. For the rest, their old condition not being disturbed, and there being no dissimilarity of customs, the people settle down quietly under their new rulers, as is seen in the case of Burgundy, Brittany, Gascony, and Normandy, which have been so long united to France; and although there may be some slight differences of language, the customs of the people are nevertheless similar, and they can get along well together. Whoever obtains possession of such territories and wishes to retain them must bear in mind two things: the one, that the blood of their old rulers be extinct; the other, to make no alteration either in their laws or in their taxes; in this way they will in a very short space of time become united with their old possessions and form one state.

But when dominions are acquired in a province differing in language, laws, and customs, the difficulties to be overcome are great, and it requires good fortune as well as great industry to retain them; one of the best and most certain means of doing so would be for the new ruler to take up his residence there. This would render possession more secure and durable, and it is what the Turk has done in Greece. In spite of all the other measures taken by him to hold that state, it would not have been possible to retain it had he not gone to live there. Being on the spot, disorders can be seen as they arise and can quickly be remedied, but living at a distance, they are only heard of when they get beyond remedy. Besides which, the province is not despoiled by your officials, the subjects being able to obtain satisfaction by direct recourse to their prince; and wishing to be loyal they have more reason to love him, and should they be otherwise inclined they will have greater cause to fear him. Any external Power who wishes to assail that state will be less disposed to do so; so that as long as he resides there he will be very hard to dispossess.

The other and better remedy is to plan colonies in one or two of those places which form as it were the keys of the land, for it is necessary either to do this or to maintain a large force of armed men. The colonies will cost the prince little; with little or no expense on his part, he can send and maintain them; he only injures those whose lands and houses are taken to give to the new inhabitants, and these form but a small proportion of the state, and those who are injured, remaining poor and scattered, can never do any harm to him, and all the others are, on the one hand, not injured and therefore easily pacified; and, on the other, are fearful of offending lest they should be treated like those who have been dispossessed. To conclude, these colonies cost nothing, are more faithful, and give less offence; and the injured parties being poor and scattered are unable to do mischief, as I have shown. For it must be noted that men must either be caressed or else annihilated; they will revenge themselves for small injuries, but cannot do so for great ones; the injury therefore that we do to a man must be such that we need not fear his vengeance. But by maintaining a garrison instead of colonists, one will spend much more, and consume all the revenues of that state in guarding it, so that the acquisition will result in a loss, besides giving much greater offence, since it injures every one in that state with the quartering of the army on it; which being an inconvenience felt by all, every one becomes an enemy, and these are enemies which can do mischief, as, though beaten, they remain in their own homes. In every way, therefore, a garrison is as useless as colonies are useful. . . .

Chapter V: The Way to Govern Cities or Dominions That, Previous to Being Occupied, Lived under Their Own Laws

When those states which have been acquired are accustomed to live at liberty under their own laws, there are three ways of holding them. The first is to despoil them; the second is to go and live there in person; the third is to allow them to live under their own laws, taking tribute of them, and creating within the country a government composed of a few who will keep it friendly to you. Because this government, being created by the prince, knows that it cannot exist without his friendship and protection, and will do all it can to keep them. What is more, a city used to liberty can be more easily held by means of its citizens than in any other way, if you wish to preserve it.

There is the example of the Spartans and the Romans. The Spartans held Athens and Thebes by creating within them a government of a few; nevertheless they lost them. The Romans, in order to hold Capua, Carthage, and Numantia, ravaged them, but did not lose them. They wanted to hold Greece in almost the same way as the Spartans held it, leaving it free and under its own laws, but they did not succeed; so that they were compelled to lay waste many cities in that province in order to keep it, because in truth there is no sure method of holding them except by despoiling them. And whoever becomes the ruler of a free city and does not destroy it, can expect to be destroyed by it, for it can always find a motive for rebellion in the name of liberty and of its ancient usages, which are forgotten neither by lapse of time nor by benefits received; and whatever one does or provides, so long as the inhabitants are not separated or dispersed, they do not forget that name and those usages, but appeal to them at once in every emergency, as did Pisa after being so many years held in servitude by the Florentines. But when cities or provinces have been accustomed to live under a prince, and the family of that prince is extinguished, being on the one hand used to obey, and on the other not having their old prince, they cannot unite in choosing one from among themselves, and they do not know how to live in freedom, so that they are slower to take arms, and a prince can win them over with greater facility and establish himself securely. But in republics there is greater life, greater hatred, and more desire for vengeance; they do not and cannot cast aside the memory of their ancient liberty, so that the surest way is either to lay them waste or reside in them.

Chapter IX: Of the Civic Principality

But we now come to the case where a citizen becomes prince not through crime or intolerable violence, but by the favour of his fellow-citizens, which may be called a civic principality. To attain this position depends not entirely on worth or entirely on fortune, but rather on cunning assisted by fortune. One attains it by help of popular favour or by the favour of the aristocracy. For in every city these two opposite parties are to be found, arising from the desire of the populace to avoid the oppression of the great, and the desire of the great to command and oppress the people. And from these two opposing interests arises in the city one of the three effects: either absolute government, liberty, or licence. The former is created either by the populace or the nobility, depending on the relative opportunities of the two parties; for when the nobility see that they are unable to resist the people they unite in exalting one of their number and creating him prince, so as to be able to carry out their own designs under the shadow of his authority. The populace, on the other hand, when unable to resist the nobility, endeavour to exalt and create a prince in order to be protected by his authority. He who becomes prince by help of the nobility has greater difficulty in maintaining his power than he who is raised by the populace, for he is surrounded by those who think themselves his equals, and is thus unable to direct or command as he pleases. But one who is raised to leadership by popular favour finds himself alone, and has no one, or very few, who are not ready to obey him. Besides which, it is impossible to satisfy the nobility by fair dealing and without inflicting injury on others, whereas it is very easy to satisfy the mass of the people in this way. For the aim of the people is more honest than that of the nobility, the latter desiring to oppress, and the former merely to avoid oppression. It must also be added that the prince can never insure himself against a hostile populace on account of their number, but he can against the hostility of the great, as they are but few. The worst that a prince has to expect from a hostile people is to be abandoned, but from hostile nobles he has to fear not only desertion but their active opposition, and as they are more far-seeing and more cunning, they are always in time to save themselves and take sides with the one who they expect will conquer. The prince is, moreover, obliged to live always with the same people, but he can easily do without the same nobility, being able to make and unmake them at any time, and improve their position or deprive them of it as he pleases.

And to throw further light on this part of my argument, I would say, that the nobles are to be considered in two different manners; that is, they are either to be ruled so as to make them entirely dependent on your fortunes, or else not. Those that are thus bound to you and are not rapacious, must be honoured and loved; those who stand aloof must be considered in two ways, they either do this through pusillanimity and natural want of courage, and in this case you ought to make use of them, and especially such as are of good counsel, so that they may honour you in prosperity and in adversity you have not to fear them. But when they are not bound to you of set purpose and for ambitious ends, it is a sign that they think more of themselves than of you; and from such men the prince must guard himself and look upon them as secret enemies, who will help to ruin him when in adversity.

One, however, who becomes prince by favour of the populace, must maintain its friendship, which he will find easy, the people asking nothing but not to be oppressed. But one who against the people's wishes becomes prince by favour of the nobles, should above all endeavour to gain the favour of the people; this will be easy to him if he protects them. And as men, who receive good from whom they expected evil, feel under a greater obligation to their benefactor, so the populace will soon become even better disposed towards him than if he had become prince through their favour. Their prince can win their favour in many ways, which vary according to circumstances, for which no certain rule can be given, and will therefore be passed over. I will only say, in conclusion, that it is necessary for a prince to possess the friendship of the people; otherwise he has no resource in times of adversity.

Nabis, prince of the Spartans, sustained a siege by the whole of Greece and a victorious Roman army, and defended his country against them and maintained his own position. It sufficed when the danger arose for him to make sure of a few, which would not have sufficed if the populace had been hostile to him. And let no one oppose my opinion in this by quoting the trite proverb, "He who builds on the people, builds on mud"; because that is true when a private citizen relies upon the people and persuades himself that they will liberate him if he is oppressed by enemies or by the magistrates; in this case he might often find himself deceived, as were in Rome the Gracchi and in Florence Messer Georgio Scali. But when it is a prince who founds himself on this basis, one who can command and is a man of courage, and does not get frightened in adversity, and does not neglect other preparations, and one who by his own valour and measures animates the mass of the people, he will not find himself deceived by them, and he will find that he has laid his foundations well.

Usually these principalities are in danger when the prince from the position of a civil ruler changes to an absolute one, for these princes either command themselves or by means of magistrates. In the latter case their position is weaker and more dangerous, for they are at the mercy of those citizens who are appointed magistrates, who can, especially in times of adversity, with great facility deprive them of their position, either by acting against them or by not obeying them. The prince is not in time, in such dangers, to assume absolute authority, for the citizens and subjects who are accustomed to take their orders from the magistrates are not ready in these emergencies to obey his, and he will always in difficult times lack men whom he can rely on. Such a prince cannot base himself on what he sees in quiet times, when the citizens have need of the state; for then every one is full of promises and each one is ready to die for him when death is far off; but in adversity, when the state has need of citizens, then he will find but few. And this experience is the more dangerous, in that it can only be had once. Therefore a wise prince will seek means by which his subjects will always and in every possible condition of things have need of his government, and then they will always be faithful to him.

Chapter X: How the Strength of All States Should Be Measured

In examining the character of these principalities it is necessary to consider another point, namely, whether the prince has such a position as to be able in case of need to maintain himself alone, or whether he has always need of the protection of others. The better to explain this I would say, that I consider those capable of maintaining themselves alone who can, through abundance of men or money, put together a sufficient army, and hold the field against any one who assails them; and I consider to have need of others, those who cannot take the field against their enemies, but are obliged to take refuge within their walls and stand on the defensive. We have already discussed the former case and will speak of it in future as occasion arises. In the second case there is nothing to be said except to encourage such a prince to provision and fortify his own town, and not to trouble about the surrounding country. And whoever has strongly fortified his town and, as regards the government of his subjects, has proceeded as we have already described and will further relate, will be attacked with great reluctance, for men are always averse to enterprises in which they foresee difficulties, and it can never appear easy to attack one who has his town stoutly defended and is not hated by the people.

The cities of Germany are absolutely free, have little surrounding country, and obey the emperor when they choose, and they do not fear him or any other potentate that they have about them. They are fortified in such a manner that every one thinks that to reduce them would be tedious and difficult, for they all have the necessary moats and bastions, sufficient artillery, and always keep food, drink, and fuel for one year in the public storehouses. Beyond which, to keep the lower classes satisfied, and without loss to the commonwealth, they have always enough means to give them work for one year in these employments which form the nerve and life of the town, and in the industries by which the lower classes live. Military exercises are still held in high reputation, and many regulations are in force for maintaining them.

A prince, therefore, who possesses a strong city and does not make himself hated, cannot be assaulted; and if he were to be so, the assailant would be obliged to retire shamefully; for so many things change, that it is almost impossible for any one to maintain a siege for a year with his armies idle. And to those who urged that the people, having their possessions outside and seeing them burnt, will not have patience, and the long siege and self-interest will make them forget their prince, I reply that a powerful and courageous prince will always overcome those difficulties by now raising the hopes of his subjects that the evils will not last long, now impressing them with fear of the enemy's cruelty, now by dextrously assuring himself of those who appear too bold. Besides which, the enemy would naturally burn and ravage the country on first arriving and at the time when men's minds are still hot and eager to defend themselves, and therefore the prince has still less to fear, for after some time, when people have cooled down, the damage is done, the evil has been suffered, and there is no remedy, so that they are the more ready to unite with their prince, as it appears that he is under an obligation to them, their houses having been burnt and their possessions ruined in his defence.

It is the nature of men to be as much bound by the benefits that they confer as by those they receive. From which it follows that, everything considered, a prudent prince will not find it difficult to uphold the courage of his subjects both at the commencement and during a state of siege, if he possesses provisions and means to defend himself.

Chapter XI: Of Ecclesiastical Principalities

It now only remains to us to speak of ecclesiastical principalities, with regard to which the difficulties lie wholly before they are possessed. They are acquired either by ability or by fortune; but are maintained without either, for they are sustained by ancient religious customs, which are so powerful and of such quality, that they keep their princes in power in whatever manner they proceed and live. These princes alone have states without defending them, have subjects without governing them, and their states, not being defended, are not taken from them; their subjects not being governed do not resent it, and neither think nor are capable of alienating themselves from them. Only these principalities, therefore, are secure and happy. But as they are upheld by higher causes, which the human mind cannot attain to, I will abstain from speaking of them; for being exalted and maintained by God, it would be the work of a presumptuous and foolish man to discuss them. However, I might be asked how it has come about that the Church has reached such great temporal powers, when, previous to Alexander VI, the Italian potentates—and not merely the really powerful ones, but every lord or baron, however insignificant—held it in slight esteem as regards temporal power; whereas now it is dreaded by a king of France, whom it has been able to drive out of Italy, and has also been able to ruin the Venetians. . . .

Chapter XIV: The Duties of a Prince with Regard to the Militia

A prince should therefore have no other aim or thought, nor take up any other thing for his study, but war and its organisation and discipline, for that is the only art that is necessary to one who commands, and it is of such virtue that it not only maintains those who are born princes, but often enables men of private fortune to attain to that rank. And one sees, on the other hand, that when princes think more of luxury than of arms, they lose their state. The chief cause of the loss of states, is the contempt of this art, and the way to acquire them is to be well versed in the same.

Francesco Sforza, through being well armed, became, from private status, Duke of Milan; his sons, through wishing to avoid the fatigue and hardship of war, from dukes became private persons. For among other evils caused by being disarmed, it renders you contemptible; which is one of those disgraceful things which a prince must guard against, as will be explained later. Because there is no comparison whatever between an armed and a disarmed man, it is not reasonable to suppose that one who is armed will obey willingly one who is unarmed, or that any unarmed man will remain safe among armed servants. For one being disdainful and the other suspicious, it is not possible for them to act well together. And therefore a prince who is ignorant of military matters, besides the other misfortunes already mentioned, cannot be esteemed by his soldiers, nor have confidence in them.

He ought, therefore, never to let his thoughts stray from the exercise of war; and in peace he ought to practise it more than in war, which he can do in two ways: by action and by study. As to action, he must, besides keeping his men well disciplined and exercised, engage continually in hunting, and thus accustom his body to hardships; and meanwhile learn the nature of the land, how steep the mountains are, how the valleys debouch, where the plains lie, and understand the nature of rivers and swamps. To all this he should devote great attention. This knowledge is useful in two ways. In the first place, one learns to know one's country, and can the better see how to defend it. Then by means of the knowledge and experience gained in one locality, one can easily understand any other that it may be necessary to observe; for the hills and valleys, plains and rivers of Tuscany, for instance, have a certain resemblance to those of other provinces, so that from a knowledge of the country in one province one can easily arrive at a knowledge of others. And that prince who is lacking in this skill is wanting in the first essentials of a leader; for it is this which teaches how to find the enemy, take up quarters, lead armies, plan battles and lay siege to towns with advantage. . . .

But as to exercise for the mind, the prince ought to read history and study the actions of eminent men, see how they acted in warfare, examine the causes of their victories and defeats in order to imitate the former and avoid the latter, and above all, do as some men have done in the past, who have imitated some one, who has been much praised and glorified, and have always kept his deeds and actions before them, as they say Alexander the Great imitated Achilles, Cæsar Alexander, and Scipio Cyrus. And whoever reads the life of Cyrus written by Xenophon, will perceive in the life of Scipio how gloriously he imitated the former, and how, in chastity, affability, humanity, and liberality Scipio conformed to those qualities of Cyrus as described by Xenophon.

A wise prince should follow similar methods and never remain idle in peaceful times, but industriously make good use of them, so that when fortune changes she may find him prepared to resist her blows, and to prevail in adversity.

Chapter XV: Of the Things for Which Men, and Especially Princes, Are Praised or Blamed

It now remains to be seen what are the methods and rules for a prince as regards his subjects and friends. And as I know that many have written of this, I fear that my writing about it may be deemed presumptuous, differing as I do, especially in this matter, from the opinions of others. But my intention being to write something of use to those who understand, it appears to me more proper to go to the real truth of the matter than to its imagination; and many have imagined republics and principalities which have never been seen or known to exist in reality; for how we live is so far removed from how we ought to live, that he who abandons what is done for what ought to be done, will rather learn to bring about his own ruin than his preservation. A man who wishes to make a profession of goodness in everything must necessarily come to grief among so many who are not good. Therefore it is necessary for a prince, who wishes to maintain himself, to learn how not to be good, and to use this knowledge and not use it, according to the necessity of the case.

Leaving on one side, then, those things which concern only an imaginary prince, and speaking of those that are real, I state that all men, and especially princes, who are placed at a greater height, are reputed for certain qualities which bring them either praise or blame. Thus one is considered liberal, another *misero* or miserly (using a Tuscan term, seeing that *avaro* with us still means one who is rapaciously acquisitive and *misero* one who makes grudging use of his own); one a free giver, another rapacious; one cruel, another merciful; one a breaker of his word, another trustworthy; one effeminate and pusillanimous, another fierce and high-spirited; one humane, another haughty; one lascivious, another chaste; one frank, another astute; one hard, another easy; one serious, another frivolous; one religious, another an unbeliever, and so on. I know that every one will admit that it would be highly praiseworthy in a prince to possess all the above-named qualities that are reputed good, but as they cannot all be possessed or observed, human conditions not permitting of it, it is necessary that he should be prudent enough to avoid the scandal of those vices which would lose him the state, and guard himself if possible against those which will not lose it him, but if not able to, he can indulge them with less scruple. And yet he must not mind incurring the scandal of those vices, without which it would be difficult to save the state, for if one considers well, it will be found that some things which seem virtues would, if followed, lead to one's ruin, and some others which appear vices result in one's greater security and wellbeing.

Chapter XVII: Of Cruelty and Clemency, and Whether It Is Better to Be Loved or Feared

Proceeding to the other qualities before named, I say that every prince must desire to be considered merciful and not cruel. He must, however, take care not to misuse this mercifulness. Cesare Borgia was considered cruel, but his cruelty had brought order to the Romagna, united it, and reduced it to peace and fealty. If this is considered well, it will be seen that he was really much more merciful than the Florentine people, who, to avoid the name of cruelty, allowed Pistoia to be destroyed. A prince, therefore, must not mind incurring the charge of cruelty for the purpose of keeping his subjects united and faithful; for, with a very few examples, he will be more merciful than those who, from excess of tenderness, allow disorders to arise, from whence spring blood-shed and rapine; for these as a rule injure the whole community, while the executions carried out by the prince injure only individuals. And of all princes, it is impossible for a new prince to escape the reputation of cruelty, new states being always full of dangers. . . .

Nevertheless, he must be cautious in believing and acting, and must not be afraid of his own shadow, and must proceed in a temperate manner with prudence and humanity, so that too much confidence does not render him incautious, and too much diffidence does not render him intolerant.

From this arises the question whether it is better to be loved more than feared, or feared more than loved. The reply is, that one ought to be both feared and loved, but as it is difficult for the two to go together, it is much safer to be feared than loved, if one of the two has to be wanting. For it may be said of men in general that they are ungrateful, voluble, dissemblers, anxious to avoid danger, and covetous of gain; as long as you benefit them, they are entirely yours; they offer you their blood, their goods, their life, and their children, as I have before said, when the necessity is remote; but when it approaches, they revolt. And the prince who has relied solely on their words, without making other preparations, is ruined; for the friendship which is gained by purchase and not through grandeur and nobility of spirit is bought but not secured, and at a pinch is not to be expended in your service. And men have less scruple in offending one who makes himself loved than one who makes himself feared; for love is held by a chain of obligation which, men being selfish, is broken whenever it serves their purpose; but fear is maintained by a dread punishment which never fails.

Still, a prince should make himself feared in such a way that if he does not gain love, he at any rate avoids hatred; for fear and the absence of hatred may well go together, and will be always attained by one who abstains from interfering with the property of his citizens and subjects or with their women. And when he is obliged to take the life of any one, let him do so when there is a proper justification and manifest reason for it; but above all he must abstain from taking the property of others, for men forget more easily the death of their father than the loss of their patrimony. Then also pretexts for seizing property are never wanting, and one who begins to live by rapine will always find some reason for taking the goods of others, whereas causes for taking life are rarer and more fleeting.

But when the prince is with his army and has a large number of soldiers under his control, then it is extremely necessary that he should not mind being thought cruel; for without this reputation he could not keep an army united or disposed to any duty. Among the noteworthy actions of Hannibal is numbered this, that although he had an enormous army, composed of men of all nations and fighting in foreign countries, there never arose any dissension either among them or against the prince, either in good fortune or in bad. This could not be due to anything but his inhuman cruelty, which together with his infinite other virtues, made him always venerated and terrible in the sight of his soldiers, and without it his other virtues would not have sufficed to produce that effect. Thoughtless writers admire on the one hand his actions, and on the other blame the principal cause of them.

And that it is true that his other virtues would not have sufficed may be seen from the case of Scipio (famous not only in regard to his own times, but all times of which memory remains), whose armies rebelled against him in Spain, which arose from nothing but his excessive kindness, which allowed more license to the soldiers than was consonant with military discipline. He was reproached with this in the senate by Fabius Maximus, who called him a corrupter of the Roman militia. Locri having been destroyed by one of Scipio's officers was not revenged by him, nor was the insolence of that officer punished, simply by reason of his easy nature; so much so, that some one wishing to excuse him in the senate said that there were many men who knew rather how not to err, than how to correct the errors of others. This disposition would in time have tarnished the fame and glory of Scipio had he persevered in it under the empire, but living under the rule of the senate this harmful quality was not only concealed but became a glory to him.

I conclude, therefore, with regard to being feared and loved, that men love at their own free will, but fear at the will of the prince, and that a wise prince must rely on what is in his power and not on what is in the power of others, and he must only contrive to avoid incurring hatred, as has been explained.

Chapter XVIII: In What Way Princes Must Keep Faith

How laudable it is for a prince to keep good faith and live with integrity, and not with astuteness, every one knows. Still the experience of our times shows those princes to have done great things who have had little regard for good faith, and have been able by astuteness to confuse men's brains, and who have ultimately overcome those who have made loyalty their foundation.

You must know, then, that there are two methods of fighting, the one by law, the other by force: the first method is that of men, the second of beasts; but as the first method is often insufficient, one must have recourse to the second. It is therefore necessary for a prince to know well how to use both the beast and the man. This was covertly taught to rulers by ancient writers, who relate how Achilles and many others of those ancient princes were given to Chiron the centaur to be brought up and educated under his discipline. The parable of this semi-animal, semi-human teacher is meant to indicate that a prince must know how to use both natures, and that the one without the other is not durable.

A prince being thus obliged to know well how to act as a beast must imitate the fox and the lion, for the lion cannot protect himself from traps, and the fox cannot defend himself from wolves. One must therefore be a fox to recognize traps, and a lion to frighten wolves. Those that wish to be only lions do not understand this. Therefore, a prudent ruler ought not to keep faith when by so doing it would be against his interest, and when the reasons which made him bind himself no longer exist. If men were all good, this precept would not be a good one; but as they are bad, and would not observe their faith with you, so you are not bound to keep faith with them. Nor have legitimate grounds ever failed a prince who wished to show colourable excuse for the non-fulfilment of his promise. Of this one could furnish an infinite number of modern examples, and show how many times peace has been broken, and how many promises rendered worthless, by the faithlessness of princes, and those that have been best able to imitate the fox have succeeded best. But it is necessary to be able to disguise this character well, and to be a great feigner and dissembler; and men are so simple and so ready to obey present necessities, that one who deceives will always find those who allow themselves to be deceived.

I will only mention one modern instance. Alexander VI did nothing else but deceive men, he thought of nothing else, and found the occasion for it; no man was ever more able to give assurances, or affirmed things with stronger oaths, and no man observed them less; however, he always succeeded in his deceptions, as he well knew this aspect of things.

It is not, therefore, necessary for a prince to have all the above-named qualities, but it is very necessary to seem to have them. I would even be bold to say that to possess them and always to observe them is dangerous, but to appear to possess them is useful. Thus it is well to seem merciful, faithful, humane, sincere, religious, and also to be so; but you must have the mind so disposed that when it is needful to be otherwise you may be able to change to the opposite qualities. And it must be understood that a prince, and especially a new prince, cannot observe all those things which are considered good in men, being often obliged, in order to maintain the state, to act against faith, against charity, against humanity, and against religion. And, therefore, he must have a mind disposed to adapt itself according to the wind, and as the variations of fortune dictate, and, as I said before, not deviate from what is good, if possible, but be able to do evil if constrained.

A prince must take great care that nothing goes out of his mouth which is not full of the above-named five qualities, and, to see and hear him, he should seem to be all mercy, faith, integrity, humanity, and religion. And nothing is more necessary than to seem to have this last quality, for men in general judge more by the eyes than by the hands, for every one can see, but very few have to feel. Everybody sees what you appear to be, few feel what you are, and those few will not dare to oppose themselves to the many, who have the majesty of the state to defend them; and in the actions of men, and especially of princes, from which there is no appeal, the end justifies the means. Let a prince therefore aim at conquering and maintaining the state, and the means will always be judged honourable and praised by every one, for the vulgar is always taken by appearances and the issue of the event; and the world consists only of the vulgar, and the few who are not vulgar are isolated when the many have a rallying point in the prince. A certain prince of the present time, whom it is well not to name, never does anything but preach peace and good faith, but he is really a great enemy to both, and either of them, had he observed them, would have lost him state or reputation on many occasions.

Chapter XXV: How Much Fortune Can Do in Human Affairs and How It May Be Opposed

It is not unknown to me how many have been and are of opinion that worldly events are so governed by fortune and by God, that men cannot by their prudence change them, and that on the contrary there is no remedy whatever, and for this they may judge it to be useless to toil much about them, but let things be ruled by chance. This opinion has been more held in our day, from the great changes that have been seen, and are daily seen, beyond every human conjecture. When I think about them, at times I am partly inclined to share this opinion. Nevertheless, that our freewill may not be altogether extinguished, I think it may be true that fortune is the ruler of half our actions, but that she allows the other half or thereabouts to be governed by us. I would compare her to an impetuous river that, when turbulent, inundates the plains, casts down trees and buildings, removes earth from this side and places it on the other; every one flees before it, and everything yields to its fury without being able to oppose it; and yet though it is of such a kind, still when it is quiet, men can make provision against it by dykes and banks, so that when it rises it will either go into a canal or its rush will not be so wild and dangerous. So it is with fortune, which shows her power where no measures have been taken to resist her, and directs her fury where she knows that no dykes or barriers have been made to hold her. And if you regard Italy, which has been the seat of these changes, and who has given the impulse to them, you will see her to be a country without dykes or banks of any kind. If she had been protected by proper measures, like Germany, Spain, and France, this inundation would not have caused the great changes that it has, or would not have happened at all.

This must suffice as regards opposition to fortune in general. But limiting myself more to particular cases, I would point out how one sees a certain prince to-day fortunate and to-morrow ruined, without seeing that he has changed in character or otherwise. I believe this arises in the first place from the causes that we have already discussed at length; that is to say, because the prince who bases himself entirely on fortune is ruined when fortune changes. I also believe that he is happy whose mode of procedure accords with the needs of the times, and similarly he is unfortunate whose mode of procedure is opposed to the times. For one sees that men in those things which lead them to the aim that each one has in view, namely, glory and riches, proceed in various ways; one with circumspection, another with impetuosity, one by violence, another by cunning, one with patience, another with the reverse; and each by these diverse ways may arrive at his aim. One sees also two cautious men, one of whom succeeds in his designs, and the other not, and in the same way two men succeed equally by different methods, one being cautious, the other impetuous, which arises only from the nature of the times, which does or does not conform to their method of procedure. From this it results, as I have said, that two men, acting differently, attain the same effect, and of two others acting in the same way, one attains his goal and not the other. On this depend also the changes in prosperity, for if it happens that time and circumstances are favourable to one who acts with caution and prudence he will be successful, but if time and circumstances change he will be ruined, because he does not change his mode of procedure. No man is found so prudent as to be able to adapt himself to this, either because he cannot deviate from that to which his nature disposes him, or else because having always prospered by walking in one path, he cannot persuade himself that it is well to leave it; and therefore the cautious man, when it is time to act suddenly, does not know how to do so and is consequently ruined; for if one could change one's nature with time and circumstances, fortune would never change.

Pope Julius II acted impetuously in everything he did and found the times and conditions so in conformity with that mode of procedure, that he always obtained a good result. Consider the first war that he made against Bologna while Messer Giovanni Bentivogli was still living. The Venetians were not pleased with it, neither was the King of Spain, France was conferring with him over the enterprise, notwithstanding which, owing to his fierce and impetuous disposition, he engaged personally in the expedition. This move caused both Spain and the Venetians to halt and hesitate, the latter through fear, the former through the desire to recover the entire kingdom of Naples. On the other hand, he engaged with him the King of France, because seeing him make this move and desiring his friendship in order to put down the Venetians, that king judged that he could not refuse him his troops without manifest injury. Thus Julius by his impetuous move achieved what no other pontiff with the utmost human prudence would have succeeded in doing, because, if he had waited till all arrangements had been made and everything settled before leaving Rome, as any other pontiff would have done, it would never have succeeded. For the King of France would have found a thousand excuses, and the others would have inspired him with a thousand fears. I will omit his other actions, which were all of this kind and which all succeeded well, and the shortness of his life did not suffer him to experience the contrary, for had times followed in which it was necessary to act with caution, his ruin would have resulted, for he would never have deviated from these methods to which his nature disposed him.

I conclude then that fortune varying and men remaining fixed in their ways, they are successful so long as these ways conform to circumstances, but when they are opposed then they are unsuccessful. I certainly think that it is better to be impetuous than cautious, for fortune is a woman, and it is necessary, if you wish to master her, to conquer her by force; and it can be seen that she lets herself be overcome by the bold rather than by those who proceed coldly. And therefore, like a woman, she is always a friend to the young, because they are less cautious, fiercer, and master her with greater audacity.

Chapter XXVI: Exhortation to Liberate Italy from the Barbarians

Having now considered all the things we have spoken of, and thought within myself whether at present the time was not propitious in Italy for a new prince, and if there was not a state of things which offered an opportunity to a prudent and capable man to introduce a new system that would do honour to himself and good to the mass of the people, it seems to me that so many things concur to favour a new ruler that I do not know of any time more fitting for such an enterprise. And if, as I said, it was necessary in order that the power of Moses should be displayed that the people of Israel should be slaves in Egypt, and to give scope for the greatness and courage of Cyrus that the Persians should be oppressed by the Medes, and to illustrate the preeminence of Theseus that the Athenians should be dispersed, so at the present time, in order that the might of an Italian genius might be recognised, it was necessary that Italy should be reduced to her present condition, and that she should be more enslaved than the Hebrews, more oppressed than the Persians, and more scattered than the Athenians; without a head, without order, beaten, despoiled, lacerated, and overrun, and that she should have suffered ruin of every kind.

And although before now a gleam of hope has appeared which gave hope that some individual might be appointed by God for her redemption, yet at the highest summit of his career he was thrown aside by fortune, so that now, almost lifeless, she awaits one who may heal her wounds and put a stop to the pillaging of Lombardy, to the rapacity and extortion in the Kingdom of Naples and in Tuscany, and cure her of those sores which have long been festering. Behold how she prays God to send some one to redeem her from this barbarous cruelty and insolence. Behold her ready and willing to follow any standard if only there be some one to raise it. There is nothing now she can hope for but that your illustrious house may place itself at the head of this redemption, being by its power and fortune so exalted, and being favoured by God and the Church, of which it is now the ruler. Now will this be very difficult, if you call to mind the actions and lives of the men I have named. And although those men were rare and marvellous, they were none the less men, and each of them had less opportunity than the present, for their enterprise was not juster than this, nor easier, nor was God more their friend than He is yours. Here is a just cause; "*iustum enim est bellum quibus necessarium, et pia arma ubi nulla nisi in armis spes est.*" [1] Here is the greatest willingness, nor can

---

[1] For war is just when it is necessary, and arms are holy where there is no hope but in arms.

there be great difficulty where there is great willingness, provided that the measures are adopted of those whom I have set before you as examples. Besides this, unexampled wonders have been seen here performed by God, the sea has been opened, a cloud has shown you the road, the rock has given forth water, manna has rained, and everything has contributed to your greatness, the remainder must be done by you. God will not do everything, in order not to deprive us of freewill and the portion of the glory that falls to our lot.

It is no marvel that none of the before-mentioned Italians have done that which it is to be hoped your illustrious house may do; and if in so many revolutions in Italy and so many warlike operations, it always seems as if military capacity were extinct, this is because the ancient methods were not good, and no one has arisen who knew how to discover new ones. Nothing does so much honour to a newly-risen man than the new laws and measures which he introduces. These things, when they are well based and have greatness in them, render him revered and admired, and there is not lacking scope in Italy for the introduction of every kind of new organisation. Here there is great virtue in the members, if it were not wanting in the heads. Look how in duels and in contests of a few the Italians are superior in strength, dexterity, and intelligence. But when it comes to armies they make a poor show; which proceeds entirely from the weakness of the leaders, for those that know are not obeyed, and every one thinks that he knows, there being hitherto nobody who has raised himself so high both by valour and fortune as to make the others yield. Hence it comes about that for so long a time, in all the wars waged during the last twenty years, whenever there has been an entirely Italian army it has always been a failure, as witness first Taro, then Alexandria, Capua, Genoa, Vailà, Bologna, and Mestri.

If your illustrious house, therefore, wishes to follow those great men who redeemed their countries, it is before all things necessary, as the true foundation of every undertaking, to provide yourself with your own forces, for you cannot have more faithful, or truer and better soldiers. And although each one of them may be good, they will united become even better when they see themselves commanded by their prince, and honoured and favoured by him. It is therefore necessary to prepare such forces in order to be able with Italian prowess to defend the country from foreigners. And although both the Swiss and Spanish infantry are deemed terrible, none the less they each have their defects, so that a third method of array might not only oppose them, but be confident of overcoming them. For the Spaniards cannot sustain the attack of cavalry, and the Swiss have to fear infantry which meets them with resolution equal to their own. From which it has resulted, as will be seen by experience, that the Spaniards cannot sustain the attack of French cavalry, and the Swiss are overthrown by Spanish infantry. And although a complete example of the latter has not been seen, yet an instance was furnished in the battle of Ravenna, where the Spanish infantry attacked the German battalions, which are organised in the same way as the Swiss. The Spaniards, through their bodily agility and aided by their bucklers, had entered between and under their pikes and were in a position to attack them safely without the Germans being able to defend themselves; and if the cavalry had not charged them they would have utterly destroyed them. Knowing therefore the defects of both these kinds of infantry, a third kind can be created which can resist cavalry and need not fear infantry, and this will be done by the choice of arms and a new organisation. And these are the things which, when newly introduced, give reputation and grandeur to a new prince.

This opportunity must not, therefore, be allowed to pass, so that Italy may at length find her liberator. I cannot express the love with which he would be received in all those provinces which have suffered under these foreign invasions, with what thirst for vengeance, with what steadfast faith, with what love, with what grateful tears. What doors would be closed against him? What people would refuse him obedience? What envy could oppose him? What Italian would withhold allegiance? This barbarous domination stinks in the nostrils of every one. May your illustrious house therefore assume this task with that courage and those hopes which are inspired by a just cause, so that under its banner our fatherland may be raised up, and under its auspices be verified that saying of Petrarch:

Valour against fell wrath

Will take up arms; and be the combat quickly sped!

For, sure, the ancient worth,

That in Italians stirs the heart, is not yet dead.

Discourses on the First Ten Books of Titus Livius

Niccolò Machiavelli to Zanobi Buondelmonti and Cosimo Rucellai,[2] Greetings.

I am sending you a gift which, even though it may not match the obligations I have to you, is, without a doubt, the best that Niccolò Machiavelli can send to you; in it I have expressed all I know and all that I have learned from long experience and continuous study of worldly affairs. And since it is not possible for you or anyone else to ask more of me, you cannot complain if I have not given you more. You may very well complain about the poverty of my wit when my arguments are weak, and about the fallacious quality of my judgment if, in the course of my reasonings, I often manage to deceive myself. This being the case, I do not know which of us should be less obliged to the other: whether I should be so to you, who have encouraged me to write what I never would have written by myself, or you to me, since I may have written without satisfying you. Take this, then, as you would accept something from a friend: there one considers the intention of the sender more than the quality of the thing which is sent. And rest assured that in this venture I have one consolation, for I believe that although I may have deceived myself in many of its particulars, in one matter I know that I have not made an error; that is, to have chosen you above all others to whom I should dedicate these *Discourses* of mine, both because in so doing I believe that I have shown my gratitude for the benefits I have received and because I felt that I had departed from the common practice of those who write and always address their works to some prince and, blinded by ambition and by avarice, praise him for all his virtuous qualities when they ought to be blaming him for all his bad qualities. So, to avoid this mistake, I have chosen not those who are princes but those who, because of their numerous good qualities, deserve to be princes; not those who might shower me with offices, honors, and wealth, but those who, although unable, would like to do so. If men wish to judge correctly, they must esteem those who are generous, not those who are potentially generous; and, in like manner, they must esteem those who know how to rule a kingdom, not those who, without knowing how, have the power to do so. Thus, historians praise Hiero the Syracusan[3] more when he was a private citizen than they do Perseus of Macedonia[4] when he was king: for Hiero lacked nothing to be prince save a kingdom, while the other had no attribute of a king except his kingdom. Therefore, enjoy this good or bad work which you yourselves have requested; and if you persist in erroneously finding pleasure in my opinions, I shall not fail to follow this with the rest of the history, as I promised you in the beginning. Farewell.

---

[2] Associates of Machiavelli in the city's chief literary circle in the Rucellai Gardens; they were implicated in a plot against the Medici regime in 1523.

[3] King of Syracuse (Sicily), 265–215 B.C.

[4] The last king of Macedon (179–168 B.C.), son of Philip V.

Book 1

Introduction

Because of the envious nature of men, it has always been no less dangerous to discover new methods and institutions than to explore unknown oceans and lands, since men are quicker to criticize than to praise the deeds of others. Nevertheless, driven by that natural desire I have always felt to work on whatever might prove beneficial to everyone, I have determined to enter a path which has not yet been taken by anyone. Although it may bring me worry and difficulty, yet I may find my reward among those who study kindly the goal of these labors of mine. And if my feeble intelligence, my limited experience of current events, and my weak knowledge of ancient ones[5] should make this attempt of mine defective and of little use, it may, at least, show the way to someone with more ability, more eloquence, and more judgment who will be able to fulfill my intention; so that if I do not earn praise, I should not receive blame.

When we consider, then, how much honor is attributed to antiquity, and how many times (leaving aside numerous other examples) a fragment of an ancient statue has been bought at a great price so that the buyer may have it near him to decorate his house or to have it imitated by those who take pleasure in that art; and when we see, on the other hand, the powerful examples which history shows us that have been accomplished by ancient kingdoms and republics, by kings, captains, citizens, and legislators who have exhausted themselves for their fatherland, examples that have been more often admired than imitated (or so much ignored that not the slightest trace of this ancient ability remains), I cannot but be at the same time both amazed and sorry. And I am even more amazed when I see that in civil disputes which arise among citizens, or in sicknesses that break out, men always have recourse to those judgments or remedies which were pronounced or prescribed by the ancients. For civil law is nothing other than the judgments given by ancient jurists which, organized into a system, instruct our jurists today. Nor is medicine anything other than the experiments carried out by ancient doctors on which the doctors of today base their diagnoses. Nevertheless, in instituting republics, maintaining states, governing kingdoms, organizing the army and administering a war, dispensing justice to subjects, and increasing an empire one cannot find a prince or a republic that has recourse to the examples of the ancients.

This, in my opinion, arises not so much from the weakness into which the present religion has brought the world or from the harm done to many Christian provinces and cities by an idle ambition as from not possessing a proper knowledge of histories, for in reading them we do not draw out of them that sense or taste that flavor which they have in themselves. Hence it happens that an infinite number of people read them and take pleasure in hearing about the variety of incidents which are contained in them without thinking to imitate them, for they consider imitation not only difficult but impossible; as if the heavens, the sun, the elements, and men had varied in their motion, their order, and their power from what they were in ancient times. Wishing, therefore, to free men of this erroneous way of thinking, I deemed it necessary to write about all those books by Livy which the malignity of time has not taken from us; I wish to write what I, according to my knowledge of ancient and modern affairs, judge necessary for a better understanding of them, so that those who read these statements of mine may more easily draw from them that practical knowledge one should seek from an acquaintance with history books. And although this undertaking is difficult, neverthe-

---

[5] A paraphrase of the corresponding passage in the dedication to *The Prince*.

less, aided by those who have encouraged me to shoulder this burden, I believe I can carry it in such a manner that only a short distance will remain for another to bring it to the destined goal.

Chapter 2. Of How Many Kinds of Republics There Are and of What Kind the Roman Republic Was

I wish to put aside a discussion of those cities which, at their beginnings, were subject to others; and I shall speak about those which have had their beginnings far from any foreign servitude and have been governed from the beginning by their own judgment, either as republics or as principalities, and which have had different laws and institutions just as they have had different origins. Some of them, either at their start or after very little time, were given laws by a single man and at one time, as Lycurgus did with the Spartans; others acquired their laws by chance, at different times and according to circumstances, as occurred in Rome. A republic can, indeed, be called fortunate if it produces a man so prudent that he gives it laws organized in such a manner that it can live securely under them without needing to revise them. And it seems that Sparta observed its laws more than eight hundred years without corrupting them or without any dangerous upheaval. Unfortunate, on the contrary, is the city which is forced to reorganize itself, not having chanced to encounter a prudent organizer. And of these cities, the one which is the furthest from order is the most unfortunate; and that one is furthest from it which in its institutions is completely off the straight path which could lead it to its perfect and true goal, because for those who find themselves in this state it is almost impossible that by any happening they can be set on the right path again. Those other cities that have had a good beginning and are capable of becoming better, even if they have not had a perfect constitution, can, by means of an unexpected course of events, become perfect. But it is very true that institutions are never established without danger; for most men never agree to a new law that concerns a new order in the city unless a necessity demonstrates to them that it is required; and since this necessity cannot arise without danger, the republic may easily be destroyed before it is brought to a perfection of organization. The Republic of Florence testifies to this: reorganized after what occurred at Arezzo in 1502, it was disorganized by what occurred at Prato in 1512.[6]

Since I wish to discuss what the institutions of the city of Rome were and the circumstances which led to their perfection, let me say that those who have written about republics declare that there are in them three kinds of governments, which they call principality, aristocracy, and democracy; and that those who organize a city most often turn to one of these, depending upon whichever seems more appropriate to them. Others—and wiser men, according to the judgment of many—are of the opinion that there are six types of government: three of these are very bad; three others are good in themselves but are so easily corruptible that they, too, can become pernicious. Those which are good are the three mentioned above; those which are bad are three others which depend upon the first three, and each of them is, in a way, similar to its good counterpart, so that they easily jump from one form to another. For the principality easily becomes tyrannical; aristocrats can very easily produce an oligarchy; democracy is converted into anarchy with no difficulty. So that if a founder of a republic organizes one of these three governments in a city, he organizes it there for a brief period of time only, since no precaution can prevent it from slipping into its contrary on account of the similarity, in such a case, of the virtue and the vice.

---

[6] Cf. Luca Landucci, *Diary*, in this volume, pp. 162–66 and 166–71.

These variations of government are born among men by chance: for in the beginning of the world, when its inhabitants were few, they lived at one time dispersed and like wild beasts; then, when their numbers multiplied, they gathered together and, in order to defend themselves better, they began to search among themselves for one who was stronger and braver, and they made him their leader and obeyed him. From this sprang the knowledge of what things are good and honorable, as distinct from the pernicious and the evil: for if someone were to harm his benefactor, this aroused hatred and compassion among men, since they cursed the ungrateful and honored those who showed gratitude; and thinking that the same injuries could also be committed against themselves, they made laws to avoid similar evils and instituted punishments for transgressors. Thus, the recognition of justice came about. The result was that, later on, when they had to elect a prince, they did not select the bravest man but rather the one who was most prudent and most just. But when they began to choose the prince by hereditary succession rather than by election, the heirs immediately began to degenerate from the level of their ancestors and, putting aside acts of valor, they thought that princes had nothing to do but to surpass other princes in luxury, lasciviousness, and in every other form of pleasure. So, as the prince came to be hated he became afraid of this hatred and quickly passed from fear to violent deeds, and the immediate result was tyranny.

From this there came next the destructions, the conspiracies, and the plots against princes, carried out not by those who were either timid or weak but by those who surpassed others in generosity, greatness of spirit, wealth, and nobility: these men could not stand the disreputable life of such a prince. The masses, therefore, following the authority of these powerful men, took up arms against the prince, and after he had been eliminated they obeyed those men as their liberators. And since those men hated the very idea of a single ruler, they constituted for themselves a government, and in the beginning, since they remembered the past tyranny, they governed according to the laws instituted by themselves, subordinating their own interests to the common good, and they managed and maintained both their private and public affairs with the greatest of care. When this administration later passed to their sons, who did not understand the changeability of Fortune, had never experienced bad times, and could not be satisfied with equality among citizens, they turned to avarice, ambition, and the violation of other men's women, and they caused a government of the aristocrats to become a government of the few, with no regard to any civil rights; so that in a short time they experienced the same fate as the tyrant, for as the masses were sick of their rule, they assisted, in any way they could, anyone who might plan to attack these rulers, and thus there soon arose someone who, with the aid of the masses, destroyed them. And since the memory of the prince and of the injuries received from him was still fresh, they turned to a democratic form of government, having destroyed the government ruled by a few men and not wishing to return to that ruled by a prince; and they organized it in such a way that neither the few powerful men nor a prince might have any authority whatsoever in it. And because all governments are, at the outset, respected, this democratic government was maintained awhile, but not for a long time, particularly after the generation that organized it passed away; it immediately turned to anarchy, where neither the individual citizen nor the public official is feared; each individual lived according to his own wishes, so that every day a thousand wrongs were done; and so, constrained by necessity, either because of the suggestion of some good man or in order to flee such anarchy, it returned again to the principality; and from that, step by step, the government moved again in the direction of anarchy, in the manner and for the reasons just given.

And this is the cycle through which all states that have governed themselves or that now govern themselves pass; but rarely do they return to the same forms of government, for virtually no state can possess so much vitality that it can sustain so many changes and remain on its feet. But it may well happen that while a state lacking counsel and strength is in difficulty, it becomes subject to a neighboring state which is better organized; but if this were not the case, then a state might be liable to pass endlessly through the cycle of these governments.

Let me say, therefore, that all the forms of government listed are defective: the three good ones because of the brevity of their lives, the three bad ones because of their inherent harmfulness. Thus, those who were prudent in establishing laws recognized this fact and, avoiding each of these forms in themselves, chose one that combined them all, judging such a government to be steadier and more stable, for when there is in the same city-state a principality, an aristocracy, and a democracy, one form keeps watch over the other.

Among those who have deserved great praise for having established such constitutions is Lycurgus, who organized his laws in Sparta in such a manner that, assigning to the king, the aristocrats, and the people their respective roles, he created a state which lasted more than eight hundred years, to his everlasting credit, and resulted in the tranquillity of that city. The contrary happened to Solon, who organized the laws in Athens: for in organizing only a democratic state there he made it of such a brief existence that before he died he saw arise the tyranny of Pisistratus; and although forty years later the latter's heirs were driven away and Athens returned to its freedom, having reestablished the democratic state according to the institutions of Solon, it did not last more than a hundred years. In spite of the fact that many laws which were not foreseen by Solon were established in Athens in order to restrain the insolence of the upper class and the anarchy of the populace, nevertheless Athens lived a very brief time in comparison to Sparta, because Solon did not mix democracy with the power of the principality and with that of the aristocrats.

But let us come to Rome. In spite of the fact that she never had a Lycurgus to organize her at the beginning so that she might exist free for a long time, nevertheless, because of the friction between the plebeians and the senate, so many circumstances attended her birth that chance brought about what a lawgiver had not acomplished. If Rome did not receive Fortune's first gift, she received the second: for her early institutions, although defective, nevertheless did not deviate from the right path that could lead them to perfection. Romulus and all the other kings passed many good laws in accordance with a free government; but since their goal was to found a kingdom and not a republic, when that city became free she lacked many institutions which were necessary to organize her under freedom, institutions which had not been set up by those kings. And when it happened that her kings lost their power for the reasons and in the ways described earlier, nonetheless those who drove them out, having immediately established two consuls in place of the king, drove out only the title of king and not royal power; so that, as there were in that republic the consuls and the senate, it came to be formed by only two of the three above-mentioned elements, that is, the principality and the aristocrats. There remained only to make a place for the democratic part of the government. When the Roman nobility became insolent, for the reasons that will be listed below, the people rose up against them; in order not to lose everything, the nobility was forced to concede to the people their own share; and on the other hand, the senate and the consuls retained enough authority so that they could maintain their rank in that republic. And thus there came about the creation of the tribunes of the plebeians, after which the government of the republic became more stable, since each of the three elements of government had its share. And Fortune was so favorable to Rome that even though she passed from a government by kings and aristocrats to one by the people, through those same steps and because of those same reasons which were discussed above, nevertheless the kingly authority was never entirely abolished to give authority to the aristocrats, nor was the authority of the aristocrats diminished completely to give it to the people; but since these elements remained mixed, Rome was a perfect state; and this perfection was produced through the friction between the plebeians and the senate, as the two following chapters will demonstrate at greater length.

Chapter 7. How the Right to Bring Public Charges is Necessary for a Republic to Preserve its Liberty

No more useful and necessary authority can be granted to those who are appointed to preserve a city's liberty than the capacity to bring before the people or before some magistrate or council charges against citizens who sin in any manner against the freedom of the government. This institution produces two very useful results in a republic: first, for fear of being accused, the citizens do not attempt anything against the government, or, if they do, they are immediately suppressed without regard to their station; second, it provides an outlet for those hatreds which grow up in cities, in whatever manner, against some particular citizen: and when these hatreds do not find a legal means of expression, they have recourse to illegal means, which cause the eventual ruin of the entire republic. And so, nothing makes a republic so stable and strong as organizing it in such a way that the agitation of the hatreds which excite it has a means of expressing itself provided for by the laws. This can be demonstrated by many examples, and especially by that which Livy brings forth concerning Coriolanus,[7] where he says that since the Roman nobility was angered at the plebeians because they felt that the plebeians had assumed too much authority as a result of the creation of the tribunes, who were to defend them, and since it happened that Rome then suffered a great scarcity of provisions and the senate had sent to Sicily for grain, Coriolanus, enemy of the popular faction, advised that the time had come to punish the plebeians by keeping them hungry and not distributing the grain, and by taking away from them the authority which they had usurped from the nobility. When this advice reached the ears of the people, they were so angry at him that he would have been murdered by the crowd as he left the senate if the tribunes had not called him to appear before them in his own defense. What was said above can be applied to this event—that is, that it is useful and necessary for republics to provide with their laws a means of expression for the wrath that the multitude feels against a single citizen, for when these legal means do not exist the people turn to illegal ones, and without a doubt the latter produced much worse effects than do the former.

For, when a citizen is legally oppressed, even if this be unjust to him, little or no disorder in the republic follows; for the execution of the act is done without private or foreign forces, which are the ones that destroy free government; but it is done with public forces and institutions which have their specific limits—nor do they transcend these limits to damage the republic. And as for corroborating this opinion with examples, that of Coriolanus from the ancients should suffice. Everyone should observe how much evil would have resulted for the Roman republic if he had been put to death by the crowd, for this would have created private grievances, which generate fear, and fear seeks defenses for which partisans are recruited, and from partisans are born the factions in cities, and form factions the ruin of the city. But since the matter was handled by

---

[7] Livy, 2.33–35.

those who had the authority to do so, all those evils which might have arisen by using private power were avoided.

We have witnessed in our own times what changes occurred in the Republic of Florence when the people were not able to vent their wrath legally against one of its citizens, as was the case when Francesco Valori[8] was almost like the prince of that city. He was regarded by many as ambitious, a man who would transgress lawful government because of his audacity and hot temper; and since there was no means within the republic's existing institutions of resisting him without establishing a rival party, it came about that he set out to enlist partisans, not fearing anything but illegal methods; on the other hand, since those who opposed him had no legal way to suppress him, they turned to illegal methods and eventually resorted to arms. Given the proper legal institutions, he might have been opposed and his authority destroyed, harming only himself, but because he had to be destroyed unlawfully, this resulted in harm not only to him but also to many other noble citizens. One could also cite, in support of the above conclusion, the incident which happened in connection with Piero Soderini, which came about entirely from the absence in that republic of any means of bringing charges against the ambition of powerful citizens. For it is not enough to accuse a powerful citizen before eight judges in a republic; there must be many judges, for the few always act in favor of the few. If these methods had existed in Florence, either the citizens would have accused him if his conduct was bad—by this means, without calling in a Spanish army, they would have vented their anger—or, if his conduct was not bad, they would not have dared to act against him for fear that they themselves might be accused; and thus, in either case the appetite for conflict, which was the cause of the quarrel, would have vanished.

The following conclusion can be drawn: whenever one finds foreign forces being called in by one faction of men living in a city, it may be taken for granted that the bad ordinances of that city are the cause, for it does not have an institution that provides an outlet for the malignant humors which are born among men to express themselves without their resorting to illegal means; adequate provision for this is made by making a number of judges available before whom public indictments may be made; and these accusations must be given proper importance. These means were so well organized in Rome that during the many conflicts between the plebeians and the senate neither the senate nor the plebeians nor any private citizen ever attempted to use outside forces; for they had a remedy at home and there was no need to search for it outside. And although the above examples are more than sufficient to prove this, I nevertheless wish to use another taken from Livy's history: there he relates how in Chiusi, a city which in those times was one of the most noble in Tuscany, a certain Lucumones raped the sister of Aruntes; unable to revenge himself because of the power of the rapist, Aruntes went to meet with the Gauls, who at that time ruled in the area which is now called Lombardy, and persuaded them to come with troops to Chiusi, showing them how they would profit by avenging the injustice he had suffered; Livy further explains how Aruntes would not have sought barbarian troops if he had seen a way to avenge himself through the city's institutions. But just as public accusations are useful in a republic, so false accusations are useless and harmful, as the discussion in the next chapter will show.

[8] The head of the pro-Savonarola party in the Florentine government between 1495 and 1498. The events mentioned below are described in detail in the *Diary* of Luca Landucci in this volume.

Chapter 9. How a Man Must Be Alone in Order to Found a New Republic or to Reform Completely Its Ancient Institutions

It may appear to some that I have gone too far along in Roman history without mentioning the founders of that republic or those institutions which are concerned with her religion and her militia; therefore, no longer wishing to keep the minds that wish to hear about this matter in suspense, let me say that many will perhaps judge it to be a bad example for a founder of a constitutional state, as Romulus was, to have first murdered his brother and then to have consented to the death of Titus Tatius, the Sabine, whom he had elected as his companion in his rule. Judging from this, the citizens might, out of ambition and a desire to rule, follow the example of their prince and oppress those who are opposed to their authority. This opinion might be correct, were we not to consider the goal that led Romulus to commit such a murder.

And this should be taken as a general rule: it rarely or never happens that a republic or kingdom is well organized from the beginning, or completely reformed, with no respect for its ancient institutions, unless it is done by one man alone; moreover, it is necessary that one man provide the means and be the only one from whose mind any such organization originates; therefore, a prudent founder of a republic, one whose intention it is to govern for the common good and not in his own interest, not for his heirs but for the sake of the fatherland, should try to have the authority all to himself; nor will a wise mind ever reproach anyone for some extraordinary action performed in order to found a kingdom or to institute a republic. It is, indeed, fitting that while the action accuses him, the result excuses him; and when this result is good, as it was with Romulus, it will always excuse him: for one should reproach a man who is violent in order to destroy, not one who is violent in order to mend things.

The founder should be so prudent and able-minded as not to bequeath the authority he has taken to his heir; for, since men are more apt to do evil than good, his successor might use for ambitious ends what the founder had employed virtuously. Besides this, though one man alone is fit for founding a government, what he has founded will not last long if it rests upon his shoulders alone; it is lasting when it is left in the care of many and when many desire to maintain it. As the many are not fit to organize a government, for they cannot recognize the best means of doing so because of the diversity of opinion among them, just so, when they have realized that they have it they will not agree to abandon it. And that Romulus was among those who deserve to be pardoned for the death of his brother and his companion, and that what he did was for the common good and not for private ambition, is demonstrated by the fact that he immediately organized a senate with whom he would consult and whose opinions he deliberated; and anyone who would examine carefully the authority that Romulus reserved for himself will see that all he kept for himself was the power to command the army during wartime and to convoke the senate. Later, when Rome became free as a result of the expulsion of the Tarquins, we can see that the city was not given any new institutions by the Romans besides their ancient ones, except that in place of a permanent king there were two yearly consuls: this testifies to the fact that all the original institutions were more suitable to a free, self-governing state than to one which was absolutist and tyrannical.

Numerous examples could be cited in support of what I have written above, such as Moses, Lycurgus, Solon, and other founders of kingdoms and republics who were able to form laws for the common good because they had taken sole authority upon themselves, but I shall omit them since they are well known; instead, I shall present only one example, not so well known but worthy of examination by those who wish to be the organizers of good laws, and the example is: Agis, King of Sparta, who wished to return the Spartans to the bounds within which the laws of Lycurgus had enclosed them, for he felt that, having departed from them, his city had lost much of its former ability and, as a result, much of its strength and empire; but at the start of his efforts he was assassinated by the Spartan Ephors as a man who wanted to become a tyrant. But when Cleomenes succeeded him on the throne, the same desire, after a time, arose in him as a result of reading the memoirs and writings of Agis which he had discovered, wherein he saw what his real intentions were, and he realized that he could not do this good for his country if he did not possess sole authority; for it seemed impossible, on account of man's ambition, for him to be able to help the many against the wishes of the few; so, when the right occasion arose he had all the Ephors killed and anyone else who might oppose him; then he completely restored the laws of Lycurgus. This action might have been enough to revive Sparta and to give Cleomenes the same reputation that Lycurgus had if it had not been for the power of the Macedonians and the weakness of the other Greek republics; for, after such institutions had been established, Cleomenes was attacked by the Macedonians, and when he discovered he was weaker in numbers and had nowhere to go for help, he was defeated.[9] This plan of his, no matter how just and praiseworthy it might have been, was not carried out.

Considering all these matters, then, I conclude that it is necessary to be alone in establishing a republic; and that, concerning the death of Remus and Titus Tatius, Romulus deserves to be excused, not blamed.

Chapter 10. Those Who Found a Republic or a Kingdom Deserve as Much Praise as Those Who Found a Tyranny Deserve Blame

Among all praiseworthy men, the most praiseworthy are those who were leaders and founders of religions; next come those who founded either republics or kingdoms; after these the most celebrated men are those who, commanding armies, have increased either their own kingdom or that of their native land; next to these may be placed men of letters, who, since they are of various types, are each praised according to their merits. To other men, whose number is infinite, some portion of praise may be attributed according to the skill they possess in their art or profession. On the other hand, men who have destroyed religions, wasted kingdoms and republics, and have been enemies of virtue, letters, and every sort of profession that brings gain and honor to the human race—such as the impious, the violent, the ignorant, the useless, the lazy, and the wicked—are considered infamous and detestable; and no one will ever be so mad or so wise, so sorry or so good that, given the choice between the two kinds of men, he will not praise those who merit praise and blame those who deserve blame.

Nevertheless, in the end nearly all men, deceived by a false appearance of good and a false sense of glory, allow themselves, either by their own choice or through their ignorance, to join the ranks of those who deserve more blame than praise; and while they have the possibility of establishing, to their perpetual honor, either a republic or a kingdom, they turn instead to tyranny, not realizing how much fame, glory, honor, security, tranquillity, and peace of mind they are losing by such a decision and, on the other hand, how much infamy, vituperation, blame, danger, and unrest they incur.

And if they read histories and make use of the records of ancient affairs, it is impossible for those who have lived as private citizens in a republic or who have become princes either because of Fortune or

---

[9] 222 B.C.

ability not to wish to live, if they are private citizens, in their native land like Scipio rather than like Caesar and, if they are princes, to live like Agesilaus, Timoleon, and Dion rather than like Nabis, Phalaris, and Dionysius;[10] for they would see how the latter are soundly condemned while the former are praised most highly; they would also see how Timoleon and the others had no less authority in their native lands than Dionysius and Phalaris had, and that they enjoyed, by far, greater security for a longer time.

Nor should anyone be deceived by Caesar's glory, so very celebrated by historians, for those who praised him were corrupted by his good fortune and amazed by the duration of the empire which, ruled in his name, did not allow writers to speak freely about him. But anyone who wishes to know what free historians would say about him should examine what they say about Catiline. And Caesar is even more blameworthy, just as a man who has committed an evil deed is more to be blamed than one who has only wished to do so; moreover, let the reader see how Brutus is so highly praised, as though, unable to criticize Caesar because of his power, they praise his enemy instead.[11]

Furthermore, let any man who has become a prince in a republic consider how much more praise those emperors deserved who lived under the laws and as good princes after Rome had become an empire than those who lived the opposite way, and he will see how Titus, Nerva, Trajan, Hadrian, Antoninus [Pius], and Marcus [Aurelius] had no need of Praetorian guards nor a multitude of legions to defend themselves, for their customs, the goodwill of the people, and the love of the senate protected them; the prince will also see how the Eastern and Western armies were not sufficient for Caligula, Nero, Vitellius, and other evil emperors to save themselves from the enemies that their wicked customs and evil lives had created for them. And if the history of these men were studied carefully, it would serve as an excellent lesson to show any prince the path to glory or to censure, to his security or to his peril, for of the twenty-six emperors between Caesar and Maximinus, sixteen were murdered and ten died a natural death; and if among those who were murdered there were several good men, like Galba and Pertinax, they were killed by the corruption which their predecessors had left behind in their soldiers; and if among those who died a natural death there was a wicked man, like Severus, this was the result of his very great fortune and ability—a combination of two things which few men enjoy. A prince will also observe, through the lesson of this history, how one can organize a good kingdom: for all the emperors who assumed the imperial throne by birth, except for Titus, were bad, and those who became emperors by adoption were all good, as were the five from Nerva to Marcus; and when the empire fell into hereditary succession, it returned again to its ruin.

Therefore, let a prince examine the times from Nerva to Marcus [Aurelius], and let him compare them with those which came before and afterward, and then let him choose during which period he would wish to be born or in which period he would like to be made emperor. In the times when good emperors governed, he will see a ruler secure in the midst of his secure citizens, and a world of peace and justice; he will see a senate with its full authority, the magistrates with their honors, the rich citizens enjoying their wealth, the nobles and ability exalted, and he will find tranquillity and well-being in everything; and on the other hand, he will see all rancor, licentiousness, corruption, and ambition extinguished; he will see a golden age in which a man can hold and defend whatever opinion he wishes. He will, in the end, see the world rejoicing: its prince endowed with respect and glory, its peoples with love and security. If next he studies carefully the times of the other emperors,

---

[10] Agesilaus (400–c. 360 B.C.) was a king of Sparta; Timoleon and Dion overthrew the tyranny of Dionysius II, who had invited Plato to Syracuse; Nabis (206–192 B.C) and Phalaris (570–555 B.C) were tyrants respectively of Sparta and Agrigento.

[11] The opposite judgment in *The Prince*, 16.

he will see them full of the atrocities of war, the conflicts of sedition, and the cruelties of both peace and war, so many princes put to death by the sword, so many civil wars, so many foreign wars, all of Italy afflicted and full of previously unknown adversities, and her cities ruined and sacked. He will see Rome burned, the Capitoline destroyed by her own citizens, her ancient temples desolate, her rituals corrupted, and the cities full of adulterous conduct; he will see the seas covered with exiles and the earth stained with blood. He will find countless cruelties in Rome and discover that nobility, wealth, past honors, and especially virtue are considered capital crimes. He will see the rewarding of those who accuse falsely, the turning of servants against their masters and freedmen against their former owners, and he will see those who, lacking enemies, are oppressed by their friends. And then he will well understand how many obligations Rome, Italy, and the world owe to Caesar!

And the prince, without a doubt, if he is a man, will be frightened away from any imitation of the bad times and will burn with an ardent desire to follow the ways of the good times. If a prince truly seeks worldly glory, he should hope to possess a corrupt city—not in order to ruin it completely as Caesar did but to reorganize it as Romulus did. And the heavens cannot truly bestow upon men a greater opportunity for obtaining glory than this, nor can men desire a greater one. And if a man who wanted to reorganize a city well had, of necessity, to renounce the principality in order to do so, he might merit some excuse if he did not reform it in order not to lose his rank; but if he were able both to retain his principality and to reform it, he would deserve no excuse whatsoever.

In conclusion, then, let those to whom the heavens grant such opportunities observe that there are two paths open to them: one allows them to live securely and makes them famous after death; the other makes them live in continuous anxiety and, after death, allows them to leave behind an eternal reputation of infamy.

Chapter 11. The Religion of the Romans

Even though Rome found its first institution builder in Romulus and, like a daughter, owed her birth and her education to him, nevertheless, as the heavens judged that the institutions of Romulus would not suffice for so great an empire, they inspired the Roman senate to elect Numa Pompilius as Romulus's successor so that those matters not attended to by Romulus could be seen to by Numa. Numa found the Roman people most undisciplined, and since he wanted to bring them to civil obedience by means of the arts of peace, he turned to religion as an absolutely necessary institution for the maintenance of a civic government, and he established it in such a way that for many centuries never was there more fear of God than in that republic—a fact which greatly facilitated any undertaking that the senate or those great Romans thought of doing.

Anyone who examines the many actions of the Roman people as a whole and of many individual Romans will discover how these citizens were more afraid of breaking an oath than of breaking the laws, since they respected the power of God more than that of man: this is most evident in the examples of Scipio and of Manlius Torquatus. After the rout inflicted upon the Romans by Hannibal at the battle of Cannae, many of the citizens assembled and, despairing for their native land, agreed to abandon Italy and to go to Sicily; when Scipio heard about this, he went to them, and with his bare sword in hand he forced them to swear not to abandon their fatherland. Lucius Manlius, the father of Titus Manlius (afterward called Torquatus), was accused of a crime by Marcus Pomponius, tribune of the plebeians; before the day of the trial arrived Titus went to Marcus and threatened to kill him if he did not swear to remove the indictment against his father; and when Marcus swore to do so, he withdrew the charge out of fear.

In this manner, those citizens whose love for the fatherland or its laws could not have kept them in Italy were restrained by an oath which they were forced to take; and that tribune set aside the hatred he had for the father and the injury he had suffered from the son and his own honor in order to obey the oath he had taken—all this came about from nothing other than the religion which Numa had introduced into that city.

Thus, anyone who examines Roman history closely will discover how much religion helped in commanding armies, encouraging the plebeians, keeping men good, and shaming the wicked. And so, if one were to argue about which prince Rome was more indebted to—whether Romulus or Numa—I believe that Numa would most easily be first choice; for where there is religion it is easy to introduce arms, but where there are arms without religion the latter can be introduced only with difficulty. It is evident that Romulus did not find divine authority necessary to found the senate and other civil and military institutions, but it was necessary for Numa, who pretended to have a relationship with a nymph who advised him what to say to the people; the reason was that he wanted to establish new and unfamiliar institutions in the city, and he doubted that his own authority would be sufficient to do so.

Actually, there never existed a person who could give unusual laws to his people without recourse to God, for otherwise such laws would not have been accepted: for the benefits they bring, although evident to a prudent man, are not self-explanatory enough to be evident to others. Therefore, wise men who wish to avoid this difficulty have recourse to God. Lycurgus did this, as did Solon and many others who had the same goal. Since the Roman people were amazed at the goodness and the prudence of Numa, they yielded to his every decision. It is, of course, true that those times were very religious ones and that the men with whom he had to deal were unsophisticated, thereby giving him a great deal of freedom to follow his own plans and to be able to impress upon them easily any new form he wished. And, without any doubt, anyone wishing to establish a republic in our present day would find it easier to do so among mountaineers, where there is no culture, than among men who are accustomed to living in cities where culture is corrupt; in like manner, a sculptor can more easily carve a beautiful statue out of a rough piece of marble than he can from one poorly blocked out by someone else.

Having considered everything, then, I conclude that the religion introduced by Numa was among the most important reasons for the success of that city, for it brought forth good institutions, and good institutions led to good fortune, and from good fortune came the felicitous successes of the city's undertakings. And as the observance of religious teaching is the reason for the greatness of republics, in like manner the disdain of the practice is the cause of their ruin; for where the fear of God is lacking a kingdom must either come to ruin or be sustained by the fear of a prince who makes up for the lack of religion. And since princes are short-lived, it is most likely that a kingdom will fail as quickly as the abilities of its prince fail; thus, kingdoms which depend upon the ability of a single man cannot last long, for such ability disappears with the life of the prince; and only rarely does it happen that this ability is revived by a successor, as Dante prudently declares:

> Not often in a family tree does virtue
> rise up to all its branches. This is what
> the Giver wills, that we may ask Him for it.[12]

The well-being, therefore, of a republic or a kingdom cannot rest upon a prince who governs prudently while he is alive, but rather upon one who organizes the government in such a way that it

---

[12] *Purgatorio*, 7.122–23.

can be maintained in the event of his death. And, while it is true that uncultured men can be more easily persuaded to adopt a new institution or opinion, it is not, however, for this reason impossible to persuade cultured men or men who do not consider themselves uncultured to do the same. The people of Florence do not consider themselves ignorant or uncultured; nevertheless, they were persuaded by Brother Girolamo Savonarola that he spoke with God. I do not wish to judge if this were true or not, for of such a man as this one must speak with respect; but I do say that very many people believed him without ever having seen anything out of the ordinary to make them believe him, and this was the case because his life, his doctrines, and the topics about which he chose to preach from the Bible were enough to persuade them to have faith in him. No one, therefore, should despair of being able to accomplish what others have accomplished, for men—as I said in my preface—are born, live, and die always in the same way.

Chapter 12. How Much Importance Must be Granted to Religion, and How Italy, Without Religion, Thanks to the Roman Church, Has been Ruined

Princes or republics that wish to maintain themselves without corruption must, above all else, maintain free of corruption the ceremonies of their religion and must hold them constantly in veneration; for there is no greater indication of the ruin of a country than to see its religious worship not respected. This is easy to understand when one realizes upon what basis the religion of the place where a man was born is founded, because every religion has the foundation of its existence in one of its main institutions. The essence of the religion of the pagans resided in the responses of oracles and upon a sect of fortune-tellers and soothsayers: all their ceremonies, sacrifices, and rites depended upon these, for it was easy for them to believe that the god who could predict your future, good or evil, could also bring it about for you. From these arose their temples, their sacrifices, their supplications, and every other ceremony used in venerating them; from this arose the oracle of Delos, the temple of Jupiter Ammon, and other famous oracles which filled the world with admiration and devotion. Then, later, as these oracles began to speak on behalf of the powerful, their falsity was discovered by the people and men became unbelievers and were willing to upset every good institution.

Therefore, it is the duty of the rulers of a republic or of a kingdom to maintain the foundations of the religion that sustains them; and if this is done it will be easy for them to keep their republic religious and, as a consequence, good and united. And they must favor and encourage all those things which arise in favor of religion, even if they judge them to be false; the more they do this the more prudent and knowledgeable in worldly affairs they will be. And because this practice has been followed by wise men, there has arisen the belief in miracles that are celebrated even in false religions; for, no matter how they originated, men always gave them greater importance than they deserved, thus causing everyone to believe in them. There were many such miracles in Rome, among them the one that happened while the Roman soldiers were sacking the city of Veii: some of them entered the temple of Juno and, approaching the image of the goddess, asked: "Do you wish to come to Rome?"[13] It seemed to some that she nodded her head as if to say "yes" and to others that she actually replied that she did. Since these men were deeply religious (this Livy demonstrates, for he describes them entering the temple without a sound, devout and full of reverence), perhaps it seemed to them that they heard the reply to their question which they had expected from the start; this opinion and belief was carefully encouraged and cultivated by Camillus and the other leaders of the city. If the

---

[13] Latin in the original, quoting from Livy, 5.22.

rulers of Christian republics had maintained this sort of religion according to the system set up by its founder, Christian states and republics would be more united and happier than they are at present. Nor can there be another, better explanation of its decline than to see how those people who are closer to the Roman church, the head of our religion, are less religious. And anyone who examines the principles upon which it was based and sees how different present practice is from these principles would conclude, without a doubt, that it is drawing near either to calamity or a scourge.

And since there are many who are of the opinion that the well-being of the Italian cities comes from the church of Rome, I wish to present some of my beliefs against such an opinion, very powerful ones which, I feel, cannot be refuted. The first is that because of the bad examples of that court of Rome this land has lost all its devotion and religion; this, in turn, brings about countless evils and countless disorders: for just as one takes for granted that all goes well where there is religion, just so, where religion is lacking one supposes the contrary. We Italians owe this first debt to the church and to the priests—we have become irreligious and wicked; but we owe them an even greater debt still, which is the second reason for our ruin: that the church has kept, and still keeps, this land of ours divided. And, in truth, no land is ever happy or united unless it is under the rule of one republic or one prince, as is the case with France and Spain. And the reason why Italy is not in the same condition and why she, too, has neither one republic nor one prince to govern her, lies solely with the Church: for although the Church possesses temporal power and has its seat in Italy, it has not been powerful enough nor has it possessed sufficient skill to be able to tyrannize Italy and make itself her ruler; and it has not been, on the other hand, so feeble that, when in fear of losing its control of temporal affairs, it has been unable to bring in a foreign power to defend itself from those Italian states which have become too powerful. There are many instances of this in ancient times: when, with Charlemagne's aid, the Lombards—who were in control of almost all of Italy—were driven out; and when, in our own day, the Church took power away from the Venetians with the aid of France, and then when it drove out the French with the help of the Swiss. Therefore, since the Church has not been strong enough to take possession of Italy, nor has she permitted anyone else to do so, Italy has not been able to unite under one ruler. Rather, Italy has been under many rulers and lords, and from this has come so much disunity and so much weakness that she has continued to be at the mercy not only of powerful barbarians but of anyone who might attack her. This is the debt we Italians owe the Church and no one else! And anyone who might wish to see the truth of this borne out by actual experience need only have sufficient power to send the Roman court, with the authority it possesses in Italy, to live in the lands of the Swiss, who are today the only peoples living under both religious and military institutions organized according to ancient practices; and he would see that in a short time the wicked customs of that court would create more disorder in that land than any other event occurring at any time could possibly cause there.

Chapter 58. The Masses[14] Are Wiser and More Constant Than a Prince

Nothing can be more unreliable and more inconstant than the masses, as our own Livy declares and as all other historians affirm. In the recounting of the actions of men, we often read that the masses condemn someone to death and then repent later, wishing that he were still alive, as is evident in what the Roman people did with Manlius Capitolinus, whom they first condemned to death and then wished to have back alive. And the words of the author are these: "As soon as he ceased to represent

---

[14] The Italian word is *moltitudine* which perhaps would be better rendered by the word multitude.—ED.

a danger, the people immediately were seized by remorse." And elsewhere, when he is explaining the events in Syracuse after the death of Hieronymus, the grandson of Hiero, he declares: "Such is the nature of the masses—either to obey humbly or to rule arrogantly."[15]

I do not know whether, in undertaking to defend an argument which, as I have mentioned, all writers have attacked, I may not be taking on a task so difficult and so full of problems that I shall either have to abandon it in shame or follow it with great pains. But be that as it may, I do not, nor shall I ever, think it wrong to defend an opinion with reasons without employing either authority or force. Let me say, therefore, that all men, and especially princes, can be accused individually of that fault for which writers blame the masses: for anyone not regulated by law will make the same errors that the uncontrolled masses will make. And this is obvious, for there are, and have been, many princes who have been able to break the bounds that could restrain them; nor shall we count among these the kings who arose in Egypt when, in that ancient time, the province was ruled by laws, nor those who arose in Sparta, nor those in our own times who arose in France, a kingdom more regulated by laws than any other kingdom that we have any knowledge of in our own day. The kings who arose under such constitutions are not to be considered among those whose individual nature we ought to consider here in order to see if it resembles that of the masses, for they should be compared to the masses regulated by laws in the same fashion as they are; and we shall find in the masses that same goodness we discover in such kings and shall see that the masses neither obey humbly nor rule arrogantly. The Roman people were like this, for while the Roman republic endured without corruption, it never obeyed humbly nor ruled arrogantly; on the contrary, it held its position honorably through its institutions and magistrates. And when it was necessary to band together against some powerful man, as in the case of Manlius, the decemvirs, and others who sought to oppress it, it did so; when it was necessary to obey the dictators and the consuls for the public welfare, it did so. And if the Roman people regretted the death of Manlius Capitolinus, it is not surprising, for they regretted the loss of his virtues, which were such that the memory of them aroused everyone's compassion; and it would have had the power to produce the same effect in a prince, since all writers declare that ability is praised and admired even in one's enemies. If Manlius had been resurrected because of such an opinion, the people of Rome would have pronounced upon him the same sentence that they did when they had him removed from prison and shortly thereafter condemned him to death; nevertheless we see princes, reputed to be wise, who have had someone executed and then wished him returned to life, as Alexander did in the case of Clitus and his other friends and as Herod did with Mariamne. But when our historian speaks of the nature of the masses, he does not mean those who are regulated by law, as the Romans were; he speaks of the uncontrolled masses, like those of Syracuse, which committed crimes typical of undisciplined and infuriated men, as did Alexander the Great and Herod in the instances mentioned. But the nature of the masses is no more to be condemned than that of princes, for both err when there is nothing to control them. There are many examples of this, in addition to the ones I have mentioned, both among the Roman emperors and other tyrants and princes; and in them we witness as much lack of stability and variation of behavior as may ever be found in any multitude.

Therefore, I come to a conclusion contrary to the common opinion, which declares that when the people hold power they are unstable, changeable, and ungrateful; I affirm, rather, that the people are no more susceptible to these sins than are individual princes. And if one were to blame both

---

[15] Latin in the original, from Livy, 6.20 and 24.25.

the people and princes alike, he might be telling the truth, but if princes are to be excluded from this charge, then he would be deceiving himself, because a people which have power and are well organized will be no less stable, prudent, and grateful than a prince. In fact, they may be more so, even though the prince is thought wise; and, on the other hand, a prince freed from the restraint of law will be more ungrateful, changeable, and imprudent than the people. And the changeability of their behavior does not arise from a different nature, for it is the same in all men, and if there is one better than the other, it is the people; it comes, rather, from having greater or lesser respect for the laws under which they both live. And anyone who considers the Roman people will see that they were opposed to the very title of king for four hundred years and were lovers of the glory and the common good of their city; and he will see many examples that testify to both characteristics. If anyone should cite, to the contrary, the ingratitude that the people showed toward Scipio, I would make the same reply I did earlier on this subject, where I showed that the people are less ungrateful than princes. But, concerning prudence and stability, let me say that the people are more prudent, more reliable, and have better judgment than a prince does. And it is not without reason that the voice of the people is likened to that of God: for it is evident that popular opinion has marvelous power in predicting, so much so that it would appear to foresee its own good and evil fortune through some occult ability. As for its judgment in various matters, when the people hear two equally able speakers, each arguing different opinions, only very rarely does it happen that they do not choose the better opinion and are incapable of understanding the truth of what they hear. And if they err in matters of courage or profit, as was mentioned above, a prince will often err because of his own passions, which are much stronger than those of the people. It is also evident that the people make better choices in electing magistrates than does a prince, for one can never persuade the people that it is good to elect to public office an infamous man of corrupt habits—something that a prince can easily be persuaded to do in a thousand ways; and when the people begin to feel an aversion for something, we see them persist in this aversion for many years—something we do not observe in a prince. For both of these characteristics I find it sufficient to cite the Roman people as evidence, for in so many hundreds of years, in so many elections of consuls and tribunes, the people did not make even four elections which they were forced to regret. And, as I have said, they so hated the very name of king that no amount of meritorious service rendered by one of their citizens seeking to gain the title could persuade the people to forget the just penalties he deserved for this ambition. Furthermore, it is evident that cities in which people are the rulers increase their territories in a very short time, much more so than cities which have always been under a prince, just as Rome did after the expulsion of the kings and Athens did after she freed herself of Pisistratus. This is the result of nothing other than the fact that government by the people is better than government by princes. Nor do I wish everything that our historian says in the aforementioned passage and elsewhere to be cited against this opinion of mine, for if we were to discuss all the faults of the people and all those of princes, all the glories of the people and all those of princes, it would be evident that the people are far superior in goodness and in glory. And if princes are superior to the people in instituting laws, forming civic communities, and establishing statutes and new institutions, then the people are so much more superior in maintaining the things thus established that they attain, without a doubt, the same glory as those who established them.

And, in short, to conclude this subject, let me say that just as the states of princes have endured for a long time, so too have the states of republics; both have needed to be regulated by laws, for a prince who is able to do what he wishes is mad, and a people that can do what it wishes is not wise. If, therefore, we are talking about a prince obedient to the laws or a people restricted by them, we shall observe more ability in the people than in the prince; if we are discussing either one or the other as being free from these restrictions, we shall observe fewer errors in the people than in the prince; moreover, they are less serious ones and easier to remedy. For a licentious and unruly people can be spoken to by one good man and can easily be brought back to the right path; however, with an evil prince there is no one who can speak to him and no other remedy than the sword. From this fact one can draw a conclusion concerning the seriousness of their respective maladies: if words are enough to cure the malady of the people and the sword to cure that of the prince, there will never be anyone who will not conclude that the greater the faults, the greater the attention required. When a people is unrestrained, neither its mad actions nor the evil at hand need be feared, but rather the evil that may arise from them, since a tyrant may emerge from so much confusion. But with an evil prince the opposite happens: present evil is feared and one hopes for the future, since men persuade themselves that ending his evil life can result in an era of freedom. So you see the difference between the two: one concerns things as they are and the other concerns things that will be. The cruelties of the masses are directed against anyone who they fear might act against the public welfare; those of the prince are directed against anyone who he fears might act against his own interests. But the prejudice against the people arises because everyone speaks ill of them freely and without fear, even when they rule; one always speaks ill of princes only with great fear and apprehension. And this seems not to be beside the point, since this subject leads me ahead to discuss, in the following chapter, whether one may place more trust in alliances made with a republic or those made with a prince.

Book 2

Introduction

Men always praise ancient times and condemn the present, but not always with good reason; they are such advocates of the past that they celebrate not merely those ages which they know only through the memory of the historians but also those that they, now being old, remember having seen in their youth. And when this opinion of theirs is mistaken, as it is most of the time, I am persuaded that there are several reasons which lead them to make this mistake. First, I believe that we do not know the complete truth about antiquity; most often the facts that would discredit those times are hidden and other matters which bestow glory upon them are reported magnificently and most thoroughly. Most writers submit to the fortune of conquerors, and in order to render their victories glorious they not only exaggerate what they have ably achieved but also embellish the deeds of their enemies in such a way that anyone born afterward in either of the two lands—that of the victor or that of the vanquished— has reason to marvel at those men and those times and is forced to praise them and to love them to the greatest degree. Besides this, since men hate things either out of fear or envy, two very powerful reasons for hatred of things in the past are eliminated, for they cannot hurt you or give you cause for envy. But the contrary applies to those things you deal with and observe: they are known to you in every detail, you see in them what is good as well as the many things that displease you, and you are obliged to judge them most inferior to things of the past; while, in truth, those of the present may deserve even more glory and fame—I am not speaking of things pertaining to the arts here, for in themselves they possess so much brilliance that the times take away from them little and cannot bestow upon them much more glory than they intrinsically merit; I am speaking rather of those matters pertaining to the lives and customs of men, about which we do not witness such clear evidence.

I repeat, then, that this aforementioned custom of praising the old and condemning the new does exist, but it is not always wrong. Sometimes such a judgment has to be correct since human affairs are always in motion, either rising or declining. And so, one city or province can be seen to possess a government that was well organized by an excellent man; and for a time it may keep improving because of the ability of the founder. Anyone, then, who is born in such a state and praises ancient times more than modern times deceives himself, and his deception is caused by those things mentioned above. But those who are born afterward in that city or region, at the time of its decline, do not, then, deceive themselves. As I reflect on why these matters proceed as they do, I believe that the world has always been in the same state and that there has always been as much good as evil in it; but this evil and this good changes from country to country, as we can see from what we know of ancient kingdoms that were different from each other according to the differences in their customs, while the world remained the same as it always had been. There is only this difference: the world's talents first found a home in Assyria, then moved to Media, later to Persia, and, in time, came into Italy and Rome; and if, after the Roman empire, no succeeding empire has lasted, nor has there been one where the world has retained all its talents in one place, nevertheless we can still see them scattered among many nations where men live ably, as in the kingdom of the Franks, the Turks—that of the Sultan—and today among the peoples of Germany; earlier there was that Turkish group which achieved so many grand things and seized so much of the world once it had destroyed the Eastern Roman Empire. In all these lands, then, after the Romans came to ruin, and in all those groups of people, such talents existed and still exist in some of them where they are desired and truly praised. And anyone who is born there and praises past times more than present ones may be deceiving himself, but anyone who is born in Italy or Greece and has not become an Ultramontane in Italy or a Turk in Greece has reason to condemn his own times and to praise others, for in them there were many things that made them marvelous, but in the present ones there is nothing to be seen but utter misery, infamy, and vituperation. There is no observance of religion, laws, or military discipline; all is stained with every kind of filth. Furthermore, these vices are the more detestable as they are found among those who sit on tribunals, command others, and expect to be worshiped.

But, returning to our subject, let me say that if the judgment of men is unfair in deciding which is better—the present age or the past—the latter of which, because of its antiquity, men cannot have as perfect a knowledge of as they can of their own times, this should not corrupt the judgment of old men in assessing the time of their youth and their old age, since they have known and observed both one and the other equally well. This would be true if men were all of the same opinion and had the same desires in all phases of their lives; but since these desires change, and the times do not, things cannot appear to men to be the same, since they have other desires, other pleasures, and other concerns in their old age than they had in their youth. For as men grow older they lose in vigor and gain in judgment and prudence, and the things that seemed acceptable and good to them in their youth become, later on, as they grow older, intolerable and bad; and although they should place the blame for this on their own judgment, they blame the times instead. Besides this, human desires are insatiable, for we are endowed by Nature with the power and the wish to desire everything and by Fortune with the ability to obtain little of what we desire. The result is an unending discontent in the minds of men and a weariness with what they possess: this makes men curse the present, praise the past, and hope in the future, even though they do this with no reasonable motive. I do not know, therefore, if I deserve to be considered among those who deceive themselves if, in these discourses of mine, I am too lavish with my praise of ancient Roman times and condemn our own. And certainly, if the excellence that existed then and the vice that rules now were not clearer than the sun, I would speak more hesitantly for fear that I might fall into the same error of which I accuse others. But since the matter is clear enough for all to see, I shall boldly declare in plain terms what I understand of those ancient times and of our own times, so that the minds of young men who read these writings of mine may be able to reject the present and prepare themselves to imitate the past whenever Fortune provides them with an occasion. For it is your duty as a good man to teach others whatever good you yourself have not been able to do, either because of the malignity of the times or because of Fortune, in order that—since many will thus be made aware of it—someone more beloved by Heaven may be prepared to put your truth into action.

In the discourse of the preceding book I have discussed the decisions the Romans made in matters concerning their internal affairs; now, in this one, I shall discuss what it was that the Roman people did concerning the expansion of their empire.

Martin Luther

Martin Luther (1483–1546) was born in Saxony, the son of a miner. In 1501 he entered the University of Erfurt intending to study jurisprudence. He distinguished himself in his studies, although remaining singularly untouched by the humanistic tendencies active in the university. Following a frightening vision and the death of a friend he abandoned the law and entered the Augustinian order, of which he was ordained a priest in 1505. In 1510–11 he went to Rome as an emissary of his Order, and there the splendor as well as the corruption of the capital of Christendom depressed him profoundly. Returning to Germany, he became a vicar of his order, supervising eleven monasteries, and professor at Wittenberg.

In 1517 the Dominican John Tetzel traveled through Germany, selling papal indulgences and advertising that the purchase of an indulgence would release from Purgatory the soul of a departed relative. Angered that the instruments of salvation should be sold, and that people already poverty-stricken should be prevailed upon by such promises, Luther attacked indulgences in his famous Ninety-five Theses, which he nailed to the door of the Castle Church in Wittenberg.

The posting of the Ninety-five Theses was the beginning of Luther's break with the Church. Although he had envisaged no schism, before he was done he had broken his monastic vows and denounced the Pope as Antichrist, and had been in turn excommunicated by Leo X and banned by the Holy Roman Emperor Charles V. Aside from its religious significance, the Lutheran movement was the occasion for widespread disorder and revolution in Germany, despite Luther's own opposition to political rebellion.

Luther hoped to exercise his influence primarily through the written and spoken word. He translated the Bible into German, giving a standard form to the language and making religion available outside the Church organization. His voluminous writings include the *Address to the Christian Nobility of the German Nation* (1520), which argues, among other things, for the independence of the civil from the ecclesiastical power; *On Christian Liberty* (1520), the basis of his "program" of reformation; *The Babylonian Captivity of the Church*; and the *De servo arbitrio*, a reply to the *De libero arbitrio* of Erasmus. In 1525 he wrote an *Exhortation to Peace* in which he made both the aristocrats and the lower classes responsible for the Peasant War, and followed it up with a tract *Against the Thievish, Murderous Hordes of Peasants*.

The following selections from the *Address* and *On Christian Liberty* are from the translations from the German by C. A. Buchheim and R. S. Grignon, respectively.

Address to the Christian Nobility of the German Nation

Introduction

The grace and might of God be with you, Most Serene Majesty! most gracious, well beloved gentlemen!

It is not out of mere arrogance and perversity that I, a single poor man, have taken upon me to address your lordships. The distress and misery that oppress all the Christian estates, more especially in Germany, have led not only myself, but every one else, to cry aloud and to ask for help, and have now forced me too, to cry out and to ask, if God would give His Spirit to any one, to reach a hand to His wretched people. Councils have often put forward some remedy, but through the cunning of certain men it has been adroitly frustrated, and the evils have become worse; whose malice and wickedness I will now, by the help of God, expose, so that, being known, they may henceforth cease to be so obstructive and injurious. God has given us a young and noble sovereign, and by this has roused hope in many hearts: now it is right that we too should do what we can, and make good use of time and grace.

The first thing that we must do is to consider the matter with great earnestness, and, whatever we attempt, not to trust in our own strength and wisdom alone, even if the power of all the world were ours; for God will not endure that a good work should be begun, trusting to our own strength and wisdom. He destroys it; it is all useless: as we read in the xxxiii Psalm. "There is no king saved by the multitude of an host: a mighty man is not delivered by much strength." And I fear it is for that reason, that those beloved Princes, the Emperors Frederick, the First and the Second, and many other German Emperors were, in former times, so piteously spurned and oppressed by the Popes, though they were feared by all the world. Perchance they trusted rather in their own strength than in God; therefore they could not but fall: and how would the sanguinary tyrant Julius II have risen so high in our own days, but, that, I fear, France, the Germans and Venice trusted to themselves? The children of Benjamin slew forty-two thousand Israelites, for this reason, that these trusted to their own strength.

That it may not happen thus to us and to our noble Emperor Charles, we must remember that in this matter we wrestle not against flesh and blood, but against the rulers of the darkness of this world, who may fill the world with war and bloodshed, but cannot themselves be overcome thereby. We must renounce all confidence in our natural strength, and take the matter in hand with humble trust in God; we must seek God's help with earnest prayer, and have nothing before our eyes but the misery and wretchedness of Christendom, irrespective of what punishment the wicked may deserve. If we do not act thus, we may begin the game with great pomp; but when we are well in it, the spirits of evil will make such confusion that the whole world will be immersed in blood, and yet nothing be done. Therefore let us act in the fear of God, and prudently. The greater the might of the foe, the greater is the misfortune, if we do not act in the fear of God, and with humility. As Popes and Romanists have hitherto, with the Devil's help, thrown Kings into confusion, so will they still do, if we attempt things with our own strength and skill, without God's help.

The Three Walls of the Romanists

The romanists have, with great adroitness, drawn three walls round themselves, with which they have hitherto protected themselves, so that no one could reform them, whereby all Christendom has fallen terribly.

Firstly, if pressed by the temporal power, they have affirmed and maintained that the temporal power has no jurisdiction over them, but on the contrary that the spiritual power is above the temporal.

Secondly, if it were proposed to admonish them with the Scriptures, they objected that no one may interpret the Scriptures but the Pope.

Thirdly, if they are threatened with a Council, they pretend that no one may call a Council but the Pope.

Thus they have secretly stolen our three rods, so that they may be unpunished, and entrenched themselves behind these three walls, to act with all wickedness and malice, as we now see. And whenever they have been compelled to call a Council, they have made it of no avail, by binding the Princes beforehand with an oath to leave them as they were. Besides this they have given the Pope full power over the arrangement of the Council, so that it is all one, whether we have many Councils, or no Councils, for in any case they deceive us with pretences and false tricks. So grievously do they tremble for their skin before a true, free Council; and thus they have overawed Kings and Princes, that these believe they would be offending God, if they were not to obey them in all such knavish, deceitful artifices.

Now may God help us, and give us one of those trumpets, that overthrew the walls of Jericho, so that we may blow down these walls of straw and paper, and that we may set free our Christian rods, for the chastisement of sin, and expose the craft and deceit of the devil, so that we may amend ourselves by punishment and again obtain God's favour.

The First Wall

Let us, in the first place, attack the first wall.

It has been devised, that the Pope, bishops, priests and monks are called the Spiritual Estate; princes, lords, artificers and peasants, are the Temporal Estate; which is a very fine, hypocritical device. But let no one be made afraid by it; and that for this reason: That all Christians are truly of the Spiritual Estate, and there is no difference among them, save of office alone. As St. Paul says, we are all one body, though each member does its own work, to serve the others. This is because we have one baptism, one gospel, one faith, and are all Christians alike; for baptism, gospel and faith, these alone make Spiritual and Christian people.

As for the unction by a pope or a bishop, tonsure, ordination, consecration, clothes differing from those of laymen—all this may make a hypocrite or an anointed puppet, but never a Christian, or a spiritual man. Thus we are all consecrated as priests by baptism, as St. Peter says: "Ye are a royal priesthood, a holy nation"; and in the book of Revelations: "and hast made us unto our God, kings and priests." For, if we have not a higher consecration in us than Pope or bishop can give, no priest could ever be made by the consecration of Pope or bishop; nor could he say the mass, or preach, or absolve. Therefore the bishop's consecration is just as if in the name of the whole congregation he took one person out of the community, each member of which has equal power, and commanded him to exercise this power for the rest; in the same way as if ten brothers, co-heirs as king's sons, were to choose one from among them to rule over their inheritance; they would, all of them, still remain kings and have equal power, although one is ordered to govern.

And to put the matter even more plainly; if a little company of pious Christian laymen were taken prisoners and carried away to a desert, and had not among them a priest consecrated by a bishop, and were there to agree to elect one of them, married or unmarried, and were to order him to baptize, to celebrate the mass, to absolve and to preach; this man would as truly be a priest, as if all the bishops and all the Popes had consecrated him. That is why in cases of necessity every man can baptize and absolve, which would not be possible if we were not all priests. This great grace and virtue of baptism and of the Christian Estate, they have almost destroyed and made us forget by their ecclesiastical law. In this way the Christians used to choose their bishops and priests out of the community; these being afterwards confirmed by other bishops, without the pomp that we have now. So was it that St. Augustine, Ambrose, Cyprian, were bishops.

Since then the temporal power is baptized as we are, and has the same faith and gospel, we must allow it to be priest and bishop, and account its office an office that is proper and useful to the Christian community. For whatever issues from baptism may boast that it has been consecrated priest, bishop, and Pope, although it does not beseem every one to exercise these offices. For, since we are all priests alike no man may put himself forward, or take upon himself, without our consent and election, to do that which we have all alike power to do. For, if a thing is common to all, no man may take it to himself without the wish and command of the community. And if it should happen that a man were appointed to one of these offices and deposed for abuses, he would be just what he was before. Therefore a priest should be nothing in Christendom but a functionary; as long as he holds his office, he has precedence of others; if he is deprived of it, he is a peasant and a citizen like the rest. Therefore a priest is verily no longer a priest after deposition. But now they have invented *characteres indelebiles,*[1] and pretend that a priest after deprivation still differs from a simple layman. They even imagine that a priest can never be anything but a priest, that is, that he can never become a layman. All this is nothing but mere talk and ordinance of human invention.

It follows then, that between layman and priests, princes and bishops, or as they call it, between spiritual and temporal persons, the only real difference is one of office and function, and not of estate: for they are all of the same Spiritual Estate, true priests, bishops and Popes, though their functions are not the same: just as among priests and monks every man has not the same functions. And this St. Paul says and St. Peter; "we being many are one body in Christ, and every one members one of another." Christ's body is not double or twofold, one temporal, the other spiritual. He is one head, and he has one body.

We see then that just as those that we call spiritual, or priests, bishops or popes, do not differ from other Christians in any other or higher degree, but in that they are to be concerned with the word of God, and the sacraments—that being their work and office—in the same way the temporal authorities hold the sword and the rod in their hands to punish the wicked and to protect the good. A cobbler, a smith, a peasant, every man has the office and function of his calling, and yet all alike are consecrated priests and bishops, and every man in his office must be useful and beneficial to the rest, that so many kinds of work may all be united into one community: just as the members of the body all serve one another.

Now see, what a Christian doctrine is this: that the temporal authority is not above the clergy, and may not punish it. This is, as if one were to say, the hand may not help, though the eye is in grievous suffering. Is it not unnatural, not to say unchristian, that one member may not help another, or guard it against harm? Nay, the nobler the member, the more the rest are bound to help it. Therefore I say: forasmuch as the temporal power has been ordained by God for the punishment of the bad, and the protection of the good, therefore we must let it do its duty throughout the whole Christian body, without respect of persons: whether it strike popes, bishops, priests, monks, or nuns. If it were sufficient reason for fettering the temporal power that it is inferior among the offices of Christianity to the offices of priest or confessor, or to the spiritual estate—if this were so, then we ought to restrain tailors, cobblers, masons, carpenters, cooks, servants, peasants, and all secular workmen, from providing the Pope, or bishops, priests and monks, with shoes, clothes, houses or victuals, or from paying them tithes. But if these laymen are allowed to do their work without restraint, what do the Romanist scribes mean by their laws? They mean that they withdraw themselves from the operation of temporal Christian power, simply in order that they may be free to do evil, and thus fulfill what St. Peter said: "There shall be false teachers among you, . . . and through covetousness shall they with feigned words make merchandise of you."

---

[1] That is, distinctive attributes not subject to change.

Therefore the temporal Christian power must exercise its office without let or hindrance, without considering whom it may strike, whether pope, or bishop, or priest: whoever is guilty let him suffer for it. Whatever the ecclesiastical law says in opposition to this, is merely the invention of Romanist arrogance. For this is what St. Paul says to all Christians: "Let every soul" (I presume including the Popes) "be subject unto the higher powers: for he beareth not the sword in vain: for he is the minister of God, a revenger to execute wrath upon him that doeth evil." Also St. Peter: "Submit yourselves to every ordinance of man for the Lord's sake . . . for so is the will of God." He has also said, that men would come, who should despise government; as has come to pass through ecclesiastical law.

Now I imagine, the first paper wall is overthrown, inasmuch as the temporal power has become a member of the Christian body, and although its work relates to the body, yet does it belong to the spiritual estate. Therefore it must do its duty without let or hindrance upon all members of the whole body, to punish or urge, as guilt may deserve, or need may require, without respect of Pope, bishops or priests; let them threaten or excommunicate as they will. That is why a guilty priest is deprived of his priesthood before being given over to the secular arm; whereas this would not be right, if the secular sword had not authority over him already by divine ordinance.

It is, indeed, past bearing that the spiritual law should esteem so highly the liberty, life and property of the clergy, as if laymen were not as good spiritual Christians, or not equally members of the Church. Why should your body, life, goods, and honour be free and not mine, seeing that we are equal as Christians, and have received alike baptism, faith, spirit and all things? If a priest is killed, the country is laid under an interdict: why not also if a peasant is killed? Whence comes all this difference among equal Christians? Simply from human laws and inventions.

It can have been no good spirit that devised these exceptions, and made sin to go unpunished. For, if as Christ and the Apostles bid us, it is our duty to oppose the evil one, and all his works and words, and to drive him away as well as may be; how then should we look on in silence, when the Pope and his followers are guilty of devilish works and words? Are we for the sake of men to allow the commandments and the truth of God to be defeated, which at our baptism we vowed to support with body and soul? Truly we should have to answer for all souls that are thus led away into error.

Therefore it must have been the archdevil himself who said, as we read in the ecclesiastical law: If the Pope were so perniciously wicked, as to be dragging souls in crowds to the devil, yet he could not be deposed. This is the accursed and devilish foundation on which they build a Rome, and think that the whole world is to be allowed to go to the devil, rather than they should be opposed in their knavery. If a man were to escape punishment simply because he is above the rest, then no Christian might punish another, since Christ has commanded each of us to esteem himself the lowest and the humblest.

Where there is sin, there remains no avoiding the punishment, as St. Gregory says: We are all equal, but guilt makes one subject to another. Now see how they deal with Christendom, depriving it of its freedom without any warrant from the Scriptures, out of their own wickedness, whereas God and the Apostles made them subject to the secular sword; so that we must fear that it is the work of Antichrist, or a sign of his near approach.

The Second Wall

The second wall is even more tottering and weak: that they alone pretend to be considered masters of the Scriptures; although they learn nothing of them all their life, they assume authority, and juggle before us with impudent words, saying that the Pope cannot err in matters of faith, whether he be evil or good; albeit they cannot prove it by a single letter. That is why the canon law contains so many heretical and unchristian, nay, unnatural laws; but of these we need not speak now. For whereas they imagine the Holy Ghost never leaves them, however unlearned and wicked they may be, they grow bold enough to decree whatever they like. But were this true, where were the need and use of the Holy Scriptures? Let us burn them, and content ourselves with the unlearned gentlemen at Rome, in whom the Holy Ghost dwells, who however can dwell in pious souls only. If I had not read it, I could never have believed that the Devil should have put forth such follies at Rome and find a following.

But not to fight them with our own words, we will quote Scriptures. St. Paul says: "If anything be revealed to another that sitteth by, let the first hold his peace." What would be the use of this commandment, if we were to believe him alone that teaches or has the highest seat? Christ Himself says: "And they shall be all taught of God." Thus it may come to pass that the Pope and his followers are wicked and not true Christians, and not being taught by God, have no true understanding, whereas a common man may have true understanding. Why should we then not follow him? Has not the Pope often erred? Who could help Christianity, in case the Pope errs, if we do not rather believe another, who has the Scriptures for him?

Therefore it is a wickedly devised fable, and they cannot quote a single letter to confirm it, that it is for the Pope alone to interpret the Scriptures or to confirm the interpretation of them: they have assumed the authority of their own selves. And though they say that this authority was given to St. Peter when the keys were given to him, it is plain enough that the keys were not given to St. Peter alone, but to the whole community. Besides, the keys were not ordained for doctrine or authority, but for sin, to bind or loose; and what they claim besides this is mere invention. But what Christ said to St. Peter: "I have prayed for thee, that thy faith fail not," cannot relate to the Pope, inasmuch as there have been many Popes without faith, as they are themselves forced to acknowledge. Nor did Christ pray for Peter alone, but for all the Apostles and all Christians, as He says, "Neither pray I for these alone, but for them also which shall believe on me through their word." Is not this plain enough?

Only consider the matter. They must needs acknowledge that there are pious Christians among us, that have the true faith, spirit, understanding, word, and mind of Christ; why then should we reject their word and understanding, and follow a Pope who has neither understanding nor Spirit? Surely this were to deny our whole faith and the Christian Church. Moreover, if the article of our faith is right: *I believe in the Holy Christian Church*, the Pope cannot alone be right; else we must say: *I believe in the Pope of Rome*, and reduce the Christian Church to one man, which is a devilish and damnable heresy. Besides that, we are all priests, as I have said, and have all one faith, one gospel, one sacrament; how then should we not have the power of discerning and judging what is right or wrong in matters of faith? What becomes of St. Paul's words: "But he that is spiritual judgeth all things, yet he himself is judged of no man"; and also, "we having the same spirit of faith." Why then should we not perceive as well as an unbelieving Pope, what agrees, or disagrees with our faith?

By these and many other texts we should gain courage and freedom, and should not let the spirit of liberty (as St. Paul has it) be frightened away by the inventions of the Popes; we should boldly judge what they do and what they leave undone, by our own understanding, and not their own. Did not Abraham in old days have to obey his Sarah, who was in stricter bondage to him than we are to any one on earth? Thus too Balaam's ass was wiser than the prophet. If God spoke by an ass against a prophet, why should He not speak by a pious man against the Pope? Besides, St. Paul withstood St. Peter as being in error. Therefore it behoves every Christian to aid the faith by understanding and defending it, and by condemning all errors.

The Third Wall

The third wall falls of itself, as soon as the first two have fallen; for if the Pope acts contrary to the Scriptures, we are bound to stand by the Scriptures, to punish and to constrain him, according to Christ's commandment; "Moreover if thy brother shall trespass against thee, go and tell him his fault between thee and him alone: if he shall hear thee, thou hast gained thy brother. But if he will not hear thee, then take with thee one or two more, that in the mouth of two or three witnesses every word may be established. And if he shall neglect to hear them, tell it unto the church: but if he neglect to hear the church, let him be unto thee as an heathen man and a publican." Here each member is commanded to take care for the other; much more then should we do this, if it is a ruling member of the community that does evil, which by its evil doing, causes great harm and offence to the others. If then I am to accuse him before the church, I must collect the church together. Moreover they can show nothing in the Scriptures giving the Pope sole power to call and confirm councils; they have nothing but their own laws; but these hold good only so long as they are not injurious to Christianity and the laws of God. Therefore, if the Pope deserves punishment, these laws cease to bind us, since Christendom would suffer, if he were not punished by a council. Thus we read, that the council of the Apostles was not called by St. Peter, but by all the Apostles and the elders. But if the right to call it had lain with St. Peter alone, it would not have been a Christian council, but a heretical *conciliabulum*.[2] Moreover the most celebrated Nicene Council was neither called nor confirmed by the Bishop of Rome, but by the Emperor Constantine; and after him many other Emperors have done the same, and yet the councils called by them were accounted most Christian. But if the Pope alone had the power, they must all have been heretical. Moreover if I consider the councils that the Pope has called, I do not find that they produced any notable results.

Therefore when need requires and the Pope is a cause of offence to Christendom, in these cases whoever can best do so, as a faithful member of the whole body, must do what he can to procure a true free council. This no one can do so well as the temporal authorities, especially since they are fellow-Christians, fellow-priests, sharing one spirit, and one power in all things; and since they should exercise the office that they have received from God without hindrance, whenever it is necessary and useful that it should be exercised. Would it not be most unnatural, if a fire were to break out in a city, and every one were to keep still and let it burn on and on, whatever might be burnt, simply because they had not the mayor's authority, or because the fire perhaps broke out at the mayor's house? Is not every citizen bound in this case to rouse and call in the rest? How much more should this be done in the spiritual city of Christ, if a fire of offence breaks out, either at the Pope's government or wherever it may! The like happens if an enemy attacks a town. The first to rouse up the rest earns glory and thanks. Why then should not he earn glory that announces the coming of our enemies from hell, and rouses and summons all Christians?

But as for their boasts of their authority, that no one must oppose it, this is idle talk. No one in Christendom has any authority to do harm, or to forbid others to prevent harm being done. There is no authority in the Church but for reformation. Therefore if the Pope wished to use his power to prevent the calling of a free council, so as to prevent the reformation of the Church, we must not respect him or his power; and if he should begin to excommunicate and fulminate, we must despise this as the ravings of a madman, and trusting in God, excommunicate and repel

---

2 The Latin word itself implies an illegitimate or heretical council.

him, as best we may. For this his usurped power is nothing; he does not possess it, and he is at once overthrown by a text from the Scriptures. For St. Paul says to the Corinthians, "That God has given us authority for edification and not for destruction." Who will set this text at naught? It is the power of the Devil and of Antichrist that prevents what would serve for the reformation of Christendom. Therefore we must not follow it, but oppose it with our body, our goods and all that we have. And even if a miracle were to happen in favour of the Pope, against the temporal power, or if some were to be stricken by a plague, as they sometimes boast has happened: all this is to be held as having been done by the Devil, for our want of faith in God, as was foretold by Christ: "There shall arise false Christs, and false prophets, and shall shew great signs and wonders; insomuch that, if it were possible, they shall deceive the very elect"; and St. Paul tells the Thessalonians that the coming of Antichrist shall be "after the working of Satan with all power and signs and lying wonders."

Therefore let us hold fast to this: that Christian power can do nothing against Christ, as St. Paul says: "for we can do nothing against Christ, but for Christ." But, if it does anything against Christ, it is the power of Antichrist and the Devil, even if it rained and hailed wonders and plagues. Wonders and plagues prove nothing, especially in these latter evil days, of which false wonders are foretold in all the Scriptures. Therefore we must hold fast to the words of God with an assured faith; then the Devil will soon cease his wonders.

And now I hope we have laid the false, lying spectre with which the Romanists have long terrified and stupefied our consciences. And we have shown that, like all the rest of us, they are subject to the temporal sword; that they have no authority to interpret the Scriptures by force without skill; and that they have no power to prevent a council, or to pledge it in accordance with their pleasure, or to bind it beforehand, and deprive it of its freedom; and that if they do this, they are verily of the fellowship of Antichrist and the Devil, and have nothing of Christ but the name.

On Christian Liberty

CHRISTIAN FAITH has appeared to many an easy thing; nay, not a few even reckon it among the social virtues, as it were; and this they do, because they have not made proof of it experimentally, and have never tasted of what efficacy it is. For it is not possible for any man to write well about it, or to understand well what is rightly written, who has not at some time tasted of its spirit, under the pressure of tribulation. While he who has tasted of it, even to a very small extent, can never write, speak, think, or hear about it sufficiently. For it is a living fountain, springing up unto eternal life, as Christ calls it in the 4th chapter of St. John.

Now, though I cannot boast of my abundance, and though I know how poorly I am furnished, yet I hope that, after having been vexed by various temptations, I have attained some little drop of faith, and that I can speak of this matter, if not with more elegance, certainly with more solidity than those literal and too subtle disputants who have hitherto discoursed upon it, without understanding their own words. That I may open, then, an easier way for the ignorant—for these alone I am trying to serve—I first lay down these two propositions, concerning spiritual liberty and servitude.

A Christian man is the most free lord of all, and subject to none; a Christian man is the most dutiful servant of all, and subject to every one.

Although these statements appear contradictory, yet when they are found to agree together, they will be highly serviceable to my purpose. They are both the statements of Paul himself, who says:

"Though I be free from all men, yet have I made myself servant unto all," and: "Owe no man anything, but to love one another." Now love is by its own nature dutiful and obedient to the beloved object. Thus even Christ, though Lord of all things, was yet made of a woman; made under the law; at once free and a servant; at once in the form of God and in the form of a servant.

Let us examine the subject on a deep and less simple principle. Man is composed of a twofold nature, a spiritual and a bodily. As regards the spiritual nature, which they name the soul, he is called the spiritual, inward, new man; as regards the bodily nature, which they name the flesh, he is called the fleshly, outward, old man. The Apostle speaks of this: "Though our outward man perish, yet the inward man is renewed day by day." The result of this diversity is, that in the Scriptures opposing statements are made concerning the same man; the fact being that in the same man these two men are opposed to one another; the flesh lusting against the spirit, and the spirit against the flesh.

We first approach the subject of the inward man, that we may see by what means a man becomes justified, free, and a true Christian; that is, a spiritual, new, and inward man. It is certain that absolutely none among outward things, under whatever name they may be reckoned, has any weight in producing a state of justification and Christian liberty, nor, on the other hand, an unjustified state and one of slavery. This can be shown by an easy course of argument.

What can it profit the soul, that the body should be in good condition, free, and full of life; that it should eat, drink, and act according to its pleasure; when even the most impious slaves of every kind of vice are prosperous in these matters? Again, what harm can ill-health, bondage, hunger, thirst, or any other outward evil, do to the soul, when even the most pious of men, and the freest in the purity of their conscience, are harassed by these things? Neither of these states of things has to do with the liberty or the slavery of the soul.

And so it will profit nothing that the body should be adorned with sacred vestments, or dwell in holy places, or be occupied in sacred offices, or pray, fast, and abstain from certain meats, or do whatever works can be done through the body and in the body. Something widely different will be necessary for the justification and liberty of the soul, since the things I have spoken of can be done by any impious person, and only hypocrites are produced by devotion to these things. On the other hand, it will not at all injure the soul that the body should be clothed in profane raiment, should dwell in profane places, should eat and drink in the ordinary fashion, should not pray aloud, and should leave undone all the things abovementioned, which may be done by hypocrites.

And, to cast everything aside, even speculations, meditations, and whatever things can be performed by the exertions of the soul itself, are of no profit. One thing, and one alone, is necessary for life, justification, and Christian liberty; and that is the most holy word of God, the Gospel of Christ, as He says: "I am the resurrection and the life; he that believeth in me shall not die eternally"; and also "If the Son shall make you free, ye shall be free indeed"; and "Man shall not live by bread alone, but by every word that proceedeth out of the mouth of God."

Let us therefore hold it for certain and firmly established, that the soul can do without everything, except the word of God, without which none at all of its wants are provided for. But, having the word, it is rich and wants for nothing; since that is the word of life, of truth, of light, of peace, of justification, of salvation, of joy, of liberty, of wisdom, of virtue, of grace, of glory, and of every good thing. It is on this account that the prophet in a whole psalm, and in many other places, sighs for and calls upon the word of God with so many groanings and words.

Again, there is no more cruel stroke of the wrath of God than when He sends a famine of hearing His words; just as there is no greater favour from Him than the sending forth of His word, as it is said: "He sent his word and healed them, and delivered them from their destructions." Christ was sent for no other office than that of the word, and the order of apostles, that of bishops, and that of the whole body of the clergy, have been called and instituted for no object but the ministry of the word.

But you will ask:—"What is this word, and by what means is it to be used, since there are so many words of God?" I answer, the Apostle Paul explains what it is, namely, the Gospel of God, concerning His son, incarnate, suffering, risen, and glorified through the Spirit, the sanctifier. To preach Christ is to feed the soul, to justify it, to set it free, and to save it, if it believes the preaching. For faith alone, and the efficacious use of the word of God, bring salvation. "If thou shalt confess with thy mouth the Lord Jesus, and shalt believe in thine heart that God hath raised him from the dead, thou shalt be saved." And again: "Christ is the end of the law for righteousness to every one that believeth"; and "The just shall live by faith." For the word of God cannot be received and honoured by any works, but by faith alone. Hence it is clear that, as the soul needs the word alone for life and justification, so it is justified by faith alone and not by any works. For if it could be justified by any other means, it would have no need of the word, nor consequently of faith.

But this faith cannot consist at all with works; that is, if you imagine that you can be justified by those works, whatever they are, along with it. For this would be to halt between two opinions, to worship Baal, and to kiss the hand to him, which is a very great iniquity, as Job says. Therefore, when you begin to believe, you learn at the same time that all that is in you is utterly guilty, sinful, and damnable; according to that saying: "All have sinned, and come short of the glory of God." And also: "There is none righteous, no, not one; they are all gone out of the way; they are together become unprofitable; there is none that doeth good, no, not one." When you have learnt this, you will know that Christ is necessary for you, since He has suffered and risen again for you, that, believing on Him, you might by this faith become another man, all your sins being remitted, and you being justified by the merits of another, namely, of Christ alone.

Since then this faith can reign only in the inward man, as it is said: "With the heart man believeth unto righteousness"; and since it alone justifies, it is evident that by no outward work of labour can the inward man be at all justified, made free, and saved; and that no works whatever have any relation to him. And so, on the other hand, it is solely by impiety and incredulity of heart that he becomes guilty, and a slave of sin, deserving condemnation; not by any outward sin or work. Therefore the first care of every Christian ought to be, to lay aside all reliance on works, and strengthen his faith alone more and more, and by it grow in the knowledge, not of works, but of Christ Jesus, who has suffered and risen again for him; as Peter teaches, when he makes no other work to be a Christian one. Thus Christ, when the Jews asked Him what they should do that they might work the works of God, rejected the multitude of works, with which He saw that they were puffed up, and commanded them one thing only, saying: "This is the work of God, that ye believe on him whom He hath sent, for him hath God the Father sealed."

Hence a right faith in Christ is an incomparable treasure, carrying with it universal salvation, and preserving from all evil, as it is said: "He that believeth not shall be damned." Isaiah, looking to this treasure, predicted: "The consumption decreed shall overflow with righteousness. For the Lord God of hosts shall make a consumption, even determined, in the midst of the land." As if he said:— "Faith, which is the brief and complete fulfilling of the law, will fill those who believe with such righteousness, that they will need nothing else for justification." Thus too Paul says: "For with the heart man believeth unto righteousness."

But you ask how it can be the fact that faith alone justifies, and affords without works so great a treasure of good things, when so many works, ceremonies, and laws are prescribed to us in the

Scriptures. I answer: before all things bear in mind what I have said, that faith alone without works justifies, sets free, and saves, as I shall show more clearly below.

Meanwhile it is to be noted, that the whole Scripture of God is divided into two parts, precepts and promises. The precepts certainly teach us what is good, but what they teach is not forthwith done. For they show us what we ought to do, but do not give us the power to do it. They were ordained, however, for the purpose of showing man to himself; that through them he may learn his own impotence for good, and may despair of his own strength. For this reason they are called the Old Testament, and are so.

For example: "thou shalt not covet," is a precept by which we are all convicted of sin; since no man can help coveting, whatever efforts to the contrary he may make. In order therefore that he may fulfil the precept, and not covet, he is constrained to despair of himself, and to seek elsewhere and through another the help which he cannot find in himself; as it is said: "O Israel, thou hast destroyed thyself; but in me is thine help." Now what is done by this one precept, is done by all; for all are equally impossible of fulfilment by us.

Now when a man has through the precepts been taught his own impotence, and become anxious by what means he may satisfy the law—for the law must be satisfied, so that no jot or tittle of it may pass away; otherwise he must be hopelessly condemned—then, being truly humbled and brought to nothing in in his own eyes, he finds in himself no resource for justification and salvation.

Then comes in that other part of Scripture, the promises of God, which declare they glory of God, and say: "If you wish to fulfil the law, and, as the law requires, not to covet, lo! believe in Christ, in whom are promised to you grace, justification, peace, and liberty." All these things you shall have, if you believe, and shall be without them, if you do not believe. For what is impossible for you by all the works of the law, which are many and yet useless, you shall fulfil in an easy and summary way through faith; because God the Father has made everything to depend on faith, so that whosoever has it, has all things, and he who has it not, has nothing. "For God hath concluded them all in unbelief, that He might have mercy upon all." Thus the promises of God give that which the precepts exact, and fulfil what the law commands; so that all is of God alone, both the precepts and their fulfilment. He alone commands. He alone also fulfils. Hence the promises of God belong to the New Testament; nay, are the New Testament.

Now since these promises of God are words of holiness, truth, righteousness, liberty, and peace, and are full of universal goodness; the soul, which cleaves to them with a firm faith, is so united to them, nay, thoroughly absorbed by them, that it not only partakes in, but is penetrated and saturated by, all their virtue. For if the touch of Christ was healing how much more does that most tender spiritual touch, nay, absorption of the word, communicate to the soul all that belongs to the word. In this way, therefore, the soul, through faith alone, without works, is from the word of God justified, sanctified, endued with truth, peace, and liberty, and filled with every good thing, and is truly made the child of God; as it is said: "To them gave he power to become the sons of God, even to them that believe on his name."

From all this it is easy to understand why faith has such great power, and why no good works, nor even all good works put together, can compare with it; since no work can cleave to the word of God, or be in the soul. Faith alone and the word reign in it; and such as is the word, such is the soul made by it; just as iron exposed to fire glows like fire, on account of its union with the fire. It is clear then that to a Christian man his faith suffices for everything, and that he has no need of works for justification. But if he has no need of works, neither has he need of the law; and, if he has no need of the law, he is certainly free from the law, and the saying is true: "The law is not made for a righteous man." This is that Christian liberty, our faith, the effect of which is, not that we should be careless or lead a bad life, but that no one should need the law or works for justification and salvation.

Let us consider this as the first virtue of faith; and let us look also to the second. This also is an office of faith, that it honours with the utmost veneration and the highest reputation him in whom it believes, inasmuch as it holds him to be truthful and worthy of belief. For there is no honour like that reputation of truth and righteousness, with which we honour him, in whom we believe. What higher credit can we attribute to any one than truth and righteousness, and absolute goodness? On the other hand, it is the greatest insult to brand any one with the reputation of falsehood and unright-eousness, or to suspect him of these, as we do when we disbelieve him. . . .

Thus the soul, in firmly believing the promises of God, holds Him to be true and righteous; and it can attribute to God no higher glory than the credit of being so. The highest worship of God is to ascribe to Him truth, righteousness, and whatever qualities we must ascribe to one in whom we believe. In doing this the soul shows itself prepared to do His whole will; in doing this it hallows His name, and gives itself up to be dealt with as it may please God. For it cleaves to His promises, and never doubts that He is true, just, and wise, and will do, dispose, and provide for all things in the best way. Is not such a soul, in this its faith, most obedient to God in all things? What command-ment does there remain which has not been amply fulfilled by such an obedience? What fulfilment can be more full than universal obedience? Now this is not accomplished by works, but by faith alone.

On the other hand, what greater rebellion, impiety, or insult to God can there be, than not to believe His promises? What else is this, than either to make God a liar, or to doubt His truth—that is, to attribute truth to ourselves, but to God falsehood and levity? In doing this, is not a man deny-ing God and setting himself up as an idol in his own heart? What then can works, done in such a state of impiety, profit us, were they even angelic or apostolic works? Rightly hath God shut up all—not in wrath nor in lust—but in unbelief; in order that those who pretend that they are fulfilling the law by works of purity and benevolence (which are social and human virtues), may not presume that they will therefore be saved; but, being included in the sin of unbelief, may either seek mercy, or be justly condemned. . . .

The third incomparable grace of faith is this, that it unites the soul to Christ, as the wife to the husband; by which mystery, as the Apostle teaches, Christ and the soul are made one flesh. Now if they are one flesh, and if a true marriage—nay, by far the most perfect of all marriages—is accom-plished between them (for human marriages are but feeble types of this one great marriage), then it follows that all they have becomes theirs in common, as well good things as evil things; so that whatsoever Christ possesses, that the believing soul may take to itself and boast of as its own, and whatever belongs to the soul, that Christ claims as his.

If we compare these possessions, we shall see how inestimable is the gain. Christ is full of grace, life, and salvation; the soul is full of sin, death, and condemnation. Let faith step in, and then sin, death, and hell will belong to Christ, and grace, life, and salvation to the soul. For, if he is a husband, he must needs take to himself that which is his wife's, and, at the same time, impart to his wife that which is his. For, in giving her his own body and himself, how can he but give her all that is his? And, in taking to himself the body of his wife, how can he but take to himself all that is hers?

In this is displayed the delightful sight, not only of communion, but of a prosperous warfare, of victory, salvation, and redemption. For since Christ is God and man, and is such a person as neither has sinned, nor dies, nor is condemned,—nay, cannot sin, die or be condemned; and since his right-eousness, life, and salvation are invincible, eternal, and almighty; when, I say, such a person, by the wedding-ring of faith, takes a share in the sins, death, and hell of his wife, nay, makes them his own, and deals with them no otherwise than as if they were his, and as if he himself had sinned; and when he suffers, dies, and descends to hell, that he may overcome all things, since sin, death, and hell cannot swallow him up, they must needs be swallowed up by him in stupendous conflict. For his righteousness rises above the sins of all men; his life is more powerful than all death; his salvation is more unconquerable than all hell.

Thus the believing soul, by the pledge of its faith in Christ, becomes free from all sin, fearless of death, safe from hell, and endowed with the eternal righteousness, life, and salvation of its husband Christ. Thus he presents to himself a glorious bride, without spot or wrinkle, cleansing her with the washing of water by the word; that is, by faith in the word of life, righteousness, and salvation. Thus he betroths her unto himself "in faithfulness, in righteousness, and in judgment, and in lovingkindness, and in mercies. . . ."

From all this you will again understand, why so much importance is attributed to faith, so that it alone can fulfil the law, and justify without any works. For you see that the first commandment, which says, "Thou shalt worship one God only," is fulfilled by faith alone. If you were nothing but good works from the soles of your feet to the crown of your head, you would not be worshipping God, nor fulfilling the first commandment, since it is impossible to worship God, without ascribing to Him the glory of truth and of universal goodness, as it ought in truth to be ascribed. Now this is not done by works, but only by faith of heart. It is not by working, but by believing, that we glorify God and confess Him to be true. On this ground faith is the sole righteousness of a Christian man, and the fulfilling of all the commandments. For to him who fulfils the first, the task of fulfilling all the rest is easy.

Works, since they are irrational things, cannot glorify God; although they may be done to the glory of God, if faith be present. But at present we are enquiring, not into the quality of the works done, but into him who does them, who glorifies God, and brings forth good works. This is faith of heart, the head and the substance of all our righteousness. Hence that is a blind and perilous doctrine which teaches that the commandments are fulfilled by works. The commandments must have been fulfilled, previous to any good works, and good works follow their fulfilment, as we shall see. . . .

Let it suffice to say this concerning the inner man and its liberty, and concerning that righteousness of faith, which needs neither laws nor good works; nay, they are even hurtful to it, if any one pretends to be justified by them.

And now let us turn to the other part, to the outward man. Here we shall give an answer to all those who, taking offence at the word of faith and at what I have asserted, say: "If faith does everything, and by itself suffices for justification, why then are good works commanded? Are we then to take our ease and do no works, content with faith?" Not so, impious men, I reply; not so. That would indeed really be the case, if we were thoroughly and completely inner and spiritual persons; but that will not happen until the last day, when the dead shall be raised. As long as we live in the flesh, we are but beginning and making advances in that which shall be completed in a future life. On this account the Apostle calls that which we have in this life, the first-fruits of the Spirit. In future we shall have the tenths, and the fulness of the Spirit. To this part belongs the fact I have stated before, that the Christian is the servant of all and subject to all. For in that part in which he is free, he does no works, but in that in which he is a servant, he does all works. Let us see on what principle this is so.

Although, as I have said, inwardly, and according to the spirit, a man is amply enough justified by faith, having all that he requires to have, except that this very faith and abundance ought to increase from day to day, even till the future life; still he remains in this mortal life upon earth, in which it is necessary that he should rule his own body, and have intercourse with men. Here then works begin; here he must not take his ease; here he must give heed to exercise his body by fastings, watchings, labour, and other moderate discipline, so that it may be subdued to the spirit, and obey and conform itself to the inner man and faith, and not rebel against them nor hinder them, as is its nature to do if it is not kept under. For the inner man, being conformed to God, and created after the image of God through faith, rejoices and delights itself in Christ, in whom such blessings have been conferred on it; and hence has only this task before it, to serve God with joy and for nought in free love.

In doing this he offends that contrary will in his own flesh, which is striving to serve the world, and to seek its own gratification. This the spirit of faith cannot and will not bear; but applies itself with cheerfulness and zeal to keep it down and restrain it; as Paul says: "I delight in the law of God after the inward man; but I see another law in my members, warring against the law of my mind, and bringing me into captivity to the law of sin." And again: "I keep under my body, and bring it into subjection, lest that by any means, when I have preached to others, I myself should be a cast-away." And: "They that are Christ's have crucified the flesh with the affections and lusts."

These works, however, must not be done with any notion that by them a man can be justified before God—for faith, which alone is righteousness before God, will not bear with this false notion—but solely with this purpose, that the body may be brought into subjection, and be purified from its evil lusts, so that our eyes may be turned only to purging away those lusts. For when the soul has been cleansed by faith and made to love God, it would have all things to be cleansed in like manner; and especially its own body, so that all things might unite with it in the love and praise of God. Thus it comes that, from the requirements of his own body, a man cannot take his ease, but is compelled on its account to do many good works, that he may bring it into subjection. Yet these works are not the means of his justification before God; he does them out of disinterested love to the service of God; looking to no other end than to do what is well-pleasing to Him whom he desires to obey most dutifully in all things.

On this principle every man may easily instruct himself in what measure, and with what distinctions, he ought to chasten his own body. He will fast, watch, and labour, just as much as he sees to suffice for keeping down the wantonness and concupiscence of the body. But those who pretend to be justified by works are looking, not to the mortification of their lusts, but only to the works themselves; thinking that, if they can accomplish as many works and as great ones as possible, all is well with them, and they are justified. Sometimes they even injure their brain, and extinguish nature, or at least make it useless. This is enormous folly, and ignorance of Christian life and faith, when a man seeks, without faith, to be justified and saved by works.

To make what we have said more easily understood, let us set it forth under a figure. The works of a Christian man, who is justified and saved by his faith out of the pure and unbought mercy of God, ought to be regarded in the same light as would have been those of Adam and Eve in Paradise, and of all their posterity, if they had not sinned. Of them it is said: "The Lord God took the man, and put him into the garden of Eden to dress it and to keep it." Now Adam had been created by God just and righteous, so that he could not have needed to be justified and made righteous by keeping the garden and working in it; but, that he might not be unemployed, God gave him the business of keeping and cultivating Paradise. These would have indeed been works of perfect freedom, being done for no object but that of pleasing God, and not in order to obtain justification, which he already had to the full, and which would have been innate in us all.

So it is with the works of a believer. Being by his faith replaced afresh in Paradise and created anew, he does not need works for his justification, but that he may not be idle, but may keep his own body and work upon it. His works are to be done freely, with the sole object of pleasing God. Only we are not yet fully created anew in perfect faith and love; these require to be increased, not however through works, but through themselves.

A bishop, when he consecrates a church, confirms children, or performs any other duty of his office, is not consecrated as bishop by these works; nay, unless he had been previously consecrated as bishop, not one of those works would have any validity; they would be foolish, childish, and ridiculous. Thus a Christian, being consecrated by his faith, does good works; but he is not by these works made a more sacred person, or more a Christian. That is the effect of faith alone; nay, unless he were previously a believer and a Christian, none of his works would have any value at all, they would really be impious and damnable sins.

True then are these two sayings: Good works do not make a good man, but a good man does good works. Bad works do not make a bad man, but a bad man does bad works. Thus it is always necessary that the substance or person should be good before any good works can be done, and that good works should follow and proceed from a good person. As Christ says: "A good tree cannot bring forth evil fruit, neither can a corrupt tree bring forth good fruit." Now it is clear that the fruit does not bear the tree, nor does the tree grow on the fruit; but, on the contrary, the trees bear the fruit and the fruit grows on the trees.

As then trees must exist before their fruit, and as the fruit does not make the tree either good or bad, but, on the contrary, a tree of either kind produces fruit of the same kind; so must first the person of the man be good or bad, before he can do either a good or a bad work; and his works do not make him bad or good, but he himself makes his works either bad or good.

We may see the same thing in all handicrafts. A bad or good house does not make a bad or good builder, but a good or bad builder makes a good or bad house. And in general, no work makes the workman such as it is itself; but the workman makes the work such as he is himself. Such is the case too with the works of men. Such as the man himself is, whether in faith or in unbelief, such is his work; good if it be done in faith, bad if in unbelief. But the converse is not true—that, such as the work is, such the man becomes in faith or in unbelief. For as works do not make a believing man, so neither do they make a justified man; but faith, as it makes a man a believer and justified, so also it makes his works good.

Since, then, works justify no man, but a man must be justified before he can do any good works, it is most evident that it is faith alone which, by the mere mercy of God through Christ, and by means of His word, can worthily and sufficiently justify and save the person; and that a Christian man needs no work, no law, for his salvation; for by faith he is free from all law, and in perfect freedom does gratuitously all that he does, seeking nothing either of profit or of salvation—since by the grace of God he is already saved and rich in all things through his faith—but solely that which is well-pleasing to God.

So too no good work can profit an unbeliever to justification and salvation; and on the other hand no evil work makes him an evil and condemned person, but that unbelief, which makes the person and the tree bad, makes his works evil and condemned. Wherefore, when any man is made good or bad, this does not arise from his works, but from his faith or unbelief, as the wise man says: "The beginning of sin is to fall away from God"; that is, not to believe, Paul says: "He that cometh to God must believe"; and Christ says the same thing: "Either make the tree good, and his fruit good; or else make the tree corrupt, and his fruit corrupt." As much as to say: He who wishes to have good fruit, will begin with the tree and plant a good one; even so he who wishes to do good works must begin, not by working, but by believing, since it is this which makes the person good. For nothing makes the person good but faith, nor bad but unbelief.

It is certainly true that, in the sight of men, a man becomes good or evil by his works; but here "becoming" means that it is thus shown and recognized who is good or evil; as Christ says: "By their fruits ye shall know them." But all this stops at appearances and externals; and in this matter very many deceive themselves, when they presume to write and teach that we are to be justified by good works, and meanwhile make no mention even of faith, walking in their own ways, ever deceived and deceiving, going from bad to worse, blind leaders of the blind, wearying themselves with many works, and yet never attaining to true righteousness; of whom Paul says: "Having a form of godliness, but denying the power thereof; ever learning, and never able to come to the knowledge fo the truth. . . ."

Here is the truly Christian life; here is faith really working by love; when a man applies himself with joy and love to the works of that freest servitude, in which he serves others voluntarily and for nought; himself abundantly satisfied in the fulness and riches of his own faith. . . .

Thus from faith flow forth love and joy in the Lord, and from love a cheerful, willing, free spirit, disposed to serve our neighbour voluntarily, without taking any account of gratitude or ingratitude, praise or blame, gain or loss. Its object is not to lay men under obligations, nor does it distinguish between friends and enemies, or look to gratitude or ingratitude, but most freely and willingly spends itself and its goods, whether it loses them through ingratitude, or gains good will. For thus did its Father, distributing all things to all men abundantly and freely; making his sun to rise upon the just and the unjust. Thus too the child does and endures nothing, except from the free joy with which it delights through Christ in God, the giver of such great gifts. . . .

Finally, for the sake of those to whom nothing can be stated so well but that they misunderstand and distort it, we must add a word, in case they can understand even that. There are very many persons, who, when they hear of this liberty of faith, straightway turn it into an occasion of licence. They think that everything is now lawful for them, and do not choose to show themselves free men and Christians in any other way than by their contempt and reprehension of ceremonies, of traditions, of human laws; as if they were Christians merely because they refuse to fast on stated days, or eat flesh when others fast, or omit the customary prayers; scoffing at the precepts of men, but utterly passing over all the rest that belongs to the Christian religion. On the other hand, they are most pertinaciously resisted by those who strive after salvation solely by their observance of and reverence for ceremonies; as if they would be saved merely because they fast on stated days, or abstain from flesh, or make formal prayers; talking loudly of the precepts of the Church and of the Fathers, and not caring a straw about those things which belong to our genuine faith. Both these parties are plainly culpable, in that, while they neglect matters which are of weight and necessary for salvation, they contend noisily about such as are without weight and not necessary.

How much more rightly does the Apostle Paul teach us to walk in the middle path, condemning either extreme, and saying: "Let not him that eateth despise him that eateth not; and let not him which eateth not judge him that eateth." You see here how the Apostle blames those who, not from religious feeling, but in mere contempt, neglect and rail at ceremonial observances; and teaches them not to despise, since this "knowledge puffeth up." Again he teaches the pertinacious upholders of these things not to judge their opponents. For neither party observes towards the other that charity which edifieth. In this matter we must listen to Scripture, which teaches us to turn aside neither to the right hand nor to the left, but to follow those right precepts of the Lord which rejoice the heart. For just as a man is not righteous, merely because he serves and devotes himself to works and ceremonial rites, so neither will he be accounted righteous, merely because he neglects and despises them.

It is not from works that we are set free by the faith of Christ, but from the belief in works, that is, from foolishly presuming to seek justification through works. Faith redeems our consciences, makes them upright and preserves them, since by it we recognise the truth that justification does not depend on our works, although good works neither can nor ought to be wanting to it; just as we cannot exist without food and drink and all the functions of this mortal body. Still it is not on them that our justification is based, but on faith; and yet they ought not on that account to be despised or neglected. Thus in this world we are compelled by the needs of this bodily life; but we are not hereby justified. "My kingdom is not hence, nor of this world," says Christ; but He does not say: "My kingdom is not here, nor in this world." Paul too says: "Though we walk in the flesh, we do not war after the flesh"; and: "The life which I now live in the flesh I live by the faith of the Son of God." Thus our doings, life, and being, in works and ceremonies, are done from the necessities of this life, and with the motive of governing our bodies; but yet we are not justified by these things, but by the faith of the Son of God. . . .

Since, then, we cannot live in this world without ceremonies and works; since the hot and inexperienced period of youth has need of being restrained and protected by such bonds; and since every one is bound to keep under his own body by attention to these things; therefore the minister of Christ must be prudent and faithful in so ruling and teaching the people of Christ in all these matters that no root of bitterness may spring up among them, and so many be defiled, as Paul warned the Hebrews; that is, that they may not lose the faith, and begin to be defiled by a belief in works, as the means of justification. This is a thing which easily happens, and defiles very many, unless faith be constantly inculcated along with works. It is impossible to avoid this evil, when faith is passed over in silence, and only the ordinances of men are taught, as has been done hitherto by the pestilent, impious, and soul-destroying traditions of our pontiffs, and opinions of our theologians. An infinite number of souls have been drawn down to hell by these snares, so that you may recognise the work of Antichrist. . . .

Hence in the Christian life ceremonies are to be not otherwise looked upon than builders and workmen look upon those preparations for building or working which are not made with any view of being permanent or anything in themselves, but only because without them there could be no building and no work. When the structure is completed, they are laid aside. Here you see that we do not contemn these preparations, but set the highest value on them; a belief in them we do contemn, because no one thinks that they constitute a real and permanent structure. If anyone were so manifestly out of his senses as to have no other object in life but that of setting up these preparations with all possible expense, diligence, and perseverance, while he never thought of the structure itself, but pleased himself and made his boast of these useless preparations and props; should we not all pity his madness, and think that, at the cost thus thrown away, some great building might have been raised?

John Calvin

(1509–1564)

━━━

JOHN CALVIN (1509–64) was a Frenchman, born in Picardy and reared by aristocratic foster parents. He studied scholastic philosophy in Paris, and later law at Bourges and Orleans, where he came under the influence of Protestant teachers. Returning to Paris, he studied the classics, Hebrew, and the Greek Testament.

By 1534 Calvin's heretical opinions were conspicuous enough to make his leaving France advisable. In 1536 he stopped in Geneva, which was already evangelical. His moralism was so extreme that he was expelled in 1538 by the town council. Calvin's reputation grew, however, and in 1541 he was recalled to Geneva to take charge of the troubled affairs of the city. He immediately instituted the theocracy which in a short time made of Geneva the center of the Protestant world. The austere puritanical regime attempted to regulate minutely the daily lives of the citizens; the basis of Calvinist rule was literal interpretation of the Bible, the power of decision being delegated to clerical authority and elders chosen by the town council. The system was copied by John Knox in Scotland and has exerted great influence in that country and North America.

The ideal which Calvin attempted to impose on Geneva was uncompromisingly otherworldly. "There is no medium between these two extremes, either the earth must become vile in our estimation, or it must retain our immoderate love. Wherefore if we have any concern about eternity, we must use our most diligent efforts to extricate ourselves from these fetters." Such a regime had its limitations, of course, "As I see that we cannot forbid men all diversions," Calvin admitted, "I confine myself to those that are really bad."

In contrast with the mystical Luther, Calvin was legalistic and rationalistic. It was Calvin rather than Luther who institutionalized the Reformation, and his theocracy contrasts starkly with Luther's pietistic version of the religious life.

Calvin's major work is the *Institutes of the Christian Religion* (1536, Basel); it came to occupy a place in informed Protestant opinion similar to that of the *Summa* within the Catholic world.

The following translation is by John Allen (Philadelphia, Presbyterian Board of Christian Education, 1928).

Institutes of the Christian Religion

God's Preservation and Support of the World by His Power, and His Government of Every Part of It by His Providence

To represent God as a Creator only for a moment, who entirely finished all his work at once, were frigid and jejune; and in this it behoves us especially to differ from the heathen, that the presence of the Divine power may appear to us no less in the perpetual state of the world than in its first origin. For although the minds even of impious men, by the mere contemplation of earth and heaven, are constrained to rise to the Creator, yet faith has a way peculiar to itself to assign to God the whole praise of creation. To which purpose is that assertion of an Apostle before cited, that it is only "through faith that we understand the worlds were framed by the word of God"; because, unless we proceed to his providence, we have no correct conception of the meaning of this article, "that God is the Creator"; however we may appear to comprehend it in our minds, and to confess it with our tongues. The carnal sense, when it has once viewed the power of God in the creation, stops there; and when it proceeds the furthest, it only examines and considers the wisdom, and power, and goodness, of the Author in producing such a work, which spontaneously present themselves to the view even of those who are unwilling to observe them. In the next place, it conceives of some general operation of God in preserving and governing it, on which the power of motion depends. Lastly, it supposes that the vigour originally infused by God into all things is sufficient for their sustentation. But faith ought to penetrate further. When it has learned that he is the Creator of all things, it should immediately conclude that he is also their perpetual governor and preserver; and that not by a certain universal motion, actuating the whole machine of the world, and all its respective parts, but by a particular providence sustaining, nourishing, and providing for every thing which he has made. . . .

But as we know that the world was made chiefly for the sake of mankind, we must also observe this end in the government of it. The Prophet Jeremiah exclaims, "I know that the way of man is not in himself: it is not in man that walketh to direct his steps." And Solomon: "Man's goings are of the Lord: how can a man then understand his own way?" Now, let them say that man is actuated by God according to the bias of his nature, but that he directs that influence according to his own pleasure. If this could be asserted with truth, man would have the free choice of his own ways. That, perhaps, they will deny, because he can do nothing independently of the power of God. But since it is evident that both the Prophet and Solomon ascribe to God choice and appointment, as well as power, this by no means extricates them from the difficulty. But Solomon, in another place, beautifully reproves this temerity of men, who predetermine on an end for themselves, without regard to God, as though they were not led by his hand: "The preparation of the heart in man," says he, "and the answer of the tongue, is from the Lord." It is, indeed, a ridiculous madness for miserable men to resolve on undertaking any work independently of God, whilst they cannot even speak a word but what he chooses. Moreover, the Scripture, more fully to express that nothing is transacted in the world but according to his destination, shows that those things are subject to him which appear most fortuitous. For what would you be more ready to attribute to chance, than when a limb broken off from a tree kills a passing traveller? But very different is the decision of the Lord, who acknowledges that he has delivered him into the hand of the slayer. Who, likewise, does not leave lots to the blindness of fortune? Yet the Lord leaves them not, but claims the disposal of them himself. He teaches us that it is not by any power of their own that lots are cast into the lap and drawn out; but the only thing which could be ascribed to chance, he declares to belong to himself. To the same purpose is another passage from Solomon: "The poor and the deceitful man meet together: the Lord enlighteneth the eyes of them both." For although the poor and the rich are blended together in the world, yet, as their respective condition are assigned to them by Divine appointment, he suggests that God, who enlightens all, is not blind, and thus exhorts the poor to patience; because those who are discontented with their lot, are endeavouring to shake off the burden imposed on them by God. Thus also another Prophet rebukes profane persons, who attribute it to human industry, or to fortune, that some men remain in obscurity, and others rise to honours: "Promotion cometh neither from the east, nor from the west, nor from the south. But God is the Judge; he putteth down one, and setteth up another." since God cannot divest himself of the office of a judge, hence he reasons, that it is from the secret counsel of God, that some rise to promotion, and others remain in contempt. . . .

The Proper Application of This Doctrine to Render It Useful to Us

. . . Those who have learned this modesty, will neither murmur against God on account of past adversities, nor charge him with the guilt of their crimes, like Agamemnon, in Homer, who says, "The blame belongs not to me, but to Jupiter and Fate." Nor will they, as if hurried away by the Fates, under the influence of despair, put an end to their own lives, like the young man whom Plautus introduces as saying, "The condition of our affairs is inconstant; men are governed by the caprice of the Fates; I will betake myself to a precipice, and there destroy my life and every thing at once." Nor will they excuse their flagitious actions by ascribing them to God, after the example of another young man introduced by the same poet, who says, "God was the cause: I believe it was the Divine will. For had it not been so, I know it would not have happened." But they will rather search the Scripture, to learn what is pleasing to God, that by the guidance of the Spirit they may strive to attain it; and at the same time, being prepared to follow God whithersoever he calls them, they will exhibit proofs in their conduct that nothing is more useful than a knowledge of this doctrine. Some profane men foolishly raise such a tumult with their absurdities, as almost, according to a common expression, to confound heaven and earth together. They argue in this manner: If God has fixed the moment of our death, we cannot avoid it; therefore all caution against it will be but lost labour. One man dares not venture himself in a way which he hears is dangerous, lest he should be assassinated by robbers; another sends for physicians, and wearies himself with medicines, to preserve his life; another abstains from the grosser kinds of food, lest he should injure his valetudinary constitution; another dreads to inhabit a ruinous house; and men in general exert all their faculties in devising and executing methods by which they may attain the object of their desires. Now, either all these things are vain remedies employed to correct the will of God, or life and death, health and disease, peace and war, and other things which, according to their desires or aversions, men industriously study to obtain or to avoid, are not determined by his certain decree. Moreover they conclude, that the prayers of the faithful are not only superfluous, but perverse, which contain petitions that the Lord will provide for those things which he has already decreed from eternity. In short, they supersede all deliberations respecting futurity, as opposed to the providence of God, who, without consulting men, has decreed whatever he pleased. And what has already happened they impute to the Divine providence in such a manner as to overlook the person, who is known to have committed any particular act. Has an assassin murdered a worthy citizen? they say he has executed the counsel of God. Has any one been guilty of theft or fornication? because he has done what was foreseen and ordained by the Lord, he is the minister of his providence. Has a son, neglecting all remedies, carelessly waited the death of his father? it was impossible for him to resist God, who had decreed this event from eternity. Thus by these persons all crimes are denominated virtues, because they are subservient to the ordination of God. . . .

The same persons inconsiderately and erroneously ascribe all past events to the absolute providence of God. For since all things which come to pass are dependent upon it, therefore, say they, neither thefts, nor adulteries, nor homicides, are perpetrated without the intervention of the Divine will. Why, therefore, they ask, shall a thief be punished for having pillaged him whom it has pleased the Lord to chastise with poverty? Why shall a homicide be punished for having slain him whose life the Lord had terminated? If all such characters are subservient to the Divine will, why shall they be punished? But I deny that they serve the will of God. For we cannot say, that he who is influenced by a wicked heart, acts in obedience to the commands of God, while he is only gratifying his own malignant passion. That man obeys God, who, being instructed in his will, hastens whither God calls him. Where can we learn his will, but in his word? Therefore in our actions we ought to regard the will of God, which is declared in his word. God only requires of us conformity to his precepts. If we do any thing contrary to them, it is not obedience, but contumacy and transgression. But it is said, if he would not permit it, we should not do it. This I grant. But do we perform evil actions with the design of pleasing him? He gives us no such command. We precipitate ourselves into them, not considering what is his will, but inflamed with the violence of our passions, so that we deliberately strive to oppose him. In this manner even by criminal actions we subserve his righteous ordination; because, in the infinite greatness of his wisdom, he well knows how to use evil instruments for the accomplishment of good purposes. . . .

Man, in His Present State Despoiled of Freedom of Will, and Subjected to a Miserable Slavery

Since we have seen that the domination of sin, from the time of its subjugation of the first man, not only extends over the whole race, but also exclusively possesses every soul, it now remains to be more closely investigated, whether we are despoiled of all freedom, and, if any particle of it yet remain, how far its power extends. But, that we may the more easily discover the truth of this question, I will first set up by the way a mark, by which our whole course must be regulated. The best method of guarding against error is to consider the dangers which threaten us on every side. For when man is declared to be destitute of all rectitude, he immediately makes it an occasion of slothfulness; because he is said to have no power of himself for the pursuit of righteousness, he totally neglects it, as though it did not at all concern him. On the other hand, he cannot arrogate any thing to himself, be it ever so little, without God being robbed of his honour, and himself being endangered by presumptuous temerity. Therefore, to avoid striking on either of these rocks, this will be the course to be pursued-that man, being taught that he has nothing good left in his possession, and being surrounded on every side with the most miserable necessity, should, nevertheless, be instructed to aspire to the good of which he is destitute, and to the liberty of which he is deprived; and should be roused from indolence with more earnestness, than if he were supposed to be possessed of the greatest strength. The necessity of the latter is obvious to every one. The former, I perceive, is doubted by more than it ought to be. For this being placed beyond all controversy, that man must not be deprived of any thing that properly belongs to him, it ought also to be manifest how important it is that he should be prevented from false boasting. For if he was not even then permitted to glory in himself, when by the Divine beneficence he was decorated with the noblest ornaments, how much ought he now to be humbled, when, on account of his ingratitude, he has been hurled from the summit of glory to the abyss of ignominy! At that time, I say, when he was exalted to the most honourable eminence, the Scripture attributes nothing to him, but that he was created after the image of God; which certainly implies that his happiness consisted not in any goodness of his own, but in a participation of God. What, then, remains for him now, deprived of all glory, but that he acknowledge God, to whose beneficence he could not be thankful, when he abounded in the riches of his favour? and that he now, at least, by a confession of his poverty, glorify him, whom he glorified not by an acknowledgment of his blessing? It is also no less conducive to our interests than to the Divine glory, that all the praise of wisdom and strength be taken away from us; so that they join sacrilege to our fall, who ascribe to us any thing more than truly belongs to us. For what else is the consequence, when we are taught to contend in our own strength, but that we are lifted into the air on a reed, which being soon broken, we fall to the ground. Though our strength is placed in too favourable a point of view, when it is compared to a reed. For it is nothing but smoke, whatever vain men have imagined and pretended concerning it. Wherefore it is not without reason, that that remarkable sentence is so frequently repeated by Augustine, that free will is rather overthrown than established even by its own advocates. It was necessary to premise these things for the sake of some, who, when they hear that human power is completely subverted in order that the power of God may be established in man, inveterately hate this whole argument, as dangerous and unprofitable; which yet appears to be highly useful to us, and essential to true religion. . . .

This being admitted will place it beyond all doubt, that man is not possessed of free will for good works, unless he be assisted by grace, and that special grace which is bestowed on the elect alone in regeneration. For I stop not to notice those fanatics, who pretend that grace is offered equally and promiscuously to all. But it does not yet appear, whether he is altogether deprived of power to do good, or whether he yet possesses some power, though small and feeble; which of itself can do nothing, but by the assistance of grace does also perform its part. Lombard, in order to establish this notion, informs us that two sorts of grace are necessary to qualify us for the performance of good works. One he calls operative, by which we efficaciously will what is good; the other cooperative, which attends as auxiliary to a good will. This division I dislike, because, while he attributes an efficacious desire of what is good to the grace of God, he insinuates that man has of his own nature antecedent, though ineffectual, desires after what is good; as Bernard asserts that a good will is the work of God, but yet allows that man is self-impelled to desire such a good will. But this is very remote from the meaning of Augustine, from whom, however, Lombard would be thought to have borrowed this division. The second part of it offends me by its ambiguity, which has produced a very erroneous interpretation. For they have supposed that we cooperate with the second sort of Divine grace, because we have it in our power either to frustrate the first sort by rejecting it, or to confirm it by our obedience to it. The author of the treatise "On the Vocation of the Gentiles" expresses it thus-that those who have the use of reason and judgment are at liberty to depart from grace, that they may be rewarded for not having departed, and that what is impossible without the cooperation of the Spirit, may be imputed to their merits, by whose will it might have been prevented. These two things I have thought proper to notice as I proceed, that the reader may perceive how much I dissent from the sounder schoolmen. For I differ considerably more from the later sophists, as they have departed much further from the judgment of antiquity. However, we understand from this division, in what sense they have ascribed free will to man. For Lombard at length pronounces, that we are not therefore possessed of free will, because we have an equal power to do or to think either good or evil, but only because we are free from constraint. And this liberty is not diminished, although we are corrupt, and the slaves of sin, and capable of doing nothing but sin.

Then man will be said to possess free will in this sense, not that he has an equally free election of good and evil, but because he does evil voluntarily, and not by constraint. That, indeed, is very true; but what end could it answer to decorate a thing so diminutive with a title so superb? Egregious liberty indeed, if man be not compelled to serve sin, but yet is such a willing slave, that his will is held in bondage by the fetters of sin. I really abominate contentions about words, which disturb the Church without producing any good effect; but I think that we ought religiously to avoid words which signify any absurdity, particularly when they lead to a pernicious error. How few are there, pray, who, when they hear free will attributed to man, do not immediately conceive, that he has the sovereignty over his own mind and will, and is able by his innate power to incline himself to whatever he pleases? But it will be said, all danger from these expressions will be removed, if the people are carefully apprized of their signification. But on the contrary, the human mind is naturally so prone to falsehood, that it will sooner imbibe error from one single expression, than truth from a prolix oration; of which we have a more certain experiment than could be wished in word. For neglecting that explanation of the fathers, almost all their successors have been drawn into a fatal self-confidence, by adhering to the original and proper signification of the word. . . .

But I am obliged to repeat here, what I premised in the beginning of this chapter-that he who feels the most consternation, from a consciousness of his own calamity, poverty, nakedness, and ignominy, has made the greatest proficiency in the knowledge of himself. For there is no danger that man will divest himself of too much, provided he learns that what is wanting in him may be recovered in God. But he cannot assume to himself even the least particle beyond his just right, without ruining himself with vain confidence, and incurring the guilt of enormous sacrilege, by transferring to himself the honour which belongs to God. And whenever our minds are pestered with this cupidity, to desire to have something of our own, which may reside in ourselves rather than in God, we may know that this idea is suggested by the same counsellor, who excited in our first parents the desire of resembling "gods, knowing good and evil." . . .

Eternal Election, or God's Predestination of Some to Salvation, and of Others to Destruction

The covenant of life not being equally preached to all, and among those to whom it is preached not always finding the same reception, this diversity discovers the wonderful depth of the Divine judgment. Nor is it to be doubted that this variety also follows, subject to the decision of God's eternal election. If it be evidently the result of the Divine will, that salvation is freely offered to some, and others are prevented from attaining it,-this immediately gives rise to important and difficult questions, which are incapable of any other explication, than by the establishment of pious minds in what ought to be received concerning election and predestination-a question, in the opinion of many, full of perplexity; for they consider nothing more unreasonable, than that, of the common mass of mankind, some should be predestinated to salvation, and others to destruction. But how unreasonably they perplex themselves will afterwards appear from the sequel of our discourse. Besides, the very obscurity which excites such dread, not only displays the utility of this doctrine, but shows it to be productive of the most delightful benefit. We shall never be clearly convinced as we ought to be, that our salvation flows from the fountain of God's free mercy, till we are acquainted with his eternal election, which illustrates the grace of God by this comparison, that he adopts not all promiscuously to the hope of salvation, but gives to some what he refuses to others. Ignorance of this principle evidently detracts from the Divine glory, and diminishes real humility. But according to Paul, what is so necessary to be known, never can be known, unless God, without any regard to works, chooses those whom he has decreed. "At this present time also, there is a remnant according to the election of grace. And if by grace, then it is no more of works; otherwise, grace is no more grace. But if it be of works, then it is no more grace; otherwise, work is no more work." If we need to be recalled to the origin of election, to prove that we obtain salvation from no other source than the mere goodness of God, they who desire to extinguish this principle, do all they can to obscure what ought to be magnificently and loudly celebrated, and to pluck humility by the roots. In ascribing the salvation of the remnant of the people to the election of grace, Paul clearly testifies, that it is then only known that God saves whom he will of his mere good pleasure, and does not dispense a reward to which there can be no claim. They who shut the gates to prevent any one from presuming to approach and taste this doctrine, do no less injury to man than to God; for nothing else will be sufficient to produce in us suitable humility, or to impress us with a due sense of our great obligations to God. Nor is there any other basis for solid confidence, even according to the authority of Christ, who, to deliver us from all fear, and render us invincible amidst so many dangers, snares, and deadly conflicts, promises to preserve in safety all whom the Father has committed to his care. Whence we infer, that they who know not themselves to be God's peculiar people will be tortured with continual anxiety; and therefore, that the interest of all believers, as well as their own, is very badly consulted by those who blind to the three advantages we have remarked, would wholly remove the foundation of our salvation. And hence the Church rises to our view, which otherwise, as Bernard justly observes, could neither be discovered nor recognized among creatures, being in two respects wonderfully concealed in the bosom of a blessed predestination, and in the mass of a miserable damnation. But before I enter on the subject itself, I must address some preliminary observations to two sorts of persons. The discussion of predestination-a subject of itself rather intricate-is made very perplexed, and therefore dangerous, by human curiosity, which no barriers can restrain from wandering into forbidden labyrinths, and soaring beyond its sphere, as if determined to leave none of the Divine secrets unscrutinized or unexplored. As we see multitudes every where guilty of this arrogance and presumption, and among them some who are not censurable in other respects, it is proper to admonish them of the bounds of their duty on this subject. First, then, let them remember that when they inquire into predestination, they penetrate the inmost recesses of Divine wisdom, where the careless and confident intruder will obtain no satisfaction to his curiosity, but will enter a labyrinth from which he will find no way to depart. For it is unreasonable that man should scrutinize with impunity those things which the Lord has determined to be hidden in himself; and investigate, even from eternity, that sublimity of wisdom which God would have us to adore and not comprehend, to promote our admiration of his glory. The secrets of his will which he determined to reveal to us, he discovers in his word; and these are all that he foresaw would concern us or conduce to our advantage. . . .

Predestination, by which God adopts some to the hope of life, and adjudges others to eternal death, no one, desirous of the credit of piety, dares absolutely to deny. But it is involved in many cavils, especially by those who make foreknowledge the cause of it. We maintain, that both belong to God; but it is preposterous to represent one as dependent on the other. When we attribute foreknowledge to God, we mean that all things have ever been, and perpetually remain, before his eyes, so that to his knowledge nothing is future or past, but all things are present; and present in such a manner, that he does not merely conceive of them from ideas formed in his mind, as things remembered by us appear present to our minds, but really beholds and sees them as if actually placed before him. And this foreknowledge extends to the whole world, and to all the creatures. Predestination we call the eternal decree of God, by which he has determined in himself, what he would have to become of every individual of mankind. For they are not all created with a similar destiny; but eternal life is foreordained for some, and eternal damnation for others. Every man, therefore, being created for one or the other of these ends, we say, he is predestinated either to life or to death. This God has not only testified in particular persons, but has given a specimen of it in the whole posterity of Abraham, which should evidently show the future condition of every nation to depend upon his decision. . . .

The True Church and the Necessity of 'Our Union with Her, Being the Mother of all the Pious

. . . Here we must regard both the secret election of God, and his internal vocation; because he alone "knoweth them that are his"; and keeps them enclosed under his "seal," to use the expression of Paul; except that they bear his impression, by which they may be distinguished from the reprobate. But because a small and contemptible number is concealed among a vast multitude, and a few grains of wheat are covered with a heap of chaff, we must leave to God alone the knowledge of his Church whose foundation is his secret election. Nor is it sufficient to include in our thoughts and minds the whole multitude of the elect, unless we conceive of such a unity of the Church, into which we know ourselves to be truly ingrafted. For unless we are united with all the other members under Christ our Head, we can have no hope of the future inheritance. Therefore the Church is called *Catholic*, or universal; because there could not be two or three churches, without Christ being divided, which is impossible. But all the elect of God are so connected with each other in Christ, that as they depend upon one head, so they grow up together as into one body, compacted together like members of the same body; being made truly one, as living by one faith, hope, and charity, through the same Divine Spirit, being called not only to the same inheritance of eternal life, but also to a participation of one God and Christ. Therefore, though the melancholy desolation which surrounds us, seems to proclaim that there is nothing left of the Church, let us remember that the death of Christ is fruitful, and that God wonderfully preserves his Church as it were in hiding-places; according to what he said to Elijah: "I have reserved to myself seven thousand men, who have not bowed the knee to Baal."

This article of the creed, however, relates in some measure to the external Church, that every one of us may maintain a brotherly agreement with all the children of God, may pay due deference to the authority of the Church, and, in a word, may conduct himself as one of the flock. Therefore we add *The Communion of Saints*-a clause which, though generally omitted by the ancients, ought not to be neglected, because it excellently expresses the character of the Church; as though it had been said that the saints are united in the fellowship of Christ on this condition, that whatever benefits God confers upon them, they should mutually communicate to each other. This destroys not the diversity of grace, for we know that the gifts of the Spirit are variously distributed; nor does it disturb the order of civil polity, which secures to every individual the exclusive enjoyment of his property, as it is necessary for the preservation of the peace of society that men should have peculiar and distinct possessions. . . .

Here are three things, therefore, worthy of our observation. First, that whatever holiness may distinguish the children of God, yet such is their condition as long as they inhabit a mortal body, that this they cannot stand before god without remission of sins. Secondly, that this benefit belongs to the Church; so that we cannot enjoy it unless we continue in its communion. Thirdly, that it is dispensed to us by the ministers and pastors of the Church, either in the preaching of the gospel, or in the administration of the sacraments; and that this is the principal exercise of the power of the keys, which the Lord has conferred on the society of believers. Let every one of us, therefore, consider it as his duty, not to seek remission of sins any where but where the Lord has placed it. Of public reconciliation, which is a branch of discipline, we shall speak in its proper place. . . .

The Council of Trent

The Council of Trent (1545–1563) was part of that movement generally called the Counter-Reformation. As a result of the Protestant Reformation a Council was necessary for the purpose of clarifying Catholic doctrine and promulgating reforms. During the course of Trent's three sessions, doctrinal decrees were passed on such subjects as the sacraments, invocation of the saints, predestination, justification, etc. Each doctrinal decree was accompanied by a decree advocating some practical reform, e.g. the improvement of preaching, the setting up of seminaries for the training of priests, the ending of pluralism, nepotism and episcopal absenteeism. The Council of Trent, in fact, made the last comprehensive review of Catholic doctrine and practice until the Second Vatican Council called by Pope John XXIII in 1963.

The following selections on justification and indulgences show clearly the essence of the doctrinal differences between the Protestant reformers and the Catholic Church.[1]

Canons on Justification

1) If anyone saith, that man may be justified before God by his own works, whether done through the teaching of human nature, or that of the law, without the grace of God through Jesus Christ; let him be anathema.

2) If anyone saith, that the grace of God, through Jesus Christ, is given only for this, that man may be able more easily to live justly, and to merit eternal life, as if, by free will without grace, he were able to do both, though hardly indeed and with difficulty; let him be anathema.

3) If anyone saith, that without the prevenient inspiration of the Holy Ghost, and without his help, man can believe, hope, love, or be penitent as he ought, so as that the grace of Justification may be bestowed upon him; let him be anathema.

4) If anyone saith, that man's free will moved and excited by God, by assenting to God exciting and calling, nowise cooperates towards disposing and preparing itself for obtaining the grace of Justification; that it cannot refuse its consent, if it would, but that, as something inanimate, it does nothing whatever and is merely passive; let him be anathema.

5) If anyone saith, that since Adam's sin, the free will of man is lost and extinguished; or, that it is a thing with only a name, yea a name without a reality, a figment, in fine, introduced into the Church by Satan; let him be anathema.

6) If anyone saith, that it is not in man's power to make his ways evil, but that the works that are evil God worketh as well as those that are good, not permissively only but properly, and of Himself, in such wise that the treason of Judas is no less His own proper work than the vocation of Paul; let him be anathema.

7) If anyone saith, that all works done before Justification, in whatsoever way they be done, are truly sins, or merit the hatred of God; or that the more earnestly one strives to dispose himself for grace, the more grievously he sins: let him be anathema.

---

[1] The passages on justification are taken, with slight alterations, from J. Waterworth, trans., *Canons and Decrees of the Council of Trent*, (London: 1848).

8) If anyone saith, that the fear of hell,—whereby, by grieving for our sins, we flee unto the mercy of God, or refrain from sinning,—is a sin, or makes sinners worse; let him be anathema.

9) If anyone saith, that by faith alone the impious is justified; in such wise as to mean, that nothing else is required to cooperate in order to the obtaining of the grace of Justification, and that it is not in any way necessary, that he be prepared and disposed by the movement of his own will; let him be anathema.

15) If anyone saith, that a man, who is born again and justified, is bound of faith to believe that he is assuredly in the number of predestinate; let him be anathema.

20) If anyone saith that a man who is justified and however perfect is not bound to observe the commandments of God and the Church, but only to believe, as if the Gospel were a bare and absolute promise of eternal life without the condition of observing the commandments: let him be anathema.

23) If anyone saith, that a man once justified can sin no more, nor lose grace, and that therefore he that falls and sins was never truly justified; or, on the other hand, that he is able, during his whole life, to avoid all sins, even those that are venial,—except by a special privilege from God, as the Church holds in regard of the Blessed Virgin; let him be anathema.

24) If anyone saith, that the justice received is not preserved and also increased before God through good works; but that the said works are merely the fruits and signs of Justification obtained, but not a cause of the increase thereof; let him be anathema.

32) If anyone saith that the good works of the one justified are in such manner the gifts of God and that they are not also the good merits of him justified: or that the one justified by the good works that he performs by the grace of God and the merit of Jesus Christ, whose living member he is, does not truly merit an increase of grace, eternal life, and in case he dies in grace, the attainment of eternal life itself and also an increase in glory; let him be anathema.

Decree Concerning Indulgences, Dec. 1563

Whereas the power of conferring Indulgences was granted by Christ to the Church; and she has, even in the most ancient times, used the said power, delivered unto her of God; the sacred holy Synod teaches, and enjoins, that the use of Indulgences, for the Christian people most salutary, and approved of by the authority of sacred Councils, is to be retained in the Church; and it condemns with anathema those who either assert, that they are useless; or who deny that there is in the Church the Power of granting them. In granting them, however, It desires that, in accordance with the ancient and approved custom in the Church, moderation be observed; lest, by excessive facility, ecclesiastical discipline be enervated. And being desirous that the abuses which have crept therein, and by occasion of which this honourable name of Indulgences is blasphemed by heretics, be amended and corrected. It ordains generally by this decree, that all evil gains for the obtaining thereof,—whence a most prolific cause of abuses amongst the Christian people has been derived,—be wholly abolished. But as regards the other abuses which have proceeded from supersition, ignorance, irreverance, or from whatsoever other source, since, by reason of the manifold corruptions in the places and provinces where the said abuses are committed, they cannot conveniently be specially prohibited. It commands all bishops, diligently to collect, each in his own church, all abuses of this nature, and to report them in the first provincial Synod; that, after having been reviewed by the opinions of the other bishops also, they may forthwith be referred to the Sovereign Roman Pontiff, by whose authority and prudence that which may be expedient for the universal Church will be ordained; that thus the gift of holy Indulgences may be dispensed to all the faithful, piously, holily, and incorruptly.

Ignatius de Loyola

(1491–1556)

IGNATIUS DE LOYOLA (1491–1556) was one of the most influential figures in the Catholic Reformation of the sixteenth century and founder of the Jesuits. Ignatius dictated the material for his autobiography in Rome towards the end of his life, calling his amanuensis—a young Portuguese Jesuit, Luis Goncalves de Câmara—to him when quiet moments presented themselves during a hectic round of engagements. The original manuscript no longer survives but there are several very old copies on the basis of which a number of modern critical editions have been made.

From *The Autobiography of Saint Ignatius Loyola*

Until the age of twenty-six he was a man given over to vanities of the world; with a great and vain desire to win fame he delighted especially in the exercise of arms.[1] Once when he was in a fortress that the French were attacking,[2] although all the others saw clearly that they could not defend themselves and were of the opinion that they should surrender provided their lives were spared, he gave so many reasons to the commander that he persuaded him at last to defend it; this was contrary to the views of all the knights, but they were encouraged by his valour and energy. When the day arrived on which the bombardment was expected, he confessed to one of his companions in arms. After the bombardment had lasted a good while, a shot hit him in the leg, breaking it completely; since the ball passed through both legs, the other one was also badly damaged.

When he fell, the defenders of the fortress surrendered immediately to the French who, having taken possession of it, treated the wounded man very well, with courtesy and kindness. After he had been in Pamplona for twelve or fifteen days, they carried him on a litter to his own country where he was very ill. All the doctors and surgeons who were summoned from many places decided that the leg ought to be broken again and the bones reset because they had been badly set the first time or had been broken on the road and were out of place and could not heal. This butchery was done again; during it, as in all the others he suffered before or since, he never spoke a word nor showed any sign of pain other than to clench his fists.

Yet he continued to get worse, not being able to eat and showing the other indications that are usually signs of death. When the feast of St John came, because the doctors had very little confidence in his health, he was advised to confess; he received the sacraments on the vigil of Sts Peter and Paul. The doctors said that if he did not feel better by midnight, he could consider himself dead. As the sick man had devotion to St Peter, Our Lord willed that he should begin to improve that very

---

[1] It is likely that Ignatius was 29–30 at the time of his conversion.
[2] The French attack on the citadel of Pamplona, May 1521.

midnight. His improvement proceeded so quickly that some days later it was decided that he was out of danger of death.

As his bones knit together, one bone below the knee remained on top of another, shortening his leg. The bone protruded so much that it was an ugly sight. He was unable to abide it because he was determined to follow the world and he thought that it would deform him; he asked the surgeons if it could be cut away. They said that indeed it could be cut away, but that the pain would be greater than all those that he had suffered, because it was already healed and it would take some time to cut it. Yet he was determined to make himself a martyr to his own pleasure. His older brother was astounded and said that he himself would not dare to suffer such pain, but the wounded man endured it with his customary patience.

After the flesh and excess bone were cut away, means were taken so the leg would not be so short; many ointments were applied to it, and, as it was stretched continually with instruments, he suffered martyrdom for many days. But Our Lord was restoring his health, and he was getting well. In everything else he was healthy except that he could not stand easily on his leg and had to stay in bed. As he was much given to reading worldly and fictitious books, usually called books of chivalry, when he felt better he asked to be given some of them to pass the time. But in that house none of those that he usually read could be found, so they gave him a Life of Christ and a book of the lives of the saints in Spanish.[3]

As he read them over many times, he became rather fond of what he found written there. Putting his reading aside, he sometimes stopped to think about the things he had read and at other times about the things of the world that he used to think about before . . . Yet there was this difference. When he was thinking about the things of the world, he took much delight in them, but afterwards, when he was tired and put them aside, he found that he was dry and discontented. But when he thought of going to Jerusalem, barefoot and eating nothing but herbs and undergoing all the other rigours that he saw the saints had endured, not only was he consoled when he had these thoughts, but even after putting them aside, he remained content and happy. He did not wonder, however, at this; nor did he stop to ponder the difference until one time his eyes were opened a little, and he began to marvel at the difference and to reflect upon it, realizing from experience that some thoughts left him sad and others happy. Little by little he came to recognize the difference between the spirits that agitated him, one from the demon, the other from God.

From this reading he obtained not a little insight, and he began to think more earnestly about his past life and about the great need he had to do penance for it. At this point the desire to imitate the saints came to him, though he gave no thought to the circumstances, but only promised with God's grace to do as they had done. All he wanted to do was to go to Jerusalem as soon as he recovered . . . performing all the disciplines and abstinences which a generous soul, inflamed by God, usually wants to do.

[After his conversion, Ignatius journeyed in March 1522 to the famous shrine of Our Lady at Montserrat in Catalonia.]

As he was going on his way . . . a Moor riding on a mule came up to him, and they went on talking together. They began to talk about Our Lady, and the Moor said it seemed to him that the Virgin had indeed conceived without a man, but he could not believe that she remained a virgin after

---

[3] *The Life of Christ* by the fourteenth-century German Carthusian Ludolph of Saxony, and *The Golden Legend* by the thirteenth-century Dominican writer Jacopo de Voragine.

[4] At this point in the biography Ignatius refers to himself as the pilgrim.

giving birth. In support of this he cited the natural reasons that suggested themselves to him. The pilgrim,[4] in spite of the many reasons he gave him, could not dissuade him from this opinion. The Moor then went on ahead so rapidly that he lost sight of him, and he was left to think about what had transpired with the Moor. Various emotions came over him and caused discontent in his soul, as it seemed to him that he had not done his duty. This also aroused his indignation against the Moor, for he thought that he had done wrong in allowing the Moor to say such things about Our Lady and that he was obliged to defend her honour. A desire came over him to go in search of the Moor and strike him with his dagger for what he had said. He struggled with this conflict of desires for a long time, uncertain to the end as to what he was obliged to do. The Moor, who had gone on ahead, had told him that he was going to a place on the same road a little farther on, very near the highway, though the highway did not pass through the place.

Tired of examining what would be best to do and not finding any guiding principle, he decided as follows, to let the mule go with the reins slack as far as the place where the road separated. If the mule took the village road, he would seek out the Moor and strike him; if the mule did not go toward the village but kept on the highway, he would let him be. He did as he proposed. Although the village was little more than thirty or forty paces away, and the road to it was very broad and very good, Our Lord willed that the mule took the highway and not the village road. Coming to a large town before Montserrat, he wanted to buy there the clothing he had decided to wear when he went to Jerusalem. He bought cloth from which sacks were usually made, loosely woven and very prickly. Then he ordered a long garment reaching to his feet to be made from it. He bought a pilgrim's staff and a small gourd and put everything up front on the mule's saddle.

He went on his way to Montserrat, thinking as always about the deeds he would do for the love of God. As his mind was full of ideas from Amadis of Gaul[5] and such books, some things similar to those came to mind. Thus he decided to watch over his arms all one night, without sitting down or going to bed, but standing a while and kneeling a while, before the altar of Our Lady of Montserrat where he had resolved to leave his clothing and dress himself in the armour of Christ. Leaving this place then he went on, thinking as usual about his intentions. After arriving at Montserrat, he said a prayer and arranged for a confessor. He made a general confession in writing which lasted three days. He arranged with the confessor[6] to take his mule and to place his sword and his dagger in the church on the altar of Our Lady. This was the first man to whom he revealed his decision, because until then he had not revealed it to any confessor.

On the eve of the feast of Our Lady in March in the year 1522, he went at night as secretly as he could to a poor man, and stripping off all his garments he gave them to the poor man and dressed himself in his desired clothing and went to kneel before the altar of Our Lady. At times in this way, at other times standing, with his pilgrim's staff in his hand he spent the whole night. He left at daybreak so as not to be recognized. He did not take the road that led straight to Barcelona, where he would encounter many who would recognize and honour him, but he went off to a town called Manresa. There he decided to stay in a hospice a few days and also to note some things in his book that he carefully carried with him and by which he was greatly consoled. After he had gone about a league from Montserrat, a man who had been hurrying after him caught up to him and asked if he had given some clothing to a poor man, as the poor man said. Answering that he had, the tears ran

---

[5] A knight and hero of a prose romance which was very popular in sixteenth-century Spain.
[6] Jean Chanon, a French Benedictine, noted for his austere spirituality.

from his eyes in compassion for the poor man to whom he had given the clothes—in compassion, for he realized they were threatening him, thinking he had stolen them. Yet as much as he avoided esteem, he could not remain long in Manresa before people were saying great things, as the story of what happened at Montserrat spread. Eventually they said more than the truth, that he had given up much wealth and so forth.

Ignatius de Loyola, *Spiritual Exercises* (1522–1538)

Between 1522 and 1523 Ignatius Loyola lived an ascetic life at Manresa and began work on *The Spiritual Exercises*, which was completed in Paris in 1538. A revised version was approved by Pope Paul III in 1548. The Spanish original of this text is lost but there survives a manuscript copy with the author's corrections. The first printed edition appeared in 1548 (Rome). This programme of meditation with its structured, well ordered procedure for prayer, meditation and self-examination, had an enormous impact amongst sixteenth-century Catholics, with figures such as St Teresa of Ávila adopting them as part of their spiritual devotions.

The work begins with an explanation of the nature of the Spiritual Exercises:

1. The name 'Spiritual Exercises' means every form of examination of conscience, of meditation, contemplation, prayer (vocal and mental) and the spiritual activities mentioned later. Going for long or short walks and running are physical exercises; so we give the name of spiritual exercises to any process which makes the soul ready and able to rid itself of all irregular attachments, so that, once rid of them, it may look for and discover how God wills it to regulate its life to secure its salvation.

2. The person who gives another the method and outline for meditation or contemplation must faithfully recount the historical subject of such a contemplation or meditation, just running over the headings in a brief and summary explanation; the reason for this is that when the person making the contemplation is given the basic facts of the story and then goes over it and thinks about it for himself, any discovery he makes which sheds light on the story, or brings it home to him more, will give him greater delight and more benefit of soul. Such discoveries may be due to his own reflection or to the divine action, but they are better than if the giver of the exercises had gone into great detail and expounded at length the significance of the story. Nor does the soul's full satisfaction come from wide knowledge so much as from the personal appreciation of and feeling for things.

3. In all the following spiritual exercises we make acts of the understanding in reasoning and acts of the will in being moved to action; we must be careful to note that, in those acts of the will in which we hold converse (in word or thought) with our Lord God or His Saints, greater reverence is required of us than when we are employing our reasoning faculties.

4. Four weeks are assigned to the following exercises, corresponding with their four divisions: first, reflection on and contemplation of sins; second, the life of Christ our Lord, up to and including Palm Sunday; third, the sufferings of Christ our Lord; fourth, the Resurrection and Ascension, with three ways of Praying, as an appendix. But these four weeks are not to be understood as each consisting of seven or eight days. In the first week some may be slower to find what they want, namely contrition and tears of sorrow for

their sins, whilst some are more earnest, or more disturbed and tried by different spiritual influences: so sometimes the first week will have to be shortened, sometimes lengthened, and so with the following weeks, having in mind all the time what the given subject-matter is meant to effect. Still, the whole course should be completed in approximately thirty days.

5. The retreatant will benefit greatly if he starts with a largehearted generosity towards his Creator and Lord, surrendering to Him his freedom of will, so that His Divine Majesty may make that use of his person and possessions which is in accordance with His most holy will . . .

[A number of additional recommendations are made for the reader to follow out in the first week.]

82. (10) *Penance.* This is divided into interior and exterior penance. Interior penance means sorrow for one's sins, with a firm intention of not committing them or any others.

Exterior penance, which is the outcome of this interior penance, consists in inflicting punishment on ourselves for the sins we have committed. It is of three main kinds:

83. (a) The first kind concerns food. When we cut out what is excessive, this is temperance, not penance.

We do penance when we cut down what is normal. The more we do this, the greater and the better is the penance, provided that the constitution is not undermined and no obvious weakness ensues.

84. (b) The second kind concerns sleep. Here again, it is not penance to do away with anything excessively luxurious or soft. Penance consists in cutting down what is normal in our sleeping habits, and the more we cut down the better, provided the constitution is not undermined and no obvious weakness ensues. But we should not shorten our normal time for sleeping, unless perhaps to reach the mean, if we have got into a bad habit of sleeping too much.

85. (c) The third form is to chastise the body by inflicting actual pain on it. This is done by wearing hairshirts or cords or iron chains, by scourging or beating ourselves and by other kinds of harsh treatment.

86. (1) The safest and most suitable form of penance seems to be that which causes pain in the flesh but does not penetrate to the bones, that is, which causes suffering but not sickness. So the best way seems to be to scourge oneself with thin cords which hurt superficially, rather than to use some other means which might produce serious internal injury.

87. (2) The chief purpose in external penances is to produce three results:

(a) satisfaction for former sins;

(b) to overcome oneself, i.e. to subject the sensual nature to reason, and in general to ensure that all our lower appetites are under the control of our higher powers;

(c) to ask for and to obtain some favour or gift which one earnestly desires: for example, one may wish to have true sorrow for sins and to grieve over them; or over the pains and sorrows which Christ our Lord endured in His Passion, or to solve some doubt one is experiencing . . .

89. (4) When the retreatant has not yet found what he is looking for, e.g., grief, comfort, etc., it often helps if he makes some change in his penances, as regards sleep, food or other things. Thus we can modify our practice by doing penance for two or three days and then omitting it for two or three more, because it suits some to do more penance, others less. Moreover, we often leave off penance out of love of bodily comfort, judging wrongly that our constitution cannot stand it without serious illness; on the other hand, we sometimes go too far, thinking that the body can bear it. As our Lord God understands our nature infinitely better than we do, He very often enables each one, through these variations, to realize what best suits him.

90. (5) The particular examination of conscience is to be made to eliminate faults and slackness in the performance of the exercises and the additional practices. This applies also to the second and third weeks . . .
[On the fourth day of the second week the reader is advised to conduct a meditation on two standards:]

136. One is that of Christ our Lord, our Commander-in-Chief; the other that of Lucifer, our human nature's deadly enemy.
The usual preparatory prayer.

137. *First preliminary.* The story. Christ invites all men, desiring them to rally to His standard, whilst Lucifer, on the other side, invites them to join his.

138. *Second preliminary.* The picture. A great plain, comprising the entire Jerusalem district, where is the supreme Commander-in-Chief of the forces of good, Christ our Lord: another plain near Babylon, where Lucifer is, at the head of the enemy.

139. *Third preliminary.* Prayer for my special need. This time it is to ask for an understanding of the tricks of the wicked leader, and for help to guard against them: also for an understanding of the life of truth exemplified by our true Commander-in-Chief; also for grace to imitate Him.

140. *First heading.* Imagine that leader of all the enemy, in that great plain of Babylon, sitting on a sort of throne of smoking flame, a horrible and terrifying sight.

141. *Second heading.* Watch him calling together countless devils, to despatch them into different cities till the whole world is covered, forgetting no province or locality, no class or single individual.

142. *Third heading.* Study the harangue he makes to them, telling them to have their traps and fetters in position, tempting men first with eagerness for money (his usual procedure) as the easiest means to acquiring some worthless position in the world, and eventually to overweening pride. Notice the three steps, money, position, pride: from these three steps he leads men on to all other vices.

143. By contrast we must make a parallel application of the imagination to our true Commander-in-Chief, Christ our Lord.

144. *First heading.* Study the attitude of Christ our Lord in that great plain in the Jerusalem country, his unostentatious manner, his attractive and delightful appearance.

145. *Second heading.* Watch the Lord of the entire world choosing so many as apostles, disciples and so on, and sending them out through the whole world, sowing the seed of His sacred teaching in the hearts of men of every rank and condition.

146. *Third heading.* Study the sermon which Christ our Lord preaches to all who serve Him and are His friends, as He sends them out on this expedition. He exhorts them to make it their aim to help everybody, leading them first to perfect poverty in the spirit, and even to poverty in reality, if this be His Divine Majesty's pleasure and He should, of His graciousness, so choose them; then to want to be laughed at and looked down on. From these two comes humility. Notice the three steps: poverty, as against money: being laughed at and looked down on as against being looked up to by men of the world: humility, as against pride. From these three steps men can be led on to all the virtues.

147. *Colloquy.* One colloquy with our Lady, asking her to get me from her Son and Lord the favour of being admitted under His standard, at first in perfect poverty in the spirit, and then in real poverty, should this be His Divine Majesty's pleasure and He should, of His graciousness, so choose me; next, in putting up with being laughed at and treated unjustly, so that I may be more like Him—so long as I can have these to bear without sin on anybody's part and offence to the Divine Majesty. I will then say a Hail Mary.[7]

   Second colloquy. I will ask the Son too to get me the same favour from the Father. I will then say the Anima Christi.[8]

Third colloquy. I will ask the Father to give me the same favour and will say the Our Father.[9]

148. *Note.* This exercise is to be made at midnight and again in the early morning. Two repetitions of it should be made at the times for Mass and Vespers, always finishing with the three colloquies with our Lady, the Son and the Father . . .

[On the seventh day of the third week the reader is given a number of recommendations aimed at achieving self-control with regard to eating:]

210. (1) There is not much point in cutting down on bread, which is not a food about which the appetite is usually so irregular or temptation so strong as it is about other foods.

211. (2) There is more point in cutting down on drink than on bread. So one should look carefully to see what is beneficial and to be taken, and what is bad for one and to be given up.

212. (3) Food, other than bread, calls for greater and more perfect abstinence. For it is here that the appetite inclines to excess more easily and temptation is liable to be more violent. To avoid disorder, then, in food there are two ways of practising abstinence: one, by making a practice of eating plainer foods; two, delicacies, if eaten at all, should be taken in small amounts . . .

[The work concludes with a set of rules reminding the reader of the mind of the Church:]

352. The following rules are to be observed in order that we may hold the opinions we should hold in the Church militant.

353. (1) We should put away completely our own opinion and keep our minds ready and eager to give our entire obedience to our holy Mother the hierarchical Church, Christ our Lord's undoubted Spouse.

---

[7] A prayer to the Virgin Mary based on the salutations to Mary of the angel Gabriel at the Annunciation and of Elizabeth at the Visitation (Luke 1:28 and 42).

[8] The prayer, beginning 'Soul of Christ, sanctify me', used especially as a private Eucharistic devotion.

[9] The prayer taught by Jesus Christ to his disciples (Matthew 6: 9-13; Luke 11: 2-4).

354. (2) We should speak with approval of confession to a priest, of the reception of Holy Communion once a year, still more once a month, most of all once a week, the requisite conditions being duly fulfilled.

355. (3) We should openly approve of the frequent hearing of Mass, and also of hymns, psalms and lengthy prayers both inside and outside the church, as well as the set times for the divine office as a whole, for prayer in general and for all the canonical hours.

356. (4) We should speak with particular approval of religious orders, and the states of virginity and celibacy, not rating matrimony as high as any of these.

357. (5) We should express approval of the vows of religion, poverty, obedience, and chastity, as well as of vows to perform other counsels of perfection. It is to be noted that a vow concerns activities conducive to the perfection of the Gospels; hence a vow should not be taken in matters far removed from those activities, such as going into business or getting married, and so on.

358. (6) We should approve of relics of the saints, showing reverence for them and praying to the saints themselves; visits to Station churches, pilgrimages, indulgences, jubilees, Crusade bulls, the lighting of candles in churches should all be commended.

359. (7) We should approve of the laws of fasting and abstinence in Lent, on Ember Days, vigils, Fridays and Saturdays, as well as mortifications both interior and exterior.

360. (8) We should praise church decoration and architecture, as well as statues, which we should venerate in view of what they portray.

361. (9) Finally, all the Church's commandments should be spoken of favourably, our minds being always eager to find arguments in her defence, never in criticism.

362. (10) We should be more inclined to approve and speak well of the regulations and instructions as well as the personal conduct of our superiors. It may well be that these are not or have not been always praiseworthy; but to criticize them, whether in public utterances or in dealing with ordinary people, is likely to give rise to complaint and scandal rather than to do good. This would arouse popular hostility towards authority both temporal and spiritual. Of course, whilst it does harm to speak ill of superiors behind their backs in the hearing of ordinary people, it can do good to point out their failings to these superiors themselves, who can correct them.

363. (11) Theology, both positive and scholastic, should be praised by us; on the one hand, the positive doctors, like St Jerome, St Augustine and St Gregory, have the special gift of moving men's hearts to a general love and service of God our Lord; the scholastics, on the other hand, like St Thomas, St Bonaventure, the Master of the Sentences and the rest, have their special gift, which is rather to give precision to and clarify, in a way suited to our age, those truths which are necessary for eternal salvation. These scholastic doctors, being nearer to our own times, not only have the advantage of a correct understanding of the Sacred Scriptures and of the positive doctors and saints but, whilst being also enlightened and assisted themselves by the power of God, they have the further assistance of the Councils, Canons and decrees of our Holy Mother the Church.

364. (12) We must be careful not to institute comparisons between our present generation and the saints of former times, for this can be a source of great error. We should not, for example,

say: 'He knows more than St Augustine'; 'He is another St Francis or even greater'; 'He is another St Paul in goodness, holiness', etc.

365. (13) To arrive at complete certainty, this is the attitude of mind we should maintain: I will believe that the white object I see is black if that should be the decision of the hierarchical Church, for I believe that linking Christ our Lord the Bridegroom and His Bride the Church, there is one and the same Spirit, ruling and guiding us for our souls' good. For our Holy Mother the Church is guided and ruled by the same Spirit, the Lord who gave the Ten Commandments.

366. (14) Whilst it is absolutely true that no man can be saved without being predestined and without faith and grace, great care is called for in the way in which we talk and argue about all these matters.

367. (15) Nor should we make a habit of talking about predestination. If we have to talk about it to some extent on occasion, our language should be such as not to lead ordinary people astray, as can happen if a man says: 'It is already settled whether I am to be saved or damned; my good or bad conduct cannot make any difference.' So they lose heart and cease to bother about the activities which make for their souls' health and spiritual profit.

368. (16) Again we must be careful lest, by over-much emphasis in talking about faith, without the necessary qualifications and clarifications, we give occasion to people to become indifferent and lazy about what they do, either before or after the acquisition of faith informed by charity.

369. (17) Nor should we talk so much about grace and with such insistence on it as to give rise to the poisonous view that destroys freedom. Thus, with the help of God, we should take every opportunity of talking about faith and grace, having in view the greater praise of His Divine Majesty; but our language and way of speaking should not be such that the value of our activities and the reality of human freedom might be in any way impaired or disregarded, especially in times like these which are full of dangers.

370. (18) It is of course true that we must esteem above all else the entire service of God out of sheer love; yet we should often speak in praise of the fear of His Divine Majesty. Not only is a childlike fear a good and holy attitude; so also is the fear proper to servants, which helps greatly to get men out of mortal sin when they are not capable of rising to the better and more effective form of love. Once they have got rid of mortal sin they can more easily rise to the childlike fear which is wholly acceptable and pleasing to God our Lord, since it is in accordance with His own love.

Teresa of Ávila

(1515–1582)

TERESA OF ÁVILA (1515–82) was one of the great mystics of the Catholic Church and originator of the Carmelite reform order. The autobiographical *Life* which conveys her remarkable personality so well and provides an insight into her moral and spiritual values, was dictated to her confessor and edited for publication by Luis de León. It was first published in 1611.

St Teresa of Ávila, Life (1565)

Now to speak of those who are beginning to be the servants of love—for this, I think, is what we become when we decide to follow along the way of prayer Him who loved us so greatly. It is so high an honour that even the thought of it brings a strange joy. Servile fear vanishes immediately, if we act as we should in this first stage . . . For the perfect possession of this true love of God brings all blessings with it. We are so niggardly and so slow to give ourselves entirely to God that we do not prepare ourselves to secure that precious thing, which His Majesty does not wish us to enjoy if we have not paid a high price first . . .

We resolve to be poor, and that is a great merit. But very often we resume our precautions and take care not to be short of necessities, also of superfluities, and even to collect friends who will supply us. In this way we take greater pains and, perhaps, expose ourselves to greater danger in our anxiety not to go short than we did before, when we had possession of our estates. Presumably we also gave up all thought of our own importance when we became nuns, or when we began to lead a spiritual life and to pursue perfection. Yet the moment our self-importance is wounded we forget that we have given ourselves to God. We want to snatch it up and tear it out of His very hands, as they say, even after we have, to all appearances, made Him lord over our will. And it is the same with everything else.

That is a fine way of seeking God's love! We expect it by the handful, as they say, and yet we want to keep our affections for ourselves! We make no attempt to carry our desires into effect, and fail to raise them above the earth, and yet we want great spiritual comforts. This is not good, for the two aims are, as I see it, irreconcilable. So, since we do not manage wholly to give ourselves up, we never receive the whole of this treasure. May it please the Lord to give it us drop by drop, even though receiving it may cost us all the labours in the world . . .

Here I shall have to make use of a comparison though, being a woman and writing only what I have been commanded to write, I should like to avoid it. But this spiritual language is so difficult to use for those like myself who have no learning, that I must find some other means of expression. It may be that my comparisons will not very often be effective, in which case your Reverence will be amused at my stupidity. It strikes me that I have read or heard this one before. But as I have a bad memory I do not know where it occurred or what it illustrated. But for the present it will serve my purpose.

A beginner must look on himself as one setting out to make a garden for his Lord's pleasure, on most unfruitful soil which abounds in weeds. His Majesty roots up the weeds and will put in good plants instead. Let us reckon that this is already done when a soul decides to practise prayer and has begun to do so. We have then, as good gardeners, with God's help to make these plants grow, and to water them carefully so that they do not die, but produce flowers, which give out a good smell, to delight this Lord of ours. Then He will often come to take His pleasure in this garden and enjoy these virtues.

Now let us see how this garden is to be watered, so that we may understand what we have to do, and what labour it will cost us, also whether the gain will outweigh the effort, or how long it will take. It seems to me that the garden may be watered in four different ways. Either the water must be drawn from a well, which is very laborious; or by a water-wheel and buckets, worked by a windlass—I have sometimes drawn it in this way, which is less laborious than the other, and brings up more water—or from a stream or spring, which waters the ground much better, for the soil then retains more moisture and needs watering less often, which entails far less work for the gardener; or by heavy rain, when the Lord waters it Himself without any labour of ours; and this is an incomparably better method than all the rest.

Now to apply these four methods of watering, by which this garden is to be maintained and without which it will fail. This is my purpose, and will, I think, enable me to explain something about the four stages of prayer, to which the Lord has, in His kindness, sometimes raised my soul. May he graciously grant that I may speak in such a way as to be of use to one of the persons who commanded me to write this,[1] whom the Lord has advanced in four months far beyond the point that I have reached in seventeen years. He prepared himself better than I, and therefore, without any labour on his part, his garden is watered by all these four means; although it only receives the last water drop by drop. But, as things are going, with the Lord's help, his garden will soon be submerged. If my way of explaining all this seems crazy to him, he is welcome to laugh at me.

We may say that beginners in prayer are those who draw the water up out of the well; which is a great labour, as I have said. For they find it very tiring to keep the senses recollected, when they are used to a life of distraction. Beginners have to accustom themselves to pay no attention to what they see or hear, and to put this exercise into practice during their hours of prayer, when they must remain in solitude, thinking whilst they are alone of their past life. Although all must do this many times, the advanced as well as the beginners, all need not do so equally, as I shall explain later. At first they are distressed because they are not sure that they regret their sins. Yet clearly they do, since they have now sincerely resolved to serve God. They should endeavour to meditate on the life of Christ, and thus the intellect will grow tired. Up to this point we can advance ourselves, though with God's help of course, for without it, as everyone knows, we cannot think one good thought.

This is what I mean by beginning to draw water from the well—and God grant there may be water in it! But at least this does not depend on us, who have only to draw it up and do what we can to water the flowers. But God is so good that when for reasons known to His Majesty—and perhaps for our greater profit—He wishes the well to be dry, we, like good gardeners, must do what we can ourselves. Meanwhile He preserves the flowers without water, and in this way He makes our virtues grow. Here by water I mean tears, or if there be none, a tenderness and inward feeling of devotion. But what shall a man do here who finds that for many days on end he feels nothing but dryness, dislike, distaste and so little desire to go and draw water that he would give it up altogether if he did

---

[1] Father Pedro Ibañez.

not remember that he is pleasing and serving the Lord of the garden; if he did not want all his service to be in vain, and if he did not also hope to gain something for all the labour of lowering the bucket so often into the well and bringing it up empty? It will often happen that he cannot so much as raise his arms to the task, or think a single good thought. For by this drawing of water I mean, of course, working with the understanding . . .

It is of especial note—and I say this because I know it from experience—that the soul which begins resolutely to tread this path of mental prayer, and can manage not greatly to care about consolations and tenderness in devotion, neither rejoicing when the Lord gives them nor being discouraged when He withholds them, has already gone a large part of the way. Though it may often stumble, it need have no fear of falling back, for its building has been begun on firm foundations. The love of the Lord does not consist in tears or in these consolations and tendernesses which we so much desire and in which we find comfort, but in our serving Him in justice, fortitude, and humility. Anything else seems to me rather an act of receiving than of giving on our part.

As for a poor woman like myself, a weak and irresolute creature, it seems right that the Lord should lead me on with favours, as He now does, in order that I may bear certain afflictions with which He has been pleased to burden me. But when I hear servants of God, men of weight, learning, and under-standing, worrying so much because He is not giving them devotion, it makes me sick to listen to them. I do not say that they should not accept it if God grants it to them, and value it too, for then His Majesty will see that it was good for them, but they should not be distressed when they do not receive it. They should realize that since the Lord does not give it to them they do not need it. They should exercise control over themselves and go right ahead. Let them take it from me that all this fuss is a mistake, as I have myself seen and proved. It is an imperfection in them; they are not advancing in freedom of spirit but hanging back through weakness . . .

I repeat my warning that it is most important not to raise the spirit if the Lord does not raise it for us; and if He does, we know it immediately. This straining is especially harmful to women, because the devil can delude them. I am quite certain, however, that the Lord will never allow anyone to be harmed who endeavours to approach Him with humility. On the contrary, such a person will derive great gain and advantage from the attack by which Satan intended to destroy him.

I have dwelt for so long on this way of prayer because it is the commonest with beginners and because the advice I offer is very important. I admit that it has been better expressed by others in other places, and that I have felt some shame and confusion in writing this, though not enough. Blessed be the Lord for it all, whose will and pleasure it is that a woman like myself should speak of things that are His, and of such a sublime nature . . .

I wish that I could explain, with God's help, the difference between union and rapture, or eleva-tion, or flight of the spirit or transport—for they are all one. I mean that these are all different names for the same thing, which is also called ecstasy. It is much more beneficial than union, its results are much greater, and it has very many other effects as well. Union seems to be the same at the begin-ning, the middle, and the end, and is altogether inward. But the ends of rapture are of a much higher nature, and their effects are both inward and outward . . .

In these raptures, the soul no longer seems to animate the body; its natural heat therefore is felt to diminish and it gradually gets cold, though with a feeling of very great joy and sweetness. Here there is no possibility of resisting, as there is in union, in which we are on our own ground. Against union, resistance is almost always possible though it costs pain and effort. But rapture is, as a rule, irresistible. Before you can be warned by a thought or help yourself in any way, it comes as a quick and violent shock; you see and feel this cloud, or this powerful eagle rising and bearing you up on its wings.

You realize, I repeat, and indeed see that you are being carried away you know not where. For although this is delightful, the weakness of our nature makes us afraid at first, and we need a much more determined and courageous spirit than for the previous stages of prayer. Come what may, we must risk everything and leave ourselves in God's hands. We have to go willingly wherever we are carried, for in fact, we are being borne off whether we like it or not. In this emergency very often I should like to resist, and I exert all my strength to do so, especially at such times as I am in a public place, and very often when I am in private also, because I am afraid of delusions. Sometimes with a great struggle I have been able to do something against it. But it has been like fighting a great giant, and has left me utterly exhausted. At other times resistance has been impossible; my soul has been carried away, and usually my head as well, without my being able to prevent it; and sometimes it has affected my whole body, which has been lifted from the ground.

This has only happened rarely. Once, however, it took place when we were all together in the choir, and I was on my knees, about to take Communion. This distressed me very much, for it seemed a most extraordinary thing and likely to arouse considerable talk. So I ordered the nuns—for it happened after I was made prioress—not to speak of it. On other occasions, when I felt that the Lord was about to enrapture me again, and once in particular during a sermon—it was our patron's feast and some great ladies were present—I lay on the ground and the sisters came to hold me down, but all the same the rapture was observed. Then I earnestly beseeched the Lord to grant me no more favours if they must have outward and visible signs. For worries on this score exhausted me, and whenever He gave me these raptures I was observed. It seems that, of His goodness, He has been pleased to hear me. For I have never had them since, although it is true that this was not long ago.

It seemed to me when I tried to resist that a great force, for which I can find no comparison, was lifting me up from beneath my feet. It came with greater violence than any other spiritual experience, and left me quite shattered. Resistance requires a great struggle, and is of little use in the end when the Lord wills otherwise, for there is no power than can resist His power.

What power the soul has when the Lord raises it to a height from which it looks down on everything and is not enmeshed in it! How ashamed it is of the time when it was so enmeshed! It is indeed amazed at its own blindness, and feels pity for those who are still blind, especially if they are men of prayer to whom God is granting consolations. It longs to cry aloud and call their attention to their delusions; and sometimes it actually does so, only to bring down a storm of persecutions on its head. Particularly if the person in question is a woman, it is accused of lacking humility, and of wishing to teach those from whom it should learn. So they condemn it, and not without reason, for they know nothing of the force that impels it. At times it cannot help itself, or refrain from enlightening those whom it loves and wishes to see freed from the prison of this life. For the state in which it has once been living is neither more nor less than a prison, and this it realizes.

The soul is weary of the time when it was concerned with points of honour, and of the delusion which led it to believe that what the world calls by that name is honour at all. It sees that this is just a great lie, and that we are all taken in by it. It understands that true honour is not illusory but real; that it esteems what has value, and despises what has none. For all transitory things are as nothing or less than nothing, and are displeasing to God. The soul laughs at itself when it thinks of the time when it valued money and desired it; though, for myself, I really do not think that I ever had to confess to being covetous. It was quite bad enough that I should have given any thought to money at all. If the blessing that I now see within me could be bought with money I should set great store by it. But I know that it can only be gained by abandoning everything . . .

Whenever the Lord told me in prayer to do one thing and my confessor said something else, the Lord would speak again and tell me to obey him. Then His Majesty would change that confessor's mind, so that he would come back and tell me to do the opposite. When a number of books in Spanish were taken away from us, and we were told not to read them,[2] I felt it deeply because some of them gave me recreation and I could not go on reading them, since now I only had them in Latin. Then the Lord said to me: 'Do not be distressed, for I will give you a living book.' I could not understand why this had been said to me, for I had not yet had visions. But a very few days afterwards I understood perfectly. What I saw before me gave me so much to think about and so many subjects for recollection, and the Lord showed me such love and taught me in so many ways, that I have had very little or no need of books since. His Majesty has been a veritable book in which I have read the truth. Blessed be this book, which imprints on our minds in an unforgettable way what we must read and do . . .

What a grand illustration God has just taken from us in the shape of the blessed friar, Peter of Alcántara. The world is not yet fit to bear such perfection. They say that people's health is poorer nowadays, and that times are not what they were. But this holy person was a man of our day, and yet he had as robust a spirit as those of the olden times, and so he trampled on the world. Now although everyone does not go about barefoot or perform such severe penances as he did, there are many ways, as I have said elsewhere, of treading the world underfoot, and the Lord teaches them to those in whom He sees courage. And what great courage His Majesty gave to this holy man, that he could perform, as is common knowledge, such severe penances for forty-six years. I should like to say something about this, for I know that it is all true.

He spoke of it to me, and to another person from whom he concealed very little. In me he confided out of love, for the Lord was pleased that he should feel love for me, and should stand up for me, and encourage me at a time when I was in great need. This I have spoken of and shall speak of again. He said, I think, that for forty years he had never slept more than an hour and a half between nightfall and morning, and that at the beginning the hardest part of his penance had been the conquering of sleep. For this reason he always remained standing or on his knees. Such sleep as he had, he took sitting down, with his head propped against a piece of wood, which he had fixed to the wall. He could not lie down to sleep even if he wished to, for his cell, as is well known, was only four and a half feet long. During all those years, however hot the sun or heavy the rain, he never wore his hood or anything on his feet. He was always clothed in a sackcloth habit with nothing between it and his skin; and this he wore as tight as he could bear it, with a cloak of the same material over it. He told me that in the bitterest cold he would take off his cloak and leave the door and window of his cell open, so as to gain some physical relief afterwards from the increased warmth, when he put it on again and closed the door. He usually ate only once in three days, and he wondered why this surprised me. He said that it was perfectly possible once one got used to it, and a companion of his told me that sometimes he would go eight days without food. This must have been when he was at prayer, for he used to have great raptures and transports of love for God, of which I was once a witness.

His poverty was extreme, and so, even in his youth, was his mortification. He told me that he had lived for three years in a house of his Order, and had not known a single friar except by his voice.

---

[2] By decree of the Inquisition, 1559

For he never raised his eyes, and so when he had to go to any part of the house, he could only do so by following the other friars; it was the same thing out of doors. For many years he had never looked at a woman. He told me that it was all one to him whether he looked at things or not; but he was very old when I came to know him, and so extremely thin that he looked like nothing more than a knotted root. With all his holiness, he was very courteous, though he used very few words except when answering questions. Then he was a delight, for he had a very lively intelligence. There are many other things about him that I should like to say, but I am afraid that your Reverence will ask me what this has to do with me—I have been afraid of that even as I have been writing. So I will stop here, adding only that he died as he had lived, preaching and admonishing his friars. As he saw that his end was approaching, he recited the psalm, *I was glad when they said unto me*.[3] Then he fell on his knees and died . . .

One day when I was at prayer, I found myself, without knowing how, plunged, as I thought, into hell. I understood that the Lord wished me to see the place that the devils had ready for me there, and that I had earned by my sins. All this happened in the briefest second; but even if I should live for many years, I do not think I could possibly forget it. The entrance seemed to me like a very long, narrow passage, or a very low, dark, and constricted furnace. The ground appeared to be covered with a filthy wet mud, which smelt abominably and contained many wicked reptiles. At the end was a cavity scooped out of the wall, like a cupboard, and I found myself closely confined in it. But the sight of all this was pleasant compared with my feelings. There is no exaggeration in what I am saying.

I do not think that my feelings could possibly be exaggerated, nor would anyone understand them. I felt a fire inside my soul, the nature of which is beyond my powers of description, and my physical tortures were intolerable. I have endured the severest bodily pains in the course of my life, the worst, so the doctors say, that it is possible to suffer and live, among them the contraction of my nerves during my paralysis, and many other agonies of various kinds, including some, as I have said, caused by the devil. But none of them was in any way comparable to the pains I felt at that time, especially when I realized that they would be endless and unceasing. But even this was nothing to my agony of soul, an oppression, a suffocation, and an affliction so agonizing, and accompanied by such a hopeless and distressing misery that no words I could find would adequately describe it. To say that it was as if my soul were being continuously torn from my body is an nothing. The fact is that I can find no means of describing that inward fire and that despair which is greater than the severest torments or pains. I could not see my torturer, but I seemed to feel myself being burnt and dismembered; and, I repeat, that interior fire and despair were the very worst of all.

In that pestilential spot, deprived of all hope of comfort, it was impossible for me to sit or lie down; there was no room to do so. I had been put in what seemed a hole in the wall, and the very walls, which are hideous to behold, pressed in on me and completely stifled me. There is no light there, only the deepest darkness. Yet, although there was no light, it was possible to see everything that brings pain to the sight; I do not know how this can be. It was not the Lord's will that I should at that time see more of hell itself; since then I have seen another vision of frightful things that are the punishment for certain vices. But although these seemed to me a much more dreadful sight, yet they alarmed me less, for then I felt no physical pain. In the first vision, however, it was the Lord's will that I really should feel these torments and afflictions of spirit, just as if my body were

---

[3] Psalm 122: 1.

actually suffering them. I do not know how it was, but I quite clearly realized that this was a great favour, and that the Lord wished me to see with my very eyes the place from which His mercy had delivered me . . . I was terrified, and though this happened six years ago, I am still terrified as I write; even as I sit here my natural heat seems to be drained away by fear. I can think of no time of trial or torture when everything that we can suffer on earth has not seemed to me trifling in comparison with this . . .

It was this vision that filled me with the very deep distress which I feel on account of the great number of souls who bring damnation on themselves—of the Lutherans in particular, since they were members of the Church by baptism. It has also given me a fervent desire to help other souls . . .

I tried to think what I could do for God, and decided that the first thing was to follow the call to a religious life that the Lord had given me, by keeping my Rule with every possible perfection. Although in the house where I was there were many servants of God and He was well served there, yet, because it was very poor, we nuns often left it for other places where we could live decently and keep our vows. Moreover the Rule was not observed there in its original strictness but, as throughout the Order, in the relaxed form permitted by the Bull of Mitigation. There were other drawbacks too, among them what seemed to me the excessive comfort that we enjoyed, for the house was a large and pleasant one. Now this habit of going on visits, though I was one who frequently indulged in it, was a serious inconvenience to me, because many people whom my superiors could not refuse liked to have me with them, and when I was invited they ordered me to go. Things reached such a pitch, indeed, that I was able to be in the convent very little; the devil must have had a hand in these frequent departures of mine, though at the same time I would always pass on to some of the nuns what I learnt from the people I met, and this was of great benefit to them.

One day, in conversation with myself and one or two other nuns, a certain person[4] asked whether we were prepared to follow the practice of the Barefoot Orders, for it would be quite possible to found a convent of Discalced nuns.[5] I had desired something of the sort myself, and so I discussed the idea with a companion who was of the same mind, that widowed lady whom I have already mentioned. She began to think out ways of finding the necessary revenue. But, as I can see now, this would not have got us very far. For my part, however, I was very happy in the house where I was. The place was pleasing to me, and so was my cell, which suited me excellently; and this held me back. Nevertheless we agreed to commend the matter most fervently to God.

One day, after Communion, the Lord earnestly commanded me to pursue this aim with all my strength. He made me great promises; that the house would not fail to be established, that great service would be done Him there, that its name should be St Joseph's; that He would watch over us at one of its doors and Our Lady at the other; that Christ would be with us; that the convent would be a star, and that it would shed the most brilliant light . . . He told me to convey His orders to my confessor,[6] With the request that he should not oppose them or in any way hinder my carrying them out . . . So I dared not do otherwise than speak to my confessor and give him a written account of all that had taken place.

---

[4] María de Ocampo, the daughter of Teresa's cousin.

[5] The order that St Teresa founded within the Carmelite Order was called the Discalced Carmelites in contrast to the Calced Carmelites, who followed a more relaxed discipline. 'Discalced' was the name traditionally given to those religious orders and congregations whose members either went barefoot or wore sandals rather than shoes as a sign of their commitment to observe a degree of asceticism.

[6] Father Balthasar Alvarez.

He did not venture definitely to tell me to abandon the project, though he saw that, humanly speaking, there was no way of carrying it out, since my companion who was to undertake it all had very small resources—indeed almost none. He told me to discuss the matter with my director, and to do as he advised me. I did not discuss these visions of mine with my director, but the lady who wanted to found the convent had a talk with him, and the Provincial,[7] who is a friend of the religious Orders, took the idea very well. He offered her all the necessary support, and told her that he would give the house his sanction. They discussed what income it would require, and for many reasons we decided that it must never contain more than thirteen nuns. Before we began these discussions, we had written to the blessed friar Peter of Alcántara, and told him all that was happening. He advised us to stick to our plans, and gave us his opinion on the whole subject.

Hardly had news of this begun to spread around the place than there fell upon us a persecution so severe that it would not be possible to describe it in a few words. They talked, they laughed at us, and they declared that the idea was absurd. Of me they said that I was in the right place where I was, and they subjected my companion to such a persecution that it quite wore her out. I did not know what to do, for they seemed to me partly right . . . There was hardly anyone among the prayerful, or indeed in the whole place, who was not against us, and did not consider our project absolutely absurd.

There was so much chatter and fuss in my own convent that the Provincial thought it would be difficult to oppose everybody, and so changed his mind. He now withdrew his backing, saying that the income was not assured, that in any case it would be insufficient, and that the plan was meeting with heavy opposition. In all this he seemed to be right. So he put the matter aside and refused to sanction it . . .

As the Provincial now refused to sanction the foundation, my confessor at once told me to let it drop, though the Lord knows what great labours and afflictions it had cost me to bring it so far. Once it was discontinued and abandoned, people were even more certain that it had all been an absurd feminine whimsy, and gossip at my expense increased, even though up to that time I had been acting on my Provincial's orders.

I was very unpopular throughout the convent for wanting to found a more strictly enclosed house. The nuns said that this was an insult to them; that I could serve God just as well where I was, since there were others there better than myself; that I had no love for my own house, and that I should have been better employed raising money for it than for founding another. Some said that I ought to be put in the prison-cell; but others, though only a few, came out on my side. I saw quite well that in many respects my opponents were right, and sometimes I could make allowances for them. But as I could not tell them my principal argument—that I had been obeying the Lord's commands—I did not know what to do and was therefore silent . . . It seemed to me that I had done everything in my power to fulfil the Lord's commands, and that I had now no further obligation. So I remained in my house, where I was quite content and happy, though at the same time I was never able to give up the conviction that the task would be fulfilled. How, when, and by what means this would be I could not say, but of its eventual accomplishment I was certain.

What greatly distressed me was that my confessor wrote to me on one occasion as if I had been acting against his instructions . . . In his letter he said that, as I ought to have realized by now, the whole matter was just a dream. He advised me henceforth to lead a better life, and not to attempt anything

---

[7] Father Nicolás de Jesús María Doria, head of the unreformed Carmelite Order in Spain.

more of the kind or even to talk about it, since I now saw what a scandal I had raised. He said some other things too, all of them most painful. This distressed me more than everything else put together, for I wondered whether I had been guilty of leading others into sin, whether these visions were illusory, whether all my prayer had been a deception, and whether I was not utterly lost and deceived. These thoughts so weighed on me that I became quite upset and was plunged into the deepest affliction . . .

For five or six months I kept quiet, making no move towards it and not even speaking about it, and the Lord did not give me a single command. I could not guess the reason for this, but was unable to rid myself of the belief that the foundation would eventually take place. At the end of that time, the then Rector of the Society of Jesus having left, His Majesty replaced him by a very spiritual man of great courage, understanding, and learning,[8] just at the moment when I was in the greatest need. For the priest who was hearing my confessions was subject to a superior, and in the Company they attach great importance to the practice of never taking the slightest action except in conformity with the will of their superiors . . .

I went to see this Rector, and my confessor told me to talk to him with all freedom and frankness. I used very much to dislike speaking about these things, and yet when I entered the confessional I felt something in my spirit that I never remember having felt before or since in the presence of anyone else. I cannot possibly describe its nature, or compare it with anything at all. It was a spiritual joy; my soul recognized that here was a soul which would understand and be in harmony with mine . . . When I began to have conversations with him, I immediately recognized what type of director he was, and saw that he had a pure and holy soul, endowed with a special gift from the Lord for the discernment of spirits. This gave me great comfort. Soon after I came under his direction, the Lord began to impress on me again that I must return to the project of the convent, and explain all my reasons and intentions to my confessor, and to the Rector as well, so that they should not stand in my way. Some of the things I said frightened them, but the Rector never doubted that I was prompted by the spirit of God, for he had considered the probable results of such a foundation with very great care. In short, after hearing my many arguments, they dared not risk standing in my way.

My confessor now gave me leave to resume the project with all my might, and I clearly saw what a task I was taking on, for I was quite alone and could do very little. We agreed that things should be done with the utmost secrecy, and so I arranged that a sister of mine,[9] who lived outside the town, should buy the necessary house and furnish it as if it were for herself, with purchase money that the Lord had provided in various ways. It would be a long story to tell how He looked after us. I made a great point of doing nothing to violate my obedience. But I knew that if I spoke of the project to my superiors all would be lost, as it had been on the last occasion; and this time things might be even worse. Getting the money, finding a house, arranging for its purchase and furnishing it was a very trying process, a part of which I had to carry through alone . . .

Once when I was in a difficulty and could not think what to do or how to pay certain workmen, St Joseph, my true lord and father, appeared to me, and told me to proceed with my arrangements, for the money would not be lacking. So I went on, without a farthing, and the Lord did provide it in ways that astonished all who heard of them. I thought the house very small, so small indeed that it did not seem possible to turn it into a convent. I wanted to buy another, but had not the means. So there was no way of buying it, and I did not know what to do. There was a

8 The Jesuit Father Gaspar de Salazar.
9 Doña Juana, St Teresa's married sister.

little house close to ours, however, also very small, which would have made a chapel. But one day, after I had taken Communion, the Lord said to me, 'I have told you already to move in as best you can', and then added, as a sort of exclamation, 'O the greed of humankind, to imagine that there will not be enough room for you! How often did I sleep in the open air, having nowhere else to lay My head!' I was amazed, and saw that He was right. So I went to survey the little house and found that it would just do for a convent, though a very small one. I did no more about adding to the property, but arranged to have the little house equipped so that we could live in it. It was very rough and ready, and no more was done to it than was necessary to make it healthy to live in. This is always the proper way of doing things.

On St Clare's day, as I was going to Communion, that saint appeared to me in great beauty and told me to take courage. She promised that she would help me if I went forward with what I had begun. I conceived a great devotion for her, and she has truly kept her word. For a convent of her Order, which is close to ours, is at present helping to maintain us. What is more, she has gradually brought this plan of mine to such perfection that the same Rule of poverty which obtains in her house is also observed in ours, and we live on alms. It was essential to get the Holy Father's approval for our existing without any revenue, and the procuring of that cost me no small labour. But the Lord is doing even greater things for us, and it may be at the request of this blessed saint that He is doing them. Without any demand on our part, His Majesty is providing most amply for our needs. May He be blessed for it all. Amen . . .

O how great God is! I am often astounded when I reflect on this, and think how particularly anxious His Majesty was to help me deal with the business of this little corner of God's kingdom—for such I think it is—or of this dwelling in which His Majesty takes His delight, as He once told me in prayer, when He spoke of this house as the paradise of His delight. So it seems that His Majesty has chosen the souls he has drawn to Himself, in whose company I live in very deep shame. For I could never have asked for better companions with whom to live this life of strict enclosure, poverty, and prayer. They live it so joyfully and contentedly that not one of them thinks herself deserving of her place in this house; and this is especially true of some whom the Lord has called from all the show and vanity of the world, whose customs they might have followed and in which they might have been happy. But here the Lord has so multiplied their happiness that, as they clearly recognize, in exchange for one thing forsaken He has rewarded them a hundredfold, and they can never give His Majesty enough thanks. Others who were good, He has made better. To those who are young He gives fortitude and knowledge, so that they may desire nothing else and understand that to live apart from all the things of this life is to live in greater peace, even here upon earth. To those who are older and poor in health, He has given—and continues to give—strength to endure the same austerities and penances as the rest . . .

When everything had been arranged, the Lord was pleased that some of the sisters should take the habit on St Bartholomew's Day, and on that day too the Most Holy Sacrament was brought to the convent. So with full sanction and authority, this convent of our most glorious father St Joseph was founded in the year 1562. I was there myself to give the habit, with two other nuns of our own house who happened to be absent from it. As the house which thus became a convent belonged to my brother-in-law—for as I have said, it was he who purchased it in order to keep things secret—my special permission allowed me to be there. I did nothing without the approval of some learned men, so as in no way to infringe my obedience. But as they saw what a benefit this was in so many ways to the whole Order, they told me to follow my wishes, even though everything was being done in secret and was being kept from my superiors' knowledge. Had they pointed to a single imperfection in all this, I would, I believe, have willingly given up a thousand convents, let alone one. I am certain of this; for although I desired the foundation to be made in order to withdraw more completely from activities and to fulfil my profession and vocation more perfectly under conditions of greater enclosure, I desired it only in so far as I believed the Lord would not be better served by my abandoning it. If I had thought that He would, I should have given it up with complete peace and tranquillity, as I had done before.

Well, it was like heaven to me to see the Blessed Sacrament in its place, and for us to be supporting four poor orphans, who were taken without dowry and were great servants of God. It was our aim from the beginning to accept only persons whose examples would be a basis on which we could effectively develop our scheme for a community of great perfection and true prayer, and perform a work which I believed would be for God's service, and would honour the habit of His glorious Mother. This is what I yearned for. But I was greatly comforted also, to have done what the Lord had so firmly commanded me, and that there was now one more church in the town than there had been, dedicated to my glorious father, St Joseph.

Sources

The Autobiography of Saint Ignatius Loyola, translated by J. O'Callaghan and edited by J. C. Olin (New York: Harper Torch Books, 1974), pp. 21–32 abridged.

Source: The Spiritual Exercises of Saint Ignatius, translated by T. Corbishley, SJ (Wheathampstead: A. Clarke, 1973), pp. 12–124 abridged.

The Life of Saint Teresa of Ávila, translated by J. M. Cohen (Harmondsworth: Penguin Books, 1957), pp. 76–267 abridged.

Tycho Brahe

(1546–1601)

<hr>

Although born into a distinguished, noble family, Tycho Brahe spurned a career in government that would probably have elevated him to the ruling Council of the Kingdoms of Denmark and Norway. Instead, he decided to become an astronomer—an unusual choice for a man of his social standing. After studying at the University of Copenhagen from 1559 to 1562, he polished his education by residing at Leipzig, Rostock, Wittenberg, Basel, and Augsburg for nearly a decade. Encouraged by the powerful Peter Oxe (the virtual ruler of Denmark during Tycho's youth and brother of Tycho's foster mother), Tycho published a treatise he had written on the new star of 1572. Upon the request of aristocratic students at the University of Copenhagen, he presented a series of lectures on planetary theory during the winter of 1574–5. In recognition of such unusual talents, King Frederick started in 1576 to endow the young nobleman with a series of fiefs and other livings, including the island of Hven across the Sound from Copenhagen where Tycho erected his observatory. In return, Tycho "served as a sort of royal consultant on astronomical and astrological matters, compiled a horoscope upon the birth of each royal son, replied to royal inquiries like the one of 1578 concerning rumors that another new star had appeared, and he apparently supplied the royal family with an almanac or prognostication in manuscript annually. He also fabricated and repaired instruments for the crown, worked on various cartographic and iconographic projects, and supplied Queen Sophie with alchemical equipment."[1] Such relatively light duties for such substantial support left Tycho free to devote a great deal of time to his own research. With instruments of his own design and with the help of learned assistants, Tycho systematically mapped the heavens with an accuracy hitherto unattained and which would remain unsurpassed until the development of accurate telescopes nearly a century later. His mature world system combined most of the mathematical advantages of the solar system proposed by Copernicus with a geostatic model of the universe; it remained the chief rival to heliocentric systems well into the late seventeenth century.

Europeans of the sixteenth century inherited a sophisticated verbal and mathematical explanation of nature from the philosophers and mathematicians of the ancient world. Early Greek thinkers, such as Pythagoras (who argued that mathematics explained all reality), Aristotle (who produced non-mathematical, descriptive treatises on physics and biology), and Euclid (who worked out a system of geometry), to name only a few, laid the foundations for a comprehensive explanation of nature, one taught at such educational institutions as Plato's Academy or Aristotle's Lyceum. Despite the differences between the Pythagorean/Platonic stress upon mathematics and the Aristotelian emphasis on verbal description, natural philosophers blended the two traditions to produce a relatively coherent, consistent view of the universe. This synthesis culminated with the work of Ptolemy in the second century A.D. Thereafter, until the late sixteenth century, the Ptolemaic model dominated European astronomy.

<hr>

[1] J.R. Christianson, "Tycho Brahe's German Treatise on the Comet of 1577: A Study in Science and Politics," *Isis*, 70 (1979), p. 118; see pp. 110–32 for a complex introduction to the context of this treatise.

Reflecting the mentality of the ancient world, the conventional learned cosmology of the middle ages and renaissance divided the universe into two qualitatively different realms, hierarchically related to each other. The fixed stars, wandering stars (planets), sun, and moon made up the superior heavenly or celestial realm, a region of being, immutability, and perfection. The lower, inferior realm encompassed all of the region below the moon and included the earth. Unsettling change—birth, death, generation, and decay—characterized this imperfect region of becoming. Following the evidence of the senses, natural philosophers argued that the earth stood motionless at the center of the universe while the entire system of the heavens revolved around it daily. Different sorts of substance made up the matter of these two regions.

Four elements, qualitatively arranged in a hierarchy according to the degree of their fineness: fire, air, water, and earth, formed all matter in the inferior Sublunary realm. All physical objects in this region consisted of a mixture of these four elements; the degree and proportion of the mixture determined the character of any given object. The element fire, for example, possessed the character of lightness (levity), moved quickly, and naturally rose towards the heavens when dominant or unmixed. Applied to objects concocted primarily of other elements, fire increased the fineness of the mixture and often changed the nature of the object, causing earthy objects to become watery (to melt), watery materials to become airy (to evaporate), and air to take on fiery qualities (to rise and expand). At the other extreme, coarseness characterized the element earth which had a heavy property (gravity), moved sluggishly, and—when not overly mixed with other elements—sank towards the center of the universe where it rested. According to this view, fiery objects naturally rose to the edges of the sublunary region and earthy objects naturally sought a place of rest at the center of the universe. Any motion of a heavy object, such as a ball of lead, away from the earth was violent and unnatural; hence, such a ball when thrown vertically or shot horizontally into the air naturally returned to the surface of the earth. Just as naturally, it sank when placed in the lighter, finer element of water. Natural motion, then, took place when an object sought a position corresponding to the mixture of elements which characterized its substance. Unnatural or violent motion happened only when external forces operated upon an object and removed it from its natural place; the latter continued only so long as such forces remained dominant. Because of the very different characters of fire, air, water, and earth, objects made of these elements naturally changed. Hence, the generation and decay of the sublunar region of becoming where such unstable mixtures dominated the world perceptible to the senses. The theory of the four elements underlay many of the explanations used in physics, medicine, and chemistry (or alchemy), as well as in astronomy. Most natural philosophers saw a correspondence between the explanations of each of these disciplines and reasoned that the movements of the heavens influenced developments of earth. Astronomy and astrology marched hand and hand, then, and both related to other branches of natural philosophy.

A fifth, incorruptible element, ether, composed the substance of heavenly bodies. These consisted of solid, crystalline spheres arranged concentrically about the earth. As perfect bodies, circular motion came naturally to the spheres. Although the spheres revolved daily about the earth, carrying all of the heavenly bodies as denser knobs or swellings of their substance, the planets, sun, and moon all appeared to change on a regular basis. Astronomers easily explained the changes in the sun and moon by their respective annual and monthly rotation around the earth.

More difficulties, however, sprang from the observation that the planets, when viewed against the background of the fixed stars, appeared to follow a regular path across the heavens, but periodically moved backwards for a short time. To account for this irregularity, ancient astronomers devised a complex geometric system that accounted for the apparent positions of the planets by a combination of different circular motions. As the sphere of a planet rotated on its regular cycle, the planet moved in the opposite direction in a smaller epicycle around a gradually moving point within the sphere. Astronomers called this point a deferent and this secondary motion an epicycle and used them to account for the retrograde movements of planets. Although the system of deferents and epicycles dated back at least to the work of Apollonius and Hipparchus in the second and third centuries B.C. and recorded observations of heavenly bodies stemmed from even earlier times, astronomical theory remained sketchy and speculative throughout most of the ancient era.

Not until about 150 A.D. did the brilliant work of the astronomer and geographer Ptolemy synthesize all of the known observations and explanations of the heavens into one comprehensive, systematic, mathematical model of the universe. His *Almagest*, after summarizing earlier theories and presenting all of the known arguments for and against a geostatic system, firmly presented a mathematical model with the heavens revolving around a stationary earth. Ptolemy computed the apparent paths of the planets, sun, and moon and reduced each to a series of perfect circular motions. While the earth stood at the center of the universe, it did not form the central point for the mathematical calculation of each of the heavenly spheres in Ptolemy's system. Nor could he reduce the paths of the heavenly bodies to a simple circle; for the sun and the planets he had to retain both cycles and epicycles. Even with these admitted difficulties, Ptolemy's achievement stood high. In addition to the world system, the *Almagest* also included a series of tables that gave the positions of the heavenly bodies, projected their movements into the future, and predicted astronomical events. The system of Ptolemy easily accommodated the theory of the four elements and it made mathematical sense out of the verbal account of nature advanced by the Aristotelians. The acknowledged flaws in his work, the need for greater mathematical simplicity and the tendency, increasingly apparent as the centuries rolled by, for the tables to get out of date because of the imperfect calendar used in Europe, inspired future astronomers to improve the system, not to discard it.

The systematic, mathematical synthesis of ancient astronomy created by Ptolemy reigned over European cosmology without a serious rival for 1,400 years. In part, this sprang from the technical competence of the author; until the sixteenth century, few, if any, Europeans could equal and none surpassed the mathematical skill and imagination displayed by Ptolemy. However, Ptolemaic astronomy also held its prevailing position because it meshed so well with the accepted physics, biology, alchemy, and medicine of the ancient world; all worked together as a unified system of natural philosophy. With no other systematic verbal or mathematical framework to draw upon, scholars found the science of the ancient world the best available account of nature. Medieval philosophers—especially the Aristotelians of the thirteenth century—Christianized the system. Astronomers recalculated the tables and those drawn up at the command of Alphonso the Wise in Spain at the end of the thirteenth century remained in use for another three hundred years. Such changes only added to the persuasiveness of the whole, however.

Major shifts in perception and thought often spring from ironic beginnings. In the case of astronomy, the interest of renaissance humanists in recovering the original texts of the writings of antiquity indirectly inspired a reexamination of Ptolemaic theory. Renewed interest in Greek texts produced a much greater familiarity in European universities with Greek natural philosophy, now made more widely available with the advent of printed editions and translations. As with other ancient Greek writings, Ptolemy's *Almagest* had come to Western Europe through Arabic translations. In the fifteenth century, humanist scholars such as George Peurbach and his disciple Regiomantanus sought Ptolemy's original text in order to make a direct translation into Latin, the learned language of their day. The *Almagest* first appeared in print in 1515 in the medieval Latin version, but a new Latin translation, based on the original Greek, soon followed, and the Greek text appeared in 1538. In addition, Peurbach, Regiomantanus, and others produced new, more sophisticated textbooks for the study of mathematics and astronomy, which helped to refine the teaching of astronomy, a prescribed subject in the university curriculum. Not only did Ptolemy's *Almagest* become more widely available in more accurate versions, but alternative explanations put forth in the ancient world also became better known. To scholars of the sixteenth century, then, astronomy appeared to present a field full of questions, problems, and calculations awaiting solution. Out of this ferment came the work of Nicholas Copernicus (1473–1543), a canon of the cathedral of Frauenburg in Poland. Copernicus trained for an ecclesiastical career by studying at the University of Cracow and at the University of Bologna in Italy. He also studied canon law and medicine at the University of Padua, and finally took a doctorate in law at the University of Ferrara. Eventually, he returned to Poland to pursue the busy life of an ecclesiastical administrator and a practicing physician.

Despite the pressures of his career, Copernicus found time to continue the study of astronomy started in Italy. In 1512 he produced a brief sketch of his system. Although this "Little Commentary" circulated in manuscript for many years, the most important astronomical writings of Copernicus remained private until a young professor from the Lutheran University of Wittenberg, Georg Joachim Rheticus, received the master's permission to assemble a selection from his astronomical manuscripts for publication as a treatise. As a result, Rheticus saw the *First Narration* (1540) through the press and persuaded an older Lutheran pastor, Andraes Osiander, to shepherd through the longer and more systematic *Six Books on the Revolution of the Celestial Orbs* (1543).[2] Both books appeared anonymously, the second shortly before the death of Copernicus. *De Revolutionibus* contained an anonymous preface by Osiander which somewhat dampened the impact of the text by suggesting that the proposed heliostatic system might work better as a mathematical hypothesis than as a literal portrayal of the order of the universe. In the vigour of its conception, the rigour of its argument, and the completeness of its detail, *de Revolutionibus* surpassed any treatise on the heavens written either before or after the *Almagest*. From the time of its publication onward, all astronomers and mathematicians had to deal seriously with the arguments put forward by Copernicus.

The power of *de Revolutionibus* lay both in its bold, systematic vision of a heliostatic system of the universe and in the sophistication of its mathematical solutions to the problems that this vision posed. Drawing upon essentially the same observational evidence as that available to Ptolemy and adding only slightly to the ancient scholar's trigonometry, Copernicus carefully argued for a changed conception and perception of the planetary system. Often attacking Aristotelian views, he drew deeply upon the Platonic, Neo-Platonic, and Pythagorean sources made available by the humanists. Still, *de Revolutionibus* cautiously followed the format of the *Almagest*. As Copernicus explained:

> In the first book I describe all the positions of the spheres together with such movements as
> I ascribe to the Earth; so that this book contains, as it were, the general system of the universe.
> Afterwards, in the remaining books, I relate the motions of the other planets and all the spheres
> to the mobility of the Earth, so that we may thus comprehend how far the motions and appearances of the remainder of the planets and spheres may be preserved, if they are related to the
> motions of the Earth. [3]

---

[2] These works appeared in Latin as *Narratio Prima* (1540) and *De Revolutionibus Orbium Coelestium Libri Sex* (1543).

[3] [Copernicus], *De Revolutionibus*, as quoted and translated in Marie Boas, The *Scientific Renaissance 1450–1630* (New York, 1962), p. 69.

Clearly Copernicus wished to have his system judged on the same basis as that of Ptolemy, for he carefully refuted Ptolemy's arguments against a heliostatic system one by one and covered all specific points as thoroughly as had the ancient astronomer.

In order to present a persuasive case for the motion of the earth (the great stumbling block in his system for contemporaries) Copernicus needed first, to assume that heavenly bodies revolved about more than one center (for the moon clearly moved about the earth); second, to argue that the sun (not the earth) stood at the center of the planetary system; and third, to assert that the magnitude of the universe must extend over vast distances for otherwise one could not account for the lack of parallax observed in the fixed stars as the earth traveled from one side of its orbit around the sun to the other. Since no one could prove these assumptions with conclusive observational evidence, they remained open to dispute for a long time; Tycho, for example, accepted the first of them and parts of the third while rejecting the second. Both verbally and mathematically, Copernicus could account for the apparent motion of the planets, including their puzzling retrograde movements, by reference to their orbits around the sun. His system attributed the daily and seasonal movements of the heavens to the daily rotation of the earth around its axis and to the annual orbits of the planets around the sun. The force of these arguments alone demonstrated the brilliance of the author. Because he accepted the old idea of circular motion as the only perfect motion, Copernicus did need to employ cycles and epicycles to explain the paths of the planets. However, the Copernican system counted as one of its glories the fact that it substantially reduced the number of motions required by the Ptolemaic system. Copernicus showed that a modern man could improve upon the mathematical clarity, simplicity, and harmony of the greatest model of the universe produced by the ancients. *De Revolutionibus*, both by its bold vision and by its sometimes untidy answers, encouraged others to question the commonplaces of the Aristotelian tradition and to work for a simpler and more accurate mathematical model of the universe.

One of the young men who took up this challenge during the sixteenth century was Tycho Brahe. Born three years after the death of Copernicus, Tycho received his astronomical education in a Lutheran geostatic Copernican tradition which accepted the Copernican system as a mathematical model, but not as a description of reality. Near the commencement of his career as a scholar, Tycho spelled out his debt to Copernicus:

In our own day, Nicholas Copernicus, who has rightly been called a second Ptolemy, realized from his own observations that Ptolemy left some things to be desired. He concluded that the hypotheses of Ptolemy were somehow not in harmony with the axioms of mathematics but actually ran contrary to them. He further found that the Alphonsine calculations were not in agreement with the movements of the heavens. His marvellous skill and genius allowed him to construct new hypotheses, with the result that he predicted the course of the planets more accurately than anyone had ever done before. Although he constructed certain things contrary to the principles of Aristotelian physics—the sun resting in the center of the universe, the earth with its mixed elements and with the moon moving about the sun in a threefold motion, and the eighth sphere resting immobile—yet he admits of nothing absurd as far as his mathematical axioms are concerned. We cannot say as much of Ptolemy and the usual hypotheses, where the motions of the planets are made irregular to the centers of their circles by means of [the device called the equant], which is absurd—in this inconvenient manner they salvage the irregularity of the planets by the very means of irregularity. Everything which we in our age consider to be thoroughly investigated and well known about the revolutions of the stars has been established and handed down to us by these two scholars, Ptolemy and Copernicus. . . .[4]

In the previous year, Tycho had published the treatise on the new star of 1572 that launched his public career as an astronomer. One can see in that treatise, in the speech of 1574 quoted above, and in the treatise on the comet of 1577 (composed as part of his new duties as royal astronomer), the great concern to observe the heavens accurately, to work out an harmonious mathematical astronomy, and to reconcile the great advantages of the Copernican system with established principles of physics and with the best observational evidence available.

Like Copernicus, Tycho boldly attacked Aristotelian commonplaces when they conflicted with observations and mathematics. In his treatise on the new star, he demonstrated that the nova of 1572 exhibited no parallax and must, therefore, exist in the highest heavens; explicitly, he rejected the Aristotelian view that no change could take place above the moon. In the treatise on the comet of 1577, Tycho again demonstrated his observational and mathematical ability by charting the path of the comet as it extended through the orbits of several planets; this time, he rejected the Aristotelian idea of the material reality of crystalline spheres. In time, Tycho would prove just as bold in rejecting the heliostatic system of Copernicus and working out his own planetary system which involved a geocentric universe in which the planets orbited the sun, and the fixed stars, the sun (with its planets), and the moon revolved around the earth. In addition, Tycho would gather the massive evidence needed to work out an accurate mathematical model of the planetary system, as Johannes Kepler would later demonstrate.

Written for astrological as well as for astronomical purposes, the German *Treatise on the Comet of 1577* both reflected and contributed to the scientific debate of the sixteenth century.[5] It carried forward the work of Copernicus and stood in that important Pythagorean/Platonic tradition which contributed so strongly to natural philosophy in early modern Europe. This tradition, with its assertion that reality lay deeper than material appearances, linked many scholars who stood divided on such important issues as religion or geostatic versus heliostatic astronomy. Mathematics provided the core of this vision of natural philosophy; as Galileo so aptly stated:

> Philosophy is written in this grand book, the universe, which stands continually open to our gaze. But the book cannot be understood unless one first learns to comprehend the language and read the letters in which it is composed *It is written in the language of mathematics*, and its characters are triangles, circles, and other . . . geometric figures without which it is humanly impossible to understand a single word of it; without these, one wanders about in a dark labyrinth.[6]

Observation could not be defined, refined, or even understood without mathematics. This assumption bound together Copernicus, Tycho, Kepler, and Galileo and provided them with their most important weapon in their assault upon almost wholly verbal Aristotelian natural philosophy. Out of their very different and often conflicting contributions sprang the new view of the world presented by the seventeenth-century scientific revolution.

---

[4] Tycho Brahe as quoted and translated in J.R. Christianson, "Copernicus and the Lutherans," *Sixteenth Century Journal*, 4 (1973), pp. 8–9; see pp. 1–10 for the full argument.

[5] The following selection is taken from Christianson, "Tycho Brahe's German Treatise," pp. 132–140.

[6] Galileo Galilei, *The Assayer* (1632) as translated by Stillman Drake in his *Discoveries and Opinions of Galileo* (Garden City, 1957), pp. 226–7.

Treatise on the Comet of 1577

On the Origin of the Comets, and What the Ancient and Modern Philosophers Opine and Maintain Concerning Them

After God Almighty had created the whole heaven with sun, moon, and all stars, and had adorned them with manifold prodigious sizes and marvelous motions, then did He also arrange the four elements under the heavens, namely that the element of fire (which we hold and believe to be none other than an ignition of the uppermost air by the rapid revolution of the heavens) would follow after the sphere of the moon, and after this is the element of air, and in the center or midpoint of the whole heaven is the earth and water, fastened together and round like a ball. We humans are placed upon it, so that we might contemplate His almighty and indescribable marvel of the heavens, investigate it by means of the discernment which He has given us, and thus also learn to know rightly the Creator of it all. Yet how the prodigious mass and depth of the heavens must rotate in rapid course in twenty-four hours, together with sun and moon and all the stars, nay moreover, how the prodigious mass of the [planets] with their marvelous courses through the heavens can go quickly now, slowly then, now behind and now ahead, sometimes even seem to stand still—these are wonders enough that a man can pass his whole life long and still not grasp and understand. But because we see such things from our youth onwards, and thereby grow accustomed to them, we give them little thought or astonishment, and we fail to perceive the swift course and vastness of the stars, mainly because our eyes are fixed more on worldly things than on heavenly. Then it comes to pass that something new is born in the heavens, contrary to the custom of nature, and all mankind holds it to be a great wonder and becomes very eager to know its meaning, but that is something which the Lord God alone knows, and [no] man, however learned, can have right knowledge of.

From the beginning of the world, those stars called comets have been held to be the greatest of all wonders seen in the heavens, All philosophers of every age have been much concerned to know the origin, nature, and attributes of such stars, since they are not always visible in the heavens, but only at certain times, and thereafter expend themselves again. Various opinions have been expressed by ancient and modern philosophers concerning' comets and their origin, the first of which was held by Pythagoras and his followers, Democritus and Anaxagoras, that comets are born in the heavens and are special stars which arise at times and then come so near the earth that they can be seen by us men, and then are charmed away from us again into the heights, and have their being and place in the heavens. But Aristotle, who came after them, has refuted and defeated their arguments, for he was of the opinion that no alteration nor any change occurred in the heavens, and also that nothing new could be born there. He therefore presented his opinion on comets, that they are not born in the heavens but in the upper part of the air, in the element Fire, below the sphere of the moon, and that they come from a dry and fatty material, drawn from the earth by the power of the stars and ignited up there, which then burns until it consumes itself. The greater part of succeeding philosophers have accepted this Aristotelian opinion, and have considered it quite impossible that comets or anything new could be born in the heavens, though some have recently doubted this, on the grounds that it was possible to observe and discover that the new star or comet, which appeared four years ago in the constellation Cassiopeia, had no parallax whatsoever and always remained in one place like the fixed stars, and therefore not only could not be under the moon in the element of fire or of air, but that it stood in the uppermost sphere of the fixed stars, among the other [stars], as I have proved and demonstrated sufficiently in my little book on that same star. Various distinguished mathematicians, both in Germany and other nations, have concurred in their observations that the same star stood in the heavens with the other fixed stars. This miracle has made it necessary for us to abandon the opinion of Aristotle and take up another: that something new can also be born in heaven. Since it could happen in the case of the aforementioned star, it is not impossible that other comets are born in the heavens and are not comprised of dryness and fattiness extracted from the earth. The Paracelsians hold and recognize the heavens to be the fourth element of fire, in which generation and corruption may also occur, and thus it is not impossible, according to their philosophy, for comets to be born in the heavens, just as occasional fabulous excrescences are sometimes found in the earth and in metals, and monsters among animals. For Paracelsus is of the opinion that the Superior Penates, which have their abode in the heavens and stars, at certain times ordained by God, fabricate such new stars and comets out of the plentiful celestial matter and display them clearly before mankind as a sign of future things which do not have their true origin in the planets but are rather caused and augured in opposition to the planets by the Pseudoplanet, as a comet is called.

It has been sufficiently demonstrated that the star which appeared four years ago had its place, not in the elemental regions, but above in the heavens, and I have also discovered by careful observation and demonstration of this present comet, that it has its place and path far above the moon, in the heavens, as hereafter will be shown. Therefore, the opinion of Aristotle is entirely false when he asserts that comets are drawn upwards from the earth into the air and that they cannot be generated in the heavens, for he has established this on the basis of his own good thoughts and not from any mathematical observation or demonstration. Because they do have their generation in the heavens, however, it should all the more be regarded as a miraculous portent that such a new birth comes forth in the heavens, which are composed of the most subtle, most transluscent and imperishable of all materials. Whether they are ordained by God and fabricated by Superior Penates unknown to us, or whether God the Almighty through His power and will and in His own good time makes such a new light in the heavens without [material] means, in order to warn us of future punishment, is not to be disputed at length here, for we humans, with our limited and earthly understanding, really have no proper grounds or conceptual framework for explaining the material of comets and how they are generated in a way which would not seem a wonder to us. We have no real knowledge of the matter of nature of the whole heavens, sun, and moon, nor what causes their wonderfully adroit motions, though they have stood and been visible since the beginning of the world. How many things there are, even here on earth, which we see with our eyes and seize with our hands, the nature of which we can never satisfactorily comprehend. Therefore, philosophers should not contend so uselessly about things they cannot resolve, but should the more readily admit to a modest ignorance and say that comets are a special creation of God which come from unknown natural causes, of which we do not know how they are born.

When This Comet First Was Seen and How Long It Shone

In the year of Christ our Savior's birth 1577, on 11 November in the evening soon after sunset, this new birth in the heavens revealed itself, namely a comet with a very long tail, and the body of the star was whitish, though not with the bright gleam of the fixed stars but somewhat darkish, almost like the star Saturn in appearance, which indeed at that time stood not far away from it. Its tail was great and long, curved over itself somewhat in the middle, of a burning reddish dark color like a flame penetrating through smoke. This comet had its true beginning, in my opinion, with the new moon which occurred shortly before, on 10 November, about an hour past midnight, though it is true that various seafaring people have reported that they saw it on the evening of 9 November in the Baltic Sea, but I cannot vouch for that. It were not clear long enough for such observations. This comet lasted for over two months and was first observed by me through my instrument on 13 November, because until then, the heavens was visible until 26 January, although it waned continually during that time, and the longer [it lasted], the smaller it became, so I could hardly observe it with my instruments on 13 January, and around 26 January, when I saw it for the last time, it had become almost unrecognizable.

On the Course of This Comet and Its Place under the Firmament

When this comet was first observed by me on 13 November at 5 o'clock in the afternoon, I found it in 7¼° of Capricorn, at a declination of 8°20' north of the ecliptic, 26°50' distant from the bright star in Aquila, and 210401 from the lowest star in the horn of Capricorn, through which its tail extended before ending. From this, by means of trigonometry, I find the location of the comet as previously indicated. On the 14th at 5 o'clock in the afternoon, it was 23°45' from the bright star in Aquila, 18°30' from the previously named star in Capricorn. From this, it follows that the comet progressed 3½° on its circle within 24 hours, and inasmuch as it moved most rapidly in the beg of its course, I imagine that in the previous days, before I began to observe it, it might have moved 4° on its circle each day. Therefore, inasmuch as it was first seen on 9 November at the time of the new light, it must have had its place or beginning near the ecliptic, under 25° of Sagittarius, at the margin of the Milky Way, from which it is believed that all comets take their origin. From this position by the ecliptic, not far from the winter solstice and the tropical circle, the comet began its course, continued and completed it, toward the north according to the succession of the signs, in the manner of the planets and stars in setting and rising with the course of the heavens, until it came to the Tropic of Cancer by that star which is called the flying horse Pegasus, sitting foremost upon the breast between the two called little and great Scheat. In this position, I found it for the last time on 26 January, grown so small that one could hardly see it, and for aught I know, it faded soon after, and was gone. This comet thus described the quarter part of a great circle of a sphere, beginning at 25° of Sagittarius at the ecliptic and intersecting the equator at 300°40' from the vernal intersection, describing an angle of 34° with the equator; when it vanished, it was 3° north of the ecliptic in the longitude of 25° of Pisces, and thus, reckoning not only from its own circle but also from the ecliptic, it had transversed a quarter circle or the fourth part of the heavens with its path. Its course on this circle was not uniform, however, for in the beginning, as we have said, it absolved 4° of proper motion in one day and thereafter became more sluggish, so that by 15 November, it progressed fin one day, on the 20th 2¼° on the 23rd exactly 2° on the last [day of November] 1 ⅓°, 5 December 1 ° the middle [of December] 50', and the end 35', 10 January 25', and at last, when it was about to go out, it progressed 20 minutes upon its circle in one day, which is the third part of one degree, and from 13 January until the 26th it progressed only 4 ⅓°. From this, it may be seen that it went as far in one day in the beginning as it did in ten toward the end, and likewise concerning its size, in this manner also did it diminish in the course of time, although it was not altered so much from day to day toward the end as in the beginning.

On the Tail of the Comet

In the beginning this comet had a very long and large tail which stretched over 22°, but it gradually grew smaller and shorter, so that by the end of January it was scarcely visible, and at all times this comet had its tail turned directly away from the sun, as all other comets, those observed many years ago by Regiomontanus, Apian, Gemma Frisius, and Fracastoro, have also done: all have turned their tails away from the sun. From this, it appears that the tail of a comet is nothing but the rays of the sun which have passed through the body of the comet, for this body, not being diaphanous like other stars, cannot transmit the rays invisibly, and not being opaque like the moon, cannot reflect the rays, but since the body of the comet is some medium between rare and dense, it holds a part of the radiance from the sun within itself, and from this comes the light of the head by reason of the resistance of celestial matter of which the head is fabricated, but because it is also somewhat rare and porous, it lets those solar rays pass through which are seen by us as a long tail hanging to the head of the comet. This is indeed so and has been demonstrated so by all comets observed at various times by mathematicians and it is no longer to be doubted. Therefore, Aristotle and all those who follow him cannot maintain their opinion, namely that the tail of a comet is a flame of the rare fattiness which is burning above the air, for if that were true, these flames would not have a relationship to the sun, and always turn themselves away from it, wheresoever it might be and howsoever the heavens might turn. But the manner in which this comet passed across the circle of the heavens, and the manner in which its tail was always turned away from the sun, cannot be completely described in words, and therefore it is made manifest in the delineation which is to be seen in the following figure.

On the Place Where This Comet Arose in the Diameter of the World, and How Far It Was Elevated above Us

However much they who still hold the Aristotelian philosophy to be the best do tenaciously and truly believe that all comets come into existence and run their course far below the lowest sphere of the moon, and can by no means admit or apprehend that any change could occur in the [aetherial] regions or among the heavenly bodies, or that anything new could be born there, yet they do not derive such knowledge and opinions from experience or any carefully conceived mathematical observations, nay rather they have it from subtle rational arguments alone, which in such matters cannot rise nearer the truth, as can manifest observations with proper instruments, from which it can be demonstrated, by means of trigonometry, what is to be believed. The other, however, be it adorned with ever so subtle arguments, is still nothing but a good thought come out of the human intelligence, which can be refuted by other arguments deriving from human understanding, as indeed, there have been philosophers both before and after Aristotle who have by no means agreed with him, but have recognized comets to be heavenly and not elemental bodies, as has been told above.

This point is that it is possible to determine how far distant the comet is from us in the firmament. This may be determined only by its parallax, if there be any, and if it have a greater parallax or change of aspect that the moon, which is the next [celestial body] to us, then the conclusion would be that it were nearer still to us than the sphere in which the moon runs.

I have taken great care actually to determine this, for the whole science of the position and character of the comet lies in this, and I have taken numerous observations through appropriate instruments and have found from these, by means of spherical trigonometry, that this comet was so far distant from us that its greatest parallax at the horizon cannot have been greater than 15 minutes, and was found to be rather less than more than that. I have thoroughly demonstrated this on the basis of the observations in the Latin treatise on this comet, which can be understood from the method. It thus follows through geometrical apportionment reckoning, that this comet was at least 230 times the earth's radius above the earth, and inasmuch as the radius of the earth is reckoned as 860 German miles, it must have been nearly two hundred thousand German miles above the earth. Inasmuch as the moon, when it is closest to us in its sphere, is 52 times the earth's radius above us, which is less than 50,000 German miles, then it is easy to conclude and understand that this comet was high above the moon in the sphere of the planet Venus, for the sphere of Venus, which astronomers place just below the sun, is reckoned as 164 times the earth's radius above the earth, reaching to the solar sphere, that is 1104 times the earth's radius. Through my observations, I have found the location of the comet to be here, between [these extremities]. Therefore, I conclude that it was in the sphere of Venus, but if one will not follow the usual order of the celestial orbs, but would rather accept as valid the opinion of certain ancient philosophers and of Copernicus in our own time, that Mercury has its orb around the sun, and Venus around Mercury with the sun approximately in the center, which reasoning is not entirely out of harmony with truth, even if the sun is not put to rest in the center of the universe as with the hypotheses of Copernicus, then it follows from this that the comet was generated between the orb of the moon and the aforementioned orb of Venus which they designated about the sun, for according to this view, Venus could not come nearer to the earth than 296 times the radius of the earth, and the moon, when it is most distant from us, is 68 times the earth's radius, thus there is 228 times the radius of the earth between the moon and Venus, according to which teaching I do regard the comet to have originated in this same space, at a height of 230 times the earth's radius, as reported above. The Aristotelian philosophy, however, which we hear so often, cannot be valid in teaching that nothing new can originate in the heavens, and that all comets are located in the upper parts of the air, for I have discovered otherwise of this comet, on the basis of diligent observation and demonstration as indicated. Likewise, the new star, which was visible for a whole year in Cassiopeia some four years past, also gave sufficient evidence that something new can be generated in the heavens, for it had its seat, not in the lower heavens, but in the uppermost eighth sphere and had neither parallax nor proper motion, for neither I nor other mathematicians were able to find any, through diligent observation from many places. Consequently, it must all the less be considered incredible, if the observations indicated that we should consider it to have had its seat in the heavenly regions, for this comet had a proper head or corpus like a star. That it also had a tail comes from the gleam of the sun which penetrates through it, therefore the tail was always turned away from the sun, as reported previously, and this comet could be in the celestial regions no less than the previous star was, which has now been asserted sufficiently and shall be demonstrated in the Latin [treatise] on the basis of geometry to the satisfaction of those who understand that art.

On the Size of This Comet

This comet was greatest and most powerful at first and then gradually grew smaller as time passed, decelerating in its course at the same time. I have taken its apparent diameter in the beginning, on 13 November, with an instrument especially designed for that purpose, namely 8 minutes, and the length of its tail was 21°40', as it then stretched or reached from the margin of the Milky Way, where the head was, to the horn of Capricorn, where it ended. It thus grew to this size immediately, and inasmuch as it stood as far from us in the heavens as the planet Venus, as mentioned previously, it had a greater immensity of size than we down here are able to grasp. Geometrical calculation and demonstration shows that the head was distant by 230 times the earth's radius, which is two hundred thousand miles, as mentioned previously, and its apparent diameter was 8 minutes, so the comet itself must have had a diameter or thickness of 465 German miles. Thus its diameter was as great as the fourth part of the diameter of the earth. The circumference of the head or corpus of the comet, derived proportionally from the diameter, was 1460 German miles, from which it follows that it was as great in corpulence as the thirtieth part of the earth, and almost the same size as the morning star called Venus. Inasmuch as its tail was 22 degrees long at first, it reached seventy six thousand German miles when it appeared, according to geometrical calculation: thus far did the beams of the sun reveal themselves through the comet. The thickness of the tail was two and a half degrees in the thickest part, which amounts to or comprises five thousand German miles, and from this follows the conclusion that this comet was a great thing in itself, no matter how small it became in our eyes.

Judicial Astrology of this Comet's Effect and Significance

Astrologers are of the opinion that all comets are born of a particular constitution of the upper stars, with which they also agree entirely in their effects and significance, and they would therefore undoubtedly assert that the past great eclipse of the moon on 27 September in Aries, which is regarded as a fiery sign, had foretold this comet, and that its significance should therefore agree with the influence of the same eclipse, but this cannot be so, because comets do not have their origin or signification from any natural course of the stars nor from any eclipse of the sun or moon, but they are rather a new and supernatural creation of God the Almighty, placed in the heavens in His good time, the significance and influence of which not only cannot have anything in common with the influence of the planets, but actually works against them and violently upsets their normal workings, for they overwhelm the natural signs of the stars with much greater powers and bring about their own effects instead. They are in all manner such a great wonder of God and a miracle in the nature of the heavens that they also have greater deeds to accomplish than all other natural courses of the heavens. What this might be, however, to which it is predestined and has to fulfill, is on good grounds known to no man but is to be revealed by God the Almighty through special means, for the works of God which shine so naturally and are before our eyes every day and which have also been studied diligently by men in various places since the beginning of the world, do yet remain unfathomable and unknown to the majority to this day, so meagre is our understanding beside the wisdom of God in His creation. How much less is it then possible for us to interpret and thoroughly understand the unnatural wonders of God, by which He means to proclaim something other than what the natural courses might signify. But because people, when they see such unaccustomed creations and great miracles in the heavens, are eager to know what the [effect] and significance of it might be, and although the right grounds for knowing future things are concealed from all men, it is still possible to derive some information from the ancient, experienced astrological authors concerning what such unnatural births in the heavens might mean, and this can be done without any superstition or mummery if one goes no further in his investigations than what is known to this art. Thus I have in the following expressed my good thoughts, on the basis of such grounds and opinions of those knowledgeable in such matters, what the effects and significance of this comet might be, and which regions of the world or what peoples might be affected, also how soon it will commence and when its end will come.

Follows Now What This Comet Signifies

Comets, which have appeared at certain times since the earliest age, always have had something great to deliver to this lower world, as all histories concerning them do testify unmistakably and would be too long to recite here. Usually, however, experience has taught that they have aroused great dryness and heat in the air, mighty and destructive wind storms, also in certain places overwhelming water courses, and in other places terrible earthquakes, in addition to spoilage of grain and fruits of the earth, from which usually follows great scarcity, and among mankind, many fiery illnesses and pestilence and also poisonings of the air by which many people lose their lives quickly, and it also signifies great disunity among reigning potentates, from which follows violent warfare and bloodshed, at times also the demise of certain mighty chieftains and secular rulers. It is regrettable that this comet, no less than former ones, brings and arouses the same evil effects and misfortunes here on earth, so much the more so because this comet has grown so very much greater than others and has a saturnine, evil appearance, which was revealed by its pallid appearance and unclearly shining color like the star Saturn. We thus conclude that this comet is of the nature of Saturn, towards which it also drew near and conjoined bodily in the beginning, which occurred in 10 of Capricorn on 14 November, when the comet was exalted over Saturn through a conjunction, soon after its first appearance. Likewise, on the evening when the comet first appeared after sunset, it was in the 8th house, which astrology ascribes to death. All of this indicates that the comet augurs an exceptionally great mortality among mankind (for it stood in the human constellation), the like of which has not occurred in many years. This will come about not only through gruesome pestilence and other deadly diseases which will gain the upper hand among mankind, but it will also ensue from great wars and bloodsheddings for the tail of the comet had a fiery, dark, and martial appearance, which also augurs martial effects as reported above, warfare, bloodshed, great disunity among potentates, great harm by fire, and all like manner of martial affairs, and great dear times and much turmoil will befall mankind on various grounds, inasmuch as this comet appears most unfortunate, both by means of the saturnine head and the martial tail. Because it had its first beginnings near the Tropic of Capricorn, and in the evening, a few days after its appearance, had advanced to the ninth house, which astrology ascribes to religion, is to be understood that this comet will bring a great alteration and turmoil in the spiritual matters of religion, which will be something more than has hitherto been experienced, all the more so because this comet, at the moment of new light, which occurred (in my opinion) on 10 November, 1 hour 20 minutes past midnight, stood in the fourth house together with Saturn, which the teaching of the ancients say will usually result in new sects and the alteration of customs with great evil. As this constitution was sent as an earthly sign, great solicitations were heard throughout the lands towards noonday, which were swallowed up or came to other remarkable harm in many places, and in some places, plagues were born such as locusts and worms which destroyed fruits and trees and whatever grew upon the earth. From this and other unnatural withering of grain and all that grows upon the earth for the nourishment of mankind, a great shortage will result, and pestilential, poisonous sicknesses will come, as well as other, unknown infirmities that bring long-lasting and incurable pains, exuded over the comet in its origin from Saturn, according to the teaching of the Ancients. Air and weather will not have their normal order, but will engender an unpleasant and saturnine nature. The sun will occasionally bring unnatural, harmful heat, then turn around and bring unpleasant cold and sharp air. In the winter, there will be gruesome cold with sharp wind, more than has usually been the case.

On the Places and Peoples of the World upon Whom the Effects of This Comet Mainly Will Be Accomplished

Concerning the significance of this comet in general, it pertains more to all those kingdoms which lie toward the west in Europe within Christendom, inasmuch as this comet first let itself be seen with the setting of the sun, from which is to be understood that the Occidental Imperium and regions pertaining thereto will be disturbed more than the Oriental (which is in Turkish and Persian subjection). It thus behooves the reigning lords of those regions to beware that they are not led into great misfortune by Spanish treachery or other secret counsels and plots, and be deprived of their peaceful life.

This comet will not only have its significance over the Spanish lands and their reigning lords, but also over others of the Spanish stem, and especially so if there be a potentate among them who has had his ascendence of birth and coronation in Sagittarius and Capricorn, where this comet first appeared, and then in particular if at that time a malevolent direction of the state of places made its entry, as when the ascendence in the direction of the corpus of Saturn of the signature of this comet, or another malevolent progression, brought them along. The prevalence of such an effect will cause great disunity to arise in Germany, until the matter is turned for the better by another means and person whose significance derives from the sign of Libra, for the planets which counteract this comet are mainly found in Libra. To predict the details of such an affair does not properly adhere to astrology, however, for it must seek out the causes in general terms and can discover no true knowledge beyond that.

Although this comet appeared in the west and will realize its greatest significance in those lands that lie toward the west, yet it will also spew its venom over those lands that lie eastward in the north, for its tail swept thence. By this is indicated the Muscovites and Tartars who lie toward the east, and all the more so because they have a great concordance with the constellation Sagittarius, in which this comet first appeared, for like the heavenly sign of the Archer, a demihuman with the hind parts of a horse, bending a bow, so they are comparable to the constellation of Sagittarius in their ruination and deeds of war. Therefore, this comet will incite great warfare and bloodshed upon these same peoples. It may even come to pass that this comet will bring about a well-deserved punishment upon those presently reigning in Muscovy, for the inhumane tyranny which they have practiced so long, and perhaps even bring about an end to their wantonness. In general, however, all who are associated with equestrian pursuits, shooting, and the armaments of warfare will be assailed, and those who are always on the prowl will cause great injury to others, though they must also expect to receive like measure upon themselves. Those who deal with the affairs and practices of political regimes, such as jurists and great lords councillor, will also be much stifled, and their honor, dignity, and goods will suffer great diminution in worth, especially those among them who have a confluence with Sagittarius. The Jews will also suffer great persecutions, for they are subject to Saturn. Monks, priests, and others of the Popish religion should fear the same, for this comet is very much opposed to them, and they might expect truly to be repaid in good measure during these coming years for the ruthlessness, murder, and pain which they have inflicted upon many pious folk. Not alone they, but many others, who seek their own honor and gain in the guise of the true religion, and as pseudo-planets, for the comet has let itself be seen as a pseudo-planet so that the children of the planets, both clerical and secular, who have mounted too high in their arrogance, and have not wandered in divine wisdom, will be punished.

On the Time When the Significance of the Comet Will Begin, and How Long It Will Last

The effects of the comet will be kindled in this year of '78 but there will be greater effects in the following years of '79 and '80, extending into the year of '83, though as I say, it will be most powerful in the years '79 and '80, thereafter when the year of '83 is past, other constellations and significations from the upper stars will set in. After that time, the new star which was visible beginning *anno* '72 for more than a year, simultaneously with the greatest conjunction of the upper planets in the begin of Aries, which can only occur once in 800 years, will begin their mighty operations. In the following years, there will occur great alterations and reformation, both of the spiritual and secular regimes, which may even bode more for the better of Christendom than for the worse. Inasmuch as this greatest conjunction is the seventh since the beginning of the world, which number adheres to the Sabbath according to the Hebrew caballa, it might be presumed that the eternal Sabbath of all Creation is at hand in this seventh maximum conjunction. It seems to me that the new star *anno* '72 was a harbinger of this maximum conjunction, for it was united across the poles of the world with the beginning of Aries, in which location this aforenamed maximum conjunction will be celebrated and held. So it seems natural to think of the maximum conjunction, which will end here, and which undoubtedly will bring greater alterations to the whole world than have ever occurred hitherto.

There are actually no reliable grounds, however, for predicting the end of the world from the heavenly constellations, for this knowledge does not come from the light of nature and its understanding, but from divine prophecy and the predestination of God's will, which is known to no man nor even to the angels of heaven. On this subject, it might be noted that the darkness upon the sun and moon, which Christ the Lord said would come to pass in the latter days, is not the sort of natural eclipse which can be augured by astronomy, for this latter has its natural causes in the course of the heavens and has occurred just as regularly since the beginning of the world as in our times, as is known to astronomers who understand the course of the heavens. Thus Christ was not speaking of such an eclipse, and his prophecy did not refer to the visible and corporeal heaven, but to the invisible of the light of divinity, and from this is to be understood that the unnatural darkness upon the sun and moon which will herald the latter days, cannot be predicted by means of astronomy as the others can. Such a darkness upon the sun occurred at the time of Christ's death upon the cross, when the sun in the time of the full moon lost its glow without any natural cause or means. I take present notice of this because it should be understood that this comet, oven though it has also been born unnaturally in the heavens, cannot signify the end of the world, for comets were seen before the birth of Christ, and they have been seen at various times ever since the beginning of the world, as history shows for as far as it reaches, and it is likely that many more have occurred than have been noted in the historiography. Therefore, although the end of the world, according to the signs of Christ and the prophets, cannot be too distant, yet the termination itself cannot reliably be foreseen, neither from a natural eclipse of the sun and moon, nor from other heavenly constellations, nor comets, and I thus assert that the end of the world is known only to God the Almighty and to no creature. It thus behooves us to use well our short life here on earth, so that we may praise Him to eternity with all the angels.

Galileo Galilei
(1564–1642)

GALILEO (1564–1642), born in Pisa, the eldest son of a cultivated but impoverished Florentine noble, studied first medicine and then science in his native city. At twenty-six he was appointed professor of mathematics at the University of Pisa. In 1592 he accepted a professorship in Padua. He remained there for eighteen years, during which time he achieved his most sensational triumphs. He constructed a telescope (1609), through which he discovered Jupiter's moons, the phases of Venus, and spots on the surface of the sun; he then publicly declared himself a Copernican. In 1610 he accepted the post of mathematician at the court of the grand duke of Tuscany, where he came under the censorship of the Church. Although Galileo was well received by Pope Paul V when he visited Rome in 1615 to explain his astronomical views, the next year Copernicus' work was declared heretical by the Inquisition. Galileo thereafter taught the heliocentric theory only as a hypothesis, but his writings made his real acceptance of the Copernican view evident. He was summoned to Rome and forced by the Inquisition to abjure his Copernican views; forbidden to teach, he went into seclusion at his estate in Arcetri, near Florence, where he continued his work.

Galileo's most brilliant literary work is his *Dialogue on the Two Chief Systems of the World* (1632), an implicit defense of the Copernican against the Ptolemaic system. His *Sidereal Messenger* (1610) presents his findings with the telescope, *The Assayer* (1623) his famous distinction between primary and secondary qualities. The *Dialogues concerning Two New Sciences* (1638), his most important work, contains the foundations upon which all subsequent work in dynamics was to be erected.

The first of the following selections is from *The Assayer* (*Il Saggiatore*), originally a series of letters to Virginio Cesarini, chamberlain to Urban VIII.

The last selection, from the First Dialogue of the *Dialogue Concerning the Two Great World-Systems*, has, like the first, been translated from the Italian of *Galileo's Opere*, Vols. V–VII (Florence, 1895–98).

The Assayer

IN ACCORDANCE with the promise which I made to Your Excellency, I shall certainly state my ideas concerning the proposition "Motion is the cause of heat," explaining in what way it appears to me to be true. But first it will be necessary for me to say a few words concerning that which we call "heat," for I strongly suspect that the commonly held conception of the matter is very far from the truth, inasmuch as heat is generally believed to be a true accident, affection, or quality which actually resides in the material which we feel to be heated.

Now, whenever I conceive of any material or corporeal substance, I am necessarily constrained to conceive of that substance as bounded and as possessing this or that shape, as large or small in relationship to some other body, as in this or that place during this or that time, as in motion or at rest, as in contact or not in contact with some other body, as being one, many, or few—and by no stretch of imagination can I conceive of any corporeal body apart from these conditions. But I do not at all feel myself compelled to conceive of bodies as necessarily conjoined with such further conditions as being red or white, bitter or sweet, having sound or being mute, or possessing a pleasant or unpleasant fragrance. On the contrary, were they not escorted by our physical senses, perhaps neither reason nor understanding would ever, by themselves, arrive at such notions. I think, therefore, that these tastes, odors, colors, etc., so far as their objective existence is concerned, are nothing but mere names for something which resides exclusively in our sensitive body (*corpo sensitivo*), so that if the perceiving creature were removed; all of these qualities would be annihilated and abolished from existence. But just because we have given special names to these qualities, different from the names we have given to the primary and real properties, we are tempted into believing that the former really and truly exist as well as the latter.

An example, I believe, will clearly explain my concept. Suppose I pass my hand, first over a marble statue, then over a living man. So far as the hand, considered in itself, is concerned, it will act in an identical way upon each of these objects; that is, the primary qualities of motion and contact will similarly affect the two objects, and we would use identical language to describe this in each case. But the living body, which I subject to this experiment, will feel itself affected in various ways, depending upon the part of the body I happen to touch; for example, should it be touched on the sole of the foot or the kneecap, or under the armpit, it will feel, in addition to simple contact, a further affection to which we have given a special name: we call it "tickling." This latter affection is altogether our own, and is not at all a property of the hand itself. And it seems to me that he would be gravely in error who would assert that the hand, in addition to movement and contact, intrinsically possesses another and different faculty which we might call the "tickling faculty," as though tickling were a resident property of the hand *per se*. Again, a piece of paper or a feather, when gently rubbed over any part of our body whatsoever, will in itself act everywhere in an identical way; it will, namely, move and contact. But we, should we be touched between the eyes, on the tip of the nose, or under the nostrils, will feel an almost intolerable titillation—while if touched in other places, we will scarcely feel anything at all. Now this titillation is completely ours and not the feather's, so that if the living, sensing body were removed, nothing would remain of the titillation but an empty name. And I believe that many other qualities, such as taste, odor, color, and so on, often predicated of natural bodies, have a similar and no greater existence than this.

A solid body and, so to speak, one that is sufficiently heavy, when moved and applied against any part of my body whatsoever, will produce in me the sensation which we call "touch." Although this sense is to be found in every part of the body, it appears principally to reside in the palm of the hand, and even more so in the fingertips, with which we can feel the minutest differences of roughness, texture, and softness and hardness—differences which the other parts of the body are less capable of distinguishing. Some amongst these tactile sensations are more pleasing than others, depending upon the differences of configuration of tangible bodies; that is to say, in accordance with whether they are smooth or irregular, sharp or dull, flexible or rigid. And the sense of touch, being more material than the other senses and being produced by the mass of the material itself, seems to correspond to the element of earth.

Since certain material bodies are continually resolving themselves into tiny particles, some of the particles, because they are heavier than air, will descend; and some of them, because they are lighter than air, will ascend. From this, perhaps, two further senses are born, for certain of the particles penetrate two parts of our body which are effectively more sensitive than the skin, which is incapable of feeling the incursion of materials which are too fine, subtle, or flexible. The descending particles are received by the upper surface of the tongue, and penetrating, they blend with its substance and moisture. Thus our tastes are caused, pleasant or harsh in accordance with variations in the contact of diversely shaped particles, and depending upon whether they are few or many, and whether they have high or low velocity. Other particles ascend, and entering the nostrils they penetrate the various nodes *(mammilule)* which are the instruments of smell; and these particles, in like manner through contact and motion, produce savoriness or unsavoriness—again depending upon whether the particles have this or that shape, high or low velocity, and whether they are many or few. It is remarkable how providently the tongue and nasal passages are situated and disposed, the former stretched beneath to receive the ingression of descending particles, and the latter so arranged as to receive those which ascend. The arrangement whereby the sense of taste is excited in us is perhaps analogous to the way in which fluids descend through the air, and the stimulation of the sense of smell may be compared to the manner in which flames ascend in it.

There remains the element of air, which corresponds to the sense of sound. Sounds come to us indiscriminately, from above and below and from either side, since we are so constituted as to be equally disposed to every direction of the air's movement; and the ear is so situated as to accommodate itself in the highest possible degree to any position in space. Sounds, then, are produced in us and felt when (without any special quality of harmoniousness or dissonance) there is a rapid vibration of air, forming minutely small waves, which move certain cartilages of a certain drum which is in our ear. The various external ways in which this wave-motion of the air is produced are manifold, but can in large part be reduced to the vibrating of bodies which strike the air and form the waves which spread out with great velocity. High frequencies give rise to high tones; low frequencies give rise to low tones. But I cannot believe that there exists in external bodies anything, other than their size, shape, or motion (slow or rapid), which could excite in us our tastes, sounds, and odors. And indeed I should judge that, if ears, tongues, and noses be taken away, the number, shape, and motion of bodies would remain, but not their tastes, sounds, and odors. The latter, external to the living creature, I believe to be nothing but mere names, just as (a few lines back) I asserted tickling and titillation to be, if the armpit or the sensitive skin inside the nose were removed. As to the comparison between the four senses which we have mentioned and the four elements, I believe that the sense of sight, most excellent and noble of all the senses, is like light itself. It stands to the others in the same measure of comparative excellence as the finite stands to the infinite, the gradual to the instantaneous, the divisible to the indivisible, the darkness to the light. Of this sense, and all that pertains to it, I can pretend to understand but little; yet a great deal of time would not suffice for me to set forth even this little bit that I know, or (to put it more exactly) for me to sketch it out on paper. Therefore I shall ponder it in silence.

I return to my first proposition, having now shown how some affections, often reputed to be indwelling properties of some external body, have really no existence save in us, and apart from us are mere names. I confess myself to be very much inclined to believe that heat, too, is of this sort, and that those materials which produce and make felt in us the sense of heat and to which we give the general name "fire" consist of a multitude of tiny particles of such and such a shape, and having such and such a velocity. These, when they encounter our body, penetrate it by means of their extreme subtlety; and it is their contact, felt by us in their passage through our substance, which is the affection we call "heat." It will be pleasantly warm or unpleasantly hot depending upon the number and the velocity (greater or lesser) of these pricking, penetrating particles—pleasant if by their penetration our necessary perspiring is facilitated, unpleasant if their penetrating effects too great a division and dissolution of our substance. In sum, the operation of fire, considered in itself, is nothing but movement, or the penetration of bodies by its extreme subtlety, quickly or slowly, depending upon the number and velocity of tiny corpuscles of flame *(ignicoli)* and upon the greater or lesser density of the bodies concerned. Many bodies dissolve in such a manner that the major part of them becomes transformed into further corpuscles of flame; and this dissolution continues as further dissolvable material is encountered. But that there exists in fire, apart from shape, number, movement, penetration, and contact, some further quality which we call "heat,"

I cannot believe. And I again judge that heat is altogether subjective, so that if the living, sensitive body be removed, what we call heat would be nothing but a simple word. Since it is the case that this affection is produced in us by passage of tiny corpuscles of flame through our substance and their contact with it, it is obvious that once this motion ceases, their operation upon us will be null. It is thus that we perceive that a quantity of fire, retained in the pores and pits of a piece of calcified stone, does not heat—even if we hold it in the palm of our hand—because the flame remains stationary in the stone. But should we swish the stone in water where, because of its weight, it has greater propensity for movement and where the pits of the stone open so mewhat, the corpuscles of flame will escape and, encountering our hand, will penetrate it, so that we will feel heat. Since, in order for heat to be stimulated in us, the mere presence of corpuscles of flame is not by itself sufficient, and since movement is required in addition, it is with considerable reason that I declare motion to be the cause of heat.

This or that movement by which a scantling or other piece of wood is burned up or by which lead and other metals are melted will continue so long as the corpuscles of flame, moved either by their own velocity or (if this be insufficient) aided by a strong blast from a bellows, continue to penetrate the body in question; the former will resolve itself into further corpuscles of flame or into ash; the latter will liquify and be rendered fluid like water. From a common-sense point of view, to assert that that which moves a stone, piece of iron, or a stick, is what *heats* it, seems like an extreme vanity. But the friction produced when two hard bodies are rubbed together, which either reduces them to fine flying particles or permits the corpuscles of flame contained in them to escape, can finally be analyzed as motion. And the particles, when they encounter our body and penetrate and tear through it, are felt, in their motion and contact, by the living creature, who thus feels those pleasant or unpleasant affections which we call "heat," "burning," or "scorching."

Perhaps while this pulverizing and attrition continue, and remain confined to the particles themselves, their motion will be temporary and their operation will be merely that of heating. But once we arrive at the point of ultimate and maximum dissolution into truly indivisible atoms, light itself may be created, with an instantaneous motion or (I should rather say) an instantaneous diffusion and expansion, capable—I do not know if by the atoms' subtlety, rarity, immateriality, or by different and as yet unspecifiable conditions—capable, I say, of filling vast spaces.

But I should not like, Your Excellency, inadvertently to engulf myself in an infinite ocean without the means to find my way back to port. Nor should I like, while removing one doubt, to give birth to a hundred more, as I fear might in part be the case even in this timid venture from shore. Therefore, I shall await a more opportune moment to re-embark.

Dialogue Concerning the Two Great World-Systems

Simplicius. However perspicacious his genius may have been, Aristotle was not one to depend upon it more than seemed advisable; and in his philosophizing, he judged that sense-experience must be preferred to any argument whatsoever, fabricated by the mind of man. He said that whoever would deny his senses ought, as punishment, to be deprived of them.... So let us proceed to the specific reasons and the sensory experiences which (how well Aristotle put it!) must be preferred to what may be supplied by human reason.

Sagredo. What has been said, then, should enable us to consider which of the two general arguments, that of Aristotle or that of Salviatus, has the greater probability. Aristotle's would persuade us that sublunary bodies are generable, corruptible, etc.; and that they are, therefore, different indeed from celestial bodies, which are impassible—that is to say, ingenerable, incorruptible, and so forth.... Salviatus, who supposes that the integral parts of the world are arranged in a perfect order, ... deems the Earth itself to be a celestial body, endowed with all the prerogatives which the latter possess. His argument, it seems to me, is much more in accord with things than Aristotle's. But be so good, Simplicius, as to produce all those particular reasons, experiments, and observations, natural as well as astronomical, on the basis of which others may remain persuaded that the Earth is different from celestial bodies, that it is immobile and located in the center of the world, and that it is otherwise prohibited from being as mobile as a planet like Jupiter or the Moon. And let Salviatus, on his part, be kind enough to answer them, point for point.

Simp. Well, to begin with, here are two powerful demonstrations which prove the Earth to be altogether different from celestial bodies. First. Bodies which are generable, corruptible, alterable, etc., are different from those which are ingenerable, incorruptible, inalterable, etc. But the Earth is generable, corruptible, alterable, etc.; and heavenly bodies are not. Therefore, the Earth is different from heavenly bodies!

Sagr. With your first argument, you merely bring back to the table that which stood there all day long, and which we just eliminated a moment back.

Simp. Just a moment, sir! Listen to the rest of it, and you shall see how really different the two sorts of bodies are. In my first argument, the minor premise was set forth *a priori*. I should like now to prove it *a posteriori*—watch if they are not the same. Since the major premise is too obviously true, I shall prove the minor premise as follows. Sensory experience shows us how on Earth there is continual generation, corruption, and change. But neither our own senses, nor the records of antiquity, have ever once witnessed these as taking place in celestial bodies. Hence the heavens are inalterable and the Earth is alterable, etc.

I base my second argument on a principal and essential property. A body which is obscure and deprived of light is different from a luminous, resplendent body. The Earth is dark and without light, but the heavenly bodies are full of light and brilliant. Therefore, they are different. Answer these arguments first, before we accumulate too many, and then I shall bring forward some others . . .

Simp. If Socrates declared himself to be the most ignorant while the oracle declared him to be the wisest, then I must point out that either Socrates or the oracle was a liar.

Salv. Neither conclusion follows, for both statements could be true. The oracle judged Socrates to be wise above all other men, whose wisdom is limited. Socrates claimed to know nothing with respect to absolute knowledge, which is infinite. With respect to infinity, any finite thing, be it large or small, is as nothing (to arrive at infinity, for example, it does not matter whether we add together thousands, tens, or units). Socrates understood well enough that the extent of his wisdom was nothing in comparison with the infinite wisdom which he lacked. Still, since there is some wisdom found in men, and this not equally distributed amongst all, Socrates could have had a greater share than all the others, and the response of the oracle would thence be verified.

Sagr. I seem to understand that point very well. Amongst men, Simplicius, there is the power to act, but it is not shared equally by all. There is no doubt that the power of an emperor is far greater than that of an ordinary person—but neither the one nor the other counts as anything in comparison with divine omnipotence. Amongst men, we find some who understand agriculture better than most others do. But to know how to plant a grape-seed in a hole—what has that to do with knowing how to make it take root, or how to draw nourishment to it, or how to select this part as good for making leaves, that for the vines, another for the clusters, another for the grapes, another for the skins! These are the workings of Nature, in all her wisdom. And yet this is only one of all the innumerable things which Nature does; and in just this one thing, we may recognize infinite wisdom. Can we not conclude that divine wisdom is infinitely infinite?

Salv. Here is another example. Would we not say that the knowledge of how to discover a beautiful statue in a piece of marble has raised the genius of Michelangelo high, high above the common wit of other men? And his work is only the imitation of a single pose and disposition of the outside parts of the external members of an immobile man. What is this, though, compared to a man made by Nature, composed of all the external and internal members, all the muscles, tendons, nerves, and bones which serve so many different motions? And what shall we say of the senses, the will, and the intellect? Can we not with good reason say that the fabrication of a statue, by an interval of infinity, falls short of the formation not only of a living man, but even of the vilest worm? . . .

Simp. Either I am not a man who understands, or else your discourse is manifestly inconsistent. You reckon understanding to be one of the greatest gifts—if not, indeed, the greatest—which have been given to man who is made by Nature. But a moment ago, you said of Socrates that his understanding was as nothing. So you must say that Nature has not understood how to make an understanding that understands!

Salv. Very sharply put! And in order to reply to your objection, I must have recourse to a philosophical distinction. Now, understanding may be interpreted in two different ways, *intensively* and *extensively*. Extensively, that is to say, with respect to the infinite number of intelligible things, the human understanding is as nothing. Even if it well understood a thousand propositions, a thousand is like zero in comparison with infinity. But intensively, that is to say, in terms of knowing some one thing perfectly, I assert that there are some propositions of which the human understanding is as absolutely certain as Nature is. I mean the sciences of pure mathematics—geometry and arithmetic. The divine intellect may well know infinitely more such propositions than we, because it knows them all. But of those few that the human intellect does knows, I believe our knowledge is equal to divine knowledge, so far as objective certainty is concerned. For we have come to understand the necessity of these propositions, and there can be no greater certainty than that.

Simp. This appears very bold to me, very rash.

Salv. These are common notions and are far from being tainted by audacity or presumptuousness. Nor do they in any way detract from the majesty of divine wisdom, any more than it would diminish God's omnipotence to assert that He cannot undo what has once been done. But I suspect, Simplicius, that you take umbrage at my words because, as you hear them, you feel them to be somewhat equivocal. Therefore, in order better to express myself, I shall say that the truth which mathematical demonstration gives us is the same truth that divine wisdom apprehends. I grant you that the manner in which God knows the infinity of propositions is utterly more excellent than is the manner by means of which we know the few that we do. We proceed by argumentation, and advance from conclusion to conclusion, while God [apprehends] through a simple, sudden intuition. . . . To conclude, then, the manner and number of propositions known to human intellect is infinitely surpassed by divine intellect. Nonetheless, I would not dishonor it. For when I consider how many, and how marvelous, are the things that human intellect has understood, discovered, and invented, I clearly know and do acknowledge that the mind of man is the work of God. And that is one of His most excellent ones.

Isaac Newton

(1642–1727)

ISAAC NEWTON (1642–1727) was born at Woolsthorpe in Lincolnshire, England. His widowed mother planned to make a country squire of him, and he was given the customary grammar school education. But the boy consistently neglected the chores required of him and showed instead a strong liking for mechanical contrivances; finally he was permitted to enter Trinity College, Cambridge. Here he rapidly revealed unusual gifts for mathematics, and won the interest and the friendship of Isaac Barrow, the first Lucasian Professor of Mathematics at the university. From Barrow, himself groping toward the methods of the differential calculus, Newton acquired a strong interest in optics, in the general problem of drawing tangents to curves, and in theology.

In 1664 he obtained his B.A., and on the outbreak of the Great Plague returned to Woolsthorpe, the scene of the famous alleged incident of the falling apple; although the story may be apocryphal, there is no question that most of his great ideas suggested themselves during the two years of enforced seclusion at Woolsthorpe. He then returned to Cambridge, and in 1699 succeeded Barrow as Lucasian Professor of Mathematics. He was presently made Fellow of the Royal Society and became involved in various controversies over his researches on such topics as the compound nature of white light and the force required to keep planets in orbit. His important works began to achieve recognition, and many honors were bestowed on him, including the presidency of the Royal Society, which he retained until his death twenty-four years later. He was made Warden, and later Master, of the Mint, with a comfortable salary; in 1705 he was knighted. Newton's duties as a Treasury official consumed much of his energy, but in his later years he gave free rein to his theological interests.

Newton's major work is the *Philosophiae Naturalis Principia Mathematica* (1687), which realized Descartes's dream of a universal mathematical science of nature, at least in astronomy and dynamics; it came to be regarded as the authoritative model of scientific method. In 1704 he published his *Opticks,* his most well-known work in the eighteenth century. His later religious works, such as *Two Notable Corruptions of Scripture* and *Observations on the Prophecies of Daniel and the Apocalypse of St. John,* reveal Newton's belief in the necessary existence of God behind the orderly world machine.

The following selections aim to explain Newton's achievements in his *Principia* and the character of his mathematical experimental method. The first is taken from a widely read book by one of his editors, Henry Pemberton's *A View of Sir Isaac Newton's Philosophy* (1728); and the second is comprised of excerpts from Newton's *Principia.*

A View of Sir Isaac Newton's Philosophy by Henry Pemberton

. . . But what surprising advancements in the knowledge of nature may be made by pursuing the true course in philosophical inquiries; when those searches are conducted by a genius equal to so divine a work, will be best understood by considering Sir Isaac Newton's discoveries. That my reader may apprehend as just a notion of these, as can be conveyed to him, by the brief account, which I intend to lay before him; I have set apart this introduction for explaining, in the fullest manner I am able, the principles, whereon Sir Isaac Newton proceeds. For without a clear conception of these, it is impossible to form any true idea of the singular excellence of the inventions of this great philosopher.

The principles then of this philosophy are: upon no consideration to indulge conjectures concerning the powers and laws of nature, but to make it our endeavour with all diligence to search out the real and true laws, by which the constitution of things is regulated. The philosopher's first care must be to distinguish, what he sees to be within his power, from what is beyond his reach; to assume no greater degree of knowledge, than what he finds himself possessed of; but to advance by slow and cautious steps; to search gradually into natural causes; to secure to himself the knowledge of the most immediate cause of each appearance, before he extends his views farther to causes more remote. This is the method, in which philosophy ought to be cultivated; which does not pretend to so great things, as the more airy speculations; but will perform abundantly more: we shall not perhaps seem to the unskilful to know so much, but our real knowledge will be greater. And certainly it is no objection against this method, that some others promise, what is nearer to the extent of our wishes: since this, if it will not teach us all we could desire to be informed of, will however give us some true light into nature; which no other can do. Nor has the philosopher any reason to think his labour lost, when he finds himself stopt at the cause first discovered by him, or at any other more remote cause, short of the original: for if he has but sufficiently proved any one cause; he has entered so far into the real constitution of things, has laid a safe foundation for others to work upon, and has facilitated their endeavours in the search after yet more distant causes; and besides, in the mean time he may apply the knowledge of these intermediate causes to *many useful purposes*. Indeed the being able to make practical deductions from natural causes, constitutes the great distinction between the true philosophy and the false. Causes assumed upon conjecture, must be so loose and undefined, that nothing particular can be collected from them. But those causes, which are brought to light by a strict examination of things, will be more distinct. Hence it appears to have been no unuseful discovery, that the ascent of water in pumps is owing to the pressure of the air by its weight or spring; though the causes, which make the air gravitate, and render it elastic, be unknown: for notwithstanding we are ignorant of the original, whence these powers of the air are derived; yet we may receive much advantage from the bare knowledge of these powers. If we are but certain of the degree of force, wherewith they act, we shall know the extent of what is to be expected from them; we shall know the greatest height, to which it is possible by pumps to raise water; and shall thereby be prevented from making any useless efforts towards improving these instruments beyond the limits prescribed to them by nature; whereas without so much knowledge as this, we might probably have wasted in attempts of this kind much time and labour. . . . It is confessed by all, that Galileo greatly improved philosophy, by shewing, as we shall relate hereafter, that the power in bodies, which we call gravity, occasions them to move downwards with a velocity equably accelerated; and that when any body is thrown forwards, the same power obliges it to describe in its motion that line, which is called by geometers a parabola: yet we are ignorant of the cause, which makes bodies gravitate. But although we are unacquainted with the spring, whence this power in nature is derived, nevertheless we can estimate its effects. When a Body falls perpendicularly, it is known, how long time it takes in descending from any height whatever: and if it be thrown forward, we know the real path, which it describes; we can determine in what direction, and with what degree of swiftness it must be projected, in order to its striking against any object desired; and we can also ascertain the very force, wherewith it will strike. Sir Isaac Newton has further taught, that this power of gravitation extends up to the moon, and causes that planet to gravitate as much towards the earth, as any of the bodies, which are familiar to us, would, if placed at the same distance: he has proved likewise, that all the planets gravitate towards the sun, and towards one another; and that their respective motions follow from this gravitation. All this he has demonstrated upon indisputable geometrical principles, which cannot be rendered precarious for want of knowing what it is, which causes these Bodies thus mutually to gravitate: any more than we can doubt of the propensity in all the bodies about us, to descend towards the earth; or can call in question the fore-mentioned propositions of Galileo, which are built upon that principle. And as Galileo has shewn more fully, than was known before, what effects were produced in the motion of bodies by their gravitation towards the earth; so Sir Isaac Newton, by this his invention, has much advanced our knowledge in the celestial motions. By discovering that the moon gravitates towards the sun, as well as towards the earth; he has laid open those intricacies in the moon's motion, which no astronomer, from observations only, could ever find out: and one kind of heavenly bodies, the comets, have their motion now clearly ascertained; whereof we had before no true knowledge at all.

Doubtless it might be expected, that such surprising success should have silenced, at once, every cavil. But we have seen the contrary. For because this philosophy professes modestly to keep within the extent of our faculties, and is ready to confess its imperfections, rather than to make any fruitless attempts to conceal them, by seeking to cover the defects in our knowledge with the vain ostentation of rash and groundless conjectures; hence has been taken an occasion to insinuate that we are led to miraculous causes, and the occult qualities of the schools.

But the first of these accusations is very extraordinary. If by calling these causes miraculous nothing more is meant than only, that they often appear to us wonderful and surprising, it is not easy to see what difficulty can be raised from thence; for the works of nature discover every where such proofs of the unbounded power, and the consummate wisdom of their author, that the more they are known, the more they will excite our admiration: and it is too manifest to be insisted on, that the common sense of the word miraculous can have no place here, when it implies what is above the ordinary course of things. The other imputation, that these causes are occult upon the account of our not perceiving what produces them, contains in it great ambiguity. That something relating to them lies hid, the followers of this philosophy are ready to acknowledge, nay desire it should be carefully remarked, as pointing out proper subjects for future inquiry. But this is very different from the proceeding of the schoolmen in the causes called by them occult. For as their occult qualities were understood to operate in a manner occult, and not apprehended by us; so they were obtruded upon us for such original and essential properties in bodies, as made it vain to seek any farther cause; and a greater power was attributed to them, than any natural appearances authorized. For instance, the rise of water in pumps was ascribed to a certain abhorrence of vacuum, which they thought fit to assign to nature. And this was so far a true observation, that the water does move, contrary to its usual course, into the space, which otherwise would be left void of any sensible matter; and, that the procuring such a vacuity was the apparent cause of the water's ascent. But while we were not in the least informed how this power, called an abhorrence of a vacuum, produced the visible effects; instead of making any advancement in the knowledge of nature, we only gave an artificial name to one of her operations: and when the speculation was pushed so beyond what any appearances required, as to have it concluded, that this abhorrence of a vacuum was a power inherent in all matter, and so unlimited as to render it impossible for a vacuum to exist at all; it then became a much greater absurdity, in being made the foundation of a most ridiculous manner of reasoning; as at length evidently appeared, when it came to be discovered, that this rise of the water followed only from the pressure of the air, and extended itself no farther, than the power of that cause. The scholastic style in discoursing of these occult qualities, as if they were essential differences in the very substances, of which bodies consisted, was certainly very absurd; by reason it tended to discourage all farther inquiry. But no such ill consequences can follow from the considering of any natural causes, which confessedly are not traced up to their first original. How shall we ever come to the knowledge of the several original causes of things, otherwise than by storing up all intermediate causes which we can discover? Are all the original and essential properties of matter so very obvious, that none of them can escape our first view? This is not probable. It is much more likely, that, if some of the essential properties are discovered by our first observations, a stricter examination should bring more to light.

But in order to clear up this point concerning the essential properties of matter, let us consider the subject a little distinctly. We are to conceive, that the matter, out of which the universe of things is formed, is furnished with certain qualities and powers, whereby it is rendered fit to answer the purposes, for which it was created. But every property, of which any particle of this matter is in itself possessed, and which is not barely the consequence of the union of this particle with other portions of matter, we may call an essential property: whereas all other qualities or attributes belonging to bodies, which depend on their particular frame and composition, are not essential to the matter, whereof such bodies are made; because the matter of these bodies will be deprived of those qualities, only by the dissolution of the body, without working any change in the original constitution of one single particle of this mass of matter. *Extension* we apprehend to be one of these essential properties, and *impenetrability* another. These two belong universally to all matter; and are the principal ingredients in the idea, which this word matter usually excites in the mind. Yet as the idea, marked by this name, is not purely the creature of our own understandings, but is taken for the representation of a certain substance without us; if we should discover, that every part of the substance, in which we find these two properties, should likewise be endowed universally with any other essential qualities; all these, from the time they come to our notice, must be united under our general idea of matter. How many such properties there are actually in all matter we know not; those, of which we are at present apprized, have been found out only by our observations on things; how many more a farther search may bring to light, no one can say; nor are we certain, that we are provided with sufficient methods of perception to discern them all. Therefore, since we have no other way of making discoveries in nature, but by gradual inquiries into the properties of bodies; our first step must be to admit without distinction all the properties, which we observe; and afterwards we must endeavour, as far as we are able, to distinguish between the qualities, wherewith the very substances themselves are indued, and those appearances, which result from the structure only of compound bodies. Some of the properties, which we observe in things, are the attributes of particular bodies only; others universally belong to all, that fall under out notice. Whether some of the qualities and powers of particular bodies, be derived from different kinds of matter entering their composition, cannot, in the present imperfect state of our knowledge, absolutely be decided; though we have not yet any reason to conclude, but that all the bodies, with which we converse, are framed out of the very same kind of matter, and that their distinct qualities are occasioned only by their structure; through the variety whereof the general powers of matter are caused to produce different effects. On the other hand, we should not hastily conclude, that whatever is found to appertain to all matter, which falls under our examination, must for that reason only be an essential property thereof, and not be derived from some unseen disposition in the frame of nature. Sir Isaac Newton has found reason to conclude, that *gravity* is a property universally belonging to all the perceptible bodies in the universe, and to every particle of matter, whereof they are composed. *But yet he no where asserts this property to be essential to matter.* And he was so far from having any design of establishing it as such, that, on the contrary, he has given some hints worthy of himself at a cause for it; and expressly says, that he proposed those hints to shew that he had no such intention.

It appears from hence, that it is not easy to determine, what properties of Bodies are essentially inherent in the matter, out of which they are made, and what depend upon their frame and composition. But certainly whatever properties are found to belong either to any particular systems of matter or universally to all, must be considered in philosophy; because philosophy will be otherwise imperfect. Whether those properties can be deduced from some other appertaining to matter, either among those, which are already known, or among such as can be discovered by us, is afterwards to be sought for the farther improvement of our knowledge. But this inquiry cannot properly have place in the deliberation about admitting any property of matter or bodies into philosophy; for that purpose it is only to be considered, whether the existence of such a property has been justly proved or not. Therefore to decide what causes of things are rightly received into natural philosophy, requires only a distinct and clear conception of what kind of reasoning is to be allowed of as convincing, when we argue upon the works of nature.

The proofs in natural philosophy cannot be so absolutely conclusive, as in the mathematics. For the subjects of that science are purely the ideas of our own minds. They may be represented to our senses by material objects, but they are themselves the arbitrary productions of our own thoughts; so that as the mind can have a full and adequate knowledge of its own ideas, the reasoning in geometry can be rendered perfect. But in natural knowledge the subject of our contemplation is without us, and not so compleatly to be known: therefore our method of arguing must fall a little short of absolute perfection. It is only here required to steer a just course between the conjectural method of proceeding, against which I have so largely spoke; and demanding so rigorous a proof, as will reduce all philosophy to mere scepticism, and exclude all prospect of making any progress in the knowledge of nature.

Newton's *Principia*

Preface

Since the ancients (as we are told by *Pappus*), made great account of the science of mechanics in the investigation of natural things; and the moderns, laying aside substantial forms and occult qualities, have endeavoured to subject the phænomena of nature to the laws of mathematics, I have in this treatise cultivated mathematics so far as it regards philosophy. The ancients considered mechanics in a twofold respect; as rational, which proceeds accurately by demonstration; and practical. To practical mechanics all the manual arts belong, from which mechanics took its name. But as artificers do not work with perfect accuracy, it comes to pass that mechanics is so distinguished from geometry, that what is perfectly accurate is called geometrical; what is less so, is called mechanical. But the errors are not in the art, but in the artificers. He that works with less accuracy is an imperfect mechanic; and if any could work with perfect accuracy, he would be the most perfect mechanic of all; for the description of right lines and circles, upon which geometry is founded, belongs to mechanics. Geometry does not teach us to draw these lines, but requires them to be drawn; for it requires that the learner should first be taught to describe these accurately, before he enters upon geometry; then it shows how by these operations problems may be solved. To describe right lines and circles are problems, but not geometrical problems. The solution of these problems is required from mechanics; and by geometry the use of them, when so solved, is shown; and it is the glory of geometry that from those few principles, brought from without, it is able to produce so many things. Therefore geometry is founded in mechanical practice, and is nothing but that part of universal mechanics which accurately proposes and demonstrates the art of measuring. But since the manual arts are chiefly conversant in the moving of bodies, it comes to pass that geometry is commonly referred to their magnitudes, and mechanics to their motion. In this sense rational mechanics will be the science of motions resulting from any forces whatsoever, and of the forces required to produce any motions, accurately proposed and demonstrated. This part of mechanics was cultivated by the ancients in the five powers which relate to manual arts, who considered gravity (it not being a manual power), no otherwise than as it moved weights by those powers. Our design not respecting arts, but philosophy, and our subject not manual but natural powers, we consider chiefly those things which relate to gravity, levity, elastic force, the resistance of fluids, and the like forces, whether attractive or impulsive; and therefore we offer this work as the mathematical principles of philosophy; for all the difficulty of philosophy seems to consist in this—from the phænomena of motions to investigate the forces of nature, and then from these forces to demonstrate the other phænomena; and to this end the general propositions in the first and second book are directed. In the third book we give an example of this in the explication of the System of the World; for by the propositions mathematically demonstrated in the former books, we in the third derive from the celestial phænomena the forces of gravity with which bodies tend to the sun and the several planets. Then from these forces, by other propositions which are also mathematical, we deduce the motions of the planets, the comets, the moon, and the sea. I wish we could derive the rest of the phænomena of nature by the same kind of reasoning from mechanical principles; for I am induced by many reasons to suspect that they may all depend upon certain forces by which the particles of bodies, by some causes hitherto unknown, are either mutually impelled towards each other; and cohere in regular figures, or are repelled and recede from each other; which forces being unknown, philosophers have hitherto attempted the search of nature in vain; but I hope the principles here laid down will afford some light either to this or some truer method of philosophy. . . .

Book III

Rules of Reasoning in Philosophy

Rule I. *We are to admit no more causes of natural things than such as are both true and sufficient to explain their appearances.*

To this purpose the philosophers say that Nature does nothing in vain, and more is in vain when less will serve; for Nature is pleased with simplicity, and affects not the pomp of superfluous causes.

Rule II. *Therefore to the same natural effects we must, as far as possible, assign the same causes.*

As to respiration in a man and in a beast; the descent of stones in Europe and in America; the light of our culinary fire and of the sun; the reflection of light in the earth, and in the planets.

Rule III. *The qualities of bodies, which admit neither intension nor remission of degrees, and which are found to belong to all bodies within the reach of our experiments, are to be esteemed the universal qualities of all bodies whatsoever.*

For since the qualities of bodies are only known to us by experiments, we are to hold for universal all such as universally agree with experiments and such as are not liable to diminution can never be quite taken away. We are certainly not to relinquish the evidence of experiments for the sake of dreams and vain fictions of our own devising; nor are we to recede from the analogy of Nature, which uses to be simple, and always consonant to itself. We no other way know the extension of bodies than by our senses, nor do these reach it in all bodies; but because we perceive extension in all that are sensible, therefore we ascribe it universally to all others also. That abundance of bodies are hard, we learn by experience; and because the hardness of the whole arises from the hardness of the parts, we therefore justly infer the hardness of the undivided particles not only of the bodies we feel but of all others. That all bodies are impenetrable, we gather not from reason, but from sensation. The bodies which we handle we find impenetrable, and thence conclude impenetrability to be an universal property of all bodies whatsoever. That all bodies are moveable, and endowed with certain powers (which we call the *vires inertiæ*) of persevering in their motion, or in their rest, we only infer the like properties observed in the bodies which we have seen. The extension, hardness, impenetrability, mobility, and *vis inertiæ* of the whole, result from the extension, hardness, impenetrability, mobility, and *vires inertiæ* of the parts; and thence we conclude the least particles of all bodies to be also all extended, and hard, and impenetrable, and moveable, and endowed with their proper *vires inertiæ*. And this is the foundation of all philosophy. Moreover, that the divided but contiguous particles of bodies may be separated from one another, is matter of observation; and, in the particles that remain undivided, our minds are able to distinguish yet lesser parts, as is mathematically demonstrated. But whether the parts so distinguished, and not yet divided, may, by the powers of Nature, be actually divided and separated from one another, we cannot certainly determine. Yet, had we the proof of but one experiment that any undivided particle, in breaking a hard and solid body, suffered a division, we might by virtue of this rule conclude that the undivided as well as the divided particles may be divided and actually separated to infinity.

Lastly, if it universally appears, by experiments and astronomical observations, that all bodies about the earth gravitate towards the earth, and that in proportion to the quantity of matter which they severally contain; that the moon likewise, according to the quantity of its matter, gravitates towards the earth; that, on the other hand, our sea gravitates towards the moon; and all the planets mutually one towards another; and the comets in like manner towards the sun; we must, in consequence of this rule, universally allow that all bodies whatsoever are endowed with a principle of mutual gravitation. For the argument from the appearances concludes with more force for the universal gravitation of all bodies than for their impenetrability; of which, among those in the celestial regions, we have no experiments, nor any manner of observation. Not that I affirm gravity to be essential to bodies: by their *vis insita* I mean nothing but their *vis inertiæ*. This is immutable. Their gravity is diminished as they recede from the earth.

Rule IV. *In experimental philosophy we are to look upon propositions collected by general induction from phænomena as accurately or very nearly true, notwithstanding any contrary hypotheses that may be imagined, till such time as other phænomena occur, by which they may either be made more accurate, or liable to exceptions.*

This rule must follow, that the argument of induction may not be evaded by hypotheses.

General Scholium

. . . Hitherto we have explained the phænomena of the heavens and of our sea by the power of gravity, but have not yet assigned the cause of this power. This is certain, that it must proceed from a cause that penetrates to the very centres of the sun and planets, without suffering the least diminution of its force; that [it] operates not according to the quantity of the surfaces of the particles upon which it acts (as mechanical causes use to do), but according to the quantity of the solid matter which they contain, and propagates its virtue on all sides to immense distances, decreasing always in the duplicate proportion of the distances. Gravitation towards the sun is made up out of the gravitations towards the several particles of which the body of the sun is composed; and in receding from the sun decreases accurately in the duplicate proportion of the distances as far as the orb of Saturn, as evidently appears from the quiescence of the aphelions of the planets; nay, and even to the remotest aphelions of the comets, if those aphelions are also quiescent. But hitherto I have not been able to discover the cause of those properties of gravity from phænomena, and I frame no hypotheses; for whatever is not deduced from the phænomena is to be called an hypothesis; and hypotheses, whether metaphysical or physical, whether of occult qualities or mechanical, have no place in experimental philosophy. In this philosophy particular propositions are inferred from the phænomena, and afterwards rendered general by induction. Thus it was that the impenetrability, the mobility, and the impulsive force of bodies, and the laws of motion and of gravitation, were discovered. And to us it is enough that gravity does really exist, and act according to the laws which we have explained, and abundantly serves to account for all the motions of the celestial bodies, and of our sea. . . .

• • • • • • • • • • • •

Newton's science was grounded in a number of metaphysical and theological assumptions concerning God and the structure of the universe. It is evident, for example, that Newton's scientific theories were influenced by an unshakable faith in an all powerful and omnipresent God who was both the creator and sustainer of nature. Accordingly, nature was interpreted as a stable, uniform and essentially harmonious order, carefully regulated by a superintendent and benevolent God.

The following selections from Newton's *Optics* illustrate the important role which his philosophical views of nature played in the formulation of his method and principles of science.[1] They show that for Newton science, like natural theology, sought to unlock the underlying mysteries of God and his universe. Hence, although Newton limited his scientific inquiries to the physical phenomena of nature, he nevertheless hoped that they would ultimately bring him nearer to the knowledge of God, the First and highest cause of all things.

From *Optics*

The main business of natural philosophy is to argue from phenomena without feigning hypotheses, and to deduce causes from effects, till we come to the very first cause, which certainly is not mechanical; and not only to unfold the mechanism of the world, but chiefly to resolve these and such like questions. What is there in places almost empty of matter, and whence is it that the sun and planets gravitate towards one another, without dense matter between them? Whence is it that Nature doth nothing in vain; and whence arises all that order and beauty which we see in the world? To what end are comets, and whence is it that planets move all one and the same way in orbs concentric, while comets move all manner of ways in orbs very excentric; and what hinders the fixed stars from falling upon one another? How came the bodies of animals to be contrived with so much art, and for what ends were their several parts? Was the eye contrived without skill in optics, and the ear without knowledge of sounds? How do the motions of the body follow from the will, and whence is the instinct in animals? Is not the sensory of animals that place to which the sensitive substance is present, and into which the sensible species of things are carried through the nerves and brain, that there

---

[1] Selections from Sir Isaac Newton, *Optics: or a Treatise of the Reflections, Refractions, Inflections and Colours of Light*, 4th ed., (London: William Innys: 1730), Queries 28 and 31, pp. 369–370, 375–376, 400–406.

they may be perceived by their immediate presence to that substance? And these things being rightly dispatched, does it not appear from phenomena that there is a being incorporeal, living, intelligent, omnipresent, who in infinite space, as it were in his sensory, sees the things themselves intimately, and thoroughly perceives them, and comprehends them wholly by their immediate presence to himself: of which things the images only carried through the organs of sense into our little sensoriums, are there seen and beheld by that which in us perceives and thinks. And though every true step made in this philosophy brings us not immediately to the knowledge of the first cause, yet it brings us nearer to it, and on that account is to be highly valued. ...

Have not the small particles of bodies certain powers, virtues, or forces, by which they act at a distance, not only upon the rays of light for reflecting, refracting, and inflecting them, but also upon one another for producing a great part of the phenomena of Nature? For it is well known, that bodies act one upon another by the attractions of gravity, magnetism, and electricity; and these instances show the tenor and course of Nature, and make it not improbable but that there may be more attractive powers than these. For Nature is very consonant and conformable to her self. How these attractions may be performed, I do not here consider. What I call attraction may be performed by impulse, or by some other means unknown to me. I use that word here to signify only in general any force by which bodies tend towards one another, whatsoever be the cause. For we must learn from the phenomena of Nature what bodies attract one another, and what are the laws and properties of the attraction, before we enquire the cause by which the attraction is performed. The attractions of gravity, magnetism, and electricity, reach to very sensible distances, and so have been observed by vulgar eyes, and there may be others which reach to so small distances as hitherto escape observation; and perhaps electrical attraction may reach to such small distances, even without being excited by friction. . . .

All these things being considered, it seems probable to me, that God in the beginning formed matter in solid, massy, hard impenetrable, moveable particles, of such sizes and figures, and with such other properties, and in such proportion to space, as most conduced to the end for which he formed them; and that these primitive particles being solids, are incomparably harder than any porous bodies compounded of them, even so very hard, as never to wear or break in pieces; no ordinary power being able to divide what God himself made one in the first creation. While the particles continue entire, they may compose bodies of one and the same Nature and texture in all ages: but should they wear away, or break in pieces, the Nature of things depending on them, would be changed. Water and earth, composed of old worn particles and fragments of particles, would not be of the same nature and texture now, with water and earth composed of entire particles in the beginning. And therefore, that Nature may be lasting, the changes of corporeal things are to be placed only in the various separations and new associations and motions of these permanent particles; compound bodies being apt to break, not in the midst of solid particles, but where those particles are laid together, and only touch in a few points.

It seems to me further, that these particles have not only a *vis inertiae*, [power of inertia] accompanied with such passive laws of motion as naturally result from that force, but also that they are moved by certain active principles, such as is that of gravity, and that which causes fermentation, and the cohesion of bodies. These principles I consider, not as occult qualities, supposed to result from the specific forms of things, but as general laws of Nature, by which the things themselves are formed; their truth appearing to us by phenomena, though their causes be not yet discovered. For these are manifest qualities, and their causes only are occult. And the *Aristotelians* gave the name of occult qualities, not to manifest qualities but to such qualities only as they supposed to lie hid in bodies, and to be the unknown causes of manifest effects: such as would be the causes of gravity, and of magnetic and electric attractions, and of fermentations, if we should suppose that these forces or actions arose from qualities unknown to us, and uncapable of being discovered and made manifest. Such occult qualities put a stop to the improvement of natural philosophy, and therefore of late years have been rejected. To tell us that every species of things is endowed with an occult specific quality by which it acts and produces manifest effects, is to tell us nothing: but to derive two or three general principles of motion from phenomena, and afterwards to tell us how the properties and actions of all corporeal things follow from those manifest principles, would be a very great step in philosophy, though the causes of those principles were not yet discovered: and therefore I scruple not to propose the principles of motion above-mentioned, they being of very general extent, and leave their causes to be found out.

Now by the help of these principles, all material things seem to have been composed of the hard and solid particles above-mentioned, variously associated in the first creation by the counsel of an intelligent agent. For it became him who created them to set them in order. And if he did so, it is unphilosophical to seek for any other origin of the world, or to pretend that it might arise out of a chaos by the mere laws of nature: though being once formed, it may continue by those laws for many ages. For while comets move in very excentric orbs in all manner of positions, blind fate could never make all the planets move one and the same way in orbs concentric, some inconsiderable irregularities excepted, which may have risen from the mutual actions of comets and planets upon one another, and which will be apt to increase, till this system wants reformation. Such a wonderful uniformity in the planetary system must be allowed the effect of choice. And so must the uniformity in the bodies of animals, they having generally a right and a left side shaped alike, and on either side of their bodies two legs behind, and either two arms, or two legs, or two wings before upon their shoulders, and between their shoulders a neck running down into a back-bone, and ahead upon it; and in the head two ears, two eyes, a nose, a mouth, and a tongue, alike situated. Also the first contrivance of those very artificial parts of animals, the eyes, ears, brain, muscles, heart, lungs, midriff, glands, larynx, hands, wings, swimming bladders, natural spectacles, and other organs of sense and motion; and the instinct of brutes and insects, can be the effect of nothing else than the wisdom and skill of a powerful ever-living agent, who being in all places, is more able by his Will to move the bodies within his boundless uniform sensorium, and thereby to form and reform the parts of the universe, than we are by our will to move the parts of our own bodies. And yet we are not to consider the world as the body of God, or the several parts thereof, as the parts of God. He is an uniform being, void of organs, members or parts, and they are his creatures subordinate to him, and subservient to his Will; and he is no more the soul of them, than the soul of Man is the soul of the species of things carried through the organs of sense into the place of its sensation, where it perceives them by means of its immediate presence, without the intervention of any third thing. The organs of sense are not for enabling the soul to perceive the species of things in its sensorium, but only for conveying them thither; and God has no need of such organs, he being every where present to the things themselves. And since space is divisible *in infinitum*, and matter is not necessarily in all places, it may be also allowed that God is able to create particles of matter of several sizes and figures, and in several proportions to space, and perhaps of different densities and forces, and thereby to vary the laws of Nature, and make worlds of several sorts in several parts of the universe. At least, I see nothing of contradiction in all this.

As in mathematics, so in natural philosophy, the investigation of difficult things by the method of analysis, ought ever to precede the method of composition. This analysis consists in making experiments and observations, and in drawing general conclusions from them by induction, and admitting of no objections against the conclusions, but such as are taken from experiments, or other certain truths. For hypotheses are not to be regarded in experimental philosophy. And although the arguing from experiments and observations by induction be no demonstration of general conclusions; yet it is the best way of arguing which the nature of things admits of, and may be looked upon as so much the stronger, by how much the induction is more general. And if no exception occur from phenomena, the conclusion may be pronounced generally. But if at any time afterwards any exception shall occur from experiments, it may then begin to be pronounced with such exceptions as occur. By this way of analysis we may proceed from compounds to ingredients, and from motions to the forces producing them; and in general, from effects to their causes, and from particular causes to more general ones, till the argument end in the most general. This is the method of analysis: and the synthesis consists in assuming the causes discovered, and established as principles, and by them explaining the phenomena proceeding from them, and proving the explanations.

In the two first books of these *Optics*, I proceeded by this analysis to discover and prove the original differences of the rays of light in respect of refrangibility, reflexibility, and colour, and their alternate fits of easy reflexion and easy transmission, and the properties of bodies, both opake and pellucid, on which their reflexions and colours depend. And these discoveries being proved, may be assumed in the method of composition for explaining the phenomena arising from them: an instance of which method I gave in the end of the first book. In this third book I have only begun the analysis of what remains to be discovered about light and its effects upon the frame of Nature, hinting several things about it, and leaving the hints to be examined and improved by the farther experiments and observations of such as are inquisitive. And if natural philosophy in all its parts, by pursuing this method, shall at length be perfected, the bounds of moral philosophy will be also enlarged. For so far as we can know by natural philosophy what is the first Cause, what power he has over us, and what benefits we receive from him, so far our duty towards him, as well as that towards one another, will appear to us by the light of Nature. And no doubt, if the worship of false Gods had not blinded the heathen, their moral philosophy would have gone farther than to the four cardinal virtues; and instead of teaching the transmigration of souls, and to worship the sun and moon, and dead heroes, they would have taught us to worship our true author and benefactor, as their ancestors did under the government of *Noah* and his sons before they corrupted themselves.

René Descartes
(1596–1650)

Descartes was born in Touraine, France, of a noble family. He received one of the best educations available at the time, at the Jesuit college of La Fleche. He then attended the University of Poitiers and, after having spent some time in the army, travelling and then living in Paris, he finally settled in Holland in 1628 to continue his work in mathematics, science and philosophy. He gained an international reputation in these fields during his lifetime by inventing, for example, analytical geometry and deducing the correct law of inertia.

Descartes, like Bacon, was concerned to find a new method by which certainty could be reached and error avoided. In *A Discourse on Method* (1637)[1] —the complete title *is A Discourse on the Method of Rightly Conducting the Reason and Seeking Truth in the Sciences*—Descartes displays his preference for a rationalistic approach. After severely criticising his own education, in a passage which sets him at odds with the Renaissance man, Descartes lays down a set of rules of procedure drawn from the study of mathematics. By applying these rules to all science and philosophy, Descartes hoped to enter onto the path of certainty, which is open to all men who follow the method. In Descartes' view, all the necessary laws of the universe can be discovered by reflection on innate ideas; experiment serves only to show us the particular instances that fall under these laws.

Descartes has often been called the Father of Modem Philosophy. Since his ambition was to replace Aristotle as the philosophical support of the Christian religion, and to do this with a system which was of his own building from the ground up, he may be said to have coveted some such position. In fact, his own views owed more to his predecessors than he cared to admit. His doctrine of innate ideas was squarely in the Platonic and Augustinian tradition; the argument "Cogito, ergo sum" (I think, therefore I am) is to be found in Augustine, even if its use in Descartes is more radical; and his ontological argument for the existence of God has an ancestor in the writings of Anselm. Indeed, Descartes often seems to attribute to the natural light of reason the origin of ideas (such as that of God) which were the product of centuries of philosophical and theological reflection, and which in fact he learned from the Jesuits at La Flèche.

Nonetheless, the emphasis, aim and method of Descartes' system was highly original, and he has left a profound mark on subsequent philosophy. His attempt to build the world which we know out of *ideas* in the mind as the sole direct object of consciousness stamps the nature of seventeenth-century epistemology, both rationalist and empiricist alike, save that the ideas stressed by Descartes and the rationalists were ideas of understanding, while those emphasized by the empiricists were ideas of sense-experience. Thus Descartes and Locke shared the view, called representationalism, that we are directly aware only of ideas in the mind which *represent* the external world to our consciousness; and they thus inaugurated the stress on the question of validating human knowledge which dominated

---

[1] Selections reprinted from John Veitch, trans., *The Method, Meditations, and Selections from the Principles of Descartes*, (London: Blackwood, 1880), pp. 2–22, 32–46, 59–64, 74–76.

philosophy up to Kant and beyond. Again, the roots of modem existentialism and phenomenology may be seen in Descartes' stress on the primacy of self-consciousness as the indubitable datum. Finally, Descartes' dualism of body and mind, which echoes Plato but is far more theoretically rigid, left the conscious self and the mechanistically-conceived body without any really intelligible connection; and after some unsuccessful attempts to explain their apparent interaction, many subsequent thinkers tended to regard either the mind or the body as alone the ultimate reality. In this way, despite himself, Descartes seems to be the progenitor both of idealism and of materialism. Thus he has been a seminal influence on almost every school of philosophy from his time to the present day.

From *A Discourse on Method*

If this Discourse appear too long to be read at once, it may be divided into six parts: and, in the first, will be found various considerations touching the Sciences; in the second, the principal rules of the Method which the Author has discovered; in the third, certain of the rules of Morals which he has deduced from this Method; in the fourth, the reasonings by which he establishes the existence of God and of the Human Soul, which are the foundations of his Metaphysic; in the fifth, the order of the Physical questions which he has investigated, and, in particular, the explication of the motion of the heart and of some other difficulties pertaining to Medicine, as also the difference between the soul of man and that of the brutes; and, in the last, what the Author believes to be required in order to greater advancement in the Investigation of Nature than has yet been made, with the reasons that have induced him to write.

Part I

Good sense is, of all things among men, the most equally distributed; for every one thinks himself so abundantly provided with it, that those even who are the most difficult to satisfy in everything else, do not usually desire a larger measure of this quality than they already possess. And in this it is not likely that all are mistaken: the conviction is rather to be held as testifying that the power of judging aright and of distinguishing truth from error, which is properly what is called good sense or reason, is by nature equal in all men; and that the diversity of our opinions, consequently, does not arise from some being endowed with a larger share of reason than others, but solely from this, that we conduct our thoughts along different ways, and do not fix our attention on the same objects. For to be possessed the prime requisite is rightly to apply it. The greatest of a vigorous mind is not enough; minds, as they are capable of the highest excellences, are open likewise to the greatest aberrations; and those who travel very slowly may yet make far greater progress, provided they keep always to the straight road, than those who, while they run, forsake it.

For myself, I have never fancied my mind to be in any respect more perfect than those of the generality; on the contrary, I have often wished that I were equal to some others in promptitude of thought, or in clearness and distinctness of imagination, or in fullness and readiness of memory. And besides these, I know of no other qualities that contribute to the perfection of the mind; for as to the reason or sense, inasmuch as it is that alone which constitutes us men, and distinguishes us from the brutes, I am disposed to believe that it is to be found complete in each individual; and on this point to adopt the common opinion of philosophers, who say that the difference of greater and less holds only among the *accidents*, and not among the *forms* or *natures* of *individuals* of the same *species*.

I will not hesitate, however, to avow my belief that it has been my singular good fortune to have very early in life fallen in with certain tracks which have conducted me to considerations and maxims, of which I have formed a method that gives me the means, as I think, of gradually augmenting my knowledge, and of raising it by little and little to the highest point which the mediocrity of my talents and the brief duration of my life will permit me to reach. For I have already reaped from it such fruits that, although I have been accustomed to think lowly enough of myself, and although when I look with the eye of a philosopher at the varied courses and pursuits of mankind at large, I find scarcely one which does not appear vain and useless, I nevertheless derive the highest satisfaction from the progress I conceive myself to have already made in the search after truth, and cannot help entertaining such expectations of the future as to believe that if, among the occupations of men as men, there is any one really excellent and important, it is that which I have chosen.

After all, it is possible I may be mistaken; and it is but a little copper and glass, perhaps, that I take for gold and diamonds. I know how very liable we are to delusion in what relates to ourselves, and also how much the judgments of our friends are to be suspected when given in our favour. But I shall endeavour in this discourse to describe the paths I have followed, and to delineate my life as in a picture, in order that each one may be able to judge of them for himself, and that in the general opinion entertained of them, as gathered from current report, I myself may have a new help towards instruction to be added to those I have been in the habit of employing.

My present design, then, is not to teach the method which each ought to follow for the right conduct of his reason, but solely to describe the way in which I have endeavoured to conduct my own. They who set themselves to give precepts must of course regard themselves as possessed of greater skill than those to whom they prescribe; and if they err in the slightest particular, they subject themselves to censure. But as this tract is put forth merely as a history, or, if you will, as a tale, in which, amid some examples worthy of imitation, there will be found, perhaps, as many more which it were advisable not to follow, I hope it will prove useful to some without being hurtful to any, and that my openness will find some favour with all.

From my childhood, I have been familiar with letters; and as I was given to believe that by their help a clear and certain knowledge of all that is useful in life might be acquired, I was ardently desirous of instruction. But as soon as I had finished the entire course of study, at the close of which it is customary to be admitted into the order of the learned, I completely changed my opinion. For I found myself involved in so many doubts and errors, that I was convinced I had advanced no farther in all my attempts at learning, than the discovery at every turn of my own ignorance. And yet I was studying in one of the most celebrated schools in Europe, in which I thought there must be learned men, if such were anywhere to be found. I had been taught all that others learned there; and not contented with the sciences actually taught us, I had, in addition, read all the books that had fallen into my hands, treating of such branches as are esteemed the most curious and rare. I knew the judgment which others had formed of me; and I did not find that I was considered inferior to my fellows, although there were among them some who were already marked out to fill the places of our instructors. And, in fine, our age appeared to me as flourishing, and as fertile in powerful minds as any preceding one. I was thus led to take the liberty of judging of all other men by myself, and of concluding that there was no science in existence that was of such a nature as I had previously been given to believe.

I still continued, however, to hold in esteem the studies of the schools. I was aware that the languages taught in them are necessary to the understanding of the writings of the ancients; that the grace of fable stirs the mind; that the memorable deeds of history elevate it; and, if read with discretion, aid in forming the judgment; that the perusal of all excellent books is, as it were, to interview with the noblest men of past ages, who have written them, and even a studied interview, in which are discovered to us only their choicest thoughts; that eloquence has incomparable force and beauty; that poesy has its ravishing graces and delights; that in the mathematics there are many refined discoveries eminently suited to gratify the inquisitive, as well as further all the arts and lessen the labour of man; that numerous highly useful precepts and exhortations to virtue are contained in treatises on morals; that theology points out the path to heaven; that philosophy affords the means of discoursing with an appearance of truth on all matters, and commands the admiration of the more simple; that jurisprudence, medicine, and the other sciences, secure for their cultivators honours and riches; and, in fine, that it is useful to bestow some attention upon all, even upon those abounding the most in superstition and error, that we may be in a position to determine their real value, and guard against being deceived.

But I believed that I had already given sufficient time to languages, and likewise to the reading of the writings of the ancients, to their histories and fables. For to hold converse with those of other ages and to travel, are almost the same thing. It is useful to know something of the manners of different nations, that we may be enabled to form a more correct judgment regarding our own, and be prevented from thinking that everything contrary to our customs is ridiculous and irrational,—a conclusion usually come to by those whose experience has been limited to their own country. On the other hand, when too much time is occupied in travelling, we become strangers to our native country; and the over curious in the customs of the past are generally ignorant of those of the present. Besides, fictitious narratives lead us to imagine the possibility of many events that are impossible; and even the most faithful histories, if they do not wholly misrepresent matters, or exaggerate their importance to render the account of them more worthy of perusal, omit, at least, almost always the meanest and least striking of the attendant circumstances; hence it happens that the remainder does not represent the truth, and that such as regulate their conduct by examples drawn from this source, are apt to fall into the extravagances of the knight-errants of romance, and to entertain projects that exceed their powers.

I esteemed eloquence highly, and was in raptures with poesy; but I thought that both were gifts of nature rather than fruits of study. Those in whom the faculty of reason is predominant, and who most skillfully dispose their thoughts with a view to render them clear and intelligible, are always the best able to persuade others of the truth of what they lay down, though they should speak only in the language of Lower Brittany, and be wholly ignorant of the rules of rhetoric; and those whose minds are stored with the most agreeable fancies, and who can give expression to them with the greatest embellishment and harmony, are still the best poets, though unacquainted with the art of poetry.

I was especially delighted with the mathematics, on account of the certitude and evidence of their reasonings; but I had not as yet a precise knowledge of their true use; and thinking that they but contributed to the advancement of the mechanical arts, I was astonished that foundations, so strong and solid, should have had no loftier superstructure reared on them. On the other hand, I compared the disquisitions of the ancient moralists to very towering and magnificent palaces with no better foundation than sand and mud: they laud the virtues very highly, and exhibit them as estimable far above anything on earth; but they give us no adequate criterion of virtue, and frequently that which they designate with so fine a name is but apathy, or pride, or despair, or parricide.

I revered our theology, and aspired as much as any one to reach heaven: but being given assuredly to understand that the way is not less open to the most ignorant than to the most learned, and that the revealed truths which lead to heaven are above our comprehension, I did not presume to subject them to the impotency of my reason; and I thought that in order competently to undertake their examination, there was need of some special help from heaven, and of being more than man.

Of philosophy I will say nothing, except that when I saw that it had been cultivated for many ages by the most distinguished men, and that yet there is not a single matter within its sphere which is not still in dispute, and nothing, therefore, which is above doubt, I did not presume to anticipate that my success would be greater in it than that of others; and further, when I considered the number of conflicting opinions touching a single matter that may be upheld by learned men, while there can be but one true, I reckoned as well-nigh false all that was only probable.

As to the other sciences, inasmuch as these borrow their principles from philosophy, I judged that no solid superstructures could be reared on foundations so infirm; and neither the honour nor the gain held out by them was sufficient to determine me to their cultivation: for I was not, thank Heaven, in a condition which compelled me to make merchandise of science for the bettering of my fortune; and though I might not profess to scorn glory as a cynic, I yet made very slight account of that honour which I hoped to acquire only through fictitious titles. And, in fine, of false sciences I thought I knew the worth sufficiently to escape being deceived by the professions of an alchemist, the predictions of an astrologer, the impostures of a magician, or by the artifices and boasting of any of those who profess to know things of which they are ignorant.

For these reasons, as soon as my age permitted me to pass from under the control of my instructors, I entirely abandoned the study of letters, and resolved no longer to seek any other science than the knowledge of myself, or of the great book of the world. I spent the remainder of my youth in travelling, in visiting courts and armies, in holding intercourse with men of different dispositions and ranks, in collecting varied experience, in proving myself in the different situations into which fortune threw me, and, above all, in making such reflection on the matter of my experience as to secure my improvement For it occurred to me that I should find much more truth in the reasonings of each individual with reference to the affairs in which he is personally interested, and the issue of which must presently punish him if he has judged amiss, than in those conducted by a man of letters in his study, regarding speculative matters that are of no practical moment, and followed by no consequences to himself, farther, perhaps, than that they foster his vanity the better the more remote they are from common sense; requiring, as they must in this case, the exercise of greater ingenuity and art to render them probable. In addition, I had always a most earnest desire to know how to distinguish the true from the false, in order that I might be able clearly to discriminate the right path in life, and proceed in it with confidence.

It is true that, while busied only in considering the manners of other men, I found here, too, scarce any ground for settled conviction, and remarked hardly less contradiction among them than in the opinions of the philosophers. So that the greatest advantage I derived from the study consisted in this, that, observing many things which, however extravagant and ridiculous to our apprehension, are yet by common consent received and approved by other great nations, I learned to entertain too decided a belief in regard to nothing of the truth of which I had been persuaded merely by example and custom; and thus I gradually extricated myself from many errors powerful enough to darken our natural intelligence, and incapacitate us in great measure from listening to reason. But after I had been occupied several years in thus studying the book of the world, and In essaying to gather some experience, I at length resolved to make myself an object of study, and to employ all the powers of my mind in choosing the paths I ought to follow, an undertaking which was accompanied with greater success than it would have been had I never quitted my country or my books.

Part II

I was then in Germany, attracted thither by the wars in that country, which have not yet been brought to a termination; and as I was returning to the army from the coronation of the emperor, the setting in of winter arrested me in a locality where, as I found no society to interest me, and was besides fortunately undisturbed by any cares or passions, I remained the whole day in seclusion,[2] with full opportunity to occupy my attention with my own thoughts. Of these one of the very first that occurred to me was, that there is seldom so much perfection in works composed of many separate parts, upon which different hands had been employed, as in those completed by a single master. Thus it is observable that the buildings which a single architect has planned and executed, are generally more elegant and commodious than those which several have attempted to improve, by making old walls serve for purposes for which they were not originally built. Thus also, those ancient cities which, from being at first only villages, have become, in course of time, large towns, are usually but ill laid out compared with the regularly constructed towns which a professional architect has freely planned on an open plain; so that although the several buildings of the former may often equal or surpass in beauty those of the latter, yet when one observes their indiscriminate juxtaposition, there a large one and here a small, and the consequent crookedness and irregularity of the streets, one is disposed to allege that chance rather than any human will guided by reason must have led to such an arrangement. And if we consider that nevertheless there have been at all times certain officers whose duty it was to see that private buildings contributed to public ornament, the difficulty of reaching high perfection with but the materials of others to operate on, will be readily acknowledged. In the same way I fancied that those nations which, starting from a semi-barbarous state and advancing to civilisation by slow degrees, have had their laws successively determined, and, as it were, forced upon them simply by experience of the hurtfulness of particular crimes and disputes, would by this process come to be possessed of less perfect institutions than those which, from the commencement of their association as communities, have followed the appointments of some wise legislator. It is thus quite certain that the constitution of the true religion, the ordinances of which are derived from God, must be incomparably superior to that of every other. And, to speak of human affairs, I believe that the past pre-eminence of Sparta was due not to the goodness of each of its laws in particular, for many of these were very strange, and even opposed to good morals, but to the circumstance that, originated by a single individual, they all tended to a single end. In the same way I thought that the sciences contained in books (such of them at least as are made up of probable reasonings, without demonstrations), composed as they are of the opinions of many different individuals massed together, are farther removed from truth than the simple inferences which a man of good sense using his natural and unprejudiced judgment draws respecting the matters of his experience. And because we have all to pass through a state of infancy to manhood, and have been of necessity, for a length of time, governed by our desires and preceptors (whose dictates were frequently conflicting, while neither perhaps always counselled us for the best), I farther concluded that it is almost impossible that our judgments can be so correct or solid as they would have been, had our reason been mature from the moment of our birth, and had we always been guided by it alone.

It is true, however, that it is not customary to pull down all the houses of a town with the single design of rebuilding them differently, and thereby rendering the streets more handsome; but it often happens that a private individual takes down his own with the view of erecting it anew, and that people are even sometimes constrained to this when their houses are in danger of falling from age, or when the foundations are insecure. With this before me by way of example, I was persuaded that it would indeed be preposterous for a private individual to think of reforming a state by fundamentally changing it throughout, and overturning it in order to set it up amended; and the same I thought

---

2 Literally, in a room heated by means of a stove.–Tr.

was true of any similar project for reforming the body of the sciences, or the order of teaching them established in the schools: but as for the opinions which up to that time I had embraced, I thought that I could not do better than resolve at once to sweep them wholly away, that I might afterwards be in a position to admit either others more correct, or even perhaps the same when they had undergone the scrutiny of reason. I firmly believed that in this way I should much better succeed in the conduct of my life, than if I built only upon old foundations, and leant upon principles which, in my youth, I had taken upon trust For although I recognised various difficulties in this undertaking, these were not, however, without remedy, nor once to be compared with such as attend the slightest reformation in public affairs. Large bodies, if once overthrown, are with great difficulty set up again, or even kept erect when once seriously shaken, and the fall of such is always disastrous. Then if there are any imperfections in the constitutions of states (and that many such exist the diversity of constitutions is alone sufficient to assure us), custom has without doubt materially smoothed their inconveniences, and has even managed to steer altogether clear of, or insensibly corrected a number which sagacity could not have provided against with equal effect; and, in fine, the defects are almost always more tolerable than the change necessary for their removal; in the same manner that highways which wind among mountains, by being much frequented, become gradually so smooth and commodious, that it is much better to follow them than to seek a straighter path by climbing over the tops of rocks and descending to the bottoms of precipices.

Hence it is that I cannot in any degree approve of those restless and busy meddlers who, called neither by birth nor fortune to take part in the management of public affairs, are yet always projecting reforms; and if I thought that this tract contained aught which might justify the suspicion that I was a victim of such folly, I would by no means permit its publication. I have never contemplated anything higher than the reformation of my own opinions, and basing them on a foundation wholly my own. And although my own satisfaction with my work has led me, to present here a draft of it, I do not by any means therefore recommend to every one else to make a similar attempt. Those whom God has endowed with a larger measure of genius will entertain, perhaps, designs still more exalted; but for the many I am much afraid lest even the present undertaking be more than they can safely venture to imitate. The single design to strip one's self of all past beliefs is one that ought not to be taken by every one. The majority of men is composed of two classes, for neither of which would this be at all a befitting resolution: in the *first* place, of those who with more than a due confidence in their own powers, are precipitate in their judgments and want the patience requisite for orderly and circumspect thinking; whence it happens, that if men of this class once take the liberty to doubt of their accustomed opinions, and quit the beaten highway, they will never be able to thread the byway that would lead them by a shorter course, and will lose themselves and continue to wander for life; in the *second* place, of those who, possessed of sufficient sense or modesty to determine that there are others who excel them in the power of discriminating between truth and error, and by whom they may be instructed, ought rather to content themselves with the opinions of such than trust for more correct to their own reason.

For my own part, I should doubtless have belonged to the latter class, had I received instruction from but one master, or had I never known the diversities of opinion that from time immemorial have prevailed among men of the greatest learning. But I had become aware, even so early as during my college life, that no opinion, however absurd and incredible, can be imagined, which has not been maintained by some one of the philosophers; and afterwards in the course of my travels I remarked that all those whose opinions are decidedly repugnant to ours are not on that account barbarians and savages, but on the contrary that many of these nations make an equally good, if not a better, use of their reason than we do. I took into account also the very different character which a person brought up from infancy in France or Germany exhibits, from that which, with the same mind originally, this individual would have possessed had he lived always among the Chinese or with savages, and the circumstance that in dress itself the fashion which pleased us ten years ago, and which may again, perhaps, be received into favour before ten years have gone, appears to us at this moment extravagant and ridiculous. I was thus led to infer that the ground of our opinions is far more custom and example than any certain knowledge. And, finally, although such be the ground of our opinions, I remarked that a plurality of suffrages is no guarantee of truth where it is at all of difficult discovery, as in such cases it is much more likely that it will be found by one than by many. I could, however, select from the crowd no one whose opinions seemed worthy of preference, and thus I found myself constrained, as it were, to use my own reason in the conduct of my life.

But like one walking alone and in the dark, I resolved to proceed so slowly and with such circumspection, that if I did not advance far, I would at least guard against falling. I did not even choose to dismiss summarily any of the opinions that had crept into my belief without having been introduced by reason, but first of all took sufficient time carefully to satisfy myself of the general nature of the task I was setting myself, and ascertain the true method by which to arrive at the knowledge of whatever lay within the compass of my powers.

Among the branches of philosophy, I had, at an earlier period, given some attention to logic, and among those of the mathematics to geometrical analysis and algebra,—three arts or sciences which ought, as I conceived, to contribute something to my design. But, on examination, I found that, as for logic, Its syllogisms and the majority of its other precepts are of avail rather in the communication of what we already know, or even as the art of Lully, in speaking without judgment of things of which we are ignorant, than in the investigation of the unknown; and although this science contains indeed a number of correct and very excellent precepts, there are, nevertheless, so many others, and these either injurious or superfluous, mingled with the former, that it is almost quite as difficult to effect a severance of the true from the false as it is to extract a Diana or a Minerva from a rough block of marble. Then as to the analysis of the ancients and the algebra of the moderns, besides that they embrace only matters highly abstract, and, to appearance, of no use, the former is so exclusively restricted to the consideration of figures, that it can exercise the understanding only on condition of greatly fatiguing the imagination; and, in the latter, there is so complete a subjection to certain rules and formulas, that there results an art full of confusion and obscurity calculated to embarrass, instead of a science fitted to cultivate the mind. By these considerations I was induced to seek some other method which would comprise the advantages of the three and be exempt from their defects. And as a multitude of laws often only hampers justice, so that a state is best governed when, with few laws, these are rigidly administered; in like manner, instead of the great number of precepts of which logic is composed, I believed that the four following would prove perfectly sufficient for me, provided I took the firm and unwavering resolution never in a single instance to fail in observing them.

The *first* was never to accept anything for true which I did not clearly know to be such; that is to say, carefully to avoid precipitancy and prejudice, and to comprise nothing more in my judgment than what was presented to my mind so clearly and distinctly s to exclude all ground of doubt.

The *second*, to divide each of the difficulties under examination into as many parts as possible, and as might be necessary for its adequate solution.

The *third*, to conduct my thoughts in such order that, by commencing with objects the simplest and easiest to know, I might ascend by little and little, and, as it were, step by step, to the knowledge of the more complex; assigning in thought a certain order even to those objects which in their own nature do not stand in a relation of antecedence and sequence.

And the *last*, in every case to make enumerations so complete, and reviews so general, that I might be assured that nothing was omitted.

The long chains of simple and easy reasonings by means of which geometers are accustomed to reach the conclusions of their most difficult demonstrations, had led me to imagine that all things, to the knowledge of which man is competent, are mutually connected in the same way, and that there is nothing so far removed from us as to be beyond our reach, or so hidden that we cannot discover it, provided only we abstain from accepting the false for the true, and always preserve in our thoughts the order necessary for the deduction of one truth from another. And I had little difficulty in determining the objects with which it was necessary to commence, for I was already persuaded that it must be with the simplest and easiest to know, and, considering that of all those who have hitherto sought truth in the sciences, the mathematicians alone have been able to find any demonstrations, that is, any certain and evident reasons, I did not doubt but that such must have been the rule of their investigations. I resolved to commence, therefore, with the examination of the simplest objects, not anticipating, however, from this any other advantage than that to be found in accustoming my mind to the love and nourishment of truth, and to a distaste for all such reasonings as were unsound. But I had no intention on that account of attempting to master all the particular sciences commonly denominated mathematics: but observing that, however different their objects, they all agree in considering only the various relations or proportions subsisting among those objects, I thought it best for my purpose to consider these proportions in the most general form possible, without referring them to any objects in particular, except such as would most facilitate the knowledge of them, and without by any means restricting them to these, that afterwards I might thus be the better able to apply them to every other class of objects to which they are legitimately applicable. Perceiving further, that in order to understand these relations I should sometimes have to consider them one by one, and sometimes only to bear them in mind, or embrace them in the aggregate, I thought that, in order the better to consider them individually, I should view them as subsisting between straight lines, than which I could find no objects more simple, or capable of being more distinctly represented to my imagination and senses; and on the other hand, that in order to retain them in the memory, or embrace an aggregate of many, I should express them by certain characters the briefest possible. In this way I believed that I could borrow all that was best both in geometrical analysis and in algebra, and correct all the defects of the one by help of the other.

And, in point of fact, the accurate observance of these few precepts gave me, I take the liberty of saying, such ease in unravelling all the questions embraced in these two sciences, that in the two or three months I devoted to their examination, not only did I reach solutions of questions I had formerly deemed exceedingly difficult, but even as regards questions of the solution of which I continued ignorant, I was enabled, as it appeared to me, to determine the means whereby, and the extent to which, a solution was possible; results attributable to the circumstance that I commenced with the simplest and most general truths, and that thus each truth discovered was a rule available in the discovery of subsequent ones. Nor in this perhaps shall I appear too vain, if it be considered that, as the truth on any particular point is one, whoever apprehends the truth, knows all that on that point can be known. The child, for example, who has been instructed in the elements of arithmetic, and has made a particular addition, according to rule, may be assured that he has found, with respect to the sum of the numbers before him, all that in this instance is within the reach of human genius. Now, in conclusion, the method which teaches adherence to the true order, and an exact enumeration of all the conditions of the thing sought includes all that gives certitude to the rules of arithmetic.

But the chief ground of my satisfaction with this method, was the assurance I had of thereby exercising my reason in all matters, if not with absolute perfection, at least with the greatest attainable by me: besides, I was conscious that by its use my mind was becoming gradually habituated to clearer and more distinct conceptions of its objects; and I hoped also, from not having restricted this method to any particular matter, to apply it to the difficulties of the other sciences, with not less success than to those of algebra. I should not, however, on this account have ventured at once on the examination of all the difficulties of the sciences which presented themselves to me, for this would have been contrary to the order prescribed in the method, but observing that the knowledge of such is dependent on principles borrowed from philosophy, in which I found nothing certain, I thought it necessary first of all to endeavour to establish its principles. And because I observed, besides, that an inquiry of this kind was of all others of the greatest moment, and one in which precipitancy and anticipation in judgment were most to be dreaded, I thought that I ought not to approach it till I had reached a more mature age (being at that time but twenty-three), and had first of all employed much of my time in preparation for the work, as well by eradicating from my mind all the erroneous opinions I had up to that moment accepted, as by amassing variety of experience to afford materials for my reasonings, and by continually exercising myself in my chosen method with a view to increased skill in its application.

Part IV

I am in doubt as to the propriety of making my first meditations in the place above mentioned matter of discourse; for these are so metaphysical, and so uncommon, as not, perhaps, to be acceptable to every one. And yet, that it may be determined whether the foundations that I have laid are sufficiently secure, I find myself in a measure constrained to advert to them. I had long before remarked that, in relation to practice, it is sometimes necessary to adopt, as if above doubt, opinions which we discern to be highly uncertain, as has been already said; but as I then desired to give my attention solely to the search after truth, I thought that a procedure exactly the opposite was called for, and that I ought to reject as absolutely false all opinions in regard to which I could suppose the least ground for doubt, in order to ascertain whether after that there remained aught in my belief that was wholly indubitable. Accordingly, seeing that our senses sometimes deceive us, I was willing to suppose that there existed nothing really such as they presented to us; and because some men err in reasoning, and fall into paralogisms, even on the simplest matters of geometry, I, convinced that I was as open to error as any other, rejected as false all the reasonings I had hitherto taken for demonstrations; and finally, when I considered that the very same thoughts (presentations) which we experience when awake may also be experienced when we are asleep, while there is at that time not one of them true, I supposed that all the objects (presentations) that had ever entered into my mind when awake, had in them no more truth than the illusions of my dreams. But immediately upon this I observed that, whilst I thus wished to think that all was false, it was absolutely necessary that I, who thus thought, should be somewhat; and as I observed that this truth, *I think, hence I am*, was so certain and of such evidence, that no ground of doubt, however extravagant, could be alleged by the sceptics capable of shaking it, I concluded that I might, without scruple, accept it as the first principle of the philosophy of which I was in search.

In the next place, I attentively examined what I was, and as I observed that I could suppose that I had no body, and that there was no world nor any place in which I might be; but that I could not therefore suppose that I was not; and that, on the contrary, from the very circumstance that I thought to doubt of the truth of other things, it most clearly and certainly followed that I was; while, on the other hand, if I had only ceased to think, although all the other objects which I had ever imagined had been in reality existent, I would have had no reason to believe that I existed; I thence concluded that I was a substance whose whole essence or nature consists only in thinking, and which, that it may exist, has need of no place, nor is dependent on any material thing; so that "I," that is to say, the mind by which I am what I am, is wholly distinct from the body, and is even more easily known than the latter, and is such, that although the latter were not, it would still continue to be all that it is.

After this I inquired in general into what is essential to the troth and certainty of a proposition; for Since I had discovered one which I knew to be true, I thought that I must likewise be able to discover the ground of this certitude. And as I observed that in the words *I think hence I am*, there is nothing at all which gives me assurance of their truth beyond this, that I see very clearly that in order to think it is necessary to exist, I concluded that I might take, as a general rule, the principle, that all the things which we very clearly and distinctly conceive are true, only observing, however, that there is some difficulty in rightly determining the objects which we distinctly conceive.

In the next place, from reflecting on the circumstance that I doubted, and that consequently my being was not wholly perfect (for I clearly saw that it was a greater perfection to know than to doubt), I was led to inquire whence I had learned to think of something more perfect than myself; and I clearly recognised that I must hold this notion from some nature which in reality was more perfect. As for the thoughts of many other objects external to me, as of the sky, the earth, light, heat, and a thousand more, I was less at a loss to know whence these came; for Since I remarked in them nothing which seemed to render them superior to myself, I could believe that, if these were true, they were dependencies on my own nature, in so far as it possessed a certain perfection, and, if they were false, that I held them from nothing, that is to say, that they were in me because of a certain imperfection of my nature. But this could not be the case with the idea of a nature more perfect than myself; for to receive it from nothing was a thing manifestly impossible; and, because it is not less repugnant that the more perfect should be an effect of, and dependence on the less perfect, than that something should proceed from nothing, it was equally impossible that I could hold it from myself: accordingly, it but remained that it had been placed in me by a nature which was in reality more perfect than mine, and which even possessed within itself all the perfections of which I could form any idea; that is to say, in a single word, which was God. And to this I added that, since I knew some perfections which I did not possess, I was not the only being in existence (I will here, with your permission, freely use the terms of the schools); but, on the contrary, that there was of necessity some other more perfect Being upon whom I was dependent, and from whom I had received all that I possessed; for if I had existed alone, and independently of every other being, so as to have had from myself all the perfection, however little, which I actually possessed, I should have been able, for the same reason, to have had from myself the whole remainder of perfection, of the want of which I was conscious, and thus could of myself have become infinite, eternal, immutable, omniscient, all-powerful, and, in fine, have possessed all the perfections which I could recognise in God. For in order to know the nature of God (whose existence has been established by the preceding reasonings), as far as my own nature permitted, I had only to consider in reference to all the properties of which I found in my mind some idea, whether their possession was a mark of perfection; and I was assured that no one which indicated any imperfection was in him, and that none of the rest was awanting. Thus I perceived that doubt, inconstancy, sadness, and such like, could not be found in God, since I myself would have been happy to be free from them. Besides, I had ideas of many sensible and corporeal things; for although I might suppose that I was dreaming, and that all which I saw or imagined was false, I could not, nevertheless, deny that the ideas were in reality in my thoughts. But, because I had already very clearly recognised in myself that the intelligent nature is distinct from the corporeal, and as I observed that all composition is an evidence of dependency, and that a state of dependency is manifestly a state of imperfection, I therefore determined that it could not be a perfection in God to be compounded of these two natures, and that consequently he was not so compounded; but that if there were any bodies in the world, or even any intelligences, or other natures that were not wholly perfect, their existence depended on his power in such a way that they could not subsist without him for a single moment.

I was disposed straightway to search for other truths; and when I had represented to myself the object of the geometers, which I conceived to be a continuous body, or a space indefinitely extended in length, breadth, and height or depth, divisible into divers parts which admit of different figures and sizes, and of being moved or transposed in all manner of ways (for all this the geometers suppose to be in the object they contemplate), I went over some of their simplest demonstrations. And, in the first place, I observed, that the great certitude which by common consent is accorded to these demonstrations, is founded solely upon this, that they are clearly conceived in accordance with the rules I have already laid down. In the next place, I perceived that there was nothing at all in these demonstrations which could assure me of the existence of their object: thus, for example, supposing a triangle to be given, I distinctly perceived that its three angles were necessarily equal to two right angles, but I did not on that account perceive anything which could assure me that any triangle existed: while, on the contrary, recurring to the examination of the idea of a Perfect Being, I found that the existence of the Being was comprised in the idea in the same way that the equality of its three angles to two right angles is comprised in the idea of a triangle, or as in the idea of a sphere, the equidistance of all points on its surface from the centre, or even still more clearly; and that consequently it is at least as certain that God, who is this Perfect Being, is, or exists, as any demonstration of geometry can be.

But the reason which leads many to persuade themselves that there is a difficulty in knowing this truth, and even also in knowing what their mind really is, is that they never raise their thoughts above sensible objects, and are so accustomed to consider nothing except by way of imagination, which is a mode of thinking limited to material objects, that all that is not imaginable seems to them not intelligible. The truth of this is sufficiently manifest from the single circumstance, that the philosophers of the schools accept as a maxim that there is nothing in the understanding which was not previously in the senses, in which however it is certain that the ideas of God and of the soul have never been; and it appears to me that they who make use of their imagination to comprehend these ideas do exactly the same thing as if, in order to hear sounds or smell odours, they strove to avail themselves of their eyes; unless indeed that there is this difference, that the sense of sight does not afford us an inferior assurance to those of smell or hearing; in place of which, neither our imagination nor our senses can give us assurance of anything unless our understanding intervene.

Finally, if there be still persons who are not sufficiently persuaded of the existence of God and of the soul, by the reasons I have adduced, I am desirous that they should know that all the other propositions, of the truth of which they deem themselves perhaps more assured, as that we have a body, and that there exist stars and an earth, and such like, are less certain; for, although we have a moral assurance of these things, which is so strong that there is an appearance of extravagance in doubting of their existence, yet at the same time no one, unless his intellect is impaired, can deny, when the question relates to a metaphysical certitude, that there is sufficient reason to exclude entire assurance, in the observation that when asleep we can in the same way imagine ourselves possessed of another body and that we see other stars and another earth, when there is nothing of the kind. For how do we know that the thoughts which occur in dreaming are false rather than those other which we experience when awake, since the former are often not less vivid and distinct than the latter? And though men of the highest genius study this question as long as they please, I do not believe that they will be able to give any reason which can be sufficient to remove this doubt, unless they presuppose the existence of God. For, in the first place, even the principle which I have already taken as a role, viz., that all the things which we clearly and distinctly conceive are true, is certain only because God is or exists, and because he is a Perfect Being, and because all that we possess is derived from him: whence it follows that our ideas or notions, which to the extent of their clearness and distinctness are real, and proceed from God, must to that extent be true. Accordingly, whereas we not unfrequently have ideas or notions in which some falsity is contained, this can only be the case with such as are to some extent confused and obscure, and in this proceed from nothing (participate of negation), that is, exist in us thus confused because we are not wholly perfect. And it is evident that it is not less repugnant that falsity or imperfection, in so far as it is imperfection, should proceed from God, than that truth or perfection should proceed from nothing, But if we did not know that all which we possess of real and true proceeds from a Perfect and Infinite Being, however clear and distinct our ideas might be, we should have no ground on that account for the assurance that they possessed the perfection of being true. But after the knowledge of God and of the soul has rendered us certain of this rule, we can easily understand that the truth of the thoughts we experience when awake, ought not in the slightest degree to be called in question on account of the illusions of our dreams. For if it happened that an individual, even when asleep, had some very distinct idea, as, for example, if a geometer should discover some new demonstration, the circumstance of his being asleep would not militate against its truth; and as for the most ordinary error of our dreams, which consists in their representing to us various objects in the same way as our external senses, this is not prejudicial, since it leads us very properly to suspect the truth of the ideas of sense; for we are not unfrequently deceived in the same manner when awake; as when persons in the jaundice see all objects yellow, or when the stars or bodies at a great distance appear to us much smaller than they are. For, in fine, whether awake or asleep, we ought never to allow ourselves to be persuaded of the truth of anything unless on the evidence of our reason. And it must be noted that I say of our *reason*, and not of our imagination or of our senses: thus, for example, although we very clearly see the sun, we ought not therefore to determine that it is only of the size which our sense of sight presents; and we may very distinctly imagine the head of a lion joined to the body of a goat, without being therefore shut up to the conclusion that a chimaera exists; for it is not a dictate of reason that what we thus see or imagine is in reality existent; but it plainly tells us that all our ideas or notions contain in them some truth; for otherwise it could not be that God, who is wholly perfect and veracious, should have placed them in us. And because our reasonings are never so clear or so complete during sleep as when we are awake, although sometimes the acts of our imagination are then as lively and distinct, if not more so than in our waking moments, reason further dictates that, since all our thoughts cannot be true because of our partial imperfection, those possessing truth must infallibly be found in the experience of our waking moments rather than in that of our dreams.

Blaise Pascal

(1623–1662)

Blaise Pascal confronts the modern reader with an apparent paradox. Although he was one of the great mathematicians and natural scientists of his time, he was also a Christian philosopher possessed of an acute Augustinian sense of human imperfection and the vanity of scientific reason.

Pascal was a man of many talents. In the course of his short life he was able to demonstrate a genius for whatever subject captured his interest. While still a boy he revealed a remarkable aptitude for geometry. At sixteen he published a treatise on conic sections. Later he did seminal work in probability theory, and some of his last geometrical studies were to inspire Gottfried Leibnitz's development of calculus. When he was eighteen he designed a rudimentary calculating machine. Turning his attention to physics, Pascal conclusively refuted the ancient Aristotelian belief that nature abhors a vacuum. From there he was led to study the properties of gases and liquids. In demonstrating that air has weight he proposed the uses of the barometer. He also formulated the theory of the elasticity of gases and experimentally established the law of the communication of pressure through a liquid, which, as he recognized, made possible the hydraulic press. In all of his scientific writing he was interested in defining precisely the procedures of the inductive experimental method.

Pascal, however, was a spiritually restless man who found that natural science and human reason were inadequate to provide consoling answers to the besetting interrogations of his soul. One evening in late 1654 he was seized by a mystic vision that convinced him of the futility of human life. Thereafter he gave up physics, though not mathematics, and devoted himself to the study of man's spiritual predicament. The *Pensées* are the fruit of his reflection on the human condition. They were designed to show the need for Christian faith by convincing men of their inescapable weakness. What is remarkable about Pascal's method is that he attempts to persuade the reader of the insufficiency of reason by means of a reasoned appeal to the patent facts of experience. In other words, by inductive argumentation that follows the logic of science, Pascal tries to demonstrate the impotence of scientific reason to solve man's ultimate problems. His method exemplifies his belief that "the last proceeding of reason is to recognise that there is an infinity of things which are beyond it." Human nature itself presents paradoxes which are impenetrable of reason. Beneath reason, and more fundamental, is intuition. Thus "the heart has its reasons, which reason does not know."

At a time when the startling accomplishments of the new sciences were beginning to encourage the belief that science possessed a secure avenue to truth, Pascal uttered a powerful warning against the pretensions of human reason. His words were aimed directly at Descartes, who believed that people could attain indubitable truths by the powers of pure reasoning. Given his critique of reason and his stress on intuition it is not surprising that in later times Enlightenment philosophers regarded Pascal as a dangerous enemy, while the Romantics in turn extolled him. In the twentieth century Pascal came to be considered a precursor to existentialism. His view of the limitations of science has also been linked to the philosophic implications of nuclear physics.

In the *Pensées*, as well as in his polemical writings against Jesuits, Pascal established the classic style of what has become modern French prose. The *Pensées* were mostly composed between 1656 and 1659.[1]

From *Pensées*

Man's disproportion

I.1. Let [man] contemplate universal nature in all the height and fulness of its majesty. Let him consider that glorious luminary, hung as an eternal lamp, to enlighten the universe. Let him consider that this earth is a mere point, compared with the vast circuit which that bright orb describes. Let him learn with wonder, that this wide orbit itself is but a speck, compared with the course of the stars, which roll in the firmament of heaven. And if here our sight is limited, let the imagination take up the inquiry and venture further. It will weary with conceiving, far sooner than nature in supplying food for thought. All that we see of the universe is but an almost imperceptible spot on the ample bosom of nature. No conception even approaches the limits of its space. Let us labour as we will with our conceptions, we bring forth mere atoms, compared with the immensity of that which really is. It is an infinite sphere, whose centre is everywhere, and whose circumference is nowhere. And, in fact, one of the most powerful sensible impressions of the omnipotence of God is that our imagination is lost in this thought.

Then let man return to himself, and consider what he is, compared with all else that is. Let him consider himself as a wanderer in this remote corner of nature; and then, from what he sees of this narrow prison in which he lies,—this visible world, let him learn to estimate rightly the earth, its kingdoms, its cities, himself, and his own real value. What is man in this infinity? Who can comprehend him?

But to show him another prodigy equally astonishing, let him search among the minutest objects around him. Let a mite, for instance, exhibit to him, in the exceeding smallness of its frame, portions yet incomparably smaller; limbs well articulated; veins in those limbs; blood in those veins; humours in that blood; globules in that humour; and gases in those globules;—and then dividing again their smallest objects, let him exhaust the powers of his conception, and then let the lowest particle that he can imagine, become the subject of our discourse. He thinks, perhaps, that this is the minutest atom of nature; but I will open to him, within it, anew and fathomless abyss. I can exhibit to him yet, not only the visible universe, but even all that he is capable of conceiving of the immensity of nature, embosomed in this imperceptible atom. Let him see there an infinity of worlds, each of which has its firmament, its planets, its earth; bearing the same proportion to the other parts in the visible world: and in this earth, animals, and even mites again, in which he shall trace the same discoveries which the first mites yielded; and then again the same in others, without end and without repose. He is lost in these wonders, equally astonishing in their minuteness, and the former by their extent. And who would not wonder to think that this body, which so lately was not perceptible in that universe, which universe was itself an imperceptible spot on the bosom of infinity, should now appear a colossus, a world, a universe, compared with that ultimate atom of minuteness to which we cannot arrive.

---

[1] The present selection is based on Edward Craig, trans., Blaise Pascal, *Thoughts on Religion and Other Subjects*, (Edinburgh: John Boyd, 1828), pp. 91–94, 113–117, adapted for this collection.

He who thus thinks of himself, will doubtless be afraid to see himself, as it were, suspended in the mass of matter that is allotted to him, between these two abysses of infinity and nothingness, and equally remote from both. He will tremble at the perception of these wonders; and I would think, that his curiosity changing into reverence, he would be more disposed to contemplate them in silence, than to scrutinize them with presumption. For what after all is man, in nature? A nothing compared with infinity,—a universe, compared with nothing,—a mean between all and nothing. Since he is infinitely distant from both extremes, the purposes of things and their beginnings are invincibly hidden from him in an impenetrable secret. His being is not less remote from the nothing out of which he was formed, than from the infinity in which he is lost.

His mind holds the same rank in the order of intelligent beings, as his body in material nature; and all that it can do, is to discern somewhat of the middle of things, in an endless despair of ever knowing their beginning or their end. All things are called out of nothing, and carried onward to infinity. Who can follow in this endless race? The Author of these wonders comprehends them. No other can. ...

By failing to contemplate these infinities, men have rashly rushed to explore nature, as if they bore some proportion to her. It is odd that they have sought to grasp the beginnings of things, and from there to proceed to the knowledge of the whole, with a presumption as infinite as their very object. For surely this project cannot be formed without presumption, or without an infinite capacity like that of nature.

III.24. The instructed mind discovers that as nature carries the imprint of its author stamped on all things, they all have a certain relation to his two-fold infinity. Thus we see that all the sciences are infinite in the extent to which their researches may be carried. Who doubts, for instance, that geometry involves in it an infinity of infinities of propositions? It is infinite also in the multitude and the delicacy of its principles; for who does not perceive that any which are proposed as the last, must rest upon themselves, which is absurd; and that in fact they are sustained by others, which have others again for their basis, and must thus eternally exclude the idea of an ultimate proposition. . . . Nevertheless, we regard some principles as ultimate for reason in the same fashion as with respect to material objects we call that point "indivisible" beyond which our senses can perceive nothing further, although by its nature it is infinitely divisible.

Of these two infinities of science that of magnitude is the most discernible, and that is why few have pretended to know everything. "I will speak of the whole," said Democritus.

But if the infinitely small is much less discernible than the infinitely great, philosophers have much more readily pretended to have attained to it; and here all have stumbled. This error has given rise to those terms so commonly in use, as "the principles of things,—the principles of philosophy;" and other similar expressions, as conceited, in fact, though not quite so obtrusively so as that insufferably disgusting title: "Of Everything Knowable: *De omni scibili.*"*

We think ourselves much more capable of reaching the centre of things, than of grasping the circumference. The visible expanse of the world, manifestly surpasses us; but as we visibly surpass little things, we think ourselves on a vantage ground for comprehending them; and yet it does not require less capacity to trace something down to nothing, than up to totality. This capacity, in either case, must be infinite; and it appears to me that he who can discover the ultimate principles of things, might reach also to the knowledge of the infinitely great. The one depends on the other; the

---

* The title of a thesis maintained at Rome by Giovanni Pico Della Mirandola

one leads to the other. These extremities touch and meet in consequence of their very distance. They meet in God, and in God only.

Let us then take our measure. We are something, we are not everything. The nature of our existence deprives us of knowledge of the first principles which are born of the nothingness; and our smallness conceals from us the sight of infinity.

I.1. This state, which occupies the mean between two extremes, shows itself in all our powers. Our senses will not admit any thing extreme. Too much noise confuses us,—too much light dazzles, —too great distance or nearness prevents vision,—too great prolixity or brevity weakens an argument, —too much pleasure gives pain,—too much accordance annoys. We relish neither extreme heat, nor extreme cold. All excessive qualities are injurious to us, and not perceptible. We do not feel them, we suffer them. Extreme youth and extreme age alike enfeeble the mind; too much or too little nourishment weakens its operation; by too much or too little instruction it becomes stupid. Extreme things are not ours, any more than if they were not; we are not made for them.

This is our real condition. It is this which confines our knowledge within certain limits that we cannot pass, being equally incapable of universal knowledge, or of total ignorance; we are placed in a vast medium; ever floating uncertainly between ignorance and knowledge: if we attempt to go farther forward, our object wavers and eludes our grasp,—it retires and flies with an eternal flight. Nothing stays for us. This is our natural condition; yet it is ever opposed to our inclination. We burn with desire to sound the utmost depth, and to raise a tower that shall reach infinity. But all we build up crumbles, and the earth opens in a fathomless abyss beneath our deepest foundation.

III.24. Let us not seek then for certainty and stability. Our reason is perpetually deceived by the variableness of appearances, nothing can fix that which is finite, between the two infinities that enclose it, and fly from it; and when this is well understood, each man will, I believe, remain quietly in the position in which nature has placed him. This medium state, which has fallen to our lot, being always infinitely distant from the extremes, what matters it whether man has, or has not a little more knowledge of the things round him? If he has, why then he traces them a degree or two higher. But is he not always infinitely distant from the extremes, and is not the longest human life infinitely short of eternity?

Compared with these infinities, all finite things are equal; and I see no reason why the imagination should occupy itself with one more than another. Even the least comparison that we institute between ourselves and that which is infinite gives us pain.

III.26. If man would begin by studying himself, he would soon see how unable he is to go further. How can a part comprehend the whole? He would aspire probably to know, at least, those parts which are similar in proportion to himself. But all parts of creation have such a relation to each other, and are so intertwined, that 1 think it is impossible to know one without knowing the other, and even the whole.

Man, for instance, has a relation to all that he knows. He needs space to contain him,—time for existence,—motion that he may live,—elements for his substance,—warmth and food to nourish him, and air to breath. He sees the light, he feels his material body. In fact, every thing is allied with him. . . . Flame will not live without air; then to comprehend the one, we must comprehend the other also.

Since, then, all things are either caused or causes, assisting or being assisted, mediately or immediately; and all are related to each other by a natural though imperceptible bond, which unites together things the most distant and dissimilar; I hold it impossible to know the parts, without knowing the whole, and equally so to know the whole, without knowing the parts in detail.

And that which completes our inability to know the essential nature of things is, that they are simple, and that we are a compound of two different and opposing natures, body and spirit; for it is impossible that the portion of us which thinks, can be other than spiritual; and as to the pretence, that we are simply corporeal, that would exclude us still more entirely from the knowledge of things; because there is nothing more inconceivable, than that matter could comprehend itself.

It is this compound nature of body and spirit which had led almost all the philosophers to confuse their ideas of things; and to attribute to matter that which belongs only to spirit, and to spirit, that which cannot consist but with matter; for, they say boldly, that bodies tend downwards; that they seek the centre; that they shrink from destruction; that they dread a vacuum; that they have inclinations, sympathies, antipathies, etc. which are all qualities that can only exist in mind. And in speaking of spirits, they consider them as occupying a place, and attribute to them motion from one place to another, etc., which are the qualities of body.

Instead, therefore, of receiving the ideas of things, simply as they are, we colour, with the qualities of our compound being, all the simple things that we contemplate.

Who would not suppose, when they see us attach to every thing the compound notions of body and spirit, that this mixture was familiarly comprehensible to us? Yet it is the thing of which we know the least. Man is, to himself, the most astonishing object in nature, for he cannot conceive what body is, still less what spirit is, and less than all, how a body and a spirit can be united; that is the climax of his difficulties, and yet it is his proper being. *Modus quo corporibus adhaeret spiritus comprehendi ab hominibus non potest, et hoc tamen homo est.* [The union of mind with matter, is a subject utterly incomprehensible to man, and yet this is man's essential nature.]

Francis Bacon
(1561–1626)

Though an active civil servant who became Lord Chancellor of England in 1618, Bacon had a profound interest in philosophy and science and was a major figure in the scientific revolution of the 17th century. His contribution to that revolution was, however, not in the realm of actual scientific research but rather in his ideas about the method by which scientific research should be pursued in order to reach truth. Bacon believed that medieval science, which he asserted was based on an unfruitful, deductive method, had to be abandoned. Instead people should turn to observation and experiment, for only by careful observation and well-directed experimentation could a true knowledge of the workings of nature be reached. This observational method, which Bacon called induction, is explained in his major work, *The Great Instauration* (1605–1621), which he described as representing a "total reconstruction of the sciences, arts and all human knowledge."[1] Bacon's attempt to formulate sound scientific methods was accompanied by an optimistic belief in the advantages that would follow from the advance of science as it gave human beings increasing power over nature. Perhaps his main defect was his failure to see the very important part that mathematics and bold conjectures were to play in the development of science. The insights of Descartes, Galileo, and Newton were a necessary corrective to Bacon's postulates.

From *The Great Instauration*

The Plan of the Work

The work is in six Parts:—

1. *The Divisions of the Sciences.*
2. *The New Organon; or Directions concerning the Interpretation of Nature.*
3. *The Phenomena of the Universe; or a Natural and Experimental History for the foundation of Philosophy.*
4. *The Ladder of the Intellect.*
5. *The Forerunners; or Anticipations of the New Philosophy.*
6. *The New Philosophy; or Active Science.*

The Arguments of the Several Parts

It being part of my design to set everything forth, as far as may be, plainly and perspicuously (for nakedness of the mind is still, as nakedness of the body once was, the companion of innocence and simplicity), let me first explain the order and plan of the work. I distribute it into six parts.

---

[1] Selection reprinted from James Spedding, Robert L. Ellis, and Douglas D. Heath, eds., *The Philosophical Works of Francis Bacon*, Vol. IV, Translations of the Philosophical Works, Vol. I, (London: Longmans and Co., 1883), pp. 22–33.

The first part exhibits a summary or general description of the knowledge which the human race at present possesses. For I thought it good to make some pause upon that which is received; that thereby the old may be more easily made perfect and the new more easily approached. And I hold the improvement of that which we have to be as much an object as the acquisition of more. Besides which it will make me the better listened to; for "He that is ignorant (says the proverb) receives not the words of knowledge, unless thou first tell him that which is in his own heart." We will therefore make a coasting voyage along the shores of the arts and sciences received; not without importing into them some useful things by the way.

In laying out the divisions of the sciences however, I take into account not only things already invented and known, but likewise things omitted which ought to be there. For there are found in the intellectual as in the terrestial globe waste regions as well as cultivated ones. It is no wonder therefore if I am sometimes obliged to depart from the ordinary divisions. For in adding to the total you necessarily alter the parts and sections; and the received divisions of the sciences are fitted only to the received sum of them as it stands now.

With regard to those things which I shall mark as omitted, I intend not merely to set down a simple title or a concise argument of that which is wanted. For as often as I have occasion to report anything as deficient, the nature of which is at all obscure, so that men may not perhaps easily understand what I mean or what the work is which I have in my head, I shall always (provided it be a matter of any worth) take care to subjoin either directions for the execution of such work, or else a portion of the work itself executed by myself as a sample of the whole: thus giving assistance in every care either by work or by counsel. For if it were for the sake of my own reputation only and other men's interests were not concerned in it, I would not have any man think that in such cases merely some light and vague notion has crossed my mind, and that the things which I desire and offer at are no better than wishes; when they are in fact things which men may certainly command if they will, and of which I have formed in my own mind a clear and detailed conception. For I do not propose merely to survey these regions in my mind, like an augur taking auspices, but to enter them like a general who means to take possession.—So much for the first part of the work.

Having thus coasted past the ancient arts, the next point is to equip the intellect for passing beyond. To the second part therefore belongs the doctrine concerning the better and more perfect use of human reason in the inquisition of things, and the true helps of the understanding: that thereby (as far as the condition of mortality and humanity allows) the intellect may be raised and exalted, and made capable of overcoming the difficulties and obscurities of nature. The art which I introduce with this view (which I call *Interpretation of Nature*) is a kind of logic; though the difference between it and the ordinary logic is great; indeed immense. For the ordinary logic professes to contrive and prepare helps and guards for the understanding, as mine does; and in this one point they agree. But mine differs from it in three points especially; viz. in the end aimed at; in the order of demonstration; and in the starting point of the inquiry.

For the end which this science of mine proposes is the invention not of arguments but of arts; not of things in accordance with principles, but of principles themselves; not of probable reasons, but of designations and directions for works. And as the intention is different, so accordingly is the effect; the effect of the one being to overcome an opponent in argument, of the other to command nature in action.

In accordance with this end is also the nature and order of the demonstrations. For in the ordinary logic almost all the work is spent about the syllogism. Of induction the logicians seem hardly to have taken any serious thought, but they pass it by with a slight notice, and hasten on to the formulae of disputation.

I on the contrary reject demonstration by syllogism, as acting too confusedly, and letting nature slip out of its hands. For although no one can doubt that things which agree in a middle term agree with one another (which is a proposition of mathematical certainty), yet it leaves an opening for deception; which is this. The syllogism consists of propositions; propositions of words; and words are the tokens and signs of notions. Now if the very notions of the mind (which are as the soul of words and the basis of the whole structure) be improperly and over-hastily abstracted from facts, vague, not sufficiently definite, faulty in short in many ways, the whole edifice tumbles. I therefore reject the syllogism; and that not only as regards principles (for to principles the logicians themselves do not apply it) but also as regards middle propositions; which, though obtainable no doubt by the syllogism, are, when so obtained, barren of works, remote from practice, and altogether unavailable for the active department of the sciences. Although therefore I leave to the syllogism and these famous and boasted modes of demonstration their jurisdiction over popular arts and such as are matter of opinion (in which department I leave all as it is), yet in dealing with the nature of things I use induction throughout, and that in the minor propositions as well as the major. For I consider induction to be that form of demonstration which upholds the sense, and closes with nature, and comes to the very brink of operation, if it does not actually deal with it.

Hence it follows that the order of demonstration is likewise inverted. For hitherto the proceeding has been to fly at once from the sense and particulars up to the most general propositions, as certain fixed poles for the argument to turn upon, and from these to derive the rest by middle terms: a short way, no doubt, but precipitate; and one which will never lead to nature, though it offers an easy and ready way to disputation. Now my plan is to proceed regularly and gradually from one axiom to another, so that the most general are not reached till the last: but then when you do come to them you find them to be not empty notions, but well defined, and such as nature would really recognize as her first principles, and such as lie at the heart and marrow of things.

But the greatest change I introduce is in the form itself of induction and the judgment made thereby. For the induction of which the logicians speak, which proceeds by simple enumeration, is a puerile thing; concludes at hazard; is always liable to be upset by a contradictory instance; takes into account only what is known and ordinary; and leads to no result.

Now what the sciences stand in need of is a form of induction which shall analyse experience and take it to pieces, and by a due process of exclusion and rejection lead to an inevitable conclusion. And if that ordinary mode of judgment practised by the logicians was so laborious, and found exercise for such great wits, how much more labour must we be prepared to bestow upon this other, which is extracted not merely out of the depths of the mind, but out of the very bowels of nature.

Nor is this all. For I also sink the foundations of the sciences deeper and firmer; and I begin the inquiry nearer the source than men have done heretofore; submitting to examination those things which the common logic takes on trust. For first, the logicians borrow the principles of each science from the science itself; secondly, they hold in reverence the first notions of the mind; and lastly, they receive as conclusive the immediate informations of the sense, when well disposed. Now upon the first point, I hold that true logic ought to enter the several provinces of science armed with a higher authority than belongs to the principles of those sciences themselves, and ought to call those putative principles to account until they are fully established. Then with regard to the first notions of the intellect; there is not one of the impressions taken by the intellect when left to go its own way, but I hold it for suspected, and no way established, until it has submitted to a new trial and a fresh judgment has been thereupon pronounced. And lastly, the information of the sense itself I sift and examine in many ways. For certain it is that the senses deceive; but then at the same time they supply the means of discovering their own errors; only the errors are here, the means of discovery are to seek.

The sense fails in two ways. Sometimes it gives no information, sometimes it gives false information. For first, there are very many things which escape the sense, even when best disposed and no way obstructed; by reason either of the subtlety of the whole body, or the of the parts, or distance of place, or slowness or else swiftness of the motion, or familiarity of the object, or other causes. And again when the sense does apprehend a thing its apprehension is not much to be relied upon. For the testimony and information of the sense has reference always to man, not to the universe; and it is a great error to assert that the sense is the measure of things.

To meet these difficulties, I have sought on all sides diligently and faithfully to provide helps for the sense—substitutes to supply its failures, rectifications to correct its errors; and this I endeavour to accomplish not so much by instruments as by experiments. For the subtlety of experiments is far greater than that of the sense itself, even when assisted by exquisite instruments; such experiments, I mean, as are skilfully and artificially devised for the express purpose of determining the point in question. To the immediate and proper perception of the sense therefore I do not give much weight; but I contrive that the office of the sense shall be only to judge of the experiment, and that the experiment itself shall judge of the thing. And thus I conceive that I perform the office of a true priest of the sense (from which all knowledge in nature must be sought, unless men mean to go mad) and a not unskilful interpreter of its oracles; and that while others only profess to uphold and cultivate the sense, I do so in fact. Such then are the provisions I make for finding the genuine light of nature and kindling and bringing it to bear. And they would be sufficient of themselves, if the human intellect were even, and like a fair sheet of paper with no writing on it. But since the minds of men are strangely possessed and beset, so that there is no true and even surface left to reflect the genuine rays of things, it is necessary to seek a remedy for this also.

Now the idols, or phantoms, by which the mind is occupied are either adventitious or innate. The adventitious come into the mind from without; namely, either from the doctrines and sects of philosophers, or from perverse rules of demonstration. But the innate are inherent in the very nature of the intellect, which is far more prone to error than the sense is. For let men please themselves as they will in admiring and almost adoring the human mind, this is certain: that as an uneven mirror distorts the rays of objects according to its own figure and section, so the mind, when it receives impressions of objects through the sense, cannot be trusted to report them truly, but in forming its notions mixes up its own nature with the nature of things.

And as the first two kinds of idols are hard to eradicate, so idols of this last kind cannot be eradicated at all. All that can be done is to point them out, so that this insidious action of the mind may be marked and reproved (else as fast as old errors are destroyed new ones will spring up out of the ill complexion of the mind itself, and so we shall have but a change of errors, and not a clearance); and to lay it down once for all as a fixed and established maxim, that the intellect is not qualified to judge except by means of induction, and induction in its legitimate form. This doctrine then of the expurgation of the intellect to qualify it for dealing with truth, is comprised in three refutations: the refutation of the Philosophies; the refutation of the Demonstrations; and the refutation of the Natural Human Reason. The explanation of which things, and of the true relation between the nature of things and the nature of the mind, is as the strewing and decoration of the bridal chamber of the Mind and the Universe, the Divine Goodness assisting; out of which marriage let us hope (and be this the prayer of the bridal song) there may spring helps to man, and a line and race of inventions that may in some degree subdue and overcome the necessities and miseries of humanity. This is the second part of the work.

But I design not only to indicate and mark out the ways, but also to enter them. And therefore the third part of the work embraces the Phenomena of the Universe; that is to say, experience of every kind, and such a natural history as may serve for a foundation to build philosophy upon. For a good method of demonstration or form of interpreting nature may keep the mind from going astray or stumbling, but it is not any excellence of method that can supply it with the material of knowledge. Those however who aspire not to guess and divine, but to discover and know; who propose not to devise mimic and fabulous worlds of their own, but to examine and dissect the nature of this very world itself; must go to facts themselves for everything. Nor can the place of this labour and search and worldwide perambulation be supplied by any genius or meditation or argumentation; no, not if all men's wits could meet in one. This therefore we must have, or the business must be for ever abandoned. But up to this day such has been the condition of men in this matter, that it is no wonder if nature will not give herself into their hands.

For first, the information of the sense itself, sometimes failing, sometimes false; observation, careless, irregular, and led by chance; tradition, vain and fed on rumour; practice, slavishly bent upon its work; experiment, blind, stupid, vague, and prematurely broken off; lastly, natural history trivial and poor;—all these have contributed to supply the understanding with very bad materials for philosophy and the sciences.

Then an attempt is made to mend the matter by a preposterous subtlety and winnowing of argument. But this comes too late, the case being already past remedy; and is far from setting the business right or sifting away the errors. The only hope therefore of any greater increase or progress lies in a reconstruction of the sciences.

Of this reconstruction the foundation must be laid in natural history, and that of a new kind and gathered on a new principle. For it is in vain that you polish the mirror if there are no images to be reflected; and it is as necessary that the intellect should be supplied with fit matter to work upon, as with safeguards to guide its working. But my history differs from that in use (as my logic does) in many things,—in end and office, in mass and composition, in subtlety, in selection also and setting forth, with a view to the operations which are to follow.

For first, the object of the natural history which I propose is not so much to delight with variety of matter or to help with present use of experiments, as to give light to the discovery of causes and supply a suckling philosophy with its first food. For though it be true that I am principally in pursuit of works and the active department of the sciences, yet I wait for harvest-time, and do not attempt to mow the moss or to reap the green corn. For I well know that axioms once rightly discovered will carry whole troops of works along with them, and produce them, not here and there one, but in clusters. And that unseasonable and puerile hurry to snatch by way of earnest at the first works which come within reach, I utterly condemn and reject, as an Atalanta's apple that hinders the race. Such then is the office of this natural history of mine.

Next, with regard to the mass and composition of it: I mean it to be a history not only of nature free and at large (when she is left to her own course and does her work her own way),—such as that of the heavenly bodies, meteors, earth and sea, minerals, plants, animals,—but much more of nature under constraint and vexed; that is to say, when by art and the hand of man she is forced out of her natural state, and squeezed and moulded. Therefore I set down at length all experiments of the mechanical arts, of the operative part of the liberal arts, of the many crafts which have not yet grown into arts properly so called, so far as I have been able to examine them and as they conduce to the end on view. Nay (to say the plain truth) I do in fact (low and vulgar as men may think it) count more upon this part both for helps and safeguards than upon the other; seeing that the nature of things betrays itself more readily under the vexations of art than in its natural freedom.

Nor do I confine the history to Bodies; but I have thought it my duty besides to make a separate history of such Virtues as may be considered cardinal in nature. I mean those original passions or desires of matter which constitute the primary elements of nature; such as Dense and Rare, Hot and Cold, Solid and Fluid, Heavy and Light, and several others.

Then again, to speak of subtlety: I seek out and get together a kind of experiments much subtler and simpler than those which occur accidentally. For I drag into light many things which no one who was not proceeding by a regular and certain way to the discovery of causes would have thought of inquiring after; being indeed in themselves of no great use; which shows that they were not sought for on their own account; but having just the same relation to things and works which the letters of the alphabet have to speech and words—which, though in themselves useless, are the elements of which all discourse is made up.

Further, in the selection of the relations and experiments I conceived I have been a more cautious purveyor than those who have hitherto dealt with natural history. For I admit nothing but on the faith of eyes, or at least of careful and severe examination; so that nothing is exaggerated for wonder's sake, but what I state is sound and without mixture of fables or vanity. All received or current falsehoods also (which by strange negligence have been allowed for many ages to prevail and become established) I proscribe and brand by name; that the sciences may be no more troubled with them. For it has been well observed and the fables and superstitions and follies which nurses instil into children do serious injury to their minds; and the same consideration makes me anxious, having the management of the childhood as if were of philosophy in its course of natural history, not to let it accustom itself in the beginning to any vanity. Moreover, whenever I come to a new experiment of any subtlety (though it be in my own opinion certain and approved), I nevertheless subjoin a clear account of the manner in which I made it; that men knowing exactly how each point was made out, may see whether there be any error connected with it, and may arouse themselves to devise proofs more trustworthy and exquisite, if such can be found; and finally, I interpose everywhere admonitions and scruples and cautions, with a religious care to eject, repress, and as it were exorcise every kind of phantasm.

Lastly, knowing how much the sight of man's mind is distracted by experience and history, and how hard it is at the first (especially for minds either tender or preoccupied) to become familiar with nature, I not unfrequently subjoin observation of my own, being as the first offers, inclinations, and as it were glances of history towards philosophy; both by way of an assurance to men that they will not be kept for ever tossing on the waves of experience, and also that when the time comes for the intellect to begin its work, it may find everything the more ready. By such a natural history then as I have described, I conceive that a safe and convenient approach may be made to nature, and matter supplied of good quality and well prepared for the understanding to work upon.

And now that we have surrounded the intellect with faithful helps and guards, and got together with most careful selection a regular army of divine works, it may seem that we have no more to do but to proceed to philosophy itself. And yet in a matter so difficult and doubtful there are still some things which it seems necessary to premise, partly for convenience of explanation, partly for present use.

Of these the first is to set forth examples of inquiry and invention according to my method, exhibited by anticipation in Some particular subjects; choosing such subjects as are at once the most noble in themselves among those under inquiry, and most different one from another; that there may be an example in every kind. I do not speak of those examples which are joined to the several precepts and rules by way of illustration (for of these I have given plenty in the second part of the work);

but I mean actual types and models, by which the entire process of the mind and the whole fabric and order of invention from the beginning to the end, in certain subjects, and those various and remarkable, should be set as it were before the eyes. For I remember that in the mathematics it is easy to follow the demonstration when you have a machine beside you; whereas without that help all appears involved and more subtle than it really is. To examples of this kind,—being in fact nothing more than an application of the second part in detail and at large,—the fourth part of the work is devoted.

The fifth part is for temporary use only, pending the completion of the rest; like interest payable from time to time until the principal be forthcoming. For I do not make so blindly for the end of my journey, as to neglect anything useful that may turn up by the way. And therefore I include in this fifth part such things as I have myself discovered, proved, or added,—not however according to the true rules and methods of interpretation, but by the ordinary use of the understanding in inquiring and discovering. For besides that I hope my speculations may in virtue of my continual conversancy with nature have a value beyond the pretensions of my wit, they will serve in the meantime for wayside inns, in which the mind may rest and refresh itself on its journey to more certain conclusions. Nevertheless I wish it to be understood in the meantime that they are conclusions by which (as not being discovered and proved by the true form of interpretation) I do not at all mean to bind myself. Nor need any one be alarmed at such suspension of judgment, in one who maintains not simply that nothing can be known, but only that nothing can be known except in a certain course and way; and yet establishes provisionally certain degrees of assurance, for use and relief until the mind shall arrive at a knowledge of causes in which it can rest. For even those schools of philosophy which held the absolute impossibility of knowing anything were not inferior to those which took upon them to pronounce. But then they did not provide helps for the sense and understanding, as I have done, but simply took away all their authority: which is quite a different thing—almost the reverse.

The sixth part of my work (to which the rest is subservient and ministrant) discloses I and sets forth that philosophy which by the legitimate, chaste, and severe course of inquiry which I have explained and provided is at length developed and established. The completion however of this last part is a thing both above my strength and beyond my hopes. I have made a beginning of the work—a beginning, as I hope, not unimportant;—the fortune of the human race will give the issue—such an issue, it may be, as in the present condition of things and men's minds cannot easily be conceived or imagined. For the matter in hand is no mere felicity of speculation, but the real business and fortunes of the human race, and all power of operation. For man is but the servant and interpreter of nature: what he does and what he knows is only what he has observed of nature's order in fact or in thought; beyond this he knows nothing and can do nothing. For the chain of causes cannot by any force be loosed or broken, nor can nature be commanded except by being obeyed. And so those twin objects, human Knowledge and human Power, do really meet in one; and it is from ignorance of causes that operation fails.

And all depends on keeping the eye steadily fixed upon the facts of nature and so receiving their images simply as they are. For God forbid that we should give out a dream of our own imagination for a pattern of the world; rather may he graciously grant to us to write an apocalypse or true vision of the footsteps of the Creator imprinted on his creatures.

Therefore do thou, O Father, who gavest the visible light as the first fruits of creation, and didst breathe into the face of man the intellectual light as the crown and consummation thereof, guard and protect this work, which coming from thy goodness returneth to thy glory. Thou when thou turnedst to look upon the works which thy hands had made, sawest that all was very good, and didst rest from the labours. But man, when he turned to look upon the work which his hands had made, saw that all was vanity and vexation of spirit, and could find no rest therein. Wherefore if we labour in thy works with the sweat of our brows thou wilt make us partakers of thy vision and thy sabbath. Humbly we pray that this mind may be steadfast in us, and that through these our hands, and the hands of others to whom thou shalt give the same spirit, thou wilt vouchsafe to endow the human family with new mercies.

John Locke

(1632–1704)

The name of Locke was, with Newton's, preeminent in the Enlightenment. The philosophers of that period, especially in France, looked up to Locke for having done for human nature what Newton had done for the physical world. These thinkers had most in mind Locke's epoch-making work, the *Essay concerning Human Understanding* (1690). To men like Voltaire in pre-Revolutionary France it seemed that Locke had liberated the human mind from the trammels of supernatural authority by demonstrating that all ideas were primarily derived from man's experience and circumstances. Although not without ambiguities, his implication was that neither innate flaws in human nature (e.g. original sin) nor accident of birth (e.g. lowly birth) were responsible for what a man came to be in life.

The influence of Locke's ideas in psychology is impossible to measure. There are few modern students of theory of knowledge, of education, and of character formation who have not, directly or indirectly been affected by the *Essay concerning Human Understanding.*

From *An Essay Concerning Human Understanding*[1]

Book II: Of Ideas

Chapter I: Of Ideas In General, and Their Origin

Every man being conscious to himself that he thinks, and that which his mind is applied about, whilst thinking, being the ideas that are there, it is past doubt, that men have in their minds several ideas, such as are those expressed by the words, Whiteness, Hardness, Sweetness, Thinking, Motion, Man, Elephant, Army, Drunkenness, and others. It is in the first place then to be inquired, how he comes by them. I know it is a received doctrine, that men have native ideas, and original characters, stamped upon their minds, in their very first being. This opinion I have, at large, examined already; and, I suppose, what I have said, in the foregoing book, will be much more easily admitted, when I have shown, whence the understanding may get all the ideas it has, and by what ways and degrees they may come into the mind; for which I shall appeal to every one's own observation and experience.

Let us then suppose the mind to be, as we say, white paper, void of all characters, without any ideas; how comes it to be furnished? Whence comes it by that vast store which the busy and boundless fancy of man has painted on it, with an almost endless variety? Whence has it all the materials of reason and knowledge? To this I answer, in one word, from experience; in that all our knowledge is founded, and from that it ultimately derives itself. Our observation employed either about external sensible objects, or about the internal operations of our minds, perceived and reflected on by ourselves, is that which supplies our understandings with all the materials of thinking. These two are the fountains of knowledge, from whence all the ideas we have, or can naturally have, do spring.

---

[1] The following selection is taken from A. C. Fraser's edition (Oxford, Clarendon Press, 1894).

First, Our senses, conversant about particular sensible objects, do convey into the mind several distinct perceptions of things, according to those various ways wherein those objects do affect them: and thus we come by those ideas we have, of Yellow, White, Heat, Cold, Soft, Hard, Bitter, Sweet, and all those which we call sensible qualities; which when I say the senses convey into the mind, I mean, they from external objects convey into the mind what produces there those perceptions. This great source of most of the ideas we have, depending wholly upon our senses, and derived by them to the understanding, I call *sensation.*

Secondly, The other fountain, from which experience furnisheth the understanding with ideas, is the perception of the operations of our own mind within us, as it is employed about the ideas it has got; which operations when the soul comes to reflect on and consider, do furnish the under-standing with another set of ideas, which could not be had from things without; and such are Perception, Thinking, Doubting, Believing, Reasoning, Knowing, Willing, and all the different act-ings of our own minds; which we being conscious of and observing in ourselves, do from these receive into our understandings as distinct ideas, as we do from bodies affecting our senses. This source of ideas every man has wholly in himself; and though it be not sense, as having nothing to do with external objects, yet it is very like it, and might properly enough be called internal sense. But as I call the other sensation, so I call this *reflection,* the ideas it affords being such only as the mind gets by reflecting on its own operations within itself. By reflection then, in the following part of this discourse, I would be understood to mean that notice which the mind takes of its own oper-ations, and the manner of them; by reason whereof there come to be ideas of these operations in the understanding. These two, I say, *viz.,* external material things, as the objects of sensation; and the operations of our own minds within, as the objects of reflection; are to me the only originals from whence all our ideas take their beginnings. The term operations here I use in a large sense, as comprehending not barely the actions of the mind about its ideas, but some sort of passions arising sometimes from them, such as is the satisfaction or uneasiness arising from any thought.

The understanding seems to me not to have the least glimmering of any ideas, which it doth not receive from one of these two. External objects furnish the mind with the ideas of sensible qualities, which are all those different perceptions they produce in us: and the mind furnishes the understanding with ideas of its own operations.

These, when we have taken a full survey of them and their several modes, combinations, and relations, we shall find to contain all our whole stock of ideas; and that we have nothing in our minds which did not come in one of these two ways. Let any one examine his own thoughts, and thoroughly search into his understanding; and then let him tell me, whether all the original ideas he has there, are any other than of the objects of his senses, or of the operations of his mind, considered as objects of his reflection: and how great a mass of knowledge soever he imagines to be lodged there, he will, upon taking a strict view, see that he has not any idea in his mind, but what one of these two have imprinted; though perhaps, with infinite variety compounded and enlarged by the understanding, as we shall see hereafter.

Chapter II: Of Simple Ideas of Sense

1. The better to understand the nature, manner, and extent of our knowledge, one thing is care-fully to be observed concerning the ideas we have; and that is, that some of them are *simple* and some *complex.*

Though the qualities that affect our senses are, in the things themselves so united and blended, that there is no separation, no distance between them; yet it is plain, the ideas they produce in the mind enter by the senses simple and unmixed. For, though the sight and touch often take in from the same object, at the same time, different ideas—as a man sees at once motion and colour; the hand feels softness and warmth in the same piece of wax: yet the simple ideas thus united in the same subject, are as perfectly distinct as those that come in by different senses. The coldness and hardness which a man feels in a piece of ice being as distinct ideas in the mind as the smell and whiteness of a lily; or as the taste of sugar, and smell of a rose. And there is nothing can be plainer to a man than the clear and distinct perception he has of those simple ideas; which, being each in itself uncompounded, contains in it nothing but *one uniform appearance* of conception in the mind, and is not distinguishable into different ideas.

2. These simple ideas, the materials of all our knowledge, are suggested and furnished to the mind only by those two ways above mentioned, viz. sensation and reflection. When the understanding is once stored with these simple ideas, it has the power to repeat, compare, and unite them, even to an almost infinite variety, and so can make at pleasure new complex ideas. But it is not in the power of the most exalted wit or enlarged understanding, by any quickness or variety of thought, to *invent* or *frame* one new simple idea in the mind, not taken in by the ways before mentioned: nor can any force of the understanding *destroy* those that are there, the dominion of man in this little world of his own understanding being muchwhat the same as it is in the great world of visible things; wherein his power, however managed by art and skill, reaches no farther than to compound and divide the materials that are made to his hand; but can do nothing towards the making the least particle of new matter, or destroying one atom of what is already in being. The same inability will every one find in himself, who shall go about to fashion in his understanding one simple idea, not received in by his senses from external objects, or by reflection from the operations of his own mind about them.

3. This is the reason why it is not possible for any one to imagine any other qualities in bodies, howsoever constituted, whereby they can be taken notice of, besides sounds, tastes, smells, visible and tangible qualities. And had mankind been made but with four senses, the qualities then which are the objects of the fifth sense had been as far from our notice, imagination, and conception, as now any belonging to a sixth, seventh, or eighth sense can possibly be. I have here followed the common opinion of man's having but five senses, though perhaps, there may be justly counted more; but either supposition serves equally to my present purpose.

Book IV: Of Knowledge, Certain and Probable

Chapter I: Of Knowledge in General

1. Since the mind, in all its thoughts and reasonings, hath no other immediate object but its own ideas, which it alone does or can contemplate, it is evident that our knowledge is only conversant about them.

2. *Knowledge* then seems to me to be nothing but *the perception of the connection of and agreement, or disagreement and repugnancy, of any of our ideas*. In this alone it consists. Where this perception is, there is knowledge, and where it is not, there, though we may fancy, guess, or believe, yet we always come short of knowledge. For when we know that white is not black, what do we else but perceive, that these two ideas do not agree? When we possess ourselves with the utmost security of the demonstration that the three angles of a triangle are equal to two right ones, what do we more but perceive, that equality to two right ones does necessarily agree to, and is inseparable from, the three angles of a triangle?

Chapter II: Of the Degrees of Our Knowledge

1. All our knowledge consisting, as I have said, in the view the mind has of its own ideas, which is the utmost light and greatest certainty we, with our faculties, and in our way of knowledge, are capable of, it may not be amiss to consider a little the degree of its evidence. The different clearness of our knowledge seems to me to lie in the different way of perception the mind has of the agreement or disagreement of any of its ideas. For if we will reflect on our own ways of thinking, we will find, that sometimes the mind perceives the agreement or disagreement of two ideas immediately by themselves, without the intervention of any other: and this I think we may call *intuitive knowledge*. For in this the mind is at no pains of proving or examining, but perceives the truth as the eye doth light, only by being directed towards it. Thus the mind perceives that *white* is not *black*, that a *circle* is not a *triangle*, that *three* are more than *two* and equal to *one and two*. Such kinds of truths the mind perceives at the first sight of the ideas together, by bare intuition; without the intervention of any other idea: and this kind of knowledge is the clearest and most certain that human frailty is capable of. This part of knowledge is irresistible, and like bright sunshine, forces itself immediately to be perceived, as soon as ever the mind turns its view that way; and leaves no room for hesitation, doubt, or examination but the mind is presently filled with the clear light of it. It is on this intuition that depends all the certainty and evidence of all our knowledge; which certainty every one finds to be so great, that he cannot imagine, and therefore not require, a greater: for a man cannot conceive himself capable of a greater certainty than to know that any idea in his mind is such as he perceives it to be; and that two ideas, wherein he perceives a difference, are different and not precisely the same. He that demands a greater certainty than this, demands he knows not what, and shows only that he has a mind to be a sceptic, without being able to do so. Certainty depends so wholly on this intuition, that in the next degree of knowledge, which I call demonstrative, this intuition is necessary in all the connections of the intermediate ideas, without which we cannot attain knowledge and certainty.

2. The next degree of knowledge is, where the mind perceives the agreement or disagreement of any ideas, but not immediately. The reason why the mind cannot always perceive presently the agreement or disagreement of two ideas, is because those ideas, concerning whose agreement or disagreement the inquiry is made, cannot by the mind be so put together as to show it. In this case then, when the mind cannot so bring its ideas together as by their immediate comparison, and as it were juxtaposition or application one to another, to perceive their agreement or disagreement, it is fain, *by the intervention of other ideas* (one or more, as it happens) to discover the agreement or disagreement which it searches; and this is that which we call *reasoning*.

Chapter X: Of the Knowledge of the Existence of a God

1. Though God has given us no innate ideas of himself; though he has stamped no original characters on our minds, wherein we may read his being; yet having furnished us with those faculties our minds are endowed with, he hath not left himself without witness; since we have sense, perception, and reason, and cannot want a clear proof of him, as long as we carry *ourselves* about us. But, though this be the most obvious truth that reason discovers, and though its evidence be (if I mistake not) equal to mathematical certainty: yet it requires thought and attention; and the mind must apply itself to a regular deduction of it from some part of our intuitive knowledge, or else we shall be as uncertain and ignorant of this as of other propositions, which are in themselves capable of clear demonstration. To show, therefore, that there is a God, and *how we may come* by this certainty, I think we need go no further than *ourselves*, and that undoubted knowledge we have of our own existence.

2. This, I think I may take for a truth, which every one's certain knowledge assures him of, beyond the liberty of doubting, viz. that he is *something that actually exists*. If any one pretends to be so sceptical as to deny his own existence (for really to doubt of it is manifestly impossible), let him for me enjoy his beloved happiness of being nothing, until hunger or some other pain convince him of the contrary.

3. In the next place, man knows, by an intuitive certainty, that bare *nothing can no more produce any real being, than it can be equal to two right angles*. If a man knows not that nonentity, or the absence of all being, cannot be equal to two right angles, it is impossible he should know any demonstration in Euclid. If, therefore, we know there is some real being, and that nonentity cannot produce any real being, it is an evident demonstration, that *from eternity there has been something*; since what was not from eternity had a beginning; and what had a beginning must be produced by something else.

4. Next, it is evident, that what had its being and beginning from another, must also have all that which is in and belongs to its being from another too. All the powers it has must be owing to and received from the same source. This eternal source, then, of all being must also be the source and original of all power; and so *this eternal Being must be also the most powerful*.

5. Again, a man finds in himself perception and knowledge. We have then got one step further; and we are certain now that there is not only some being, but some knowing, intelligent being in the world. There was a time, then, when there was no knowing being, and when knowledge began to be; or else there has been also a *knowing being from eternity*. If it be said, there was a time when no being had any knowledge, when that eternal being was void of all understanding; I reply, that then it was impossible there should ever have been any knowledge; it being as impossible that things wholly void of knowledge, and operating blindly, and without any perception, should produce a knowing being, as it is impossible that a triangle should make itself three angles bigger than two right ones. For it is as repugnant to the idea of senseless matter, that it should put into itself sense, perception, and knowledge, as it is repugnant to the idea of a triangle, that it should put into itself greater angles than two right ones.

6. Thus, from the consideration of ourselves, and what we infallibly find in our own constitutions, our reason leads us to the knowledge of this certain and evident truth—*that there is an eternal, most powerful, and most knowing Being*; which whether any one will please to call God, it matters not. The thing is evident; and from this idea duly considered, will easily be deduced all those other attributes, which we ought to ascribe to this eternal Being.

7. How far the *idea* of a most perfect being, which a man may frame in his mind, does or does not prove the *existence* of a God, I will not here examine. For in the different make of men's tempers and application of their thoughts, some arguments prevail more on one, and some on another, for the confirmation of the same truth. But yet, I think, this I may say, that it is an ill way of establishing this truth, and silencing atheists, to lay the whole stress of so important a point as this upon that sole foundation: and take some men's having that idea of God in their minds (for it is evident some men have none, and some worse than none, and the most very different), for the only proof of a Deity.

8. It being, then, unavoidable for all rational creatures to conclude that *something* has existed from eternity, let us next see *what kind of thing* that must be.

9. There are but two sorts of being in the world that man knows or conceives.

First, Such as are purely material, without sense, perception, or thought, as the clippings of our beards, and parings of our nails.

Secondly, Sensible, thinking, perceiving beings, such as we find ourselves to be. Which, if you please, we will hereafter call *cogitative* and *incogitative* beings; which to our present purpose, if for nothing else, are perhaps better terms than material and immaterial.

10. If, then, there must be something eternal, let us see what sort of being it must be. And to that it is very obvious to reason, that it must necessarily be a cogitative being. For it is as impossible to conceive that ever bare incogitative matter should produce a thinking intelligent being, as that nothing should of itself produce matter. Let us suppose any parcel of matter eternal, great or small, we shall find it, in itself, able to produce nothing. For example: let us suppose the matter of the next pebble we meet with eternal, closely united, and the parts firmly at rest together; if there were no other being in the world, must it not eternally remain so, a dead inactive lump? Is it possible to conceive it can add motion to itself, being purely matter, or produce anything? Matter, then, by its own strength cannot produce in itself so much as motion: the motion it has must also be from eternity, or else be produced, and added to matter by some other being more powerful than matter; matter, as is evident, having not power to produce motion in itself. But let us suppose motion eternal too: yet matter, *incogitative* matter and motion, whatever changes it might produce of figure and bulk, could never produce thought: knowledge will still be as far beyond the power of motion and matter to produce, as matter is beyond the power of nothing or nonentity to produce. So that, if we will suppose *nothing* first or eternal, matter can never begin to be: if we suppose bare matter without motion, eternal, motion can never begin to be: if we suppose only matter and motion first, or eternal, thought can never begin to be.

11. If, therefore it be evident, that something necessarily must exist from eternity, it is also as evident, that that something must necessarily be a cogitative being: for it is as impossible that incogitative matter should produce a cogitative being, as that nothing, or the negation of all being, should produce a positive being or matter.

12. Though this discovery of the *necessary existence of an eternal Mind* does sufficiently lead us into the knowledge of God; since it will hence follow, that all other knowing beings that have a beginning must depend on him, and have no other ways of knowledge or extent of power than what he gives them; and, therefore, if he made those, he made also the less excellent pieces of this universe—all inanimate beings, whereby his omniscience, power, and providence will be established, and all his other attributes necessarily follow: yet, to clear up this a little further, we will see what doubts can be raised against it.

13. First, Perhaps it will be said, that, though it be as clear as demonstration can make it, that there must be an eternal Being, and that Being must also be knowing: yet it does not follow but that thinking Being may also be material. There being no way to avoid the demonstration that there is an eternal knowing Being, men, devoted to matter, would willingly have it granted that this knowing being is material; and then, letting slide out of their minds, or the discourse, the demonstration whereby an eternal *knowing* Being was proved necessarily to exist, would argue all to be matter, and so deny a God, that is, an eternal cogitative Being: whereby they are so far from establishing that they destroy their own hypothesis.

14. But now let us see how they can satisfy themselves, or others, that this eternal thinking Being is material. I would ask them, whether they imagine that all matter, *every particle of matter*, thinks. This, I suppose, they will scarcely say; since then there would be as many eternal thinking beings as there are particles of matter, and so an infinity of gods. And yet, if they will not allow matter as matter, that is, every particle of matter, to be as well cogitative as extended, they will have as hard a task to make out to their own reasons a cogitative being out of incogitative particles, as an extended being out of unextended parts, if I may so speak.

15. If all matter does not think, I next ask, whether it be *only one atom* that does so. This has as many absurdities as the other; for then this atom of matter must be alone eternal or not. If this alone be eternal, then this alone, by its powerful thought or will, made all the rest of matter. And so we have the creation of matter by a powerful thought, which is that the materialists stick at; for if they suppose one single thinking atom to have produced all the rest of matter, they cannot ascribe that pre-eminency to it upon any other account than that of its thinking, the only supposed difference. To suppose all matter eternal, and yet one small particle in knowledge and power infinitely above all the rest, is without any the least appearance of reason to frame an hypothesis. Every particle of matter, as matter, is capable of all the same figures and motions of any other; and I challenge any one, in his thoughts, to add anything else to one above another.

16. If then neither one peculiar atom alone can be this eternal thinking being; nor all matter, as matter, i.e. every particle of matter, can be it; it only remains, that it is some certain *system* of matter, duly put together, that is this thinking eternal Being. This is that which, I imagine, is that notion which men are aptest to have of God; who would have him a material being as most readily suggested to them by the ordinary conceit they have of themselves and other men, which they take to be material thinking beings. But this imagination, however more natural, is no less absurd than the other. For unthinking particles of matter, however put together can have nothing thereby added to them, but a new relation of position, which it is impossible should give thought and knowledge to them.

18. Secondly, Others would have matter to be eternal, notwithstanding that they allow an eternal, cogitative, immaterial Being. This, though it take not away the being of a God, yet since it denies one and the first great piece of his workmanship, the creation, let us consider it a little. Matter must be allowed eternal: Why? because you cannot conceive how it can be made out of nothing: why do you not also think yourself eternal? You will answer, perhaps, Because, about twenty or forty years since, you began to be. But if I ask you, what that *you* is, which began then to be, you can scarce tell me. The matter whereof you are made began not then to be: for if it did, then it is not eternal: but it began to be put together in such a fashion and frame as makes up your body; but yet that frame of particles is not you, it makes not that thinking thing you are (for I have now to do with one who allows an eternal, immaterial, thinking Being, but would have unthinking matter eternal too); therefore, when did that thinking thing begin to be? If it did never begin to be, then have you always been a thinking thing from eternity; the absurdity whereof I need not confute, till I meet with one who is so void of understanding as to own it. If, therefore, you can allow a thinking thing to be made out of nothing (as all things that are not eternal must be) why also can you not allow it possible for a material being to be made out of nothing by an equal power, but that you have the experience of the one in view, and not of the other?

19. But you will say, Is it not impossible to admit of the making anything out of nothing, since we cannot possibly conceive it? I answer, No. Because it is not reasonable to deny the power of an infinite Being, because we cannot comprehend its operations. We do not deny other effects upon this ground, because we cannot possibly conceive the manner of their production. For example: my right hand writes, whilst my left hand is still: What causes rest in one, and motion in the other? Nothing but my will—a thought of my mind; my thought only changing, the right hand rests, and the left hand moves. This is matter of fact, which cannot be denied: explain this and make it intelligible, and then the next step will be to understand creation.

. . . .

Of Civil Government is the second of *Two Treatises of Government*, which appeared in 1690, and which Locke prefaced with these words: "These . . . I hope are sufficient to establish the Throne of our great Restorer, our present King *William*, to make good his title, in the Consent of the People; which being the only one of all lawful Governments, he has more fully and clearly, than any Prince in *Christendom*, and to justify to the World the People of *England*, whose love of their just and natural Rights, with their Resolution to preserve them, saved the Nation when it was on the very birth of Slavery and Ruin." Such a justification rested first on Locke's refutation of the doctrine of absolute monarchy, and the first *Treatise* is devoted to an attack upon Sir Robert Filmer's defense of that form of government.

David Hume

(1711–1776)

The Scottish philosopher David Hume reformulated Locke's empiricist philosophy to take account of criticisms levelled by Bishop Berkeley in *A Treatise Concerning the Principles of Human Knowledge* (1710). Berkeley had argued that, on Locke's own premises, it was impossible to prove the existence of a material world independent of human perception. External reality, Berkeley admitted, could be known only through the senses—on this crucial point Locke had been correct and Descartes in error. But, he added, sense impressions ("sensations" or "ideas") gained through perception were always interpreted and structured by the human mind before they became intelligible and meaningful. So, he concluded, there was necessarily a "subjective" element in perception and cognition, and "reality" was, in part, a mental construct.

Samuel Johnson, objecting to what he regarded as Berkeley's specious logic-chopping, vindicated the reality of the external world by kicking a rock and exclaiming, "I refute him thus!". Hume, on the other hand, accepted Berkeley's argument, and generalised the latter's epistemological insight into a thorough-going analysis of the underlying assumptions of empirical science. In two major works, *A treatise of Human Nature* (1740) and *An Enquiry Concerning the Human Understanding* (1748, revised edition 1777), Hume claimed that although empirical procedures were the only means of obtaining factual knowledge, it was impossible—strictly speaking—to deduce universal causal laws from the evidence of the senses. The order which natural scientists believed they had detected underlying the universe, he suggested, was a product of the concepts and assumptions they brought to their researches. All inferences from experience, he pointed out, were "effects of custom, not reasoning," induction was, at best, an imperfect form of logic, and scientists assumed two *a priori* principles (causal determinism and the uniformity of nature) which could neither be demonstrated rationally nor verified experimentally. Natural science, he asserted, was therefore built on faith and habit, and the only position which a philosopher could honestly adopt was one of complete scepticism regarding both the possibility of human knowledge and the existence of an ordered, law-governed, material universe.

Naturally Hume recognised that this extreme scepticism (Pyrrhonism) flew in the face of common sense. In practice, he thought, there was no alternative to accepting as provisionally valid the "laws" of physics, and, for that matter, those of Lockean psychology and classical political economy. But it was worthwhile retaining an attitude of "mitigated scepticism," he counselled, because much that had previously been claimed as "knowledge" was no more than unsubstantiated speculation. In fact there were only two kinds of knowledge, he maintained in the *Enquiry*, "matters of fact" and "relations of ideas," and whereas the latter category of truths were demonstrable by formal logic or mathematics, the former were always subject to verification through sensory experience. No proposition which could not be validated by one or other of these two procedures should be admitted into the corpus of human knowledge, Hume concluded, and he intransigently insisted that most traditional theology, metaphysical philosophy, ethics, and political theory should be condemned as so much "sophistry and illusion."

The following extract from *An Enquiry Concerning the Human Understanding* illustrates Hume's epistemology, his analysis of the explanatory categories of scientific thinking, his ambivalent attitude to philosophical scepticism, and his attack on "metaphysics."[1] It should be recognized, however, that Hume himself regarded his later writings on ethics, religion, politics and history as equally important as his early epistemology. His views on these topics may be found in *An Enquiry Concerning the Principles of Morals* (1752), *Political Discourses* (1752), *History of England* (1754), and *Dialogues Concerning Natural Religion* (published posthumously in 1779).

From *An Enquiry Concerning the Human Understanding*

Section IV: Sceptical Doubts Concerning the Operations of the Understanding

20. All the objects of human reason or enquiry may naturally be divided into two kinds to wit, *relations of ideas* and *matters of fact*. Of the first kind are the sciences of geometry, algebra, and arithmetic and in short, every affirmation which is either intuitively or demonstratively certain. That the square of the hypotenuse is equal to the squares of the two sides, is a proposition which expresses a relation between these figures. That three times five is equal to the half of thirty, expresses a relation between these numbers. Propositions of this kind are discoverable by the mere operation of thought, without dependence on what is anywhere existent in the universe. Though there never were a circle or triangle in nature the truths demonstrated by Euclid would for ever retain their certainty and evidence.

21. Matters of fact, which are the second objects of human reason, are not ascertained in the same manner; nor is our evidence of their truth, however great, of a like nature with the foregoing. The contrary of every matter of fact is still possible; because it can never imply a contradiction and is conceived by the mind with the same facility and distinctness, as if ever so conformable to reality. That the sun will not rise tomorrow is no less intelligible a proposition, and implies no more contradiction than the affirmation, that it will rise. We should in vain, therefore, attempt to demonstrate its falsehood. Were it demonstratively false, it would imply a contradiction, and could never be distinctly conceived by the mind.

It may, therefore, be a subject worthy of curiosity, to enquiry what is the nature of that evidence which assures us of any real existence and matter of fact, beyond the present testimony of our senses or the records of our memory. . . .

22. All reasonings concerning matter of fact seem to be founded on the relation of *cause and effect*. By means of that relation alone we can go beyond the evidence of our memory and senses. If you were to ask a man, why he believes any matter of fact, which is absent; for instance, that his friend is in the country, or in France; he would give you a reason; and this reason would be some other fact; as a letter received from him, or the knowledge of his former resolutions and promises. A man finding a watch or any other machine on a desert island, would conclude that there had once been men on that island. All our reasonings concerning fact are of the same nature. And here it is constantly supposed that there is a connexion between the present fact and that which is inferred from it. Were there nothing to bind them together, the inference would be entirely precarious.

---

[1] Selection reprinted from L.A. Selby-Bigge, ed., David Hume, *An Enquiry concerning the Human Understanding, and An Enquiry concerning the Principles of Morals*, posthumous edition of 1777, edited by (Oxford: The Clarendon Press, 1894), pp. 25–27, 32, 34, 37–39, 42–47, 49–50, 60–62, 73–77, 149–155, 159–165.

The hearing of an articulate voice and rational discourse in the dark assures us of the presence of some person: Why? because these are the effect of the human make and fabric, and closely connected with it. If we anatomize all the other reasonings of this nature, we shall find that they are founded on the relation of cause and effect, and that this relation is either near or remote, direct or collateral. Heat and light are collateral effects of fire and the one effect may justly be inferred from the other.

23. If we would satisfy ourselves, therefore, concerning the nature of that evidence, which assures us of matters of fact, we must enquiry how we arrive at the knowledge of cause and effect.

I shall venture to affirm, as a general proposition, which admits of no exception, that the knowledge of this relation is not, in any instance, attained by reasonings a Priori; but rises entirely from experience, when we find that any particular objects are constantly conjoined with each other. . . .

28. . . . I say then, that, even after we have experience of the operations of cause and effect, our conclusions from that experience are *not* founded on reasoning, or any process of understanding. This answer we must endeavour both to explain and to defend. . . .

29. . . . These two propositions are far from being the same, *I have found that such an object has always been attended with such effect,* and *I foresee, that other objects which are, in appearance, similar, will be attended with similar effects.* I shall allow, if you please, that the one proposition may justly be inferred from the other: I know, in fact, that it is always inferred. But if you insist that the inference is made by a chain of reasoning, I desire you to produce that reasoning. The connexion between these propositions is not intuitive. There is required a medium, which may enable the mind to draw such an inference, if indeed it be drawn by reasoning and argument. What that medium is, I must confess, passes my comprehension; and it is incumbent on those to produce it, who assert that it really exists, and is the origin of all our conclusions concerning matter of fact. . . .

32. . . . You say that the one proposition is an inference from the other. But you must confess that the inference is not intuitive; neither is it demonstrative. Of what nature is it, then? To say it is experimental, is begging the question. For all inferences from experience suppose, as their foundation, that the future will resemble the past, and that similar powers will be conjoined with similar sensible qualities. If there be any suspicion that the course of nature may change, and that the past may be no rule for the future, all experience becomes useless, and can give rise to no inference or conclusion. It is impossible, therefore, that any arguments from experience can prove this resemblance of the past to the future; since all these arguments are founded on the supposition of that resemblance. Let the course of things be allowed hitherto ever so regular; that alone, without some new argument or inference, proves not that, for the future, it will continue so. In vain do you pretend to have learned that nature of bodies from your past experience. Their secret nature, and consequently all their effects and influence may change, without any change in their sensible qualities. This happens sometimes, and with regard to some objects: Why may it not happen always, and with regard to all objects? What logic, what process of argument secures you against this supposition? My practice, you say, refutes my doubts. But you mistake the purport of my question. As an agent, I am quite satisfied in the point; but as a philosopher, who has some share of curiosity, I will not say scepticism, I want to learn the foundation of this inference. . . .

33. . . . It is certain that the most ignorant and stupid peasants—nay infants, nay even brute beasts—improve by experience, and learn the qualities of natural objects, by observing the effects which result from them. When a child has felt the sensation of pain from touching the flame of a candle, he will be careful not to put his hand near any candle, but will expect a similar effect from a cause which is similar in its sensible qualities and appearance. If you assert, therefore, that the understanding of the child is led into this conclusion by any process of argument or ratiocination, I may justly require you to produce that argument; nor have you any pretense to refuse so equitable a demand. You cannot say that the argument is abstruse, and may possibly escape your enquiry; since you confess that it is obvious to the capacity of a mere infant. If you hesitate therefore, a moment, or if, after reflection. you produce any intricate or pro- found argument, you, in a manner, give up the question, and confess that it is not reasoning which engages us to suppose the past resembling the future, and to expect similar effects from causes which are, to appearance, similar. This is the proposition which I intended to enforce in the present section. . . .

Section V: Sceptical Solution of These Doubts

35. Suppose a person, though endowed with the strongest faculties of reason and reflection, to be brought on a sudden into this world; he would, indeed, immediately observe a continual succession of objects, and one event following another; but he would not be able to discover anything farther. He would not, at first, by any reasoning, be able to reach the idea of cause and effect; since the particular powers, by which all natural operations are performed, never appear to the senses; nor is it reasonable to conclude, merely because one event, in one instance, precedes another, that therefore the one is the cause, the other the effect. Their conjunction may be arbitrary and casual. There may be no reason to infer the existence of one from the appearance of the other. And in a word, such a person, without more experience, could never employ his conjecture or reasoning concerning any matter of fact, or be assured of anything beyond what was immediately present to his memory and senses.

Suppose, again, that he has acquired more experience, and has lived so long in the world as to have observed familiar objects or events to be constantly conjoined together; what is the consequence of this experience? He immediately infers the existence of one object from the appearance of the other. Yet he has not, by all his experience, acquired any idea or knowledge of the secret power by which the one object produces the other; nor is it, by any process of reasoning, he is engaged to draw this inference. But still he finds himself determined to draw it: And though he should be convinced that his understanding has no part in the operation, he would nevertheless continue in the same course of thinking. There is some other principle which determines him to form such a conclusion.

36. This principle is *Custom* or *Habit*. For wherever the repetition of any particular act or operation produces a propensity to renew the same act or operation, without being impelled by any reasoning or process of the understanding, we always say, that this propensity is the effect of Custom. . . . All inferences from experience, therefore, are effects of custom, not reasoning.

Custom, then, is the great guide of human life. It is that principle alone which renders our experience useful to us, and makes us expect, for the future, a similar train of events with those which have appeared in the past. Without the influence of custom, we should be entirely ignorant of every matter of fact beyond what is immediately present to the memory and senses. We should never know how to adjust means to ends, or to employ our natural powers in the production of any effect. There would be an end at once of all action, as well as of the chief part of speculation. . . .

38. What, then, is the conclusion of the whole matter? A simple one; though, it must be confessed, pretty remote from the common theories of philosophy. All belief of matter of fact or real existence is derived merely from some object, present to the memory or senses, and a customary conjunction between that and some other object. Or in other words; having found, in many instances, that any two kinds of objects—flame and heat, snow and cold—have always been conjoined together; if flame or snow be presented anew to the senses, the mind is carried by custom to expect heat or cold, and to *believe* that such a quality does exist, and will discover itself upon a nearer approach. This belief is the necessary result of placing the mind in such circumstances. It is an operation of the soul, when we are so situated, as unavoidable as to feel the passion of love, when we receive benefits; or hatred, when we meet with injuries. All these operations are a species of natural instincts, which no reasoning or process of the thought and understanding is able either to produce or to prevent.

At this point, it would be very allowable for us to stop our philosophical researches. In most questions we can never make a single step farther; and in all questions we must terminate here at last, after our most restless and curious enquiries. But still our curiosity will be pardonable, perhaps commendable, if it carries us on to still farther researches, and make us examine more accurately the nature of this *belief*, and of the *customary conjunction*, whence it is derived. . . .

And in philosophy, we can go no farther than assert that *belief* is something felt by the mind, which distinguishes the ideas of the judgement from the fictions of the imagination. It gives them more weight and influence; makes them appear of greater importance; enforces them in the mind; and renders them the governing principle of our actions. I hear at present, for instance, a person's voice, with whom I am acquainted; and the sound comes as from the next room. This impression of my senses immediately conveys my thought to the person, together with all the surrounding objects. I paint them out to myself as existing at present, with the same qualities and relations, of which I formerly knew them possessed. These ideas take faster hold of my mind than ideas of an enchanted castle. They are very different to the feeling, and have a much greater influence of every kind, either to give pleasure or pain, joy or sorrow.

Let us, then, take in the whole compass of this doctrine, and allow, that the sentiment of belief is nothing but a conception more intense and steady than what attends the mere fictions of the imagination, and that this *manner* of conception arises from a customary conjunction of the object with something present to the memory or senses: I believe that it will not be difficult, upon these suppositions, to find other operations of the mind analogous to it, and to trace up these phenomena to principles still more general.

41. We have already observed that nature has established connexions among particular ideas, and that no sooner one idea occurs to our thoughts than it introduces its correlative, and carries our attention towards it, by a gentle and insensible movement. These principles of connexion or association we have reduced to three, namely *Resemblance, Contiguity*, and *Causation*; which are the only bonds that unite our thoughts together, and beget that regular train of reflection or discourse, which in a greater or less degree, takes place among mankind. . . .

Section VII: Of the Idea of Necessary Connexion

48. The great advantage of the mathematical sciences above the moral consists in this, that the ideas of the former, being sensible, are always clear and determinate, the smallest distinction between them is immediately perceptible, and the same terms are still expressive of the same ideas, without ambiguity or variation. An oval is never mistaken for a circle, nor a hyperbola for an ellipsis. The isosceles and scalenum are distinguished by boundaries more exact than vice and virtue, right and wrong. If any term be defined in geometry, the mind readily, of itself substitutes, on all occasions, the definition for the term defined: Or even when no definition is employed, the object itself may be presented to the senses, and by that means be steadily and clearly apprehended. But the finer sentiments of the mind, the operations of the understanding, the various agitations of the passions, though really in themselves distinct, easily escape us, when surveyed by reflection; nor is it in our power to recall the original object, as often as we have occasion to contemplate it. Ambiguity, by this means, is gradually introduced into our reasonings: Similar objects are readily taken to be the same: And the conclusion becomes at last very wide of the premises. . . .

. . . The chief obstacle, therefore, to our improvement in the moral or metaphysical sciences is the obscurity of the ideas, and the ambiguity of the terms. . . .

49. There are no ideas which occur in metaphysics, more obscure and uncertain than those of *power, force, energy* or *necessary connexion*, of which it is every moment necessary for us to treat in all our disquisitions. . . .

58. But to hasten to a conclusion of this argument, which is already drawn out to too great a length: We have sought in vain for an idea of power or necessary connexion in all the sources from which we could suppose it to be derived. It appears that, in single instances of the operation of bodies, we never can, by our utmost scrutiny, discover anything but one event following another, without being able to comprehend any force or power by which the cause operates, or any connexion between it and its supposed effect. The same difficulty occurs in contemplating the operations of the mind on body—where we observe the motion of the latter to follow upon the volition of the former, but are not able to observe or conceive the tie which binds together the motion and the volition, or the energy by which the mind produces this effect. The authority of the will over its own faculties and ideas is not a whit more comprehensible: So that, upon the whole, there appears not, throughout all nature, anyone instance of connexion which is conceivable by us. All events seem entirely loose and separate. One event follows another; but we never can observe any tie between them. They seem *conjoined*, but never *connected*. And as we can have no idea of anything which never appeared to our outward sense or inward sentiment, the necessary conclusion *seems* to be that we have no idea of connexion or power at all, and that these words are absolutely without any meaning, when employed either in philosophical reasonings or common life. . . .

59. . . . But when one particular species of event has always, in all instances, been conjoined with another, we make no longer any scruple of foretelling one upon the appearance of the other, and of employing that reasoning, which can alone assure us of any matter of fact or existence. We then call the one object, *Cause*; the other, *Effect*. We suppose that there is some connexion between them; some power in the one, by which it infallibly produces the other, and operates with the greatest certainty and strongest necessity.

It appears, then, that this idea of a necessary connexion among events arises from a number of similar instances which occur of the constant conjunction of these events; nor can that idea ever be suggested by anyone of these instances, surveyed in all possible lights and positions. But there is nothing in a number of instances, different from every single instance, which is supposed to be exactly similar; except only, that after a repetition of similar instances, the mind is carried by habit, upon the appearance of one event, to expect its usual attendant, and to believe that it will exist. The connexion, therefore, which we *feel* in the mind, this customary transition of the imagination from one object to its usual attendant, is the sentiment or impression from which we form the idea of power or necessary connexion. Nothing farther is in the case. Contemplate the subject on all sides; you will never find any other origin of that idea. This is the sole difference between one instance, from which we can never receive the idea of connexion, and a number of similar instances, by which it is suggested. The first time a man saw the communication of motion by impulse, as by the shock of two billiard balls, he could not pronounce that the one event was *connected*; but only that it was *conjoined* with the other. After he has observed several instances of this nature, he then pronounces them to be *connected*. What alteration has happened to give rise to this idea of *connexion*? Nothing but that he now *feels* these events to be *connected* in his imagination, and can readily foretell the existence of one from the appearance of the other. When we say, therefore, that one object is connected with another, we mean only that they have acquired a connexion in our thought, and give rise to this inference, by which they become proofs of each other's existence: A conclusion which is somewhat extraordinary, but which seems founded on sufficient evidence. Nor will its evidence be weakened by any general diffidence of the understanding or sceptical suspicion concerning every conclusion which is new and extraordinary. No conclusions can be more agreeable to scepticism than such as make discoveries concerning the weakness and narrow limits of reason and capacity.

60. And what stronger instance can be produced of the surprising ignorance and weakness of the understanding than the present? For surely, if there be any relation among objects which it imports to us to know perfectly, it is that of cause and effect. On this are founded all our reasonings concerning matter of fact or existence. By means of it alone we attain any assurance concerning objects which are removed from the present testimony of our memory and senses. The only immediate utility of all sciences, is to teach us, how to control and regulate future events by their causes. Our thoughts and enquiries are, therefore, every moment, employed about this relation: Yet so imperfect are the ideas which we form concerning it, that it is impossible to give any just definition of cause, except what is drawn from something extraneous and foreign to it. Similar objects are always conjoined with similar. Of this we have experience. Suitably to this experience, therefore, we may define a cause to be an *object, followed by another, and where all the objects similar to the first are followed by objects similar to the second.* Or in other words *where, if the first object had not been, the second never had existed.* The appearance of a cause always conveys the mind, by a customary transition, to the idea of the effect. Of this we also have experience. We may therefore, suitably to this experience, form another definition of cause, and call it, *an object followed by another, and whose appearance always conveys the thought to that other.* But though both these definitions be drawn from circumstances foreign to the cause, we cannot remedy this inconvenience, or attain any more perfect definition, which may point out that circumstance in the cause, which gives it a connexion with its effect. We have no idea of this connexion, nor even any distinct notion what it is we desire to know, when we endeavour at a conception of it. . . .

Section XII: Of the Academical or Sceptical Philosophy

116. What is meant by a sceptic? And how far is it possible to push these philosophical principles of doubt and uncertainty?

There is a species of scepticism, *antecedent* to all study and philosophy, which is much inculcated by Descartes and others, as a sovereign preservative against error and precipitate judgement. It recommends an universal doubt, not only of all our former opinions and principles, but also of our very faculties; of whose veracity, say they, we must assure ourselves, by a chain of reasoning, deduced from some original principle, which cannot possibly be fallacious or deceitful. But neither is there any such original principle, which has a prerogative above others, that are self-evident and convincing: or if there were, could we advance a step beyond it, but by the use of those very faculties, of which we are supposed to be already diffident. The Cartesian doubt, therefore, were it ever possible to be attained by any human creature (as it plainly is not) would be entirely incurable; and no reasoning could ever bring us to a state of assurance and conviction upon any subject. . . .

117. There is another species of scepticism, *consequent* to science and enquiry, when men are supposed to have discovered, either the absolute fallaciousness of their mental faculties, or their unfitness to reach any fixed determination in all those curious subjects of speculation, about which they are commonly employed. Even our very senses are brought into dispute by a certain species of philosophers; and the maxims of common life are subjected to the same doubt as the most profound principles or conclusions of metaphysics and theology. As these paradoxical tenets (if they may be called tenets) are to be met with in some philosophers, and the refutation of them in several, they naturally excite our curiosity, and make us enquiry into the arguments, on which they may be founded. . . .

118. It seems evident, that men are carried, by a natural instinct or prepossession, to repose faith in their senses; and that, without any reasoning, or even almost before the use of reason, we always suppose an external universe, which depends not on our perception, but would exist, though we and every sensible creature were absent or annihilated. Even the animal creation are governed by a like opinion, and preserve this belief of external objects, in all their thoughts, designs, and actions.

It seems also evident, that, when men follow this blind and powerful instinct of nature, they always suppose the very images, presented by the senses, to be the external objects, and never entertain any suspicion, that the one are nothing but representations of the other. This very table, which we see white and feel hard, is believed to exist, independent of our perception, and to be something external to our mind, which perceives it. Our presence bestows not being on it: our absence does not annihilate it. It preserves its existence uniform and entire, independent of the situation of intelligent beings, who perceive or contemplate it.

But this universal and primary opinion of all men is soon destroyed by the slightest philosophy, which teaches us, that nothing can ever be present to the mind but an image or perception, and that the senses are only the inlets, through which these images are conveyed, without being able to produce any immediate intercourse between the mind and the object. The table, which we see, seems to diminish, as we remove farther from it: but the real table, which exists independent of us, suffers no alteration: it was, therefore nothing but its image, which was present to the mind. These are the obvious dictates of reason; and no man, who reflects, ever doubted, that the existences, which we consider, when we say, *this house* and *that tree*, are nothing but perceptions in the mind, and fleeting copies or representations of other existences, which remain uniform and independent.

119. So far, then, are we necessitated by reasoning to contradict or depart from the primary instincts of nature, and to embrace a new system with regard to the evidence of our senses. But here philosophy finds herself extremely embarrassed, when she would justify this new system, and obviate the cavils and objections of the sceptics. She can no longer plead the infallible and irresistible instinct of nature: for that led us to a quite different system, which is acknowledged fallible and even erroneous. And to justify this pretended philosophical system, by a chain of clear and convincing argument, or even any appearance of argument, exceeds the power of all human capacity.

By what argument can it be proved, that the perceptions of the mind must be caused by external objects, entirely different from them, though resembling them (if that be possible) and could not arise either from the energy of the mind itself, or from the suggestion of some invisible and unknown spirit, or from some other cause still more unknown to us? It is acknowledged, that, in fact, many of these perceptions arise not from anything external, as in dreams, madness, and other diseases. And nothing can be more inexplicable than the manner, in which body should so operate upon mind as ever to convey an image of itself to a substance, supposed of so different, and even contrary a nature.

It is a question of fact, whether the perceptions of the senses be produced by external objects, resembling them: how shall this question be determined? By experience surely; as all other questions of a like nature. But here experience is, and must be entirely silent. The mind has never anything present to it but the perceptions, and cannot possibly reach any experience of their connexion with objects. The supposition of such a connexion is, therefore, without any foundation in reasoning.

120. To have recourse to the veracity of the supreme Being, in order to prove the veracity of our senses, is surely making a very unexpected circuit. If his veracity were at all concerned in this matter, our senses would be entirely infallible; because it is not possible that he can ever deceive. Not to mention, that, if the external world be once called in question, we shall be at a loss to find arguments, by which we may prove the existence of that Being or any of his attributes.

121. This is a topic, therefore, in which the profounder and more philosophical sceptics will always triumph, when they endeavour to introduce an universal doubt into all subjects of human knowledge and enquiry. Do you follow the instincts and propensities of nature, may they say, in assenting to the veracity of sense? But these lead you to believe that the very perception or sensible image is the external object. Do you disclaim this principle, in order to embrace a more rational opinion, that the perceptions are only representations of something external? You here depart from your natural propensities and more obvious sentiments; and yet are not able to satisfy your reason, which can never find any convincing argument from experience to prove, that the perceptions are connected with any external objects.

122. There is another sceptical topic of a like nature, derived from the most profound philosophy; which might merit our attention, were it requisite to dive so deep, in order to discover arguments and reasonings, which can so little serve to any serious purpose. It is universally allowed by modern enquiryrs, that all the sensible qualities of objects, such as hard, soft, hot, cold, white, black, &c. are merely secondary, and exist not in the objects themselves, but are perceptions of the mind, without any external archetype or model, which they represent. If this be allowed, with regard to secondary qualities, it must also follow, with regard to the supposed primary qualities of extension and solidity; nor can the latter be any more entitled to that denomination than the former. The idea of extension is entirely acquired from the senses of sight and feeling; and if all the qualities, perceived by the senses, be in the mind, not in the object, the same conclusion must reach the idea of extension, which is wholly dependent on the sensible ideas of secondary qualities. Nothing can save us from this conclusion, but the asserting, that the ideas of those primary qualities are attained by Abstraction, an opinion, which, if we examine it accurately, we shall find to be unintelligible, and even absurd. An extension, that is neither tangible nor visible, cannot possibly be conceived: and a tangible or visible extension, which is neither hard nor soft, black nor white, is equally beyond the reach of human conception. Let any man try to conceive a triangle in general, which is neither Isosceles nor Scalenum, nor has any particular length or proportion of sides; and he will soon perceive the absurdity of all the scholastic notions with regard to abstraction and general ideas.

123. Thus the first philosophical objection to the evidence of sense or to the opinion of external existence consists in this, that such an opinion, if rested on natural instinct, is contrary to reason, and if referred to reason, is contrary to natural instinct, and at the same time carries no rational evidence with it, to convince an impartial enquiryer. The second objection goes farther, and represents this opinion as contrary to reason: at least, if it be a principle of reason, that all sensible qualities are in the mind, not in the object. Bereave matter of all its intelligible qualities, both primary and secondary, you in a manner annihilate it, and leave only a certain unknown, inexplicable *something*, as the cause of our perceptions; a notion so imperfect, that no sceptic will think it worth while to contend against it.

127. The sceptic, therefore . . . seems to have ample matter of triumph; while he justly insists, that all our evidence for any matter of fact, which lies beyond the testimony of sense or memory is derived entirely from the relation of cause and effect; that we have no other idea of this relation than that of two objects, which have been frequently *conjoined* together; that we have no argument to convince us, that objects, which have, in our experience, been frequently conjoined, will likewise, in other instances, be conjoined in the same manner; and that nothing leads us to this inference but custom or a certain instinct of our nature; which it is indeed difficult to resist, but which, like other instincts, may be fallacious and deceitful. While the sceptic insists upon these topics, he shows his force, or rather, indeed, his own and our weakness; and seems, for the time at least, to destroy all assurance and conviction. These arguments might be displayed at greater length, if any durable good or bene-fit to society could ever be expected to result from them.

128. For here is the chief and most confounding objection to *excessive* scepticism, that no durable good can ever result from it; while it remains in its full force and vigor. We need only ask such a sceptic, *What his meaning is? And what he proposes by all these curious researches?* He is imme-diately at a loss, and knows not what to answer. . . .

129. There is indeed, a more *mitigated* scepticism or *academical* philosophy, which may be both durable and useful, and which may, in part, be the result of this Pyrrhonism, or *excessive* scepticism, when its undistinguished doubts are, in some measure, corrected by common sense and reflection. The greater part of mankind are naturally apt to be affirmative and dogmatical in their opinions; and while they see objects only on one side, and have no idea of any counter-poising argument, they throw themselves precipitately into the principles, to which they are inclined nor have they any indulgence for those who entertain opposite sentiments. To hesitate or balance perplexes their understanding, checks their passion, and suspends their action. They are, therefore, impatient till they escape from a state, which to them is so uneasy: and they think, that they could never remove themselves far enough from it, by the violence of their affirmations and obstinacy of their belief. But could such dogmatical reasoners become sensible of the strange infirmities of human understanding, even in its most perfect state, and when most accurate and cautious in its determinations; such a reflection would naturally inspire them with more modesty and reserve, and diminish their fond opinion of themselves, and their prejudice against antagonists. . . .

130. . . . Another species of *mitigated* scepticism which may be of advantage to mankind, and which may be the natural result of the Pyrrhonian doubts and scruples, is the limitation of our enquiries to such subjects as are best adapted to the narrow capacity of human understanding. The imagination of man is naturally sublime, delighted with whatever is remote and extraordinary, and running, without control, into the most distant parts of space and time in order to avoid the objects, which custom has rendered too familiar to it. A correct *Judgement* observes a contrary method, and avoiding all distant and high enquiries, confines itself to common life, and to such subjects as fall under daily practice and experience; leaving the more sublime topics to the embellishment of poets and orators, or to the arts of priests and politicians. To bring us to so salutary a determination, nothing can be more serviceable, than to be once thoroughly convinced of the force of the Pyrrhonian doubt, and of the impossibility, that anything, but the strong power of natural instinct, could free us from it. Those who have a propensity to philosophy, will still continue their researches; because they reflect, that, besides the immediate pleasure, attending such an occupation, philosophical decisions are nothing but the reflections of common life methodized and corrected. But they will never be tempted to go beyond common life, so long as they consider the imperfection of those faculties which they employ, their narrow reach, and their inaccurate operations. While we cannot give a satisfactory reason, why we believe, after a thousand experiments, that a stone will fall, or fire burn; can we ever satisfy ourselves concerning any determination, which we may form, with regard to the origin of worlds, and the situation of nature, from, and to eternity?

This narrow limitation, indeed, of our enquiries, is, in every respect, so reasonable, that it suffices to make the slightest examination into the natural powers of the human mind and to compare them with their objects, in order to recommend it to us. We shall then find what are the proper subjects of science and inquiry.

131. It seems to me, that the only objects of the abstract science or of demonstration are quantity and number, and that all attempts to extend this more perfect species of knowledge beyond these bounds are mere sophistry and illusion. . . .

132. All other enquiries of men regard only matter of fact and existence; and these are evidently incapable of demonstration. Whatever *is* may *not be*. No negation of a fact can involve a contradiction. The non-existence of any being, without exception, is as clear and distinct an idea as its existence. The proposition, which affirms it not to be, however false, is no less conceivable and intelligible, than that which affirms it to be. The case is different with the sciences, properly so-called. Every proposition, which is not true, is there confused and unintelligible. That the cube root of 64 is equal to the half of 10, is a false proposition, and can never be distinctly conceived. But that Caesar, or the angel Gabriel, or any being never existed, may be a false proposition, but still is perfectly conceivable, and implies no contradiction.

The existence, therefore, of any being can only be proved by arguments from its cause or its effect; and these arguments are founded entirely on experience. If we reason a *priori*, anything may appear able to produce anything. The falling of a pebble may, for aught we know, extinguish the sun; or the wish of a man control the planets in their orbits. It is only experience, which teaches us the nature and bounds of cause and effect, and enables us to infer the existence of one object from that of another. Such is the foundation of moral reasoning, which forms the greater part of human knowledge, and is the source of all human action and behaviour.

Moral reasonings are either concerning particular or general facts. All deliberations in life regard the former; as also all disquisitions in history, chronology, geography and astronomy.

The sciences, which treat of general facts, are politics, natural philosophy, physic, chemistry; etc., where the qualities, causes and effect of the whole species of objects are inquired into.

Divinity or Theology, as it proves the existence of a Deity, and the immortality of souls, is composed partly of reasonings concerning particular, partly concerning general facts. It has a foundation in reason, so far as it is supported by experience. But its best and most solid foundation is *faith* and divine revelation.

Morals and criticism are not so properly objects of the understanding as of taste and sentiment. Beauty, whether moral or natural, is felt, more properly than perceived. Or if we reason concerning it, and endeavour to fix its standard, we regard a new fact, to wit, the general taste of mankind, or some such fact, which may be the object of reasoning and enquiry.

When we run over libraries, persuaded of these principles, what havoc must we make? If we take in our hand any volume; of divinity or school metaphysics, for instance; let us ask, *Does it contain any abstract reasoning concerning quantity or number?* No. *Does it contain any experimental reasoning concerning matter of fact and existence?* No. Commit it then to the flames: for it can contain nothing but sophistry and illusion.